Rave reviews for
Bed & Breakfast U.S.A.:

"A valuable source of information."—*The New York Times*

"A best-selling travel book."—*Reader's Digest*

"An excellent readable guide."—*Washington Post*

"The best source of nationwide information."—*Changing Times*

"The most comprehensive B&B guide."—*Sylvia Porter's Personal Finance*

"Your best bet."—*Philadelphia Inquirer*

"Makes enjoyable reading."—*Country Living*

"Extremely useful, well-organized guide."—*American Library Association Booklist*

"Many a first-time B&B guest vows never again to stay in a motel . . . business travelers—particularly women traveling alone—have found this personal touch just the ticket."—*Karen Cure, TWA Ambassador*

"*Bed & Breakfast U.S.A.* is one of the bibles of the business."—*Chicago Tribune*

"Squeezed budgets get relief at B&Bs. . . . *Bed & Breakfast U.S.A.* [is] an extensive list of establishments. . . ."—*United Press International*

"The best overall view . . . Betty Rundback is so enthusiastic that she even gives readers pointers on how to start their own B&Bs."—*Detroit News*

"Especially helpful . . . especially valuable."—*New York Daily News*

"For those who have embraced the B&B way to travel, there is no going back to hotel highrises and motel monotony."—*Time*

"America's newest and hottest accommodations trend is B&B."—*Boston Globe*

Bed & Breakfast U.S.A. 1991

Betty Revits Rundback
Assisted by Leslie Jay and Michael Ackerman

Tourist House Association of America

℗

A PLUME BOOK

With love to Bob Rundback
because this whole project was his idea;
and to Ann Revits,
ever the proud mother and grandma

Front cover photo: The Feather Bed Inn, Quincy, California,
by John and Naomi Brazier.
Back cover photos: Breakfast Room, Sweet Basil Hill Farm, Gurnee, Illinois;
Bedroom, The Palmer House Inn, Falmouth, Massachusetts, by Ron Havey.

PLUME
Published by the Penguin Group
Penguin Books USA Inc., 375 Hudson Street,
New York, New York 10014, U.S.A.
Penguin Books Ltd, 27 Wrights Lane,
London W8 5TZ, England
Penguin Books Australia Ltd, Ringwood,
Victoria, Australia
Penguin Books Canada Ltd, 2801 John Street,
Markham, Ontario, Canada L3R 1B4
Penguin Books (N.Z.) Ltd, 182–190 Wairau Road,
Auckland 10, New Zealand

Penguin Books Ltd, Registered Offices:
Harmondsworth, Middlesex, England

Published by Plume, an imprint of New American Library,
a division of Penguin Books USA Inc.

Library of Congress Number: 86-649303

ISBN: 0-452-26571-1

First Printing, February, 1991

10 9 8 7 6 5 4 3 2 1

 REGISTERED TRADEMARK—MARCA REGISTRADA

Printed in the United States of America
Set in Palatino and Optima
Designed by Stanley S. Drate/Folio Graphics Co. Inc.

Contents

Reservation service organizations appear here in boldface type.

Reservation service organizations appear here in boldface type.

Reservation service organizations appear here in boldface type.

Reservation service organizations appear here in boldface type.

Reservation service organizations appear here in boldface type.

Reservation service organizations appear here in boldface type.

Reservation service organizations appear here in boldface type.

Reservation service organizations appear here in boldface type.

Reservation service organizations appear here in boldface type.

Reservation service organizations appear here in boldface type.

Reservation service organizations appear here in boldface type.

Reservation service organizations appear here in boldface type.

Reservation service organizations appear here in boldface type.

Reservation service organizations appear here in boldface type.

Reservation service organizations appear here in boldface type.

Reservation service organizations appear here in boldface type.

Reservation service organizations appear here in boldface type.

Reservation service organizations appear here in boldface type.

Reservation service organizations appear here in boldface type.

Reservation service organizations appear here in boldface type.

Reservation service organizations appear here in boldface type.

Reservation service organizations appear here in boldface type.

Reservation service organizations appear here in boldface type.

Reservation service organizations appear here in boldface type.

Reservation service organizations appear here in boldface type.

Reservation service organizations appear here in boldface type.

Reservation service organizations appear here in boldface type.

Reservation service organizations appear here in boldface type.

Reservation service organizations appear here in boldface type.

Reservation service organizations appear here in boldface type.

Reservation service organizations appear here in boldface type.

Preface

If you are familiar with earlier editions of *Bed & Breakfast U.S.A.*, you know that this book has always been a labor of love. It is personally gratifying to see how it has grown from the first 16-page edition, titled *Guide to Tourist Homes and Guest Houses*, which was published in 1975 and contained 40 individual listings. Fifteen years later, the fourteenth revised edition lists 1012 homes and 122 reservation agencies, giving travelers access to over 11,000 host homes. This spectacular success indicates how strongly the revived concept of the guest house has recaptured the fancy of both travelers and proprietors.

On the other hand, what was welcomed as a reasonably priced alternative to the plastic ambience of motel chains has, in some instances, lost its unique qualities. Our mailbox is crammed with letters from grand hotels, condominium rental agencies, campground compounds, and chic inns with nightly tariffs topping the $100 mark. All share a common theme—they all serve breakfast and they all want to be listed in *Bed & Breakfast U.S.A.* Who can blame them? Since 1976, over 500,000 people have bought this best-selling guide.

We also receive a substantial amount of mail from our readers, and we have tailored our book to meet their needs. We have given a great deal of thought to what we feel a B&B should be, and are again focusing on our original definition: an owner-occupied residence with breakfast included at a fair rate, where the visitor is made to feel more like a welcome guest than a paying customer.

Based on personal experience, and comments from our readers, several key problems are apparent in some B&Bs: Waiting your turn to use a bathroom shared with five other guests is unpleasant, especially when you're paying upward of $40 a night. Nor is it enjoyable to pay $90 and up simply for staying in someone's home, no matter how exquisite the decor. Finally, when paying $35 or $40, no one wants to go out to a restaurant for breakfast—no matter how close it may be, it's just not the same as breakfast "at home."

As a result of these problems, we have regretfully deleted several listings that have been on our roster for years. This does not imply, in any way, that these B&Bs aren't nice; it simply means that, *in our opinion*, they do not fit the traditional B&B

experience. We've had a goodly share of irate letters from several "old friends" disputing our opinion and pointing out that rising operating expenses must be reflected in their charges. Newcomers to the business decry our stand and tell us of their high costs that must somehow be recouped. While we sympathize and understand fully their positions, we must, in all fairness, be firm.

This is not a project for which listings have been compiled just for the sake of putting a book together; bigger isn't necessarily better. *Bed & Breakfast U.S.A.* is a product of a membership organization whose credo is "Comfort, cleanliness, cordiality, and fairness of cost." We solicit and rely on the comments of readers. For this purpose, we include a tear-out form on page 677. If we receive negative reports, that member is dropped from our roster. We genuinely appreciate comments from guests— negative if necessary, positive when warranted. *We want to hear from you!*

All of the B&Bs described in this book are members of the Tourist House Association of America, RD 2, Box 355A Greentown, Pennsylvania 18426. THAA dues are $25 annually. We share ideas and experiences by way of our newsletter, and sometimes arrange regional seminars and conferences. To order a list of B&Bs that joined after this edition went to press, use the form at the back of this book.

BETTY R. RUNDBACK
PEGGY ACKERMAN
Tourist House Association of America

January 1991

Even after careful editing and proofreading, errors occasionally occur. We regret any inconvenience to our readers and members.

Acknowledgments

With great pride, our entire family remembers the love and enthusiasm Betty Revits Rundback put into this book every year. She touched many hearts. May her warmth and wisdom never be forgotten.

A special thanks to Michael Frome, who saw promise in the first 16-page Guide and verbally applauded our growth with each subsequent edition. And many thanks to all of the other travel writers and reporters who have brought us to the attention of their audiences.

Many hugs to family and friends who lovingly devoted time to the "office" chores: Justin Ackerman, Karen Zane, Travis Kali, the Shepard family, and the Schweisguth family. We are most grateful to Joyce and James McGhee for their artwork.

Our appreciation goes to our editor, Sandy Soule. She exhausted her supply of blue pencils, but never her patience. And to Leslie Jay for her special input and able assistance.

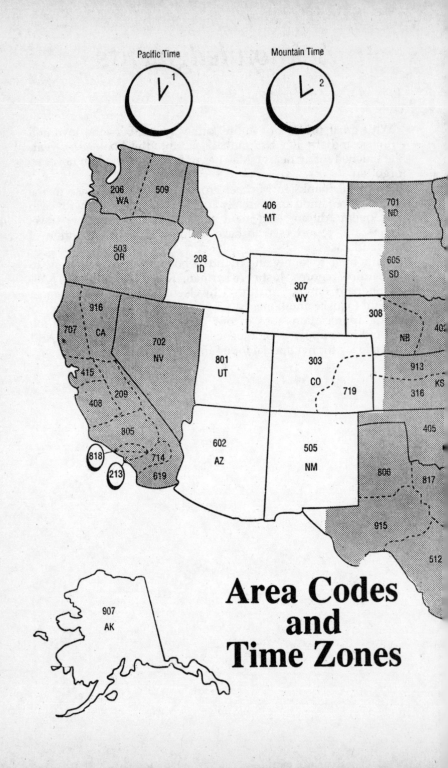

**Area Codes
and
Time Zones**

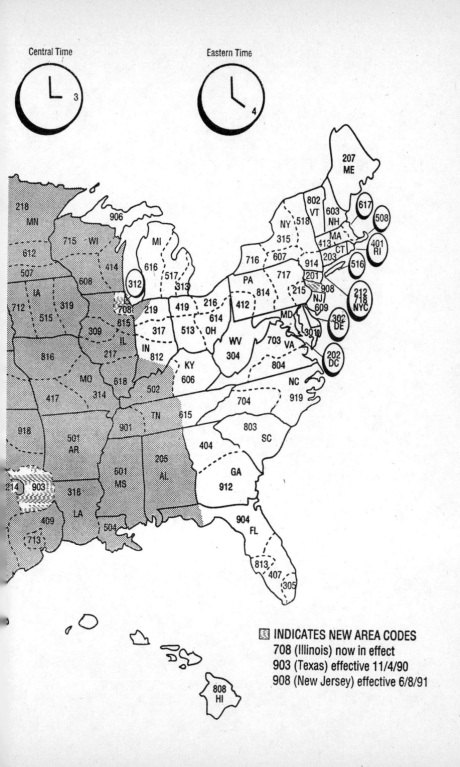

Central Time

Eastern Time

207
ME

218
MN

906

802
VT

603
NH

617

518

508

NY

315

MA

413

401
RI

715   WI

MI

716

607

203

CT

612

507

616

517

914

516

608

313

312

PA

717

201

212
718
NYC

712

319

708

219

419

216

412

814

215

908

NJ

609

302
DE

515

614

309

IA

317

513

OH

WV

304

703

VA

301

MD

816

217

IN

812

KY

606

804

202
DC

618

502

NC

417

314

MO

TN

615

704

919

918

901

803

SC

501
AR

404

214   903

318

601
MS

205
AL

GA
912

409

LA

504

904
FL

713

813

407

305

808
HI

INDICATES NEW AREA CODES
708 (Illinois) now in effect
903 (Texas) effective 11/4/90
908 (New Jersey) effective 6/8/91

1

Introduction

Bed and Breakfast is the popular lodging alternative to hotel high rises and motel monotony. B&Bs are either private residences where the owners rent spare bedrooms to travelers, or small, family-operated inns offering a special kind of warm, personal hospitality. Whether large or small, B&Bs will make you feel more like a welcome guest than a paying customer.

The custom of opening one's home to travelers dates back to the earliest days of Colonial America. Hotels and inns were few and far between in those days, and wayfarers relied on the kindness of strangers to provide a bed for the night. Which is why, perhaps, there is hardly a Colonial-era home in the mid-Atlantic states that does not boast: "George Washington Slept Here!"

During the Depression, the tourist home provided an economic advantage to both the traveler and the host. Travelers always drove through the center of town; there were no superhighways to bypass local traffic. A house with a sign in the front yard reading "Tourists" or "Guests" indicated that a traveler could rent a room for the night and have a cup of coffee before leaving in the morning. The usual cost for this arrangement was $2. The money represented needed income for the proprietor as well as the opportunity to chat with an interesting visitor.

In the 1950s, the country guest house became a popular alternative to the costly hotels in resort areas. The host compensated for the lack of hotel amenities, such as private bathrooms, by providing comfortable bedrooms and bountiful breakfasts at a modest price. The visitors enjoyed the home-away-from-home atmosphere; the hosts were pleased to have paying houseguests.

The incredible growth in international travel that has occurred over the past 30 years has provided yet another stimulus. Millions of Americans now vacation annually in Europe, and travelers have become enchanted with the bed and breakfast concept so popular in England, Ireland, and other parts of the continent. In fact, many well-traveled Americans are delighted to learn that we "finally" have B&Bs here. But, as you now know, they were always here—just a rose by another name.

Bed and breakfasts are for

- **Parents of college kids:** Tuition is costly enough without the added expense of Parents' Weekends. Look for a B&B near campus.
- **Parents traveling with children:** A family living room, play room, or backyard is preferable to the confines of a motel room.
- **"Parents" of pets:** Many proprietors will allow your well-behaved darling to come, too. This can cut down on the expense and trauma of kenneling Fido.
- **Business travelers:** Being "on the road" can be lonely and expensive. It's so nice, after a day's work, to return to a home-away-from-home.
- **Women traveling alone:** Friendship and conversation are the natural ingredients of a guest house.
- **Skiers:** Lift prices are lofty, so it helps to save some money on lodging. Many mountain homes include home-cooked meals in your room rate.
- **Students:** A visit with a family is a pleasant alternative to camping or the local "Y."
- **Visitors from abroad:** Cultural exchanges are often enhanced by a host who can speak your language.
- **Carless travelers:** If you plan to leave the auto at home, it's nice to know that many B&Bs are convenient to public transportation. Hosts will often arrange to meet your bus, plane, or train for a nominal fee.
- **Schoolteachers and retired persons:** Exploring out-of-the-way places is fun and will save you money.
- **History buffs:** Many B&Bs are located in areas important to our country's past. A number have the distinction of being listed on the National Register of Historic Places.
- **Sports fans:** Tickets to championship games are expensive. A stay at a B&B helps to defray the cost of attending out-of-town events.
- **Antique collectors:** Many hosts have lovely personal collections, and nearby towns are filled with undiscovered antique shops.
- **House hunters:** It's a practical way of trying out a neighborhood.
- **Relocating corporate executives:** It's more comfortable to stay in a real home while you look for a permanent residence. Hosts will often give more practical advice than professional realtors.

- **Relatives of hospitalized patients:** Many B&Bs are located near major hospitals. Hosts will offer tea and sympathy when visiting hours are over.
- **Convention and seminar attendees:** Staying at a nearby B&B is less expensive than checking into a hotel.

And everyone else who has had it up to here with plastic motel monotony!

What It Is Like to Be a Guest in a B&B

The B&B descriptions provided in this book will help you choose the places that have the greatest appeal to you. A first-hand insight into local culture awaits you; imagine the advantage of arriving in New York City or San Francisco and having an insider to help you sidestep the tourist traps and direct you to that special restaurant or discount store. Or explore the countryside, where fresh air and home-cooked meals beckon. Your choice is as wide as the U.S.A.

Each bed and breakfast listed offers personal contact, a real advantage in unfamiliar environments. You may not have a phone in your room or a TV on the dresser. You may even have to pad down the hall in robe and slippers to take a shower, but you'll discover that little things count.

- In Williamsburg, Virginia, a visitor from Germany opted to stay at a B&B to help improve her conversational English. When the hostess saw that she was having difficulty understanding directions, she personally escorted her on a tour of Old Williamsburg.
- In Pennsylvania, the guests mistakenly arrived a week prior to their stated reservation date and the B&B was full. The hostess made a call to a neighbor who accommodated the couple. (By the way, the neighbor has now become a B&B host!)
- In New York City, a guest was an Emmy Award nominee and arrived with his tuxedo in need of pressing. The hostess pressed it; when he claimed his award over nationwide TV, he looked well groomed!

Expect the unexpected, such as a pot of brewed coffee upon your arrival, or fresh flowers on a nightstand. At the very least, count on our required standard of cleanliness and comfort. Although we haven't personally visited all of the places listed, they have all been highly recommended by chambers of commerce or former guests. We have either spoken to or corresponded with all of the proprietors; they are a friendly group of people who enjoy having visitors. They will do all in their power to make your stay memorable.

Our goal is to enable the traveler to crisscross the country and stay only at B&Bs along the way. To achieve this, your help is vital. Please take a moment to write us of your experiences; we will follow up on every suggestion. Your comments will serve as the yardstick by which we can measure the quality of our accommodations. For your convenience, an evaluation form is included at the back of this book.

Cost of Accommodations

Bed and Breakfast, in the purest sense, is a private home, often referred to as a "homestay," where the owners rent their spare bedrooms to travelers. These are the backbone of this book.

However, American ingenuity has enhanced this simple idea to include more spectacular homes, mansions, small inns, and intimate hotels. With few exceptions, the proprietor is the host and lives on the premises.

There is a distinction between B&B homestays and B&B inns. Inns are generally defined as a business and depend upon revenue from guests to pay expenses. They usually have six or more guest rooms, and may have a restaurant that is open to the public. The tariff at inns is usually higher than at a homestay because the owners must pay the mortgage, running expenses, and staff, whether or not guests come.

Whether plain or fancy, all B&Bs are based on the concept that people are tired of the plastic monotony of motels and are disappointed that even the so-called budget motels can be quite expensive. Travelers crave the personal touch, and they sincerely enjoy "visiting" rather than just "staying."

Prices vary accordingly. There are places listed in this book where lovely lodging may be had for as low as $10 a person a night, and others that feature an overnight stay with a gourmet breakfast in a canopied bed for $85. Whatever the price, if you see the sign ✪, it means that the B&B has guaranteed its rates through 1991 to holders of this book, so be sure to mention it when you call or write! (If there is a change in ownership, the guarantee may not apply. Please notify us in writing if any host fails to honor the guaranteed rate.)

Accommodations vary in price depending upon the locale and the season. Peak season usually refers to the availability of skiing in winter and water sports in summer; in the Sunbelt states, winter months are usually the peak season. Some B&Bs require a two-night weekend minimum during peak periods, and three nights on holiday weekends. Off-season rate schedules are usually reduced. Resorts and major cities are generally more expensive than out-of-the-way places. However, B&Bs are always less expensive than hotels and motels of equivalent caliber in the same area. A weekly rate is usually less expensive than a daily rate. Special reductions are sometimes given to families (occupying two rooms) or senior citizens. Whenever reduced rates are available, you will find this noted in the individual listings.

Meals

Breakfast: *Continental* refers to fruit or juice, rolls, and a hot beverage. Many hosts pride themselves on home-baked breads, homemade preserves, as well as imported teas and cakes, so their Continental breakfast may be quite deluxe. Several hosts have regular jobs outside the home, so you may have to adjust your schedule to theirs. A "full" breakfast includes fruit, cereal and/or eggs, breakfast meats, breads, and a hot beverage. The table is set family-style and is often the highlight of a B&B's hospitality. Either a Continental breakfast or full breakfast is included in the room rate unless otherwise specified.

Other Meals: If listed as "available," you can be assured that the host takes pride in his or her cooking skills. The prices for lunch or dinner are usually reasonable but are not included in the quoted room rate unless clearly specified as "included."

Making Reservations

• Reservations are a MUST or you may risk missing out on the accommodations of your choice. Reserve *early* and confirm with a deposit equal to one night's stay. If you call to inquire about reservations, please remember the difference in time zones. When dialing outside of your area, remember to dial the digit "1" before the area code.

- Many individual B&Bs now accept charge cards. This information is indicated in the listings by the symbols MC for MasterCard, AMEX for American Express, etc. A few have a surcharge for this service, so inquire as to the policy.
- Cash or traveler's checks are the accepted method of paying for your stay. Be sure to inquire whether or not tax is included in the rates quoted so that you will know exactly how much your lodging will cost.
- Rates are based on single or double occupancy of a room as quoted. Expect that an extra person(s) in the room will be charged a small additional fee. Inquire when making your reservation what the charge will be.
- If a listing indicates that children or pets are welcome, it is expected that they will be well behaved. All of our hosts take pride in their homes and it would be unfair to subject them to circumstances in which their possessions might be abused or the other houseguests disturbed by an unruly child or animal.
- Please note that many hosts have their own resident pets. If you are allergic or don't care to be around animals, inquire before making a reservation.
- In homes where smoking is permitted, do check to see if it is restricted in any of the rooms. Most hosts object to cigars.
- Where listings indicate that social drinking is permitted, it usually refers to your bringing your own beverages. Most hosts will provide ice; many will allow you to chill mixers in the refrigerator, and others offer complimentary wine and snacks. A few B&B inns have licenses to sell liquor. Any drinking should not be excessive.
- If Yes is indicated in the listings for airport/station pickup, it means that the host will meet your plane, bus, or train for a fee.
- Feel free to request brochures and local maps so that you can better plan for your visit.
- Do try to fit in with the host's house rules. You are on vacation; he or she isn't!
- A reservation form is included at the back of this book for your convenience; just tear it out and sent it in to the B&B of your choice.

Cancellations

Cancellation policies vary from one B&B to another, so be sure to read the fine print on the reservation form. Many require a 15-day notice to refund the entire deposit, after which they will refund only if the room is rebooked. When a refund is due, most keep a processing fee and return the balance. A few keep the deposit and apply it to a future stay.

While these policies may seem harsh, please keep in mind that B&Bs are not hotels, which commonly overbook and where no-show guests can easily be replaced. Your host may have turned down a prospective guest, and may have bought special breakfast food in anticipation of your visit and should not be penalized. If you feel you've been unfairly treated in a cancellation situation, please do let us know.

B&B Reservation Services

There are many host families who prefer not to be individually listed in a book, and would rather have their houseguests referred by a coordinating agency. The organizations listed in this book are all members of the Tourist House Association. They all share our standards regarding the suitability of the host home as to cordiality, cleanliness, and comfort.

The majority do a marvelous job of matching host and guest according to age, interests, language, and any special require-ments. To get the best match, it is practical to give them as much time as possible to find the host home best tailored to your needs.

Many have prepared descriptive pamphlets describing the homes on their rosters, the areas in which the homes are located, and information regarding special things to see and do. *Send a self-addressed, stamped, business-size envelope to receive a descriptive directory by return mail along with a reservation form for you to complete.* When returning the form, you will be asked to select the home or homes listed in the brochure that most appeal to you. (The homes are usually given a code number for reference.) The required deposit should accompany your reservation. Upon receipt, the coordinator will make the reservation and advise you of the name, address, telephone number, and travel instructions for your host.

A few agencies prepare a descriptive directory and *include* the host's name, address, and telephone number so that you can contact the host and make your arrangements directly. They charge anywhere from $2 to $5 for the directory.

Several agencies are *membership* organizations, charging guests an annual fee ranging from $5 to $25 per person. Their descriptive directories are free to members and a few of them maintain toll-free telephone numbers for reservations.

Most reservation services have a specific geographic focus. The coordinators are experts in the areas they represent. They can often make arrangements for car rentals, theater tickets, and touring suggestions, and offer information in planning a trip best suited to your interests.

Most work on a commission basis with the host, and that fee is included in the room rates quoted in each listing. Some make a surcharge for a one-night stay; others require a two- or three-night minimum stay for holiday periods or special events. Some will accept a credit card for the reservation but the balance due must be paid to the host in cash or traveler's checks.

All of their host homes offer a Continental breakfast, and some may include a full breakfast.

Many reservation services in the larger cities have, in addition to the traditional B&Bs, a selection of apartments, condominiums, and houses *without hosts in residence*. This may be appealing to those travelers anticipating an extended stay in a particular area.

Statewide services are listed first in the section for each state. City or regionally based organizations are listed first under the heading for that area. For a complete description of their services, look them up under the city and state where they're based.

NOTE: When calling, do so during normal business hours (for that time zone), unless otherwise stated. Collect calls are not accepted.

2

How to Start Your Own B&B

What It's Like to Be a Host

Hosts are people who like the idea of accommodating travelers and sharing their home and the special features of their area with them. They are people who have houses too large for their personal needs and like the idea of supplementing their income by having people visit. For many, it's a marvelous way of meeting rising utility and maintenance costs. For young families, it is a way of buying and keeping that otherwise-too-large house, as well as a way of furnishing it, since many of the furnishings may be tax deductible. Another advantage is that many state and local governments have recognized the service that some host families perform. In browsing through this book you will note that some homes are listed on the National Historic Register. Some state governments allow owners of landmark and historical houses a special tax advantage if they are used for any business purpose. Check with the Historical Preservation Society in your state for details.

If you have bedrooms to spare, if you sincerely like having overnight guests, if your home is clean and comfortable, this is an opportunity to consider. It is a unique business because *you* set the time of the visit and the length of stay. (Guest houses are not boarding homes.) You invite the guests at *your* convenience, and the extras, such as meals, are entirely up to you. You can provide a cup of coffee, complete meals, or just a room and shared bath. Remember that your income may be erratic and should not be depended upon to pay for monthly bills. However, it can afford you some luxuries.

Although the majority of hosts are women, many couples are

finding pleasure in this joint venture. The general profile of a typical host is a friendly, outgoing, flexible person who is proud of his or her home and hometown. The following information and suggestions represent a guideline to consider in deciding whether becoming a B&B host is really for you.

There are no set rules for the location, type, or style of a B&B. Apartments, condos, farmhouses, town houses, beach houses, vacation cottages, houseboats, mansions, as well as the traditional one-family dwelling are all appropriate. The important thing is for the host to be on the premises. The setting may be urban, rural, or suburban, near public transportation or in the hinterlands. Location is only important if you want to have guests every night. Areas where tourism is popular, such as resort areas or major cities, are often busier than out-of-the-way places. However, if a steady stream of visitors is not that important or even desirable, it doesn't matter where you are. People will contact you if your rates are reasonable and if there is something to see and do in your area, or if it is near a major transportation route.

Setting Rates

Consider carefully four key factors in setting your rates: location, private versus shared bath, type of breakfast, and your home itself.

Location: If you reside in a traditional resort or well-touristed area, near a major university or medical center, or in an urban hub or gateway city, your rates should be at least 40% lower than those of the area's major motels or hotels. If you live in an out-of-the-way location, your rates must be extremely reasonable. If your area has a "season"—snow sports in winter, water sports in summer—offer off-season rates when these attractions are not available. Reading through this book will help you to see what is the going rate in a situation similar to yours.

The Bath: You are entitled to charge more for a room with private bath. If the occupants of two rooms share one bath, the rate should be less. If more than five people must share one bathroom, you may have complaints, unless your rates are truly inexpensive.

The Breakfast: Figure the approximate cost of your ingredients, plus something for your time. Allow about $1 to $2 for a Continental breakfast, $2 to $3 for a full American breakfast, and then *include* it in the rate.

Your Home: Plan on charging a fair and reasonable rate for a typical B&B home, one that is warm and inviting, clean and comfortable. If your home is exceptionally luxurious, with king-size beds, Jacuzzi baths, tennis courts, or hot tubs, you will find guests who are willing to pay a premium. If your home is over 75 years old, well restored, with lots of antiques, you may also be able to charge a higher rate.

The Three Bs—Bed, Breakfast, and Bath

The Bedroom: The ideal situation for a prospective host is the possession of a house too large for current needs. The children may be away at college most of the year or may have left permanently, leaving behind their bedrooms and, in some cases, an extra bath. Refurbishing these rooms does not mean refurnishing; an extraordinary investment need not be contemplated for receiving guests. Take a long, hard look at the room. With a little imagination and a little monetary outlay, could it be changed into a bedroom *you'd* be pleased to spend the night in? Check it out *before* you go any further. Are the beds comfortable? Is the carpet clean? Are the walls attractive? Do the curtains or shades need attention? Are there sturdy hangers in the closet? Would emptying the closet and bureau be an impossible task? Is there a good light to read by? A writing table and comfortable chair? Peek under the bed to see if there are dust balls or old magazines tucked away. While relatives and friends would "understand" if things weren't perfect, a paying guest is entitled to cleanliness and comfort.

Equip the guest bureau or dresser with a good mirror, and provide a comfortable chair and good reading light. The clothes closet should be free from your family's clothing and storage items, and stocked with firm, plastic hangers, a few skirt hangers, and some hooks. Sachet hung on the rod will chase musty odors. Provide room darkening shades or blinds on the windows. And, if your house is located on a busy street, it is wise to have your guest bedrooms in the rear. Paying guests are entitled to a good night's rest! If your tap water is not tasty, it is thoughtful to supply bottled water.

If the idea of sprucing up the room has you overwhelmed, forget the idea and continue to be a guest rather than a host! If, however, a little "spit and polish," replacement of lumpy mattresses, sagging springs, and freshening the room in general presents no problem, continue!

Mattresses should be firm, covered with a mattress pad, attractive linens, and bedspread. Although seconds are OK, good-quality linens are a wise investment, since cheap sheets tend to pill. Offer a selection of pillows of various firmnesses—a choice of down or fiberfill is the ultimate in consideration! Twin beds are often preferred, since many people do not wish to share a bed. Sofa beds are really not comfortable and should be avoided. Is there a bedside lamp and night table on each side of the bed? Bulbs should be at least 75 watts for comfortable reading. A luggage rack is convenient for guests and keeps the bedspread clean. Provide a varied assortment of books, current magazines in a rack, a local newspaper, and some information on what's doing in your town along with a map. If yours is a shared-bath accommodation, do provide a well-lit mirror and convenient electric outlet for makeup and shaving purposes. It will take the pressure off the bathroom! A fresh thermos of ice water and drinking glasses placed on an attractive dresser tray is always appreciated. Put it in the room while the guest is out to dinner, right next to the dish of hard candy or fruit. A fancy candlestick is a pretty accessory and a useful object in case of a power failure. Dresser drawers should be clean and lined with fresh paper. A sachet, flashlight, and a pad and pencil are thoughtful touches. For safety's sake, prohibit smoking in the bedroom. Besides, the odor of tobacco clings forever. Always spray the bedroom with air freshener a few minutes before the guest arrives. On warm or humid days, turn on the air conditioner as well.

From time to time sleep in each guest room yourself. It's the best test.

The Breakfast: Breakfast time can be the most pleasant part of a guest's stay. It is at the breakfast table with you and the other guests that suggestions are made as to what to see and do, and exchanges of experiences are enjoyed. From a guest's point of view, the only expected offering is what is known as a Continental breakfast, which usually consists of juice, roll, and coffee or tea.

Breakfast fare is entirely up to you. If you are a morning person who whips out of bed at the crack of dawn with special recipes for muffins dancing in your head, muffins to be drenched with your homemade preserves followed by eggs Benedict, an assortment of imported coffees or exotic teas—hop to it! You will play to a most appreciative audience. If, however, morning represents an awful intrusion on sleep, and the idea of talking to anyone before noon is difficult, the least you should do is to prepare the breakfast table the night before with the necessary mugs, plates, and silverware. Fill the electric coffee pot and leave instructions that the first one up should plug it in; you can even hook it up to a timer so that it will brew automatically!

Most of us fall somewhere in between these two extremes. Remember that any breakfast at "home" is preferable to getting dressed, getting into a car, and driving to some coffee shop. Whether you decide upon a Continental breakfast or a full American breakfast, consisting of juice or fruit, cereal or eggs, possibly bacon or sausage, toast, rolls, and coffee or tea, is up to you. It is most important that whatever the fare, it be included in your room rate. It is most awkward, especially after getting to know and like your guests, to present an additional charge for breakfast.

With so many of us watching calories, caffeine, and cholesterol, be prepared to offer unsweetened and/or whole grain breads, oat-bran cereals and muffins, and brewed decaf coffee or tea. It is also thoughtful to inquire about your guests' dietary restrictions and allergies. Whatever you serve, do have your table attractively set.

Some Suggestions

- Don't have a messy kitchen. If you have pets, make sure their food dishes are removed after they've eaten. If you have cats, make sure they don't walk along the counter tops, and be certain that litter boxes are cleaned without fail. Sparkling clean surroundings are far more important than the decor.
- Let guests know when breakfast will be served. Check to see if they have any allergies, diet restrictions, or dislikes. Vary the menu if guests are staying more than one night.
- Do offer one nonsweet bread for breakfast.
- Consider leaving a breakfast order sheet in each room with a request that it be returned before guests retire. It might read:

We serve breakfast between 7 AM and 10 AM. Please check your preference and note the time at which you plan to eat.

☐ Coffee ☐ Tea ☐ Decaf ☐ Milk ☐ Toast ☐ Muffins
☐ Sweet Rolls ☐ Orange Juice ☐ Tomato Juice ☐ Fruit Cup

The Bath: This really is the third B in B&B. If you are blessed with an extra bathroom for the exclusive use of a guest, that's super. If guests will have to share the facilities with others, that really presents no problem. If it's being shared with your family, the family must always be "last in line." Be sure that they are aware of the guest's importance; the guest, paying or otherwise, always comes first. No retainers, used Band-Aids, or topless toothpaste tubes are to be carelessly left on the sink. The tub, shower, floor, and toilet bowl are to be squeaky clean. The mirrors and chrome should sparkle, and a supply of toilet tissue, fresh soap, and unfrayed towels goes a long way in reflecting a high standard of cleanliness. Make sure that the grout between tiles is free of mildew and that the shower curtain is unstained; add nonskid tape to the tub. Cracked ceilings should be repaired. Paint should be free of chips, and if your bath is wallpapered, make certain no loose edges mar its beauty.

Although it is your responsibility to check out the bath at least twice a day, most guests realize that in a share-the-bath situation they should leave the room ready for the next person's use. It is a thoughtful reminder for you to leave tub cleanser, a cleaning towel or sponge, and bathroom deodorant handy for this purpose. A wastepaper basket, paper towels, and paper cups should be part of your supplies. Needless to say, your hot water and septic systems should be able to accommodate the number of guests you'll have without being overtaxed. Call the plumber to fix any clogged drains or dripping faucets. Make sure that there are enough towel bars and hooks to accommodate the towels of all guests. Extra bathroom touches:

- Use liquid soap dispensers in lieu of bar soap on the sink.
- Provide a place for guests' personal toilet articles; shelves add convenience and eliminate clutter.
- Give different colored towels to each guest.
- Supply each guest room with its own bath soap in a covered soap dish.
- Provide guests with one-size-fits-all terry robes.

The B&B Business

Money Matters: Before embarking upon any business, it's a good idea to discuss it with an accountant and possibly an attorney. Since you'll be using your home for a business enterprise there are things with which they are familiar that are important for you to know. For instance, you may want to incorporate, so find out what the pros and cons are. Ask about depreciation. Deductible business expenses may include refurbishing, furnishings, supplies, printing costs, postage, etc. An accountant will be able to guide you with a simple system of record keeping. Accurate records will help you analyze income and expense, and show if you are breaking even or operating at a profit or a loss.

Taxes: Contact your state department of taxation requesting specific written information regarding tax collection and payment schedules. Get a sales tax number from your county clerk. If you rent rooms less than 15 days a year, you need not report the B&B income on your federal return. Income after the fourteenth day is taxable, and you can take deductions and depreciation allowances against it. If the revenues from running the B&B are insignificant, you can call it "hobby income" and avoid taxes. However, you can't qualify as a business and may lose other tax advantages.

Record Keeping: Open a B&B checking account and use it to pay expenses and to deposit all income, including sales tax associated with the B&B. Write checks whenever possible for purchases; get dated receipts when you can. Estimate the cost of serving breakfast and multiply it by the number of guests you feed annually; keep track of extra expenses for household supplies and utilities.

The Case for Credit Cards: Many guests prefer to stay now and pay later; business travelers like the easy record keeping for their expense sheets. Even if you don't wish to accept them on a regular basis, credit cards give you the opportunity to take a deposit over the phone when there isn't time to receive one by mail. The cost is negligible, generally 4%.

If you do accept a last-minute reservation without a credit card number to guarantee it, make certain the caller understands that if they don't show up, and you have held the room for them, you will have lost a night's rent. You may also remind them that if they aren't there by a mutually agreed upon time, you may rent the room to someone else. Needless to say, it is equally important for you to remain at home to receive the guests or to be on hand for a phone call should they get lost en route to your home.

Insurance: It is important to call your insurance broker. Some homeowner policies have a clause covering "an occasional overnight paying guest." See if you will be protected under your existing coverage and, if not, what the additional premium would be. As a member of the THAA, you may participate in our group liability policy under the auspices of Brown, Schuck, Townshend, and Associates.

Every home should be equipped with smoke detectors and fire extinguishers. All fire hazards should be eliminated; stairways and halls should be well lit and kept free of clutter. If you haven't already done so, immediately post prominently the emergency numbers for the fire department, police, and ambulance service.

Safety Reminders: Equip guest bedrooms and bathrooms with nightlights. Keep a flashlight (in working order!) in each bedroom, in case of power failure. Bathrooms should have nonslip surfaces in the tub and shower, and hand-holds should be installed in bathtubs. Keep a well-stocked first aid kit handy and know how to use it. Learn the Heimlich Maneuver and CPR (cardiopulmonary resuscitation). Periodically test smoke detectors and fire extinguishers to make certain they are in working order.

Regulations: If you have read this far and are still excited about the concept of running a B&B, there are several steps to take at this point. As of this writing, there don't seem to be any specific laws governing B&Bs. Since guests are generally received on an irregular basis, B&Bs do not come under the same laws governing hotels and motels. And since B&Bs aren't inns where emphasis is on food rather than on lodging, no comparison can really be made in that regard either. As the idea grows, laws and regulations will probably be passed. Refer to the back of *Bed & Breakfast U.S.A.* to write to your state's office of tourism for information. The address and phone number are listed for your convenience. You might even call or write to a few B&Bs in your state and ask the host about his or her experience in this regard. Most hosts will be happy to give you the benefit of their experience, but keep in mind that they are busy people and it would be wise to limit your intrusion upon their time.

If you live in a traditional, residential area and you are the first in your neighborhood to consider operating a B&B, it would be prudent to examine closely the character of houses nearby. Do physicians, attorneys, accountants, or psychologists maintain offices in their residences? Do dressmakers, photographers, cosmeticians, or architects receive clients in their homes? These professions are legally accepted in the most prestigious communities as "customary house occupations." Bed and breakfast has been tested in many communities where the question was actually brought to court. In towns from La Jolla, California, to Croton-on-Hudson, New York, bed and breakfast has been approved and accepted.

Zoning boards are not always aware of the wide acceptance of the B&B concept. Possibly the best evidence that you could present to them is a copy of *Bed & Breakfast U.S.A.*, which indicates that it is an accepted practice throughout the entire country. It illustrates the caliber of the neighborhoods, the beauty of the homes, and the fact that many professionals are also hosts. Reassure the zoning board that you will accept guests only by advance reservation. You will not display any exterior signs to attract attention to your home. You will keep your home and grounds properly maintained, attractive, and in no way detract from the integrity of your neighborhood. You will direct guests to proper parking facilities and do nothing to intrude upon the privacy of your neighbors.

After all, there is little difference between the visit of a family friend and a B&B guest, because that is the spirit and essence of a B&B. Just as a friend would make prior arrangements to be a houseguest, so will a B&B guest make a reservation in advance. Neither would just drop in for an overnight stay. We are happy to share letters from hosts attesting to the high caliber, honesty, and integrity of B&B guests that come as a result of reading about their accommodations in this book. There are over 12,000 B&Bs extending our kind of hospitality throughout the United States, and the number is increasing geometrically every day.

You should also bring along a copy of *Bed & Breakfast U.S.A.* when you go to visit the local chamber of commerce. Most of them are enthusiastic, because additional visitors mean extra business for local restaurants, shops, theaters, and businesses.

This is a good time to inquire what it would cost to join the chamber of commerce.

The Name: The naming of your B&B is most important and will take some time and consideration because this is the moment when dreams become reality. It will be used on your brochures, stationery, and bills. (If you decide to incorporate, the corporation needs a name!) It should somehow be descriptive of the atmosphere you wish to convey.

Brochure: Once you have given a name to your house, design a brochure. The best ones include a reservation form and can be mailed to your prospective guests. The brochure should contain the name of your B&B, address, phone number, best time to call, your name, a brief description of your home, its ambience, a brief history of the house if it is old, the number of guest rooms, whether or not baths are shared, the type of breakfast served, rates, required deposit, minimum stay requirement if any, dates when you'll be closed, and your cancellation policy. Although widely used, the phrase "Rates subject to change without notice" should be avoided. Rather, state the specific dates when the rates will be valid. A deposit of one night's stay is acceptable, and the promise of a full refund if cancellation is received at least two weeks prior to arrival is typical. If you have reduced rates for a specific length of stay, for families, for senior citizens, etc., mention it.

The Rate Sheet should be a separate insert so that if rates change, the entire brochure need not be discarded. Mention your smoking policy. If you do allow smoking inside the house, do you reserve any bedrooms for nonsmokers? Don't forget to mention the ages of your children, and describe any pets in residence. If you don't accept a guest's pet, be prepared to supply the name, address, and phone number of a reliable local kennel.

If you can converse in a foreign language, say so, because many visitors from abroad seek out B&Bs; it's a marvelous plus to be able to chat in their native tongue. Include your policy regarding children, pets, or smokers, and whether you offer the convenience of a guest refrigerator or barbecue. It is helpful to include directions from a major route and a simple map for finding your home. It's a good idea to include a line or two about yourself and your interests, and do mention what there is to see and do in the area as well as proximity to any major university. A line drawing of your house is a good investment since the picture can be used not only on the brochure but on your stationery, postcards, and greeting cards as well. If you can't have this taken care of locally, write the Tourist House Association. We have a service that can handle it for you.

Take your ideas to a reliable printer for his professional guidance. Don't forget to keep the receipt for the printing bill since this is a business expense.

Confirmation Letter: Upon receipt of a paid reservation, do send out a letter confirming it. You can design a form letter and have it offset printed by a printer, since the cost of doing so is usually nominal. Include the dates of the stay; number of people expected; the rate, including tax; the cancellation policy; as well as explicit directions by car and, if applicable, by public transportation. A simple map reflecting the exact location of your home in relation to major streets and highways is most useful. It is a good idea to ask your guests to call you if they will be traveling and unavailable by phone for the week prior to their expected arrival. You might even want to include any of the house rules regarding smoking, pets, or whatever.

Successful Hosting

The Advantage of Hosting: The nicest part of being a B&B host is that you aren't required to take guests every day of the year. Should there be times when having guests would not be convenient, you can always say you're full and try to arrange an alternate date. But most important, keep whatever date you reserve. It is an excellent idea at the time reservations are accepted to ask for the name and telephone number of an emergency contact should you have to cancel unexpectedly. However, *never* have a guest come to a locked door. If an emergency arises and you cannot reach your prospective guests in time, do make arrangements for someone to greet them, and make alternate arrangements so that they can be accommodated.

House Rules: While you're in the thinking stage, give some thought to the rules you'd like your guests to adhere to. The last thing you want for you or your family is to feel uncomfortable in your own home. Make a list of House Rules concerning arrival and departure during the guests' stay, and specify when breakfast is served. If you don't want guests coming home too late, say so. Most hosts like to lock up at a certain hour at night, so arrange for an extra key for night owls. If that makes you uncomfortable, have a curfew on your House Rules list. If smoking disturbs you, confine the area where it's permitted.

Some guests bring a bottle of their favorite beverage and enjoy a drink before going out to dinner. Many hosts enjoy a cocktail hour too, and often provide cheese and crackers to share with guests. B&Bs cannot sell drinks to guests since this would require licensing. If you'd rather no drinks be consumed in your home, say so.

Many hosts don't mind accommodating a well-behaved pet. If you don't mind, or have pets of your own, discuss this with your guests before they pack Fido's suitcase. Your House Rules can even be included in your brochure. That way, both host and guest are aware of each other's likes and dislikes, and no hard feelings are made.

Entertaining: One of the most appealing features of being a guest at a B&B is the opportunity to visit in the evening with the hosts. After a day of sightseeing or business, it is most relaxing and pleasant to sit around the living room and chat. For many hosts, this is the most enjoyable part of having guests. However, if you are accommodating several people on a daily basis, entertaining can be tiring. Don't feel you'll be offending anyone by excusing yourself to attend to your own family or personal needs. The situation can be easily handled by having a room to which you can retreat, and offering your guests the living room, den, or other area for games, books, magazines, and perhaps the use of a television or bridge table. Most guests enjoy just talking to one another since this is the main idea of staying at a B&B.

The Telephone: This is a most important link between you and your prospective guests. As soon as possible, have your telephone number included under your B&B name in the white pages. It is a good idea to be listed in the appropriate section in your telephone directory yellow pages. If your home phone is used for a lot of personal calls, ask the local telephone company about call-waiting service, or think about installing a separate line for your B&B. If you are out a lot, give some thought to using a telephone answering device to explain your absence and time of return, and record the caller's message. There is nothing more frustrating to a prospective guest than to call and get a constant busy signal, or no answer at all. Request that the caller leave his or her name and address so that you can mail a reservation form. This will help eliminate the necessity of having to return long-distance calls. If the caller wants further information, he or she will call again at the time you said you'd be home.

B&B guests don't expect a phone in the guest room. However, there are times when they might want to use your phone for a long-distance call. In your House Rules list, suggest that any such calls be charged to their home telephone. Business travelers often have telephone charge cards for this purpose. In either case, you should keep a telephone record book and timer near your instrument. Ask the caller to enter the city called, telephone number, and length of call. Thus, you will have an accurate record should a charge be inadvertently added to your bill. Or, if you wish, you can add telephone charges to the guest bill. A telephone operator will quote the cost of the per-minute charge throughout the country for this purpose.

Maid Service: If you have several guest rooms and bathrooms, you may find yourself being a chambermaid as part of the business. Naturally, each guest gets fresh linens upon arrival. If a guest stays up to three days, it isn't expected that bed linen be changed every day. What is expected is that the room be freshened and the bath be cleaned and towels replaced every day. If you don't employ a full-time maid you may want to investigate the possibility of hiring a high school student on a part-time basis to give you a hand with the housekeeping. Many guests, noticing the absence of help, will voluntarily lend a hand, although they have the right to expect some degree of service, particularly if they are paying a premium rate.

Keys: A great many hosts are not constantly home during the day. Some do "hosting" on a part-time basis, while involved with regular jobs. There are times when even full-time hosts have to be away during the day. If guests are to have access to the house while you are not on the premises, make extra keys and attach them to an oversize key chain. It is also wise to take a key deposit of $50 simply to assure return of the key. Let me add that in the 11 years of my personal experience, as well as in the opinions of other hosts, B&B guests are the most honest people you can have. No one has ever had even a washcloth stolen, let alone the family treasures. In fact, it isn't unusual for the guest to leave a small gift after a particularly pleasant visit. On the other hand, guests are sometimes forgetful and leave belongings behind. For this reason it is important for you to have their names and addresses so that you can return their possessions. They will expect to reimburse you for the postage.

Registering Guests: You should keep a regular registration ledger for the guest to complete before checking in. The information should include the full name of each guest, home address, phone number, business address and telephone, and auto license number. It's a good idea to include the name and phone number of a friend or relative in case of an emergency. This information will serve you well for other contingencies, such as the guest leaving some important article behind, an unpaid long-distance phone call, or the rare instance of an unpaid bill. You may prefer to have this information on your guest bill, which should be designed as a two-part carbon form. You will then have a record and the guest has a ready receipt. (Receipts are very important to business travelers!)

Settling the Bill: The average stay in a B&B is two nights. A deposit equal to one night's lodging is the norm, when to collect the balance is up to you. Most guests pay upon leaving, but if they leave so early that the settling of the bill at that time is inconvenient, you can request the payment the previous night. You might want to consider the convenience of accepting a major credit card, but contact the sponsoring company first to see what percentage of your gross is expected for this service. If you find yourself entertaining more business visitors than vacationers, it might be something you should offer. Most travelers are aware that cash or traveler's checks are the accepted modes of payment. Accepting a personal check is rarely risky, but again, it's up to you. You might include your preference in your brochure.

Other Meals: B&B means that only breakfast is served. If you enjoy cooking and would like to offer other meals for a fee, make sure that you investigate the applicable health laws. If you have to install a commercial kitchen, the idea might be too expensive for current consideration. However, allowing guests to store fixings for a quick snack or to use your barbecue can be a very attractive feature for families traveling with children or for people watching their budget. If you can offer this convenience, be sure to mention it in your brochure. (And be sure to add a line to your House Rules that the guest is expected to clean up.) Some hosts keep an extra guest refrigerator on hand for this purpose.

It's an excellent idea to keep menus from your local restaurants on hand. Try to have a good sampling, ranging from moderately priced to expensive dining spots, and find out if reservations are required. Your guests will always rely heavily upon your advice and suggestions. After all, when it comes to your town, you're the authority! It's also a nice idea to keep informed of local happenings that might be of interest to your visitors. A special concert at the university or a local fair or church supper can add an extra dimension to their visit. If parents are visiting with young children they might want to have dinner out without them; try to have a list of available baby-sitters. A selection of guide books covering your area is also a nice feature.

The Guest Book: These are available in most stationery and department stores, and it is important that you buy one. It should contain designated space for the date, the name of the guest, home address, and a blank area for the guest's comments. They generally sign the guest book before checking out. The guest book is first of all a permanent record of who came and went. It will give you an idea of what times during the year you were busiest and which times were slow. Second, it is an easy way to keep a mailing list for your Christmas cards and future promotional mailings. You will also find that thumbing through it in years to come will recall some very pleasant people who were once strangers but now are friends.

Advertising: Periodically distribute your brochures to the local university, college, and hospital, since out-of-town visitors always need a place to stay. Let your local caterers know of your existence since wedding guests are often from out of town. If you have a major corporation in your area, drop off a brochure at the personnel office. Even visiting or relocating executives and salespeople enjoy B&Bs. Hotels and motels are sometimes overbooked; it wouldn't hurt to leave your brochure with the manager for times when there's no room for their last-minute guests. Local residents sometimes have to put up extra guests, so it's a good idea to take an ad out in your local school or church newspaper. The cost is usually minimal. Repeat this distribution process from time to time so that you can replenish the supply of brochures.

Check the back of this book for the address of your state tourist office. Write to them, requesting inclusion in any brochures listing B&Bs in the state.

The best advertising is being a member of the Tourist House Association since all member B&Bs are fully described in this book, which is available in bookstores, libraries, and B&Bs throughout the United States and Canada. In addition, it is natural for THAA members to recommend one another when guests inquire about similar accommodations in other areas. The most important reason for keeping your B&B clean, comfortable, and cordial is that we are all judged by what a guest experiences in any individual Tourist House Association home. The best publicity will come from your satisfied guests, who will recommend your B&B to their friends.

Additional Suggestions

Extra Earnings: You might want to consider a few ideas for earning extra money in connection with being a host. If guests consistently praise your muffins and preserves, you might sell attractively wrapped extras as take-home gifts. If you enjoy touring, you can plan and conduct a special outing, off the beaten tourist track, for a modest fee. In major cities, you can do such things as acquiring tickets for theater, concert, or sports events. A supply of *Bed & Breakfast U.S.A.* for sale to guests is both a source of income and gives every THAA member direct exposure to the B&B market. Think about offering the use of your washer and dryer. You may, if you wish, charge a modest fee to cover the service. Guests who have been traveling are thrilled to do their wash or have it done for them "at home" rather than wasting a couple of hours at the laundromat.

Several hosts tell me that a small gift shop is often a natural offshoot of a B&B. Items for sale might include handmade quilts, pillows, potholders, and knitted items. One host has turned his hobby of woodworking into extra income. He makes lovely picture frames, napkin rings, and footstools that many guests buy as souvenirs to take home. If you plan to do this, check with the Small Business Administration to inquire about such things as a resale license and tax collection; a chamber of commerce can advise in this regard.

Transportation: While the majority of B&B guests arrive by car, there are many who rely on public transportation. Some hosts, for a modest fee, are willing to meet arriving guests at airports, train depots, or bus stations. Do be knowledgeable about local transportation schedules in your area, and be prepared to give explicit directions for your visitors' comings and goings. Have phone numbers handy for taxi service, as well as information on car rentals.

Thoughtful Touches: Guests often write to tell us of their experiences at B&Bs as a result of learning about them through this book. These are some of the special touches that made their visit special: fresh flowers in the guest room; even a single flower in a bud vase is pretty. One hostess puts a foil-wrapped piece of candy on the pillow before the guest returns from dinner. A small decanter of wine and glasses, or a few pieces of fresh fruit in a pretty bowl on the dresser are lovely surprises. A small sewing kit in the bureau is handy. Offer guests the use of your iron and ironing board, rather than having them attempt to use the bed or dresser. Writing paper and envelopes in the desk invite the guest to send a quick note to the folks at home. If your house sketch is printed on it, it is marvelous free publicity. A pre-bed cup of tea for adults and cookies and milk for children are always appreciated.

By the way, keep a supply of guest-comment cards in the desk, both to attract compliments as well as to bring to your attention the flaws in your B&B that should be corrected.

Join the Tourist House Association: If you are convinced that you want to be a host, and have thoroughly discussed the pros and cons with your family and advisers, complete and return the membership application found at the back of this book. Our dues are $25 annually. The description of your B&B will be part of the next edition of *Bed & Breakfast U.S.A.*, as well as in the interim supplement between printings. Paid-up members receive a complimentary copy of *Bed & Breakfast U.S.A.* You will also receive the THAA's newsletter; regional seminars and conferences are held occasionally and you might enjoy attending. And, as an association, we will have clout should the time come when B&B becomes a recognized industry.

Affiliating with a B&B Reservation Agency: Over 122 agencies are listed in *Bed & Breakfast U.S.A.* If you do not care to advertise your house directly to the public, consider joining one in your area. Membership and reservation fees, as well as the degree of professionalism, vary widely from agency to agency, so do check carefully.

Prediction of Success: Success should not be equated with money alone. If you thoroughly enjoy people, are well organized, enjoy sharing your tidy home without exhausting yourself, then the idea of receiving compensation for the use of an otherwise dormant bedroom will be a big plus. Your visitors will seek relaxing, wholesome surroundings, and unpretentious hosts who open their hearts as well as their homes. Being a B&B host or guest is an exciting, enriching experience.

3

B&B Recipes

The recipes that follow are not to be found in standard cookbooks. Some are B&B host originals, and the measurements are sometimes from the school of "a smidgen of this," "according to taste," and "till done." But they all indicate the host's desire to pamper guests with something special. The most important ingredient is the heartful of love that is as unmeasured as the handful of flour.

We had an overwhelming response to our request for host-contributed favorite breakfast recipes. Although we could not publish them all this time, we will use most of them in future editions. The following represent, as much as possible, regional or ethnic recipes that impart the flavor and variety of B&Bs across the country.

BREADS AND CAKES

Any Fruit Coffee Cake

4 c. chopped apples, apricots, peaches, pineapples, blueberries, or raspberries
1 c. water
2 tbsp. lemon juice
1½ c. sugar
⅓ c. cornstarch

3 c. flour
1 c. sugar
1 tbsp. baking powder
1 tsp. cinnamon

¼ tsp. mace
1 tsp. salt
1 c. butter/margarine
2 slightly beaten eggs
1 c. milk
1 tsp. vanilla

Topping
½ c. sugar
½ c. flour
¼ c. butter
½ c. walnuts

In covered saucepan combine and simmer fruit and water for five minutes. Stir in lemon juice. Stir sugar and cornstarch slowly into fruit mixture; cook, stirring continuously until mixture thickens. Cool. Add and stir together flour, sugar, baking powder, cinnamon, mace, and salt. Cut in butter until mixture is crumbly. Combine eggs, milk, and vanilla, and add to flour mixture and blend. Spread half the batter into one or two pans. Spread fruit mixture over batter. Spread rest of batter over fruit. Combine first three topping ingredients until crumbly, then add nuts and sprinkle over batter. Bake at 350° for 45 to 50 minutes in a 13" × 9" × 2" pan, or 40 to 45 minutes in two 8" × 8" × 2" pans. Cool and remove from pans.

Isaiah B. Hall House, Dennis, Massachusetts

Apple Phyllo Tart

6 sheets phyllo dough
¼ c. unsalted butter, melted
2 apples, peeled, cored, and sliced
  into eighths
2 tbsp. sugar
2 tbsp. butter
Dash of nutmeg or cinnamon

Filling
¾ c. toasted hazelnuts
½ c. sugar
2 tbsp. butter
1 egg

Sauté the apples in the butter and sugar. Add a dash of freshly grated nutmeg (or cinnamon). Set aside. To prepare filling: in food processor, put sugar and hazelnuts in work bowl and process until well blended. Add butter and egg, process until smooth and creamy. Set aside. Place 1 sheet of phyllo dough in a tart pan and brush on melted butter. Continue in this fashion until you have used all the sheets of dough. Spoon nut filling into tart pan and then arrange sautéed apples on top. Fold phyllo edges over top and brush on butter. Bake at 325° for 25 minutes or until golden brown. Sift powdered sugar on top when cool.

The Carter House, Eureka, California

Cranberry Coffee Cake

½ c. margarine
1 c. sugar
2 eggs
1 c. sour cream
1 tsp. vanilla

1 tsp. baking powder
1 tsp. baking soda
½ c. flour
16 oz. cooked whole cranberries,
  canned or homemade

Cream margarine and sugar. Add eggs, one at a time, then sour cream and vanilla. Beat well. Add dry ingredients and mix well. Put ½ batter into greased tube pan. Spoon cranberries on top. Pour remaining batter and spoon more berries on top. Bake at 375° for 45 minutes. May be topped with a mixture of powdered sugar, warm water, and almond flavoring.

The Marlborough, Woods Hole, Massachusetts

Cream Cheese Braid

1 c. sour cream
½ c. sugar
1 tsp. salt
½ c. butter
2 pkg. dry yeast
½ c. water
2 eggs, beaten
4 c. bread flour

Cream Cheese Filling
2 8-oz. packages cream cheese, softened
¾ c. sugar
1 egg, beaten
⅛ tsp. salt
2 tsp. vanilla

Glaze
2 c. powdered (10X) sugar
4 tbsp. milk (maybe less)
2 tsp. vanilla

Heat sour cream over low heat. Stir in sugar, salt, and butter, and cool to lukewarm. In a large bowl, sprinkle yeast over the water, stirring well to dissolve. Add sour cream mixture, eggs, and flour. Mix well. Cover tightly and refrigerate overnight. Divide dough into 4 equal parts. On a well-floured work surface, roll each into a 12″ × 18″ rectangle, flouring work surface well. Make cream cheese filling: blend cheese and sugar together; add remaining ingredients and mix well. Spread one-fourth of the filling onto each rectangle and then roll up, jelly roll fashion, starting with long side. Pinch edges together, fold ends under slightly, and place seam side down on greased baking sheet. Slit each roll at 1″ intervals, ⅔ through dough, to resemble braid. Cover and let rise for 1 hour or more until double in size. Bake at 375° for 12 to 15 minutes. Combine glaze ingredients in small bowl and mix until smooth. Spread glaze while bread is still hot. May be frozen or refrigerated.

The Graustein Inn, Knoxville, Tennessee

Grandma Nettie's Bread Pudding

4 kaiser rolls or half-loaf challah
4 eggs, beaten
½ c. golden raisins
1 tart apple, grated
5 tsp. cinnamon sugar

1 quart milk
6 c. corn flakes
½ c. sugar
1½ tsp. vanilla
boiling and cold water

Soak bread in water and cover. Pour boiling water over raisins and cover. Squeeze water from bread and add eggs. Add sugar, milk, corn flakes, grated apple, and vanilla. Drain raisins and add. Mix together. Spread into 9″ × 13″ well-greased baking pan. Sprinkle with cinnamon sugar and bake for one hour at 350°. Serve warm with sweet cream.

A Bit o' the Apple, New York City

Plum Nut Bread

1 c. butter
1 tsp. vanilla
3 c. flour
1 tsp. cream of tartar
¾ c. plain yogurt
2 c. diced purple or prune plums in
    ½″ pieces

1 c. chopped walnuts
2 c. sugar
4 eggs
1 tsp. salt
½ tsp. baking soda
1 tsp. grated lemon rind

Cream butter with sugar and vanilla until fluffy. Add eggs, one at a time; beat after each egg. Sift flour, salt, cream of tartar, and baking soda. Blend yogurt and lemon rind. Add to creamed mixture, alternating with dry ingredients. Stir until well blended. Add plums and nuts, mix. Place in 2 greased and floured bread pans. Bake at 350°, 50 to 55 minutes, or until done. Loosen sides of bread from pan with a knife and let cool 10 minutes in pan before turning out.

The Colonial House, Weston, Vermont

Apple Bread

½ c. butter, softened
1 c. brown sugar
2 eggs
3 tbsp. vanilla yogurt
1 tsp. vanilla

1 tsp. baking powder
1 tsp. baking soda
½ tsp. cinnamon
1¾ c. unbleached flour
2 medium apples, unpeeled

Cream butter and sugar; beat in eggs. Stir in yogurt and vanilla. In a separate bowl combine flour, baking powder, baking soda, cinnamon. Gradually add to butter mixture. Do not peel apples! Slice thinly and gently stir into batter. Spoon into greased 9" × 5" × 3" loaf pan. Bake at 350° for one hour.

Applewood Manor, Asheville, North Carolina

Vermont Honey Loaf

1½ c. flour
½ c. brown sugar
½ tsp. salt
½ tsp. baking powder
1 tsp. baking soda
1 tsp. cinnamon

¼ tsp. cloves
½ c. honey, mixed with 1 tbsp. hot water
1 tbsp. molasses
½ c. buttermilk
1 egg

Mix all ingredients together until "satiny." Pour into greased bread pan. Bake at 325° for one hour. Slice and toast before serving.

The Little Lodge at Dorset, Dorset, Vermont

Zucchini Bread

3 eggs
1¼ c. oil
1½ c. sugar
1 tsp. vanilla extract
2 c. grated, unpeeled, raw zucchini
2 c. flour
2 tsp. baking soda

1 tsp. baking powder
1 tsp. salt
1 tsp. cinnamon
½ tsp. cloves
¼ tsp. nutmeg
1 c. raisins
1 c. walnuts (optional)

Preheat oven to 350°. Butter five miniloaf pans. Beat eggs, oil, sugar, and vanilla until light and thick. Fold grated zucchini into egg/oil mixture. Sift dry ingredients; stir into zucchini mixture. Fold in raisins and nuts. Pour batter into pans. Bake for 1¼ hours. Cool slightly. Remove and cool completely on racks. Serve with butter, marmalade butter, or whipped cream cheese.

The Kingsleigh, Southwest Harbor, Maine

EGGS AND CASSEROLES

Apple-Sausage Ring

2 lbs. bulk sausage, cooked and
   drained
2 eggs, slightly beaten
½ c. milk

1½ c. herb stuffing
¼ c. minced onion
1 c. apples, pared and finely chopped

Preheat oven to 350°. Combine sausage, eggs, milk, stuffing,
onion, and apples. Mix thoroughly and press into greased mold.
Bake 1 hour. This can be made the day before and partially
baked for 30 minutes. Finish baking before serving. Serves 8 to
10.

The Oakwood Inn, Raleigh, North Carolina

Four Cheese and Herb Quiche

1 10″ partially baked quiche shell
¾ c. sharp cheddar cheese, shredded
¾ c. Swiss cheese, shredded
¾ c. Jack or Mozzarella cheese,
   shredded
½ c. ricotta or cottage cheese
4 eggs

1 tbsp. fresh, or 1 tsp. dried
   marjoram
1 tbsp. fresh, or 1 tsp. dried thyme
1 tbsp. fresh, or 1 tsp. dried dill or
   basil
¼ c. parsley, minced
1 c. half-and-half

Toss together shredded cheese and place in pie shell. *Optional:*
add 1 cup chopped, cooked asparagus, broccoli or carrots on top
of cheese. Beat together ricotta (or cottage) cheese, eggs,
marjoram, thyme, dill (or basil), parsley, and half-and-half. Pour
over cheese and vegetables. Bake at 400° for 35 to 45 minutes
until golden and set. Makes 8 servings.

Corner Oak Manor, Asheville, North Carolina

Chili Cheese Casserole

4 eggs
¼ c. flour
½ tsp. baking powder
1½ tsp. dry mustard
1 c. cottage cheese

1 c. Monterey Jack cheese, shredded
1 c. cheddar cheese, shredded
¼ c. margarine, melted
1 4-oz. can chopped green chilies

Beat eggs. Add dry ingredients and beat well. Blend in
remaining ingredients. Batter will be lumpy. Lightly grease

casserole dish and bake at 350° for 25 to 35 minutes, or until center is firm and top is nicely browned.

La Posada de Chimayó, Chimayó, New Mexico

Mel's Asparagus Cordon Bleu

16 fresh asparagus spears	¼ tsp. black pepper
4 slices Swiss cheese	1 c. flour
4 slices boiled ham	2 eggs, beaten
3 c. fine bread crumbs	½ c. butter, melted
3 tbsp. parsley	

Top each ham slice with a slice of cheese, then 4 asparagus spears. Wrap ham and cheese around asparagus and trim protruding ends of asparagus to fit. Combine bread crumbs with parsley and pepper. Dredge each ham/cheese/asparagus roll in flour, pressing together. Dip each in egg, then bread crumbs. Sauté in melted butter at medium heat for 4 minutes each side, or until golden brown. Serve at once. Top with hollandaise sauce if desired.

Tide Watch Inn, Waldoboro, Maine

Pain Perdue (Custard-Soaked French Toast)

Custard

4 eggs	8 oz. orange marmalade
2 c. milk	⅓ c. orange juice concentrate
⅓ c. sugar	½ oz. brandy extract

Cut French bread into 1" thick slices and place in flat pan. Mix custard ingredients together and cover bread slices with mixture. Refrigerate overnight, turning once. Bake in an electric skillet at low temperature (about 225°) for one hour, turning after 30 minutes. Serve with maple syrup or orange cream.

Orange Cream

Beat together until thick:

1 c. heavy cream	⅓–½ c. sugar
⅓ c. orange juice concentrate	

Palmer House Inn, Falmouth, Massachusetts

Green Eggs and Ham

1 bell pepper, thinly sliced
½ onion, sliced
1 clove garlic, sliced
⅓ lb. sliced prosciutto ham, to taste

7 eggs, beaten
3 tbsp. fresh pesto
grated Parmesan cheese, to taste

Sauté pepper, onion, and garlic in frying pan. Add ham and eggs. When eggs begin to set, add pesto and Parmesan cheese. Cook eggs until desired consistency. Serve with more Parmesan cheese, a bit of sour cream, and tomato garnish. Toast Dr. Seuss with fresh orange juice. Serves 4 to 5.

Road's End at Poso Creek, Posey, California

Shaw Casserole

1 c. hot cooked grits
1 box Jiffy cornbread mix
4 eggs, beaten
2 lbs. hot bulk sausage, cooked, drained

1 c. grated cheese
1¾ c. hot milk
1 stick butter
salt and pepper to taste

Mix all ingredients. Layer sausage and grits mixture; top with cheese. Bake 45 minutes at 325°.

Shaw House, Georgetown, South Carolina

Smoked Salmon Crêpes

3 eggs
water
⅛ tsp. cream of tartar
butter

4 oz. smoked salmon
¼ c. sour cream
¼ small onion, chopped
salt and pepper, to taste

Crêpes

Combine eggs with 1 tbsp. water and cream of tartar. Butter a crêpe pan, and heat until hot. Place 1 tbsp. egg batter into pan and cook until crêpe is done on one side (about 1 minute). Turn and cook other side for about ½ minute. Remove from pan and keep warm. Continue with rest of batter.

Filling

In a food processor, process salmon, sour cream, onion, salt, and pepper until smooth. Place about 1 tbsp. of filling in center of crêpe, pull crêpe up around filling and tie with a blanched chive stem. Makes 8 crêpes, to serve 4.

Carter House, Eureka, California

Seafood-Stuffed Eggs

8 eggs, hard-boiled
6-oz. can crabmeat, drained and
  flaked
¼ c. sour cream
1 tsp. lemon juice
Dash hot pepper sauce
4 oz. mushrooms, sliced
½ c. butter
⅓ c. flour

⅛ tsp. pepper
⅛–¼ tsp. salt
2 c. milk
½ c. chicken broth
¼–½ c. cooking sherry
1 c. fresh or frozen shrimp, thawed
2-oz. jar sliced pimiento, drained
½ c. dry bread crumbs

Preheat oven to 350°. Shell and halve eggs lengthwise. Remove yolks. Combine crabmeat, sour cream, lemon juice, and hot pepper sauce with yolks in a small bowl and blend well. Fill egg white halves with yolk mixture. In a saucepan over medium heat, sauté mushrooms in butter. Stir in flour, pepper, and salt. Cook 1 minute, stirring constantly, until smooth and bubbly. Gradually stir in milk, chicken broth, and sherry. Cook over medium heat until slightly thickened and bubbly, stirring constantly. Stir in shrimp and pimiento. Spoon about 1 cup sauce into a 12″ × 8″ baking pan. Arrange eggs over sauce. Spoon remaining sauce over eggs. In a small bowl combine 2 tbsp. melted butter and dry bread crumbs. Sprinkle evenly over eggs. Bake for 20 to 25 minutes at 350°, or until bubbly. Let stand 5 minutes before serving. Serves 8.

Casa de Flores, San Clemente, California

MUFFINS

Bran Muffins

½ package All-Bran cereal, crushed
2 c. honey
5 c. unbleached white flour or
  combined whole wheat
5 tsp. baking soda

1 tsp. salt
3 tsp. cinnamon
4 eggs, beaten
1 c. vegetable oil
3 c. buttermilk

Combine first 6 ingredients in large bowl. Mix. Add remaining ingredients. Mix. Bake in preheated oven 15 to 20 minutes at 375°. Store in tight container for up to 6 weeks. Makes about 60 muffins.

Watercourse Way, South Strafford, Vermont

Hearty Blueberry Muffins

1½ c. unsifted all-purpose flour
½ c. unsifted whole wheat flour
½ c. brown sugar, packed
1 tbsp. baking powder
½ tsp. salt
½ tsp. ground cinnamon

1 c. fresh or frozen (unthawed) blueberries
½ c. (1 stick) butter, melted
½ c. milk
2 large eggs
1 tsp. vanilla

Preheat oven to 425°. Grease 12 muffin cups (or use muffin papers). Makes about a dozen. Combine all dry ingredients in a bowl and blend well. In a separate small bowl, toss 1 tablespoon of the dry ingredients with berries. Cool melted butter a little, then add milk, eggs, and vanilla, and stir. Add wet mixture to dry mixture and stir until just moist. Stir in berries. Spoon batter into muffin cups and sprinkle sugar on top. Bake about 15 minutes until brown on top.

White Lace Inn, Sturgeon Bay, Wisconsin

Jalapeño Muffins

3 c. corn bread mix
2½ c. milk
½ c. salad oil
3 eggs, beaten
1 large onion, grated
2 tbsp. sugar

½ c. finely chopped peppers
1½ c. sharp cheese, shredded
¼ lb. bacon, fried and crumbled
¼ c. chopped pimientoes
½ clove garlic, crushed

Mix first four ingredients, then add remainder. Bake in heavily greased or lined muffin tins. Bake at 400° for approximately 35 minutes. (Yields 4 dozen muffins; freezes well.) Variation for supper use: Decrease milk by ¼ cup and add 2 cups cream-style corn.

Betty Hyde, Dallas, Texas

Pookie Muffins

Sift together:

2 c. all-purpose flour
2 c. whole wheat flour
4 tsp. baking soda

1 tsp. salt
4 tsp. ground cinnamon

Combine in a large bowl:

6 eggs, beaten
¾ c. sugar
¾ c. brown sugar

1 c. buttermilk
1 c. vegetable oil
2 tsp. vanilla

Slowly stir dry ingredients into egg mixture (it will be lumpy). Fold in gently the following fruit mixture:

3 c. shredded apple
3 c. shredded carrot
1½ c. shredded coconut

1 c. nuts, chopped
1 c. dates, chopped
1 tbsp. grated orange rind

Spoon batter into greased muffin tins. Bake at 375° for 15 to 20 minutes. Yield: 4 dozen muffins; they freeze well.

Babbling Brook Inn, Santa Cruz, California

Peach Mountain Muffins

2 c. flour
⅓ c. brown sugar
1 tbsp. baking powder

¼ tsp. baking soda
⅛ tsp. nutmeg
¼ tsp. salt

Stir together in bowl; make well in center.

Combine:

1 egg
¼ c. cooking oil

1 c. chopped peaches (fresh, frozen, or canned)

Add peach mixture all at once to flour mixture. Stir until just moistened. Spoon into greased muffin pan. Temperature: 400°. Bake: 20 to 25 minutes. Yield: 12 muffins.

The Bayberry Inn B&B, Peebles, Ohio

Popovers

2 eggs
1 c. milk

1 c. flour
Dash salt

Grease a 12-cup muffin tin and place in freezer to chill. Mix batter; it will be lumpy. Fill muffin cups approximately three-quarters full. Put in cold oven. Turn oven to 450° and bake 20 to 30 minutes. Do not open door for 20 minutes. Serve immediately.

Elizabeth Street Guest House, Fort Collins, Colorado

Sara's French Puffs

3 c. flour
1 tbsp. baking powder
1 tsp. salt
½ tsp. ground nutmeg
1 c. sugar
⅔ c. shortening

2 eggs
1 c. milk

Topping
¾ c. melted butter
2 tsp. cinnamon mixed with 1 c. sugar

Stir together flour, baking powder, salt, and nutmeg and set aside. In mixer bowl, cream together the first cup of sugar, shortening, and eggs. Add flour mixture to creamed mixture alternately with milk, beating well after each addition. Fill greased muffin cups ⅔ full. Bake at 350° for 20 to 25 minutes. Dip in melted butter, then in cinnamon-sugar mixture.

Stranahan House, Mercer, Pennsylvania

PANCAKES

Apple Rings

Pancake batter
4 McIntosh apples
Maple syrup

Prepare one recipe pancake batter (regular or whole wheat). Peel (if desired) and core 4 McIntosh or other soft apples; cut the apples into slices about ¼-inch thick. Use a fork in the center of each apple piece to dip the ring into the pancake batter. Let any excess drip off. Fry the apple rings in butter, margarine, or vegetable oil in a skillet until golden brown on one side. Turn and brown on the other side. Serve hot with maple syrup.

Goose Creek Guesthouse, Southold, New York

Blueberry Pancakes

Have available: frozen wild (small) blueberries. Combine in a large bowl:

1¾ c. milk		1 c. milk
¼ c. plain yogurt	OR	1 c. buttermilk

Add to milk mixture, mixing together well:

3 tbsp. vegetable oil	½ tsp. salt
2 eggs	¼ tsp. cinnamon
3 tbsp. sugar	1 tsp. vanilla

Combine:

2 c. flour	1 tbsp. baking powder

Add dry ingredients to milk mixture, stirring just until moistened (batter will be slightly lumpy). Pour onto hot griddle and sprinkle top of each pancake with frozen blueberries. When top has bubbled up, turn over to cook other side. Serve hot with syrup and fresh yogurt.

Milligan's Bed & Breakfast, Seeleys Bay, Ontario

Gingerbread Pancakes

Combine in a large bowl:

2½ c. flour	1 tsp. baking powder
1 tsp. baking soda	½ tsp. salt
1½ tsp. cinnamon	1½ tsp. ginger
1 tsp. nutmeg	⅛–¼ tsp. ground cloves

Beat together:

3 eggs
¼ c. brown sugar

Add to egg mixture, mixing together well:

1 c. buttermilk
¼ c. brewed coffee

1 c. water
¼ c. butter, melted

Add buttermilk mixture to dry ingredients, stirring just until moistened (batter will be slightly lumpy). For each pancake, pour about ¼ c. batter onto a hot, lightly greased griddle. Turn pancakes over when the tops are covered with bubbles and edges appear slightly dry. Serve with warm applesauce, maple syrup, or strawberry sauce.

Strawberry Sauce

1 pint strawberries, hulled
½ c. sugar

2 tbsp. lemon juice

In blender or food processor process all ingredients until smooth. Heat to boiling and cook until thickened. Add additional whole or halved berries and serve warm over Gingerbread Pancakes.

Lambsgate, Swoope, Virginia

Strawberry Blintzes

1 c. all-purpose flour
3 tbsp. granulated sugar
¼ tsp. salt
5 eggs
1⅓ c. milk

2 8-oz. cartons strawberry yogurt
½ c. strawberry preserves
Butter or margarine
Powdered sugar
Strawberry preserves

In medium bowl, mix flour, sugar, and salt. In another medium bowl, mix 3 eggs and milk. Gradually add milk mixture to flour mixture. Beat with electric mixer (medium speed) until blended. Cover and chill 2 to 3 hours. Prepare crêpe pan or shallow skillet. Brush with oil, use 2 tbsp. batter for each crêpe. Cook until brown on bottom. Remove crêpe, stack crêpe between waxed paper. In medium bowl, slightly beat 2 eggs with fork. Stir in yogurt and strawberry preserves. Place crêpe brown side up and spoon 1½ tbsp. yogurt mix on center of crêpe. Fold crêpe over—first bottom, then sides and top—envelope-style. Melt butter in pan. Brown blintzes over medium heat on both sides. Sprinkle blintzes with powdered sugar and top with spoonful of strawberry preserves. Makes 10 servings.

The Brafferton Inn, Gettysburg, Pennsylvania

SCONES

Maine Blueberry Scones

2 c. flour	½ stick sweet butter
2 tbsp. sugar	1 egg, beaten
3 tsp. baking powder	1 c. blueberries
Dash nutmeg	½ c. medium cream
¾ tsp. salt	½–¾ c. milk

Sift dry ingredients. Cut in shortening. Add berries. Combine egg with milk. Add to dry ingredients. Stir just enough to moisten. Pat out dough quickly and gently into a circle about ¾" thick. Cut into pie-shaped wedges. Brush with cream and sprinkle with sugar. Place on cookie sheet and bake in 450° oven for 15 minutes or until golden brown. Serve warm.

Bed & Breakfast Down East, Eastbrook, Maine

Scottish Oat Scones

⅔ c. butter or margarine, melted	⅓ c. sugar
⅓ c. milk	1 tbsp. baking powder
1 egg	1 tsp. cream of tartar
1½ c. all-purpose flour	½ tsp. salt
1¼ c. quick Quaker oats, uncooked	½ c. raisins or currants

Add butter, milk, and egg to combined dry ingredients; mix until just moist. Stir in raisins. Shape dough to form ball; pat out on lightly floured surface to form 8" circle. Cut into 8 to 12 wedges; bake on greased cookie sheet in preheated 425° oven 12 to 15 minutes or until golden brown. Serve warm with butter, preserves, or honey.

Oak Shores, Swampscott, Massachusetts

FRUITS

Baked Pears

d'Anjou pears
Brown or cinnamon sugar
Cream

Peel and halve small d'Anjou pears. Generously butter baking dish just large enough to hold desired number of pears. Sprinkle dish with ½ tablespoon brown sugar or cinnamon sugar per pear. Put pears cut side down in dish and sprinkle with additional ½ tablespoon sugar per pear. Bake in 375° oven for 20 minutes. Remove and pour one tablespoon cream over each pear half. Bake an additional 15 minutes. Serve hot or warm.

The Heirloom, Ione, California

Fruit Crisp

1 qt. berries (or any mixture of fruit
   sliced thinly)
⅓ c. water
⅓ c. flour

⅓ c. brown sugar
¾ c. oatmeal
¼ c. lemon juice (over the fruit)
6 tbsp. butter

Cream sugar and butter. Beat in oatmeal. Toss fruit in flour and water. Place in greased baking dish. Crumble oatmeal mixture over the top. Bake 40 minutes at 375°. Serves 4 to 6.

The Whistling Swan, Stanhope, New Jersey

Granola

Mix together:

12 c. rolled oats, old-fashioned
1½ c. wheat germ
1 lb. shredded coconut

1 c. sesame seeds
3 c. nuts, chopped

Combine in a saucepan:

1½ c. brown sugar
1½ c. water
1¼ c. safflower oil
½ c. honey

¾ c. molasses
1 tsp. vanilla
1 tsp. salt
1 tbsp. cinnamon

Heat saucepan mixture on low until sugar has dissolved (do not boil). Pour over dry ingredients, mixing well. In a 9" × 13" pan, bake at 250° for 25 to 30 minutes per batch. (This recipe makes 4 to 6 batches.) After cooking add 3 c. (or more) mixed dried fruit (chopped). Serve with milk or yogurt. Makes a good snack. Freezes well.

Bluebird Haven, Williamsburg, Virginia

4

State-by-State Listings

ALABAMA

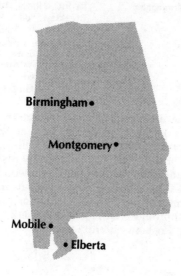

Birmingham •

Montgomery •

Mobile •

• Elberta

Bed & Breakfast—Birmingham ✪
RTE. 2, BOX 275, LEEDS, ALABAMA 35094

Tel: **(205) 699-9841**
Coordinator: **Kay Rice**
States/Regions Covered: **Anniston,
Auburn, Birmingham, Decatur, Ft.
Payne, Hartford, Hoover, Huntsville,
Tuscumbia**

Descriptive Directory: **$2**
Rates (Single/Double):
  Modest: **$35–$40**
  Average: **$40–$50**
  Luxury: **$50–$75**
Credit Cards: **MC, VISA**

Kay specializes in making compatible placements in host homes where
southern hospitality is assured. Her listings range from an exquisite
cottage to a classic contemporary. There are Federalist homes, Victorian farmhouses, or cozy vacation hideaways. They are located in a
variety of settings: close to lakes or rivers, downtown, in suburbs, or
convenient to I-65. All are comfortable accommodations in homes
where hosts balance friendliness with respect for privacy. There's a $5
surcharge for one-night stays.

Roses and Lace Country Inn ✪
P.O. BOX 852, FIFTH STREET AT NINTH AVENUE SOUTH, ASHVILLE, ALABAMA 35953

Tel: (205) 594-4366, 594-4660	Suites: $75
Hosts: Mark and Shirley Sparks	Open: All year
Location: 40 mi. NE of Birmingham	Reduced Rates: 10%, after 4 nights
No. of Rooms: 4	Breakfast: Full
No. of Private Baths: 2	Other Meals: Available
Max. No. Sharing Bath: 4	Credit Cards: MC, VISA
Double/pb: $65	Pets: Sometimes
Single/pb: $55	Children: Welcome, over 12
Double/sb: $55	Smoking: No
Single/sb: $45	Social Drinking: Permitted

A friendly greeting awaits you at this handsome two-story Victorian with a wraparound porch and stained-glass windows. As you cross the threshold, your hosts Mark and Shirley will invite you to relax with a beverage and snack. Their home, lovingly restored over a two-year period by the entire family, contains fine woodwork and many antiques. Ask about other landmark buildings in the area; St. Clair County is an old, historic part of Alabama. For modern pleasures, visit Birmingham's thoroughbred racetrack, or take a day trip to the Huntsville Space and Rocket Center.

Dunrovan B&B ✪
27475 COUNTY ROAD 20, ELBERTA, ALABAMA 36530

Tel: (205) 986-7119	Open: All year
Best Time to Call: Mornings, evenings	Reduced Rates: 10%, Nov. 1–Apr. 30
Hosts: Val and Jack Holtz	Breakfast: Full
Location: 19 mi. W of Pensacola, FL	Other Meals: Available
No. of Rooms: 3	Pets: No
No. of Private Baths: 1	Children: Welcome, over 5
Max. No. Sharing Bath: 4	Smoking: Permitted
Double/pb: $65	Social Drinking: Permitted
Double/sb: $45	Airport/Station Pickup: Yes
Single/sb: $35	Foreign Languages: German

Minutes away from Alabama's Gulf Shore, Dunrovan B&B is a haven for fishermen, swimmers, and beachcombers; duffers can choose from several nearby golf courses. After a day in the sun, watch TV in the den while savoring a complimentary glass of Jack's homemade Muscadine wine. The bedrooms of this brick ranch house are decorated in soft pastel tones, with wicker and rattan furniture, and fresh flowers. Guests have use of a swimming pool, refrigerator, and gas grill. Val's full breakfast—served in the sunroom overlooking the pool—includes country ham, homemade Danish and breads, strawberry butter, and freshly ground Colombian or Southern pecan coffee.

Hill-Ware-Dowdell Mansion ✪
203 SECOND AVENUE SOUTHWEST, LAFAYETTE, ALABAMA 36862

Tel: (205) 864-7861
Hosts: Nick and Althea Mendaloff
Location: 24 mi. NE of Auburn
No. of Rooms: 4
No. of Private Baths: 4
Double/pb: $55–$125
Open: All year
Reduced Rates: 25%, Sun.–Tues.;
  20%, business travelers; 15%,
  seniors

Breakfast: Full
Pets: Sometimes
Credit Cards: MC, VISA
Children: Welcome, over 10
Smoking: Permitted
Social Drinking: Permitted
Minimum Stay: 2 nights on weekends
Airport/Station Pickup: Yes

Scarlett O'Hara would feel right at home in this exquisite Greek Revival mansion listed on the National Register of Historic Places. The large, airy rooms, furnished with period reproductions and fine linens, offer parklike views from every window. The mansion features an impressive billiard room, an outdoor pool, and nine working fireplaces. There's also a gift shop—Nick and Althea are avid craftspeople who enjoy sharing their hobby with others.

Bed & Breakfast—Montgomery
P.O. BOX 886, MILLBROOK, ALABAMA 36054

Tel: (205) 285-5421
Best Time to Call: 7 AM–9 PM
Coordinator: Helen Maier
States/Regions Covered: Millbrook,
  Montgomery, Prattville

Rates (Single/Double):
  Average: $36 $40
  Luxury: $46 $40–$85
Credit Cards: No

If you are a history buff, you are sure to love Montgomery, the Cradle of the Confederacy. Helen Maier can put you within easy reach of the sights as a guest in one of her 15 homes. Accommodations range from antebellum to country contemporaries, with a typical farmhouse in between. Southern hospitality abounds in each of these diverse homes. All accommodations have private baths, and a hearty breakfast is served at every B&B. It is also the home of the Alabama Shakespeare Festival Theater and the Civil Rights Memorial.

Vincent-Doan Home ✪
1664 SPRINGHILL AVENUE, MOBILE, ALABAMA 36604-1428

Tel: (205) 433-7121
Host: Betty M. Doan
No. of Rooms: 3
No. of Private Baths: 3
Double/pb: $70
Single/pb: $50
Open: All year

Breakfast: Full
Credit Cards: MC, VISA
Pets: Welcome
Children: Welcome
Smoking: Permitted
Social Drinking: Permitted
Airport/Station Pickup: Yes

The Vincent-Doan Home, built circa 1827, is one of the area's last period "summer houses," and the only known example of French Creole architecture in the city. The area, known as the Old Dauphin Way District, is listed on the National Register of Historic Places. The furnishings and decor are subtle but elegant, and reflect the history of the home. It is 15 minutes to Bellingrath Gardens, 10 minutes to Battleship Park, and 30 minutes to deep-sea fishing. Betty will welcome you with a refreshing beverage.

For key to listings, see inside front or back cover.

○ This star means that rates are guaranteed through December 31, 1991, to any guest making a reservation as a result of reading about the B&B in *BED & BREAKFAST U.S.A.—1991* edition.

Important! To avoid misunderstandings, always ask about cancellation policies when booking.

Please enclose a self-addressed, stamped, business-size envelope when contacting reservation services.

For more details on what you can expect in a B&B, see Chapter 1.

Always mention *Bed & Breakfast U.S.A.* when making reservations!

If no B&B is listed in the area you'll be visiting, use the form on page 675 to order a copy of our "List of New B&Bs."

We want to hear from you! Use the form on page 677.

ALASKA

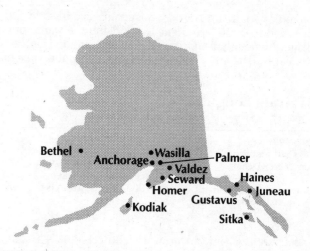

Accommodations Alaska Style—Stay with a Friend
3605 ARCTIC BOULEVARD, SUITE 173, ANCHORAGE, ALASKA 99503

Tel: **(907) 278-8800**
Coordinator: **Jean Parsons**
States/Regions Covered: **Anchorage,
Denali, Fairbanks, Gustavus, Homer,
Juneau, Palmer, Seward, Sitka,
Soldotna, Valdez, Wasilla**

Descriptive Directory: **$2**
Rates (Single/Double):
  Modest: **$40–$50**
  Average: **$45–$60**
  Luxury: **$55–$95**
Credit Cards: **MC, VISA**

Anchorage is an eclectic mix, and its frontier spirit and contemporary
style always take visitors by surprise. Accommodations include a B&B
near a small park with views of the port and Sleeping Lady Mountain;
another overlooks Cook Inlet; a third is an elegant suite where breakfast may be enjoyed on a large deck. Friendly, personal attention is
how Jean has built this agency's reputation since 1981.

Alaska Bed and Breakfast Association ✪
P.O. BOX 21890, JUNEAU, ALASKA, 99802

Tel: **(800) 627-0382**
Best Time to Call: **9 AM–5 PM**
Coordinator: **Mavis Hanna**
States/Regions Covered: **Alaska, the Yukon**

Rates (Single/Double):
Luxury: **$40–$55**

Visitors can enjoy southeast Alaskan hospitality in a historic inn, a log cabin in the woods, a modern home overlooking the water, or an old Indian village. Mendenhall Glacier, Glacier Bay, and the University of Alaska are nearby. The area is known for fine fishing and great hiking.

Alaska Private Lodgings
P.O. BOX 200047, ANCHORAGE, ALASKA 99520

Tel: **(907) 248-2292**
Best Time to Call: **Mornings**
Coordinator: **Mercy Dennis**
States/Regions Covered: **Anchorage, Fairbanks, Homer, Kenai, Palmer, Seward, Talkeetna, Valdez, Wasilla, Willow**

Rates (Single/Double):
Modest: **$35–$43**
Average: **$40–$45**
Luxury: **$50–$60**
Credit Cards: **MC, VISA**

Alaskan hosts are this state's warmest resource! Mary's accommodations range from an original log house of a pioneer's homestead, where the host is in the antique-doll business, to a one-bedroom apartment with a view of Mt. Denali. Many are convenient to the University of Alaska and Alaska Pacific University. There's a $5 surcharge for one-night stays.

The Green Bough ✪
3832 YOUNG STREET, ANCHORAGE, ALASKA 99508

Tel: **(907) 562-4636**
Best Time to Call: **7 AM–10 AM; 4 PM–8 PM**
Hosts: **Jerry and Phyllis Jost**
Location: **20 min. from airport**
No. of Rooms: **3**
Max. No. Sharing Bath: **4**
Double/sb: **$35–$45**

Single/sb: **$35–$45**
Open: **All year**
Reduced Rates: **Families**
Breakfast: **Continental**
Pets: **Sometimes**
Children: **Welcome**
Smoking: **No**
Social Drinking: **No**

Even on the coldest days, you'll forget about the outside temperature in this comfortable home filled with family furnishings, needlework, and local artifacts. Breakfast features a choice of homemade breads, muffins, and scones served with seasonal fruit and plenty of hot coffee. The Green Bough is located in a quiet residential area close to colleges, shopping, bike trails, and buses. A large yard and deck are available for reading and relaxing. Your hosts have 20 years of experience in this part of the country, and they will gladly help you discover its charms. Special arrangements can be made for storing fishing and camping gear.

Snug Harbor Inn ✪
1226 WEST 10TH AVENUE, ANCHORAGE, ALASKA 99501

Tel: **(907) 272-6249**	Other Meals: **Available**
Hosts: **Kenneth and Laurine "Sis" Hill**	Credit Cards: **MC, VISA**
Location: **Downtown Anchorage**	Pets: **Sometimes**
No. of Rooms: **3**	Children: **Yes**
No. of Private Baths: **3**	Smoking: **Permitted**
Double/pb: **$60**	Social Drinking: **Permitted**
Single/pb: **$60**	Minimum Stay: **2 nights**
Open: **All year**	Airport/Station Pickup: **Yes**
Reduced Rates: **Families**	Foreign Languages: **Spanish**
Breakfast: **Full**	

This homey cottage is minutes from bus routes serving downtown Anchorage, with its parks, sports facilities, shopping areas, museum, and performing arts center. Entrance to the Coastal Bike Path—which leads to Earthquake Park—is only three blocks away; your hosts will supply bicycles. Ken, an avid outdoorsman and private pilot, likes taking guests on private tours of Alaska's mountains and glaciers. You'll get energy for these expeditions from Laurine's ample breakfasts; the menu ranges from eggs and pancakes to homemade muffins, with juice and coffee or tea.

Wilson's Hostel ✪
BOX 969, BETHEL, ALASKA 99559

Tel: **(907) 543-3841**	Reduced Rates: **Weekly**
Best Time to Call: **Before 8 PM**	Breakfast: **Full**
Hosts: **Gail and Tom Wilson**	Credit Cards: **DC, MC, VISA**
No. of Rooms: **5**	Pets: **Sometimes**
Max. No. Sharing Bath: **4**	Children: **Welcome**
Double/sb: **$79**	Smoking: **No**
Single/sb: **$59**	Social Drinking: **No**
Open: **All year**	Airport/Station Pickup: **Yes**

A third *B* could be added to this B&B: banana splits! because Tom and Gail frequently serve them at bedtime as an example of the pampering guests receive here. This is in addition to refrigerator raiding, access to the family library, TV and stereo, laundry facilities, safety pins, and writing paper. You are encouraged to make yourself at home with all the privileges and responsibilities that implies. "Home," accessible only by air to the Bethel jetport, is a chalet made cozy by a fire in the wood stove and comfortable furnishings. Your hearty breakfast might be shared with a family from an Eskimo village, a business traveler, or a vacationer en route to the salmon streams along the nearby Kuskokwim River.

Kodiak Bed & Breakfast ✪
308 COPE STREET, KODIAK, ALASKA 99615

Tel: **(907) 486-5367**
Coordinator: **Mary Monroe**
States/Regions Covered: **Kodiak**

Rates (Single/Double):
Average: **$55–$66**
Credit Cards: **MC, VISA**

Kodiak is one of the nation's top fishing ports, a hunting and sport fishing paradise, and the home of the first Russian settlement in America and of the famous Kodiak bear. The people are warm and friendly, and look forward to receiving you.

Mat-Su Valley B&B Association ✪
HCO1 BOX 6229-R, PALMER, ALASKA 99645

Tel: **(907) 376-7662; Fax (907) 376-3036**
Best Time to Call: **8 AM–8 PM**
Coordinator: **Evelyn Russell**
States/Regions Covered: **Alaska, Mat-Su Valley, Palmer, Talkeetna, Wasilla**

Descriptive Directory of B&Bs: **Free**
Rates (Single/Double):
Modest: **$35**   **$45**
Average: **$45**   **$55**
Luxury: **$70**   **$80**

Whether you are housed in a remote lodge or a modern two-story home with spectacular views, Evelyn will do all she can to ensure you a pleasant holiday in the 23,000-square-mile Mat-Su Valley. It's a photographer's paradise of mountains, glaciers, parks, and farms. You can have an accessible wilderness experience by day, and all the creature comforts at a cozy B&B at night. This is the gateway to Mt. McKinley and Independence Mine. Visit a reindeer farm, take a llama pack trip, go dog mushing, or do the traditional: golf, tennis, or skiing.

Ede Den
BOX 870365, DAVIS ROAD, WASILLA, ALASKA 99687

Tel: **(907) 376-2162**
Hosts: **Jim and Julie Ede**
Location: **45 mi. NE of Anchorage**
No. of Rooms: **2**
No. of Private Baths: **1**
Max. No. Sharing Bath: **4**
Double/pb: **$65**
Single/pb: **$55**
Double/sb: **$55**

Single/sb: **$45**
Open: **All year**
Breakfast: **Full**
Credit Cards: **MC, VISA**
Pets: **Welcome**
Children: **Welcome**
Smoking: **Permitted**
Social Drinking: **Permitted**
Airport/Station Pickup: **Yes**

Guests enjoy the privacy and charm of this scenic Matanuska Valley homestead, furnished with antiques and Alaskan art. A private entrance opens into a cozy bedroom adjoining a luxurious bath that features an artistic rock wall with a waterfall cascading into a hot tub. Breakfast includes sourdough hotcakes, local honey, and homegrown berries in season. Jim and Julie are longtime Alaskan village teachers who collect and sell antiques. They'll be happy to arrange sightseeing, fishing, river rafting, and winter dog-team trips to Mt. McKinley.

For key to listings, see inside front or back cover.

✪ This star means that rates are guaranteed through December 31, 1991, to any guest making a reservation as a result of reading about the B&B in *BED & BREAKFAST U.S.A.*—1991 edition.

Important! To avoid misunderstandings, always ask about cancellation policies when booking.

Please enclose a self-addressed, stamped, business-size envelope when contacting reservation services.

For more details on what you can expect in a B&B, see Chapter 1.

Always mention *Bed & Breakfast U.S.A.* when making reservations!

If no B&B is listed in the area you'll be visiting, use the form on page 675 to order a copy of our "List of New B&Bs."

We want to hear from you! Use the form on page 677.

ARIZONA

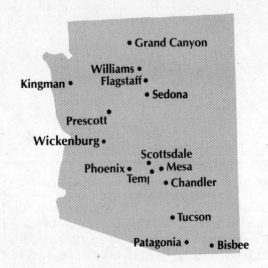

Grand Canyon

Williams •
Flagstaff •
Kingman •
• Sedona

Prescott •

Wickenburg •

Scottsdale
Phoenix • • • Mesa
Tempe • Chandler

• Tucson

Patagonia • • Bisbee

Bed & Breakfast in Arizona ✪
P.O. BOX 8628, SCOTTSDALE, ARIZONA 85252

Tel: **(602) 995-2831 or (800) 266-7829**
Best Time To Call: **10 AM–6 PM**
Coordinator: **Tom Thomas**
States/Regions Covered: **Ajo, Bisbee, Flagstaff, Lake Havasu City, Lakeside, Oracle, Page, Phoenix, Prescott, Scottsdale, Sedona, Tucson**

Descriptive Directory: **$2**
Rates (Single/Double):
  Modest: **$35–$50**
  Average: **$51–$75**
  Luxury: **$76–$150**
Credit Cards: **AMEX, MC, VISA**
Minimum Stay: **Holidays: 2 nights**

Claiming more mountains than Switzerland and more forests than Minnesota, Arizona boasts spectacular scenery. It is the home of the Grand Canyon, Lake Powell, London Bridge, famous museums, and sporting opportunities. Tom's choices range from a modestly priced town house with a swimming pool to a historic ranch with a spa, gardens, and a pool that was used as the locale for a western film. In business for ten years, this service takes pride in their growing roster

56

of friendly hosts. They require two days advance notice for reservations; seven days notice for cancellation.

Mi Casa–Su Casa Bed & Breakfast ✪
P.O. BOX 950, TEMPE, ARIZONA 85281

Tel: **(602) 990-0682; (800) 456-0682**
Best Time to Call: **8 AM–8 PM**
Coordinator: **Ruth T. Young**
States/Regions Covered: **Arizona—
Ajo, Bisbee, Cave Creek, Flagstaff,
Fountain Hills, Mesa, Page, Prescott,
Scottsdale, Sedona, Tempe, Tucson,
Wickenburg, Yuma; New Mexico;
Utah**

Rates (Single/Double):
Modest: **$25–$35**
Average: **$40–$60**
Luxury: ' **$75–$120**

Ruth's guest houses are located statewide; the cities listed above are only a partial listing. They are located in cities, suburbs, and rural settings, all of which are within easy driving range of canyons, national parks, Indian country, Colorado River gem country, the Mexican border area, historic mining towns, and water recreation areas. Send $5 for her detailed directory. Arizona State University and the University of Arizona are convenient to many B&Bs. There is a $5 surcharge for one-night stays.

The Judge Ross House ✪
605 SHATTUCK STREET, BISBEE, ARIZONA 85603

Tel: **(602) 432-5376 days; 432-4120
evenings and weekends**
Best Time to Call: **Evenings**
Hosts: **Jim and Bonnie Douglass**
Location: **25 mi. SE of Tombstone**
No. of Rooms: **2**
Max. No. Sharing Bath: **4**
Double/sb: **$65**
Single/sb: **$55**

Open: **All year**
Breakfast: **Full**
Other Meals: **Available**
Credit Cards: **MC, VISA**
Pets: **No**
Children: **Welcome, over 12**
Smoking: **No**
Social Drinking: **Permitted**
Airport/Station Pickup: **Yes**

A two-story, brick home built at the turn of the century and named for its first owner, a superior court judge, the Judge Ross House has a charmingly old-fashioned look enhanced by decorative moldings, lavish wood trim, and period furniture. Jim and Bonnie are gracious hosts, welcoming visitors with fresh flowers, wine, candy, and magazines. Breakfast varies from day to day, with specialties such as Belgian waffles and eggs Benedict. Bisbee was once the southwest's largest copper mining area, and the open pit mine remains a major attraction. Browsers will enjoy visiting the town's galleries and antique stores.

Cone's Tourist Home ✪
2804 WEST WARNER, CHANDLER, ARIZONA 85224

Tel: **(602) 839-0369**
Best Time to Call: **After 5 PM**
Hosts: **Howard and Beverly Cone**
Location: **18 mi. SE of Phoenix**
No. of Rooms: **1**
No. of Private Baths: **1**
Double/pb: **$35**

Single/pb: **$35**
Open: **Sept. 1–May 31**
Breakfast: **Continental**
Pets: **Sometimes**
Children: **Welcome**
Smoking: **Permitted**
Social Drinking: **Permitted**

This beautiful contemporary home is situated on two acres. Howard and Beverly offer a large guest room with phone and television, a large parlor for relaxing, and kitchen and barbecue facilities. It is 2 miles from fine restaurants, and 12 miles from Sky Harbor airport.

Dierker House ✪
423 WEST CHERRY, FLAGSTAFF, ARIZONA 86001

Tel: **(602) 774-3249**
Host: **Dorothea Dierker**
No. of Rooms: **3**
Max. No. Sharing Bath: **5**
Double/sb: **$40**
Single/sb: **$30**

Open: **All year**
Breakfast: **Full**
Pets: **Sometimes**
Children: **Welcome, over 12**
Smoking: **No**
Social Drinking: **Permitted**

After a day of touring the Grand Canyon and Indian sites, return to Dorothea's Victorian home and enjoy a glass of wine and fresh fruit in the evening, by the fire in winter, or in the pretty garden room in warmer months. You are welcome to borrow a good book and snuggle in bed under a cozy down comforter. Activities might include a Colorado River raft trip in summer, and skiing in winter.

The Little House ✪
P.O. BOX 461, PATAGONIA, ARIZONA 85624

Tel: **(602) 394-2493**
Hosts: **Don and Doris Wenig**
Location: **60 mi. S of Tucson**
No. of Rooms: **2**
No. of Private Baths: **2**
Double/pb: **$60**
Single/pb: **$50**

Open: **All year**
Breakfast: **Full**
Pets: **No**
Children: **Sometimes**
Smoking: **No**
Social Drinking: **Permitted**

The Wenig's home is located close to the Mexican border in a small mountain town at an elevation of 4,000 feet. Comfort and privacy are assured in the adobe guest house separated from the main house by a charming courtyard. One of the bedrooms has a queen-size bed; the other has twin beds and is wheelchair accessible. Each bedroom has a fireplace, sitting area, and adjacent patio. Coffee or tea is brought to your room to start the day. Afterwards, join Don and Doris for a breakfast of sausage and waffles, eggs from local hens, and home-baked breads. Birdwatching, a visit to a ghost town or silver mine, and shopping in Nogales, Mexico, are pleasant pastimes available.

Bed 'n' Breakfast in Arizona ✪
5995 EAST ORANGE BLOSSOM LANE, PHOENIX, ARIZONA 85018

Tel: **(602) 994-3759**	Single/sb: **$45**
Best Time to Call: **Anytime**	Suite: **$75**
Host: **Marjorie Ann Lindmark**	Open: **All year**
Location: **15 minutes from Phoenix**	Reduced Rates: **Weekly**
airport	Breakfast: **Full**
No. of Rooms: **3**	Pets: **No**
Max. No. Sharing Bath: **4**	Children: **Welcome**
Double/pb: **$55**	Smoking: **Yes**
Single/pb: **$50**	Social Drinking: **Permitted**
Double/sb: **$50**	

Marjorie's charming, trilevel home is located in the exclusive Arizona Country Club area. It is furnished in eclectic contemporary mixtures. You are welcome to use the swimming pool. The delicious breakfast often features fresh fruit or unusual waffles and crêpes. Arizona State University and the fashionable 5th Avenue Scottsdale shops are nearby. There is a $5 surcharge for one-night stays.

Gerry's Bed & Breakfast ✪
5150 NORTH 37TH AVENUE, PHOENIX, ARIZONA 85019

Tel: **(602) 973-2542**	Single/sb: **$35**
Best Time to Call: **8 AM–8 PM**	Open: **All year**
Hosts: **Gerry and Lynn Snodgres**	Breakfast: **Full**
Location: **1½ mi. W from I-17**	Pets: **No**
No. of Rooms: **3**	Children: **Welcome, over 12**
Max. No. Sharing Bath: **3**	Smoking: **No**
Double/sb: **$40**	Social Drinking: **Permitted**

The Snodgreses welcome guests to their contemporary two-story stucco with crackers, cheese, and home-baked goodies. Bring a bathing suit so you can make use of the swimming pool; your hosts will provide terry cover-ups so you can lounge in comfort. Indoor diversions include TV, pool, and other games. Lynn's full breakfasts feature specialties like cinnamon French toast and a salsa-garnished egg-and-cheese casserole.

Bed & Breakfast Scottsdale and the West
P.O. BOX 3999, PRESCOTT, ARIZONA 86302-3999

Tel: **(602) 776-1102**
Best Time to Call: **9 AM–6 PM**
Coordinators: **Joyce and George Thomson**
States/Regions Covered: **Arizona**
Descriptive Directory: Free

Rates (Single/Double):
  Modest: **$40**   **$55**
  Average: **$50**   **$65–$75**
  Luxury: **$65**   **$75–$150**
Credit Cards: **No**

The Thomsons have a roster of friendly hosts with homes that have a relaxed atmosphere to complement the easygoing Southwestern life style. Many are close to Paolo Soleri's Bell Foundry, Taliesin West, fine restaurants, shops, galleries, and lively entertainment. Take along plenty of color film to capture the panoramic desert sunsets.

Casa de Mariposa ✪
6916 EAST MARIPOSA, SCOTTSDALE, ARIZONA 85251

Tel: **(602) 947-9704, 994-9599**
Hosts: **Jo and Jim Cummings**
Location: **15 mi. N of I-10**
No. of Rooms: **1**
No. of Private Baths: **1**
Double/pb: **$60**
Single/pb: **$50**
Open: **All year**
Reduced Rates: **20%, May 30–Sept. 30**

Breakfast: **Full**
Credit Cards: **MC, VISA**
Pets: **No**
Children: **Welcome; must know how to swim**
Smoking: **No**
Social Drinking: **Permitted**
Airport/Station Pickup: **Yes**

Casa de Mariposa is in a quiet residential neighborhood within walking distance of parks, golf courses, stores, and restaurants. Visitors can avail themselves of the pool, the Cummingses' golf clubs, and, in season, box seats at Giants' spring-training games. If you're nostalgic for the nifty fifties, you'll appreciate your hosts' collection of period memorabilia. The guest suite has its own kitchenette, but you'll want to leave breakfast to Jo—her specialties include baked grapefruit.

Valley o' the Sun Bed & Breakfast ✪
P.O. BOX 2214, SCOTTSDALE, ARIZONA 85252

Tel: **(602)941-1281**
Best Time to Call: **After 5 PM**
Host: **Kay Curtis**
Location: **Tempe**
No. of Rooms: **3**
No. of Private Baths: **1**
Max. No. Sharing Bath: **4**
Double/pb: **$40**
Double/sb:**$35**
Single/sb: **$25**

Open: **All year**
Reduced Rates: **Weekly; monthly; seniors**
Breakfast: **Full, except Sunday**
Pets: **No**
Children: **Welcome, over 8**
Smoking: **Permitted**
Social Drinking: **Permitted**
Minimum Stay: **2 nights**
Airport/Station Pickup: **Yes**

The house is ideally located in the college area of Tempe, but is close enough to Scottsdale to enjoy its fine shops and restaurants. From the patio, you can enjoy a beautiful view of the Papago Buttes and McDowell Mountains. Local attractions include swimming at Big Surf, the Phoenix Zoo, and the Scottsdale Center for the Arts.

Cathedral Rock Lodge ✪
STAR RTE. 2, BOX 856, SEDONA, ARIZONA 86336

Tel: **(602) 282-7608**	Reduced Rates: **Available**
Host: **Carol Shannon**	Breakfast: **Full**
Location: **2.7 mi. from Rte. 89A**	Credit Cards: **MC, VISA**
No. of Rooms: **3**	Pets: **No**
No. of Private Baths: **3**	Children: **Welcome (crib)**
Double/pb: **$65**	Smoking: **No**
Suites: **$90**	Social Drinking: **Permitted**
Open: **All year**	

Set in rock terrace gardens surrounded by tall shade trees, this rambling country home boasts spectacular views of the surrounding mountains. The suite has its own deck, built against a giant pine tree. Guest bedrooms feature family treasures and handmade quilts. Each day starts with Carol's hot breads and homemade jams; fresh fruits from local orchards are summertime treats. Lovers of the great outdoors will delight in the natural scenic beauty of the area, and browsers will enjoy the many galleries and shops. In the evening, curl up in front of the fireplace, borrow a book, or select a videotape from your host's collection.

Sipapu Lodge ✪
65 PIKI DRIVE, P.O. BOX 552, SEDONA, ARIZONA 86336

Tel: **(602) 282-2833**	Open: **All year**
Hosts: **Lea Pace and Vince Mollan**	Reduced Rates: **After 4 nights**
Location: **100 mi. N of Phoenix**	Breakfast: **Full**
No. of Rooms: **3**	Pets: **Sometimes**
No. of Private Baths: **2**	Children: **Welcome, over 5**
Max. No. Sharing Bath: **4**	Smoking: **No**
Double/sb: **$55**	Social Drinking: **Permitted**
Suites: **$80**	Airport/Station Pickup: **Yes**

Constructed of local red rock and timber, the house is surrounded by blooming vegetation. The influence of the Anasazi Indian culture is evident with the decor of each spacious room reflecting its artifacts and memorabilia. Explore the Indian ruins or art galleries; hike Oak Creek Canyon; visit a ghost town; or just commune with nature. Lea is a former school teacher who loves to celebrate special occasions, and offers wine, tea, or spiced cider in the evening. Son Vince is a massage technician, craftsman, and potter.

Old Pueblo Homestays, R.S.O.
P.O. BOX 13603, TUCSON, ARIZONA 85711

Tel: **(602) 790-2399**	Rates (Single/Double):
Best Time to Call: **9 AM–5 PM**	Modest: **$25**　**$40**
Coordinator: **Rena Kiekebusch**	Average: **$35**　**$50**
States/Regions Covered: **Ajo, Green Valley, Tucson**	Luxury: **$45**　**$85**

There is a wide variety of homes in Tucson proper, close to the desert, in outlying towns, and in more remote desert locations, ranging from "nothing pretentious" to foothills elegance and charm. Most fall into the comfortable middle range. Rena will match you with a host home where you'll feel perfectly at home. The weather is almost always good, and you'll find many interests to keep you busy, from playing golf, to visiting Indian missions, to taking a trip south of the border to Nogales, Mexico. The University of Arizona is nearby.

Mesquite Retreat ○
3770 NORTH MELPOMENE WAY, TUCSON, ARIZONA 85749

Tel: **(602) 749-4884**	Open: **All year**
Best Time to Call: **Evening**	Breakfast: **Full**
Hosts: **Jan and Curt Albertson**	Pets: **No**
No. of Rooms: **2**	Children: **Welcome, over 12**
Max. No. Sharing Bath: **4**	Smoking: **Permitted**
Double/sb: **$50**	Social Drinking: **Permitted**
Single/sb: **$45**	Airport/Station Pickup: **Yes**

At the base of Mt. Lemmon sits this spacious ranch-style house, shaded by mesquite trees in the serene quiet of the desert. Traditional furnishings are accented with antiques and collectibles. All of the sights of Tucson—interesting caves, missions, monuments, and museums—are not far, and fine dining is just 10 minutes away. Save time to enjoy the Albertson's beautiful pool and spa surrounded by lush vegetation and mountain views. Perfect days end with a cup of tea and Jan's homemade treats.

Myers' Blue Corn House ○
4215 EAST KILMER, TUCSON, ARIZONA 85711

Tel: **(602) 327-4663**	Reduced Rates: **Families, seniors**
Hosts: **Barbara and Vern Myers**	Breakfast: **Full**
Location: **5 mi. from I-10**	Pets: **Sometimes**
No. of Rooms: **2**	Children: **Welcome (crib)**
Max. No. Sharing Bath: **4**	Smoking: **No**
Double/sb: **$42–$50**	Social Drinking: **Permitted**
Single/sb: **$30–$40**	Airport/Station Pickup: **Yes**
Open: **Sept. 15–May 15**	

Located on a quiet residential street, the house is convenient to downtown Tucson via city buses. The family room, decorated with Indian arts and crafts, and filled with history books, has bumper pool and TV. Close to seasonal recreation, it is also handy for tours of Old Tucson, Saguaro National Monument, Kitt Peak Observatory, and Nogales, Mexico. You may use the kitchen for light snacks, and the washing machine, dryer, and barbecue. The University of Arizona is nearby.

Redbud House Bed & Breakfast ✪
7002 EAST REDBUD ROAD, TUCSON, ARIZONA 85715

Tel: (602) 721-0218
Hosts: Ken and Wanda Mayer
Location: 7 mi. from Rte. 10
No. of Rooms: 2
No. of Private Baths: 2
Double/pb: $42
Single/pb: $37

Open: All year
Breakfast: Full
Pets: No
Children: No
Smoking: No
Social Drinking: Permitted

The Mayers' comfortable ranch-style brick home is on a residential street bordered by tall pines and palm trees. There is a view of the Catalina Mountains from the porch. Local attractions are the Saguaro National Monument, the Arizona Sonora Desert Museum, Kitt Peak National Observatory, and Sabino Canyon. You are welcome to use the bicycles, barbeque, and TV, or to just relax on the patio. Several fine restaurants and a theater are nearby.

La Vista del Oro Guest House ✪
56851 NORTH VULTURE MINE ROAD, WICKENBURG, ARIZONA 85390

Tel: (602) 684-3198
Hosts: Ed and Fran Barton, John and
    Cheryl Roberts
Location: 55 mi. NW of Phoenix
No. of Rooms: 3
No. of Private Baths: 2
Max. No. Sharing Bath: 3
Double/pb: $75
Single/pb: $60

Single/sb: $25
Open: All year
Breakfast: Full
Wheelchair-Accessible: Yes
Pets: No
Children: Welcome, over 10
Smoking: No
Social Drinking: No

Befitting its name, this is a handsome adobe villa overlooking the Vulture Peak mountain range. The location is ideal for history buffs and recreational athletes; gold mines, a museum, desert tours, golf courses, tennis courts, and bridle paths are all within a three-mile radius, and there's a pool in the backyard. A full breakfast of fresh-squeezed juice, eggs Benedict, homemade muffins, and fruit—straight from your hosts' trees—will give you energy to start the day.

The Johnstonian B&B ✪
321 WEST SHERIDAN AVENUE, WILLIAMS, ARIZONA 86046

Tel: **(602) 635-2178**
Best Time to Call: **Before 8 AM, after 1 PM**
Hosts: **Bill and Pidge Johnston**
Location: **55 mi. S. of Grand Canyon National Park**
No. of Rooms: **4**
Max. No. Sharing Bath: **4**
Double/pb: **$65**
Single/pb: **$60**

Double/sb: **$50**
Single/sb: **$45**
Suites: **$108**
Open: **All year**
Breakfast: **Full**
Pets: **No**
Children: **Welcome**
Smoking: **No**
Social Drinking: **No**

As old as the century, this two-story Victorian has been carefully restored and decorated in period style. You'll admire the antique oak furniture and the lovely floral wallpapers. In the winter, guests cluster around the wood-burning stove. Pidge's breakfast specialties include Ukrainian potato cakes, blueberry pancakes, and homemade breads.

ARKANSAS

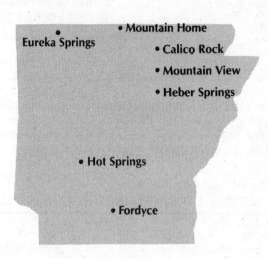

• Eureka Springs

• Mountain Home

• Calico Rock

• Mountain View

• Heber Springs

• Hot Springs

• Fordyce

Arkansas and Ozarks Bed & Breakfast ✪
ROUTE 1, BOX 38, CALICO ROCK, ARKANSAS 72519

Tel: (501) 297-8764 or 297-8211
Coordinator: Carolyn S. Eck
States/Regions Covered: Batesville,
Calico Rock, Des Arc, Fayetteville,
Fort Smith, Harrison, Hot Springs,
Mountain Home, Mountain View,
Norfolk

Rates (Single/Double):
Modest:	$25	$35
Average:	$30	$65
Luxury:	$65	$95
Credit Cards: No		

North-central Arkansas boasts an enviable combination of natural scenic beauty in its forests, rivers, and caves, as well as the homespun fun of hootenannies, square dancing, and craft shops. Carolyn's homes include contemporary houses, restored Victorians, Colonials, and log cabins in the mountains.

Bridgeford Cottage B&B ✪
263 SPRING STREET, EUREKA SPRINGS, ARKANSAS 72632

Tel: (501) 253-7853
Best Time to Call: 10 AM–10 PM
Hosts: Ken and Nyla Sawyer
No. of Rooms: 4
No. of Private Baths: 4
Double/pb: $65–$85
Single/pb: $55
Open: All year
Reduced Rates: 10% less, Jan.–Mar.

Breakfast: Full
Pets: No
Children: No
Smoking: Permitted
Social Drinking: Permitted
Minimum Stay: 2 nights weekends, holidays
Airport/Station Pickup: Yes

A stay at the cottage is a step into the quiet elegance of yesterday. It is located in the historic district, where Victorian homes line charming streets, and old-fashioned trolleys carry guests to and fro. Ken and Nyla will pamper you with coffee or tea in the afternoon or evening. Breakfast is a real eye-opener of fresh fruit, homemade cinnamon rolls, Ozark ham, and delicious egg casseroles.

Crescent Cottage Inn ✪
211 SPRING STREET, EUREKA SPRINGS, ARKANSAS 72632

Tel: (501) 253-6022
Best Time to Call: 9 AM–8 PM
Hosts: Ron and Brenda Bell
Location: On Rte. 62
No. of Rooms: 4
No. of Private Baths: 4
Double/pb: $65–$85

Open: Apr.–Dec.
Breakfast: Full
Credit Cards: MC, VISA
Pets: No
Children: No
Smoking: No
Social Drinking: Permitted

Crescent Cottage Inn was built in 1881 by Powell Clayton, the first governor of Arkansas. He would still be pleased today with the antique-filled rooms overlooking breathtaking scenes of the valley and East Mountain. Ron and Brenda provide special extras, such as nightly turndown service, fresh flowers, and surprise snacks. In the morning they serve homemade rolls, jams, and jellies with a variety of egg dishes. Historic downtown Eureka Springs is just a short walk from here, past lovely springs and shade trees.

Harvest House ✪
104 WALL STREET, EUREKA SPRINGS, ARKANSAS 72632

Tel: (501) 253-9363
Host: Lynne Goble
No. of Rooms: 3
No. of Private Baths: 3
Double/pb: $45–$65
Open: All year

Breakfast: Full
Pets: Sometimes
Children: Welcome
Smoking: No
Social Drinking: Permitted

This green-and-white Victorian house is furnished with antiques, collectibles, and family favorites. The guest rooms are downstairs, with private entrances. Located in the Ozark Mountains, the scenery is lovely. Homemade surprise snacks are always available. Lynne will do everything possible to make your stay pleasant.

Singleton House Bed & Breakfast ✪
11 SINGLETON, EUREKA SPRINGS, ARKANSAS 72632

Tel: **(501) 253-9111**	Reduced Rates: **After 3rd night**
Host: **Barbara Gavron**	Breakfast: **Full**
No. of Rooms: **4**	Credit Cards: **MC, VISA**
No. of Private Baths: **4**	Pets: **No**
Double/pb: **$55–$65**	Children: **Welcome**
Single/pb: **$55**	Smoking: **No**
Suites: **$55–$65**	Social Drinking: **Permitted**
Open: **All year**	

On a hillside overlooking Eureka Springs' historic district, Singleton House is whimsically decorated with an eclectic collection of comfortable antiques and folk art. Each guest room is decorated with brass-and-iron bedsteads, ceiling fans, and fresh flowers. Breakfast is served on a balcony overlooking a garden with stony paths, a lily-filled fish pond, and flower-covered arches and arbors. This enchanting setting is credited to a one-of-a-kind designer who claims to be an elf. A secluded footpath leads through the woods to quaint shops, cafés, and an active artists' colony. A convenient trolley provides transportation, and guided walking tours are available. Your hostess will help you discover all the best buys, and will gladly direct you to popular local attractions, including Beaver Lake.

Wynne Phillips House ✪
412 WEST FOURTH STREET, FORDYCE, ARKANSAS 71742

Tel: **(501) 352-7202**	Open: **All year**
Best Time to Call: **Morning**	Breakfast: **Full**
Hosts: **Colonel and Mrs. James H.**	Credit Cards: **MC, VISA**
Phillips	Pets: **No**
Location: **60 mi. S of Little Rock**	Children: **Yes**
No. of Rooms: **4**	Smoking: **No**
No. of Private Baths: **4**	Social Drinking: **Permitted**
Double/pb: **$55**	Airport/Station Pickup: **No**

A gracious Colonial Revival mansion listed on the National Register of Historic Places, the Wynne Phillips House is filled with antiques and Oriental rugs. Mrs. Phillips grew up here, and the bedrooms are furnished with family heirlooms. This is a place where you can enjoy old-fashioned pleasures, such as singing around the piano, or watch-

ing the sunset from the wrap-around porch. A swimming pool is on premises; tennis courts are nearby. The generous, southern-style breakfasts feature fresh fruit, homemade biscuits, eggs, sausage, and grits.

Stillmeadow Farm ✪
111 STILLMEADOW LANE, HOT SPRINGS, ARKANSAS 71913

Tel: **(501) 525-9994**	Suites: **$80**
Hosts: **Gene and Jody Sparling**	Open: **All year**
Location: **4 mi. S of Hot Springs**	Breakfast: **Continental**
No. of Rooms: **4**	Pets: **No**
No. of Private Baths: **2**	Children: **Welcome, over 6**
Max. No. Sharing Bath: **4**	Smoking: **No**
Double/pb: **$50**	Social Drinking: **Permitted**
Single/pb: **$40**	

Stillmeadow Farm is a reproduction of an 18th-century New England saltbox, set in 75 acres of pine forest with walking trails and an herb garden. The decor is of early country antiques. Your hosts provide homemade snacks and fruit in the guest rooms. For breakfast, freshly baked pastries and breads are served. Hot Springs National Park, Lake Hamilton, the Mid-America Museum, and a racetrack are nearby.

Vintage Comfort B&B Inn ✪
303 QUAPAW AVENUE, HOT SPRINGS, ARKANSAS 71901

Tel: **(501) 623-3258**	No. of Rooms: **4**
Host: **Helen Bartlett**	No. of Private Baths: **4**

Double/pb: **$55–$65**
Single/pb: **$50–$55**
Open: **All year**
Reduced Rates: **15% less Nov. 1–Feb.
1; 10% seniors**
Breakfast: **Full**

Credit Cards: **MC, VISA**
Pets: **No**
Children: **Welcome, over 6**
Smoking: **No**
Social Drinking: **Permitted**
Airport/Station Pickup: **Yes**

This handsome turn-of-the-century Queen Anne–style home has been faithfully restored, attractively appointed, and air-conditioned. The theme here is comfort and southern hospitality. Breakfast treats include biscuits and sausage gravy, grits, and regional hot breads. Afterwards, enjoy a short stroll to the famed Bath House Row or a brisk walk to the park, where miles of hiking trails will keep you in shape. Helen will be happy to direct you to the studios and shops of local artists and craftspeople. You are welcome to relax in the Old World sitting room and parlor or on the lovely veranda shaded by magnolia trees.

Williams House Bed & Breakfast Inn ✪
420 QUAPAW AVENUE, HOT SPRINGS, ARKANSAS 71901

Tel: **(501) 624-4275**
Hosts: **Mary and Gary Riley**
Best Time to Call: **9–11 AM; evenings**
Location: **50 mi. SW of Little Rock**
No. of Rooms: **6**
No. of Private Baths: **4**
Max. No. Sharing Bath: **4**
Double/pb: **$65–$80**
Single/pb: **$60–$75**
Double/sb: **$55**

Single/sb: **$50**
Suites: **$75–$80**
Open: **All year**
Breakfast: **Full**
Credit Cards: **MC, VISA**
Pets: **No**
Children: **Welcome, over 7**
Smoking: **Permitted**
Social Drinking: **Permitted**

This Victorian mansion, with its stained-glass and beveled-glass windows, is a nationally registered historical place. The atmosphere is friendly, and the marble fireplace and grand piano invite congeniality. Breakfast menu may include quiche, toast amandine, or exotic egg dishes. Gary and Mary will spoil you with special iced tea, snacks, and mineral spring water. World health experts recognize the benefits of the hot mineral baths in Hot Springs National Park. The inn is within walking distance of Bath House Row. There's a two-night minimum stay on weekends during March and April.

Mountain Home Country Inn ○
1501 HIGHWAY 201 NORTH, MOUNTAIN HOME, ARKANSAS 72653

Tel: **(501) 425-7557**	Reduced Rates: **10% less for business**
Hosts: **Ellen and Robert Ritlinger**	**travelers**
Location: **100 mi. N of Little Rock**	Breakfast: **Continental**
No. of Rooms: **4**	Pets: **No**
No. of Private Baths: **4**	Children: **Welcome, over 5**
Double/pb: **$35–$45**	Smoking: **Permitted**
Open: **March–Dec.**	Social Drinking: **Permitted**

Located just south of the Missouri border, this 80-year-old Colonial-style home is surrounded by huge oak trees and lush green lawns. Centrally air-conditioned, the guest rooms are attractively furnished in a country motif, with a lot of wicker, pretty quilts, and craft accessories. Ellen and Robert offer a snack and beverage upon your arrival. Robert, an avid angler, willingly shares his secrets about where the fish are biting. Most months feature activities of special interest, ranging from special fairs and flower festivals to music shows. Ellen graciously offers the use of her laundry facility to freshen your travel duds.

Patton House Bed & Breakfast Inn ○
P.O. BOX 61, WOOSTER, ARKANSAS 72181

Tel: **(501) 679-2975**	Single/pb: **$40**
Best Time to Call: **After 5 PM**	Open: **All year**
Host: **Mary Lee Patton Shirley**	Breakfast: **Full**
Location: **40 mi. N of Little Rock**	Credit Cards: **MC, VISA**
No. of Rooms: **3**	Pets: **Yes**
No. of Private Baths: **1**	Children: **Welcome**
Max. No. Sharing Bath: **4**	Smoking: **Permitted**
Double/pb: **$50**	Social Drinking: **Permitted**

Since its construction in 1918, Patton House has remained in the Patton family. Mary Lee, niece of the original builders, invites you to relax and be pampered while you use her home as a base for the many activities nearby. Beaver Fork Lake, only four miles away, offers fishing, swimming, and boating, while a picnic or hike at Woolly Hollow State Park lets you commune with nature. Many antique and craft shops are in the area, and the local restaurants are excellent. After a day of sightseeing, settle in the front porch swing with a cool beverage. Each morning, awake to the aroma of freshly brewed coffee served in your room while a full breakfast buffet awaits you in the formal dining room.

For key to listings, see inside front or back cover.

❂ This star means that rates are guaranteed through December 31, 1991, to any guest making a reservation as a result of reading about the B&B in *BED & BREAKFAST U.S.A.*—1991 edition.

Important! To avoid misunderstandings, always ask about cancellation policies when booking.

Please enclose a self-addressed, stamped, business-size envelope when contacting reservation services.

For more details on what you can expect in a B&B, see Chapter 1.

Always mention *Bed & Breakfast U.S.A.* when making reservations!

If no B&B is listed in the area you'll be visiting, use the form on page 675 to order a copy of our "List of New B&Bs."

We want to hear from you! Use the form on page 677.

CALIFORNIA

Mendocino/
Wine Country/
North Coast

Sacramento Area

San Francisco Area

Gold Country/High Sierra

Monterey Peninsula

Sequoia Area

San Joaquin Valley

San Luis Obispo Area

Santa Barbara Area

Desert Area

Los Angeles Area

San Diego and
Orange County Area

DESERT AREA

Travellers Repose ✪
P.O. BOX 655, 66920 FIRST STREET, DESERT HOT SPRINGS,
CALIFORNIA 92240

Tel: **(619) 329-9584**
Hosts: **Marian and Sam Relkoff**
Location: **12 mi. N of Palm Springs**
Double/pb: **$75**
Double/sb: **$50–$60**

Single/sb: **$45–$54**
Open: **Oct. 1–June 30**
Reduced Rates: **Weekly; 10% families
  on second room**
Breakfast: **Continental**

No. of Rooms: **3**
No. of Private Baths: **1**
Max. No. Sharing Bath: **4**
Pets: **No**
Children: **Welcome, over 12**

Smoking: **No**
Social Drinking: **Permitted**
Airport/Station Pickup: **Yes**
Foreign Languages: **Russian**

Bay windows, gingerbread trim, stained-glass windows, and a white picket fence decorate this charming Victorian home. The warm look of oak predominates in floors, wainscoting, and cabinetry. Guest rooms are decorated with hearts, dolls, and teddy bears everywhere. There's a rose bedroom with antiques and lace, a blue-and-white room with a heart motif, and a green room decorated with pine furniture hand-crafted by Sam. A patio, pool, and spa complete the amenities. Golf, tennis, museums, galleries, and posh Palm Springs are nearby. Marian graciously serves tea at 4 PM.

Hotel Nipton ✪
72 NIPTON ROAD, NIPTON, CALIFORNIA 92364

Tel: **(619) 856-2335**
Best Time to Call: **9 AM–6 PM**
Hosts: **Jerry and Roxanne Freeman**
Location: **10 mi. from I-15**
No. of Rooms: **4**
Max. No. Sharing Bath: **4**
Double/sb: **$45**
Open: **All year**
Reduced Rates: **Group**

Breakfast: **Continental**
Other Meals: **Available**
Credit Cards: **MC, VISA**
Pets: **No**
Children: **Welcome**
Smoking: **Permitted**
Social Drinking: **Permitted**
Foreign Languages: **Spanish**

The population of Nipton is 30! The recently restored hotel, with its foot-thick adobe walls, was built in 1904 and is located in the East Mohave National Scenic Area. Nipton is in the heart of gold-mining territory, 30 minutes from Lake Mohave's Cottonwood Cove. You are welcome to relax on the porch or in the outdoor Jacuzzi. Continental breakfast is served in the lobby at your convenience.

Inn at Palm Valley Ranch ✪

67 698 PALM VALLEY SCHOOL ROAD, P.O. BOX 4364, PALM SPRINGS, CALIFORNIA 92263

Tel: **(619) 328-5743**	Open: **Oct. 1–July 4**
Best Time to Call: **9 AM–5 PM**	Reduced Rates: **15% weekly; 10% seniors**
Host: **Loris O'Leary**	Breakfast: **Continental**
Location: **5 mi. from I-10**	Pets: **Sometimes**
No. of Rooms: **6**	Children: **Welcome**
No. of Private Baths: **6**	Smoking: **Permitted**
Double/pb: **$80–$90**	Social Drinking: **Permitted**
Single/pb: **$70**	Minimum Stay: **2 nights on weekends**
Guest Cottages: **$100–$120 (sleeps 2–4)**	Airport/Station Pickup: **Yes**
Suites: **$150**	Foreign Languages: **Spanish**

The Inn at Palm Valley Ranch is a restored adobe ranch house nestled in a two-acre date grove. The main house has two master bedrooms and a room with twin beds, all furnished with Colonial and contemporary Southwestern furniture. There are several patios for relaxing, in addition to the sun room and large living room with fireplace. Those seeking more privacy can choose from two guest houses, each with its own living room, kitchen, queen-size bed, private phone, and patio. The spacious grounds are landscaped with citrus trees and gardens, and feature a heated pool, spa, outdoor fireplace, and a lighted tennis court. Breakfast is served outside on the spa patio, and your host offers cool refreshments by the pool in the afternoon. The inn is just a few blocks from the municipal golf course, and is a convenient drive from the Bob Hope Cultural Center and the Oasis Water Park.

GOLD COUNTRY/HIGH SIERRA

The Matlick House ✪

1313 ROWAN LANE, BISHOP, CALIFORNIA 93514

Tel: **(619) 873-3133**	Reduced Rates: **Corporate discounts**
Best Time to Call: **7 AM–9 PM**	Breakfast: **Full**
Host: **Nanette Robidart**	Pets: **No**
Location: **1 mi. N of Bishop**	Children: **Welcome, over 10**
No. of Rooms: **5**	Smoking: **No**
No. of Private Baths: **5**	Social Drinking: **Permitted**
Suites: **$55–$65**	Airport/Station Pickup: **Yes**
Open: **All year**	

Hikers, backpackers, fishermen, and skiers are drawn to this turn-of-the-century ranch house in Owens Valley, which separates the White Mountains from the Sierra Nevadas. Energetic guests can reserve bicycles and picnic lunches and explore the area on their own. Of course, you may not be hungry for hours after a full breakfast of eggs, bacon, sausage, fresh-squeezed orange juice, sweet bread, homemade biscuits, and coffee or tea. Nanette has deftly combined authentic antiques with modern amenities to assure you a comfortable stay. A gallery showcasing local artists and a fine dinner restaurant are within walking distance.

The Heirloom ✪
P.O. BOX 322, 214 SHAKLEY LANE, IONE, CALIFORNIA 95640

Tel: **(209) 274-4468**	Single/sb: **$45–$60**
Hosts: **Melisande Hubbs and Patricia Cross**	Open: **All year**
	Reduced Rates: **Weekly**
Location: **35 mi. E of Sacramento**	Breakfast: **Full**
No. of Rooms: **6**	Pets: **No**
No. of Private Baths: **4**	Children: **Welcome, over 10**
Max. No. Sharing Bath: **2**	Smoking: **Permitted**
Double/pb: **$65–$80**	Social Drinking: **Permitted**
Single/pb: **$60–$80**	Airport/Station Pickup: **Yes**
Double/sb: **$50–$70**	

Nestled in the Sierra foothills, yet close to the historic gold mines, wineries, antique shops, and museums, this 1863 mansion, with its lovely balconies and fireplaces, is a classic example of antebellum architecture. It is furnished with a combination of family treasures and period pieces. Patricia and Melisande's hearty breakfast includes such delights as quiche, crêpes, soufflé, and fresh fruits. Afternoon refreshments are always offered.

Chaney House ✪
4725 WEST LAKE BOULEVARD, P.O. BOX 7852, TAHOE CITY, CALIFORNIA 95730

Tel: **(916) 525-7333**	Guest Apartment: **$100**
Hosts: **Gary and Lori Chaney**	Open: **All year**
Location: **50 mi. W of Reno, Nevada**	Breakfast: **Full**
No. of Rooms: **3**	Pets: **No (hosts have a cat and a dog)**
No. of Private Baths: **2**	Children: **Welcome, over 12**
Max No. Sharing Bath: **4**	Smoking: **No**
Double/pb: **$75**	Social Drinking: **Permitted**
Double/sb: **$75**	Minimum Stay: **2 nights**
Suites: **$85**	

Built on the Lake Tahoe shore by Italian stonemasons, Chaney House has an almost medieval quality, with its dramatically arched windows,

extra thick walls, and enormous fireplace. The rear of the house faces the waterfront, where the Chaneys' private beach and pier beckon to guests. A water-skiing boat will even be placed at your disposal, by advance arrangement. Winter visitors can choose from 19 nearby ski areas. All the bedrooms have wood paneling and antique furniture. Breakfasts feature such foods as French toast and quiche.

LOS ANGELES AREA

Bed & Breakfast of Los Angeles ✪
32074 WATERSIDE LANE, WESTLAKE VILLAGE, CALIFORNIA 91361

Tel: **(818) 889-8870**	Rates: (Single/Double):
Best Time to Call: **9–11 AM; 6–9 PM**	Modest: **$30** **$50**
Coordinator: **Angie Kobabe**	Average: **$45** **$60**
States/Regions Covered: **Los Angeles,**	Luxury: **$50** **$150**
San Diego, San Francisco	Credit Cards: **MC, VISA**

Angie can provide accommodations for you from Ventura in the north to Laguna Beach in the south. There's a guest house in Hollywood, a luxury suite in Beverly Hills, and a contemporary loft in Balboa, to name a few choices. Please send $2 for her directory. B&Bs are located near major colleges in Los Angeles, Orange, and Ventura counties. A $5 booking fee is imposed.

California Houseguests International ✪
6051 LINDLEY AVENUE—#6, TARZANA, CALIFORNIA 91356

Tel: (818) 344-7878
Best Time to Call: **Before 8 AM**
Coordinator: **Trudi Alexy**
States/Regions Covered: **Anaheim, the beach cities, Los Angeles, La Jolla, San Diego, Carmel, Monterey, Wine Country, California statewide**

Rates (Single/Double):
Modest: **$30–$45 $35–$50**
Average: **$50–$60 $55–$65**
Luxury: **$65–$150 $70–$155**
Credit Cards: MC, VISA
Minimum Stay: **2 nights**

Trudi has been reserving rooms for visitors for more than 11 years. Her host homes number 1,000, so she'll probably have the one you're looking for. Her "modest" accommodations are not centrally located, but are clean and pleasant. Her "average" category is more convenient to the freeways and tourist attractions, with such amenities as air-conditioning and private baths. The "luxury" tag applies to those that have exceptional decor and a swimming pool on premises. There is a $5 annual membership fee, and a $20 surcharge for one-night stays; acceptance of credit cards varies with the individual B&B.

El Camino Real Bed & Breakfast ✪
P.O. BOX 7155, NORTHRIDGE, CALIFORNIA 91327-7155

Tel: (818) 363-6753
Best Time to Call: **Evenings**
Coordinator: **Claire Reinstein**
States/Regions Covered: **Anaheim, Beverly Hills, Malibu, Palm Springs, San Diego, San Fernando Valley; Sun Valley, ID**

Rates (Single/Double):
Modest: **$40 $40–45**
Average: **$45–$55 $50–$75**
Luxury: **N/A $115**
Credit Cards: No
Minimum Stay: **2 nights**

This service brings the tradition of California hospitality begun with the Franciscan missions to the present-day traveler. Homes are in beach communities conveniently located to such attractions as Disneyland, Knotts Berry Farm, and the movie studios. Average accommodations are in upper-middle-class homes with swimming pools/spas, except in hilly areas. Claire offers modest apartments with simple furnishings and a luxurious private guest house on an estate with a hot tub and swimming pool. All hosts are longtime residents of California, familiar with the restaurants, tourist attractions, and the best ways of getting to them.

Casablanca Villa ✪
449 NORTH DETROIT STREET, LOS ANGELES, CALIFORNIA 90036

Tel: (213) 938-4794
Host: **Suzanne Moultout**

No. of Rooms: 2
Max. No. Sharing Bath: 3

Double/sb: **$50**   Children: **No**
Single/sb: **$40**   Smoking: **No**
Open: **All year**   Social Drinking: **No**
Breakfast: **Continental**   Foreign Languages: **French**
Pets: **No**

Suzanne Moultout welcomes you to her Spanish-style house located on a quiet, attractive street. Here, guests can enjoy the convenience of being close to West Hollywood, downtown, and Beverly Center, while having a comfortable home base. Your hostess offers an attractive guest room and a shady yard with fruit trees. She will gladly direct you to such nearby sights as Hollywood Hills, CBS Studios, and the beaches. Even if you don't have a car, the area is quite convenient, with a bus stop located within walking distance. This home is not wheelchair accessible.

Casa Larronde ✪
P.O. BOX 86, MALIBU, CALIFORNIA 90265-0086

Tel: **(213) 456-9333**   Open: **All year**
Best Time to Call: **Mornings**   Breakfast: **Full**
Hosts: **Jim and Charlou Larronde**   Pets: **Sometimes**
Location: **40 mi. NW of Los Angeles** Children: **Sometimes**
No. of Rooms: **1 suite**   Smoking: **Permitted**
No. of Private Baths: **1**   Social Drinking: **Permitted**
Suite: **$100**

The guest suite has a fireplace and color TV, but if you walk down the beach you may get to see the stars live; Rich Little, Ann-Margaret, and the McEnroes are the neighborhood people here on Millionaires' Row. This house is 4,000 square feet of spectacular living space. It has floor-to-ceiling glass, ocean decks, a private beach, and a planter that's two stories high. Jim and Charlou, world travelers, enjoy entertaining, and their gourmet breakfast ranges from Scotch eggs to French toast made with Portuguese sweet bread. Champagne, cocktails, and snacks are complimentary refreshments. Pepperdine College is two miles away. The Getty Museum is a five-minute drive away.

Hideaway House ✪
8441 MELVIN AVENUE, NORTHRIDGE, CALIFORNIA 91324

Tel: **(818) 349-5421**   Open: **All year**
Best Time to Call: **6–10 PM**   Breakfast: **Full**
Hosts: **Dean and Dorothy Dennis**   Other Meals: **Available**
Location: **20 mi. NW of Los Angeles** Pets: **Sometimes**
No. of Rooms: **1**   Children: **No**
No. of Private Baths: **1**   Smoking: **No**
Double/pb: **$55**   Social Drinking: **Permitted**
Single/pb: **$50**   Airport/Station Pickup: **Yes**

Located in a beautiful Los Angeles suburb, this country ranch home on over an acre in the San Fernando Valley is a good base for exploring southern California. It's 30 minutes to the beach, and 50 minutes to Disneyland. Freeways, shops, and restaurants are nearby. Dean and Dorothy welcome you to their art- and antiques-filled home, and will provide local guide service by prior arrangement.

The Exley House "By-the-Sea" ○
4273 PALOS VERDES DRIVE SOUTH, RANCHO PALOS VERDES, CALIFORNIA 90274

Tel: **(213) 377-2113**	Reduced Rates: **10% seniors**
Hosts: **Ruth and Earl Exley**	Breakfast: **Full**
Location: **5 mi. SW of Los Angeles**	Other Meals: **Available**
No. of Rooms: **2**	Pets: **Sometimes**
No. of Private Baths: **2**	Children: **Welcome**
Double/pb: **$50**	Smoking: **Permitted**
Single/pb: **$35**	Social Drinking: **Permitted**
Open: **All year**	Airport/Station Pickup: **Yes**

This gracious ranch-style home in suburban Los Angeles has an unobstructed ocean view. Ruth and Earl belong to a private beach club across the road, and you can use the facilities there. It is close to Marineland, Disneyland, and Hollywood. Ruth's breakfast specialties include honey-baked ham, French toast, and quiche. Your hosts offer you hors d'oeuvres with other pre-dinner refreshments. California State–Dominguez Hills is close by.

Sea Breeze Bed & Breakfast ○
122 SOUTH JUANITA, REDONDO BEACH, CALIFORNIA 90277

Tel: **(213) 316-5123**	Open: **All year**
Best Time to Call: **6–10 PM**	Reduced Rates: **10% senior citizens**
Hosts: **Norris and Betty Binding**	Breakfast: **Continental**
Location: **19 mi. S of Los Angeles**	Pets: **No**
No. of Rooms: **2**	Children: **Welcome, over 5**
No. of Private Baths: **2**	Smoking: **Permitted**
Double/pb: **$40–$50**	Social Drinking: **Permitted**
Single/pb: **$30–$35**	Airport/Station Pickup: **Yes**

The welcome mat is out in front of the lovely stained-glass Colonial doors at Norris and Betty's modest home. A patio-garden is just outside the large guest room, where you may relax after seeing the sights in the area. The Getty Museum and the Pasadena Rose Bowl are within easy reach. Their beach is the start of 22 miles of the Redondo-to-Pacific Palisades bicycle path, and tennis courts are within walking distance. Provisions are available if you prefer to fix breakfast yourself. You are welcome to use the Jacuzzi and TV. UCLA, USC, and Loyola Marymount University are nearby.

Channel Road Inn ✪
219 WEST CHANNEL ROAD, SANTA MONICA, CALIFORNIA 90402

Tel: (213) 459-1920	Reduced Rates: 12%, after 1 week
Best Time to Call: 7 AM–10 PM	Breakfast: Continental
Host: Susan Zolla	Wheelchair-Accessible: Yes
Location: 2½ mi. N of Hwy. 10	Credit Cards: MC, VISA
No. of Rooms: 14	Pets: No
No. of Private Baths: 14	Children: Welcome
Double/pb: $85–$145	Smoking: No
Suites: $165	Social Drinking: Permitted
Open: All year	Foreign Languages: Spanish

The Channel Road Inn, a 1910 colonial-revival mansion that has been lovingly restored, seems light-years away from southern California. The service is as agreeably old-fashioned as the furniture—you'll find fresh fruit in your bedroom and thick robes in the bathroom. In the morning, you'll breakfast on fruit juice and homebaked muffins; wine and cheese are served in the afternoon. Bike paths, nature trails, and the John Paul Getty Museum are among the local attractions.

The Whites' House ✪
17122 FAYSMITH AVENUE, TORRANCE, CALIFORNIA 90504

Tel: (213) 324-6164	Open: All year
Host: Margaret White	Reduced Rates: Weekly, monthly
Location: 5 mi. S of Los Angeles Intl.	Breakfast: Continental
Airport	Pets: No
No. of Rooms: 2	Children: No
No. of Private Baths: 2	Smoking: No
Double/pb: $30–$35	Social Drinking: Permitted
Single/pb: $25	

This contemporary home, with its fireplaces, deck, and patio, is located on a quiet street in an unpretentious neighborhood. The airport and lovely beaches are 15 minutes away. Disneyland, Knotts Berry Farm, Universal Studio Tours, and Hollywood are 30 minutes from the door. Use the laundry facilities or kitchen; Margaret wants you to feel perfectly at home.

MENDOCINO/WINE COUNTRY/NORTH COAST

Bed & Breakfast Exchange ✪
1458 LINCOLN AVENUE, CALISTOGA, CALIFORNIA 94515

Tel: (707) 942-5900; in Cal. (800) 654-2992; Fax (707) 942-0825	States/Regions Covered: Napa and Sonoma counties, northern
Best Time to Call: 9 AM–5 PM	California coast, Gold Rush country
Coordinators: Larry M. Paladini and Diane Byrne	

Rates (Single/Double):
   Modest: $65–$85
   Average: $85–$135
   Luxury: $135–$595

Credit Cards: **MC, VISA**

Some homes are located convenient to the wineries and vineyards. Wine-tasting tours are popular pastimes. Others are in the historic area, where gold was discovered, and others are in the spectacular locale of the Pacific. The more expensive accommodations are on fabulous estates with pools, spas, and special services. You may also call Saturday, from 10 AM–5 PM.

Seashore B&B of Marin ✪
P.O. BOX 1239, OLD CREAMY BUILDING, PT. REYES, CALIFORNIA 94956

Tel: **(415) 663-9373**
Best Time to Call: **9 AM–8 PM**
States/Regions Covered: **Bolinas, Inverness, Pt. Reyes Staion, Stinson Beach**

Rates (Single/Double):
   Modest: **$45**
   Average: **$75–$85**
   Luxury: **$125–$135**

This association of innkeepers, serving the Point Reyes National Seashore and Recreational Area, offers a wide range of amenities. Various hosts provide massages, facials, hot tubs, saunas, hypnosis for relaxation, boat excursions, and child care, so be sure to specify your needs. The California coast's natural beauty makes it a wonderful vacation spot. There are miles of beaches, and hiking, biking, and horseback-riding trails; bird and whale watchers should bring along binoculars.

Big Yellow Sunflower Bed & Breakfast ✪
235 SKY OAKS DRIVE, ANGWIN, CALIFORNIA 94508

Tel: **(707) 965-3885**
Best Time to Call: **Evenings**
Hosts: **Dale and Betty Clement**
Location: **60 mi. N of San Francisco**
No. of Rooms: **1 suite**
No. of Private Baths: **1**
Double/pb: **$65**
Single/pb: **$55**

Open: **All year**
Breakfast: **Full**
Other Meals: **Available**
Pets: **Sometimes**
Children: **Welcome**
Smoking: **No**
Social Drinking: **Permitted**

Located near the center of the Napa Valley wine area, the guest duplex—a completely private, air conditioned suite with kitchenette, fireplace, TV, videos, and sun deck—is part of Betty and Dale's wood-and-brick Colonial home. Charmingly decorated with some antiques, lots of plants, and flower baskets, it accommodates seven people.

Complimentary snacks and beverages are offered when you arrive. They pride themselves on serving a more-than-you-can-eat breakfast.

Hillcrest B&B ○

3225 LAKE COUNTY HIGHWAY, CALISTOGA, CALIFORNIA 94515

Tel: (707) 942-6334
Best Time to Call: After 8 PM
Host: Debbie O'Gorman
Location: 2 mi. N of Calistoga
No. of Rooms: 4
No. of Private Baths: 1
Max. No. Sharing Bath: 4
Double/pb: $80–$90

Double/sb: $50–$70
Open: All year
Breakfast: Continental
Pets: Sometimes
Children: No
Smoking: Permitted
Social Drinking: Permitted

Despite its name, Hillcrest is located near the base—not the top—of Mt. St. Helena, in an area famed for its wineries and spas. Without leaving the B&B's 36-acre property, guests can hike, swim, fish, or stay indoors and play the Steinway grand piano. The house was built by Debbie's great-great grandfather, and you'll see cherished family heirlooms at every turn. An elegant continental breakfast of juice, coffee, fresh fruit, and baked goods is served on antique china and silver.

Scarlett's Country Inn ○

3918 SILVERADO TRAIL NORTH, CALISTOGA, CALIFORNIA 94515

Tel: (707) 942-6669
Best Time to Call: 9 AM–5 PM
Host: Scarlett Dwyer
Location: 75 mi. N of San Francisco;
   30 mi. from I-80, Napa exit
No. of Rooms: 3
No. of Private Baths: 3
Double/pb: $85
Single/pb: $70
Suites: $95–$125

Guest Cottage: $220; sleeps 6
Open: All year
Breakfast: Continental
Credit Cards: MC, VISA
Pets: No
Children: Welcome
Smoking: Permitted
Social Drinking: Permitted
Foreign Languages: Spanish

This inn is an intimate retreat tucked away in a small canyon in the heart of the famed Napa Valley, just minutes away from wineries and spas. Tranquillity, green lawns, and a refreshing swimming pool await you in this peaceful woodland setting. An ample breakfast, featuring freshly squeezed juice, sweet rolls, and freshly ground coffee, is served on the deck, at poolside, or in your own sitting room. All rooms have separate entrances, queen-size beds, and luxurious linens.

Muktip Manor ✪
12540 LAKESHORE DRIVE, CLEARLAKE, CALIFORNIA 95422

Tel: **(707) 994-9571**	Breakfast: **Full**
Hosts: **Elisabeth and Jerry Schiffman**	Pets: **Welcome**
Location: **101 mi. N of San Francisco**	Children: **Sometimes**
No. of Rooms: **1 suite**	Smoking: **Permitted**
No. of Private Baths: **1**	Social Drinking: **Permitted**
Suite: **$50**	Foreign Languages: **French, Spanish**
Open: **All year**	

Elisabeth and Jerry have traded the often-frenzied San Francisco life-style for an uncomplicated existence by the largest lake in the state. They do not offer Victoriana, priceless antiques, or gourmet food. They do provide comfortable accommodations in their unpretentious beach house, a place to relax on the deck, and the use of their private beach and bicycles. They enjoy windsurfing and canoeing, and have been known to give instruction to interested guests. Their motto is, "If you wish company, we're conversationalists; if you wish privacy, we're invisible."

Chalet de France
17687 KNEELAND ROAD, EUREKA, CALIFORNIA 95549

Tel: **(707) 443-6512; 444-3144**	Breakfast: **Full**
Best Time to Call: **9 AM–10 PM**	Other Meals: **Available**
Hosts: **Doug and Lili Vieyra**	Pets: **No**
Location: **20 mi. from Hwy. 101**	Children: **No**
No. of Rooms: **2**	Smoking: **No**
Max. No. Sharing Bath: **4**	Social Drinking: **Permitted**
Double/sb: **$90 up**	Airport/Station Pickup: **Yes**
Open: **All year**	

Awesome describes the breathtaking view of the sun setting over the Pacific and a thousand square miles of wilderness as seen from this secluded, mountain-top retreat. The unique sculptured wood architecture and elaborately tole-painted folk scenes enhance this traditional Swiss-Tyrolian chalet. Breakfast is always a gourmet's delight, often featuring eggs Benedict, stuffed crêpes, or special quiche. Be sure to take your camera and hiking attire so that you can properly explore the area. Closer to "home," diversions include swimming, fishing, Swedish massage, croquet, horse-shoe pitching, reading old books, and listening to selections from old radio shows. If you tire of "Shangri-la," the nightlife of Eureka is only 20 miles away.

Avalon House
561 STEWART STREET, FORT BRAGG, CALIFORNIA 95437

Tel: **(707) 964-5555**
Best Time to Call: **9 AM–noon**
Host: **Anne Sorrells**
Location: **One block off Hwy. 1, Fir St. exit**
No. of Rooms: **6**
No. of Private Baths: **6**
Double/pb: **$70–$115**
Open: **All year**

Reduced Rates: **20%, Mon.–Thurs.**
Breakfast: **Full**
Credit Cards: **AMEX, DISC, MC, VISA**
Pets: **No**
Children: **Welcome**
Smoking: **Permitted**
Social Drinking: **Permitted**
Airport/Station Pickup: **Yes**

Located three blocks from the ocean and one block from the Skunk Train depot, this redwood California Craftsman house makes a great home base for visitors to Mendocino County. Anne, a designer who specializes in historic renovations, drew on her own travels to create an appealing B&B. Her furniture is an eclectic mix of antiques and wicker pieces. The more luxurious rooms have fireplaces and whirlpool baths. Breakfasts are ample: a typical meal might consist of hominy grits with eggs, ham, fried apples, and biscuits or perhaps sour cream pancakes.

Campbell Ranch Inn ✪
1475 CANYON ROAD, GEYSERVILLE, CALIFORNIA 95441

Tel: **(707) 857-3476**
Hosts: **Mary Jane and Jerry Campbell**
Location: **1.6 mi. from Rte. 101, Exit Canyon Road**
No. of Rooms: **5**
No. of Private Baths: **5**
Double/pb: **$90–$125**

Single/pb: **$80–$115**
Guest Cottage: **$125; sleeps 4**
Open: **All year**
Reduced Rates: **Weekly**
Breakfast: **Full**
Credit Cards: **DISC, MC, VISA**
Pets: **No**

Children: **Welcome, over 10**	Minimum Stay: **2 nights on weekends,**
Smoking: **No**	**Mar. 1–Nov. 30**
Social Drinking: **Permitted**	Airport/Station Pickup: **Yes**

"Spectacular!" and "charming!" are expressions most often used when guests describe their stay at this picture-perfect hilltop home surrounded by 35 acres. The spacious bedrooms, each with a king-size bed, are handsomely furnished; several have balconies where views of mountains and vineyards are a backdrop to the colorful flower gardens. Breakfast, beautifully served, features a selection of fresh fruit, choice of gourmet egg dishes, homemade breads and cakes, and a variety of beverages. You can burn off the calories on the Campbells' tennis court or in their swimming pool, or borrow a bike to tour the wineries. Water sports and fishing are less than four miles away. Jerry will be happy to make your dinner reservations at one of the area's fine restaurants, but leave room for Mary Jane's dessert, always served "at home."

Camellia Inn
211 NORTH STREET, HEALDSBURG, CALIFORNIA 95448

Tel: **(707) 433-8182**	Suite: **$95**
Best Time to Call: **Mornings**	Open: **All Year**
Hosts: **Ray and Del Lewand**	Reduced Rates: **Available**
Location: **65 mi. N of San Francisco**	Breakfast: **Full**
No of Rooms: **9**	Credit Cards: **MC, VISA**
No. of Private Baths: **7**	Pets: **No**
Max. No. Sharing Bath: **4**	Children: **Welcome, over 10**
Double/pb: **$85–$115**	Smoking: **No**
Double/sb: **$65–$75**	Social Drinking: **Permitted**
Single/sb: **$65**	

This elegant Italianate Victorian town house (circa 1869) is an architectural delight. It is convenient to the Russian River, wineries, golf, tennis, and more. Ray and Del serve a hearty breakfast buffet in the dining room, and refreshments are served in the afternoon in the grand parlor or on the pool terrace. For romantics, there are three gas fireplaces and three whirlpool tubs for two.

Frampton House ✪
489 POWELL AVENUE, HEALDSBURG, CALIFORNIA 95448

Tel: **(707) 433-5084**	Breakfast: **Full**
Host: **Paula Bogle**	Credit Cards: **MC, VISA**
Location: **70 mi. N of San Francisco**	Pets: **No**
No. of Rooms: **3**	Children: **Welcome, over 12**
No. of Private Baths: **3**	Smoking: **No**
Double/pb: **$70–$95**	Social Drinking: **Permitted**
Open: **All year**	Airport/Station Pickup: **Yes**

This turn-of-the-century redwood home is in the heart of wine country. The guest rooms offer a choice of queen-size beds or extra-long beds, and two of the baths have tubs-for-two. On chilly evenings, a fire crackles in the fireplace; complimentary wines and cheese are served in the sitting room. Breakfast may be enjoyed in the solarium. The Napa and Sonoma valleys are within an easy drive. You are welcome to use the pool and spa in summer, the sauna in winter.

Moorings ✪
8 PINE HILL DRIVE, P.O. BOX 35, INVERNESS, CALIFORNIA 94937

Tel: **(415) 669-1464**
Hosts: **John and Lee Boyce-Smith**
Location: **45 mi. N of San Francisco**
No. of Rooms: **1**
No. of Private Baths: **1**
Double/pb: **$75**
Single/pb: **$70**

Open: **All year**
Breakfast: **Full**
Pets: **No**
Children: **No**
Smoking: **No**
Social Drinking: **Permitted**
Foreign Language: **German**

Sailors and hikers will feel right at home here. From the open-air decks of this modern, cedar-shingled home, visitors can admire both Tomales Bay and Inverness Ridge. Your hosts will be glad to tell you about nearby parks and beaches. You'll have the stamina to explore the area after a hearty breakfast, served in the dining room overlooking the bay. Standard offerings range from Belgian waffles and Dutch babies to scrambled eggs with chopped ham.

The Swiss Chalet ✪
5128 SWEDBERG ROAD, LOWER LAKE, CALIFORNIA 95457

Tel: **(707) 994-7313**
Hosts: **Robert and Ingrid Hansen**
Location: **60 mi. NE of Santa Rosa**
No. of Rooms: **2**
No. of Private Baths: **1**
Max. No. Sharing Bath: **2**
Double/pb: **$65**
Single/pb: **$55**
Double/sb: **$65**
Single/sb: **$55**
Open: **Apr.–Dec.**
Reduced Rates: **$5 less after 2 nights**
Breakfast: **Full**
Pets: **No**
Children: **Welcome, up to 2 years old**
Smoking: **Permitted**
Social Drinking: **Permitted**
Airport/Station Pickup: **Yes**
Foreign Languages: **French, German, Italian, Spanish**

Stained-glass windows enhance this Bavarian gem that overlooks an 85-square-mile mountain lake. The interior is immaculate and tastefully furnished with handpainted tole pieces and antiques. The stone fireplace, deck, and private beach are fine sites for relaxation. All seasonal sports are available. Robert and Ingrid will spoil you with such goodies as eggs Benedict and blueberry pancakes. By the way, the second bedroom is available only to friends traveling together.

Wine Country Cottage ✪
400 MEADOWWOOD LANE, ST. HELENA, CALIFORNIA 94574

Tel: **(707) 963-0852**	Breakfast: **Continental**
Best Time to Call: **Evenings**	Pets: **Sometimes**
Host: **Jan Strong**	Children: **Sometimes**
Location: **In the Napa Valley**	Smoking: **Permitted**
Guest Cottage: **$95; sleeps 2**	Social Drinking: **Permitted**
Open: **All year**	

The cottage is a private woodland retreat for two, with a patio under the pines, a comfortable bed-sitting room, private bath with shower, and complete kitchen. Jan will make reservations for you at the nearby spas. Napa Valley wineries, hot-air ballooning, tennis, golf, and swimming facilities are all close by. There are many galleries and renowned restaurants for you to enjoy.

Hilltop House B&B
9550 ST. HELENA ROAD, SANTA ROSA, CALIFORNIA 95404

Tel: **(707) 944-0880**	Breakfast: **Continental**
Hosts: **Annette and Bill Gevarter**	Credit Cards: **MC, VISA**
Location: **5 mi. from Rte. 29**	Pets: **No**
No. of Rooms: **3**	Children: **Welcome**
No. of Private Baths: **3**	Smoking: **No**
Double/pb: **$90–$145**	Social Drinking: **Permitted**
Open: **All year**	Minimum Stay: **2 nights on weekends,**
Reduced Rates: **10%, Jan. 1–Apr. 15**	**Apr. 15–Nov. 30**

Annette and Bill built their contemporary country retreat to follow the contours of the Mayacama Mountains. The house is surrounded by 135 acres at the top of the ridge separating the wine regions of Napa and Sonoma. The unspoiled wilderness includes a garden of native plants, shrubs, and the sounds of hummingbirds and other wildlife. A 2,000-square-foot deck with hot tub provides the perfect spot for enjoying the panoramic views. The airy guest rooms are comfortably decorated with a combination of antiques and contemporary pieces, and each has spectacular views and a private entrance onto the deck. Your hosts serve a generous breakfast of fresh fruit, eggs, cheese, and yogurt, with fresh baked breads and muffins. They also welcome you for afternoon snacks and a glass of sherry in the evening. Hilltop

House is 12 minutes from St. Helena, and 30 minutes from Napa. The historic town of Calistoga, popular for its restorative hot mineral water, mud baths, massages, and fine restaurants, is located nearby.

The Hidden Oak
214 EAST NAPA STREET, SONOMA, CALIFORNIA 95476

Tel: **(707) 996-9863**
Best Time to Call: **9 AM–5 PM**
Host: **Catherine Cotchett**
Location: **45 mi. N of San Francisco**
No. of Rooms: **3**
No. of Private Baths: **3**
Double/pb: **$85–$105**
Single/pb: **$85**

Open: **All year**
Reduced Rates: **10%, weekly**
Breakfast: **Full**
Pets: **No**
Children: **Welcome, over 12**
Smoking: **On front porch only**
Social Drinking: **Permitted**
Airport/Station Pickup: **No**

This brown-shingled bungalow makes a great home base for forays into wine country. In fact, Catherine will lend you a bicycle to discover several wineries just a short ride away. Upon your return, you can select a book from the library and sit by the fire. The spacious bedrooms are furnished with antiques and wicker pieces. Breakfasts, served at 9:30, include egg entrées, fresh fruit, and baked goods hot out of the oven; early risers will find coffee and a newspaper in the parlor after 7:30. Feel free to specify what you cannot eat. Catherine will happily create a meal that adheres to your dietary restrictions.

Oak Knoll Bed & Breakfast ✪
858 SANEL DRIVE, UKIAH, CALIFORNIA 95482

Tel: **(707) 468-5646**
Best Time to Call: **8 AM–noon; 3–6 PM**

Host: **Shirley Wadley**
Location: **½ mi. from Hwy. 101**
No. of Rooms: **2**

Max. No. Sharing Bath: **4**
Double/sb: **$60**
Single/sb: **$50**
Open: **All year**
Breakfast: **Full**

Pets: **No**
Children: **No**
Smoking: **No**
Social Drinking: **Permitted**

Every window of this redwood contemporary offers breathtaking views of the valley and vineyards of Mendocino wine country. Your host, Shirley Wadley, has decorated her lovely home with a mixture of modern elegance and rustic charm. The rooms feature exquisite chandeliers and colorful wall coverings. Bedrooms have queen-size beds and fresh flowers to enjoy. Relax on the spacious deck with some cheese, crackers, and a glass of local wine. Guests are welcome to unwind in the large solar spa, play the piano in the living room, or enjoy a movie on a 40-inch screen in the family room. Oak Knoll offers easy access to the coast, the redwoods, Lake Mendocino, and the wineries of Ukiah and Mendocino counties.

MONTEREY PENINSULA

Happy Landing Inn ✪
P.O. BOX 2619, CARMEL, CALIFORNIA 93921

Tel: **(408) 624-7917**
Best Time to Call: **8:30 AM–9 PM**
Hosts: **Bob Alberson and Dick Stewart**
Location: **120 mi. S of San Francisco**
No. of Rooms: **7**
No. of Private Baths: **7**
Double/pb: **$90–135**
Open: **All year**

Breakfast: **Continental**
Credit Cards: **MC, VISA**
Pets: **Sometimes**
Children: **Welcome, over 12**
Smoking: **No**
Social Drinking: **Permitted**
Minimum Stay: **2 nights weekends**
Foreign Languages: **Japanese**

Located on Monte Verde between 5th and 6th, this Hansel and Gretel–style inn is a charming and romantic place to stay. Rooms with cathedral ceilings open onto a beautiful garden with gazebo, pond, and flagstone paths. Lovely antiques and personal touches, including breakfast served in your room, make your stay special.

Unicorn ✪
BOX 1540, PEBBLE BEACH, CALIFORNIA 93953

Tel: **(408) 624-5717**
Best Time to Call: **After 6 PM**
Host: **Ingo**
Location: **3 mi. W of Carmel**
No. of Rooms: **1**
No. of Private Baths: **1**
Double/pb: **$85**

Open: **All year**
Breakfast: **Continental**
Pets: **No**
Children: **No**
Smoking: **No**
Social Drinking: **Permitted**
Foreign Languages: **German**

Located in an exclusive area on the magnificent Monterey Peninsula, this lovely home on two acres is just a quarter-mile from the beach. The guest bedroom has ocean and forest views, and it is quite private because it is separated by two hallways from the main section of the house. The only thing you'll hear is the sound of the ocean, and seals.

Babbling Brook Inn ✪
1025 LAUREL STREET, SANTA CRUZ, CALIFORNIA 95060

Tel: **(408) 427-2437**
Best Time to Call: **12–3 PM**
Host: **Helen King**
Location: **2 blocks from Hwy. 1**
No. of Rooms: **12**
No. of Private Baths: **12**
Double/pb: **$85–$125**
Open: **All year**
Reduced Rates: **Available**

Breakfast: **Full**
Credit Cards: **AMEX, DISC, MC, VISA**
Pets: **No**
Children: **Welcome, over 12**
Smoking: **No**
Minimum Stay: **2 nights weekends**
Foreign Languages: **French, Spanish**

Cascading waterfalls, a brook, gardens, and redwood trees surround this country inn. The oldest part of the house was built in 1909 on what was once a tannery and flour mill. Over the years, the house was changed by a number of owners, including the counsel to a czar and a woman known as the countess, who added several rooms and a balcony. It is a rustic, rambling retreat decorated in French country furnishings. Most rooms have a cozy fireplace, private deck, and outside entrance. Your hosts have owned restaurants and hotels in South America and are experts in making 2 people or 100 feel equally at home. Helen is a gourmet cook, as you will see from her breakfast repertoire of omelets, stratas, and fritattas. This historic inn is walking distance from the ocean, boardwalk, shops, and tennis courts.

Chateau Victorian—A Bed & Breakfast Inn ✪
118 FIRST STREET, SANTA CRUZ, CALIFORNIA 95060

Tel: **(408) 458-9458**
Best Time to Call: **9 AM–noon; 3:30–9 PM**
Hosts: **Franz and Alice-June Benjamin**
Location: **90 mi. S of San Francisco**
No. of Rooms: **7**
No. of Private Baths: **7**
Double/pb: **$90–$120**

Open: **All year**
Breakfast: **Continental**
Credit Cards: **AMEX, MC, VISA**
Pets: **No**
Children: **No**
Smoking: **No**
Social Drinking: **Permitted**

Chateau Victorian is a cheerful, red turn-of-the-century mansion with a gabled roof, white trim, and a lot of gingerbread. Rooms are decorated in period antiques, each has a fireplace. It's an easy walk from this B&B to the beach, the boardwalk, and the municipal pier (where you can feed Santa Cruz's resident seals). A generous continental breakfast of coffee, tea, juice, fresh fruit, croissants, and muffins is available from 9 to 10:30 AM; guests may dine indoors, on the deck, or on the terrace. Complimentary snacks are served in the early evening.

SACRAMENTO AREA

Annie Horan's ✪
415 WEST MAIN STREET, GRASS VALLEY, CALIFORNIA 95945

Tel: **(916) 272-2418**	Breakfast: **Full**
Best Time to Call: **Mornings**	Credit Cards: **MC, VISA**
Hosts: **Tom and Pat Kiddy**	Pets: **No**
Location: **45 mi. NW of Sacramento**	Children: **Welcome**
No. of Rooms: **4**	Smoking: **No**
No. of Private Baths: **4**	Social Drinking: **Permitted**
Double/pb: **$55–$85**	Airport/Station Pickup: **Yes**
Open: **All year**	

Annie Horan's is an elegant Victorian of splendid design and workmanship. Its parlor, entry hall, and guest quarters appear as they did in the opulent Gold Rush days. Tom and Pat have furnished this treasure with antiques that best depict that era. They invite you to enjoy the mountain air on the spacious deck. Nearby activities include panning for gold, swimming, golf, hiking, and nature trails.

The Inn at Shallow Creek Farm ✪
ROUTE 3, BOX 3176, ORLAND, CALIFORNIA 95963

Tel: **(916) 865-4093**	Open: **All year**
Best Time to Call: **Evenings**	Reduced Rates: **$10 less after 3 nights**
Hosts: **Mary and Kurt Glaeseman**	Breakfast: **Continental**
Location: **3 mi. from I-5**	Pets: **No**
No. of Rooms: **4**	Children: **Sometimes**
No. of Private Baths: **2**	Smoking: **No**
Max. No. Sharing Bath: **4**	Social Drinking: **Permitted**
Double/pb.: **$60**	Airport/Station Pickup: **Yes**
Double/sb: **$45**	Foreign Languages: **French, German,**
Guest Cottage: **$75; sleeps 2–4**	**Spanish**

The orchards of Shallow Creek Farm are known for mandarin and navel oranges and sweet grapefruit. Luscious berries, fresh garden produce, and a collection of exotic poultry, including rare silver guinea hens and African geese, are quite extraordinary. The inn, a gracious 89-year-old farmhouse, offers airy, spacious rooms furnished with carefully chosen antiques and family heirlooms, combining nostalgia with country comfort. Breakfast features homemade baked goods and jams, and a generous assortment of fresh fruits or juices and hot beverages.

The Feather Bed ✪
542 JACKSON STREET, QUINCY, CALIFORNIA 95971

Tel: **(916) 283-0102**	Open: **All year**
Hosts: **Chuck and Dianna Goubert**	Reduced Rates: **10% less on 3rd night**
Location: **70 mi. NW of Reno, Nevada**	Breakfast: **Full**
No. of Rooms: **7**	Credit Cards: **AMEX, MC, VISA**
No. of Private Baths: **7**	Pets: **No**
Double/pb: **$60**	Children: **Welcome**
Single/pb: **$55**	Smoking: **No**
Suite: **$65**	Social Drinking: **Permitted**
Separate Cottage: **$90; sleeps 3**	Airport/Station Pickup: **Yes**

This charming Queen Anne was built in 1893 and renovated at the turn of the century. The rooms feature vintage wallpaper, antique furnishings, and charming baths; most have clawfoot tubs. Enjoy a glass of cider in the parlor, or a cool iced tea on the front porch. A breakfast of blended coffee, fresh juices, fruits, and home-baked breads can be served in your room, on the patio, or in the dining room. The inn is convenient to water sports, snowmobiling, hiking, tennis, and skiing. Your hosts offer complimentary bicycles to help you explore beautiful Plumas National Forest and historic downtown Quincy.

The Feather Bed is pictured on our front cover.

SAN DIEGO AND ORANGE COUNTY AREA

American Historic Homes Bed & Breakfast
P.O. BOX 388, SAN JUAN CAPISTRANO, CALIFORNIA 92693

Tel: **(714) 496-6953**	Rates (Single/Double):
Coordinator: **Deborah Sakach**	Modest: **$35–$40**
States/Regions Covered: **all beach**	Average: **$45–$60**
cities, Anaheim, Dana Point, Laguna	Luxury: **$75–$125**
Beach, Los Angeles, Napa, San	Credit Cards: **No**
Diego, San Francisco, Yosemite	

All of the homes on Deborah's roster are historically significant, from a three-story Victorian in San Francisco to an oceanfront mansion in Carmel. Many are national landmarks, and all share the element of warmth and hospitality. Ask about her special romantic hideaways.

The Blue Door ✪
13707 DURANGO DRIVE, DEL MAR, CALIFORNIA 92014

Tel: **(619) 755-3819**	No. of Rooms: **1 suite**
Best Time to Call: **7 AM–10 PM**	No. of Private Baths: **1**
Hosts: **Bob and Anna Belle Schock**	Suite: **$50**
Location: **20 mi. N of San Diego**	Open: **All year**

Reduced Rates: **After 5 nights**
Breakfast: **Full**
Pets: **No**

Children: **No**
Smoking: **No**
Social Drinking: **Permitted**

Enjoy New England charm in a quiet southern California setting overlooking exclusive Torrey Pines State Reserve. A garden-level two-room suite with wicker accessories and king or twin bed is yours. The sitting room has a couch, a desk, and a color TV. Breakfast is served in the spacious country kitchen or in the dining room warmed by the fire on chilly days. Anna Belle prides herself on creative breakfast menus featuring homemade baked goods. Breakfast specialties include blueberry muffins, Swedish oatmeal pancakes, and Blue Door orange french toast. Your hosts will gladly direct you to the nearby racetrack, beach, zoo, or University of California at San Diego. There is a $10 surcharge for one-night stays.

Gulls Nest
P.O. BOX 1056, DEL MAR, CALIFORNIA 92014

Tel: **(619) 259-4863**
Best Time to Call: **Before 8:30 AM**
Hosts: **Connie and Mike Segel**
Location: **20 mi. N of San Diego**
No. of Rooms: **2**
No. of Private Baths: **2**
Double/pb: **$60**

Suite: **$75**
Open: **All year**
Breakfast: **Full**
Pets: **No**
Children: **Welcome, over 6**
Smoking: **No**
Social Drinking: **Permitted**

Gulls Nest is a contemporary wood home surrounded by pine trees. The house boasts a beautiful view of the ocean and a bird sanctuary from two upper decks. Guest accommodations consist of a comfortable, quiet room with queen-size bed, TV, private bath, and patio. The suite has a king-size bed and a sitting room that can accommodate a third person for $10 more. Breakfast is served outdoors, weather permitting, and features fresh-squeezed juice, eggs, homemade breads, and coffee cake. Great swimming and surfing are three blocks away at Torrey State Beach. Golf, shops, and restaurants are a 5-minute drive, and Tijuana and the international border are 40 minutes away.

Inncline B&B ✪
121 NORTH VULCAN, ENCINITAS, CALIFORNIA 92024

Tel: **(619) 944-0318**
Hosts: **Richard and Kirsten Cline**
Location: **23 mi. N of San Diego**
No. of Rooms: **4**
No. of Private Baths: **4**
Double/pb: **$75**

Double/sb: **$85**
Suite: **$95**
Open: **All year**
Reduced Rates: **10%, weekly, seniors,**
 families
Breakfast: **Continental**

Pets: **No**
Children: **Welcome (playpen)**
Smoking: **Permitted**

Social Drinking: **Permitted**
Airport/Station Pickup: **Yes**

Choose between a separate apartment or three queen bedrooms in this contemporary two-story home filled with furniture the Clines built themselves. Sunbathe in privacy on the deck overlooking the Pacific, or stroll down to Moonlight Beach for a refreshing ocean dip. It's a short walk to downtown Encinitas, which boasts many fine restaurants. Mt. Palomar Observatory, Sea World, Del Mar Race Track, and the Mexican border are about a half hour away by car. Guests have use of a kitchenette. Continental breakfasts consist of muffins, fresh fruit, yogurt, and coffee, tea, or hot chocolate.

Hidden Village Bed & Breakfast ○
9582 HALEKULANI DRIVE, GARDEN GROVE, CALIFORNIA 92641

Tel: **(714) 636-8312**
Best Time to Call: **8 AM–9 PM**
Hosts: **Dick and Linda O'Berg**
Location: **3 mi. S of Anaheim**
No. of Rooms: **4**
No. of Private Baths: **2**
Max. No. Sharing Bath: **2**
Double/pb: **$55**
Single/pb: **$45**
Double/sb: **$50**
Single/sb: **$40**

Suites: **$75**
Open: **All year**
Reduced Rates: **$10 less, Sun.–Thurs.**
Breakfast: **Full**
Wheelchair-Accessible: **Yes**
Pets: **Sometimes**
Children: **Welcome (crib)**
Smoking: **No**
Social Drinking: **Permitted**
Airport/Station Pickup: **Yes**

Linda has decorated this large colonial home with lacy draperies and handmade quilts; she's a professional weaver, and guests are welcome to browse in her studio. When you're done looking at fabrics, Disneyland, the Anaheim Convention Center, and Orange County's lovely beaches are just minutes away. Couch potatoes can watch tapes on the VCR, while the energetic can borrow the O'Berg's bicycles and go for a spin. In the mornings, you'll savor a full breakfast of fresh fruit, homemade apple muffins, and quiche or omelets.

Country Comfort Bed and Breakfast ○
5104 EAST VALENCIA DRIVE, ORANGE, CALIFORNIA 92669

Tel: **(714) 532-2802**
Best Time to Call: **Evenings**
Hosts: **Geri Lopker and Joanne Angell**
Location: **5 mi. E of Anaheim**
No. of Rooms: **4**
No. of Private Baths: **2**
Max. No. Sharing Bath: **4**

Open: **All year**
Double/pb: **$60**
Single/pb: **$55**
Double/sb: **$50**
Single/sb: **$45**
Reduced Rates: **20% less after 3 nights**

Breakfast: **Full**
Other Meals: **Available**
Pets: **Sometimes**
Children: **Welcome**

Smoking: **No**
Social Drinking: **Permitted**
Airport/Station Pickup: **Yes**

Located in a quiet residential area, Geri and Joanne have furnished their home with your comfort and pleasure in mind. It is handicapped-accessible with adaptive equipment available. Amenities include a swimming pool, cable TV and VCR, an atrium, fireplace, and the use of bicycles, including one built for two. Breakfast often features delicious Scotch eggs, stuffed French toast and hash, along with fruits and assorted beverages. Vegetarian selections are also available. Disneyland and Knotts Berry Farm are less than seven miles away.

Christmas House B&B Inn ✪
9240 ARCHIBALD AVENUE, RANCHO CUCAMONGA, CALIFORNIA 91730

Tel: **(714) 980-6450**
Hosts: **Jay and Janice Ilsley**
Location: **37 mi. E of Los Angeles**
No. of Rooms: **7**
No. of Private Baths: **4**
Max. No. Sharing Bath: **3**
Double/sb: **$55–$75**
Suites: **$105–$125**

Open: **All year**
Reduced Rates: **10%, Sun.–Thur.**
Breakfast: **Full**
Pets: **No**
Children: **Welcome, over 13**
Smoking: **No**
Social Drinking: **Permitted**

H. D. Cousins built this late Queen Anne Victorian so that he could raise horses, and his wife could entertain their prominent friends, in style. Party-giving came naturally here amid the elegant furnishings, red-and-green stained-glass windows, and intricate wood carvings. Yuletide galas became a tradition, and so the name Christmas House endured. Your hosts spent two years carefully restoring the rooms and filling them with Old World antiques. Breakfast is served on fine china and linen in the dining room or in your bedroom, where thick terry cloth robes are provided for late morning lounging. On weekend mornings the meal is more elaborate, with choices such as sweet cheese crêpes with fruit sauce, and unique fresh fruit dishes. Afternoon tea is served in the parlor. Southern California's attractions are within easy reach, and your hosts will help with touring plans, picnics, and dinner reservations.

Casa de Flores B&B ✪
184 AVENUE LA CUESTA, SAN CLEMENTE, CALIFORNIA 92672

Tel: **(714) 498-1344**
Best Time to Call: **10 AM–10 PM**
Hosts: **Marilee and Robert Arsenault**

Location: **60 mi. S of Los Angeles, 60 mi. N of San Diego**
No. of Rooms: **3**

No. of Private Baths: **1**
Max. No. Sharing Bath: **4**
Double/pb: **$85**
Double/sb: **$65**
Open: **All year**
Breakfast: **Full**

Pets: **No**
Children: **Welcome**
Smoking: **Permitted**
Social Drinking: **Permitted**
Airport/Station Pickup: **Yes**

Casa de Flores is aptly named; this Spanish stucco house is surrounded by stunning banks of bougainvillea that bloom year round. Then there are the orchids—more than 200 plants—that fill the Arsenault's greenhouses. (You'll find an orchid bloom and a chocolate mint on your pillow.) Indoors, you can screen movies from the video library, shoot pool, or play the organ. San Clemente's beaches are just five minutes away. Breakfasts are elegant, featuring such dishes as crab-stuffed eggs, and "Casa Crêpes"—cottage cheese pancakes wrapped around spiced, sliced apples. Coffee and tea are served all day; complimentary snacks are offered in the afternoon.

Betty S. Bed & Breakfast ✪
3742 ARIZONA STREET, SAN DIEGO, CALIFORNIA 92104

Tel: **(619) 692-1385**
Host: **Betty Spiva Simpson**
No. of Rooms: **2**
Max. No. Sharing Bath: **2**
Single/sb: **$25–$30**
Open: **All year**
Reduced Rates: **Long-term stay**

Breakfast: **Full**
Pets: **No**
Children: **No**
Smoking: **Permitted**
Social Drinking: **Permitted**
Airport/Station Pickup: **Yes**

Betty offers clean, comfortable accommodations in an attractive bungalow. The guest rooms are furnished comfortably with tasteful pieces, carpeting, and a ceiling fan. You are welcome to relax in the den or the patio, and can feel free to store snacks and beverages in the guest refrigerator. Betty will gladly direct you to nearby Balboa Park, San Diego Zoo, and tennis courts.

The Cottage ✪
P.O. BOX 3292, SAN DIEGO, CALIFORNIA 92103

Tel: (619) 299-1564
Best Time to Call: 9 AM–5 PM
Hosts: Robert and Carol Emerick
Location: 1 mi. from Rte. 5
No. of Rooms: 1
No. of Private Baths: 1
Double/pb: $45–$55
Guest Cottage: $60–$70; sleeps 3

Open: All year
Breakfast: Continental
Credit Cards: MC, VISA
Pets: No
Children: Welcome
Smoking: No
Social Drinking: Permitted

Located in the Hillcrest section, where canyons and old houses dot the landscape, this private hideaway offers a cottage with a king-size bed in the bedroom, a single bed in the living room, full bath, and fully equipped kitchen. Decorated with turn-of-the-century furniture, the wood-burning stove and oak pump organ evoke memories of long ago. It's two miles to the zoo, less to Balboa Park, and it is within easy walking distance of restaurants, shops, and theater. The University of California and the University of San Diego are nearby.

E's Inn
3776 HAWK STREET, SAN DIEGO, CALIFORNIA 92103

Tel: (619) 295-5622
Host: Erene Rallis
Location: ½ mi. from US 5 and 8
No. of Rooms: 2
No. of Private Baths: 2
Double/pb: $45
Single/pb: $35
Open: All year
Reduced Rates: Weekly; 10%, seniors

Breakfast: Continental
Other Meals: Available
Pets: Sometimes
Children: Welcome
Smoking: Porch and patio only
Social Drinking: Permitted
Airport/Station Pickup: Yes
Foreign Languages: Greek

On a quiet street in Mission Hills, this gray-and-white cedar-sided home welcomes the visitor with its inviting pillared porch and French doors. The house is decorated with a blend of Greek antiques, armoires, and modern Dansk pieces, complemented by original paintings, ceramics, and enamels. Your host loves to cater to her guests, and provides baskets of fresh fruit and flowers in each room. In the evening, she places a tiny surprise under each pillow. Breakfast specialties include seven-grain breads. On weekends Greek and Mexican omelets are served. E's is close to Balboa Park, the Gaslight District, and beautiful beaches.

Vera's Cozy Corner
2810 ALBATROSS STREET, SAN DIEGO, CALIFORNIA 92103

Tel: **(619) 296-1938**
Best Time to Call: **Before 10 AM;**
  after 5 PM
Host: **Vera V. Warden**
No. of Rooms: **1**
No. of Private Baths: **1**
Double/pb: **$45**
Single/pb: **$35**

Open: **All year**
Reduced Rates: **Weekly; 10%, seniors**
Breakfast: **Continental**
Pets: **No**
Children: **No**
Smoking: **No**
Social Drinking: **Permitted**
Foreign Languages: **French, German**

This crisp white Colonial with black shutters sits on a quiet cul-de-sac overlooking San Diego Bay. Guest quarters consist of a separate cottage with private patio entrance. Vera offers fresh-squeezed juice from her own fruit trees in season as a prelude to breakfast, served in the Wardens' Old World dining room. The house is convenient to local shops and restaurants, and is a mile from the San Diego Zoo.

Loma Vista Bed & Breakfast ✪
33350 LA SERENA WAY, TEMECULA, CALIFORNIA 92390

Tel: **(714) 676-7047**
Best Time to Call: **Mornings**
Hosts: **Betty and Dick Ryan**
Location: **50 mi. N of San Diego**
No. of Rooms: **6**
No. of Private Baths: **6**
Double/pb: **$75–$115**
Open: **All year**

Reduced Rates: **Sun.–Thurs.; 10%,**
  corporate rate
Breakfast: **Full**
Pets: **No**
Children: **No**
Smoking: **No**
Social Drinking: **Permitted**

Temecula is a state historic site dating back to the settling of the West. This imposing white Mission-style home, with its red tile roof and numerous arches, sits high on a hill surrounded by lush citrus groves and premium vineyards. Air conditioned for summer comfort, the beautifully decorated guest rooms are named after local wines, and most have private balconies. A museum, winery tours, shopping, fine dining, boating, fishing, and hot-air ballooning are all favorite pastimes. After a day of pursuing your interests, join your hosts on the patio for a panoramic view, some award-winning Temecula wine, and hors d'oeuvres.

SAN FRANCISCO AREA

American Family Inn ✪
P.O. BOX 349, SAN FRANCISCO, CALIFORNIA 94101

Tel: **(415) 931-3083**
Best Time to Call: **9:30 AM–5 PM**

Coordinators: **Susan and Richard**
  Kreibich

States/Regions Covered: **Carmel, Marin County, Monterey, Napa, San Francisco, Sonoma (wine country)**
Descriptive Directory: **$2**
Rates (Single/Double):
Modest:	**$45**	**$55**
Average:	**$50**	**$65**
Luxury:	**$65**	**$75–200**

Credit Cards: **AMEX, DC, MC, VISA**
Minimum Stay: **2 nights**

The San Francisco locations are near all of the famous sights, such as Fisherman's Wharf and Chinatown. Many are historic Victorian houses. Some homes offer hot tubs and sun decks; a few are on yachts and houseboats.

Bed & Breakfast International—San Francisco ✪
1181-B SOLANO AVENUE, ALBANY, CALIFORNIA 94706

Tel: **(415) 525-4569**
Best Time to Call: **8:30 AM–5 PM**
Coordinator: **Jean Brown**
States/Regions Covered: **California— Berkeley, Los Angeles, Palo Alto, San Francisco and the Bay Area, Monterey, Napa Valley, Palm Springs, Lake Tahoe; San Diego, Santa Barbara, Hawaii; Las Vegas; N.Y.C.**

Rates (Single/Double):
Modest:	**$38–$46**	**$44–$58**
Average:	**$54–$72**	**$60–$78**
Luxury:	**$74 and up**	**$80 and up**

Credit Cards: **AMEX, DC, MC, VISA**
Minimum Stay: **2 nights, generally**

Jean was the first to bring the concept of a bed and breakfast reservation service to America. Her accommodations range from a town house apartment to a villa, with a private pool, above an ocean beach. Others are located near the seashore, at a marina, in a redwood forest, by a mountain stream, in the middle of a vineyard, as well as in city neighborhoods and downtown areas. A $10 surcharge is made by those who accept one-night stays.

Burlingame B&B ✪
1021 BALBOA AVENUE, BURLINGAME, CALIFORNIA 94010

Tel: **(415) 344-5815**
Hosts: **Joe and Elnora Fernandez**
Location: **½ mi. from Rte. 101**
No. of Rooms: **1**
No. of Private Baths: **1**
Double/pb: **$50**
Single/pb: **$35**
Open: **All year**

Breakfast: **Continental**
Pets: **No**
Children: **Welcome**
Smoking: **No**
Social Drinking: **No**
Airport/Station Pickup: **Yes**
Foreign Languages: **Italian, Spanish**

Located in a pleasantly quiet neighborhood, with San Francisco only minutes away by good public transportation. The house offers the privacy of upstairs guest quarters with a view of a creek and native flora and fauna. It's all very clean and cheerfully decorated. Joe and Elnora will direct you to restaurants and shops to suit your budget.

Lore's Haus ✪
22051 BETLEN WAY, CASTRO VALLEY, CALIFORNIA 94546

Tel: (415) 881-1533	Open: All year
Host: Lore Bergman	Breakfast: Full
Location: 25 mi. SE of San Francisco	Pets: No
No. of Rooms: 2	Children: Welcome, over 14
No. of Private Baths: 1	Smoking: Permitted
Max. No. Sharing Bath: 4	Social Drinking: Permitted
Double/pb: $60	Airport/Station Pickup: Yes
Single/pb: $55	Foreign Languages: French, German
Double/sb: $55	Minimum Stay: 2 nights
Single/sb: $50	

Lore's Haus is an attractive ranch home on a quiet street, with a large, beautiful garden. Lore was born in Germany and has spent the last 30 years in Castro Valley. She prides herself on offering Americans a true European atmosphere, with a lot of plants, books, comfortable furnishings, and Oriental rugs. Breakfast includes French Brie, fresh German black bread, homemade jams, cold cuts, and eggs. If you like, tours of the Bay Area, Napa Valley, or anyplace else are available in German, French, or English. If you'd like to venture out on your own, the city center is 25 minutes away via car or rapid transit. After a day of touring, come back to Lore's and enjoy a glass of wine.

The Village Green Inn ✪
89 AVENIDA PORTOLA, EL GRANADA, CALIFORNIA 94018

Tel: (415) 726-3690	Breakfast: Full
Best Time to Call: 9 AM–3 PM	Other Meals: Available
Host: Susan Hayward	Credit Cards: MC, VISA
Location: 20 mi. S of San Francisco	Pets: No
No. of Rooms: 2 suites	Children: Welcome
No. of Private Baths: 2	Smoking: No
Suites: $102.60	Social Drinking: Permitted
Open: All year	

Modeled after an English Tudor country inn, each guest suite has a private entrance, a refrigerator for storing snacks, a view of the Pacific Ocean, and, of course, a teakettle. Both are decorated in the traditional British style, with an abundance of brass, white wicker, hand-rubbed woods, and lace accents. Susan, formerly of Bath, England, serves such British fare as bangers, bacon, scones, and crumpets at breakfast. A half-hour drive from San Francisco, and 100 years behind in time, this coastal village offers fishing, hiking, whale-watching, beach strolling, and the nearby historic town of Half Moon Bay. Excellent restaurants abound, and Prohibition-era speakeasies are now operated as colorful cafés. Closed Wednesdays.

Montara Bed & Breakfast ✪
P.O. BOX 493, MONTARA, CALIFORNIA 94037

Tel: (415) 728-3946	Open: All year
Best Time to Call: Evenings	Reduced Rates: Weekly
Hosts: Bill and Peggy Bechtell	Breakfast: Full
Location: 20 mi. S of San Francisco	Credit Cards: MC, VISA
No. of Rooms: 1	Pets: Sometimes
No. of Private Baths: 1	Children: No
Double/pb: $70	Smoking: No
Single/pb: $60	Social Drinking: Permitted

Relax in a California-style contemporary set in a coastal hamlet on scenic Highway 1. Montara is a rural area, yet it's just 20 miles from San Francisco. Guest accommodations are newly remodeled and feature a private entrance that opens onto a redwood deck. Guests have exclusive use of an adjacent sitting room with a fireplace and an ocean view. Breakfast is served in a solarium overlooking the garden. Your hosts serve a variety of specialties along with honey from their beehives. Local activities include playing in the waves at the state beach, wandering the hiking trails at McNee Ranch State Park, or riding on Miramar Beach. There are numerous seafood restaurants to choose from, as well as cuisine from Italy, Germany, and Mexico.

Casa Arguello
225 ARGUELLO BOULEVARD, SAN FRANCISCO, CALIFORNIA 94118

Tel: (415) 752-9482	Open: All year
Best Time to Call: 10 AM–6 PM	Breakfast: Continental
Host: Emma Baires	Pets: No
No. of Rooms: 4	Children: Welcome, over 7
No. of Private Baths: 2	Smoking: No
Max. No. Sharing Bath: 3	Social Drinking: Permitted
Double/pb: $63–$73	Minimum Stay: 2 nights
Double/sb: $50	Foreign Languages: Spanish
Suites: $97 for 4	

This spacious duplex has an elegant living room, dining room, and cheerful bedrooms that overlook neighboring gardens. Tastefully decorated with modern and antique furnishings, it is convenient to Golden Gate Park, Golden Gate Bridge, Union Square, and fine shops and restaurants. The University of California Medical School is nearby. Excellent public transportation is close by.

Rancho San Gregorio ✪
ROUTE 1, BOX 54, SAN GREGORIO, CALIFORNIA 94074

Tel: **(415) 747-0810**	Reduced Rates: **Available**
Hosts: **Bud and Lee Raynor**	Breakfast: **Full**
Location: **35 mi. S of San Francisco**	Pets: **No**
No. of Rooms: **4**	Children: **Welcome**
No. of Private Baths: **4**	Smoking: **No**
Double/pb: **$60–$95**	Social Drinking: **Permitted**
Open: **All year**	Airport/Station Pickup: **Yes**

Graceful arches and bright stucco characterize this Spanish Mission home set on 15 wooded acres. Rooms are decorated with American antiques and family pieces. Your hosts, Bud and Lee, are glad to share a snack and a beverage. On weekdays they serve a Continental breakfast; on Saturdays and Sundays a full feast features eggs or pancakes, fresh fruit and breads, and a variety of meats. The atmosphere is relaxing, and guests are welcome to borrow a book from the library, or play the organ. Rancho San Gregorio is close to the beach, horseback riding, and golf. San Francisco, Half Moon Bay, and a variety of state parks and recreational areas are within an hour's drive.

Mrs. "K's" Retreat ✪
14497 NEW JERSEY AVENUE, SAN JOSE, CALIFORNIA 95124

Tel: **(408) 371-0593/559-3828**	Open: **All year**
Hosts: **Barbara and George Kievlan**	Reduced Rates: **Weekly**
Location: **3 mi. E of Hwy. 17**	Breakfast: **Continental**
No. of Rooms: **3**	Pets: **No**
No. of Private Baths: **3**	Children: **Welcome**
Double/pb: **$47.50**	Smoking: **No**
Single/pb: **$37.50**	Social Drinking: **Permitted**

This sprawling ranch-style home is nestled at the base of Blossom Valley, once famous for its orchards. Guest rooms are furnished with flair and boast separate entrances. Your hosts invite you to enjoy the living room fireplace, family room, spa, and adjacent patio, with pool and spacious yard. Those interested in stained glass will surely want to visit the studio on the premises. Handicap facilities are available.

Madison Street Inn ✪
1390 MADISON STREET, SANTA CLARA, CALIFORNIA 95050

Tel: **(408) 249-5541**	Location: **1½ mi. from Rte. 880**
Hosts: **Theresa and Ralph Wigginton**	No. of Rooms: **5**

No. of Private Baths: **3**
Max. No. Sharing Bath: **4**
Double/pb: **$75–$85**
Double/sb: **$60**
Single/sb: **$60**
Open: **All year**
Reduced Rates: **15%, seniors**
Breakfast: **Full**

Other Meals: **Available**
Credit Cards: **AMEX, DC, MC, VISA**
Pets: **No**
Children: **Welcome**
Smoking: **No**
Social Drinking: **Permitted**

This restored, vintage Queen Anne is furnished with Oriental rugs and museum-quality antiques, including brass beds and tubs-for-two. Landscaped gardens, a swimming pool, and a hot tub grace the grounds, and a sunny meeting room is available for business gatherings. Belgian waffles or eggs Benedict are often on the breakfast menu. Exciting dinners can be arranged, prepared by Ralph, an accomplished cook. It is convenient to Santa Clara University and San Jose State University.

SAN LUIS OBISPO AREA

Megan's Friends B&B Reservation Service
1776 ROYAL WAY, SAN LUIS OBISPO, CALIFORNIA 93405

Tel: **(805) 544-4406**
Best Time to Call: **11 AM–4 PM; 6–10 PM**
Coordinator: **Joyce Segor**
States/Regions Covered: **Baywood Park, Cambria, King City, Los Osos, Paso Robles, San Luis Obispo, Solvang, Sunset Palisades**

Rates (Single/Double):
Average: **$45–$60 $50–$65**
Luxury: **$65–$85 $75–$95**
Credit Cards: **No**

Joyce has exclusive listings that no other reservation agency has. She is certain to accommodate you in a B&B best suited to your interests and purse; these range from a contemporary showplace to a cozy country cottage. A $10 one-time membership is required, for which you receive a detailed list describing the accommodations. Local attractions include the beaches, wineries, farmers market, and Hearst Castle.

The Village Inn ✪
407 EL CAMINO REAL, ARROYO GRANDE, CALIFORNIA 93420

Tel: **(805) 489-5926; (800) 767-0083**
Best Time to Call: **9 AM–8 PM**
Hosts: **John and Gina Glass**
Location: **15 mi. S of San Luis Obispo**
No. of Rooms: **7**
No. of Private Baths: **7**
Double/pb: **$95–$135**

Single/pb: **$85–$125**
Open: **All year**
Reduced Rates: **Commercial rate and packages Sun.–Thurs.**
Breakfast: **Full**
Credit Cards: **AMEX, DISC, MC, VISA**
Pets: **No**
Children: **Welcome, over 8**

Smoking: **No**
Social Drinking: **Permitted**

Minimum Stay: **2 nights on holiday weekends**

Each of the inn's spacious, air conditioned guest rooms is decorated with Laura Ashley bed linens and wall coverings, overstuffed pillows, antique dressers or dressing tables, and attractive bay windows with window seats. Breakfast often features apple pancakes, fluffy omelets, potato latkes with applesauce, or French toast with apple slices and caramel sauce. The sand dunes of Pismo Beach, Hearst Castle, the Great American Melodrama Theater, and 30 wineries are within easy reach.

Gerarda's Bed & Breakfast ✪
1056 BAY OAKS DRIVE, LOS OSOS, CALIFORNIA 93402

Tel: **(805) 528-3973**
Host: **Gerarda Ondang**
Location: **10 mi. from Hwy. 101**
No. of Rooms: **3**
No. of Private Baths: **1**
Max. No. Sharing Bath: **4**
Double/pb: **$41.34**
Single/pb: **$26.50**
Double/sb: **$41.34**
Single/sb: **$26.50**

Open: **All year**
Breakfast: **Full**
Pets: **Welcome**
Children: **Welcome**
Smoking: **No**
Social Drinking: **Permitted**
Airport/Station Pickup: **Yes**
Foreign Languages: **Dutch, Indonesian**

When you stay at Gerarda's, you are in for a veritable Dutch treat! Located in a pleasant, quiet neighborhood, the house is surrounded by interesting landscaping and lovely flower beds. This is a simple home comfortably furnished, with charm and warmth. Breakfast features Dutch delicacies such as honeycake, jams, and breads. Hearst

Castle, Morrow Bay, and San Luis Obispo are within a half hour's drive. Gerarda has thoughtfully placed a TV in each guest bedroom.

SANTA BARBARA AREA

George and Jean Harris ✪
1483 ANITA STREET, CARPINTERIA, CALIFORNIA 93013

Tel: (805) 684-5629	Open: **All year**
Hosts: **George and Jean Harris**	Breakfast: **Full**
Location: **11 mi. E of Santa Barbara**	Pets: **No**
No. of Rooms: 1	Children: **Welcome, over 11**
No. of Private Baths: 1	Smoking: **No**
Double/pb: **$45**	Social Drinking: **Permitted**
Single/pb: **$40**	

George and Jean have a one-story stucco home at the end of a quiet court. The guest room is decorated in Early American style and features a king-size bed. Special touches, such as a cookie jar filled with homemade goodies, and fresh flowers in your room, are sure to help you feel at home. Outside, a spa surrounded by ferns awaits you in the garden. Breakfast includes a choice of whole wheat pancakes, eggs, sausages, and fresh seasonal fruit. Carpinteria is known for its flower production, both in greenhouses and in open fields. The Harrises are one mile from the beach.

Long's Seaview Bed & Breakfast ✪
317 PIEDMONT ROAD, SANTA BARBARA, CALIFORNIA 93105

Tel: (805) 687-2947	Open: **All year**
Best Time to Call: **Before 6 PM**	Breakfast: **Full**
Host: **LaVerne Long**	Pets: **No**
Location: **1½ mi. from Hwy. 101**	Children: **No**
No. of Rooms: 1	Smoking: **No**
No. of Private Baths: 1	Social Drinking: **Permitted**
Double/pb: **$65–$69**	Airport/Station Pickup: **Yes**
Single/pb: **$60**	

Overlooking Santa Barbara's prestigious north side, this ranch-style home is in a quiet, residential neighborhood. Breakfast is usually served on the patio, where you can see the ocean, Channel Islands, and citrus orchards. Convenient to the beach, Solvang, and Santa Ynez Valley, the large, airy bedroom is cheerfully furnished, with antiques and king-size bed. The breakfast menu varies from Southern dishes to Mexican specialties.

Ocean View House ✪

P.O. BOX 20065, SANTA BARBARA, CALIFORNIA 93102

Tel: **(805) 966-6659**
Best Time to Call: **8 AM–5 PM**
Hosts: **Bill and Carolyn Canfield**
Location: **2 mi. from Fwy. 101**
No. of Rooms: **2**
No. of Private Baths: **1**
Double/pb: **$50**
Suites: **$70 for 4**

Open: **All year**
Breakfast: **Continental**
Pets: **Sometimes**
Children: **Welcome**
Smoking: **No**
Social Drinking: **Permitted**
Airport/Station Pickup: **Yes**
Minimum Stay: **2 nights**

This California ranch house features a guest room furnished with a queen-size bed and antiques. The adjoining paneled den, with double-bed divan and TV, is available together with the guest room as a suite. While you relax on the patio, you can look out at the sailboats on the ocean. It's a short walk to the beach and local shops. There is a $10 surcharge for one-night stays.

SEQUOIA AREA
Road's End at Poso Creek ✪
RR 1, P.O. BOX 450, POSEY, CALIFORNIA 93260

Tel: **(805) 536-8668**
Best Time to Call: **9 AM–9 PM**
Host: **Jane Baxter**
Location: **55 mi. NE of Bakersfield**
No. of Rooms: **2**
No. of Private Baths: **1**
Max. No. Sharing Bath: **3**
Double/pb: **$120**
Single/pb: **$60**
Double/sb: **$110**

Single/sb: **$50**
Open: **All year**
Reduced Rates: **Weekly**
Breakfast: **Full**
Other Meals: **Available**
Pets: **No**
Children: **Yes**
Smoking: **No**
Social Drinking: **Permitted**
Minimum Stay: **Weekends; holidays**

Road's End is a restful streamside hideaway tucked into Sequoia National Forest. In this rustic setting, you can soak in a hot tub, fish for trout, and hike wilderness trails; in the winter, sledding and cross-country skiing await you. Jane prepares sumptuous meals, flavored with herbs and vegetables from her hillside garden. Her breakfast specialties include orange pecan waffles and, in homage to Dr. Seuss, green eggs and ham (the coloring comes from pesto).

COLORADO

Fort Collins• •Eaton
Estes Park • •Berthoud
Boulder •
Glenwood Springs • Central City• •Golden
•Denver
Vail • • •
Georgetown Pine Winter Park
Grand Junction Aspen• •Minturn
•
Manitou Springs
Hotchkiss • •Crested Butte Buena • •Colorado Springs
Olathe• Vista
Salida •
•Ouray
Yellow Jacket • •Silverton
Dolores •
•Durango • Pagosa Springs

Bed and Breakfast of Colorado, Ltd. ✪
BOX 12206, BOULDER, COLORADO 80303

Tel: (303) 494-4994	Rates (Single/Double):
Coordinators: **Kate and Jim Carey**	Modest: **$30** $38
States/Regions Covered: **Colorado**	Average: **$32** $50
Statewide	Luxury: $75–$95
Descriptive Directory: **$5**	Credit Cards: **MC, VISA**

The Careys' accommodations are quite select; listings range from a "modest" huge bedroom with a double bed, private bath, and separate entrance at the garden level to an "average" one with a living room with a fireplace and a deck overlooking the city. One "luxury" offering is a honeymoon cottage with fireplace, sauna, and hot tub. Don't miss Rocky Mountain National Park, the Shakespeare Festival, and great skiing. There is a $5 surcharge for one-night stays.

Bed & Breakfast—Rocky Mountains ✪
P.O. BOX 804, COLORADO SPRINGS, COLORADO 80901

Tel: (719) 630-3433
Best Time to Call: 9 AM–5 PM
Coordinator: Betty Ann Field
States/Regions Covered: Colorado,
   New Mexico, Utah
Descriptive Directory: $4.50

Rates (Single/Double):
   Modest: $20 $35
   Average: $28 $65
   Luxury: $50 $120
Credit Cards: MC, VISA

Kate's roster runs the gamut, from modest homes to elegant mansions, log cabins to working cattle ranches, ski chalets to lakeside homes. She will be pleased to arrange special interest accommodations, where the emphasis might be on romance, river rafting, bird watching, skiing, or gourmet breakfasts.

Parrish's Country Squire ✪
2515 PARRISH ROAD, BERTHOUD, COLORADO 80513

Tel: (303) 772-7678
Hosts: Donna and Jess Parrish
Location: 30 mi. NW of Denver
No. of Rooms: 2
No. of Private Baths: 2
Double/pb: $55
Single/pb: $45
Open: Jan. 16–Dec. 14

Reduced Rates: 10%, seniors
Breakfast: Full
Pets: No
Children: Welcome, over 5
Smoking: Permitted
Social Drinking: Permitted
Airport/Station Pickup: Yes

Donna and Jess invite you to relax at their comfortable log ranch home located near Estes Park and Carter Lake. You are certain to enjoy the serenity and breathtaking scenery of this 1,500-acre cattle ranch. Breakfast features homemade breads, wild plum or chokecherry jellies, as well as other delicious morsels. Horseback riding is available, or try your luck fishing in their stocked trout pond. No license required!

Trout City Inn ✪
BOX 431, BUENA VISTA, COLORADO 81211

Tel: (719) 495-0348
Best Time to Call: After 6 PM
Hosts: Juel and Irene Kjeldsen
Location: 5 mi. E of Buena Vista on
   Hwy. 24
No. of Rooms: 5
No. of Private Baths: 5
Double/pb: $36–40
Open: June 1–Oct. 15

Reduced Rates: 10%, seniors over 65
Breakfast: Full
Other Meals: Available
Credit Cards: MC, VISA
Pets: No
Children: Welcome, over 10
Smoking: No
Social Drinking: Permitted

Trout City Inn is a historic site on the famous South Park Narrow Gauge Railroad, and is located at the edge of a trout stream. It is an accurate reconstruction of a mountain railroad depot, with authentic private rail cars containing Pullman berths. The depot rooms feature Victorian decor, high ceilings, and four-poster or brass beds. Glass doors open onto a deck with views of the 14,000-foot peaks of the Continental Divide. Hiking, biking, panning for gold, and fly-fishing are within steps of the front door; white-water rafting is minutes away. Social-hour snacks are served in the depot "waiting room."

Griffin's Hospitality House ✪
4222 NORTH CHESTNUT, COLORADO SPRINGS, COLORADO 80907

Tel: **(719) 599-3035**
Best Time to Call: **Mornings, after 6 PM**
Hosts: **John and Diane Griffin**
Location: **5 mi. N of Colorado Springs**
No. of Rooms: **3**
No. of Private Baths: **1**
Max. No. Sharing Bath: **4**
Double/pb: **$45**
Single/pb: **$25**
Double/sb: **$35**
Open: **All year**
Breakfast: **Full**
Pets: **No**
Children: **Welcome (crib)**
Smoking: **No**
Social Drinking: **Permitted**
Airport/Station Pickup: **Yes**
Minimum Stay: **2 nights**

The welcome mat is always out at Diane and John's house. It's close to Pike's Peak, the Air Force Academy, and the Garden of the Gods. You can use the picnic table, TV, washing machine, and dryer. You will enjoy a fine view of Pike's Peak while eating a bountiful breakfast. In the evening, you are invited to relax in the living room with wine and good conversation. The University of Colorado is four miles away.

Holden House—1902 Victorian Bed & Breakfast Inn
1102 WEST PIKES PEAK AVENUE, COLORADO SPRINGS, COLORADO 80904

Tel: **(719) 471-3980**
Best Time to Call: **AM and after 4 PM**
Hosts: **Sallie and Welling Clark**
No. of Rooms: **3**
No. of Private Baths: **3**
Double/pb: **$57–$59**
Suite: **$85**
Open: **All year**
Reduced Rates: **$5/day after 2 days**
Breakfast: **Full**
Credit Cards: **AMEX, MC, VISA**
Pets: **No**
Children: **No**
Smoking: **No**
Social Drinking: **Permitted**

Built in 1902, this storybook Victorian is centrally located near historic Old Colorado City. The inn was lovingly restored by the Clarks in 1985 and is filled with antiques and family heirlooms. Guest rooms are furnished with queen-size brass or iron beds, period furnishings, and down pillows. The romantic Aspen suite also boasts an 80-gallon "tub for two" and open Victorian turret! Gourmet breakfasts—served on summer mornings on the veranda, with its mountain views— might include carob-chip muffins, Sallie's famous Eggs Fiesta, fresh fruit, gourmet coffee, tea, and juice. Complimentary sherry, coffee, and tea, turn-down service, and Sunday champagne breakfasts are a few of Holden House's amenities. Sallie and Welling are happy to help in planning your itinerary around the Pikes Peak region. Friendly cat Mingtoy in residence.

Queen Anne Inn ✪
2147 TREMONT PLACE, DENVER, COLORADO 80205

Tel: **(303) 296-6666**	Open: **All year**
Best Time to Call: **Afternoon**	Breakfast: **Continental**
Hosts: **Ann and Charles Hillestad**	Credit Cards: **AMEX, MC, VISA**
No. of Rooms: **10**	Pets: **No**
No. of Private Baths: **10**	Children: **Welcome, over 15**
Double/pb: **$69–$119**	Smoking: **No**
Single/pb: **$59–$109**	Social Drinking: **Permitted**

Located in the residential Clements Historic District, this three-story house, built in 1879, faces Benedict Fountain and Park. Decorated in the Queen Anne style, the luxurious bedrooms offer a choice of mountain or city views along with such touches as heirloom antiques, air conditioning, and writing desks. Fine art, good books, and unobtrusive chamber music provide a lovely backdrop. The Hillestads offer a generous breakfast, including seasonal fruits, assorted breads, homemade granola, and a special blend of coffee. The Central Business District, museums, shopping, and diverse restaurants are within walking distance. You are always welcome to help yourself to fruit, candy, soft drinks, and a glass of sherry. Ann and Charles will be happy to lend you their bikes for local touring.

Country Sunshine B&B ✪
35130 HIGHWAY 550 NORTH, DURANGO, COLORADO 81301

Tel: **(303) 247-2853; 247-4559**	Open: **All year**
Best Time to Call: **Before 9 AM; after 3 PM**	Reduced Rates: **Multiday stays and groups**
Hosts: **Jim and Jill Anderson**	Breakfast: **Full**
No. of Rooms: **5**	Credit Cards: **AMEX, MC, VISA**
No. of Private Baths: **3**	Pets: **Sometimes**
Max. No. Sharing Bath: **4**	Children: **Welcome (crib)**
Double/pb: **$65**	Smoking: **No**
Single/pb: **$60**	Social Drinking: **Permitted**
Double/sb: **$50**	Airport/Station Pickup: **Yes**
Single/sb: **$45**	

Nestled below rocky bluffs, there's a spectacular view of the San Juan Mountains from this spacious ranch home. In summer, breakfast of homemade breads, jams, and blackberry pancakes with pure maple syrup is served on the large deck in view of the narrow-gauge train. In cooler weather, it is set family style in front of the dining room's wood stove.

Logwood B&B ✪
35060 HIGHWAY 550, DURANGO, COLORADO 81301

Tel: (303) 259-4396
Best Time to Call: After 11 AM
Host: Hal Jackson
Location: 212 mi. NE of Albuquerque, New Mexico
No. of Rooms: 5
No. of Private Baths: 5
Double/pb: $55–$75
Single/pb: $50–$70
Suites: $95; sleeps four

Open: All year
Breakfast: Full
Credit Cards: DISC, MC, VISA
Pets: No (hosts have two cats)
Children: Yes, over 9
Smoking: No
Social Drinking: Permitted
Minimum Stay: During holidays
Airport/Station Pickup: Yes

An appealing, rough-hewn retreat with a wraparound porch, the Logwood B&B is constructed of red cedar logs. In keeping with the western spirit, the furniture is simple, attractive, and sturdy. Hal is an accomplished do-it-yourselfer: he built the bedframes himself. Logwood is a few yards away from a stream, and guests can watch wildlife year round. The generous breakfasts range from egg dishes and pancakes to quiche.

Scrubby Oaks Bed & Breakfast ✪
P.O. BOX 1047, DURANGO, COLORADO 81302

Tel: (303) 247-2176
Best Time to Call: Early AM or PM
Hosts: Mary Ann Craig
Location: 4 mi. from junction 160 and 550
No. of Rooms: 7
No. of Private Baths: 3
Max. No. Sharing Bath: 4
Double/pb: $65

Single/pb: $50
Double/sb: $55
Single/sb: $40
Open: All year
Breakfast: Full
Pets: No
Children: Welcome
Smoking: No
Social Drinking: Permitted

There's a quiet country feeling to this two-story home set on 10 acres overlooking the spectacular Animas Valley and surrounding mountains. Trees and gardens frame the patios where breakfast is apt to be served. All breads and preserves are homemade, and strawberry Belgian waffles are a specialty. On chilly mornings, the kitchen fireplace is the cozy backdrop for your wake-up cup of coffee or cocoa.

You are made to feel part of the family and are welcome to play pool, take a sauna, read a book, watch a VCR movie, or simply take in the crisp air.

The Victorian Veranda ✪
P.O. BOX 361, 515 CHEYENNE AVENUE, EATON, COLORADO 80615

Tel: **(303) 454-3890**	Single/sb: **$30**
Best Time to Call: **After 6 PM**	Double/pb: **$55**
Host: **Nadine J. White**	Open: **All year**
Location: **60 mi. N of Denver**	Breakfast: **Full**
No. of Rooms: **3**	Pets: **No**
No. of private baths: **1**	Children: **Welcome**
Max. No. Sharing Bath: **4**	Smoking: **No**
Double/sb: **$40**	Social Drinking: **No**

Nadine's Queen Anne home spells relaxation in this quaint agricultural town of 2,000. Each of the bedrooms is romantically furnished with antiques. One has a fireplace and balcony, the other a window seat flanked by bookcases. Weather permitting, breakfast, which includes juice, cereal, hard-boiled eggs, muffins, and beverages, is served on the veranda in view of the Rocky Mountains. You are welcome to borrow a bicycle built for two for local touring.

Cottenwood House ✪
P.O. BOX 1208, ESTES PARK, COLORADO 80517

Tel: **(303) 586-5104**	Open: **All year**
Best Time to Call: **Mornings; evenings**	Reduced Rates: **Weekly**
Hosts: **Kathleen and Ron Cotten**	Breakfast: **Full**
Location: **70 mi. NW of Denver**	Pets: **No**
No. of Rooms: **1 suite**	Children: **Welcome, over 8 years old**
No. of Private Baths: **1**	Smoking: **Permitted**
Suites: **$52–$75**	Social Drinking: **Permitted**

A prominent businessman built this three-story mountain home in 1929. The house is set on a quiet, residential street, surrounded by towering spruce and pine. The rooms boast mountain views, and have been lovingly restored right down to the oak floors. The Cottens have decorated 1930s-style, with a combination of antique and country furnishings, and welcome you to a guest suite privately located on the second floor. The suite consists of a bedroom with a queen-size brass bed, and a sitting room with a maple daybed, TV, telephone, and refrigerator. Relax with a lemonade on the porch, or by a cozy fire with a warm drink. Freshly baked muffins, rolls, and a choice of main dishes such as three-cheese quiche and apple-and-sausage crêpes are served each morning. In warm weather, breakfast can be enjoyed on a

sun porch, with its white wicker furnishings and plants. Cottenwood House is five miles from Rocky Mountain National Park, and is convenient to golf, tennis, shops, and restaurants.

Emerald Manor ✪
441 CHIQUITA LANE, P.O. BOX 3592, ESTES PARK, COLORADO 80517

Tel: **(303) 586-8050**
Best Time to Call: **8 AM–8 PM**
Hosts: **Reggie and Maura Fowler**
Location: **65 mi. NW of Denver**
No. of Rooms: **4**
Max. No. Sharing Bath: **4**
Double/sb: **$55–$65**
Single/sb: **$50–$60**

Open: **All year**
Breakfast: **Full**
Pets: **No**
Children: **No**
Smoking: **No**
Social Drinking: **Permitted**
Airport/Station Pickup: **Yes**

Every window of this Tudor pioneer home affords a beautiful view of the Rocky Mountains. The house is set on two acres in a quiet estate neighborhood within walking distance of downtown. Your hosts have decorated with comfortable wood furnishings, antiques, fine china, and crystal. Guest rooms are furnished in a variety of styles, from western to Victorian, and all have fine linens and lace-trimmed towels. Your hosts invite you to relax in a beamed living room in front of a cozy fire, or in a tropical room with indoor heated pool and sauna. They serve a complete Irish breakfast, including eggs and bacon or sausage accompanied by grilled tomatoes and soda bread.

Wanek's Lodge at Estes ✪

P.O. BOX 898, 560 PONDEROSA DRIVE, ESTES PARK, COLORADO 80517

Tel: (303) 586-5851
Best Time to Call: **Evenings**
Hosts: **Jim and Pat Wanek**
Location: **71 mi. NW of Denver**
No. of Rooms: **3**
Max. No. Sharing Bath: **4**
Double/sb: **$44–$49**
Single/sb: **$37–$40**

Open: **All year**
Breakfast: **Continental**
Other Meals: **Available**
Pets: **No**
Children: **Welcome, over 10**
Smoking: **No**
Social Drinking: **Permitted**

Jim and Pat invite you to share their modern mountain inn, located on a ponderosa pine-covered hillside just minutes away from Rocky Mountain National Park. The wood beams, stone fireplace, plants, and beautiful scenery provide a comfortable and relaxed atmosphere. Former educators, your hosts are people-oriented, and staying with them is like being with old friends.

Elizabeth Street Guest House ✪

202 EAST ELIZABETH, FORT COLLINS, COLORADO 80524

Tel: (303) 493-BEDS
Hosts: **John and Sheryl Clark**
Location: **65 mi. N of Denver**
No. of Rooms: **3**
Max. No. Sharing Bath: **4**
Double/sb: **$41**
Single/sb: **$35**
Double/pb: **$51**
Single/pb: **$45**

Open: **All year**
Breakfast: **Full**
Credit Cards: **AMEX, MC, VISA (for deposits only)**
Pets: **No**
Children: **Welcome, over 8**
Smoking: **No**
Social Drinking: **Permitted**

This completely renovated and restored 1905 brick American four-square has leaded windows and oak woodwork. Family antiques, plants, old quilts, and handmade touches add to its charm. All of the bedrooms have sinks. It is close to historic Old Town Square, Estes Park, Rocky Mountain National Park, and a block away from Colorado State University. John and Sheryl will spoil you with their special brand of hospitality and homemade treats.

Hardy House

P.O. BOX 0156, GEORGETOWN, COLORADO 80444

Tel: (303) 569-3388
Best Time to Call: **After 10 AM**
Host: **Sarah M. Schmidt**
Location: **50 mi. W of Denver**
No. of Rooms: **4**
No. of Private Baths: **4**

Double/pb: **$45–$65**
Single/pb: **$35**
Suites: **$45–$65**
Open: **All year**
Breakfast: **Full**
Other Meals: **Available**

Pets: **No**   Smoking: **No**
Children: **Welcome, over 10**   Social Drinking: **Permitted**

Back in the 1870s this bright red Victorian, surrounded by a white picket fence, was the home of a blacksmith. Inside you can relax by the potbelly parlor stove, sleep under feather comforters, and wake up to savory breakfast dishes such as waffle cheese strata and coffee cake. Guest quarters range from a two-bedroom suite to rooms with queen-size or twin beds. If you have a special birthday to celebrate, you can stay in the Victorian Suite and be served a candlelight dinner along with champagne, cake, and breakfast the next morning, for $125. In the evening, Sarah serves coffee and tea. Hardy House is located in the heart of the Historic District, half a block from the shops of Main Street. It is also close to hiking, skiing, and is walking distance from the Loop Railroad. Perhaps the best way to explore the town is on Sarah's six-speed tandem mountain bike, which she will gladly lend.

Bedsprings ✪
830 BLAKE, GLENWOOD SPRINGS, COLORADO 81601

Tel: **(303) 945-0350**
Best Time to Call: **8 AM–8 PM**
Host: **Emmy Hesse**
Location: **170 mi. W of Denver**
No. of Rooms: **2**
No. of Private Baths: **2**
Double/pb: **$50–$52.50**
Single/pb: **$40**

Open: **All year**
Breakfast: **Full**
Credit Cards: **MC, VISA**
Pets: **No**
Children: **Welcome**
Smoking: **Permitted**
Social Drinking: **Permitted**
Airport/Station Pickup: **Yes**

With its generous wrap-around porch, this big, gabled home says welcome. Glenwood Springs is a resort community famous for its hot-springs pool. Depending on the season, visitors may ski, hike, or go river rafting. And the stores and restaurants are open year round. Of course, after a full breakfast of fresh fruit, Belgian waffles, and home-made muffins, you may not be hungry for hours.

Sojourner's Inn ✪
1032 COOPER AVENUE, GLENWOOD SPRINGS, COLORADO 81601

Tel: **(303) 945-7162**
Best Time to Call: **After 5 PM**
Hosts: **Clay and Darlene Carrington**
Location: **160 mi. W of Denver**
No. of Rooms: **4**
No. of Private Baths: **4**
Max. No. Sharing Bath: **4**
Double/pb: **$35–$55**
Single/pb: **$27**

Open: **All year**
Reduced Rates: **Available**
Breakfast: **Full**
Credit Cards: **MC, VISA**
Pets: **No**
Children: **Permitted**
Smoking: **No**
Social Drinking: **Permitted**
Airport/Station Pickup: **Yes**

Sojourner's Inn is a large, turn-of-the-century home in a quiet, residential neighborhood. The house is a blending of different styles, but the prevailing one is comfort. Guest rooms are individually designed, featuring TVs and comfortable queen-size beds. Each morning, the cheerful dining room is the setting for a tempting breakfast, including homemade breads, fresh fruit, and specialty dishes. Hosts Clay and Darlene love their country surroundings and will gladly direct you to skiing, rafting, fishing, and hiking. Downtown Glenwood Springs and the world's largest hot springs pool are just a short walk from the house.

Talbott House ✪
928 COLORADO AVENUE, GLENWOOD SPRINGS, COLORADO 81601

Tel: (303) 945-1039
Host: **Cherry Talbott**
Location: **1 mi. from I-70, Exit 116**
No. of Rooms: **4**
Max. No. Sharing Bath: **4**
Double/sb: **$42**
Single/sb: **$27**
Open: **All year**

Breakfast: **Full**
Credit Cards: **MC, VISA**
Pets: **No**
Children: **Welcome**
Smoking: **No**
Social Drinking: **Permitted**
Airport/Station Pickup: **Yes**

This Victorian dates back to the beginning of the century. It's been lovingly restored and features an assortment of accessories collected from all over the world. Breakfast is served, family-style, in the dining room, and typically includes homemade breads, burritos, potatoes, and fresh fruit. Cherry invites you to use the solar-powered, outdoor hot tub in all seasons. Walk to the Hot Springs Pool, Vapor Caves, interesting shops, and restaurants.

The Dove Inn ✪
711 14TH STREET, GOLDEN, COLORADO 80401

Tel: (303) 278-2209
Hosts: **Sue and Guy Beals**
Location: **10 mi. W of downtown Denver**
No. of Rooms: **6**
No. of Private Baths: **6**
Double/pb: **$46–$59**
Single/pb: **$41–$54**
Open: **All year**

Reduced Rates: **10%, weekly**
Breakfast: **Full**
Credit Cards: **AMEX, DC, MC, VISA**
Pets: **No**
Children: **Welcome (crib)**
Smoking: **No**
Social Drinking: **Permitted**
Airport/Station Pickup: **Yes**

The Dove Inn is a charming Victorian on grounds beautifully landscaped with decks, walkways, and huge trees. The house has many bay windows, dormers, and angled ceilings; each room is individually decorated with pretty wallpapers and Victorian touches. Breakfast specialties such as cinnamon rolls and fresh fruit compotes are served. This delightful inn is located in the foothills of West Denver in one of the state's most beautiful valleys, yet it is just minutes from downtown Denver, historic Golden, and many other Rocky Mountain attractions. No unmarried couples, please.

The Cider House ✪
1126 GRAND AVENUE, GRAND JUNCTION, COLORADO 81501

Tel: **(303) 242-9087**
Host: **Helen Mills**
Location: **2 mi. from I-70**
No. of Rooms: **3**
No. of Private Baths: **1**
Max. No. Sharing Bath: **4**
Double/pb: **$42**
Single/pb: **$32**
Double/sb: **$38**
Single/sb:**$28**

Open: **All year**
Reduced Rates: **Available**
Breakfast: **Full**
Other Meals: **Available**
Credit Cards: **MC**
Pets: **Sometimes**
Children: **Welcome**
Smoking: **Permitted**
Social Drinking: **Permitted**
Airport/Station Pickup: **Yes**

Nestled in the heart of Grand Junction is this two-story frame house built at the start of the century. It is comfortably decorated with period furnishings, old-fashioned wallpapers, and nostalgic touches. Lace curtains and French doors add to the elegance of the living room. Sumptuous breakfasts of locally grown fruit, homemade breads, jams, special waffles, and beverages are served in the adjoining dining room. Nearby attractions include the Grand Mesa, river rafting, dinosaur digs, and some of the best winter skiing in the country.

The Gate House B&B
2502 NORTH FIRST STREET, GRAND JUNCTION, COLORADO 81501

Tel: (303) 242-6105	Single/sb: $28–$36
Best Time to Call: 9–11 AM; 5–9 PM	Open: All year
Hosts: Julie Susemihl and Rhonda McClary	Reduced Rates: 10% after 2 nights; 5%, seniors
Location: 250 mi. W of Denver	Breakfast: Full
No. of Rooms: 4	Credit Cards: MC, VISA
No. of Private Baths: 2	Pets: No
Max. No. Sharing Bath: 4	Children: Welcome, over 10
Double/pb: $52	Smoking: No
Single/pb: $40	Social Drinking: Permitted
Double/sb: $34–$42	Airport/Station Pickup: Yes

Originally built in 1889 as a gatekeeper's house to a castle estate, this Tudor-style home was moved, stone by stone, to its present site in 1945 and was recently restored. The living room is enhanced by solid oak floors, French love seats, and a large window overlooking the rose garden. The bedrooms are large and tastefully furnished. Stroll the spacious grounds, complete with the original wrought-iron gate, past the vine-covered arbor, and relax under giant sycamore trees. Breakfast treats often include fruit-filled French toast and delicious crêpes and coffee cakes. It's less than an hour to the Grand Mesa, Dinosaur Museum, the Center for the Arts, and seasonal sports.

Ye Ole Oasis Bed and Breakfast ✪
3142 J ROAD, P.O. BOX 609, HOTCHKISS, COLORADO 81419

Tel: (303) 872-3794	Open: Oct.–Aug.
Best Time to Call: Mornings; late evenings	Reduced Rates: Available
	Breakfast: Full
Hosts: Dwight and Rosemarie Ward	Other Meals: Available
Location: 1 mi. from Rte. 92	Credit Cards: MC, VISA
No. of Rooms: 3	Pets: Sometimes
Max. No. Sharing Bath: 4	Children: Welcome, over 6
Double/sb: $40–$45	Smoking: No
Single/sb: $30–$35	Social Drinking: Permitted

The Wards welcome you to their restored farmhouse set on the Rodgers Mesa at an elevation of 5,200 feet. They have a 17-acre working farm complete with buggy rides and a turkey named Hillary. The house is filled with antiques of all types, including many family heirlooms. Bedrooms have hand-crocheted and quilted spreads, wood furnishings, and period wallpapers. Before retiring, you can take a long soak in the claw-foot tub. On winter mornings, Rosemarie uses an antique wood stove to prepare special dishes such as Swedish-style French toast and New England fruit duffy. The farm is close to swimming at Glenwood Springs, skiing at Powderhorn and Aspen, and over 80 lakes for swimming and fishing.

Onaledge Bed & Breakfast Inn ✪
336 EL PASO BOULEVARD, MANITOU SPRINGS, COLORADO 80829

Tel: **(719) 685-4265**
Best Time to Call: **Afternoons**
Hosts: **Mel and Shirley Podell**
Location: **4 mi. from I-25, Exit 141**
No. of Rooms: **3**
No. of Private Baths: **3**
Double/pb: **$70–$90**
Single/pb: **$70**
Suites: **$90**
Open: **All year**

Reduced Rates: **Oct. 15–Apr. 15**
  (except holidays); 10%, seniors
Breakfast: **Full**
Credit Cards: **AMEX, DC, MC, VISA**
Pets: **No**
Children: **Welcome (crib)**
Smoking: **Permitted**
Social Drinking: **Permitted**
Airport/Station Pickup: **Yes**

Located on a hill overlooking historic Manitou Springs, this rock-and-frame Tudor-style home was built by a millionaire in 1912. Approximately $75,000 was spent on the garden area alone. The inn boasts unusual copper hardware and light fixtures, a large copper fireplace, and lovely hardwood floors. The spacious bedrooms have large windows framing lovely views of the mountains and Pike's Peak. In warm weather, breakfast may be enjoyed on one of the flowery patios. The cranberry muffins are legend, and guests have been known to give Michael's Western Omelet a standing ovation. For those watching their diet, a Heart's Delight low-fat breakfast may be ordered. Downtown Manitou Springs and Garden of the Gods Park are within walking distance.

The Eagle River Inn ✪
145 NORTH MAIN, BOX 100, MINTURN, COLORADO 81645

Tel: **(303) 827-5761 or (800) 344-1750**
Best time to Call: **8 AM–noon; 3–10 PM**
Hosts: **Beverly Rude and Richard Galloway**
Location: **100 mi. W of Denver**
No. of Rooms: **12**
No. of Private Baths: **12**
Double/pb: **$69–$120**
Single/pb: **$59–$110**

Open: **All year**
Reduced Rates: **$10 less in April**
Breakfast: **Continental**
Credit Cards: **AMEX, MC, VISA**
Pets: **No**
Children: **Welcome, over 12**
Smoking: **No**
Social Drinking: **Permitted**
Minimum Stay: **5 nights Dec. 26– Jan. 2**

The inn's adobe facade and decor are fashioned after the historic inns of Santa Fe. The living room is warm and cozy, accented by an authentic beehive fireplace and a view of the river. The guestrooms are furnished in a southwestern mode, each with a king bed. Minutes away are the slopes of Vail and Beaver Creek. A free ski shuttle stops across the street. You are invited to join your hosts for wine and cheese each afternoon.

Uncompahgre Cabin
8454 5700 ROAD, OLATHE, COLORADO 81425

Tel: **(303) 323-6789**
Best Time to Call: **Before 8 AM; after 8 PM**
Hosts: **Dean and Ellen Mosher**
Location: **15 mi. N of Montrose**
No. of Rooms: **2**
Max. No. Sharing Bath: **4**
Double/sb: **$27.50**

Single/sb: **$15**
Open: **All year**
Breakfast: **Continental**
Other Meals: **Available**
Pets: **Sometimes**
Children: **Welcome, over 2**
Smoking: **No**
Social Drinking: **Permitted**

This log cabin home is surrounded by the magnificent vistas of the Grand Mesa, the San Juan Mountains, and the Uncompahgre Plateau. Your hosts have created a rustic hunting lodge atmosphere overlooking the surrounding countryside. Natural, wholesome foods are served here, and guests are welcome to BYOB to a reasonably priced dinner topped off with a homemade dessert. In the morning, choose from a Continental or full breakfast with home-baked breads. There is much to do close to home, such as fishing in the stocked ponds or visiting the many farm animals. Dean and Ellen will gladly pack a lunch for those who like to spend the day hunting, bird-watching, hiking, or skiing. After a busy day, watch the sunset from a porch rocker, or unwind in the hot tub.

The Main Street House ✪
334 MAIN STREET, OURAY, COLORADO 81427

Tel: (303) 325-4317
Host: **David Vince**
Location: **80 mi. from I-70**
No. of Rooms: **3**
No. of Private Baths: **3**
Double/pb: **$50–$60**
Single/pb: **$35**

Suites: **$60**
Open: **All year**
Breakfast: **Continental**
Pets: **Sometimes**
Children: **Welcome**
Smoking: **Permitted**
Social Drinking: **Permitted**

The second-floor suite occupies an entire floor and features a fully equipped kitchen and two decks. The bedroom has a king-size bed and antique dresser. The living room is decorated in wood tones and the sofa converts to a queen bed. One ground-floor suite has a studio room, small greenhouse, and a large deck overlooking Oak Creek Canyon. The other suite contains a queen bed and futon couch that can sleep two. It is surrounded by a large deck with views of the San Juan Mountains. All guests are welcome to use the courtyard and children's play area. David is an avid outdoor enthusiast and will be happy to recommend ways for you to best enjoy his hometown.

Ouray 1898 House ✪
322 MAIN STREET, P.O. BOX 641, OURAY, COLORADO 81427

Tel: (303) 325-4871
Best Time to Call: **Afternoon**
Hosts: **Kathy and Lee Bates**
Location: **On Hwy. 550**
No. of Rooms: **3**
No. of Private Baths: **3**
Double/pb: **$50–$70**
Open: **June 1–Oct. 1**

Reduced Rates: **Singles, off season**
Breakfast: **Full**
Credit Cards: **MC, VISA**
Pets: **No**
Children: **Welcome, over 5**
Smoking: **No**
Social Drinking: **Permitted**

This 90-year-old house has been carefully renovated and combines the elegance of the 19th century with the comfortable amenities of the 20th. Each guest room features a spectacular view of the San Juan Mountains from its private deck. Breakfast is beautifully served on antique china. Jeep trips, horseback riding, hiking, browsing in the many quaint shops, and relaxing in the hot springs are but a few of the local diversions.

Davidson's Country Inn ✪
BOX 87, PAGOSA SPRINGS, COLORADO 81147

Tel: **(303) 264-5863**
Hosts: **The Davidson Family**
Location: **On US Hwy. 160**
No. of Rooms: **8**
No. of Private Baths: **3**
Max. No. Sharing Bath: **2**
Double/pb: **$55**
Single/pb: **$38**
Double/sb: **$43.50**

Single/sb: **$36**
Open: **All year**
Breakfast: **Full**
Credit Cards: **MC, VISA**
Pets: **Welcome**
Children: **Welcome**
Smoking: **No**
Social Drinking: **No**

You're sure to enjoy the beautiful Rocky Mountain scenery surrounding the 32 acres of this log inn's grounds. Some months bring the deer and elk to graze neaby. There's a natural hot spring in town and the San Juan River flows close by. You are invited to play horseshoes, or use the solarium and library. For the children, there's a full toy chest and sandbox. Family heirlooms, handmade quilts, and lovely paintings enhance the comfortable decor. Wolf Creek ski area is 18 miles away.

Echo Manor Inn ✪
3366 HIGHWAY 84, PAGOSA SPRINGS, COLORADO 81147

Tel: **(303) 264-5646**
Hosts: **Sandy and Virginia Northcutt**
No. of Rooms: **10**
No. of Private Baths: **6**
Max. No. Sharing Bath: **4**
Double/pb: **$59**
Single/pb: **$50**
Double/sb: **$49**
Single/sb: **$40**
Guest Cottage: **$125 for 4**

Suites: **$75**
Open: **All year**
Reduced Rates: **Weekly; families**
Breakfast: **Full**
Pets: **Sometimes**
Children: **Welcome, over 11**
Smoking: **No**
Social Drinking: **Permitted**
Airport/Station Pickup: **Yes**

Known to many locals as The Castle on 84, Echo Manor is a labyrinth of alcoves, bay windows, and turrets. The house draws from the Queen Anne and Dutch styles, and is framed on all sides by the San Juan Mountains. The Royal Suite has a fireplace, a brass bed, and complimentary champagne, while the Courtyard Suite—with living room, stone fireplace, kitchen, and wet bar—is perfect for families. Relax in the wood-beamed game room, where you can enjoy satellite TV and a crackling fire. Just across the way is Echo Lake, where you can bring a picnic lunch or take your chances with the rainbow trout. The healing waters of Pagosa Springs and the slopes of Wolf Creek Ski Area are located within a half-hour's drive. After a day of activity, sit back in the hot tub or enjoy the sunset from the deck. The Northcutts will serve a gourmet breakfast and offer the kind of hospitality that will make your visit feel like a holiday.

Meadow Creek B&B Inn ✪
13438 HIGHWAY 285, PINE, COLORADO 80470

Tel: (303) 838-4167; 4899
Best Time to Call: 10 AM–6 PM
Hosts: Pat and Dennis Carnahan
Location: 25 mi. SW of Denver
No. of Rooms: 6
No. of Private Baths: 6
Double/pb: $59–$79
Open: All year
Reduced Rates: 6th night free; 5%,
   seniors

Breakfast: Full
Other Meals: Available
Credit Cards: MC, VISA
Pets: No
Children: Welcome, over 12
Smoking: Permitted
Social Drinking: Permitted
Minimum Stay: 2 nights on weekends

Nestled in a secluded meadow surrounded by stone outcroppings and aspen and pine trees, along a spring-fed creek, this rustic mountain retreat is balm for stress. Don't forget your camera as you wander the 35 acres, home to elk, birds, and other wildlife. The historically significant house, barn, and outbuildings have been faithfully restored. Omelets and fresh baked cinnamon bread are breakfast specialties. The relaxing hot tub and the parlor fireside are both favorite gathering spots; fruit, beverages, homemade treats, and sherry are graciously served.

The Alma House ✪
220 EAST 10TH STREET, SILVERTON, COLORADO 81433

Tel: (303) 387-5336
Hosts: Don and Jolene Stott
Location: 50 mi. N of Durango
No. of Rooms: 10
Max. No. Sharing Bath: 3
Double/sb: $32
Open: June 1–Labor Day

Suite: $49
Breakfast: Continental
Credit Cards: AMEX, MC, VISA
Pets: No
Children: No
Smoking: No
Social Drinking: Permitted

This 1898 stone-and-frame building has been lovingly restored and comfortably updated. Each spacious room has a deluxe queen-size bed, luxurious linens, antique dresser, and special touches. The plumbing in the bathrooms is up-to-date, but the brass-and-walnut fixtures are faithful to a day gone by. Don and Jolene have a large videotape library for your evening entertainment. Ride the Durango-Silverton Narrow Gauge Railroad. Silverton retains the flavor of the old Western town it is.

Engelmann Pines ✪
P.O. BOX 1305, WINTER PARK, COLORADO 80482

Tel: (303) 726-4632
Hosts: **Heinz and Margaret Engel**
Location: **67 mi. W of Denver**
No. of Rooms: **6**
No. of Private Baths: **2**
Max. No. Sharing Bath: **4**
Double/pb: **$35–$85**
Single/pb: **$30–$80**
Double/sb: **$35–$75**
Single/sb: **$30–$70**

Open: **All year**
Reduced Rates: **10%, seniors and families**
Breakfast: **Full**
Pets: **Sometimes**
Children: **Welcome**
Smoking: **No**
Social Drinking: **Permitted**
Airport/Station Pickup: **Yes**
Foreign Languages: **German**

From its Rocky Mountain perch, this spacious modern lodge offers spectacular views of the continental divide. Bathrooms are equipped with Jacuzzis, and there is a complete kitchen for guests' use. A free bus ferries skiers from the front door to some of Colorado's best ski slopes; cross-country ski aficionados will find a trail just across the road. When the snow melts, it's time to go golfing, hiking, fishing, and horseback riding. In the morning, eager sportsmen and -women can fill up on marzipan cake, muesli, and fresh fruit crêpes.

CONNECTICUT

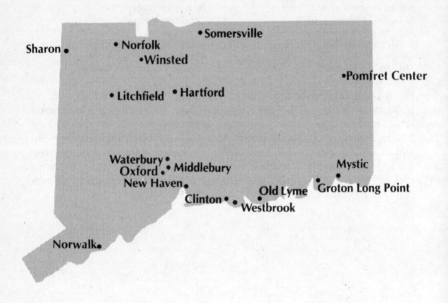

Sharon • Norfolk •Winsted •Somersville •Pomfret Center • Litchfield • Hartford Waterbury• Oxford •• Middlebury New Haven• Clinton • • Westbrook Old Lyme •Groton Long Point Mystic Norwalk•

Bed and Breakfast, Ltd. ✪
P.O. BOX 216, NEW HAVEN, CONNECTICUT 06513

Tel: **(203) 469-3260**
Best Time to Call:**after 5 PM
  weekdays; Summer: anytime**
Coordinator: **Jack Argenio**
States/Regions Covered: **Statewide;
  Rhode Island—Providence, Newport**

Rates (Single/Double):
  Modest: **$40**   **$50**
  Average: **$45**   **$60**
  Luxury: **$50**   **$75 and up**
Credit Cards: **No**

Whether you plan to visit one of Connecticut's many fine colleges—including Trinity, Yale, Wesleyan, or the Coast Guard Academy—the Mystic Seaport, picturesque country villages, theater, opera, fine restaurants, it is always pleasant to return to one of Jack's homes-away-from-home with congenial hosts ready to extend warmth and hospitality. They now have 125 listings statewide and offer great variety in host homes and personalized service to guests.

Covered Bridge Bed & Breakfast ✪
P.O. BOX 447A, MAPLE AVENUE, NORFOLK, CONNECTICUT 06058

Tel: (203) 542-5944
Best Time to Call: 9 AM–6 PM
Coordinator: Diane Tremblay
States/Regions Covered:
   Connecticut—Statewide; New
   York—Amenia, Cherry Plains, Dover
   Plains; Massachusetts—The
   Berkshires

Descriptive Directory: $3
Rates (Single/Double):
   Modest: $50–$65 $50–$65
   Average: $65–$85 $65–$85
   Luxury: $85–$150 $85–$150
Credit Cards: AMEX, MC, VISA
Minimum Stay: 3 nights, holidays
   weekends

If you enjoy historic homes, charming farmhouses, Victorian estates, picture-postcard New England scenery, unsurpassed fall foliage, music festivals, theater, antiquing, auto racing, skiing, white-water rafting, or hiking, call Diane.

Captain Dibbell House ✪
21 COMMERCE STREET, CLINTON, CONNECTICUT 06413

Tel: (203) 669-1646
Hosts: Ellis and Helen Adams
Location: 21 mi. E of New Haven
No. of Rooms: 3
No. of Private Baths: 3
Double/pb: $75
Single/pb: $60
Open: All year, except Jan.
Reduced Rates: Weekly; 10% seniors,
   3 or more nights

Breakfast: Full
Credit Cards: MC, VISA
Pets: No
Children: Welcome, over 14
Smoking: Permitted
Social Drinking: Permitted
Airport/Station Pickup: Yes

Ellis and Helen fell in love with this piece of Connecticut shore years ago when they used to come from their home in New York to spend the weekend sailing. They liked it so much, in fact, that they bought this sea captain's home, located just one-half mile from the shore and marinas and a short drive from the town beach, and converted it into a B&B. Clinton is ideally situated for exploring the Connecticut coast; not far away you'll find Hammonasset State Beach, Mystic Seaport and Aquarium, Gillette Castle, the Goodspeed Opera House, the Essex Steam Train, Long Wharf Theater, and Yale. In order to help you enjoy the Connecticut shore they love so much, the Adamses are happy to lend you their bicycles and beach chairs.

Tucker Hill Inn ✪
96 TUCKER HILL ROAD, MIDDLEBURY, CONNECTICUT 06762

Tel: (203) 758-8334
Best Time to Call: 9 AM–noon; after 4
   PM

Hosts: Richard and Susan Cebelenski
Location: 5 mi. W of Waterbury
No. of Rooms: 4

No. of Private Baths: **2**
Max. No. Sharing Bath: **4**
Double/pb: **$65–$75**
Double/sb: **$55**
Open: **All year**
Reduced Rates: **Weekly**

Breakfast: **Full**
Credit Cards: **MC, VISA**
Pets: **No**
Children: **Welcome**
Smoking: **Permitted**
Social Drinking: **Permitted**

Built in 1920, this large Colonial-style home, just down from the village green, exemplifies warm hospitality and charm. The spacious guest rooms are bright and airy, decorated with fine linens and pretty accessories. Breakfast features such caloric creations as pancakes, waffles, and omelets. Facilities for antiquing, music, theater, golf, tennis, water sports, and cross-country skiing are nearby.

Comolli's House ✪
36 BRUGGEMAN PLACE, MYSTIC, CONNECTICUT 06355

Tel: **(203) 536-8723**
Host: **Dorothy M. Comolli**
Location: **1 mi. from I-95, Exit 90**
No. of Rooms: **2**
No. of Private Baths: **2**
Double/pb: **$70–$85**
Single/pb: **$65–$75**

Open: **All year**
Breakfast: **Continental**
Pets: **No**
Children: **Welcome, over 12**
Smoking: **Permitted**
Social Drinking: **Permitted**
Airport/Station Pickup: **Yes**

This immaculate home on a quiet hill overlooking Mystic Seaport is convenient to the sights of Olde Mistick Village and the Aquarium. Dorothy caters to discriminating adults who appreciate a simple, homey atmosphere. The guest rooms are cozy in winter and cool in summer. She is pleased to provide information on sightseeing, sporting activities, shopping, and restaurants.

Weaver's House ✪
GREENWOODS ROAD, NORFOLK, CONNECTICUT 06058

Tel: **(203) 542-5108**
Hosts: **Judy and Arnold Tsukroff**
Location: **39 mi. NW of Hartford**
No. of Rooms: **4**
Max. No. Sharing Bath: **4**
Double/sb: **$45**
Single/sb: **$40**

Open: **All year**
Breakfast: **Full**
Pets: **No**
Children: **Welcome**
Smoking: **No**
Social Drinking: **Permitted**
Foreign Languages: **German**

Weaver's House is a turn-of-the-century Victorian facing the Yale Summer School of Music and Art Estate. In the 1930s, it was used as an annex to the Norfolk Inn. The guest rooms are simply decorated with handwoven rag rugs. Your hostess is a talented weaver, who will gladly display her loom for you. There are concerts and art shows in the summer, and two state parks are nearby with blazed hiking trails. Judy offers vegetarian choices at breakfast.

Janse Bed and Breakfast **○**
11 FLAT ROCK HILL ROAD, OLD LYME, CONNECTICUT 06371

Tel: **(203) 434-7269**	Reduced Rates: **10%, seniors**
Best Time to Call: **Evenings**	Breakfast: **Full**
Hosts: **Helen and Donald Janse**	Credit Cards: **MC, VISA**
Location: **1 mi. SW of New London**	Pets: **No**
No. of Rooms: **1**	Children: **Welcome, over 5**
No. of Private Baths: **1**	Smoking: **Permitted**
Double/pb: **$68**	Social Drinking: **Permitted**
Open: **All year**	Airport/Station Pickup: **Yes**

This Williamsburg-style saltbox is set on a quiet country road lined with vintage stone walls and century-old maples. The one-acre property includes a back patio and beautifully maintained gardens. Inside you'll find fresh flower arrangements, original art, Oriental rugs, and many antiques. Guest quarters feature pretty wallpaper, carpeting, wooden bed and bureau, and a sitting area with a Victorian love seat. Guests are welcome to relax in the library or living room with fireplace and grand piano. Your hosts serve fruit juice, ham or bacon, eggs, freshly baked muffins, and homemade jams for breakfast. Nearby points of interest include Mystic Seaport, the Goodspeed Opera House, and the Coast Guard Academy, home of the tall ship *Eagle*.

Butterbrooke Farm **○**
78 BARRY ROAD, OXFORD, CONNECTICUT 06483

Tel: **(203) 888-2000**	Reduced Rates: **15%, after 1 week;**
Best Time to Call: **4–10 PM**	**10%, seniors; $10 less per night,**
Host– **Tom Butterworth**	**Sun–Thurs.**
Location: **10 mi. SW of Waterbury**	Breakfast: **Full**
No. of Rooms: **1**	Pets: **Yes**
No. of Private Baths: **1**	Children: **Welcome, over 2**
Double/pb: **$65**	Smoking: **Permitted**
Single/pb: **$55**	Social Drinking: **Permitted**
Open: **All year**	Foreign Languages: **German**
	Airport/Station Pickup: **Yes**

Butterbrooke Farm, a colonial saltbox dating to 1711, has been restored and furnished in period style. From the guest-suite windows, you can survey the four-acre property, which boasts authentic 18th-century plantings: Tom, a biology professor at Connecticut State University, is interested in both historic and organic gardening. He'll also direct you to the best antique outlets. But first, he'll whip up a batch of multigrain pancakes, topped by freshly picked, home-grown berries.

Wintergreen ✪
ROUTE 169, BOX 87–AA, POMFRET CENTER, CONNECTICUT 06259

Tel: **(203) 928-5741**
Best Time to Call: **Before 10 AM, after 4 PM**
Hosts: **Doris and Stan Geary**
Location: **75 mi. W of Boston**
No. of Rooms: **4**
No. of Private Baths: **2**
Max. No. Sharing Bath: **4**
Double/pb: **$65**
Single/pb: **$60**

Double/sb: **$60**
Single/sb: **$55**
Open: **All year**
Breakfast: **Full**
Credit Cards: **MC, VISA**
Pets: **No**
Children: **Welcome**
Smoking: **No**
Social Drinking: **Permitted**

Wintergreen is a generous Victorian home set back from the road on 6½ acres. Feel free to stroll around the property, with its carefully tended rose and vegetable gardens. Pomfret offers small-town pleasures: evening walks, picnics, and hunting for antiques. You'll start the day right with a full breakfast of fruit, homemade muffins and croissants, and bacon and eggs.

The Old Mill Inn ✪
63 MAPLE STREET, SOMERSVILLE, CONNECTICUT 06072

Tel: **(203) 763-1473**
Best Time to Call: **9 AM–9 PM**
Hosts: **Ralph and Phyllis Lumb**
Location: **10 mi. S of Springfield, Mass.**
No. of Rooms: **4**
No. of Private Baths: **2**

Max. No. Sharing Bath: **4**
Double/pb: **$55**
Single/pb: **$55**
Double/sb: **$50**
Single/sb: **$50**
Open: **All year**
Reduced Rates: **10%, seniors**

Breakfast: **Continental**
Pets: **No**
Children: **Welcome**

Smoking: **No**
Social Drinking: **Permitted**
Airport/Station Pickup: **Yes**

Originally built in the 1850s, this comfortable home was enlarged and renovated many years later by the owner of the woolen mill next door. Today the old mill is a place to shop for gifts and furniture, while the house provides cozy lodgings for the traveler. Guest quarters are located on the second floor with bedrooms, baths, and a sitting room with cable TV, books, and a refrigerator. Bedrooms feature twin or full-size beds and comfortable furnishings. Downstairs in the gracious guest living room, you may relax by the fire, read, or listen to the stereo. Breakfast is served in a beautiful dining room with hand-painted walls overlooking the lawn. The Old Mill Inn is minutes from golf, the Basketball Hall of Fame, museums, restaurants, and shops.

Captain Stannard House ✪
138 SOUTH MAIN STREET, WESTBROOK, CONNECTICUT 06498

Tel: **(203) 399-7565**
Hosts: **Ray and Elaine Grandmaison**
Location: **25 mi. E of New Haven**
No. of Rooms: **9**
No. of Private Baths: **9**
Double/pb: **$65–$85**
Single/pb: **$60–$80**
Open: **All year**

Reduced Rates: **10%, seniors; AAA or Mobil clubs**
Breakfast: **Continental**
Credit Cards: **AMEX, DC, MC, VISA**
Pets: **No**
Children: **Welcome, over 6**
Smoking: **Permitted**
Social Drinking: **Permitted**

This Georgian Federal house with its fan window is the former home of a sea captain. Relax with a book, or browse through the on-premises antique shop. The village and the beach are close by. It is convenient to Mystic Seaport, Goodspeed Opera House, river cruises, fine restaurants, and charming shops. The U.S. Coast Guard Academy, Yale, and Wesleyan are nearby.

B&B By the Lake ✪
19 DILLON BEACH ROAD, WINSTED, CONNECTICUT 96098

Tel: **(203) 738-0230 in season; (914) 232-4535 other times**
Host: **Gayle Holt**
Location: **25 mi. W of Hartford**
No. of Rooms: **3**
No. of Private Baths: **1**
Max: No. Sharing Bath: **4**
Double/pb: **$60–$70**
Single/pb: **$55–65**
Double/sb: **$50–$60**
Single/sb: **$45–$55**
Nursery/Dorm: **$25–$45**

Open: **May 15–Oct. 15**
Reduced Rates: **Seniors; $10 less, midweek**
Breakfast: **Continental**
Credit Cards: **MC, VISA**
Pets: **Sometimes**
Children: **Welcome**
Smoking: **Permitted**
Social Drinking: **Permitted**
Airport/Station Pickup: **Yes**
Foreign Languages: **German, Dutch**

Make yourself at home in this rustic, turn-of-the-century lodge overlooking West Hill Lake. Feel free to borrow Gayle's canoe or fishing boat—the lake is well stocked with fish—or just loll about on the private beach. In the evening you can watch TV in your room, or screen a movie on the living room VCR. For a change of pace, your host will schedule a door-to-door Big Apple tour, since she is a licensed New York City guide. Fresh-fruit compote and bran muffins are served for breakfast; full breakfasts can be arranged.

DELAWARE

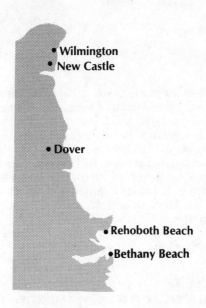

• Wilmington
• New Castle

• Dover

• Rehoboth Beach

• Bethany Beach

William Penn Guest House ✪
206 DELAWARE STREET, NEW CASTLE, DELAWARE 19720

Tel: **(302) 328-7736**
Best Time to Call: **After 5 PM**
Hosts: **Mr. and Mrs. Richard Burwell**
Location: **2 mi. from I-95**
No. of Rooms: **4**
Max. No. Sharing Bath: **4**
Double/sb: **$40**
Single/sb: **$40**

Open: **All year**
Breakfast: **Continental**
Credit Cards: **MC, VISA**
Pets: **No**
Children: **Welcome, over 3**
Smoking: **No**
Social Drinking: **Permitted**
Foreign Languages: **Italian**

If you're a history buff, perhaps a stay in a 1682 house named for William Penn is what you've been seeking. Located in the heart of New Castle's historic district, the accommodations here are most comfortable. A lovely park for strolling and for the children to play in borders the Delaware shore, just two blocks away. The University of Delaware is 15 minutes from the house.

Tembo Guest House ✪
100 LAUREL STREET, REHOBOTH BEACH, DELAWARE 19971

Tel: (302) 227-3360
Hosts: **Don and Gerry Cooper**
Location: ¾ **mi. from US 1**
No. of Rooms: **6**
Max. No. Sharing Bath: **4**
Double/pb: **$90**
Double/sb: **$60–75**
Open: **All year**

Reduced Rates: **Seasonal**
Breakfast: **Continental**
Pets: **Sometimes**
Children: **Welcome, over 6**
Smoking: **No**
Social Drinking: **Permitted**
Airport/Station Pickup: **Yes**

This white two-story frame beach cottage, set among old shade trees, is one block from the Atlantic Ocean. The house is surrounded by brick walks and gardens, and a private yard with chaise lounges for relaxing. The living room has a fireplace, hand-braided rugs, and an unusual collection of hand-carved shore birds and elephants. Each bedroom has an antique bureau, rocking chair, and either twin or full-size beds. Breakfast is served on a large enclosed front porch with rockers and swing. In colder weather, homemade muffins and scones are served in the kitchen, with its antique chandelier, butter churn, and coffee grinder. Don and Gerry will gladly direct you to local sights, such as the restored Homestead, historic Port Lewes, and the Zwaanendael Museum.

Alford's B&B ✪
3650 SILVERSIDE ROAD, BOX 177, WILMINGTON, DELAWARE 19810

Tel: (302) 479-9500
Best Time to Call: **9 AM–9 PM Mon.,**
  Wed., Fri.
Hosts: **Jack and Millie Alford**
No. of Rooms: **2**
No. of Private Baths: **2**
Double/pb: **$55**
Single/pb: **$45**

Open: **All year**
Breakfast: **Full**
Credit Cards: **MC, VISA**
Pets: **No**
Children: **Yes**
Smoking: **No**
Social Drinking: **No**
Airport/Station Pickup: **Yes**

Alford's, a two-story brick Colonial with black shutters, is an easy drive from world-class institutions such as the Winterthur Museum and Longwood Gardens. Millie, an avid gardener, fills the house with plants and flower arrangements. You'll savor refreshments upon arrival; in addition, you'll find a fruit basket in your room. For breakfast, you'll savor such dishes as French toast and eggs Benedict.

The Boulevard Bed & Breakfast ✪
1909 BAYNARD BOULEVARD, WILMINGTON, DELAWARE 19802

Tel: (302) 656-9700
Hosts: **Charles and Judy Powell**

Location: ½ **mi. from I-95, Exit 8**
No. of Rooms: **6**

No. of Private Baths: **4**
Max. No. Sharing Bath: **3**
Double/pb: **$65–$70**
Single/pb: **$60**
Double/sb: **$55**
Single/sb: **$50**
Open: **All year**

Reduced Rates: **Corporate; 10%, seniors**
Breakfast: **Full**
Credit Cards: **AMEX, MC, VISA**
Pets: **No**
Children: **Welcome**
Smoking: **Permitted**
Social Drinking: **Permitted**
Airport/Station Pickup: **Yes**

This beautifully restored city mansion was built in 1913 and has earned a place on the National Register of Historic Places. Upon entering, you'll be struck by the impressive foyer and magnificent staircase, leading to a landing complete with a window seat and large leaded-glass windows flanked by 15-foot-tall fluted columns. Breakfast is served in the formal dining room or on the screened-in porch. Although Baynard Boulevard is a quiet and peaceful street, it's just a short walk away from the downtown business district. Parks are close by, and it's just a short drive to Hagley, Winterthur, the Delaware Natural History or Art Museum; or head for nearby Chadds Ford, Pennsylvania, and the famous Brandywine River Museum.

The Pink Door ✪
8 FRANCIS LANE, WILMINGTON, DELAWARE 19803

Tel: **(302) 478-8325**
Best Time to Call: **Noon–9 PM**
Hosts: **Frank and Mary Wehner**
Location: **4½ mi. N of Wilmington**
No. of Rooms: **2**
No. of Private Baths: **1**
Max. No. Sharing Bath: **3**
Double/pb: **$45–$55**

Single/pb: **$40–$45**
Open: **All year**
Breakfast: **Full**
Pets: **Sometimes**
Children: **Welcome, over 3**
Smoking: **Permitted**
Social Drinking: **Permitted**
Airport/Station Pickup: **Yes**

The Pink Door is a contemporary ranch home on a wooded cul-de-sac. Guests are welcomed with a carafe of wine or pot of tea, and a tray of cookies. The decor is eclectic, ranging from the romantic Queen Anne period to today's modern designs. After a long day of touring the Brandywine Valley, you will appreciate returning to the sounds of crickets and awakening to the chirping of the many birds. Breakfast is served in the dining room or on the screened deck facing the woods. Your hosts will gladly direct you to the nearby Brandywine River Museum, Longwood Gardens, Winterthur, and the Hagley Museum.

Small Wonder B&B ✪
213 WEST CREST ROAD, WILMINGTON, DELAWARE 19803

Tel: **(302) 764-0789**
Best Time to Call: **After 4 PM**

Hosts: **Dot and Art Brill**
Location: **½ mi. from I-95, Exit 9**

No. of Rooms: **2**
No. of Private Baths: **2**
Double/pb: **$65**
Single/pb: **$55**
Open: **All year**
Breakfast: **Full**
Other Meals: **Available**

Credit Cards: **AMEX, MC, VISA**
Pets: **No**
Children: **Welcome, over 9**
Smoking: **No**
Social Drinking: **Permitted**
Airport/Station Pickup: **Yes**

The Brills describe their area as "a microcosm of American history and cosmopolitan trends." They live in a quiet suburb surrounded by things they enjoy—piano, organ, books, paintings, plants, outdoor swimming pool, and spa set in an award-winning garden—all of which they share with guests. Learn of historic New Castle, Winterthur, Longwood, Bellevue, Nemours, Hagley, and Eleutherian Mills, Rockwood, the Wyeths, Pyle, and more at breakfast, by the pool, or over drinks by the fire. The Brills' warm, considerate style has earned a national award for B&B comfort and hospitality. There's a $5 surcharge for one-night stays.

DISTRICT OF COLUMBIA

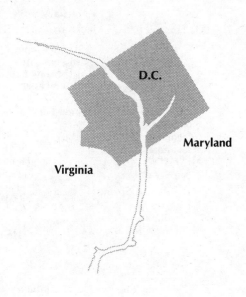

Bed 'n' Breakfast Ltd. of Washington, D.C.
P.O. BOX 12011, WASHINGTON, D.C. 20005

Tel: **(202) 328-3510**
Best Time to Call: **10 AM–5 PM**
   Mon.–Fri.; 10 AM–1 PM Sat.
Coordinator: **Michael Dale**
States/Regions Covered: **Washington,**
   D.C.; Virginia and Maryland suburbs

Rates (Single/Double):
   Average: **$40–$150 $50–$150**
Credit Cards: **AMEX, DC, MC, VISA**
Minimum Stay: **2 nights**

This service has a network of 75 homes, apartments, guesthouses, and inns. Most of the accommodations are convenient to public transportation. Several of the homes are historic properties. There is a wide range of accommodations, from budget to luxury.

FLORIDA

Amelia Island
Jacksonville
Tallahassee
Pensacola
St. Augustine
Sunnyside
Crescent City
Gainesville
Daytona Beach
Eastlake Weir
Lake Helen
DeLand
Orlando
Winter Park
Tarpon Springs
Clearwater
Tampa
Stuart
Indian Shores
Palmetto
Hobe Sound
St. Petersburg
Madeira Beach
Jupiter
Sarasota
Zolfo Lake Worth
Palm Beach
Springs
Lantana
West Palm Beach
Fort Myers
Delray Beach
Estero
Fort Lauderdale
Naples
Hollywood
Miami Beach
Big Pine Key
Marathon
Summerland Key

A & A Bed & Breakfast of Florida, Inc. ✪
P.O. BOX 1316, WINTER PARK, FLORIDA 32790

Tel: **(407) 628-3233**
Best Time to Call: **9 AM–6 PM**
Coordinator: **Brunhilde (Bruni) Fehner**
States/Regions Covered: **Orlando area—Disney World, Epcot;** Altamonte Springs, Cape Canaveral (Kennedy Space Center), Maitland, New Smyrna Beach, Sea World, Winter Park; Delray Beach, Ft. Myers, St. Augustine

Rates (Single/Double):
Modest:	**$35**	**$40**
Average:	**$40**	**$55**
Luxury:	**$50**	**$75**

Credit Cards: **No**
Minimum Stay: **2 nights**

You should allow several days to really savor all this area has to offer. Bruni's hosts will suggest hints on getting the most out of the major attractions, wonderful un-touristy restaurants, and tips on where to shop for unique gifts to take home. All of her homes have a certain "touch of class" to make you delighted with your visit. Rollins College is close by. There is a surcharge of $5 for one-night stays.

Bed & Breakfast Co.—Tropical Florida ✪
P.O. BOX 262, SOUTH MIAMI, FLORIDA 33243

Tel: (305) 661-3270	Rates (Single/Double):
Best Time to Call: 9 AM–5 PM, Mon.– Fri.	Modest: $27–$35 $32–$40
	Average: $35–$55 $40–$60
Coordinator: Marcella Schaible	Luxury: $55–$145 $60–$150
States/Regions Covered: Florida, statewide	Credit Cards: AMEX, MC, VISA

Native Floridians, Marcella's hosts live in mansions on historic properties, in homes along the ocean and Gulf of Mexico, in woodland retreats, and on private residential islands. They exude southern hospitality and want you to come stay in their accommodations that range from a charming cottage to a contemporary condo to unhosted accommodations. The decor may be simple or wildly extravagant. They are ready to direct you to famous attractions or to an undiscovered, special restaurant or shop that only a resident knows about. There is a $5 surcharge for each night stayed less than three.

Bed & Breakfast Registry of Volusia County
P.O. BOX 573, DE LEON SPRINGS, FLORIDA 32130

Tel: (904) 985-5068	Rates (Single/Double):
Coordinator: Robin Johnstone	Average: $35 $40
States/Regions Covered: Astor, Daytona Beach, De Bary, De Land, De Leon Springs, Deltona, Sanford	Luxury: $40 $45
	Credit Cards: No

Area attractions include the famed Daytona International Speedway (where the auto is king) and beach, Spring Garden Ranch (where harness horses are trained), De Leon Springs State Park, and Blue Springs State Park (which is home to the manatee, an aquatic mammal). It's also a fine fishing area. Summer rates are reduced by $10 nightly. Keep this in mind should you care to visit Disney World, Sea World, and Epcot, since they are an hour's drive from most host homes.

Central Florida B&B Reservations ✪
719 SOUTHEAST 4TH STREET, OCALA, FLORIDA 32671

Tel: (904) 351-1167
Coordinator: **Marcie Gauntlett**
States/Regions Covered: **Cocoa
Beach, Gainesville, Lakeland,
McIntosh, Melbourne, Micanopy,
Naples, Ocala, Oklawaha, Orange
Springs, Orlando, Tampa, Winter
Park**

Rates (Single/Double):
   Modest: **$40**   **$45**
   Average: **$45**   **$50**
   Luxury: **$50**   **$125**
Credit Cards: **No**

One of Marcie's B&Bs is decorated with antiques and Oriental rugs bought in the Middle East and Europe. The hostess has a most interesting doll collection as well. Another is a farm located on Lake Fay, where you are welcome to try your hand at fishing. The owner, a former horse trainer, has Arabians. Silver Springs, Wild Waters, the Museum of Drag Racing, and Cross Creek, the home of Marjorie Kinnan Rawlings, are some of the local attractions.

Open House Bed & Breakfast Registry—Gold Coast ✪
P.O. BOX 3025, PALM BEACH, FLORIDA 33480

Tel: (407) 842-5190
Best Time to Call: **Evenings; weekends**
Coordinator: **Peggy Maxwell**
States/Regions Covered: **Boca Raton,
Boynton Beach, Delray, Jupiter, Lake
Worth, Lantana, Palm Beach, Stuart,
West Palm Beach**

Rates (Single/Double):
   Average: **$35**   **$55**
   Luxury: **$60**   **$85**

Peggy's roster includes many homes within a short walk to ocean beaches. They are all within easy reach of fine restaurants, shops, galleries, museums, theaters, and sports arenas. The service is closed from August 1 to September 30. Rates are reduced for weekly and off-season stays.

The 1735 House ✪
584 SOUTH FLETCHER, AMELIA ISLAND, FLORIDA 32034

Tel: (904) 261-5878 or (800) 872-8531
Hosts: **Gary and Emily Grable**
Location: **35 mi. NE of Jacksonville**
No. of Rooms: **5 suites**
No. of Private Baths: **5**
Suites: **$55–$85**
Guest Cottage: **$95–$125; sleeps 4**
Open: **All year**

Reduced Rates: **Weekly; 5%, seniors**
Breakfast: **Continental**
Credit Cards: **AMEX, MC, VISA**
Pets: **No**
Children: **Welcome, over 3**
Smoking: **Permitted**
Social Drinking: **Permitted**
Airport/Station Pickup: **Yes**

This century-old country inn is situated right on the beach of a beautiful North Florida barrier island; each of the suites has an ocean view. A special treat is the free-standing lighthouse with four levels of living area, including two bedrooms and two baths. The decor throughout is wicker and rattan accented with nautical antiques. Breakfast, complete with freshly baked treats from the Grable's galley, is delivered to your suite along with the morning newspaper. Historic Fernandina Beach, with its lovely restored Victorian homes and shops, is nearby. Gary and Emily can suggest boat charters for those who wish to try their skill at landing a big one.

The Barnacle
ROUTE 1, BOX 780 A, LONG BEACH ROAD, BIG PINE KEY, FLORIDA 33043

Tel: **(305) 872-3298**	Open: **All year**
Best Time to Call: **Before 9 PM**	Breakfast: **Full**
Hosts: **Wood and Joan Cornell**	Pets: **No**
Location: **Mile marker 33**	Children: **No**
No. of Rooms: **4**	Smoking: **Permitted**
No. of Private Baths: **4**	Social Drinking: **Permitted**
Double/pb: **$70–$100**	Foreign Languages: **French**

The ultimate in privacy is the self-contained cottage—a tropical tree house with stained-glass windows and private terrace. Rooms overlook the ocean or the atrium, with its hot tub and lush plants. One room has a private entrance and opens onto the beach. Every detail in and around their home reflects Wood and Joan's taste, attention to detail, and artistic flair. The structure was built to frame their eclectic collection of statuary, tapestries, and art. Their emphasis is on the sun and sea, with warm hospitality offered in abundance. You can snorkel or fish right off "your own" beach. Bahia Honda State Park and Key West are close by.

Bed & Breakfast-on-the-Ocean "Casa Grande" ✪
P.O. BOX 378, BIG PINE KEY, FLORIDA 33043

Tel: **(305) 872-2878**	Open: **All year**
Hosts: **Jon and Kathleen Threlkeld**	Breakfast: **Full**
Location: **30 mi. E of Key West**	Pets: **No**
No. of Rooms: **3**	Children: **No**
No. of Private Baths: **3**	Smoking: **Permitted**
Double/pb: **$75**	Social Drinking: **Permitted**

This spectacular Spanish-style home, facing the ocean, was custom-designed to suit the natural beauty of the Keys. The large landscaped garden patio, with panoramic beach views, is where you'll enjoy Jon

and Kathleen's bountiful breakfast. It is also the site of the hot tub/ Jacuzzi for relaxing by day or under a moonlit sky. The large and airy guest rooms are comfortably cooled by Bahama fans or air-conditioning. Key deer and birds abound. From the private beach, you'll enjoy swimming, fishing, snorkeling, bicycling, and jogging. There's a picnic table, gas grill, hammock, and Windsurfer for guests to use, compliments of the gracious hosts.

Canal Cottage Bed & Breakfast
P.O. BOX 266, BIG PINE KEY, FLORIDA 33043

Tel: **(305) 872-3881**	Breakfast: **Full**
Best Time to Call: **Evenings**	Pets: **No**
Hosts: **Dean and Patti Nickless**	Children: **Welcome**
No. of Rooms: **1 suite**	Smoking: **Permitted**
No. of Private Baths: **1**	Social Drinking: **Permitted**
Suites: **$75 for 2**	Minimum Stay: **2 nights**
Open: **All year**	

You can be self-sufficient in this unusual wood stilt house. Your accommodations are nestled in the trees and consist of a bedroom with a queen-size bed, a bathroom, a living room with sleep space for two, and a kitchen stocked for your breakfast, which you can prepare at leisure and enjoy on the porch. You can dive, snorkel, and fish in the Gulf or the Atlantic. You can launch your boat at the neighborhood ramp and tie it up at your backyard dock, where you may also enjoy swimming. Dean and Patti live on the premises and will make every effort to ensure you a comfortable, enjoyable stay.

Deer Run ✪

LONG BEACH ROAD, P.O. BOX 431, BIG PINE KEY, FLORIDA 33043

Tel: (305) 872-2015; 872-2800
Best Time to Call: **Anytime before 10 PM**
Host: **Sue Abbott**
Location: **33 mi. E of Key West**
No. of Rooms: **2**
No. of Private Baths: **2**
Double/pb: **$75–$85**
Single/pb: **$65**

Open: **All year**
Breakfast: **Full**
Pets: **No**
Children: **No**
Smoking: **No**
Social Drinking: **Permitted**
Airport/Station Pickup: **Yes**
Minimum Stay: **2 nights**

Deer Run is a Florida Cracker-style home nestled among lush native trees on the ocean. The house is beautifully designed, with skylights, high ceilings, central air-conditioning, and Bahama fans. The decor boasts many paintings, artifacts, and antiques to compliment wicker and rattan furnishings. Upstairs each room has French doors that open onto a large veranda. Breakfast is served outside overlooking the ocean, where you may spot Key deer walking along the beach. Looe Key Coral Reef, Bahia Honda State Park, and Key West are all within easy reach, or you can relax and soak up the rays in the free-form deep spa, where there's room for eight.

Bed & Breakfast of Tampa Bay ✪

3234 TERN WAY, FEATHERSOUND, CLEARWATER, FLORIDA 34622

Tel: (813) 573-5825
Best Time to Call: **Before 10 AM; after 6 PM**
Hosts: **Vivian and David Grimm**
Location: **7 mi. W of Tampa**
No. of Rooms: **3**
No. of Private Baths: **1**
Max. No. Sharing Bath: **4**
Double/pb: **$45**

Single/pb: **$35**
Double/sb: **$35**
Single/sb: **$25**
Open: **All year**
Breakfast: **Full**
Pets: **Sometimes**
Children: **Welcome**
Smoking: **Permitted**
Social Drinking: **Permitted**

The lovely gardens of this fine stucco home have an Oriental flair, and the interior is graced with fine Oriental and European art. Whenever Vivian and David travel, they bring home souvenirs to enhance their decor. Busch Gardens, St. Petersburg Fine Arts Museum, and Tarpon Springs are 15 miles away; Disney World, Dali Museum, and Sea World are 65 miles away. If you want to stay close to home, the Grimms will lend you their bikes. You're welcome to use the pool, play the piano, or use the kitchen for light snacks. It's close to the University of South Florida and the University of Tampa.

Sprague House Inn ✪
125 CENTRAL AVENUE, CRESCENT CITY, FLORIDA 32012

Tel: **(904) 698-2430**
Hosts: **Terry, Edith, and baby Sarah Moyer**
Location: **75 mi. N of Orlando**
No. of Rooms: **5**
No. of Private Baths: **5**
Double/pb: **$45–$65**
Single/pb: **$40–$60**
Open: **All year**

Breakfast: **Full**
Other Meals: **Available**
Credit Cards: **MC, VISA**
Pets: **No**
Children: **Welcome**
Smoking: **Permitted**
Social Drinking: **Permitted**
Airport/Station Pickup: **Yes**

A Steamboat Gothic inn, Sprague House Inn has been welcoming guests since 1905. The comfortably air-conditioned guest rooms are highlighted in antiques. Accents of stained glass and handsome woods are found throughout. The wrap-around porches both upstairs and down boast rockers and swings from which you may enjoy the views of the lake. A public boat ramp and dock are a stone's throw away. You are welcome to borrow a cane fishing pole (no license required) or grab your net and try your luck at blue crabs. This one-stoplight town, unspoiled by plastic and neon, claims to be "the bass capital of the world." Edith does the baking; Terry is the gourmet cook for their on-premises restaurant.

Bed'n Breakfast of Greater Daytona Beach ✪
P.O. BOX 1081, ORMOND BEACH, FLORIDA 32175

Tel: **(904) 673-2232**
Coordinator: **Rusty Reed**
States/Regions Covered: **Daytona Beach, Ormond Beach, Pt. Orange, Wilbur-by-the-Sea**

Rates (Single/Double):
  Average: **$35–$75**
Credit Cards: **No**
Minimum Stay: **2 nights Speed/Bike weeks in Feb. and Mar.**

The host homes, each with its own special amenities and charm, are located throughout the greater Daytona area and pride themselves on catering to the needs of each guest. The Space Center and Disney World are within 60 miles. Closer to home, Daytona offers deep-sea fishing, golf, tennis, jai alai, dog racing, theater, and Halifax River cruises. A Daytona International Speedway tour and a drive on "the world's most famous beach" are a must. Yacht enthusiasts will be interested in the new 600-slip Halifax Marina, where they can dock, and then bed-and-breakfast nearby.

DeLand County Inn ✪
228 WEST HOWRY AVENUE, DELAND, FLORIDA 32720

Tel: **(904) 736-4244**
Best Time to Call: **Mornings**

Hosts: **Raisa and Bill Lilly**
Location: **20 mi. N of Daytona Beach**

No. of Rooms: **4**
No. of Private Baths: **3**
Max. No. Sharing Bath: **4**
Double/pb: **$59**
Single/pb: **$49**
Dugle/sb: **$49**
Single/sb: **$39**
Suites: **$79**
Open: **All year**
Reduced Rates: **10%, seniors**

Breakfast: **Full or continental**
Wheelchair-Accessible: **Yes**
Credit Cards: **MC, VISA**
Pets: **No**
Children: **Welcome, over 7**
Smoking: **Permitted**
Social Drinking: **Permitted**
Foreign Languages: **French**
Airport/Station Pickup: **Yes**

The Lillys pride themselves on giving guests "a little bit of country, close to town." Their home, built in 1903, features rich woodwork and Victorian-style floral wallpapers. The local library, museum, gallery, and flea market are within walking distance, and the pool is even closer—behind the house. Continental breakfast is laid out in the dining room every morning from 8:00 to 9:30 AM.

Lakeside Inn Bed and Breakfast ❂
P.O. BOX 71, EASTLAKE WEIR, FLORIDA 32133-0071

Tel: **(904) 288-1396**
Best Time to Call: **Mornings, evenings**
Hosts: **Bill and Sandy Bodner**
Location: **20 mi. S of Ocala**
No. of Rooms: **4**
No. of Private Baths: **3**
Max. No. Sharing Bath: **3**
Double/pb: **$50–$55**
Single/pb: **$35–$40**
Double/sb: **$40–$45**

Single/sb: **$30**
Open: **All year**
Reduced Rates: **5%, families**
Breakfast: **Full**
Pets: **Sometimes**
Children: **Welcome, over 5**
Smoking: **On porch only**
Social Drinking: **Permitted**
Airport/Station Pickup: **Yes**
Minimum Stay: **Holidays, 2 nights**

If you enjoy historic country homes filled with antiques and collectibles, this may be the vacation spot for you. This lovely Victorian Gothic home was built in the 1880s as a hotel. The house is set on beautiful Lake Weir and is complete with dock and sun deck. A huge veranda overlooks the lake on the first floor, as does the screened-in porch upstairs. The rooms are quaint and comfortable, featuring cypress paneling and five fireplaces. Enjoy a hearty Southern breakfast, complete with home-baked goodies, then grab a fishing pole or go swimming right off their dock. Lakeside Inn is located in the Silver Springs area, which abounds with numerous lakes, streams, and rollings hills.

Dolan House ❂
1401 NORTHEAST 5 COURT, FT. LAUDERDALE, FLORIDA 33301

Tel: **(305) 462-8430**
Hosts: **Tom and Sandra Dolan**

Location: **5 mi. from I-95**
No. of Rooms: **4**

No. of Private Baths: **2**
Max. No. Sharing Bath: **4**
Double/pb: **$60**
Single/pb: **$50**
Double/sb: **$60**
Single/sb: **$50**
Open: **Oct. 1–July 31**
Reduced Rates: **20% less, May–July;**
    Oct.

Breakfast: **Continental**
Pets: **No**
Children: **Welcome**
Smoking: **Permitted**
Social Drinking: **Permitted**
Airport/Station Pickup: **Yes**

All the comforts of home—if your home has a hot tub large enough to fit 19! Set right in the heart of Fort Lauderdale, and only two miles from the city's famed beach, the Dolan House offers privacy (it's completely fenced in) and convenience. When the weather's balmy, guests sit out on the large deck; when the nights are cool, they can move indoors and enjoy the large coquina fireplace. The Dolans have lived in the area for 30 years, and they're eager to tell you all about it. Ask them about the Galleria Shopping Center, the new Riverwalk historic section, Holiday Park, and all the nearby theaters and museums.

Windsong Garden & Art Gallery ✪
5570–4 WOODROSE COURT, FORT MYERS, FLORIDA 33907

Tel: **(813) 936-6378**
Host: **Embe Burdick**
No. of Rooms: **2**
No. of Private Baths: **2**
Double/pb: **$55**
Suite: **$55**
Open: **All year**

Breakfast: **Continental**
Pets: **No**
Children: **No**
Smoking: **No**
Social Drinking: **Permitted**
Minimum Stay: **2 nights**

This modern clear-shake-and-brick town house has a private courtyard and balcony for your enjoyment. The spacious combination bedroom-and-sitting room is most comfortable. Embe's varied interests include arts, crafts, music, and her household cats. It's close to Sanibel and Captiva islands, Ft. Myers Beach, fine shopping, good restaurants, and the University of Florida. You are welcome to use the pool.

Country Meadows ✪
9506 SOUTH WEST 81 WAY, GAINESVILLE, FLORIDA 32608

Tel: **(904) 495-2699**
Best Time to Call: **3–11 PM**
Hosts: **Allene and Orville Higgs**
Location: **10 mi. SW of Gainesville**
No. of Rooms: **2**
No. of Private Baths: **2**
Double/pb: **$38–$40**
Single/pb: **$32–$35**

Open: **All year**
Breakfast: **Continental**
Other Meals: **Available**
Pets: **No**
Children: **Welcome**
Smoking: **Permitted**
Social Drinking: **Permitted**
Airport/Station Pickup: **Yes**

Country Meadows is a Colonial-style home set on an acre and a half. The house is surrounded by pine trees, and has a fenced-in yard for relaxing. The country-style decor consists of comfortable furnishings and lots of handmade craft items. The Higgses enjoy entertaining and are glad to prepare either a Continental breakfast or a larger meal for guests. They will gladly direct you to nearby nature parks, horse farms, and museums.

Gaver's Bed & Breakfast ✪
301 EAST SIXTH AVENUE, HAVANA, FLORIDA 32333

Tel: **(904) 539-5611**	Breakfast: **Full**
Hosts: **Shirley and Bruce Gaver**	Credit Cards: **VISA**
Location: **12 mi. N of Tallahassee**	Pets: **No**
No. of Rooms: **1**	Children: **Welcome, over 8**
No. of Private Baths: **1**	Smoking: **No**
Double/pb: **$55**	Social Drinking: **Permitted**
Open: **All year**	Airport/Station Pickup: **Yes**
Reduced Rates: **15%, after 3 nights Mon.–Thurs.**	

This B&B, situated on a quiet residential street two blocks from the center of town, is a likely stop for collectors—at last count, Havana had twelve antique shops. Tallahassee, the state capital and home of Florida State University, is only ten minutes away by car. A restored 1907 frame house, Gaver's has two large screened porches, and guests are welcome to watch cable TV or play the piano. For breakfast, your hosts will design a menu to suit your preferences.

Meeks B&B on the Gulf Beaches ✪
19506 GULF BOULEVARD 8, INDIAN SHORES, FLORIDA 34635

Tel: **(813) 596-5424**	Single/sb: **$35**
Best Time to Call: **7 AM–10 PM**	Open: **All year**
Hosts: **Greta and Bob Meeks**	Breakfast: **Full**
Location: **10 mi. NW of St. Petersburg**	Pets: **No**
No. of Rooms: **2**	Children: **Welcome**
No. of Private Baths: **1**	Smoking: **No**
Double/pb: **$50**	Social Drinking: **Permitted**
Single/pb: **$45**	Airport/Station Pickup: **Yes**
Double/sb: **$40**	

These lovely beach accommodations are located directly on the Gulf of Mexico. From the cottage or condo you can step right onto lovely white sand beaches. A bountiful breakfast is served on the sun porch overlooking the pool and Gulf. This B&B is close to seafood restaurants and within walking distance of the Tiki Gardens.

Bed & Breakfast of Islamorada
81175 OLD HIGHWAY, ISLAMORADA, FLORIDA 33036

Tel: (305) 664-9321
Host: **Dottie Saunders**
Location: **87 mi. S of Miami**
No. of Rooms: **2**
No. of Private Baths: **2**
Double/pb: **$50–$55**
Single/pb: **$45**
Wheelchair-Accessible: **Yes**
Open: **All year**

Reduced Rates: **10%, families; $5 less, May–Dec.**
Breakfast: **Full**
Credit Cards: **MC, VISA**
Pets: **Sometimes**
Children: **Welcome**
Smoking: **Permitted**
Social Drinking: **Permitted**
Airport/Station Pickup: **Yes**

Make the most of the Florida Keys while staying in this one-story beach house. Bicycles, snorkeling gear, and a hot tub are at your disposal, and sailing trips on a historic old boat can be arranged. John Pennecamp Coral Reef State Park, 40 minutes away, is a great place for snorkeling and diving, and the whole family can ride in the glass-bottomed boats. Your hostess has had a varied career, from cooking on a freighter to selling real estate; she enjoys waterfront activities, gardening, and photography.

Innisfail ✪
134 TIMBER LANE, JUPITER, FLORIDA 33458

Tel: (407) 744-5905
Best Time to Call: **Evening**
Hosts: **Katherine and Luke van Noorden**
Location: **20 mi. N of Palm Beach**
No. of Rooms: **1**
No. of Private Baths: **1**
Double/pb: **$51–$60**
Open: **All year**

Reduced Rates: **10%, weekly; 10%, seniors**
Breakfast: **Continental**
Other Meals: **Available**
Pets: **Welcome**
Children: **Yes**
Smoking: **No**
Social Drinking: **Permitted**
Airport/Station Pickup: **Yes**

A contemporary ranch framed by palm trees, Innisfail—Gaelic for "the abode of peace and harmony"—doubles as a gallery. The van Noorden's are sculptors, and guests are welcome to watch them work in their home studio. While you don't have to be an art lover to visit, it helps to be a pet lover; Katherine and Luke's four-footed family comprises four dogs and two cats. Jupiter has wonderful beaches, but you can get an equally good tan lounging by the van Noorden's swimming pool. In the morning, a Continental breakfast of coffee or tea, fresh citrus fruit, and muffins or cereal is served.

Clauser's Bed & Breakfast ✪
201 EAST KICKLIGHTER ROAD, LAKE HELEN, FLORIDA 32744

Tel: (904) 228-0310
Best Time to Call: 7 AM–10 PM
Hosts: Marge and Tom Clauser
Location: 30 mi. NE of Orlando, 20
  mi. W of Daytona Beach
No. of Rooms: 2
No. of Private Baths: 2
Double/pb: $70–$75
Single/pb: $60–$65
Open: Sept. 1–July 31
Reduced Rates: 10%, seniors; $10
  less, midweek

Breakfast: Full
Credit Cards: MC, VISA
Pets: No
Children: No
Smoking: No
Social Drinking: Permitted
Minimum Stay: Required during
  special events
Airport/Station Pickup: Yes

Clauser's, a two-and-half-story, tin-roofed Victorian home with a porch wrapping around three sides, was described by a local journalist as "everybody's grandmother's house." Heirlooms, quilts, and comforters make the interior warm and cozy. Beach and state parks are nearby, but you may never want to leave; right on the property you can play croquet, badminton, volleyball, and horseshoes, or admire horses—Tom's passion—in the family's corral. Full country breakfasts feature Marge's homemade breads, pastries, jams, and jellies.

The Matthews B&B ✪
3150 GULFSTREAM ROAD, LAKE WORTH, FLORIDA 33461

Tel: (407) 965-0068
Best Time to Call: 9 AM–noon, 6–10
  PM
Hosts: Vern and Beryl Matthews
Location: 2 mi. off I-95, 10th Ave. N.
  exit
No. of Rooms: 1
No. of Private Baths: 1
Double/pb: $55

Single/pb: $45
Open: Nov. 1–Apr. 30
Reduced Rates: Weekly
Breakfast: Full
Pets: No
Children: Welcome, under 2
Smoking: No
Social Drinking: No
Airport/Station Pickup: Yes

As you enter this contemporary stucco ranch house, you'll be greeted with coffee and a light snack. A bowl of candies or fresh fruit will await you in the bedroom. Bicycles are at guests' disposal, but Vern and Beryl suggest renting a car for maximum enjoyment of such area attractions as jai alai, greyhound races, the Royal Poinciana Playhouse, and of course, the beach. Full breakfasts always feature Florida's famed citrus fruits and juices. You have a choice of eating areas—the kitchen, the dining room, and the sun room.

Lighthouse Bed & Breakfast ✪
13355 SECOND STREET EAST, MADEIRA BEACH, FLORIDA 33708

Tel: (813) 391-0015
Hosts: Norm and Maggie Lucore
Location: 4 mi. W of St. Petersburg
No. of Rooms: 5
No. of Private Baths: 5
Double/pb: $45–$85
Open: All year

Breakfast: Full or continental
Credit Cards: MC, VISA
Pets: Sometimes
Children: Welcome
Smoking: Permitted
Social Drinking: Permitted

This contemporary two-story home is just 300 steps, count them, from the Gulf of Mexico's sandy beaches; to the rear of the house is a classic white lighthouse. Feel free to loll about on the private sun deck, soak in the Jacuzzi, and grill dinner on the gas barbecue. Epcot Center, Busch Gardens, Sea World, and MGM tours are among the local attractions. Breakfast offerings, served either in the lighthouse or outside in the gazebo, range from fruit and pastry in summer to omelets and waffles in winter.

Inn by the Sea ✪
287 11TH AVENUE SOUTH, NAPLES, FLORIDA 33940

Tel: (813) 649-4124
Best Time to Call: 9 AM–9 PM
Host(s): Elise Sechrist
Location: 30 mi. S of Ft. Myers
No. of Rooms: 6
No. of Private Baths: 4
Max. No. Sharing Bath: 4
Double/pb: $70–$105
Double/sb: $45–$80
Suites: $80–$115

Open: All year
Reduced Rats: 10%, weekly
Breakfast: Continental
Credit Cards: MC, VISA
Pets: No
Children: Welcome, over 16
Smoking: No
Social Drinking: Permitted
Airport/Station Pickup: Yes

This inn, a beautifully appointed guest house on the National Register of Historic Places, has a tropical setting just two blocks from the beach. Decor is casually elegant, with abundant wicker, floral-print fabrics, white-iron and brass beds, and romantic ceiling fans. Much of the artwork is done by local artists; all of it is for sale to guests. Naples offers seven miles of white sand beaches, swimming, sailing, boating, and tennis. Grab a fishing pole and head for the Naples Pier, a local landmark that extends 1,000 feet into the Gulf of Mexico. Jump on one of the inn's beach cruisers and pedal through prestigious Port Royal, a neighborhood of million-dollar homes. Fabulous shopping, award-winning restaurants, and art galleries are all within walking distance.

Action Center of Orlando ✪
6638 CONWAY LAKES DRIVE, ORLANDO, FLORIDA 32812

Tel: **(407) 859-8333**
Best Time to Call: **8 AM–noon; 3–10 PM**
Hosts: **Trish and Rob Kershner**
Location: **1 mi. from Beeline 528**
No. of Rooms: **2**
Max. No. Sharing Bath: **4**
Double/pb: **$55**
Single/pb: **$40**

Suites: **$75 for 4**
Open: **All year**
Breakfast: **Full**
Pets: **Welcome**
Children: **Welcome**
Smoking: **Permitted**
Social Drinking: **Permitted**
Minimum Stay: **2 nights**
Airport/Station Pickup: **Yes**

Rob and Trish's contemporary home is furnished in a pleasant mix of past and present accented by unusual silk flower arrangements. It is accessible to all of the area's attractions, including Disney World, Epcot, and Sea World. Cape Canaveral, home of the United States space program, is less than an hour's drive; Orlando International Airport is minutes away.

Brass Bed Room & Breakfast ✪
816 NORTH SUMMERLIN AVENUE, ORLANDO, FLORIDA 32803

Tel: **(407) 896-5477**
Best Time to Call: **5–10 PM**
Host: **Lil Leddon and Janet Wing**
No. of Rooms: **1**
No. of Private Baths: **1**
Double/pb: **$55**
Single/pb: **$45**

Open: **All year**
Breakfast: **Full**
Pets: **No**
Children: **No**
Smoking: **No**
Social Drinking: **Permitted**

This charming two-story Dutch Colonial home, located in a proposed historic district near downtown, has been tastefully renovated to retain its 1920s character. The upstairs guest room features a queen-size Victorian brass bed. Guests can relax in the adjacent sitting room with color TV, or on the sun deck or shady patio. If there are more than two in your party, the sitting room, with its comfortable sofa-sleeper, is available at a reduced rate. Your hosts are Orlando natives who offer a hearty breakfast and can point you in the right direction for dining, shopping, and area attractions.

Esther's B&B ✪
2411 VIRGINIA DRIVE, ORLANDO, FLORIDA 32803

Tel: **(407) 896-9916**
Best Time to Call: **5:30–9:30 PM**
Host: **Esther Allen**
Location: **2½ mi. from I-4**
No. of Rooms: **2**
Max. No. Sharing Bath: **4**
Double/sb: **$45**

Single/sb: **$35**
Open: **All year**
Breakfast: **Continental**
Pets: **No**
Children: **Welcome, over 10**
Smoking: **No**
Social Drinking: **Permitted**

The house is attractively furnished, and features lovely needlepoint "paintings" by the Old Masters. In the morning, enjoy a special array of homemade muffins, breads, or coffee cake along with cheese, fruit, and beverages. It's close to the famous attractions of Disney World, Epcot, and Cypress Gardens. The Loch Haven Art Center, Winter Park shops, and Harry Leu Gardens are also nearby. You are welcome to enjoy the swimming pool.

Jarman's Friendly Inn ✪
567 HEWETT DRIVE, ORLANDO, FLORIDA 32807

Tel: **(407) 282-6388**
Best Time to Call: **Evenings**
Hosts: **Jo Ellen and Bert Jarman**
Location: **1 block from Hwy. 436**
No. of Rooms: **3**
No. of Private Baths: **1**
Max. No. Sharing Bath: **4**
Double/pb: **$55–$65**
Single/pb: **$45–$55**
Double/sb: **$45–$55**

Single/sb: **$35–$45**
Open: **All year**
Reduced Rates: **10%, families, seniors**
Breakfast: **Continental**
Pets: **No**
Children: **Welcome (crib)**
Smoking: **No**
Social Drinking: **Permitted**
Minimum Stay: **Two nights**
Airport/Station Pickup: **Yes**

Six children grew up in this ranch-style home, and the Jarmans say there is plenty of love left to welcome your kids. There is also plenty of space. The house spans 5,100 square feet, plus a large screened-in pool with patio area. A contemporary Florida room with hanging plants and spa is available for your enjoyment. The Victorian Rose Room has an old-fashioned wooden bed with floral spread and ceiling fan. The Gold Room has a canopy bed with handmade spread, antique dresser, and Oriental rug. If you're traveling with a small child, a third bedroom features a three-quarter oak bed, baby bed, and changing table. House specialties such as sausage-mushroom casserole and homemade biscuits are served on the patio or in a cheery breakfast room. The Jarmans are within 45 minutes of Sea World, Disney World, and Epcot.

PerriHouse B&B ✪
10417 ROAD 535, ORLANDO, FLORIDA 32819

Tel: **(800) 780-4830; (407) 876-4830**
Best Time to Call: **11 AM–11 PM**
Host(s): **Nick and Angi Perretti**
Location: **3 mi. N of I-4 on Rd. 535 N, Lake Buena Vista exit**
No. of Rooms: **6**
No. of Private Baths: **6**
Double/pb: **$65–$85**
Single/pb: **$50**

Open: **All year**
Reduced Rates: **10%, weekly, seniors**
Breakfast: **Continental**
Credit Cards: **MC, VISA**
Pets: **Sometimes**
Children: **Welcome (crib)**
Smoking: **No**
Social Drinking: **Permitted**

From its convenient location in Disney Village, PerriHouse provides easy access to Disney World, Epcot Center, MGM, Universal Studios, Sea World, and the Orlando Convention Center. Cowboys and cowgirls can sit tall in the saddle at the Grand Cypress Equestrian Center, while hot-air balloons sweep passengers up, up, and away for a different kind of ride. Each guest room has its own entrance; inside, you'll find two queen-size beds, a TV, and a telephone. Continental breakfast consists of toast, muffins, croissants, pastries, and your choice of beverage.

The Rio Pinar House ✪
532 PINAR DRIVE, ORLANDO, FLORIDA 32825

Tel: **(407) 277-4903**	Single/pb: **$40**
Best Time to Call: **7–9 AM; 9–11 PM**	Double/sb: **$40**
Hosts: **Victor and Delores**	Single/sb: **$35**
Freudenburg	Suites: **$70 (family)**
Location: **½ mi. from E-W Expy.,**	Open: **All year**
Goldenrod exit	Breakfast: **Full**
No. of Rooms: **3**	Pets: **No**
No. of Private Baths: **2**	Children: **Welcome**
Max. No. Sharing Bath: **4**	Smoking: **No**
Double/pb: **$45**	Social Drinking: **Permitted**

This home is located in a quiet neighborhood across from the Rio Pinar Golf Course. The rooms are furnished comfortably with both antiques and Americana. Breakfast is served on the porch overlooking a garden and trees. The house is a 30-minute drive from Disney World, and nine miles from downtown Orlando. Your hosts recommend an outing to the nearby Church Street Station Complex and the new Universal Studio tours.

The Spencer Home ✪
313 SPENCER STREET, ORLANDO, FLORIDA 32809

Tel: **(407) 855-5603**	Breakfast: **Full**
Hosts: **Neal and Eunice Schattauer**	Other Meals: **Available**
Location: **2 mi. from I-4**	Pets: **No**
No. of Rooms: **1 suite, 2 bedrooms**	Children: **Welcome**
No. of Private Baths: **1**	Smoking: **No**
Suites: **$50–$60; sleeps 2–4**	Social Drinking: **Permitted**
$90–$100; sleeps 4–6	Airport/Station Pickup: **Yes**
Open: **All year**	

The guest suite of this comfortable neat, ranch-style house has a private entrance and consists of a bedroom with a double bed, one with a queen bed, a living room with a sleeper for two, and a full bathroom. It is completely air-conditioned. You are welcome to freshen your traveling duds in the laundry room and yourselves in the swimming pool. Eunice will start your day with breakfast, and Neal will be pleased to direct you to Central Florida's attractions within a half hour from "home."

Five Oaks Inn ✪
1102 RIVERSIDE DRIVE, PALMETTO, FLORIDA 34221

Tel: **(813) 723-1236**
Hosts: **Bette and Chet Kriessier**
Location: **5 mi. N of Sarasota**
No. of Rooms: **4**
No. of Private Baths: **4**
Double/pb: **$45–$85**
Suites: **$90–$100**
Open: **All year**
Reduced Rates: **10%, seniors; $10 less, May–Nov.**

Breakfast: **Full**
Credit Cards: **MC, VISA**
Pets: **No**
Children: **Welcome, over 12**
Smoking: **Permitted**
Social Drinking: **Permitted**
Foreign Languages: **German**
Airport/Station Pickup: **Yes**

A local luminary built this sprawling home with plans from a Sears Roebuck catalogue; the result is a fascinating architectural hybrid with pillars and a gabled red-tile roof. Inside, antiques set off the lavish oak woodwork. Guests can borrow bicycles and fishing equipment and take advantage of the Florida coast. For sophisticated urban pleasures, it's an easy drive to either Sarasota or St. Petersburg. Whatever your plans, you'll breakfast on dishes like Cajun toast and eggs Benedict, with fresh fruits plucked from the Kriessiers' trees.

Sunshine Inn
508 DECATUR AVENUE, PENSACOLA, FLORIDA 32507

Tel: **(904) 455-6781**
Best Time to Call: **Evenings**
Hosts: **The Jablonskis**
Location: **8 mi. from I-10**
No. of Rooms: **1 suite**
No. of Private Baths: **1**
Suite: **$35**
Open: **All year**

Breakfast: **Full**
Pets: **No**
Children: **Welcome**
Smoking: **No**
Social Drinking: **Permitted**
Airport/Station Pickup: **Yes**
Foreign Languages: **German**

Sun yourself on the whitest sand, swim in the Gulf of Mexico, and return to the Sunshine Inn for a dip in the pool. Or, walk a block to the bayou for fishing. Feel free to relax in the living room and seek touring advice from your knowledgeable hostess Renate. The University of West Florida is nearby.

Carriage Way Bed & Breakfast ✪
70 CUNA STREET, ST. AUGUSTINE, FLORIDA 32084

Tel: **(904) 829-2467**
Best Time to Call: **8:30 AM–4:30 PM**
Host: **Karen Burkley**
No. of Rooms: **7**
No. of Private Baths: **7**
Double/pb: **$49–$97**
Single/pb: **$49–$97**
Open: **All year**
Reduced Rates: **10%, seniors; Sun.– Thurs., off-season**

Breakfast: **Continental**
Other Meals: **Available**
Credit Cards: **MC, VISA**
Pets: **Sometimes**
Children: **Sometimes**
Smoking: **No**
Social Drinking: **Permitted**
Airport/Station Pickup: **Yes**

This B&B, located in the heart of the historic district, is a restored Victorian built in 1883. Unique shops, museums, Castillo de San Marcos, fine restaurants, carriage tours, and the waterfront are within an easy walk. The atmosphere is leisurely and casual, in keeping with the feeling of Old St. Augustine. In addition to breakfast, Karen generously includes newspapers, wine, cookies, cordials, and dessert on Friday and Saturday evenings.

Casa de la Paz ✪
22 AVENIDA MENENDEZ, ST. AUGUSTINE, FLORIDA 32084

Tel: **(904) 829-2915**
Best Time to Call: **10 AM–4 PM**
Hosts: **Brenda and Harry Stafford**

Location: **7 mi. from I-95**
No. of Rooms: **5**
No. of Private Baths: **5**

Double/pb: **$75–$105**
Suites: **$105–$150**
Open: **All year**
Breakfast: **Continental**
Credit Cards: **AMEX, MC, VISA**
Pets: **No**

Children: **Welcome, over 9**
Smoking: **No**
Social Drinking: **Permitted**
Airport/Station Pickup: **Yes**
Foreign Languages: **French**

Overlooking historic Matanzas Bay in the heart of Old St. Augustine is this three-story Mediterranean-style stucco home. The rooms are comfortably furnished in a pleasant blend of the old and new. Amenities in each room include ceiling fans, central air-conditioning and heat, high-quality linens, cable TV, and complimentary sherry or wine. The veranda rooms have private entrances. Guests are welcome to use the private, walled courtyard, well-stocked library, and delightful parlor. It is central to all attractions and convenient to fine restaurants and shops.

Casa de Solana ✪
21 AVILES STREET, ST. AUGUSTINE, FLORIDA 32084

Tel: **(904) 824-3555**
Best Time to Call: **9 AM–6 PM**
Hosts: **Faye and Jim McMurry**
No. of Rooms: **4 suites**
No. of Private Baths: **4**
Suites: **$100–$125**
Open: **All year**

Breakfast: **Full**
Credit Cards: **AMEX, MC, VISA**
Pets: **No**
Children: **No**
Smoking: **No**
Social Drinking: **Permitted**

This is a gorgeous Colonial home built in 1763. It is located in the heart of the historic area, within walking distance of restaurants, museums, and quaint shops. Some of the antique-filled suites have fireplaces, while others have balconies that overlook the lovely garden, or a breathtaking view of Matanzas Bay. Jim and Faye include cable TV, chocolates, a decanter of sherry, and the use of their bicycles.

Kenwood Inn
38 MARINE STREET, ST. AUGUSTINE, FLORIDA 32084

Tel: **(904) 824-2116**
Best Time to Call: **11 AM–10 PM**
Hosts: **Mark, Kerrianne, and Caitlin Constant**
Location: **40 mi. S of Jacksonville**
No. of Rooms: **12**
No. of Private Baths: **12**
Double/pb: **$55–$85**

Single/pb: **$45**
Open: **All year**
Breakfast: **Continental**
Credit Cards: **DISC, MC, VISA**
Pets: **No**
Children: **Welcome, over 8**
Smoking: **No**
Social Drinking: **Permitted**

If you are to discover a Victorian building in Florida, how appropriate that it should be in the historic section of St. Augustine, the oldest city in the U.S. This New England-style inn is a rarity in the South; this one has old-fashioned beds with color-coordinated touches right down to the sheets and linens. Breakfast may be taken in your room, in the courtyard surrounded by trees, or by the swimming pool. Tour trains, waterfront shops, restaurants, and museums are within walking distance. Flagler College is three blocks away.

Old Powder House Inn ✪
38 CORDOVA STREET, ST. AUGUSTINE, FLORIDA 32084

Tel: **(904) 824-4149**	Reduced Rates: **$15 less, Sun.–Thurs.**
Hosts: **Michael and Connie Emerson**	Breakfast: **Full**
Location: **30 mi. S of Jacksonville**	Credit Cards: **MC, VISA**
No. of Rooms: **6**	Pets: **No**
No. of Private Baths: **6**	Children: **Welcome, over 2**
Double/pb: **$65–$85**	Smoking: **No**
Suite: **$95**	Social Drinking: **Permitted**
Open: **All year**	Airport/Station Pickup: **Yes**

High ceilings, spacious verandas, and elaborate woodwork distinguish this winter cottage, built in 1899 on the site of an 18th-century Spanish powder magazine. Cordova Street is in St. Augustine's historic district, and you're likely to see visitors surveying the neighborhood from a horse and buggy. If you want to take your own tour, your hosts can supply bicycles and guide maps. Of course, you're never far from the beach. The Emersons set out tea every afternoon; mornings, you'll savor juice, muffins or croissants, soufflé, fruit, cereal, and tea or coffee.

St. Francis Inn ✪
279 ST. GEORGE STREET, ST. AUGUSTINE, FLORIDA 32084

Tel: **(904) 824-6068**	Breakfast: **Continental**
Host: **Marie Register**	Credit Cards: **MC, VISA**
Location: **2 mi. from US 1**	Pets: **No**
No. of Rooms: **11**	Children: **Welcome (crib)**
No. of Private Baths: **11**	Smoking: **Permitted**
Double/pb: **$49–$85**	Social Drinking: **Permitted**
Guest Cottage: **$110; sleeps 4–6**	Airport/Station Pickup: **Yes**
Open: **All year**	

Built in 1791, the inn is a Spanish Colonial structure with a private courtyard and garden, located in the center of the restored part of town. Balconies are furnished with rocking chairs, and the swimming pool is a great cooling-off spot. The building is made of coquina, a limestone made of broken shells and coral. Due to its trapezoidal shape, there are no square or rectangular rooms. All of St. Augustine's historic and resort activities are within a three-mile radius.

Victorian House Bed & Breakfast ✪
11 CADIZ STREET, ST. AUGUSTINE, FLORIDA 32084

Tel: **(904) 824-5214**
Host: **Daisy Morden**
No. of Rooms: **8**
No. of Private Baths: **8**
Double/pb: **$55–$85**
Open: **All year**

Breakfast: **Continental**
Credit Cards: **AMEX, MC, VISA**
Pets: **No**
Children: **In cottage only**
Smoking: **Permitted**
Social Drinking: **Permitted**

From its location in the heart of the historic district, it's a short walk to fine restaurants, the waterfront, shops, museums, and the plaza. The rooms are charming, with brass and canopy beds, hand-woven coverlets, handmade quilts, and stenciled walls and floors. The house is comfortably air-conditioned, but the warmth of your hostess is quite special.

Bayboro House on Old Tampa Bay ✪
1719 BEACH DRIVE SOUTHEAST, ST. PETERSBURG, FLORIDA 33701

Tel: **(813) 823-4955**
Hosts: **Gordon and Antonia Powers**
Location: **½ mi. from I-275, Exit 9**
No. of Rooms: **3**
No. of Private Baths: **3**
Double/pb: **$55–$70**
Open: **All year**

Breakfast: **Continental**
Credit Cards: **MC, VISA**
Pets: **No**
Children: **No**
Smoking: **No**
Social Drinking: **Permitted**

A unique three-story Queen Anne with airy, high-ceilinged rooms, and a wraparound veranda in view of Tampa Bay, Bayboro House is graced with antique furniture plus tropical plants and flowers. It is the ideal spot for sunning, and beachcombing. Visit unusual shops, fine restaurants, the Sunken Gardens, or the Salvador Dali museum. Tampa is 20 minutes away; Walt Disney World and Epcot are 1½ hours away. The Suncoast Dome is five minutes from the door. A self-contained apartment is also available.

Crescent House
459 BEACH ROAD, SIESTA KEY, SARASOTA, FLORIDA 34242

Tel: **(813) 346-0857**
Hosts: **Patricia and Jean-Marc Murre**
Location: **10 mi. from Sarasota**
No. of Rooms: **3**
No. of Private Baths: **3**
Double/pb: **$90**
Double/sb: **$55**
Open: **All year**

Reduced Rates: **April–Dec.**
Breakfast: **Continental**
Pets: **No**
Children: **Welcome**
Smoking: **No**
Social Drinking: **Permitted**
Airport/Station Pickup: **Yes**
Foreign Languages: **French, Spanish**

This lovely, 70-year-old home has been fully restored and furnished with comfortable antiques. Breakfast specialties include freshly squeezed Florida orange juice, homemade muffins, scones, and freshly ground coffee. Sunbathe on a spacious wood deck, or step across the street to a white sandy beach and cool off in the Gulf of Mexico. The house is located within a short walk of Siesta Village and Pavilion, with its many restaurants, quaint shops, tennis courts, and public beach. Your hosts specialize in European service and hospitality, and will gladly guide you to fine dining and sailboat and watersporting gear rentals.

The Pepperberry House
P.O. BOX 841, SARASOTA, FLORIDA 34240

Tel: **(813) 951-0405**	Suites: **$75**
Best Time to Call: **Early AM; PM**	Open: **All year**
Host: **Lorraine Yerdonek**	Reduced Rates: **30–40%, Apr. 17–**
Location: **60 mi. S of Tampa**	**Dec. 14**
No. of Rooms: **4**	Breakfast: **Continental**
No. of Private Baths: **2**	Pets: **Yes**
Max. No. Sharing Bath: **2**	Children: **Welcome**
Double/pb: **$75**	Smoking: **No**
Double/sb: **$55**	Social Drinking: **Permitted**

This two-story Key West house right on the Hudson Bayou has its own dock for launching boating and fishing expeditions. Landlubbers can catch rays on the spacious sun deck. Inside, the house is light and airy, with coral fireplaces, honey oakwood floors, and pickled cypress walls hung with Lorraine's own artwork. In addition to beaches, Sarasota's attractions include the Ringling Mansion and Museum, the Selby Botanical Gardens, the Van Wetzel Performing Arts Center, and many excellent restaurants. Continental breakfasts consist of freshsqueezed juice, locally grown fruit, cereal, yogurt, and muffins and breads hot from the oven.

Knightswood
P.O. BOX 151, SUMMERLAND KEY, FLORIDA 33042

Tel: **(305) 872-2246**	Open: **All year**
Hosts: **Chris and Herb Pontin**	Breakfast: **Full**
Location: **26 mi. E of Key West**	Pets: **No**
No. of Rooms: **2**	Children: **No**
No. of Private Baths: **2**	Smoking: **No**
Double/pb: **$75**	Social Drinking: **Permitted**
Single/pb: **$65**	Minimum Stay: **2 nights**

Knightswood boasts one of the loveliest water views in the Keys. The guest apartment is self-contained and very private. Snorkeling, fishing, and boating can be enjoyed right from the Pontin's dock. You are welcome to swim in the fresh-water pool, relax in the spa, or sunbathe on the white sand beach. Trips to protected Looe Key Coral Reef can be arranged. Fine dining and Key West nightlife are within easy reach.

Cobb's Gulf View Inn ✪
21722 WEST HIGHWAY 98, P.O. BOX 199, SUNNYSIDE, FLORIDA 32461

Tel: (904) 234-6051 Mar. 1–Sept. 10;
  (912) 435-0178 Sept. 11–Apr. 30
Hosts: **Bill and Tina Cobb**
Location: **2 mi. W of Panama City
  Beach**
No. of Rooms: **5**
No. of Private Baths: **5**
Double/pb: **$55**
Single/pb: **$50**
Suite: **$75**

Open: **Mar. 1–Sept. 10**
Reduced Rates: **Available**
Breakfast: **Continental**
Pets: **No**
Children: **Welcome**
Smoking: **Permitted**
Social Drinking: **Permitted**
Minimum Stay: **3 nights, holiday
  weekends**

Cobb's Gulf View Inn is a new two-story beach house painted Cape Cod blue with cream lattice trim. The decor is eclectic, with white wicker furnishings on the downstairs porches and modern touches in the bedrooms. Guest quarters have private entrances, TV, carpeting, and ceiling fans. In the morning, dine on the upstairs sun deck or porch overlooking the panoramic Gulf of Mexico. Homemade breads and jellies are specialties of the house. It's just 200 feet across the road to the white, sandy beaches of Sunnyside. Bill and Tina are located convenient to fishing, sailing, golf, tennis, and restaurants. Water parks for the children are within easy reach.

Fiorito's Bed & Breakfast ✪
421 OLD EAST LAKE ROAD, TARPON SPRINGS, FLORIDA 34689

Tel: (813) 937-5487
Best Time to Call: **8 AM–9 PM**
Hosts: **Dick and Marie Fiorito**
Location: **2 mi. E of US 19**
No. of Rooms: **1**
No. of Private Baths: **1**
Double/pb: **$40**
Single/pb: **$35**

Open: **All year**
Breakfast: **Full**
Pets: **No**
Children: **No**
Smoking: **Permitted**
Social Drinking: **Permitted**
Airport/Station Pickup: **Yes**

Just off a quiet road that runs along Lake Tarpon's horse country, this meticulously maintained home on 2½ acres offers respite for the visitor. The guest room and bath are decorated in tones of blue, enhanced with beautiful accessories. Fresh fruit, cheese omelet, homemade bread and jam, and choice of beverages are the Fioritos' idea of breakfast. It is beautifully served on the tree-shaded, screened terrace.

They'll be happy to direct you to the Greek Sponge Docks, deep sea fishing opportunities, golf courses, beaches, and great restaurants.

Spring Bayou Inn ✪
32 WEST TARPON AVENUE, TARPON SPRINGS, FLORIDA 34689

Tel: **(813) 938-9333**	Single/sb: **$45–$50**
Best Time to Call: **11 AM–9 PM**	Open: **Oct. 1–Aug. 15**
Hosts: **Ron and Cher Morrick**	Breakfast: **Continental**
Location: **2 mi. W of US 19**	Reduced Rates: **$10 less, May 1–Dec.**
No. of Rooms: **5**	**31**
No. of Private Baths: **4**	Pets: **No**
Max. No. Sharing Bath: **2**	Children: **No**
Double/pb: **$50–$75**	Smoking: **No**
Single/pb: **$45–$70**	Social Drinking: **Permitted**
Double/sb: **$50–$55**	

This large, comfortable Victorian was built in 1905. Located in the Historic District, it has architectural details of the past combined with up-to-date conveniences. You will enjoy relaxing on the porch or in the courtyard to take in the sun. The parlor is a favorite gathering place, offering informal atmosphere, complimentary wine, music, books, and games, and the opportunity to make new friends. The fireplace chases the chill on winter evenings. Tarpon Springs is the sponge capital of the world, and the nearby sponge docks are interesting to visit. The area is known for its excellent restaurants and variety of shops.

West Palm Beach B&B ✪
P.O. BOX 078581, WEST PALM BEACH, FLORIDA 33407

Tel: **(407) 848-4064**	Reduced Rates: **$10 less, weekly or**
Hosts: **Dennis Keimel and Ron Seitz**	**May–Nov.**
Location: **3 mi. from Palm Beach**	Breakfast: **Continental**
International Airport	Pets: **Sometimes**
No. of Rooms: **2**	Children: **Welcome**
No. of Private Baths: **2**	Smoking: **Permitted**
Double/pb: **$65**	Social Drinking: **Permitted**
Open: **All year**	Airport/Station Pickup: **Yes**

Because it's just a block from the intracoastal waterway and minutes from the ocean, the West Palm Beach B&B is an ideal spot. And visitors won't be culture-starved: the Norton Gallery, Flagler Museum, and Drehre Park Zoo are minutes away. Palm Beach, with its fabulous mansions and boutiques, is well worth a visit. Plan your excursions over a continental breakfast that features fresh Florida fruits.

Double M Ranch Bed & Breakfast ✪
ROUTE 1, BOX 292, ZOLFO SPRINGS, FLORIDA 33890

Tel: **(813) 735-0266**
Best Time to Call: **After 6 PM**
Hosts: **Mary Jane and Charles Matheny**
Location: **60 mi. W of Bradenton**
No. of Rooms: **1**
No. of Private Baths: **1**
Double/pb: **$50**
Single/pb: **$45**

Open: **All year**
Breakfast: **Continental**
Pets: **No**
Children: **Welcome, over 13**
Smoking: **No**
Social Drinking: **Permitted**
Minimum Stay: **Two nights**
Airport/Station Pickup: **Yes**

This contemporary stone-and-wood ranch home is divided into two parts, one for the Mathenys, the other for their guests. Charles, a cattleman, likes to show visitors around the property. The area's main recreational options are fishing, waterskiing, and golfing—choose from among thirteen local courses. Continental breakfast includes oven-fresh muffins and fresh-squeezed orange juice.

GEORGIA

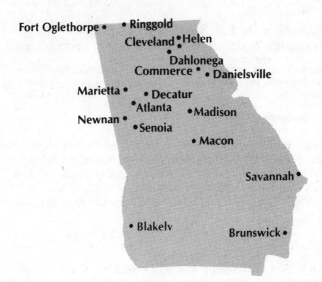

Fort Oglethorpe • • Ringgold
Cleveland •Helen
Dahlonega
Commerce • • Danielsville
Marietta • • Decatur
•Atlanta • Madison
Newnan • • Senoia
• Macon
Savannah •
• Blakely
Brunswick •

Bed & Breakfast—Atlanta ✪
1801 PIEDMONT AVENUE NORTHEAST, SUITE 208, ATLANTA, GEORGIA 30324

Tel: **(404) 875-0525**
Best Time to Call: **9 AM–noon; 2–5 PM**
Coordinators: **Madalyne Eplan and Paula Gris**
States/Regions Covered: **Alpharetta, Atlanta, Brookhaven, Buckhead, Decatur, Dunwoody, Marietta, Roswell, Sandy Springs, Smyrna, Stone Mountain, Tucker**

Rates (Single/Double):
  Modest: **$32–$40**   **$40–$44**
  Average: **$44–$56**   **$48–$56**
  Luxury: **$60–$80**   **$60–$100**
Credit Cards: **AMEX, MC, VISA**
Descriptive Directory: **$3**

Visit one of America's most gracious cities, with the advantage of being a houseguest. Madalyne and Paula have been carefully selecting accommodations for fortunate travelers since 1979. They consider transportation and language needs as well as other personal preferences in making your reservation. Lodging is offered in the city's most desirable locations. There is an $8 surcharge for one-night stays. Georgia Tech, Emory University, Georgia State University, Georgia World Congress Center, and Peachtree Center are close by. Major educational, industrial, medical, and convention complexes are conveniently served by hospitable hosts.

Quail Country Bed & Breakfast, Ltd. ✪
1104 OLD MONTICELLO ROAD, THOMASVILLE, GEORGIA 31792

Tel: **(912) 226-7218; 226-6882**	Rates (Single/Double):
Coordinators: **Mercer Watt and Kathy**	Average: **$30** **$40**
Lanigan	Luxury: **$40** **$50**
States/Regions Covered: **Thomas**	Credit Cards: **No**
County, Thomasville	

Mercer and Kathy have a wide selection of homes, several with swimming pools, in lovely residential areas. There's a lot to see and do, including touring historic restorations and plantations. Enjoy the Pebble Hill Plantation museum, historic Glen Arven Country Club, and the April Rose Festival. There is a $5 surcharge for one-night stays.

Layside ✪
611 RIVER STREET, BLAKELY, GEORGIA 31723

Tel: **(912) 723-8932**	Open: **All year**
Best Time to Call: **8:30 AM–11 PM**	Reduced Rates: **10%, seniors over 60**
Hosts: **Ted and Jeanneane Lay**	Breakfast: **Continental**
Location: **1½ mi. from US 27**	Pets: **No**
No. of Rooms: **3**	Children: **Welcome, over 10**
Max. No. Sharing Bath: **4**	Smoking: **Permitted**
Double/sb: **$35**	Social Drinking: **Permitted**
Single/sb: **$25**	

Layside is a southern Colonial dating back to the turn of the century. Spend the night in a queen-size bed and wake up to homemade muffins, jams, and coffee. State parks, Indian burial grounds, good fishing, and boating are all nearby attractions. The 60-foot-long front porch is a fine place to relax after a day of touring.

The Pittman House ✪
103 HOMER STREET, COMMERCE, GEORGIA 30529

Tel: **(404) 335-3823**	No. of Rooms: **4**
Best Time to Call: **7 AM–9 PM**	Max. No. Sharing Bath: **4**
Hosts: **Tom and Dot Tomberlin**	Double/sb: **$50**
Location: **60 mi. NE of Atlanta**	Single/sb: **$45**

Open: **All year**
Breakfast: **Full**
Credit Cards: **MC, VISA**
Pets: **No**

Children: **Welcome**
Smoking: **No**
Social Drinking: **No**

This gracious white colonial, built in 1890, is decorated throughout with period pieces. If the furniture inspires you, visit Granny's Old Things, an antique shop right next door. Other points of interest include Chateau Elan Winery, in neighboring Braselton, and the Crawford W. Long Museum—honoring the doctor who discovered ether—in the town of Commerce. Swimmers and sailors have their choice of Lake Lanier and Lake Hartwell; Hurricane Shoals is another lovely outdoor recreational area.

The Mountain Top Lodge ✪
ROUTE 7, BOX 150, DAHLONEGA, GEORGIA 30533

Tel: **(404) 864-5257**
Best Time to Call: **10–2 PM**
Host: **David Middleton**
Location: **70 mi. N of Atlanta**
No. of Rooms: **12**
No. of Private Baths: **12**
Double/pb: **$65–$75**
Single/pb: **$45–$55**

Suites: **$80–$125**
Open: **All year**
Breakfast: **Full**
Pets: **No**
Children: **Welcome, over 12**
Smoking: **Permitted**
Social Drinking: **Permitted**

Flanked by porches and decks, this gambrel-roofed, rustic cedar lodge is a secluded rural retreat on 40 acres, with a 360-degree mountain view. Decorated with art and antiques, the pine furniture and accessories made by mountain craftsmen add to the charm. Dahlonega was the site of America's first gold rush, and nature buffs will appreciate the Chattahoochee National Forest and Amicalola Falls State Park. Rafting, hiking, and horseback riding are all nearby. Don't miss the "Alpine village" of Helen, Georgia, only 30 minutes away.

Honey Bear Hideaway Farm ✪
ROUTE 4, BOX 4106, ROGERS MILL ROAD, DANIELSVILLE, GEORGIA 30633

Tel: **(404) 789-2569**
Best Time to Call: **After 4 PM**
Hosts: **Ray and Natachia Dodd**
Location: **12 mi. N of Athens**
No. of Rooms: **5**
No. of Private Baths: **5**
Double/pb: **$50**
Single/pb: **$45**
Open: **Mar. 1–Dec. 31**

Breakfast: **Full**
Other Meals: **Available**
Credit Cards: **MC, VISA**
Pets: **No**
Children: **Welcome, over 12**
Smoking: **No**
Social Drinking: **Permitted**
Airport/Station Pickup: **Yes**

This 125-year-old farmhouse is nestled among pecan and walnut trees, with a lake nearby. Ray and Natachia are artists who converted the property's two barns into studios. The house is a virtual gallery of antiques and curios; one bedroom is decorated with old-fashioned purses. Visitors will wake up to a Southern, country-style breakfast, with farm-fresh eggs, ham or sausage, and homemade breads and jellies.

Captain's Quarters B&B Inn
13 BARNHARDT CIRCLE, FORT OGLETHORPE, GEORGIA 30742

Tel: **(404) 858-0624**
Hosts: **Ann Gilbert and Pam Humphrey**
Location: **5 mi. S of Chattanooga, Tenn.**
No. of Rooms: **3**
No. of Private Baths: **3**
Double/pb: **$60–$75**

Open: **All year**
Reduced Rates: **10%, seniors**
Breakfast: **Full**
Credit Cards: **MC, VISA**
Pets: **No**
Children: **No**
Smoking: **No**
Social Drinking: **No**

This grand home, with its twin porches and winding staircase, was originally built for two army officers and their families when Ft. Oglethorpe was regarded as one of the army's most elite posts. Ann and Pam have transformed and restored it to a vision that could easily grace the pages of any magazine. A charming sitting room with TV is a comfortable spot to spend a relaxing evening. Breakfast is served in the large dining room, where one can imagine officers and their ladies being graciously served. Museums, Chickamauga battlefield, and Lookout Mountain are close by.

Hilltop Haus ✪
P.O. BOX 154, CHATTAHOOCHEE STREET, HELEN, GEORGIA 30545

Tel: **(404) 878-2388**
Hosts: **Frankie Tysor and Barbara Nichols**
Location: **60 mi. from I-85**
No. of Rooms: **5**
No. of Private Baths: **3**
Max. No. Sharing Bath: **3**
Double/pb: **$40–$65**
Single/pb: **$35–$50**
Double/sb: **$35–$60**

Single/sb: **$30–$45**
Suite: **$50–$75**
Open: **All year**
Breakfast: **Full**
Credit Cards: **MC, VISA**
Reduced Rates: **10%, seniors**
Pets: **No**
Children: **Welcome, over 12**
Smoking: **Permitted**
Social Drinking: **Permitted**

This contemporary split-level overlooks the Alpine town of Helen and the Chattahoochee River. It is near the foothills of the Smoky Mountains, six miles from the Appalachian Trail. Rich wood paneling and fireplaces create a homey atmosphere for the traveler. Guests may choose a private room or the efficiency cottage with separate entrance. Each morning a hearty breakfast includes homemade biscuits and preserves. Your hostess will direct you to many outdoor activities and sights.

Boat House Bed & Breakfast ✪
383 PORTER STREET, MADISON, GEORGIA 30650

Tel: **(404) 342-3061**
Best Time to Call: **Early AM, late PM**
Hosts: **Ron and Rhonda Erwin**
Location: **55 mi. E of Atlanta**
No. of Rooms: **4**
No. of Private Baths: **2**
Max. No. Sharing Bath: **4**
Double/pb: **$75**
Double/sb: **$60**

Open: **All year**
Reduced Rates: **10%, business travelers; 3-night stays**
Breakfast: **Full**
Pets: **No**
Children: **Welcome, over 5**
Smoking: **No**
Social Drinking: **Permitted**

A two-room retreat built by a sea captain in 1850, the Boat House was expanded into a proper Victorian home fifty years later. The Erwins bought the house in 1984 and enlarged it further, utilizing Ron's carpentry and restoration skills. The hardwood floors, high ceilings, and decorative moldings provide an ideal setting for the Erwins' vast antique collection. For guests' use, the second-floor library has a TV, a VCR, and a refrigerator stocked with cold drinks. The buffet-style breakfasts may include cognac-marinated French toast or fluffy eggs-and-cheese, fruit platters, muffins, and a variety of gourmet coffees.

Parrott-Camp-Soucy House ✪
155 GREENVILLE STREET, NEWNAN, GEORGIA 30263

Tel: **(404) 253-4846**	Double/sb: **$65**
Hosts: **Chuck and Doris Soucy**	Single/sb: **$50**
Location: **25 mi. SW of Atlanta**	Open: **All year**
No. of Rooms: **3**	Breakfast: **Full**
No. of Private Baths: **1**	Pets: **No**
Max. No. Sharing Bath: **4**	Children: **No**
Double/pb: **$75**	Smoking: **Permitted**
Single/pb: **$60**	Social Drinking: **Permitted**

This extraordinary Second Empire mansion, listed on the National Register of Historic Places, is a brilliant example of Victorian–French Mansard architecture. It took two years to restore it to its original elegance. For example, the fireplace in the front hall is surrounded by tiles that depict characters from the Robin Hood legend, and the magnificent grand staircase is lit by beautiful stained-glass windows. It is no surprise that the house is furnished entirely in antiques. The surprise is that it is so comfortable. You are certain to enjoy the formal gardens, swimming pool and spa, and the game room with its 1851 Brunswick pool table. If you can tear yourself away, Warm Springs, Callaway Gardens, and Atlanta are within easy reach.

Buckley's Cedar House B&B ✪
PIERCE ROAD, ROUTE 10, BOX 161, RINGGOLD, GEORGIA 30736

Tel: **(404) 935-2619**	Open: **All year**
Hosts: **Betty and Bill Buckley**	Breakfast: **Continental**
Location: **12 mi. S of Chattanooga**	Pets: **No**
No. of Rooms: **2**	Children: **No**
Max. No. Sharing Bath: **5**	Smoking: **No**
Double/sb: **$40**	Social Drinking: **Permitted**
Single/sb: **$35**	Airport/Station Pickup: **Yes**

Just fifteen minutes from Tennessee's Lookout Mountain, Chattanooga, and Chickamauga Battlefield National Park, Buckley's Cedar House is a likely stop for tourists and Civil War buffs. Of course, you should give yourself time to amble around this B&B's woodsy eight-acre property. In the morning, you'll wake up to fresh-baked muffins and scones, accompanied by homemade jams and locally grown fruit.

R.S.V.P. Savannah—B&B Reservation Service ✪
417 EAST CHARLTON STREET, SAVANNAH, GEORGIA 31401

Tel: **(912) 232-7787 or (800) 729-7787**
Best Time to Call: **9:30 AM–5:30 PM Mon.–Fri.**
Coordinator: **Alan Fort**
States/Regions Covered: **Georgia— Brunswick, Darien, Macon, Savannah, St. Simons Island, Tybee Island; South Carolina—Beaufort, Charleston; Florida—Amelia Island, Jacksonville, St. Augustine**

Rates (Single/Double):
Modest: **$50**   **$65**
Average: **$60**   **$80**
Luxury: **$90**   **$125**
Credit Cards: **AMEX, MC, VISA**

Alan's accommodations include elegantly restored inns, guest houses, private homes, and even a villa on the water. They're located in the best historic districts as well as along the coast, from South Carolina's Low Country to Georgia's Sea Islands and northern Florida. A special blend of cordial hospitality, comfort, and services is provided. All are air-conditioned in the summer. Facilities for children and the handicapped are often available. Please note that while some hosts accept credit cards, most do not.

Bed & Breakfast Inn ✪
117 WEST GORDON AT CHATHAM SQUARE, SAVANNAH, GEORGIA 31401

Tel: **(912) 238-0518**
Host: **Robert McAlister**
No. of Rooms: **13**
No. of Private Baths: **4**
Max. No. Sharing Bath: **4**
Double/pb: **$65–$70**
Single/pb: **$50–$55**
Double/sb: **$38–$42**
Single/sb: **$30–$34**

Open: **All year**
Breakfast: **Full**
Credit Cards: **AMEX, MC, VISA**
Pets: **No**
Children: **Welcome (crib)**
Smoking: **Permitted**
Social Drinking: **Permitted**
Foreign Languages: **German, Spanish**

Located in the heart of the historic district, the inn is a Federalist row house built in 1853. It is decorated with a few period pieces and many appropriate reproductions. Some of the bedrooms have poster beds, and all rooms are air-conditioned. The outstanding courtyard, with its profusion of trees and colorful flowers, has twice been photographed by *Southern Living* magazine. Bob is active in a variety of historical organizations and Scottish Heritage groups. He is also the Budget Director of Savannah.

The Culpepper House
P.O. BOX 462, BROAD AT MORGAN, SENOIA, GEORGIA 30276

Tel: **(404) 599-8182**
Best Time to Call: **7 AM–10 PM**
Host: **Mary A. Brown**
Location: **37 mi. S of Atlanta**
No. of Rooms: **4**
No. of Private Baths: **1**
Max. No. Sharing Bath: **4**
Double/pb: **$60**
Double/sb: **$55**
Single/sb: **$50**

Open: **All year**
Reduced Rates: **10%, families**
Breakfast: **Full**
Credit Cards: **No**
Pets: **No**
Children: **Welcome, over 10 and infants**
Smoking: **Permitted**
Social Drinking: **Permitted**
Airport/Station Pickup: **Yes**

This Queen Anne Victorian was built in 1871. Gingerbread trim, stained glass, sliding doors, bay windows, and provincial furnishings re-create that turn-of-the-century feeling. Snacks and setups are offered. Your host will gladly direct you to surrounding antique and craft shops, state parks, and gardens.

HAWAII

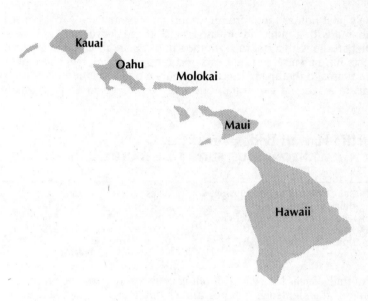

Kauai

Oahu

Molokai

Maui

Hawaii

Bed & Breakfast—Hawaii ✪
P.O. BOX 449, KAPAA, HAWAII 96746

Tel: **(808) 822-7771 or (800) 733-1632**
Best Time to Call: **8:30 AM–4:30 PM**
Coordinators: **Evie Warner and Al Davis**
States/Regions Covered: **All of the Hawaiian Islands**

Rates (Single/Double):

Modest:	**$35**	**$35**
Average:	**N/A**	**$45–$55**
Luxury:	**N/A**	**$80**

Credit Cards: **MC, VISA**
Minimum Stay: **2 nights**

Hawaii is a group of diverse islands offering traditional warmth and hospitality to the visitor through this membership organization. Some are separate units; others are in the main house. Most have private baths. The University of Hawaii at Oahu is convenient to many B&Bs.

171

Bed and Breakfast "Maui Style" ✪
P.O. BOX 886, KIHEI, HAWAII 96753

Tel: (808) 879-7865 or (800) 848-5567	Rates (Single/Double):
Best Time to Call: 9 AM–5 PM	Average: $35 $45–$55
Coordinator: Sue Rominger	Luxury: $65 $95
States/Regions Covered: Kauai,	Credit Cards: No
Hawaii, Maui, Molokai, Oahu	

Sue's host homes range from tranquil, up-country spots to a house in Lahaina with a pool and private lanais off the bedroom. Another is a quiet studio with a hot tub; another an old plantation home in Haiku. Hosts have a variety of interests and range from an avid chess player to a massage therapist. There is no public transportation on Maui, so plan to arrange a car rental. Sue will be pleased to arrange this for you.

Pacific-Hawaii Bed & Breakfast ✪
970 N. KALAHEO AVENUE, SUITE A-218, KAILUA, OAHU, HAWAII 96734

Tel: (808) 261-5030 or (800) 999-6026	Rates (Single/Double):
Coordinator: Doris E. Epp	Modest: $25 $35
States/Regions Covered: All of the	Average: $35 $35–$50
Hawaiian Islands	Luxury: $75 $75–$150
Descriptive Directory of B&Bs: $3	Credit Cards: No
	Minimum Stay: 3 nights

Waterfalls, secluded beaches, rolling countryside, and lush forests are some of the sightseeing opportunities you'll enjoy when staying at a B&B home on Doris' roster. Currently, there are over 300 hosted or unhosted accommodations, most close to the ocean, from which to choose your version of paradise. There is a $5 surcharge for one-night stays.

Adrienne's Bed & Breakfast Paradise ✪
RR 1, BOX 8E, CAPTAIN COOK, BIG ISLAND, HAWAII 96704

Tel: (808) 328-9726 or (800) 328-9726	Single/sb: $30
Hosts: Adrienne and Reg Ritz-Batty	Open: All year
Location: 18 mi. S of Kailua-Kona	Reduced Rates: Families; weekly
No. of Rooms: 4	Breakfast: Continental
No. of Private Baths: 3	Pets: No
Max. No. Sharing Bath: 4	Children: Welcome (crib)
Double/pb: $45–$70	Smoking: No
Single/pb: $35–$60	Social Drinking: Permitted
Double/sb: $40	

This custom cedar home, surrounded by gardens, has an unobstructed view of the ocean that can even be seen from the lanai's hot tub. The light and airy rooms are decorated with local artwork. Breakfast of Kona coffee, local fruits, and home-baked muffins and popovers is served on a covered lanai. Adrienne and Reg are former New Yorkers who feel they've found paradise and are pleased to share their special discoveries with you. She's an international archery champion who will direct you to places for swimming and snorkeling.

Haena Hideaway ✪

P.O. BOX 826, HANALEI, KAUAI, HAWAII 96714

Tel: **(808) 826-9522**	Reduced Rates: **10%, seniors**
Best Time to Call: **Before 10 PM**	Breakfast: **Continental**
Hosts: **Becky Swan and Bill Gillette**	Wheelchair-Accessible: **Yes**
No. of Rooms: **2**	Credit Cards: **No**
No. of Private Baths: **2**	Pets: **No**
Double/pb: **$50**	Children: **Welcome**
Single/pb: **$45**	Smoking: **No**
Guest Cottage: **$65**	Social Drinking: **Permitted**
Open: **All year**	Minimum Stay: **2 nights**

At Haena Hideaway, guests may choose between the guest room in the main house or enjoying the extra privacy of a separate cottage with full cooking facilities. The sandy white beaches of Kauai's northern shore are just a block away; your hosts love watersports and can tell you the best sites for snorkeling and Windsurfing. At the end of the day, soak your sore muscles in the Jacuzzi, or just sit on the deck and watch the sunset. Continental breakfasts feature Kona coffee, homemade bread, and fresh local fruit.

Holualoa Inn

P.O. BOX 222A, HOLUALOA, BIG ISLAND, HAWAII 96725

Tel: **(808) 324-1121**	Open: **All year**
Best Time to Call: **8 AM–5 PM**	Breakfast: **Continental**
Host: **Desmond Twigg-Smith**	Credit Cards: **CB, DC, MC, VISA**
Location: **4 mi. E of Kailua-Kona**	Pets: **No**
No. of Rooms: **4**	Children: **Welcome, over 12**
No. of Private Baths: **4**	Smoking: **No**
Double/pb: **$75–$125**	Social Drinking: **Permitted**
Single/pb: **$50**	

Experience country elegance on a private, 30-acre estate overlooking Kailua and the Kona Coast of the Big Island. The house is constructed entirely of cedar, with beautiful red eucalyptus floors. During your visit, feel free to take a swim in the pool, shoot a game of billiards, sip a drink from the wet bar, or simply stroll in the garden. When the sun sets, you'll want to be in the rooftop gazebo overlooking the pastures, coffee orchards, and ocean. Your host offers delicious Kona coffee and fresh fruit each morning. He will gladly show you the way to the beach, galleries, restaurants, entertainment, and a full range of water sports.

Bev & Monty's Bed & Breakfast
4571 UKALI STREET, HONOLULU, OAHU, HAWAII 96818

Tel: **(808) 422-9873**
Best Time to Call: **7 AM–9 PM**
Hosts: **Bev and Monty Neese**
Location: **4½ mi. from airport**
No. of Rooms: **2**
Max. No. Sharing Bath: **4**
Double/sb: **$45**
Single/sb: **$35**

Open: **All year**
Reduced Rates: **Weekly**
Breakfast: **Continental**
Pets: **No**
Children: **Welcome**
Smoking: **Permitted**
Social Drinking: **Permitted**
Airport/Station Pickup: **Yes**

This typical Hawaiian home is convenient to many of Hawaii's most popular attractions. Bev and Monty are just a mile above historic Pearl Harbor, and the Arizona Memorial can be seen from their veranda. They enjoy sharing a Hawaiian aloha, for a convenient overnight stay or a long vacation where they can share their favorite places with you. This comfortable home is just off the access road leading east to Honolulu and Waikiki, or west to the North Shore beaches, sugar plantations, and pineapple fields. Good hiking country as well as city entertainment and shopping centers are located nearby.

Papaya Paradise ✪
395 AUWINALA ROAD, KAILUA, OAHU, HAWAII 96734

Tel: **(808) 261-0316**
Best Time to Call: **7 AM–8 PM**
Hosts: **Bob and Jeanette Martz**
Location: **10 mi. E of Honolulu**
No. of Rooms: **2**
Double/pb: **$60**
Open: **All year**

Breakfast: **Full**
Pets: **No**
Children: **No**
Smoking: **Permitted**
Social Drinking: **Permitted**
Minimum Stay: **3 nights**

The Martz paradise is on the windward side of Oahu, miles from the high rise hotels, but just 20 miles from the Waikiki/Honolulu airport. Their one-story home is surrounded by a papaya grove, and tropical plants and flowers. Each guest room has two beds, a ceiling fan, air-conditioning, cable TV, and its own private entrance. Bob loves to cook, and serves breakfast on the lanai overlooking the pool and Jacuzzi. Kailua Beach, a beautiful white sandy beach four miles long, is within easy walking distance.

Kauai Calls B&B ✪
5972 HEAMOI PLACE, KAPAA, KAUAI, HAWAII 96746

Tel: **(808) 822-9699**
Hosts: **Earle and Joy Schertell**
Location: **About 5 mi. NE of Lihue
     airport**

No. of Rooms: **2**
No. of Private Baths: **2**
Double/pb: **$50–$60**
Single/pb: **$45–$55**

Guest Apartment: **$60 double, $55
  single**
Open: **All year**
Reduced Rates: **10%, senior, weekly**
Breakfast: **Full**

Pets: **No**
Children: **Welcome, over 13**
Smoking: **No**
Social Drinking: **Permitted**

Whether you choose to stay in the main house or the apartment, you'll be minutes away from beaches and mountain hiking trails; your hosts will lend you beach mats and towels. Earle, a dedicated shell collector, will tell you his favorite haunts. The studio apartment has a microwave oven and refrigerator, so you can be self-sufficient. At the end of the day, you can survey the stunning Hawaiian landscape while relaxing in the hot tub. Joy's Aloha Breakfasts feature locally-grown fruit, macadamia nut pastries, and, of course, freshly brewed Kona coffee.

The Orchid Hut
6402 KAAHELE STREET, KAPAA, HAWAII 96746

Tel: **(808) 822-7201**
Hosts: **Norm and Leonora Ross**
Location: **10 mi. E of Lihue**
No. of Rooms: **1**
No. of Private Baths: **1**
Double/pb: **$75**
Open: **All year**
Reduced Rates: **10%, weekly**

Breakfast: **Continental**
Pets: **No**
Children: **No**
Smoking: **No**
Social Drinking: **Permitted**
Minimum Stay: **3 nights**
Foreign Languages: **French, Dutch,
  Indonesian, Malaysian**

Bring your camera and escape to tropical tranquillity at a romantic, private hideaway on Kauai, known as "The Garden Island." Norm and Leonora offer the use of their completely equipped three-room contemporary cottage perched high above the Wailua River, encompassing spectacular island and water views. It's a short drive to the beach, shopping, golf, tennis, and fine dining. Local tropical fruit, a variety of cold cereals, tea, and coffee are stocked in your kitchen so you can enjoy breakfast at your own pace and leisure. Guests fly into Lihue Airport, where a car can be rented for the 15-minute drive to the "hut."

Whaler's Way
541 KUPULAU DRIVE, KIHEI, MAUI, HAWAII 96753

Tel: **(808) 879-7984**
Hosts: **Kenneth and Carol Svenson**
Location: **12 mi. S of Kahului**
No. of Rooms: **2**
No. of Private Baths: **2**
Double/pb: **$60**
Single/pb: **$55**
Open: **All year**

Breakfast: **Full**
Pets: **No**
Children: **Welcome, over 6**
Smoking: **No**
Social Drinking: **Permitted**
Minimum Stay: **3 nights**
Airport/Station Pickup: **Yes**

Nestled at the base of Mt. Haleakala—Hawaii's largest dormant volcano—Whaler's Way enjoys spectacular views of the West Maui Mountains. From November to April, you can see humpback whales swimming in the ocean below. Lush tropical gardens surround this airy, island-style home. Guests are encouraged to pick bananas, papayas, and citrus fruits to accompany the coconut pancakes and freshly baked breads served for breakfast.

Hale Ho'o Maha ✪
P.O. BOX 422, KILAUEA, HAWAII 96754

Tel: **(808) 826-1130**
Best Time to Call: **7 AM–7 PM**
Hosts: **Kirby and Toby Searles**
Location: **28 mi. N of Lihue, Kauai**
No. of Rooms: **2**
No. of Private Baths: **1**
Max. No. Sharing Bath: **4**
Double/pb: **$65**
Double/sb: **$50**

Open: **All year**
Reduced Rates: **10%, after 5 nights**
Breakfast: **Continental**
Pets: **No**
Children: **No**
Smoking: **Permitted**
Social Drinking: **Permitted**
Foreign Languages: **Spanish**

Escape to a B&B that lives up to its name, which means "house of rest" in Hawaiian. This single-story home is perched on the cliffs along Kauai's north shore. Sandy beaches, rivers, waterfalls, and riding stables are five minutes away. Ask your hosts to direct you to "Queens Bath"—a natural saltwater whirlpool. Guests have full use of the kitchen, gas grill, cable TV, and Boogie boards. When in Rome, do as the Romans: Kirby will teach you to dance the hula and make leis, and Toby will instruct you in scuba diving.

Poipu Bed and Breakfast Inn ✪
2720 HOONANI ROAD, POIPU BEACH, KOLOA, KAUAI, HAWAII 96756

Tel: **(800) 552-0095**
Best Time to Call: **7 AM–9 PM**
Hosts: **Dotti Cichon and B. Young**
Location: **12 mi. SW of Lihue airport**
No. of Rooms: **8**
No. of Private Baths: **8**
Double/pb: **$90–$125**
Single/pb: **$85–$120**
Open: **All year**

Reduced Rates: **10%, weekly**
Breakfast: **Continental**
Credit Cards: **AMEX, MC, VISA**
Pets: **No**
Children: **Welcome**
Smoking: **No**
Social Drinking: **Permitted**
Foreign Languages: **French, German**

You are invited to play tennis and swim at Dotti's private club. Back at the inn, afternoon tea and an evening of video movies (with popcorn!) are daily events. Your hosts will be happy to arrange a car rental, boat or helicopter tours, and restaurant reservations for you.

Kilohana ✪
378 KAMEHAMEIKI ROAD, KULA, MAUI, HAWAII 96790

Tel: **(808) 878-6086**
Best Time to Call: **8 AM–6 PM**
Host: **Jody Baldwin**
Location: **16 mi. NW of Kahului airport**
No. of Rooms: **3**
Double/sb: **$65**

Single/sb: **$55**
Open: **All year**
Breakfast: **Continental**
Pets: **No**
Children: **No**
Smoking: **No**
Social Drinking: **Permitted**

Drive up, up, up, along the slopes of Haleakala, past cabbage and flower fields, and you will come to Jody's home—a 55-year-old English country-style house surrounded by 3 acres, with a sweeping view of the islands of Lanai and Molokai. "The quiet and coolness of the countryside bring our visitors back again and again." Must-sees while you're in the Kula district are the sunrise from the summit of the crater, the Tedeschi Winery, and exotic Protea Farms. The beach and windsurfing are a half-hour away, and restaurants just 5 to 15 minutes by car. You'll be greeted with refreshments when you arrive, and in the morning, after the sun enters your spacious guest room, you'll get up to a breakfast of fresh fruit, homemade pastry, coffee, tea, and fresh Hawaiian juice.

Victoria Place ✪
P.O. BOX 930, LAWAI, KAUAI, HAWAII 96765

Tel: **(808) 332-9300**
Host: **Edee Seymour**
No. of Rooms: **4**
No. of Private Baths: **4**
Double/pb: **$65–$95**
Single/pb: **$55**
Open: **All year**

Reduced Rates: **$10 less, Easter–Dec. 14**
Breakfast: **Continental**
Pets: **No**
Children: **No**
Smoking: **No**
Social Drinking: **Permitted**

Perched high in the lush hills of southern Kauai, overlooking the thick jungle, cane fields, and the Pacific, Victoria Place promises an oasis of pampered comfort and privacy. The guest rooms, located in one wing of this spacious skylit home, open directly through glass doors onto the pool area, which is surrounded by flower gardens. Edee, a former Michigan native, will direct you to nearby attractions, including the resort beaches of Poipu, the National Tropical Botanical Gardens, Spouting Horn geyser, open-air markets, boutiques, and ethnic restaurants, all within minutes of the house. There is a $5 surcharge for one-night stays.

Chalet Kilauea at Volcano ✪
P.O. BOX 998, VOLCANO, HAWAII 96785

Tel: **(808) 967-7786**
Hosts: **Lisha Haan and Brian Crawford**
Location: **2 mi. NE of Volcanoes National Park**
No. of Rooms: **2**
Max. No. Sharing Bath: **4**
Double/sb: **$55**
Single/sb: **$45**
Guest Cottage: **$75**
Open: **All year**

Reduced Rates: **20%, if using both rooms; 10%, seniors; 10%, weekly**
Breakfast: **Continental**
Credit Cards: **AMEX, MC, VISA**
Pets: **Sometimes**
Children: **Welcome**
Smoking: **No**
Social Drinking: **Permitted**
Foreign Languages: **Dutch, French, Portuguese, Spanish**

Chalet Kilauea sits on an acre of rain forest just a few miles from Volcanoes National Park; visitors from the mainland have been known to spend hours looking at the area's exotic birds and plants. This B&B's interior is scarcely less fascinating, because Lisha and Brian have decorated their home with furniture and art collected from their travels around the world. Breakfasts are highlighted by Kona coffee, Hawaiian fruit shakes, and assorted breads and jams.

IDAHO

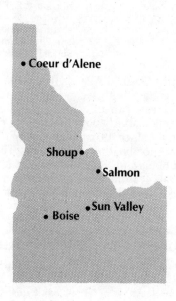

• Coeur d'Alene

Shoup•

•Salmon

•Sun Valley

• Boise

Bed and Breakfast of Idaho ✪
109 WEST IDAHO, BOISE, IDAHO 83702

Tel: **(208) 342-8066**
Best Time to Call: **9 AM–5 PM**
Coordinators: **Tom and Phyllis Lupher**
States/Regions Covered: **Idaho, statewide**

Rates (Single/Double):
Modest:	**$35**	**$45**
Average:	**$50**	**$65**
Luxury:	**$70**	**$135**

Credit Cards: **AMEX, MC, VISA**

Tom and Phyllis are prepared to arrange a stay to suit your purse and preference. In the "modest" classification, you might stay in a contemporary home with a mountain view; an "average" selection might be an inn located close to a lovely lake; and a "luxury" setting is a large suite with a sunken tub in the bathroom and a fireplace in the sitting area. All of the hosts have a genuine desire to share their knowledge of where to eat and what to do in their area. A $5 surcharge is imposed for one-night stays.

Cricket on the Hearth ✪
1521 LAKESIDE AVENUE, COEUR d'ALENE, IDAHO 83814

Tel: **(208) 664-6926**
Best Time to Call: **9 AM–8 PM**
Hosts: **Al and Karen Hutson**
Location: **30 mi. E of Spokane**
No. of Rooms: **4**
No. of Private Baths: **2**
Max. No. Sharing Bath: **4**
Double/pb: **$55**

Double/sb: **$40–$50**
Open: **All year**
Reduced Rates: **$5 less after 2 nights**
Breakfast: **Full**
Pets: **No**
Children: **Welcome, over 10**
Smoking: **Permitted**
Social Drinking: **Permitted**

Cricket on the Hearth, Coeur d'Alene's first bed-and-breakfast inn, is a comfortable 1920s cottage with second-story dormer windows and a large front porch. Guests can unwind in the library and the game room; musicians should ask Al about the antique pump organ, which has been in his family since 1916. Lake Coeur d'Alene, just a mile away, is a great place for boating and fishing. The area's many golf courses will lure duffers, and the snow-covered slopes will challenge skiers. Morning meals feature fruit, oven-fresh muffins and breads, and main courses like deep-dish French toast with huckleberry sauce.

Inn the First Place ✪
509 NORTH 15TH STREET, COEUR d'ALENE, IDAHO 83814

Tel: **(208) 667-3346**
Best Time to Call: **7 AM–11:30 PM**
Hosts: **Tom and Lois Knox**
Location: **30 mi. E of Spokane, Wash.**
No. of Rooms: **3**
Max. No. Sharing Bath: **4**
Double/sb: **$35**
Open: **All year**
Reduced Rates: **Available**

Breakfast: **Full**
Other Meals: **Available**
Credit Cards: **MC, VISA**
Pets: **No**
Children: **Welcome, over 12**
Smoking: **Permitted**
Social Drinking: **Permitted**
Airport/Station Pickup: **Yes**

Tom and Lois welcome you to their unusual home, which was once a grocery store. The guest rooms, located on the second floor, are decorated attractively, with wood paneling or country wallpaper, coordinating quilts, and a smattering of crafts and collectibles. The large living room and fully equipped kitchen are available to guests. In the morning, you can look forward to Lois's specialties, such as stuffed French toast or quiche. The inn is a mile away from beautiful Lake Coeur d'Alene, famous for fishing, swimming, and day cruises.

The Sleeping Place of the Wheels ✪
3308 LODGEPOLE ROAD, COEUR d'ALENE, IDAHO 83814 (MAIL ADDRESS: P.O. BOX 5273)

Tel: **(208) 765-3435**	Open: **May 1–Sept. 30**
Host: **Donna Bedord**	Breakfast: **Full**
Location: **1 mi. from I-90**	Pets: **No**
No. of Rooms: **2**	Children: **Welcome**
Max. No. Sharing Bath: **4**	Smoking: **No**
Double/sb: **$35**	Social Drinking: **No**
Single/sb: **$22.50**	Airport/Station Pickup: **Yes**

Wagon wheels mark the entrance to Donna's home, which is surrounded by tall pines and pretty flower gardens. Raspberries, strawberries, plums, and cherries are yours for the picking. Children will delight in the special playhouse with its fireman's slide, swing, and sandbox. Donna enjoys quilting, gardening, and reading.

Heritage Inn ✪
510 LENA STREET, SALMON, IDAHO 83467

Tel: **(208) 756-3174**	Suites: **$40**
Best Time to Call: **Until 9 PM**	Open: **All year**
Host: **Audrey Nichols**	Breakfast: **Continental**
Location: **½ mi. from Hwy. 93**	Credit Cards: **MC, VISA**
No. of Rooms: **5**	Pets: **No**
Max. No. Sharing Bath: **3**	Children: **Welcome**
Double/sb: **$25**	Smoking: **No**
Single/sb: **$20**	Social Drinking: **Permitted**

This 100-year-old Victorian farmhouse is set in a valley, surrounded by mountains and pine trees. In the old days, this was a cozy stopover for those traveling by stagecoach. The Heritage has since been lovingly restored and decorated with many antiques. Enjoy a cool drink on the glassed-in sun porch while you enjoy the quiet of this pretty neighborhood. The River of No Return is just half a mile away, and it's just a mile to the city park and swimming pool. Your hostess serves homemade muffins and jams in the sunny dining room or on the porch each morning. She is a native of Salmon and can gladly direct you to restaurants within walking distance, nearby ghost towns, and other places of historic or cultural interest.

Smith House Bed & Breakfast ✪
49 SALMON RIVER ROAD, SHOUP, IDAHO 83469

Tel: **(208) 394-2121**	Location: **50 mi. N of Salmon**
Best Time to Call: **9 AM–5 PM**	No. of Rooms: **6**
Hosts: **Aubrey and Marsha Smith**	No. of Private Baths: **2**

Max. No. Sharing Bath: **4**
Double/pb: **$54**
Double/sb: **$35–$42**
Single/sb: **$35**
Open: **All year**
Reduced Rates: **Weekly; groups**
Breakfast: **Full**

Other Meals: **Available**
Credit Cards: **MC, VISA**
Pets: **No**
Children: **Welcome**
Smoking: **No**
Social Drinking: **Permitted**
Airport/Station Pickup: **Yes**

Located on the Salmon River and adjoining a wilderness area, Smith House is a dream come true. Aubrey and Marsha vacationed here 11 years ago and fell in love with the constantly changing scenery. They sold their Florida house and built their dream log home, which they enjoy sharing with their guests. Marsha enjoys pampering people with such breakfast creations as hash-brown quiche, buttermilk scones, or wheat French toast with homemade fruit topping. Meals are served underneath the dining room skylight. Recreational opportunities include white-water rafting, fishing, hunting, and hiking. Visit the nearby ghost town or restored gold mine, then come "home" to relax in the hot tub.

ILLINOIS

```
                        Mundelein
                Rockford | .Gurnee
        Galena •      •    • Winnetka
                Sycamore.Oak Park
                    • ••Chicago
        Rock Island • St. Charles • • Lyons
                            Naperville
                            •Dwight

    Quincy •              • Champaign
            Petersburg  .Cisco
            •
        Springfield •  • Decatur
                        • Arcola
```

Bed & Breakfast/Chicago, Inc. ✪
P.O. BOX 14088, CHICAGO, ILLINOIS 60614

Tel: **(312) 951-0085**
Coordinator: **Mary Shaw**
States/Regions Covered: **Arlington Heights, Chicago, Deerfield, Evanston, Glencoe, Northfield, Oak Park, Wilmette**

Rates: (Single/Double):
  Modest: **$45**   **$55**
  Average: **$55–$65**   **$65–$75**
Credit Cards: **AMEX, MC, VISA**
Minimum Stay: **2 nights**

Mary welcomes you to midwestern hospitality in the "windy city" and its North Shore suburbs. Discover, on foot, Chicago's outdoor sculpture plazas, shop world-famous Marshall Fields, or observe the skyline from the top of the Sears Tower. Follow the happenings on the campuses of Northwestern, the University of Chicago, Loyola, and the University of Illinois. There is a three-night minimum stay for apartments without hosts in residence, and a $10 surcharge if you stay only one night in hosted B&Bs.

B&B Northwest Suburban—Chicago ✪
P.O. BOX 95503, HOFFMAN ESTATES, ILLINOIS 60195-0503

Tel: **(708) 310-9010**
Coordinator: **Martha McDonald-Swan**
States/Regions Covered: **Galena,
Geneva, Gurnee, Hinsdale,
Mundelein, Naperville, Oregon,
Palatine, West Dundee**

Descriptive Directory of B&Bs: **Free**
Rates: (Single/Double):
   Modest: **$40**   **$45**
   Average: **$45**   **$65**
   Luxury: **$60**   **$150**
Credit Cards: **DISCOVER, MC, VISA**

Martha's hosts have a lot of good advice and information to offer about events, points of interest, restaurants, and special shops in their suburban town. Each of Martha's listings has been carefully selected to meet her high standards of cleanliness and neatness. One home is in a 115-year-old villa with fireplaces in three bedrooms; another is a restored farmhouse.

Curly's Corner ✪
RR 2, BOX 85B, ARCOLA, ILLINOIS 61910

Tel: **(217) 268-3352**
Best Time to Call: **Mornings; after 5 PM**
Hosts: **Warren and Maxine Arthur**
Location: **35 mi. S of Champaign; 5 mi. from I-57**
No. of Rooms: **3**
No. of Private Baths: **2**
Max. No. Sharing Bath: **3**

Double/pb: **$40–$50**
Single/sb: **$30**
Open: **March–Nov.**
Breakfast: **Full**
Pets: **No**
Children: **Welcome, over 10**
Smoking: **No**
Social Drinking: **No**
Airport/Station Pickup: **Yes**

This ranch-style farmhouse is located in a quiet Amish community. Your hosts are dedicated to cordial hospitality and will gladly share information about the area or even take you on a tour. They offer comfortable bedrooms, one with a king-size water bed. In the morning, enjoy a wonderful breakfast of homemade biscuits, apple butter, fresh country bacon, and eggs. Curly's Corner is a half mile from beautiful Rockome Gardens.

The Golds ✪
RR 3, BOX 69, CHAMPAIGN, ILLINOIS 61821

Tel: **(217) 586-4345**
Best Time to Call: **Evenings**
Hosts: **Bob and Rita Gold**
Location: **6 mi. W of Champaign**
No. of Rooms: **2**
Max. No. Sharing Bath: **4**
Double/sb: **$40**
Single/sb: **$35**

Open: **All year**
Reduced Rates: **15% weekly**
Breakfast: **Continental**
Pets: **No**
Children: **Welcome**
Smoking: **No**
Social Drinking: **Permitted**
Airport/Station Pickup: **Available**

One of the most beautiful views in Champaign County is yours from the deck of this restored farmhouse. The house is set on six acres surrounded by prime central Illinois farmland. Inside you'll find country antiques, complemented by beautiful wainscoting. An open walnut stairway leads to bedrooms decorated with four-poster beds, handmade quilts, and Oriental rugs. Guests can relax by the living room wood stove or enjoy a glass of wine on the deck. Bob and Rita offer garden fruits and cider for breakfast, served with homemade jams, muffins, and coffee cakes. The Golds is two miles from Lake of the Woods, and 20 minutes from the University of Illinois campus. Shopping and restaurants are also within easy reach.

Country House ✪
ROUTE 1, BOX 61, CISCO, ILLINOIS 61830

Tel: **(217) 669-2291**	Suites: **$45**
Hosts: **Carol and Don Padgett**	Open: **Apr.–Dec.**
Location: **17 mi. E of Decatur**	Breakfast: **Full**
No. of Rooms: **2**	Pets: **No**
No. of Private Baths: **1**	Children: **No**
Max. No. Sharing Bath: **4**	Smoking: **No**
Double/sb: **$35**	Social Drinking: **No**
Single/sb: **$30**	

This 100-year-old country home is located in the heart of prairie farmland. Your hosts, Carol and Don, have decorated the rooms with a blend of traditional, wicker, and antique furnishings. In warmer weather, a leisurely breakfast may be served on the porch overlooking the flower garden. During cooler months, guests are served in the rustic family room or gracious dining room. The city of Monticello is not far and offers shopping and dining. The Country House is a short distance from Robert Allerton Park for picnicking, skiing, and biking. The University of Illinois at Champaign is close by.

Hamilton House ✪
500 WEST MAIN STREET, DECATUR, ILLINOIS 62522

Tel: **(217) 429-1669**	Open: **All year**
Best Time to Call: **Anytime**	Reduced Rates: **10%, seniors**
Host: **Nancy Phillips**	Breakfast: **Full**
Location: **30 mi. E of Springfield**	Credit Cards: **AMEX, MC, VISA**
No. of Rooms: **5**	Pets: **Sometimes**
No. of Private Baths: **1**	Children: **Welcome (crib)**
Max. No. Sharing Bath: **4**	Smoking: **Permitted**
Double/pb: **$45–$50**	Social Drinking: **Permitted**
Double/sb: **$45**	Airport/Station Pickup: **Yes**

Hamilton House is a brick Victorian mansion located in the Abraham Lincoln historic area. It was built in 1892 and is listed on the National Register of Historic Places. The house has been beautifully maintained and still boasts its original woodwork fireplaces. The guest rooms are decorated with period furnishings and each has a different style antique bed. Nancy and Dave also specialize in simple, elegant lunches. Their gift shop specializes in fine treasures of Victorian and American design.

La Petite Voyageur B&B ✪
116 EAST SOUTH STREET, DWIGHT, ILLINOIS 60420

Tel: **(815) 584-2239**	Breakfast: **Continental**
Host: **Pat Zolla**	Credit Cards: **DISC, MC, VISA**
Location: **60 mi. N of Bloomington**	Pets: **No**
No. of Rooms: **1**	Children: **No**
Max. No. Sharing Bath: **3**	Smoking: **Permitted, except in guest**
Double/sb: **$35**	**rooms**
Single/sb: **$32.50**	Social Drinking: **Permitted**
Open: **All year**	Airport/Station Pickup: **Yes**
Reduced Rates: **10%, seniors; 10%,**	
after 1 week	

La Petite Voyageur is on a quiet, tree-lined street filled with stately homes. Dwight is a small, friendly prairie town. Pat greets guests with coffee or tea and an assortment of baked goods. If you still have an appetite, stroll down the block to Country Manor, a wonderful old mansion that houses an excellent restaurant. In the morning, Pat sets out a generous continental breakfast of juice, baked goods, cereals, and a hot entrée.

Aldrich Guest House
900 THIRD STREET, GALENA, ILLINOIS 61036

Tel: **(815) 777-3323**	Single/sb: **$60–$65**
Host: **Judy Green**	Suites: **$135–$155**
Location: **¼ mi. from Rte. 20**	Open: **All year**
No. of Rooms: **5**	Breakfast: **Full**
No. of Private Baths: **3**	Credit Cards: **DISC, MC, VISA**
Max. No. Sharing Bath: **4**	Pets: **No**
Double/pb: **$70–$90**	Children: **Welcome, over 6**
Single/pb: **$65–$85**	Smoking: **Permitted**
Double/sb: **$65–$70**	Social Drinking: **Permitted**

George Washington didn't sleep here, but Ulysses S. Grant was entertained in the spacious double parlors of this elegant 1845 home. Throughout the house, period decor, antiques, and some reproductions harmonize effectively. Centrally air-conditioned for summer

comfort, the house is convenient to all of the historic sites. Judy's hearty breakfasts include fresh fruit salads and entrées such as pancakes or egg dishes.

Avery Guest House ✪
606 SOUTH PROSPECT STREET, GALENA, ILLINOIS 61036

Tel: **(815) 777-3883**
Best Time to Call: **9 AM–9 PM**
Hosts: **Flo and Roger Jensen**
Location: **15 mi. E of Dubuque, Iowa**
No. of Rooms: **4**
Max. No. Sharing Bath: **4**
Double/sb: **$55**
Single/sb: **$50**
Open: **All year**

Reduced Rates: **10%, seniors; $10 less weekdays**
Breakfast: **Continental**
Credit Cards: **MC, VISA**
Pets: **No**
Children: **Welcome (crib, high chair)**
Smoking: **No**
Social Drinking: **Permitted**
Airport/Station Pickup: **Yes**

This spacious, 140-year-old home is located two blocks from historic downtown Galena. Enjoy the view of bluffs and Victorian mansions from an old-fashioned porch swing overlooking the Galena River Valley. Your hosts welcome you to use the piano or bring your own instrument and join them in chamber music. Enjoy delicious homemade muffins and breads along with cheeses and jams each morning. Flo and Roger will gladly direct you to Grant's home, antique shops, and other interesting sights in the historic district.

Sweet Basil Hill Farm ☉
15937 WEST WASHINGTON STREET, GURNEE, ILLINOIS 60031

Tel: **(708) 244-3333**	Open: **All year**
Hosts: **Teri and Bob Jones**	Breakfast: **Continental**
Location: **48 mi. N of Chicago**	Credit Cards: **MC, VISA**
No. of Rooms: **5**	Pets: **No**
No. of Private Baths: **1**	Children: **Welcome in cottage**
Max. No. Sharing Bath: **4**	Smoking: **No**
Double/pb: **$85**	Social Drinking: **Permitted**
Double/sb: **$65–$75**	Airport/Station Pickup: **Yes**
Guest Cottage: **$100, sleeps 6**	Foreign Languages: **French**

Teri and Bob's informal Cape Cod is situated on 7½ acres of groomed hiking trails, herb gardens, and a picnic grove. If you are interested in the art of spinning wool, you can observe Teri firsthand, as there are fourteen sheep and two llamas to accommodate her hobby. Each guest room is individually decorated with lush feather comforters, plump pillows, and fine linen to ensure a restful night's sleep. You'll awake to the aroma of freshly brewed coffee and homemade breads. Afternoon tea and evening snacks are hallmarks of your gracious hosts' hospitality.

The Breakfast Room of Sweet Basil Hill Farm is shown on the back cover.

Round-Robin Guesthouse ☉
231 EAST MAPLE AVENUE, MUNDELEIN, ILLINOIS 60060

Tel: **(708) 566-7664**	Open: **All year**
Hosts: **George and Laura Loffredo**	Reduced Rates: **10%, seniors, families**
Location: **38 mi. NW of Chicago**	Breakfast: **Full**
No. of Rooms: **5**	Credit Cards: **MC, VISA**
No. of Private Baths: **2**	Pets: **Sometimes**
Max. No. Sharing Bath: **4**	Children: **Welcome**
Double/pb: **$60**	Smoking: **Permitted**
Double/sb: **$35–$50**	Social Drinking: **Permitted**
Suite: **$80**	Airport/Station Pickup: **Yes**

This handsome red Victorian with white trim takes its name from the letters circulated by your hosts' relatives for more than 70 years; to encourage you to write friends and family, George and Laura will provide you with paper, pen, and stamps. The many local diversions ensure that you'll have plenty to write about. Six Flags Great America, the Volo Auto Museum, and the antique village of Long Grove are barely fifteen minutes away by car, and you're never far from golf, swimming, and horseback riding. During the summer, the Chicago Symphony is in residence at nearby Ravinia Park. Or you can enjoy Laura's renditions of classical and ragtime music on the piano. You'll wake up to the aroma of fresh-brewed coffee; coffee cake, muffins, and homemade jam are served between 7:30 and 9:00 AM.

Toad Hall Bed & Breakfast House
301 NORTH SCOVILLE AVENUE, OAK PARK, ILLINOIS 60302

Tel: **(708) 386-8623**	Suites: **$65 for 2; $75 for 3**
Host: **Cynthia Mungerson**	Open: **All year**
Location: **5 mi. from Chicago Loop**	Breakfast: **Full**
No. of Rooms: **3**	Pets: **No**
No. of Private Baths: **3**	Children: **No**
Double/pb: **$50–$55**	Smoking: **No**
Single/pb: **$45–$50**	Social Drinking: **Permitted**

Built in 1909, and carefully maintained and restored, this gracious home is furnished with Victorian antiques, Oriental rugs, and Laura Ashley wallpapers. Guest rooms have comfortable reading chairs, luxurious linens, television, and air-conditioning. You are welcome to relax in the wicker on the porches, picnic on the sun deck, or curl up near a fireplace with a book. Breakfast, a British-style feast, is served in the oak-paneled dining room; in the same tradition, afternoon tea and evening brandy and sweets are offered. Centrally located in the Frank Lloyd Wright Historic District, it is within walking distance of 25 Wright masterpieces, dozens of architecturally significant buildings, the Ernest Hemingway home, and lovely shops and restaurants.

Carmody's Clare Inn ❂
207 SOUTH TWELFTH STREET, PETERSBURG, ILLINOIS 62675

Tel: **(217) 632-2350**	Reduced Rates: **10%, families renting**
Hosts: **Pat and Mike Carmody**	**2 rooms or more**
Location: **20 mi. NW of Springfield**	Breakfast: **Full**
No. of Rooms: **3**	Pets: **No**
Max. No. Sharing Bath: **3**	Children: **Welcome, over 10**
Double/sb: **$50**	Smoking: **No**
Single/sb: **$40**	Social Drinking: **Permitted**
Open: **All year**	Airport/Station Pickup: **Yes**

Built in 1874, and lovingly restored, this mansion approaches the 21st century with its ceiling medallions, marble mantels, and hand-grained woodwork gloriously intact. Antique furnishings re-create the ambience of yesteryear. While golf clubs and tennis courts are nearby, Petersburg is notable for its proximity to New Salem, where Abraham Lincoln served as postmaster and wooed Ann Rutledge. To visit Lincoln's home, law office, and tomb, drive just a few miles farther to Springfield. Complimentary snacks are served in the early evening. Breakfasts consist of fruit, juice, cereal, and a hot entrée.

The Kaufmann House
1641 HAMPSHIRE, QUINCY, ILLINOIS 62301

Tel: **(217) 223-2502**	Single/sb: **$30**
Best Time to Call: **Noon–9 PM**	Reduced Rates: **10%, 3 nights or more**
Hosts: **Emery and Bettie Kaufmann**	
Location: **100 mi. W of Springfield**	Open: **All year**
No. of Rooms: **3**	Breakfast: **Continental**
No. of Private Baths: **1**	Pets: **No**
Max. No. Sharing Bath: **4**	Children: **Welcome (crib)**
Double/pb: **$60**	Smoking: **No**
Single/pb: **$50**	Social Drinking: **No**
Double/sb: **$40–$50**	Airport/Station Pickup: **Yes**

History buffs will remember Quincy, set right on the Mississippi River, as the scene of the famous Lincoln-Douglas debates, while architecture buffs will be attracted to the town's feast of Victorian styles—Greek Revival, Gothic Revival, Italianate, and Richardsonian. The Kaufmann House was built 100 years ago, and the owners have been careful to maintain its "country" feeling. Guests may enjoy breakfast in the Ancestor's Room, on a stone patio, or at a picnic table under the trees. They are invited to play the piano, watch TV, or enjoy popcorn by the fire. The Kaufmanns describe themselves as "Christians who have a love for God, people, nature, and life."

Top o' the Morning ✪
1505 19TH AVENUE, ROCK ISLAND, ILLINOIS 61201

Tel: **(309) 786-3513**	Double/pb: **$40–$50**
Best Time to Call: **After 5 PM**	Open: **All year**
Hosts: **Sam and Peggy Doak**	Breakfast: **Full**
Location: **1½ mi. from Rte. 92, 18th Ave. exit**	Pets: **No**
	Children: **Welcome**
No. of Rooms: **2**	Smoking: **Permitted**
No. of Private Baths: **2**	Social Drinking: **Permitted**

Sam and Peggy welcome you to their country estate, set on a bluff overlooking the Mississippi River, near the center of the Quad Cities area. The 18-room mansion is situated at the end of a winding drive on three acres of lawn, orchards, and gardens. The guest rooms, graced with lovely chandeliers and Oriental rugs, command a spectacular view of the cities and river. The parlor, with its grand piano and fireplace, is an inviting place to relax. Local attractions are Mississippi River boat rides, harness racing, Rock Island Arsenal, Black Hawk State Park, Augustana College, and St. Ambrose University.

The Stagecoach Inn
41 WEST 278 WHITNEY ROAD, ST. CHARLES, ILLINOIS 60175

Tel: **(708) 584-1263**	Open: **All year**
Hosts: **Pat and Bud Koecher**	Reduced Rates: **Available**
Location: **41 mi. W of Chicago**	Breakfast: **Continental**
No. of Rooms: **2**	Pets: **No**
No. of Private Baths: **2**	Children: **Welcome (high chair)**
Double/pb: **$45–$50**	Smoking: **No**
Single/pb: **$35**	Social Drinking: **Permitted**

The Stagecoach Inn is situated on picturesque Lake Campton in a scenic area five miles west of St. Charles. The house is a spacious ranch with a porch for sunning and relaxing. Year-round activities such as ice skating and fishing can be enjoyed just steps from your door. Biking, riding, and antiquing are also within easy reach. Your hosts, Pat and Bud, serve assorted muffins, toast, or sweet rolls, with plenty of coffee and tea for breakfast. They also are glad to offer snacks and soft drinks later in the day.

The Country Charm Inn ✪
ROUTE 2, P.O. BOX 154, SYCAMORE, ILLINOIS 60178

Tel: **(815) 895-5386**	Breakfast: **Full**
Hosts: **Howard and Donna Petersen**	Pets: **No**
Location: **55 mi. W of Chicago**	Children: **Welcome, over 3**
No. of Rooms: **3**	Smoking: **No**
No. of Private Baths: **3**	Social Drinking: **Permitted**
Double/pb: **$35–$55**	Minimum Stay: **Only for local**
Open: **Apr.–Dec.**	**weekend events**
Reduced Rates: **20%, weekly**	

This rambling, three-story stucco farmhouse is a great place to bring kids—they can wander around the grounds and pet all the animals. The Petersens are happy to put Champ, the resident trick horse, through his paces. Meanwhile, adults can borrow a title from the 2,000-book library, or play golf and tennis at a nearby park. In good weather, a hearty country breakfast is served on the front porch. House specialties range from egg-and-cheese dishes to peach cobbler, with special designer pancakes for youthful visitors.

Chateau des Fleurs ✪
552 RIDGE ROAD, WINNETKA, ILLINOIS 60093

Tel: **(312) 256-7272**	No. of Rooms: **3**
Best Time to Call: **Early mornings**	No. of Private Baths: **3**
Host: **Sally Ward**	Double/pb: **$80**
Location: **15 mi. N of Chicago**	Single/pb: **$70**

Open: **All year**
Reduced Rates: **15%, weekly**
Breakfast: **Continental**
Pets: **No**

Children: **Welcome, over 16**
Smoking: **No**
Social Drinking: **Permitted**
Foreign Languages: **Limited Spanish**

At Chateau des Fleurs, guests may enjoy the elegance of a French country home and still be only 30 minutes from Chicago's Loop. Antique shops, Lake Michigan, and commuter trains are within walking distance. But there's so much to do at this luxurious B&B, you may not want to leave. Swim in the pool, screen movies on Sally's 50-inch television, tickle the ivories of a Steinway baby grand, or admire the terraced yard and carefully tended gardens. You'll enjoy the generous Continental breakfasts of muffins, fresh fruit, yogurt, toast, and hot and cold cereals. The Chateau's garden is pictured on our back cover.

INDIANA

Chesterton

Peru

Westfield
Indianapolis • • Knightstown

• Decatur
Morgantown •
• Nashville

• Madison
Paoli •

Grandview
Evansville • • Rockport • Corydon

Indiana Homes Bed & Breakfast, Inc.
1431 ST. JAMES COURT, LOUISVILLE, KENTUCKY 40208

Tel: (502) 635-7341
Best Time to Call: 8 AM–noon
Coordinators: Lillian Marshall and
  John Dillehay
States/Regions Covered: Indiana—
  Corydon, Indianapolis, Paoli,
  Washington, West Baden

Descriptive Directory: $1
Rates (Single/Double):
Average: $40–$85 $45–$90
Reduced Rates: After 1 night
Credit Cards: AMEX, MC, VISA
  (deposit only)

Moving south from the Indianapolis Museum of Art and the Indy 500 racetrack, leave the Interstate for a true view of Middle America. Traverse rolling hills past the famous stone quarries in Bedford and head for historic Corydon, the state's original capital city. Tour the cave systems, canoe the Blue River, and explore Wyandotte Woods. Wherever you decide to stop, you can be assured of a hearty welcome and pleasant surroundings.

Gray Goose Inn ✪
350 INDIAN BOUNDARY ROAD, CHESTERTON, INDIANA 46304

Tel: (219) 926-5781
Hosts: Tim Wilk and Charles Ramsey
Location: 60 mi. E of Chicago
No. of Rooms: 5
No. of Private Baths: 5
Double/pb: $65–$75
Single/pb: $60–$70
Suites: $75
Open: All year

Reduced Rates: 10%, seniors
Breakfast: Full
Credit Cards: AMEX, DISC, MC, VISA
Pets: No
Children: Welcome, over 12
Smoking: Permitted
Social Drinking: Permitted

Elegant accommodations await you in this English country-style home overlooking a 30-acre lake. Guest rooms feature canopied four-poster beds; fine linens; and thick, fluffy towels. Some rooms are decorated in Williamsburg style, and some have a fireplace. Enjoy a quiet moment in the common room, or relax with a cup of coffee on the screened-in porch. Take long walks beside the shady oaks, or feed the Canada geese and wild ducks. The Gray Goose is five minutes from Dunes State and National Lakeshore parks. Swimming, canoeing down the Little Calumet River, hiking, and fishing on Lake Michigan are all within easy reach. Dining, weekend entertainment, and minia-ture golf are within walking distance.

Cragwood Inn B&B ✪
303 NORTH SECOND STREET, DECATUR, INDIANA 46733

Tel: (219) 728-2000
Hosts: George and Nancy Craig
Location: 15 mi. S of Ft. Wayne
No. of Rooms: 4
No. of Private Baths: 2
Max. No. Sharing Baths: 4
Double/pb: $55
Single/pb: $50
Double/sb: $45–$55
Single/sb: $40–$50
Suites: $75, sleeps four
Open: All year
Reduced Rates: Weekdays; extended
  stays; families

Breakfast: Continental on weekdays,
  full on weekends
Other Meals: Available
Credit Cards: MC, VISA
Pets: No
Children: Welcome, over 12
Smoking: No
Social Drinking: Permitted
Airport/Station Pickup: Yes
Foreign Languages: Limited Spanish
  and German

Built in 1900, this Queen Anne home is distinguished by red oak woodwork, parquet floors, tin ceilings, and stained and beveled glass. If this whets your appetite for antiques, good shops are within walking distance. With ready access to a golf course, a fitness center, a swimming pool, a lake, bike paths, and tennis courts, fitness buffs won't be bored. Also of note are the Swiss Amish settlements in Berne and Amishville. The Continental breakfast consists of juice, coffee or tea, fruit, and homemade breads and muffins; the weekend menu includes French toast or strata. George and Nancy host several murder mystery parties during the year.

Brigadoon Bed & Breakfast Inn
1201 SOUTH EAST 2ND STREET, EVANSVILLE, INDIANA 47713

Tel: **(812) 422-9635**	Open: **All year**
Host: **Kathee Forbes**	Reduced Rates: **Families**
Location: **1 mi. from Hwy. 41**	Breakfast: **Full**
No. of Rooms: **4**	Other Meals: **Sometimes**
No. of Private Baths: **2**	Credit Cards: **MC, VISA**
Max. No. Sharing Bath: **4**	Pets: **Sometimes**
Double/pb: **$40**	Children: **Welcome (baby-sitter)**
Single/pb: **$35**	Smoking: **Permitted**
Double/sb: **$40**	Social Drinking: **Permitted**
Single/sb: **$35**	Airport/Station Pickup: **Yes**

Brigadoon is a white frame Victorian with a gingerbread porch. The inn was built in 1892 and has been thoroughly renovated by the Forbes family. Four fireplaces, original parquet floors, and beautiful stained-glass windows have been lovingly preserved. Modern baths and a country eat-in kitchen have been added. Bedrooms are large and sunny, with accents of lace and ruffles, floral wallpapers, and antique furnishings. Guests are welcome to relax in the parlor or library. Breakfast specialties change daily, and can include a soufflé or quiche served with a lot of homemade breads, jams, and apple butter. This charming Victorian getaway is close to the Historic Preservation area, restaurants, the riverfront, antique shops, the University of Southern Indiana, and the University of Evansville.

The River Belle Bed & Breakfast
P.O. BOX 669, HIGHWAY 66, GRANDVIEW, INDIANA 47615

Tel: **(812) 649-2500**	Guest Cottage: **$60, sleeps 4**
Host(s): **Don and Pat Phillips**	Open: **All year**
Location: **33 mi. E of Evansville**	Reduced Rates: **Weekly**
No. of Rooms: **6**	Breakfast: **Continental**
No. of Private Baths: **2**	Credit Cards: **MC, VISA**
Max. No. Sharing Bath: **4**	Pets: **No**
Double/pb: **$65**	Children: **Welcome**
Single/pb: **$60**	Smoking: **No**
Double/sb: **$45–$55**	Social Drinking: **Permitted**
Single/sb: **$40**	

Guests may choose from a selection of accommodations in an 1866 white painted brick steamboat-style house, an 1898 red-brick Italianate house, or an 1860 cottage with full kitchen. These adjacent beauties on the Ohio River have been carefully restored by Pat and Don to serve as their B&B complex. The guest rooms are large and airy, furnished with timeless heirlooms and graced by lace curtains and Oriental rugs. You may choose to walk along the riverfront, sit quietly and watch the white squirrels play among the magnolia, pecan, and dogwood trees, or take a side trip to the nearby Lincoln Boyhood National Memorial, Lincoln State Park, the "Young Abe Lincoln" Drama, and Holiday World (the nation's oldest theme amusement park).

Old Hoosier House ✪
ROUTE 2, BOX 299-1, KNIGHTSTOWN, INDIANA 46148

Tel: **(317) 345-2969**	Single/sb: **$42**
Hosts: **Tom and Jean Lewis**	Open: **May 1–Nov. 1**
Location: **30 mi. E of Indianapolis**	Reduced Rates: **10%, seniors**
No. of Rooms: **4**	Breakfast: **Full**
No. of Private Baths: **3**	Pets: **No**
Max. No. Sharing Bath: **3**	Children: **Welcome (crib)**
Double/pb: **$62**	Smoking: **No**
Single/pb: **$52**	Social Drinking: **Permitted**
Double/sb: **$52**	Airport/Station Pickup: **Yes**

The Old Hoosier House takes you back more than 100 years, when the livin' was easier. The rooms are large, with high ceilings, arched windows, antiques, and mementos. A library and patio are available for your pleasure. In the morning you'll wake to the aroma of homemade rolls and coffee. Golfers will enjoy the adjoining golf course, while antique buffs will be glad to know there are hundreds of local dealers in the area. The cities of Anderson and Richmond are close by, and the Indianapolis 500 is within an hour's drive.

Old Madison House ✪
517 MULBERRY STREET, MADISON, INDIANA 47250

Tel: **(812) 265-6874**	Single/sb: **$30**
Hosts: **Sherley and Jack Baugh**	Open: **All year**
Location: **50 mi. SW of Cincinnati, Ohio**	Breakfast: **Full**
	Pets: **Sometimes**
No. of Rooms: **2**	Children: **Welcome**
Max. No. Sharing Bath: **4**	Smoking: **Permitted**
Double/sb: **$40**	Social Drinking: **Permitted**

Located a block away from Main Street, this three-story Federal-style house dates back to 1900. It is comfortably furnished and accented with cherished antiques. Sherley prides herself on her country breakfast of eggs, hashed brown potatoes or grits, and fried apples. Jack will be happy to show you his collection of beer cans. Madison, situated on the banks of the Ohio River, is known for its splendid examples of Federal, Classic Revival, and Italian villa–inspired architecture.

The Rock House ✪
380 WEST WASHINGTON STREET, MORGANTOWN, INDIANA 46160

Tel: (812) 597-5100	Single/sb: $45
Hosts: Doug and Marcia Norton	Open: All year
Location: 32 mi. S of Indianapolis	Reduced Rates: 10%, seniors
No. of Rooms: 6	Breakfast: Full
No. of Private Baths: 2	Pets: No
Max. No. Sharing Bath: 4	Children: Welcome
Double/pb: $65	Smoking: Permitted
Single/pb: $55	Social Drinking: Permitted
Double/sb: $55	

The Rock House was built in the 1890s by James Smith Knight. He used concrete blocks years before they were popular, but it's the way he used them that made him an innovator. Before the concrete dried, Knight embedded in it rocks, seashells, dishes, and jewelry collected as souvenirs from 48 states. The result is spectacular, drawing many sightseers to the house. Inside, guests will find a homey atmosphere and comfortable furnishings. Your hosts will gladly direct you to such local attractions as Lake Monroe, Ski World, and Little Nashville Opry.

Allison House ✪
90 SOUTH JEFFERSON STREET, P.O. BOX 546, NASHVILLE, INDIANA 47448

Tel: (812) 988-0814	Open: All year
Best Time to Call: 9 AM–9 PM	Reduced Rates: 10% after 2 nights
Hosts: Tammy and Bob Galm	Breakfast: Continental
Location: 50 mi. S of Indianapolis	Pets: No
No. of Rooms: 5	Children: Welcome, over 12
No. of Private Baths: 5	Smoking: No
Double/pb: $85	Social Drinking: No

Allison House is a fully restored Victorian located in the heart of Nashville. Tammy and Bob have filled the house with a blend of old mementos and new finds from the local arts and crafts colony. The artisans are quite famous in this area, and they are located within walking distance. Tammy and Bob offer a light breakfast of home-baked goods.

Sunset House ✪

RR 3, BOX 127, NASHVILLE, INDIANA 47448

Tel: **(812) 988-6118**	Open: **Apr.–Nov.**
Host: **Mary Margaret Baird**	Breakfast: **Continental**
Location: **18 mi. from I-65**	Pets: **No**
No. of Rooms: **3**	Children: **Welcome (crib)**
No. of Private Baths: **3**	Smoking: **Permitted**
Double/pb: **$55**	Social Drinking: **Permitted**
Suites: **$65**	

Mary's home is a magnificent contemporary house with a deck and patio for relaxing. The guest rooms have separate entrances, and all are furnished in fine cherry wood. The master suite has a handsome stone fireplace. Although there are many things to keep you busy, the Little Nashville Opry is a major attraction each Saturday, with country-and-western stars entertaining. Indiana University is nearby.

Braxtan House Inn B&B ✪

210 NORTH GOSPEL STREET, PAOLI, INDIANA 47454

Tel: **(812) 723-4677**	Reduced Rates: **10%, seniors**
Best Time to Call: **6–8 PM**	Breakfast: **Full**
Hosts: **Terry and Brenda Cornwell**	Pets: **Sometimes**
Location: **45 mi. S of Bloomington**	Children: **Welcome, over 10**
No. of Rooms: **6**	Smoking: **Permitted**
No. of Private Baths: **6**	Social Drinking: **Permitted**
Double/pb: **$50–$60**	Minimum Stay: **2 nights ski season**
Single/pb: **$45–$55**	**and Kentucky Derby weekend**
Open: **All year**	

This Queen Anne Victorian was built in 1893. The original cherry, oak, and walnut woodwork is still evident in many of the 21 rooms. Terry and Brenda have carefully refurbished the mansion and decorated with lovely antiques, many of which are for sale. The dining room, with its original wainscoting and wide-plank floors, is where pecan pancakes with a variety of fruit toppings are on the breakfast menu. Paoli Peaks, a ski resort, is 2 miles away, and it's 15 miles to Patoka, the second largest lake in the state. Coffee, tea, and snacks are graciously offered.

Rosewood Mansion ✪

54 NORTH HOOD, PERU, INDIANA 46970

Tel: **(317) 472-7151**	Max. No. Sharing Bath: **4**
Best Time to Call: **8 AM–5 PM**	Double/pb: **$65**
Hosts: **Carm and Zoyla Henderson**	Single/pb: **$55**
No. of Rooms: **5**	Double/sb: **$60**
No. of Private Baths: **2**	Single/sb: **$50**

Suites: **$60–$68**
Open: **All Year**
Reduced Rates: **15%, weekly; 10%,**
   seniors, families, business travelers
   (midweek)
Breakfast: **Full**
Other Meals: **Available**

Credit Cards: **AMEX, MC, VISA**
Pets: **Sometimes**
Children: **Welcome, over 12**
Smoking: **Permitted**
Social Drinking: **Permitted**
Airport/Station Pickup: **Yes**
Foreign Languages: **Spanish**

Rosewood Mansion is a stately brick Georgian residence constructed in 1862. A winding wooden staircase connects each floor, and stained-glass windows accent each landing. The house is decorated in period style, with floral wallpaper and antique furniture. Because this B&B is located four blocks from downtown Peru, restaurants, shops, public parks, and numerous sports facilities are just minutes away. Guests breakfast on coffee, tea, juice, fresh fruit, freshly baked breads or muffins, and quiche or eggs Benedict. Snacks are served in the afternoon, with a round of hot chocolate at bedtime.

The Rockport Inn ✪
THIRD AT WALNUT, ROCKPORT, INDIANA 47635

Tel: **(812) 649-2664**
Best Time to Call: **8 AM–6PM**
Hosts: **Emil and Carolyn Ahnell**
Location: **40 mi. E of Evansville**
No. of Rooms: **6**
No. of Private Baths: **6**
Double/pb: **$35–$45**
Single/pb: **$25–$35**
Open: **All year**

Reduced Rates: **30%, weekly**
Breakfast: **Continental**
Other Meals: **Available**
Pets: **Sometimes**
Children: **Welcome (crib)**
Smoking: **Permitted**
Social Drinking: **Permitted**
Foreign Languages: **German, Swedish**

Built in 1855, this white frame two-story residence has a porch and landscaped yard. It's furnished with antiques; plants and flowers add to its cozy atmosphere. Lincoln State Park, Santa Claus Land, and Kentucky Wesleyan College are nearby.

Country Roads Guesthouse ✪
2731 WEST 146TH STREET, WESTFIELD, INDIANA 46074

Tel: (317) 846-2376
Host: **Nancy Litz**
Location: **15 mi. N of Indianapolis; 10 mi. from I-465**
No. of Rooms: **2**
No. of Private Baths: **2**
Double/pb: **$58**

Single/pb: **$38**
Open: **All year**
Breakfast: **Continental**
Pets: **No**
Children: **Welcome**
Smoking: **No**
Social Drinking: **No**

This 100-year-old farmhouse is situated on four acres, has high ceilings, a kitchen fireplace, and is furnished with antiques. It's air-conditioned for your summer comfort, and guests are welcome to use the swimming pool and basketball court. The country setting is fine for walking, jogging, or bicycling, and the area is filled with antique shops, historic sites, and fine restaurants. The Herb Barn Country Store and Gardens, and Conner Prairie, a pioneer settlement, are nearby attractions.

IOWA

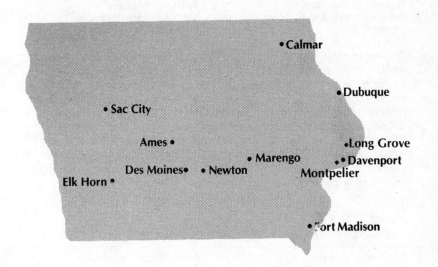

- •Calmar
- •Dubuque
- • Sac City
- Ames •
- •Long Grove
- • Marengo •• Davenport
- Des Moines• • Newton
- Montpelier
- Elk Horn •
- •Fort Madison

Bed and Breakfast in Iowa, Ltd. ✪
BOX 430, PRESTON, IOWA 52069

Tel: **(319) 689-4222**
Coordinator: **Wilma Bloom**
States/Regions Covered: **Statewide**
Descriptive Directory: **$2**

Rates (Single/Double):
Modest: **$25**   **$35**
Average: **$30**   **$50**
Luxury: **$50**   **$65**
Credit Cards: **No**

Wilma has a vast variety of accommodations, some of which are on the National Register of Historic Places. Travelers' interests, including cultural, historic, sports, and crafts, as well as fairs and festivals, can be easily satisfied. The University of Iowa, Iowa State, and Drake University are close to several homes. Some B&Bs impose a surcharge for one-night stays.

Calmar Guesthouse
RR 1, BOX 206, CALMAR, IOWA 52132

Tel: (319) 562-3851	Open: **All year**
Hosts: **Art and Lucille Kruse**	Breakfast: **Full**
Location: **10 mi. S of Decorah**	Pets: **No**
No. of Rooms: 5	Children: **Welcome**
Max. No. Sharing Bath: 5	Smoking: **Permitted**
Double/sb: **$35–$40**	Social Drinking: **Permitted**
Single/sb: **$30**	Airport/Station Pickup: **Yes**

A recent guest reports that "The Calmar Guesthouse is a spacious, lovely, newly remodeled Victorian home located on the edge of town. The atmosphere is enhanced by the friendly, charming manner of Lucille, who made us feel right at home. The rooms were comfortable, private, and pretty. After a peaceful night's sleep, we were served a delicious breakfast of fresh farm eggs with ham and cheeses, croissants with butter and jam, homemade cinnamon rolls, and coffee. I would recommend it to anyone visiting the area." Nearby points of interest include Lake Meyer, the world's smallest church, and Spillville, where the hand-carved Billy Bros. Clocks are made.

River Oaks Inn ✪
1234 EAST RIVER DRIVE, DAVENPORT, IOWA 52803

Tel: (319) 326-2629	Reduced Rates: **Available**
Best Time to Call: **8 AM–8 PM**	Breakfast: **Full**
Hosts: **Bill and Suzanne Pohl; Ron and**	Credit Cards: **MC, VISA**
Mary Jo Pohl	Pets: **Sometimes**
Location: **2 mi. from I-80**	Children: **Welcome**
No. of Rooms: 5	Smoking: **In designated areas**
No. of Private Baths: 5	Social Drinking: **Permitted**
Double/pb: **$49**	Airport/Station Pickup: **Yes**
Suites: **$69**	Foreign Languages: **Spanish**
Open: **All year**	

Abner Davison combined Italianate, Victorian, and Prairie architecture when he built his home back in the 1850s. The house is situated on a rolling lot that still shows evidence of the original carriage drive. Choose from a suite with king-size bed, sun porch, and dressing room; the Ambrose Fulton Room, with double bed and garden view; the Mississippi Room, with queen-size bed and window seat; or the Abner Davison Room, which has twin beds and a bay window. Breakfast is served in the dining room, or out on the deck in warm weather. High tea is served in the afternoon, and guests are welcome to enjoy it outside in the gazebo. The inn is located one block from river boat rides, and is convenient to many area attractions, such as Historic Rock Island Arsenal and the village of East Davenport.

The Richards House
1492 LOCUST STREET, DUBUQUE, IOWA 57001

Tel: (319) 557-1492
Host: **Michelle Delaney**
No. of Rooms: 5
No. of Private Baths: 4
Max. No. Sharing Bath: 2
Double/pb: **$45–$75**
Single/pb: **$40–$70**
Double/sb: **$45–$75**
Single/sb: **$40–$70**
Suites: **$70–$85, $120–$130**

Guest Cottage: **$45**
Open: **All Year**
Reduced Rates: **10%, Nov.–Apr.**
Breakfast: **Full**
Credit Cards: **AMEX, MC, VISA**
Pets: **Sometimes**
Children: **Welcome (crib)**
Smoking: **No**
Social Drinking: **Permitted**
Airport/Station Pickup: **Yes**

Inside and out, this four-story Victorian is a feast for the eyes, with its gabled roof, stained-glass windows, gingerbread trim, and elaborate woodwork. Rooms are furnished in period style. Guests can continue their journey back in time with a ride on the Fenelon Place Cable Car, the shortest inclined railway in the country. Then it's time to pay respects to another form of transportation at the Woodward Riverboat Museum. You're welcome to use the kitchen for light snacks; in the morning, Michelle takes over, setting out fresh fruit, waffles, pancakes, sausage, and homemade breads.

Rainbow H Ranch and Lodginghouse ✪
ROUTE 1, ELK HORN, IOWA 51531

Tel: **(712) 764-8272**
Best Time to Call: **Mornings; after
  6 PM**
Hosts: **Mark and Cherie Hensley**
Location: **60 mi. E of Omaha, Neb.**
No. of Rooms: 2
No. of Private Baths: 2
Double/sb: **$35**

Single/sb: **$26**
Open: **All year**
Breakfast: **Full**
Pets: **Sometimes**
Children: **Welcome**
Smoking: **Permitted**
Social Drinking: **No**

Enjoy the charm of the Iowa countryside as a guest in this grand brick home. The decor is country French and features a spacious recreation room with fireplace and beamed ceilings. The bedrooms have full or twin-size beds and color TVs; there is a private entrance and outdoor patio for your use. Your hosts raise longhorn cattle and will gladly give you and the kids a tour of the farm. The Elk Horn community is home to the largest Danish settlement in the United States. The town has a working windmill and is home to the National Danish Museum and the Tivoli Festival.

A Night on the Farm ✪
29375 162 AVENUE, LONG GROVE, IOWA 52756

Tel: (319) 285-4377	Single/sb: **$22**
Best Time to Call: **7–11 AM; after 6 PM**	Open: **Apr.–Sept.**
Hosts: **Alice and Bud De Schepper**	Breakfast: **Full**
Location: **15 mi. N of Davenport**	Pets: **Sometimes**
No. of Rooms: **2**	Children: **Welcome**
Max. No. Sharing Bath: **4**	Smoking: **No**
Double/sb: **$32**	Social Drinking: **No**

As its name indicates, this B&B is a comfortable, old-fashioned farm on 142 acres where your hosts raise sheep and rabbits. Scott County Park—with its swimming pool, hiking trails, picnic area, and petting zoo—is only ten minutes away. The Iowa-Illinois metropolitan area of the Quad Cities has a full schedule of summer events, notably the Bix Beiderbecke Jazz Festival and the Quad City Blues Festival. Full country breakfasts consist of omelets, buttermilk pancakes, muffins, and fruit your hostess canned herself.

Loy's Bed and Breakfast ✪
RR 1, BOX 82, MARENGO, IOWA 52301

Tel: (319) 642-7787	Single/pb: **$30**
Best Time to Call: **7 AM, noon, 6 PM**	Double/sb: **$45**
Hosts: **Loy and Robert Walker**	Open: **All year**
Location: **3 mi. from I-80 Exit 216**	Pets: **If caged**
No. of Rooms: **3**	Children: **Welcome**
No. of Private Baths: **2**	Smoking: **No**
Max. No. Sharing Bath: **4**	Social Drinking: **Permitted**
Double/pb: **$45–$50**	

The Walkers invite you to visit their contemporary farmhouse in the heartland of rural Iowa. Enjoy the peaceful surroundings of a large lawn, gardens, and patio. The rooms are furnished in modern and refinished pieces. Guests are welcome to relax in the family room by the fire or to stop by the rec room for a game of shuffleboard or pool, and a treat from the snack bar. If they are not busy with the harvest, your hosts will gladly take you on day trips. Tours may include Plum Grove, Iowa City, Brucemore Mansion, and Herbert Hoover's birthplace. A visit to the nearby lakes is recommended, and a take-along lunch can be arranged. The Amana Colonies is right here and shouldn't be missed.

Varners' Caboose Bed & Breakfast

204 EAST SECOND STREET, P.O. BOX 10, MONTPELIER, IOWA 52759

Tel: **(319) 381-3652**	Open: **All year**
Best Time to Call: **Afternoon**	Breakfast: **Full**
Hosts: **Bob and Nancy Varner**	Pets: **Sometimes**
Location: **11 mi. W of Davenport**	Children: **Welcome**
No. of Rooms: **1**	Smoking: **No**
No. of Private Baths: **1**	Social Drinking: **Permitted**
Double/pb: **$55**	Airport/Station Pickup: **Yes**

Bob and Nancy offer their guests the unique experience of staying in a genuine Rock Island Line caboose. Their home, located close to the Mississippi, was the original Montpelier Depot, and the caboose is a self-contained unit with bath, shower, and kitchen set on its own track behind the house. It sleeps four, with a queen-size bed and two singles in the cupola. The rate is increased to $65 when more than two occupy the caboose. A fully prepared egg casserole, fruit, homemade breads, juice, and coffee or tea are left in the kitchen to be enjoyed at your leisure. Enjoy this quiet town while being a few minutes downstream from the heart of the Quad Cities.

LaCorsette Maison Inn ✪

629 FIRST AVENUE EAST, NEWTON, IOWA 50208

Tel: **(515) 792-6833**	Breakfast: **Full**
Host: **Kay Owen**	Other Meals: **Available**
Location: **25 mi. E of Des Moines**	Pets: **Sometimes**
No. of Rooms: **4**	Children: **Yes**
No. of Private Baths: **4**	Smoking: **No**
Double/pb: **$55–$60**	Social Drinking: **Permitted**
Suites: **$100**	Airport/Station Pickup: **Yes**
Open: **All year**	

Bringing a touch of Spanish architecture to the American heartland, this 21-room mansion has all the hallmarks of the Mission style, from its stucco walls and red-tiled roof to its interior oak woodwork. Six nights a week, Kay doubles as a chef, preparing elaborate six-course dinners for as many as 48 scheduled guests; the first caller to make reservations selects the entrée, and a house tour precedes the meal. Overnight guests wake up to a full breakfast accented by the herbs and vegetables Kay grows in the backyard. If you want to work off the calories, tennis courts and a pool are in the area.

KANSAS

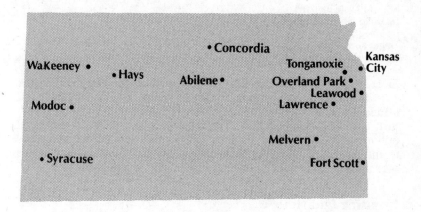

Balfours' House
ROUTE 2, ABILENE, KANSAS 67410

Tel: **(913) 263-4262**
Best Time to Call: **After 5 pm**
Hosts: **Gilbert and Marie Balfour**
Location: **2¼ mi. S of Abilene**
No. of Rooms: **2**
No. of Private Baths: **1**
Max. No. Sharing Bath: **4**
Double/pb: **$40**
Single/pb: **$35**
Double/sb: **$35**

Single/sb: **$30**
Open: **All year**
Breakfast: **Continental**
Credit Cards: **MC, VISA**
Pets: **Sometimes**
Children: **Welcome**
Smoking: **Permitted**
Social Drinking: **Permitted**
Airport/Station Pickup: **Sometimes**

Gilbert and Marie Balfour welcome you to their modern, cottage-style home, set on a hillside. The house is located on just over two acres, and has a spacious yard. Guests have their own private entrance into the family room, which includes a fireplace, piano, and TV. The main attraction of the house is a hexagonal recreation room that has a built-in swimming pool, spa, and dressing area with shower. Your hosts will gladly direct you to the Eisenhower Museum, Greyhound Hall of Fame, and old historic mansions.

Crystle's Bed and Breakfast ✪
508 WEST 7TH, CONCORDIA, KANSAS 66901

Tel: **(913) 243-2192**
Host: **Carrie Lee Warren-Gully**
Location: **50 mi. N of Salina**
No. of Rooms: **5**
No. of Private Baths: **1**
Max. No. Sharing Bath: **4**
Double/pb: **$45**
Single/pb: **$40.50**
Double/sb: **$35–$40**

Single/sb: **$31–$36**
Open: **All year**
Breakfast: **Full**
Credit Cards: **MC, VISA**
Pets: **No**
Children: **Welcome**
Smoking: **No**
Social Drinking: **Permitted**
Airport/Station Pickup: **Yes**

Erected in 1880, this spacious home boasts decorative trim on the outside and antique furniture, Victorian wallpapers, and stained and leaded glass on the inside. Concordia is full of beautifully restored, turn-of-the-century buildings. For sports-minded guests, recreational options include hunting, fishing, golf, tennis, swimming, and visits to the local health club. Discuss the possibilities with your hostess over a breakfast of fruit puffs, egg dishes, and lots of muffins.

Country Quarters ✪
ROUTE 5, BOX 80, FORT SCOTT, KANSAS 66701

Tel: **(316) 223-2889**
Host: **Marilyn McQuitty**
Location: **2 mi. S of Fort Scott**
No. of Rooms: **2**
Max. No. Sharing Bath: **4**
Double/sb: **$25**

Open: **All year**
Breakfast: **Full**
Pets: **No**
Children: **Welcome**
Smoking: **Permitted**
Social Drinking: **Permitted**

Marilyn McQuitty welcomes you to a real working farm located outside a charming Victorian town. Her 100-year-old farmhouse is furnished with comfortable family pieces. While you're sitting by the fire, ask to hear the story behind the 100-year-old hearth and hand-carved mantelpiece. Guests are welcome to relax on the porch or visit the ceramic shop located on the premises. There is easy access to the Fort Scott Lake, Gunn Park, and the Fort Scott National Historic Site, an authentically restored military fort dating back to 1892. Downtown you can drive past the magnificent old homes, browse through antiques stores, and visit a one-room schoolhouse.

Butterfield Bed & Breakfast ✪
RR1, BOX 200, HAYS, KANSAS 67601

Tel: **(913) 625-9978; (913) 628-3908**
  evenings
Best Time to Call: **9 AM–9 PM**
Hosts: **Carol and Bob Redger**

Location: **2 mi. NW of Hays**
No. of Rooms: **2**
Max. No. Sharing Bath: **4**
Double/sb: **$45**

Single/sb: **$35**
Guest Cottage: **$35–$90**
Open: **All year**
Reduced Rates: **20%, families**
Breakfast: **Full**
Credit Cards: **MC, VISA**

Pets: **Sometimes**
Children: **Welcome, over 4**
Smoking: **Permitted**
Social Drinking: **Permitted**
Airport/Station Pickup: **Yes**

An 1890s farmhouse furnished in period style, Butterfield Bed & Breakfast is part of Frontier City, a living museum that recreates the Wild West. Guests have full access to Frontier City's historic buildings, craft shop, and petting zoo. On Sundays from May through September, the Hays City Gunfighters ride into town, rob the freight office, and battle over the saloon "girls." Even a hungry gunslinger would be sated after full breakfasts featuring blueberry pancakes, French toast, or Western omelets.

Schoolhouse Inn ❂

106 EAST BECK, BOX 175, MELVERN, KANSAS 66510

Tel: **(913) 549-3473**
Best Time to Call: **After 5 PM**
Hosts: **Bill and Mary Fisher**
Location: **80 mi. SW of Kansas City, Mo.**
No. of Rooms: **4**
No. of Private Baths: **2**
Max. No. Sharing Bath: **4**
Double/pb: **$40**
Single/pb: **$35**

Double/sb: **$37.50**
Single/sb: **$32.50**
Open: **All year**
Credit Cards: **AMEX, MC, VISA**
Reduced Rates: **10%, seniors**
Breakfast: **Full**
Pets: **Sometimes**
Children: **Welcome, over 5**
Smoking: **No**
Social Drinking: **Permitted**

The Schoolhouse was built in 1870 of heavy timbers, and stone from nearby quarries. It is on the National Register of Historic Places. Today the house has been completely restored to serve as an elegant retreat in a pastoral setting. The second-floor guest rooms are large, with high ceilings, queen-size beds, and comfortable furnishings. The Schoolhouse is four miles from Melvern Lake and is convenient to state and federal parks and antique shops.

Krause House ❂

ROUTE 1, BOX 9, MODOC, KANSAS 67866

Tel: **(316) 379-4627**
Hosts: **Paul and Merilyn Krause**
Location: **13 mi. W of Scott City**
No. of Rooms: **2**
No. of Private Baths: **1**
Max. No. Sharing Bath: **4**
Double/pb: **$35**
Single/pb: **$25**
Double/sb: **$35**
Single/sb: **$25**

Open: **All year**
Reduced Rates: **Families**
Breakfast: **Full**
Other Meals: **Available**
Pets: **Sometimes**
Children: **Welcome**
Smoking: **No**
Social Drinking: **No**
Airport/Station Pickup: **Available**

Experience a working grain farm in the western Kansas countryside. Paul and Merilyn Krause have a remodeled farmhouse surrounded by tall shade trees. Guest rooms are located on the second floor and are decorated with country furnishings. Breakfast specialties such as egg casseroles, homemade breads, and cinnamon rolls are served on the glassed-in patio overlooking the flowers and greenery. On weekends, you're invited to a full-course dinner in the formal dining room. Krause House is 25 miles from Scott County State Park, where you may fish, boat, hunt for fossils, and see Indian ruins.

Braddock Ames Bed and Breakfast Hotel ○
AVENUE B AND NORTH MAIN, SYRACUSE, KANSAS 67878

Tel: **(316) 384-5218**
Hosts: **Dorothy Braddock Fouts and Mary Ruth Houdyshell**
Location: **54 mi. W of Garden City**
No. of Rooms: **3**
No. of Private Baths: **3**
Double/pb: **$35–$45**
Single/pb: **$30–$40**

Open: **All year**
Breakfast: **Continental**
Pets: **No**
Children: **Welcome, over 12**
Smoking: **No**
Social Drinking: **Permitted**
Airport/Station Pickup: **Yes**

Really a modest residential hotel, the Braddock Ames has three rooms set aside for short-term visitors. Syracuse is a small midwestern town about one mile north of the Arkansas River, which attracts canoeists in the summer and hunters in the winter. Within city limits you'll find a museum, a swimming pool, a movie theater, and reportedly the best pizzeria in southwest Kansas.

Almeda's Inn ○
BOX 103, 220 SOUTH MAIN, TONGANOXIE, KANSAS 66086

Tel: **(913) 845-2295**
Best Time to Call: **Before 9 AM; after 6 PM**
Hosts: **Almeda and Richard Tinberg**
Location: **20 mi. W of Kansas City**
No. of Rooms: **7**
No. of Private Baths: **2**
Max. No. Sharing Bath: **4**
Double/pb: **$40**

Single/sb: **$30**
Double/sb: **$30**
Suite: **$60**
Open: **All year**
Breakfast: **Continental**
Pets: **No**
Children: **Welcome, over 10**
Smoking: **Permitted**
Social Drinking: **Permitted**

Located in a picturesque small town, and made a designated Historical Site in 1983, the inn dates back to World War I. You are welcome to sip a cup of coffee at the unique stone bar in the room once used as a bus stop in 1930. In fact, this room was the inspiration for *Bus Stop*. Almeda and Richard will be happy to direct you to the golf course, swimming facilities, the Starlight Theatre, or the University of Kansas at Lawrence.

Thistle Hill ✪
ROUTE 1, BOX 93, WAKEENEY, KANSAS 67672

Tel: **(913) 743-2644**
Best Time to Call: **6–8 AM; evenings**
Hosts: **Dave and Mary Hendricks**
Location: **1½ mi. from I-70, Exit 120**
No. of Rooms: **3**
No. of Private Baths: **2**
Max. No. Sharing Bath: **4**
Double/pb: **$40**
Single/pb: **$35**
Double/sb: **$40**

Single/sb: **$35**
Open: **All year**
Reduced Rates: **Families**
Breakfast: **Full**
Pets: **Sometimes**
Children: **Welcome**
Smoking: **Permitted**
Social Drinking: **Permitted**
Airport/Station Pickup: **Yes**

The entry of this weathered wood country house sets the hospitable tone of this B&B located 325 miles west of Kansas City, or the same distance east of Denver, Colorado. Seasonal wreaths, an Early American bench, antique lanterns, and a big sign saying, "Welcome to Thistle Hill" are the Hendrickses way of saying they're glad you've come to visit. They're anxious to share with you the pleasures of their rural life, which include cooking, restoring antiques, and working with their team of draft horses. A varied breakfast often includes country fresh eggs, breakfast meats, fresh baked breads, or hotcakes made with whole wheat from their own wheat fields. On chilly mornings it is served near the fireplace. Cedar Bluff Reservoir, for fishing, is 30 miles away; pheasant, waterfowl, and deer roam 10,000 acres of public hunting land nearby.

KENTUCKY

Carrollton •
Louisville •
Frankfort • • Georgetown
Bardstown • •Springfield

• Mammoth Cave
•Paducah Cadiz •Bowling Green
• Grays Knob •

Bluegrass Bed & Breakfast ✪
ROUTE 1, BOX 263, VERSAILLES, KENTUCKY 40383

Tel: (606) 873-3208
Coordinator: **Betsy Pratt**
States/Regions Covered:
Georgetown, Harrodsburg,
Lexington, Midway, Versailles

Rates (Single/Double):
Modest: **$45**
Average: **$54**
Luxury: **$100**

Most of Betsy's B&Bs are in beautiful old houses that grace the country roads of the area. You may choose among a stone house built in 1796, a turreted Victorian in downtown Lexington, or a country home where your bedroom windows look out on thoroughbred horses. Visit Shakertown, where weavers, smiths, and woodworkers display their skills in an 1839 restored village. Take a ride on the winding Kentucky River in a paddlewheel boat. Tour exquisite historic mansions or see the picturesque homes of such Derby winners as Secretariat and Seattle Slew. And don't miss the 1,000-acre Kentucky Horse Park that includes a theater, museum, track, barns, and hundreds of horses. You may even take a horseback ride, because this place will inspire you.

Kentucky Homes Bed & Breakfast, Inc.
1431 ST. JAMES COURT, LOUISVILLE, KENTUCKY 40208

Tel: (502) 635-7341
Best Time to Call: **8 AM–noon**
Coordinators: **Lillian Marshall and John Dillehay**
States/Regions Covered: **Kentucky— Bardstown, Danville, Lexington, Louisville; S. Indiana—Corydon, Indianapolis, Paoli**

Descriptive Directory: **$1**
Rates (Single/Double):
  Average: **$40–$50 $45–$90**
Reduced Rates: **For 3 nights**
Credit Cards: **MC, VISA (deposit only)**

Lillian and John cordially invite you to be a guest in friendly Kentucky at one of dozens of host homes. Fish in spectacular lakes, visit Mammoth Cave, drop in on Shakertown at Pleasant Hill, or reserve early and assure yourself of a spot at the next running of the Kentucky Derby (held the first Saturday in May). Stay in a gorgeous turn-of-the-century home in restored old Louisville, or a dairy farm that boards and trains racehorses, or many comfortable choices in between. Ask about their unique "prepaid voucher" plan.

Jailer's Inn ✪
111 WEST STEPHEN FOSTER AVENUE, BARDSTOWN, KENTUCKY 40004

Tel: (502) 348-5551
Best Time to Call: **10 AM–5 PM**
Hosts: **Challen and Fran McCoy**
Location: **35 mi. S of Louisville**
No. of Rooms: **5**
No. of Private Baths: **3**
Max. No. Sharing Bath: **4**
Double/sb: **$60**
Single/sb: **$55**

Guest Cottage: **$40; sleeps 3**
Open: **Mar.–Dec.**
Reduced Rates: **Available**
Breakfast: **Continental**
Credit Cards: **MC, VISA**
Pets: **No**
Children: **Welcome**
Smoking: **No**
Social Drinking: **Permitted**

For the ultimate in unusual experiences, spend the night in "jail" without having committed a crime. Built in 1819, this former jailer's residence originally housed prisoners upstairs, and has been completely remodeled and furnished with fine antiques and Oriental rugs. An adjacent building, once used as the women's cell, has been transformed into a charming suite, where bunkbeds are suspended from a brick wall and the decor is black and white checks instead of stripes. The town is famous for The Stephen Foster Story, an outdoor musical production. Take time to visit the Getz Museum of Whiskey History and a Civil War museum, and take a tour of My Old Kentucky Home conducted by guides in antebellum costumes.

Alpine Lodge ✪

5310 MORGANTOWN ROAD, BOWLING GREEN, KENTUCKY 42101

Tel: **(502) 843-4846**
Best Time to Call: **9 AM–9 PM**
Hosts: **Dr. and Mrs. David Livingston**
Location: **60 mi. N of Nashville, Tenn.**
No. of Rooms: **5**
No. of Private Baths: **3**
Max. No. Sharing Bath: **4**
Double/pb: **$50**
Single/pb: **$40**
Double/sb: **$45**
Single/sb: **$35**
Guest Cottage: **$150; sleeps 6**

Suites: **$75**
Open: **All year**
Reduced Rates: **Weekly**
Breakfast: **Full**
Other Meals: **Available**
Pets: **Dogs welcome**
Children: **Welcome, over 3**
Smoking: **Permitted**
Social Drinking: **Permitted**
Airport/Station Pickup: **Yes**
Foreign Languages: **Spanish**

The lush bluegrass area of Kentucky is the setting for this spacious Swiss chalet-style home that's situated on four lovely acres and furnished with many antiques. A typical Southern breakfast of eggs, sausage, biscuits and gravy, fried apples, grits, coffee cake and beverage starts your day. If you can manage to get up from the table, stroll the grounds complete with nature trails and gardens. Afterwards, take in the sights and sounds of Opryland, Mammoth Cave, or the battlefields of historic Bowling Green. In the evening, relax in the living room, where Dr. Livingston, a music professor, may entertain you with selections played on the grand piano.

Bowling Green Bed & Breakfast ✪

659 EAST 14TH AVENUE, BOWLING GREEN, KENTUCKY 42101

Tel: **(502) 781-3861**
Best Time to Call: **Early AM; evenings**
Hosts: **Dr. and Mrs. Norman Hunter**
Location: **4 mi. from I-65, Exit 22**
No. of Rooms: **3**
No. of Private Baths: **1**
Max. No. Sharing Bath: **4**
Double/pb: **$45**
Single/pb: **$35**

Double/sb: **$40**
Single/sb: **$30**
Open: **All year**
Breakfast: **Full**
Pets: **No**
Children: **Welcome, over 14**
Smoking: **No**
Social Drinking: **Permitted**
Airport/Station Pickup: **Yes**

This trim, gray-shingled, comfortably furnished, two-story home is situated on a wooded lot. You are welcome to watch TV, select a book from the library, crank out a tune on the old Victrola, or play Ping-Pong in the recreation room. It is an easy drive to state parks, Opryland, and Mammoth Cave. Ronna Lee and Norman teach at nearby Western Kentucky University.

Tenderfoot Farms ✪
3205 OLD DOVER ROAD, CADIZ, KENTUCKY 42211

Tel: **(502) 522-3398**
Hosts: **Jay and Gayle Witty**
Location: **18 mi. W of Hopkinsville**
No. of Rooms: **2**
No. of Private Baths: **1**
Max. No. Sharing Bath: **4**
Single/pb: **$30**
Double/sb: **$50**
Suites: **$70–$90**

Open: **June–Oct.; other times by reservation**
Breakfast: **Full or continental**
Pets: **No**
Children: **Welcome**
Smoking: **Permitted on porch**
Social Drinking: **Permitted on porch**
Airport/Station Pickup: **Yes**

This spacious brick Cape Cod is fifteen minutes away from the main entrance to Land Between the Lakes, a 270,000-acre national recreation area boasting hundreds of miles of hiking, biking, and horseback-riding trails. There are plenty of waterways, too, so canoeists shouldn't feel slighted. To start off the day, guests have their choice of either a continental or a full breakfast.

P.T. Baker House Bed & Breakfast ✪
406 HIGHLAND AVENUE, CARROLLTON, KENTUCKY 41008

Tel: **Weekends: (502) 732-4210;**
Weekdays: (606) 525-7088
Hosts: **Bill and Judy Gants**
Location: **5 mi. from I-71, Exit 44**
No. of Rooms: **3**
No. of Private Baths: **3**
Double/pb: **$60**
Single/pb: **$45**
Open: **All year**

Guest Cottage: **$110; sleeps 6**
Reduced Rates: **10% Seniors**
Breakfast: **Full**
Credit Cards: **MC, VISA**
Pets: **No**
Children: **Welcome, over 8**
Smoking: **Permitted**
Social Drinking: **Permitted**
Airport/Station Pickup: **Yes**

Upon entering this large Victorian home, listed on the National Register of Historic Places, one gets the feeling of having stepped back to the 1800s. The high ceilings, heavy walnut doors, hand-carved cherry staircase, oil lamp chandeliers, and elegant antiques embellish the careful restoration of this ornate house. Upon arrival, you are graciously welcomed wth a snack and beverage. A bowl of fresh fruit in your room, a potpourri gift, and breakfast served on antique china and crystal are just some of the special touches. Recreational diversions abound in this area located midway between Cincinnati and Louisville.

Olde Kantucke Bed and Breakfast ✪
210 EAST FOURTH STREET, FRANKFORT, KENTUCKY 40601

Tel: **(502) 227-7389**
Best Time to Call: **9 AM–7 PM**

Hosts: **Patty and Dan Smith**
Location: **30 mi. W of Lexington**

No. of Rooms: **5**
No. of Private Baths: **5**
Double/pb: **$45**
Single/pb: **$35**
Open: **All year**
Reduced Rates: **3rd night free with advance reservations (excluding Derby weekend)**

Breakfast: **Continental**
Credit Cards: **MC, VISA**
Pets: **No**
Children: **No**
Smoking: **Permitted**
Social Drinking: **Permitted**
Airport/Station Pickup: **Available**

Guests often say that visiting this 100-year-old white frame home is like going back to Grandma's house. Two large maple trees shade the porch, where tea is served each afternoon beside the tall white columns. Inside, you'll find touches of the Victorian era in the lovingly restored rooms. Each bedroom overlooks the Capitol dome and is cooled by a ceiling fan. Homemade muffins and biscuits, fresh fruit, and a choice of hot drinks are served in an open kitchen–dining area. The Olde Kantucke is one block from the Frankfort Walking Tour, 15 minutes from the beautiful bluegrass and horse country, and half an hour from Lexington.

Log Cabin Bed and Breakfast ✪
350 NORTH BROADWAY, GEORGETOWN, KENTUCKY 40324

Tel: **(502) 863-3514**
Hosts: **Clay and Janis McKnight**
Location: **10 mi. N of Lexington**
No. of Rooms: **2**
No. of Private Baths: **1**
Guest Cottage: **$64 for 2**

Open: **All year**
Breakfast: **Continental**
Pets: **Welcome**
Children: **Welcome**
Smoking: **Permitted**
Social Drinking: **Permitted**

This rustic log cabin was built, circa 1809, with a shake shingle roof and chinked logs. Inside, the living room is dominated by a huge fieldstone fireplace. The master bedroom and bath are on the ground floor and a loft bedroom will sleep additional people with ease. The house has been fully restored and air-conditioned by the McKnights, and is filled with period furnishings. The dining-kitchen wing is equipped with all new appliances and modern amenities. The Log Cabin is located in a quiet neighborhood close to Kentucky Horse Park, Keeneland, and many other historic places. This is the perfect spot to bring the kids and give them a taste of authentic American tradition.

Three Deer Inn ✪
P.O. DRAWER 299, GRAYS KNOB, KENTUCKY 40829

Tel: **(606) 573-6666**
Best Time to Call: **8 AM–5 PM**
Hosts: **C. V. and Blanche Bennett, and Addie Huff**

Location: **10 mi. N of Harlan**
No. of Rooms: **6**
No. of Private Baths: **6**
Double/pb: **$49**

Single/pb: **$39**
Suites: **$45**
Open: **All year**
Reduced Rates: **20%, seniors, families**
Breakfast: **Continental**
Other Meals: **Available**

Credit Cards: **AMEX, MC, VISA**
Pets: **Sometimes**
Children: **Welcome**
Smoking: **Permitted**
Social Drinking: **Permitted**
Airport/Station Pickup: **Yes**

Three Deer Inn is nestled in the base of Black Mountain and is surrounded by forest. The house is a newly built cedar A-frame with beautiful workmanship that includes a lovely cathedral ceiling. Your hosts want you to learn firsthand about the beauty, splendor, and hospitality found in the mountains of eastern Kentucky. They want to share good food, clean surroundings, and friendliness. Among the local attractions are the Little Shepard trail, a beautiful mountaintop gravel road that offers tremendous views of eastern Kentucky, the Hensley Settlement, a village located on the top of Stone Mountain, Daniel Boone National Forest, and Stone Canyon.

The Victorian Secret Bed & Breakfast ✪
1132 SOUTH FIRST STREET, OLD LOUISVILLE, KENTUCKY 40203

Tel: **(502) 581-1914**
Hosts: **Nan and Steve Roosa**
Location: **1 mi. S of downtown Louisville**
No. of Rooms: **3**
No. of Private Baths: **1**
Max. No. Sharing Bath: **4**
Double/pb: **$53**

Double/sb: **$53**
Open: **All year**
Reduced Rates: **Weekly**
Breakfast: **Continental**
Pets: **No**
Children: **Welcome**
Smoking: **Permitted**
Social Drinking: **Permitted**

An elegant brick Victorian with lavish woodwork, this B&B has modern amenities like an exercise room with a bench press and a rowing machine, and color TVs in guest rooms. The Louisville area is rich in historic homes. Railbirds and would-be jockeys will want to make pilgrimages to the famous tracks at Churchill Downs (site of the Kentucky Derby) and Louisville Downs (home of harness races).

Ehrhardt's B&B ✪
285 SPRINGWELL LANE, PADUCAH, KENTUCKY 42001

Tel: **(502) 554-0644**
Best Time to Call: **7–9 AM; 4–6 PM**
Hosts: **Eileen and Phil Ehrhardt**
Location: **1 mi. from I-24**
No. of Rooms: **2**
Max. No. Sharing Bath: **4**
Double/sb: **$35**
Single/sb: **$30**
Open: **All year**

Reduced Rates: **10%, seniors**
Breakfast: **Full**
Other Meals: **Available**
Pets: **No**
Children: **Welcome, over 12**
Smoking: **Permitted**
Social Drinking: **Permitted**
Airport/Station Pickup: **Yes**

This brick Colonial ranch home is just a mile off I-24, which is famous for its beautiful scenery. Your hosts hope to make you feel at home in antique-filled bedrooms and a den with a fireplace. Homemade biscuits and jellies, and country ham and gravy are breakfast specialties. Enjoy swimming in the Ehrhardts' pool and boating at nearby Lake Barkley, Ky Lake, and Land Between the Lakes. Paducah features quarterhorse racing from June through November, and the National Quilt Show in April.

Maple Hill Manor B&B ❂
ROUTE 3B, BOX 20, PERRYVILLE ROAD, SPRINGFIELD, KENTUCKY 40069

Tel: **(606) 336-3075**	Breakfast: **Full**
Hosts: **Bob and Kay Carroll**	Credit Cards: **MC, VISA**
No. of Rooms: **7**	Pets: **No**
No. of Private Baths: **7**	Children: **Welcome**
Double/pb: **$55**	Smoking: **No**
Single/pb: **$45**	Social Drinking: **Permitted**
Open: **All year**	Minimum Stay: **2 nights Derby**
Reduced Rates: **After 1 night; 10%,**	**weekend**
families	

This hilltop manor house built in 1851 is situated on 14 tranquil acres in the scenic Bluegrass Region of Kentucky. Listed on the National Historic Register, its Italianate design features 13-foot ceilings, 9-foot windows and doors, a profusion of fireplaces, and a solid cherry spiral staircase. The bedrooms are large, airy, and beautifully decorated with carefully chosen antique furnishings. The romantic honeymoon bed chamber has a canopy bed and Jacuzzi bath. In the evening, Bob and Kay graciously offer complimentary beverages and homemade dessert. Within an hour of Lexington and Louisville, you can visit Perryville Battlefield and Shaker Village and take a tour of distilleries.

LOUISIANA

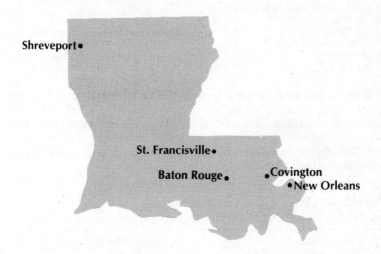

Shreveport•

St. Francisville•

Baton Rouge•

•Covington
•New Orleans

Southern Comfort Bed & Breakfast
2856 HUNDRED OAKS, BATON ROUGE, LOUISIANA 70808

For Information: **(504) 346-1928;**
  928-9815; (800) 749-1928
For Reservation: **800-523-1181, #,**
  Dial Tone, 722 (Outside Louisiana)
Best Time to Call: **8 AM–8 PM**
Coordinators: **Susan Morris and Helen
  Heath**
States/Regions Covered: **Florida—
  Kissimmee, Melbourne; Louisiana—
  statewide; Mississippi—Natchez,
  Vicksburg, Port Gibson**

Descriptive Directory: **$3.50**
Rates (Single/Double):
  Modest: **$37.50–45 $40–$50**
  Average: **$50–$60 $55–$65**
  Luxury: **$65–$90 $70–$155**
Credit Cards: **AMEX, MC, VISA**
Minimum Stay: **3–5 nights in New
  Orleans during Mardi Gras, Jazz
  Festival, Sugar Bowl, Super Bowl**

Susan and Helen offer you the best of the old and the new South with
hosts in urban and rural areas. The above is only a sample list. Special
attractions are Civil War and other historic sites; fabulous New Orleans; Acadian (Cajun) country; sports, deep-sea fishing, and race-
tracks in Louisiana; thoroughbred horse farms, Disney World, and the
Space Center in Florida. There's a $5 surcharge for one-night stays.

Joy's B&B ✪
4920 PERKINS ROAD, BATON ROUGE, LOUISIANA 70808

Tel: (504) 766-2291
Best Time to Call: 6 AM–noon
Host: Joy Robinson
Location: 85 mi. from New Orleans
No. of Rooms: 2
No. of Private Baths: 1
Max. No. Sharing Bath: 4
Double/sb: $55
Single/sb: $47.50

Open: All year
Reduced Rates: 15%, seniors
Breakfast: Full
Pets: No
Children: Welcome, over 12
Smoking: Permitted
Social Drinking: Permitted
Airport/Station Pickup: Yes

This charming stucco home is furnished with antiques and collectibles. Guest quarters are on the second floor and feature a family room, TV, and kitchen facilities. Joy serves a hearty, Southern breakfast with pride. She will gladly direct you to interesting nearby sites, including the Atchafalaya basin, the largest hardwood swamp in the South. Louisiana State University is five minutes away.

Plantation Bell Guest House ✪
204 WEST 24TH AVENUE, COVINGTON, LOUISIANA 70433

Tel: (504) 893-7693
Best Time to Call: Before 8 AM
Host: Lila Rapier
Location: 35 mi. N. of New Orleans
No. of Rooms: 2
No. of Private Baths: 2
Double/pb: $35–$40

Single/pb: $30–$35
Open: All year
Breakfast: Full
Pets: Sometimes
Children: Welcome
Smoking: Permitted
Social Drinking: Permitted

This late Victorian house has an old-fashioned porch with rocking chairs overlooking a quiet street. Inside, the ceilings are 13 feet high, and the old-time fans add to the nostalgic motif. The guest rooms are decorated with cheerful wallpapers and are comfortably air-conditioned. You are welcome to use the kitchen for light snacks. Local possibilities include canoeing, cycling, and shopping in Covington. New Orleans, St. Francisville, and the Mississippi Gulf Coast are within easy reach.

Bed & Breakfast, Inc.—New Orleans ✪
1360 MOSS STREET, BOX 52257, NEW ORLEANS, LOUISIANA 70152-2257

Tel: (504) 525-4640 or (800) 749-4640
Coordinator: Hazell Boyce
States/Regions Covered: New
  Orleans
Descriptive Directory: Free

Rates (Single/Double):
  Modest: $25–$35 $35–$40
  Average: $35–$60 $40–$60
  Luxury: $50 and up $60 and up
Credit Cards: No

New Orleans is called The City That Care Forgot. You are certain to be carefree, visiting the French Quarter, taking Mississippi riverboat rides, taking plantation tours, as well as dining in fine restaurants and attending jazz concerts. Hazell's hosts, many with historic properties along the streetcar line and in the French Quarter, will help you get the most out of your stay.

New Orleans Bed & Breakfast ✪
P.O. BOX 8163, NEW ORLEANS, LOUISIANA 70182

Tel: (508) 838-0071; 0072; 0073
Best Time to Call: 8:30 AM–4:30 PM
Coordinator: Sarah-Margaret Brown
States/Regions Covered: Louisiana—
  Covington, Jeanerette, Lafayette,
  Mandeville, New Iberia, New
  Orleans

Rates (Single/Double):
  Modest: $35–$45 $40–$45
  Average: $45–$50 $50–$55
  Luxury: $65–$200
Credit Cards: AMEX, MC, VISA (for
  deposits only)
Minimum Stay: 5 nights Mardi Gras,
  Jazz Festival; 3 nights Sugar Bowl

Sarah-Margaret offers a range from the youth-hostel type for the backpacker crowd, to modest accommodations in all areas of the city, to deluxe B&Bs in lovely and historic locations. If the past intrigues you, treat yourself to an overnight stay in a great Louisiana plantation home. Rates increase during Mardi Gras, Jazz Fest, Sugar Bowl; decrease for longer stays.

Bougainvillea House
841 BOURBON STREET, NEW ORLEANS, LOUISIANA 70116

Tel: (504) 525-3983
Best Time to Call: 9 AM–5 PM
Host: Flo Cairo
No. of Rooms: 3
No. of Private Baths: 3
Double/pb: $90
Single/pb: $75
Guest Cottage: $125; sleeps 4

Open: All year
Breakfast: Continental
Pets: No
Children: No
Smoking: No
Social Drinking: Permitted
Minimum Stay: 2 nights

Located in the heart of the French Quarter, this 1820 house has been beautifully restored to its former elegance. Furnished with rare antiques and richly decorated with color-coordinated accessories, one of the bedrooms features a canopied bed suited for royalty, a gilt-trimmed fireplace, and lovely balcony. The courtyard and patio are contained within a privacy wall and locked gates assure guests' security. The French Market, paddle wheelers on the Mississippi, antique shops, and the restaurants and music cafés of Bourbon Street are nearby.

Jensen's Bed & Breakfast ✪
1631 SEVENTH STREET, NEW ORLEANS, LOUISIANA 70115

Tel: (504) 897-1895
Best Time to Call: 6–9 PM
Hosts: Shirley, Joni, and Bruce Jensen
No. of Rooms: 5
Max. No. Sharing Bath: 4
Double/sb: $50
Single/sb: $50

Open: All year
Breakfast: Continental
Pets: No
Children: Welcome
Smoking: Permitted
Social Drinking: Permitted

Your hosts have drawn on their backgrounds as an interior decorator, piano teacher, and renovator of vintage homes, to restore this Victorian mansion. Stained glass, 12-foot-high alcove ceilings, antiques, a grand piano, raised-panel-pocket doors, and carefully chosen furnishings enhance the mansion. Located across the street from the Garden District, an area famed for its lovely homes, it is just a block to the trolley, which will whisk you to the French Quarter, Audubon Park, the zoo, or Tulane University. Breakfast is likely to feature banana cornbread or fried bananas, seasonal fruit, and Louisiana-style coffee. The mansion is air-conditioned for your summer comfort, and there's a TV in each bedroom. Rates increase during Mardi Gras, the Jazz Festival, and other special events.

The Levee View ✪
39 HENNESEY COURT, NEW ORLEANS, LOUISIANA 70123

Tel: (504) 737-5471
Hosts: Jack and Clemmie Devereux
No. of Rooms: 2
No. of Private Baths: 1
Max. No. Sharing Bath: 4
Double/pb: $35
Single/pb: $30
Double/sb: $25
Single/sb: $20
Suites: $50

Open: All year
Reduced Rates: 20%, seniors; 10%, weekly
Breakfast: Continental
Pets: No
Children: Welcome
Smoking: Permitted
Social Drinking: Permitted
Airport/Station Pickup: Yes

The Devereuxs welcome you to their contemporary home, located in a convenient residential suburb of New Orleans. The house is large and attractive, with comfortable family furnishings. Guest quarters are located in a two-story wing with separate entrance, ensuring visitors plenty of privacy and quiet. Breakfast specialties include homemade breads, croissants, and plenty of hot coffee. If you like, you can relax outside on the patio or sip a drink in the gazebo. The levee bordering the Mississippi River is less than 100 feet from the house; many lovely plantation homes are also located nearby. Your hosts will gladly guide you to the best restaurants and shops, and will occasionally baby-sit for the kids while you go out on the town.

Terrell House ✪
1441 MAGAZINE STREET, NEW ORLEANS, LOUISIANA 70130

Tel: (504) 524-9859
Host: Harry Lucas/Sally Cates
Location: ½ mi. from I-10
No. of Rooms: 9
No. of Private Baths: 9
Double/pb: $60–$90
Suites: $100

Open: All year
Breakfast: Continental
Credit Cards: AMEX, MC, VISA
Pets: No
Children: Welcome
Smoking: Permitted
Social Drinking: Permitted

Built in 1858, this faithfully restored mansion offers antique furnishings and modern conveniences. The twin parlors and the formal dining room, with gas chandeliers, gold mirrors, marble mantels, and period furnishings, capture the grace of yesteryear. All of the guest rooms open onto balconies and the landscaped courtyard. They all have telephones, color television, and central air-conditioning. Located in the historic Lower Garden District, it's convenient to public transportation. The French Quarter is five minutes away. Complimentary cocktails and other refreshments are graciously offered.

Barrow House B&B ✪
P.O. BOX 1461, 524 ROYAL STREET, ST. FRANCISVILLE, LOUISIANA 70775

Tel: (504) 635-4791
Hosts: Lyle and Shirley Dittloff
Location: 25 mi. N of Baton Rouge
No. of Rooms: 5
No. of Private Baths: 3
Max. No. Sharing Bath: 4
Double/pb: $65
Single/pb: $50

Suites: $75–$95
Open: All year, except Dec. 21–25
Breakfast: Continental
Wheelchair Accessible: Yes
Pets: No
Children: Welcome
Smoking: Permitted
Social Drinking: Permitted

A saltbox erected in 1809, with a Greek Revival wing that was added some four decades later, Barrow House is listed on the National Register of Historic Places. Appropriately enough, Lyle and Shirley have furnished their B&B with 19th-century pieces from the American South. Other notable homes are in the area; the Dittloffs like to send guests on a cassette walking tour of the neighborhood. Afterward, sit on the screened front porch and sip a glass of wine or iced tea. Breakfast options range from a simple continental meal to a full-course New Orleans spread. Shirley is a fabulous cook, and private candlelight dinners, featuring Cajun and Creole specialties, can also be arranged.

The St. Francisville Inn ☉

118 NORTH COMMERCE, DRAWER 1369, ST. FRANCISVILLE,
LOUISIANA 70775

Tel: **(504) 635-6502**
Hosts: **Florence and Dick Fillet**
Location: **24 mi. N of Baton Rouge**
No. of Rooms: **9**
No. of Private Baths: **9**
Double/pb: **$59**
Single/pb: **$49**
Suite: **$59**
Open: **All year**

Reduced Rates: **10%, seniors**
Breakfast: **Continental**
Other Meals: **Available**
Credit Cards: **AMEX, MC, VISA**
Pets: **No**
Children: **Welcome (crib)**
Smoking: **Permitted**
Social Drinking: **Permitted**

The St. Francisville Inn is located in the heart of plantation country in a town that is listed on the National Register of Historic Places. The inn is a Victorian Gothic known as the Wolf-Schlesinger House, built circa 1880. The air-conditioned guest rooms are furnished in lovely antiques, and each opens onto a New Orleans–style courtyard out back. Breakfast includes fabulous pastries from a local bakery. Florence is an antique-print dealer whose specialty is Audubon.

Fairfield Place

2221 FAIRFIELD AVENUE, SHREVEPORT, LOUISIANA 71104

Tel: **(318) 222-0048**
Host: **Janie Lipscomb**
Location: **½ mi. from I-20**
No. of Rooms: **6**
No. of Private Baths: **6**
Double/pb: **$75–$105**
Single/pb: **$65–$75**
Suite: **$145**

Open: **All year**
Breakfast: **Continental**
Credit Cards: **AMEX, MC, VISA**
Pets: **No**
Children: **Sometimes**
Smoking: **No**
Social Drinking: **Permitted**

You will enjoy this elegant 1900s inn, where the legendary hospitality of the Deep South rings true. Begin your day with New Orleans coffee, croissants and strawberry butter, and French pastries. Janie's home features lambskin rugs, king-size beds, 19th-century paintings, Swedish crystal, designer sheets and linens, and allergy-proofed European feather beds. It is located in the beautiful Highland Historical Restoration District, convenient to the business district, medical center, and airport. Louisiana Downs Racetrack is minutes away.

MAINE

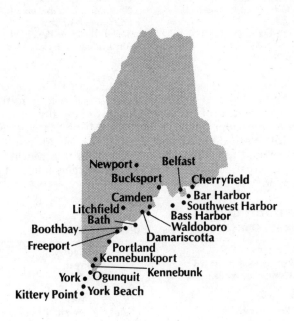

Newport •   **Belfast**
Bucksport   **Cherryfield**
Camden   • **Bar Harbor**
Litchfield •   • **Southwest Harbor**
Bath   **Bass Harbor**
Boothbay   **Waldoboro**
Freeport   **Damariscotta**
Portland
• **Kennebunkport**
York • **Ogunquit**   **Kennebunk**
Kittery Point • **York Beach**

Bed & Breakfast Down East, Ltd.
BOX 547, MACOMBER MILL ROAD, EASTBROOK, MAINE 04634

Tel: **(207) 565-3517**
Coordinator: **Sally B. Godfrey**
States/Regions Covered: **Maine,**
  statewide

Rates (Single/Double):
  Modest: **$40**   **$45**
  Average: **$45–$50**   **$60–$70**
  Luxury: **$70–$80**   **$80–$140**
Credit Cards: **AMEX, MC, VISA**

There are delightful accommodations waiting for you, from Eliot near the New Hampshire border to "way down East" in Eastport, near F.D.R.'s Campobello Island in New Brunswick, Canada. You are certain to enjoy Bar Harbor, Acadia National Park, the rugged coastline, and inland forests and streams. All of Sally's hosts will make you feel welcome.

Elizabeth's Bed and Breakfast ✪
360 FRONT STREET, BATH, MAINE 04530

Tel: (207) 443-1146
Best Time to Call: 10 AM–9 PM
Host: Elizabeth Lindsay
Location: 35 mi. N of Portland
No. of Rooms: 5
Max. No. Sharing Bath: 4
Double/sb: $42–$57
Single/sb: $35–$40

Open: Apr. 15–Jan. 1
Breakfast: Full
Pets: No
Children: Welcome, over 12
Smoking: Permitted
Social Drinking: Permitted
Airport/Station Pickup: Yes

Elizabeth's Bed and Breakfast is a fine old Federalist house, painted a traditional white with green shutters. Each bedroom is furnished in country antiques; two of the rooms have working fireplaces. Bath is famed as a shipbuilding center, and the Maine Maritime Museum merits a visit. It's also fun to walk around the downtown area, which has been restored to its 19th-century glory. Breakfast includes juice, an egg dish, cereal, muffins, and jam. During the summer, Elizabeth prepares Sunday brunches.

Fairhaven Inn ✪
RR 2, BOX 85, NORTH BATH ROAD, BATH, MAINE 04530

Tel: (207) 443-4391
Hosts: George and Sallie Pollard
Location: 35 mi. N of Portland
No. of Rooms: 7
No. of Private Baths: 3
Max. No. Sharing Bath: 4
Double/pb: $60–$70
Double/sb: $50–$60

Single/sb: $40–$45
Open: All year
Breakfast: Full
Pets: Yes
Children: Yes
Smoking: Permitted in tavern only
Social Drinking: Permitted

An 18th-century Colonial mansion on a hill above the Kennebec River, Fairhaven Inn is furnished with antique and country pieces. Shaded by hemlock, birch, and pine trees, the 27-acre grounds lure cross-country skiers in the winter, and strollers year round. Around the bend, Bath Country Club is open to the public for golfing, and beaches are nearby. Bird-watchers can study migratory waterfowl at Merry-meeting Bay. You'll get stamina for the day's activities from ample breakfasts of juice, fresh fruit, home-baked breads, and main courses such as blintzes, eggs Benedict, and orange honey French toast.

"Glad II"
60 PEARL STREET, BATH, MAINE 04530

Tel: (207) 443-1191
Host: Gladys Lansky
Location: 7–10 mi. from US 1

No. of Rooms: 3
Max. No. Sharing Bath: 3
Double/sb: $40–$45

Open: **All year**
Breakfast: **Continental**
Credit Cards: **MC, VISA**
Pets: **No**

Children: **Welcome, over 8 (in own room)**
Smoking: **No**
Social Drinking: **Permitted**

This spic-and-span white house, with its crisp green trim, is comfortable and attractively furnished. Gladys delights in pleasing her guests with breakfasts featuring fresh, homemade treats. You are welcome to play the piano, borrow a book from her library, and visit or watch TV in the parlors. It's an easy walk to the Maritime Museum, a short drive to Popham Beach, Reid State Park, Boothbay Harbor, L. L. Bean, and the Brunswick Naval Air Station. Bowdoin College is eight miles away.

Horatio Johnson House ✪
36 CHURCH STREET, BELFAST, MAINE 04915

Tel: **(207) 338-5153**
Hosts: **Helen and Gene Kirby**
Location: **30 mi. S of Bangor**
No. of Rooms: **3**
No. of Private Baths: **3**
Double/pb: **$45**
Single/pb: **$40**

Open: **All year**
Breakfast: **Full**
Pets: **No**
Children: **No**
Smoking: **Permitted**
Social Drinking: **Permitted**

While the rest of the world is rushing ahead, the small seafaring town of Belfast is rediscovering its past. The waterfront and old town buildings are being refurbished to reflect the way things used to be. Your hosts offer good company and comfortable lodging in a 19th-century home five minutes from the ocean. The Kirbys offer a variety of breakfast specialties, such as Belgian waffles and blueberry pancakes. They will gladly recommend flea markets, antique shops, and restaurants galore.

Kenniston Hill Inn
ROUTE 27, BOOTHBAY, MAINE 04537

Tel: **(207) 633-2159**
Hosts: **Paul and Ellen Morissette**
Location: **50 mi. N of Portland**
No. of Rooms: **8**
No. of Private Baths: **8**
Double/pb: **$60–$80**
Open: **Apr.–Nov.**

Breakfast: **Full**
Credit Cards: **MC, VISA**
Pets: **No**
Children: **Welcome, over 12**
Smoking: **No**
Social Drinking: **Permitted**

Kenniston Hill Inn is a white clapboard mansion dating back to 1786. The house is warm and gracious, with a large front porch and open-hearth fireplace. The bedrooms, four with fireplaces, are tastefully decorated with handmade quilts, delicately colored wallpapers, and fresh flowers. Your hosts are former restaurant owners from Vermont. They offer sumptuous breakfast specialties, such as zucchini-and-walnut pancakes and a vegetable frittata. The inn is surrounded by woods and gardens, but is within easy reach of shops, restaurants, boat rides, horseback riding, and tennis.

Harbour Towne Inn ✪
71 TOWNSEND AVENUE, BOOTHBAY HARBOR, MAINE 04538

Tel: (207) 633-4300
Best Time to Call: 8 AM–8 PM
Hosts: Rob and Marilyn Crisp
Location: 60 mi. N of Portland
No. of Rooms: 12
No. of Private Baths: 12
Single/pb: $50
Double/pb: $50–$175
Suites: $175
Open: All year

Reduced Rates: 10%, seniors; 10%, off-season
Breakfast: Continental
Wheelchair Accessible: Yes
Credit Cards: MC, VISA
Pets: No
Children: Welcome
Smoking: Permitted
Social Drinking: Permitted

This turn-of-the-century mansion is so close to the waterfront that you can stand on the deck and take a deep breath of invigorating salt air. Boothbay's shops, galleries, and restaurants are just a few steps away; would-be sailors can rent boats and spend the day at sea. Breakfast includes juice, muffins, and breads.

L'ermitage ✪
219 MAIN STREET, BUCKSPORT, MAINE 04416

Tel: (207) 469-3361
Hosts: Ginny and Jim Conklin
Location: 19 mi. E of Bangor; 1 block from US 1
No. of Rooms: 3
Max. No. Sharing Bath: 2
Double/sb: $50
Single/sb: $40
Open: All year

Reduced Rates: 20%, off season
Breakfast: Full
Other Meals: Available
Credit Cards: MC, VISA
Pets: Sometimes
Children: No
Smoking: Permitted
Social Drinking: Permitted
Airport/Station Pickup: Yes

L'ermitage is a 19th-century white Colonial with black shutters, dating back to the 1830s. Your hosts have patterned their inn after those found in Europe. The spacious rooms are furnished in period antiques, Oriental carpets, and collectibles. A small gourmet restaurant is on the premises and features an extensive wine list. L'ermitage is on Penobscot Bay, near Ft. Knox.

Blue Harbor House ✪
67 ELM STREET, ROUTE 1, CAMDEN, MAINE 04843

Tel: **(207) 236-3196**
Hosts: **Dennis Hayden and Jody Schmoll**
Location: **85 mi. NE of Portland**
No. of Rooms: **9**
No. of Private Baths: **7**
Max. No. Sharing Bath: **4**
Double/pb: **$70–$110**
Double/sb: **$70**

Open: **All year**
Reduced Rates: **$50–$90, Nov.–May**
Breakfast: **Full**
Credit Cards: **MC, VISA**
Pets: **Sometimes**
Children: **Welcome**
Smoking: **No**
Social Drinking: **Permitted**
Airport/Station Pickup: **Yes**

Camden is one of the prettiest coastal villages in New England. This 1835 Cape Cod house has been completely renovated and captures the essence of a bygone era. Each room is decorated in country antiques, stenciled walls, and handmade quilts. Guests enjoy visiting with each other in the common room, furnished with comfortable chairs and accented by antique stoneware, samplers, and folk art. The spacious dining room, with its views of Mt. Battie, is the setting for the generous breakfast that features homemade breads, delicious egg dishes, and Maine blueberries. It's a few minutes' walk to many fine restaurants, unique shops, and the famous Windjammer fleet.

Camden Maine Stay ✪
22 HIGH STREET, CAMDEN, MAINE 04843

Tel: **(207) 236-9636**
Best Time to Call: **8 AM–9 PM**
Hosts: **Peter and Donny Smith, Diana Robson**
Location: **85 mi. NE of Portland**
No. of Rooms: **8**
Max. No. Sharing Bath: **4**
Double/sb: **$72**
Single/sb: **$40–$62**

Open: **All year**
Reduced Rates: **Off-season**
Breakfast: **Full**
Credit Cards: **MC, VISA**
Pets: **No**
Children: **Welcome, over 10**
Smoking: **No**
Social Drinking: **Permitted**

A comfortable bed, a hearty breakfast, and a friendly innkeeper are found in this treasured old colonial home. Listed on the National Register of Historic Places and located in Camden's historic district, the inn is a five-minute walk from the harbor, shops, and restaurants. Whether you relax by a crackling log fire, sit on the deck, overlooking a wooded glen, or stroll by the brook behind the barn, you will find the Maine Stay to be the perfect base from which to explore midcoast Maine.

The Elms Bed and Breakfast ✪
84 ELM STREET, ROUTE 1, CAMDEN, MAINE 04843

Tel: **(207) 236-6250**
Best Time to Call: **9:30 AM–9:30 PM**
Host: **Joan A. James**
Location: **150 mi. N of Boston, MA**
No. of Rooms: **6**
No. of Private Baths: **3**
Max. No. Sharing Bath: **4**
Double/pb: **$85**
Double/sb: **$65**

Suite: **$75**
Open: **All year**
Reduced Rates: **Off-season**
Breakfast: **Full**
Credit Cards: **MC, VISA**
Pets: **No**
Children: **Welcome, over 12**
Smoking: **No**
Social Drinking: **Permitted**

Joan keeps candles burning in the windows to welcome you to her lovingly restored colonial home, built in 1806. Inside, period-style furnishings will take you back two centuries. Camden offers sailing, hiking, and skiing, and the fall foliage is spectacular. Or just stroll over to the city harbor, with its shops, galleries, and restaurants. Breakfast always consists of home-baked breads and such memorable entrées as French toast stuffed with puréed peaches and sour cream.

Hawthorn Inn ✪
9 HIGH STREET, CAMDEN, MAINE 04843

Tel: **(207) 236-8842**
Best Time to Call: **9 AM–8 PM**
Hosts: **Pauline and Brad Staub**
Location: **On Rte. 1, 150 mi. N of Boston**
No. of Rooms: **9**
No. of Private Baths: **5**
Max. No. Sharing Bath: **4**
Double/pb: **$65–$135**
Double/sb: **$55–$75**
Suites and 2 apartments: **$135–$200**

Open: **All year**
Reduced Rates: **$10 less daily, Nov. 1–May 25**
Breakfast: **Full**
Credit Cards: **MC, VISA**
Pets: **No**
Children: **Welcome, over 10**
Smoking: **Permitted**
Social Drinking: **Permitted**
Airport/Station Pickup: **Yes**

The airy rooms of this Victorian inn are an elegant mixture of the old and the new. Guests are welcome to coffee while relaxing on the deck or getting warm by the fire. Tea is served at 4:00. All rooms overlook either Mt. Battie or Camden Harbor. A score of sports can be enjoyed in the area, and shops and restaurants are a short walk away.

The Cape Neddick House ✪
1300 ROUTE 1, P.O. BOX 70, CAPE NEDDICK, MAINE 03902

Tel: **(207) 363-2500**
Hosts: **The Goodwin family**
Location: **12 mi. N of Portsmouth, NH**
No. of Rooms: **6**

Max. No. Sharing Bath: **4**
Double/sb: **$49–$69**
Single/sb: **$44–$64**
Open: **All year**

Reduced Rates: **Weekly**
Breakfast: **Full or continental**
Pets: **No**

Children: **Welcome, over 5**
Smoking: **Permitted**
Social Drinking: **Permitted**

The Goodwins inherited this late-nineteenth-century farmhouse from a relative. While cleaning up the place for resale, they fell in love with it and decided to move in. The bedrooms are furnished with anitque pieces, handmade quilts, and family keepsakes. If you want a souvenir or two, there's a craft shop on the premises. Whatever your interest, Cape Neddick has something to tempt you, from swimming, biking, and cross-country skiing to browsing in numerous local boutiques, antique shops, and factory outlets. Dianne is so proud of her cooking that she prints up recipe cards; cinnamon popovers, strawberry scones and ham apple biscuits are a few of her specialties.

Ricker House ✪
PARK STREET, P.O. BOX 256, CHERRYFIELD, MAINE 04622

Tel: **(207) 546-2780**
Hosts: **William and Jean Conway**
Location: **32 mi. E of Ellsworth**
No. of Rooms: **3**
Max. No. Sharing Bath: **5**
Double/sb: **$45**
Single/sb: **$40**
Open: **All year**

Reduced Rates: **Available**
Breakfast: **Full**
Pets: **No**
Children: **Welcome (crib)**
Smoking: **No**
Social Drinking: **Permitted**
Airport/Station Pickup: **Yes**

Built in 1803, this comfortable Federal Colonial has grounds that border the Narraguagus River, one of the best salmon rivers in the States. The village is quaint and historic, and it is fun to tour it on foot or by bike. Reasonable restaurants offer great menus, and all feature fabulous local lobster. Your hosts will be pleased to direct you to a fresh water lake and the best places to canoe and mountain climb.

Brannon-Bunker Inn ✪
HCR 64, BOX 045L, DAMARISCOTTA, MAINE 04543

Tel: **(207) 563-5941**
Hosts: **Jeanne and Joseph Hovance**
No. of Rooms: **7**
No. of Private Baths: **4**
Max. No. Sharing Bath: **3**
Double/pb: **$60**
Single/pb: **$55**
Double/sb: **$45–$50**
Single/sb: **$40–$45**

Suites: **$70–$110**
Open: **All year**
Breakfast: **Continental**
Credit Cards: **MC, VISA**
Pets: **No**
Children: **Welcome**
Smoking: **No**
Social Drinking: **Permitted**

The Brannon-Bunker Inn is an informal, relaxing inn, ideally situated in rural, coastal Maine. Guests may choose from accommodations in the main 1820 Cape House, the 1900 converted barn, or the carriage house across the stream. Each room is individually decorated in styles ranging from Colonial to Victorian. Hosts Jeanne and Joseph Hovance will help you plan your days over breakfast. Nearby activities include golf, ocean swimming at Pemaquid Beach Park, and fishing on the Damariscotta River.

Isaac Randall House
INDEPENDENCE DRIVE, FREEPORT, MAINE 04032

Tel: (207) 865-9295	Open: **All year**
Best Time to Call: **10 AM–10 PM**	Reduced Rates: **Off season**
Hosts: **Glynrose and Jim Friedlander**	Breakfast: **Full**
Location: **16 mi. NE of Portland**	Pets: **Sometimes**
No. of Rooms: **8**	Children: **Welcome (crib)**
No. of Private Baths: **6**	Smoking: **Limited**
Max. No. Sharing Bath: **4**	Social Drinking: **Permitted**
Double/pb: **$60–$100**	Airport/Station Pickup: **Yes**
Double/sb: **$$45–65**	Foreign Languages: **Spanish**

One hundred seven years ago, this Federal-style farmhouse was built as a wedding gift for Isaac Randall, Jr., and his young bride. It later became a stopover on the underground railroad, and then a Depression-era dance hall. Today, guests are welcomed to a charming, air-conditioned, antique-filled home set on five wooded acres. The grounds include a spring-fed pond, perfect for ice skating. Hiking and cross-country ski trails start at the front door. Breakfast specialties such as fruit compote, homemade breads, blueberry pancakes, coffee, and assorted teas are served in the country kitchen. Downtown Freeport, home of L. L. Bean, is within walking distance. Maine's beautiful coast, summer theater, Bowdoin College, and Freeport Harbor are just a short drive away. After a day of activity, join your hosts for an evening snack back at the inn.

Arundel Meadows Inn
P.O. BOX 1129, KENNEBUNK, MAINE 04043

Tel: (207) 985-3770	Suites: **$90–$135**
Best Time to Call: **Before 5 PM**	Open: **All year**
Hosts: **Mark Bachelder and Murray**	Breakfast: **Full**
Yaeger	Pets: **Sometimes**
Location: **2 mi. N of Kennebunk**	Children: **Welcome, over 11**
No. of Rooms: **7**	Smoking: **Permitted**
No. of Private Baths: **7**	Social Drinking: **Permitted**
Double/pb: **$70–$95**	

The Arundel Meadows Inn is situated on three and a half acres next to the Kennebunk River. Murray, a retired professor, and Mark, a professional chef, have always loved this area, and it is a dream come true for them to watch others enjoy it. They renovated this 165-year-old house themselves, and meticulously planned the decor. Several guest rooms have fireplaces and two suites sleep four. Mark's beautifully prepared breakfast specialties are the perfect start for your day. It's just three minutes to the center of town, and about ten to Kennebunk Beach. In the afternoon, come back to the inn for tea and enjoy pâtés, homemade sweets, and beverages.

1802 House Bed & Breakfast Inn ✪
LOCKE STREET, P.O. BOX 646-A, KENNEBUNKPORT, MAINE 04046

Tel: **(207) 967-5632**	Reduced Rates: **10%, weekly**
Best Time to Call: **8 AM–9 PM**	Breakfast: **Full**
Host: **Pat Ledda**	Credit Cards: **AMEX, MC, VISA**
Location: **22 mi. S of Portland**	Pets: **No**
No. of Rooms: **6**	Children: **Welcome, over 12**
No. of Private Baths: **6**	Smoking: **Permitted**
Double/pb: **$95–$125**	Social Drinking: **Permitted**
Single/pb: **$90–$120**	Minimum Stay: **2 nights on weekends**
Open: **All year**	

Tastefully decorated in Colonial style, some of the bedrooms have working fireplaces. The sound of a ship's bell will beckon you to a sumptuous breakfast that might feature sesame French toast or a stack of pancakes with blueberry sauce. In spring, visit the Rachel Carson Wildlife Refuge; in fall, the foliage is glorious; in winter, cross-country ski from the doorstep and return for mulled cider by the fireside; in summer, take in the theater, or swim at the shore. Pat will pamper you in all seasons.

The Green Heron Inn
P.O. BOX 2578, OCEAN AVENUE, KENNEBUNKPORT, MAINE 04046

Tel: **(207) 967-3315**	Guest Cottage: **$90–$100; sleeps 4**
Best Time to Call: **Noon–8 PM**	Reduced Rates: **Weekly**
Hosts: **Charles and Elizabeth Reid**	Breakfast: **Full**
Location: **4½ mi. from US 1**	Pets: **Sometimes**
No. of Rooms: **10**	Children: **Welcome (crib)**
No. of Private Baths: **10**	Smoking: **Permitted**
Double/pb: **$58–$84**	Social Drinking: **Permitted**
Single/pb: **$44–$65**	

This immaculate inn (circa 1908), with its inviting porch and striped awnings, furnished simply and comfortably, is located between the river and the ocean in this Colonial resort village. The full Yankee breakfast is a rib-buster! This is a saltwater fisherman's heaven, with boating, golf, swimming, and tennis all nearby, close to shops and galleries.

Lake Brook Guest House ✪

RR3, BOX 218, WESTERN AVENUE, KENNEBUNKPORT, MAINE 04046

Tel: (207) 967-4069	Double/sb: $65
Best Time to Call: 9 AM–9 PM	Single/sb: $50
Host: Carolyn A. McAdams	Open: All year
Location: 25 mi. S of Portland	Breakfast: Full
No. of Rooms: 4	Pets: No
No. of Private Baths: 1	Children: Welcome
Max. No. Sharing Bath: 4	Smoking: No
Double/pb: $75	Social Drinking: Permitted
Single/sb: $60	Foreign Languages: Spanish

Lake Brook is an appealing turn-of-the-century New England farm-house. Its wraparound porch is equipped with comfortable rocking chairs, and flower gardens stretch right down to the tidal brook that feeds the property. The shops and restaurants of Dock Square are within easy walking distance, and Kennebunk Beach is a little more than one mile away. Breakfasts include such main dishes as quiche, baked French toast, and Mexican chili eggs and cheese.

Harbour Watch ✪

FOLLETT LANE, RFD 1, BOX 42, KITTERY POINT, MAINE 03905

Tel: (207) 439-3242	Open: May–Oct.
Hosts: Marian and Robert Craig	Breakfast: Continental
Location: 50 mi. N of Boston	Pets: No
No. of Rooms: 4	Children: Welcome, over 14
Max. No. Sharing Bath: 4	Smoking: No
Double/sb: $60	Social Drinking: Permitted

This charming sea captain's house has been in Marian's family since the 1700s. Recently recommended by *New York Times* travel writers, Harbour Watch presents an ever-changing panorama of sailboat races, lobstermen pulling their traps, and cocktail cruises (either in the harbor or to the historic Isles of Shoals). For your added pleasure, your hostess often presents an evening of baroque music with harpsi-chord and recorders. While nearby beaches abound, you should save time to see the Strawberry Banks restoration in Portsmouth and the Prescott Park Art and Theater Series.

Black Friar Inn ✪

10 SUMMER STREET, BAR HARBOR, MT. DESERT ISLAND, MAINE 04609

Tel: (207) 288-5091	Double/pb: $75–$95
Hosts: Barbara and Jim Kelly	Single/pb: $70–$90
No. of Rooms: 6	Double/sb: $75
No. of Private Baths: 4	Single/sb: $70
Max. No. Sharing Bath: 4	Open: May–Oct.

Reduced Rates: **May 1–June 15**	Smoking: **No**
Breakfast: **Full**	Social Drinking: **Permitted**
Credit Cards: **MC, VISA**	Minimum Stay: **2 nights July and Aug.**
Pets: **No**	Airport/Station Pickup: **Yes**
Children: **Welcome, over 12**	

Fine woodwork, mantels, bookcases, and tasteful furnishings enhance the fine restoration of this vintage Victorian. The full English breakfast, afternoon tea, and refreshments are graciously served in the Greenhouse, a room paneled in cypress and embossed tin salvaged from an old Maine church. Opportunities for hiking, biking, swimming, boating, photography, nature watching, and antiquing abound.

Hearthside B&B ✪
7 HIGH STREET, BAR HARBOR, MT. DESERT ISLAND, MAINE 04609

Tel: **(207) 288-4533**	Reduced Rates: **Before June 15**
Hosts: **Susan and Barry Schwartz**	Breakfast: **Continental**
No. of Rooms: **9**	Credit Cards: **MC, VISA**
No. of Private Baths: **7**	Pets: **No**
Max. No. Sharing Bath: **4**	Children: **Welcome, over 10**
Double/pb: **$70–$95**	Smoking: **No**
Double/sb: **$65**	Social Drinking: **Permitted**
Open: **All year**	

On a quiet street, just a short walk to town, is this gracious home, recently redecorated in the manner of a country cottage. Breakfast is served buffet-style, featuring home-baked muffins and cakes, home-made granola or hot cereal, a fresh fruit bowl, and beverages. You are invited to share the special ambience of a living room with a cozy fireplace and brimming with books. Some rooms have a balcony or a fireplace. Complimentary iced tea, cheese, crackers, and wine are offered.

Holbrook House ✪
74 MOUNT DESERT STREET, BAR HARBOR, MT. DESERT ISLAND, MAINE 04609

Tel: **(207) 288-4970**
Hosts: **Dorothy and Mike Chester**
Location: **15 mi. from Rte. 1, Exit Rte. 3**
No. of Rooms: **10**
No. of Private Baths: **10**
Double/pb: **$90–$105**
Guest Cottage: **Available**
Open: **June 15–Oct. 15**
Reduced Rates: **$15 less after Labor Day, and before July 1**

Breakfast: **Full**
Credit Cards: **MC, VISA**
Pets: **No**
Children: **Welcome, over 8**
Smoking: **No**
Social Drinking: **Permitted**
Minimum Stay: **2 nights**
Airport/Station Pickup: **Yes**

In 1876, Nathan Ash built Holbrook House to provide lodging for wealthy Easterners seeking the social diversions of Bar Harbor. The 19-room house has been fully restored, but summer still brings the guests, who seek many of the same things: afternoon tea in china cups, evenings on an 80-foot porch, and conversations in the parlor. Victorian floral wallpapers, lace, chintz, and flowers complement the period furnishings and memorabilia found throughout the house. After spending the night in a four-poster bed, you'll waken in time for breakfast in the sun room. House specialties include fruit flans, blueberry buckle, French toast, cheese-and-egg pudding, and eggs Holbrook. In the afternoon, Dorothy and Mike serve cheese, tea, and other refreshments. Holbrook House is located in the historic part of town, a five-minute walk from restaurants, shops, and the seashore. Acadia National Park is just one mile away.

The Kingsleigh
P.O. BOX 1426, 100 MAIN STREET, SOUTHWEST HARBOR, MT. DESERT ISLAND, MAINE 04679

Tel: **(207) 244-5302**
Hosts: **Nancy and Tom Cervelli**
Location: **45 mi. E of Bangor**
No. of Rooms: **8**
No. of Private Baths: **8**
Double/pb: **$85–$95**
Suite: **$145**
Open: **All year**

Reduced Rates: **$15–$20 less, May 1– June 30, Sept. 8–Oct. 30**
Breakfast: **Full**
Pets: **No**
Children: **Welcome, over 8**
Smoking: **No**
Social Drinking: **Permitted**

Built at the turn of the century, the Kingsleigh is a shingled and pebble-dash Colonial revival. The house is set high on a knoll overlooking magnificent Southwest Harbor, where generations of boatbuilders and fishermen have earned their living. Waverly wall coverings, lace window treatments, plush carpeting, and period furnishings provide a comfortable blend of the old and new. Afternoon tea is served on a wraparound porch overlooking the harbor, while you relax in a white wicker chair. Your hosts serve fresh coffee, imported teas, country omelets, oatmeal pancakes, and other specialties for breakfast. They take pleasure in welcoming you to Mt. Desert Island, and will gladly direct you to swimming, hiking, fishing expeditions, whale-watching, restaurants, and shopping.

The Lamb's Ear ✪
P.O. BOX 30, CLARK POINT ROAD, SOUTHWEST HARBOR, MT. DESERT ISLAND, MAINE 04679

Tel: **(207) 244-9828**	Breakfast: **Full**
Hosts: **Elizabeth and George Hoke**	Wheelchair Accessible: **Yes**
Location: **45 mi. E of Bangor**	Credit Cards: **MC, VISA**
No. of Rooms: **6**	Pets: **No**
No. of Private Baths: **6**	Children: **Welcome, over 10**
Double/pb: **$65–$85**	Smoking: **No**
Suite: **$125**	Social Drinking: **Permitted**
Open: **All year**	Minimum Stay: **Two days**
Reduced Rates: **10%, Nov.–May**	

A stately home that dates to the mid-nineteenth century, the Lamb's Ear Inn overlooks the waterfront of Southwest Harbor, a quaint fishing village. While swimming, sailing, and fishing are the primary activities here, you'll want to set aside time to explore nearby galleries, museums, and Acadia National Park. After a full breakfast of eggs, Belgian waffles, fresh fruit, and muffins, you'll be ready for the day's adventures.

Lindenwood Inn ✪
P.O. BOX 1328, SOUTHWEST HARBOR, MT. DESERT ISLAND, MAINE 04679

Tel: **(207) 244-5335**	Open: **All year**
Hosts: **Gardiner and Marilyn Brower**	Reduced Rates: **Nov. 1—June 1**
No. of Rooms: **7**	Breakfast: **Full**
No. of Private Baths: **3**	Pets: **No**
Max. No. Sharing Bath: **4**	Children: **Welcome, over 12 in inn;**
Double/pb: **$75–$115**	**over 6 in cottage**
Double/sb: **$55–$70**	Smoking: **No**
Guest Cottage: **$105 for 2; $145 for 4**	Social Drinking: **Permitted**

Built at the turn of the century as a sea captain's home, the inn derives its name from the stately linden trees that line the front lawn. Most rooms have fine harbor views, and all are comfortably furnished. Cool mornings are warmed by the glowing fireplace in the dining room, where you can enjoy a hearty breakfast. You are welcome to relax on the shaded porch, enjoy the pleasures of a good book, or play the harpsichord in the parlor. You can explore the wonders of Acadia National Park by car, bicycle, hiking, or sailing.

Penury Hall ✪
BOX 68, MAIN STREET, SOUTHWEST HARBOR, MT. DESERT ISLAND, MAINE 04679

Tel: **(207) 244-7102**	Breakfast: **Full**
Hosts: **Gretchen and Toby Strong**	Pets: **No**
No. of Rooms: **3**	Children: **Welcome, over 16**
Max. No. Sharing Bath: **3**	Smoking: **Permitted**
Double/sb: **$55**	Social Drinking: **Permitted**
Single/sb: **$45**	Minimum Stay: **2 nights June 15–**
Open: **All year**	**Oct. 1**
Reduced Rates: **Oct. 1–June 1**	Airport/Station Pickup: **Yes**

This gray frame house is on the quiet side of Mt. Desert Island. Built in 1830, it is comfortably furnished with traditional pieces, antiques, and original art. Gretchen and Toby are cosmopolitan and cordial. Their motto is: "Each guest is an honorary member of the family," and you'll soon feel at home. Knowledgeable about the area's highlights, they'll direct you to special shops and restaurants and all of the best things to see and do. Breakfast often features eggs Benedict, and blueberry pancakes or cinnamon waffles. You are welcome to use the canoe or sail the 19-foot day sailor. There's a $10 surcharge for one-night stays.

Pointy Head Inn ✪
ROUTE 102A, BASS HARBOR, MT. DESERT ISLAND, MAINE 04653

Tel: **(207) 244-7261**	Single/sb: **$40**
Best Time to Call: **9:30 AM–3 PM**	Open: **May 15–Oct.**
Hosts: **Doris and Warren Townsend**	Breakfast: **Full**
Location: **18 mi. S of Bar Harbor**	Pets: **No**
No. of Rooms: **6**	Children: **Welcome, over 10**
No. of Private Baths: **1**	Smoking: **No**
Max. No. Sharing Bath: **4**	Social Drinking: **Permitted**
Double/pb: **$65**	Airport/Station Pickup: **Yes**
Double/sb: **$55**	

In Colonial times a sea captain made his home here, overlooking beautiful Bass Harbor. Today, this sprawling inn is a haven for artists and photographers who appreciate the quiet side of Mount Desert

Island. The house is decorated with nautical accents and homey furnishings. One of its special qualities is the beautiful sunsets that can be enjoyed from your room or the comfortable porch. The inn is set in a quaint fishing village bordering Acadia State Park. Swimming, canoeing, nature trails, fishing, and mountain climbing are just a few of the activities that can be enjoyed locally. A variety of restaurants, shops, and galleries are within walking distance.

Two Seasons ✪

BOX 829, SOUTHWEST HARBOR, MT. DESERT ISLAND, MAINE 04679

Tel: **(207) 244-9627**	Open: **June 15–Oct. 31**
Host: **Dorothy M. Lazareth**	Reduced Rates: **$10 less June, Oct.**
No. of Rooms: **4**	Breakfast: **Continental**
No. of Private Baths: **2**	Pets: **No**
Max. No. Sharing Bath: **4**	Children: **Welcome, in separate room**
Double/pb: **$60–$70**	Smoking: **No**
Double/sb: **$50–$60**	Social Drinking: **Permitted**

Dorothy offers bright, airy rooms in a spacious Colonial home overlooking the harbor. Southwest Harbor is a small fishing village; locally, this B&B is called the "doctor's house," and its blue shutters still bear the caduceus symbol. Breakfast, served in the sun room, consists of fresh fruit, cereal, local breads, muffins, homemade jams, and beverages. Shops and restaurants are within an easy stroll; yacht builders, golf courses, and Acadia National Park are a few miles away. Guests always remark on the comfortable beds and spic-and-span condition of the house.

Lake Sebasticook B&B ✪

P.O. BOX 502, 8 SEBASTICOOK AVENUE, NEWPORT, MAINE 04953

Tel: **(207) 368-5507**	Open: **May–Oct.**
Hosts: **Bob and Trudy Zothner**	Breakfast: **Full**
Location: **1 mi. off I-95, Exit 39**	Pets: **No**
No. of Rooms: **3**	Children: **No**
Max. No. Sharing Bath: **3**	Smoking: **No**
Double/sb: **$50**	Social Drinking: **No**
Single/sb: **$37.50**	Airport/Station Pickup: **Yes**

This gracious white Victorian, with its front wraparound porch and screened-in second-story sun porch, stands so near to Lake Sebasticook that guests can hear the calls of ducks and loons. In summer, the lake is a haven for swimmers and fishermen; in winter, it freezes, providing an outlet for cross-country skiers. Bob and Trudy, who love the outdoors, will direct you to the best locations. Full country breakfasts, with homemade breads and jams, will supply you with the energy to enjoy the great outdoors.

Morning Dove Bed and Breakfast
30 BOURNE LANE, OGUNQUIT, MAINE 03907

Tel: (207) 646-3891
Hosts: Peter and Eeta Schon
Location: 75 mi. N of Boston
No. of Rooms: 6
No. of Private Baths: 4
Max. No. Sharing Bath: 4
Double/pb: $70–$105
Double/sb: $55–$80
Open: All year

Reduced Rates: Off season
Breakfast: Continental
Credit Cards: AMEX, MC, VISA
Pet: No
Children: Welcome, over 12
Smoking: Permitted
Social Drinking: Permitted
Minimum Stay: 2 nights, July, Aug.,
    holiday weekends

The Morning Dove is a restored farmhouse dating back to the 1860s. The airy rooms feature antiques, luxurious towels, and fresh garden flowers. At night, handmade chocolates are placed on the pillows. Breakfast is served on the Victorian porch or in the elegant dining room. The house is within walking distance of beaches, a busy harbor for fishing and boating, and the Marginal Way, a cliff-top path along the edge of the ocean. Restaurants, art galleries, and the trolley stop are just a few steps away.

Broad Bay Inn & Gallery ✪
MAIN STREET, P.O. BOX 607, WALDOBORO, MAINE 04572

Tel: (207) 832-6668
Hosts: Jim and Libby Hopkins
Location: 80 mi. N of Portland
No. of Rooms: 5
Max. No. Sharing Bath: 4
Double/sb: $40–$65
Single/sb: $35–$60
Open: All year

Breakfast: Full
Other Meals: Dinner available Sat.
Credit Cards: MC, VISA
Pets: No
Children: Welcome, over 12
Smoking: Permitted
Social Drinking: Permitted
Foreign Languages: French

The inn, located in a charming mid-coast village, is a classic Colonial (circa 1830) with light, airy, handsomely decorated rooms. Some of the guest rooms have canopy beds, and all have Victorian furnishings. There's a large deck on which to enjoy afternoon tea or sherry. This is a convenient base from which to enjoy the quaint fishing villages, the Camden Shakespeare Theatre, and the Maine Seafood Festival. A sumptuous breakfast often includes crêpes and herbed cheese omelets. Jim and Libby are retired commercial artists and theater buffs.

Tide Watch Inn ✪
P.O. BOX 94, PINE STREET, WALDOBORO, MAINE 04572

Tel: (207) 832-4987
Best Time to Call: Before 10 AM;
    after 2 PM

Hosts: Mel and Cathy Hanson
Location: 62 mi. N of Portland; 1⁷⁄₁₆
    mi. from Rte. 1

No. of Rooms: **3**	Open: **All year**
No. of Private Baths: **1**	Breakfast: **Full**
Max. No. Sharing Bath: **4**	Pets: **No**
Double/pb: **$60**	Children: **Welcome**
Single/pb: **$50**	Smoking: **Permitted**
Double/sb: **$50**	Social Drinking: **Permitted**
Single/sb: **$40**	

Built in 1850, this twin Colonial home is located on the shore of the Medomac River. The first five-masted schooners were crafted right by the inn. You are welcome to bring your boat or canoe, or just watch the local fishermen sail with the tide. Catherine's forte is keeping the inn ship-shape, and guests comment on the comfortable ambience she's created. Mel's talent as a retired chef is evident in the ambitious and delicious breakfasts that might include asparagus cordon bleu.

The Wild Rose of York B&B ✪
78 LONG SANDS ROAD, YORK, MAINE

Tel: **(207) 363-2532**	Open: **All year**
Best Time to Call: **Afternoon, evening**	Reduced Rates: **Oct. 16–May 31**
Hosts: **Fran and Frank Sullivan**	Breakfast: **Full**
No. of Rooms: **3**	Pets: **No**
No. of Private Baths: **3**	Children: **Welcome**
Double/pb: **$60**	Smoking: **No**
Single/pb: **$50**	Social Drinking: **Permitted**
Suites: **$80 for 3**	Airport/Station Pickup: **Yes**

This handsome house, built in 1814, sits high on a hill within easy range of the ocean breezes. The bedrooms are cozy, with antique beds, patchwork quilts, fireplaces, and Fran's special artistic touches. Breakfast is special and may feature peach pancakes or nut waffles. In summer, an old-fashioned trolley will take you to the beach. Deep-sea fishing, golf, hiking, shops, galleries, and factory outlets are nearby diversions. Frank, a biology professor, often conducts nature and tidepool walks. In winter, sledding, skating, and cross-country skiing are all fun. An art gallery, featuring works by local artists, is literally on the drawing board for this B&B. Complimentary tea, cookies, and sherry are always offered.

Canterbury House
432 YORK STREET, P.O. BOX 881, YORK HARBOR, MAINE 03911

Tel: **(207) 363-3505**	Breakfast: **Full**
Best Time to Call: **Early morning**	Other Meals: **Available**
Hosts: **James T. Pappas and Jim S. Hager**	Credit Cards: **MC, VISA**
Location: **50 mi. N of Boston, MA**	Pets: **No**
No. of Rooms: **7**	Children: **Welcome, over 12**
No. of Private Baths: **2**	Smoking: **Permitted**
Max. No. Sharing Bath: **4**	Social Drinking: **Permitted**
Double/pb: **$75**	Minimum Stay: **2 nights in season**
Double/sb: **$55–$69**	Airport/Station Pickup: **Yes**
Open: **All year**	Foreign Languages: **French, Greek, German**
Reduced Rates: **7th night free**	

A lovely white Victorian overlooking unspoiled York Harbor, Canterbury House is within walking distance from the beach and other local attractions. Guests enjoy large hotel amenities while being pampered in a homey atmosphere. A scrumptious breakfast, served on fine Royal Albert china in either the dining room or, weather permitting, the scenic front porch, features hot muffins fresh from your hosts' own bakery.

MARYLAND

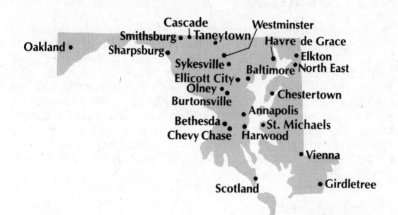

The Traveller in Maryland ☉
P.O. BOX 2277, ANNAPOLIS, MARYLAND 21404

Tel: (301) 269-6232	Rates (Single/Double):
Best Time to Call: **9 AM–5 PM**	Modest: **$55** **$60**
Coordinator: **Greg Page**	Average: **$60** **$70**
States/Regions Covered: **Annapolis,**	Luxury: **$80** **$100**
Baltimore, Bethesda, Easton, Ellicott	Credit Cards: **AMEX, MC, VISA**
City, St. Michael, Taneytown	

Maryland is the home of Annapolis, site of the United States Naval Academy; Baltimore, home to the restored Inner Harbor and locale of historic Fort McHenry of Star Spangled Banner fame; and Chesapeake Bay, known for its excellent harbors and fabulous fishing. Greg's carefully selected hosts are anxious to show off their expertise in helping you discover all of those special places that will make your visit memorable.

Betsy's Bed and Breakfast
1428 PARK AVENUE, BALTIMORE, MARYLAND 21217

Tel: (301) 383-1274	No. of Rooms: **3**
Best Time to Call: **9:30 AM–10 PM**	No. of Private Baths: **1**
Host: **Betsy Grater**	Max. No. Sharing Bath: **4**

Double/pb: **$65**
Single/pb: **$60**
Double/sb: **$60**
Single/sb: **$50**
Open: **All year**
Reduced Rates: **10–15%, weekly**

Breakfast: **Full**
Credit Cards: **AMEX, MC, VISA**
Pets: **No**
Children: **Welcome**
Smoking: **No**
Social Drinking: **Permitted**

This four-story B&B is located in Bolton Hill, a neighborhood listed on the National Register of Historic Places. This is a charming 115-year-old town house, with elegant features such as a hallway floor inlaid with alternating strips of oak and walnut. There are six marble fireplaces, the most elaborate of which is in the dining room. Other decorations include heirloom quilts, displayed on the walls, and an interesting assortment of antique kitchen tools. Guests are welcome to relax in the spacious, high-ceilinged living room with French doors opening out to the garden. Betsy's is convenient to Meyerhoff Symphony Hall, the Lyric Opera House, the Inner Harbor, and some of the city's finest restaurants.

Mulberry House
111 WEST MULBERRY STREET, BALTIMORE, MARYLAND 21201

Tel: **(301) 576-0111**
Hosts: **Charlotte and Curt Jeschke**
No. of Rooms: **4**
Max. No. Sharing Bath: **4**
Double/sb: **$65**
Open: **All year**
Breakfast: **Full**

Pets: **No**
Children: **Welcome, over 16 (in separate room)**
Smoking: **No**
Social Drinking: **Permitted**
Foreign Languages: **German**

Mulberry House, in downtown Baltimore, was built circa 1830 as a Federal-period town house. Over the years a fourth floor and a courtyard were added, and a painstaking restoration has now taken place. The owners have added special touches, such as leaded glass in first-floor transoms, fan windows, and needlepoint cushions from 19th-century wallpaper designs. Guests may choose from the Victorian, Far East, Federal, and Pineapple rooms, all professionally decorated. Guests are treated like old friends, and are welcome to relax in the sitting room with its grand piano, sofa, and fireplace. A sumptuous breakfast is served at an 18th-century banquet table each morning. The house is within walking distance of many shops, museums, restaurants, historic sights, and the waterfront area.

The Winslow Home ✪
8217 CARAWAY STREET, CABIN JOHN, BETHESDA, MARYLAND 20818

Tel: **(301) 229-4654**	Open: **All year**
Best Time to Call: **After 5PM**	Reduced Rates: **Seniors; families**
Host: **Jane Winslow**	Breakfast: **Full**
Location: **7 mi. W of D.C.**	Pets: **Welcome**
No. of Rooms: **2**	Children: **Welcome**
Max. No. Sharing Bath: **4**	Smoking: **No**
Double/sb: **$40**	Social Drinking: **No**
Single/sb: **$30**	Airport/Station Pickup: **Yes**

You may enjoy the best of two worlds while staying at Jane's. This comfortable home is located in a lovely residential section of Bethesda, just 20 minutes from downtown Washington, D.C. Imagine touring the capital with some extra pocket money saved on high hotel costs. You are welcome to use the kitchen, laundry facilities, and piano. Georgetown, George Washington, and American universities are close by. There's a $5 surcharge for one-night stays.

The Taylors' B&B ✪
P.O. BOX 238, BURTONSVILLE, MARYLAND 20866-0238

Tel: **(301) 236-4318**	Open: **All year**
Best Time to Call: **9–11 AM; 7–9 PM**	Breakfast: **Continental**
Hosts: **Ruth and Fred Taylor**	Pets: **No**
Location: **10 mi. N-NE of Washington, D.C.**	Children: **No**
No. of Rooms: **1**	Smoking: **No**
No. of Private Baths: **1**	Social Drinking: **Permitted**
Double/pb: **$60**	Foreign Languages: **French**

This gracious two-story Colonial home offers a breath of fresh country air just 45 minutes from Washington, D.C., and Baltimore's Inner Harbor district. Guests can enjoy the grand piano, the extensive collection of books in the library, and Ruth's paintings. In warm weather, cool drinks are served in the gazebo; in winter, guests gather by the fireplace in the family room. Both of your hosts are retired. Ruth likes to read, sew, paint, and cook; Fred enjoys reading, writing, history, and music. They've traveled extensively and know how to make guests feel welcome. Tennis courts, horseback riding, and nature trails are nearby.

Bluebird on the Mountain
14700 EYLER AVENUE, CASCADE, MARYLAND 21719

Tel: **(301) 241-4161**	Location: **65 mi. N of Washington, D.C.**
Best Time to Call: **8 AM–9 PM**	No. of Rooms: **4**
Host: **Edie Smith-Eley**	

No. of Private Baths: **4**
Suites: **$85–$105**
Open: **All year**
Reduced Rates: **10%, seniors; $10 less, Mon.–Thurs.**
Breakfast: **Continental**
Wheelchair Accessible: **Yes**

Credit Cards: **MC, VISA**
Pets: **No**
Children: **Welcome, over 12**
Smoking: **Permitted in common rooms and on porches**
Social Drinking: **Permitted**

Lovingly restored to its former elegance, this 1890 Georgian colonial mansion has four separate guest suites. Your host is an award-winning nature photographer; her work—and that of her friends—is displayed throughout the house. Once a fashionable resort area, Blue Ridge Summit remains in appealing hideaway year-round. Depending on the season, you can ski, golf, or take foliage tours. You can plan your itinerary over such breakfast fare as apple dumplings, cranberry nut bread, and other home-baked goodies brought right to your suite.

Inn at Mitchell House
BOX 329, RD 2, ROUTE 21, CHESTERTOWN, MARYLAND 21620

Tel: **(301) 778-6500**
Best Time to Call: **Anytime**
Hosts: **Tracy and Jim Stone**
Location: **78 mi. E of Washington**
No. of Rooms: **6**
No. of Private Baths: **5**
Max. No. Sharing Bath: **2**
Double/pb: **$75–$85**
Single/pb: **$70–$80**
Suite: **$90**

Open: **All year**
Breakfast: **Full**
Credit Cards: **MC, VISA**
Pets: **No**
Children: **Sometimes**
Smoking: **Permitted**
Social Drinking: **Permitted**
Minimum Stay: **2 nights on holiday weekends**

This brick Federal-style inn is known as the Mitchell Mansion, and is listed on the Maryland Register of Historic Homes. The house, set on 10 acres, dates back to 1743, and boasts seven fireplaces, guest parlors, and a dining room with the original beamed ceiling and exposed brick floors. Tracy and Jim enjoy providing extra touches such as wine and cheese at cocktail time. They want you to have a restful night amid period antiques, designer sheets, and authentic rope beds. Breakfast is always a hearty offering that often includes homemade granola and unusual French toast. Guests have bathing privileges at a private beach on Chesapeake Bay, just one-half mile from the house.

Radcliffe Cross ✪
QUAKER NECK ROAD, ROUTE 3, BOX 360, CHESTERTOWN, MARYLAND 21620

Tel: **(301) 778-5540**
Hosts: **Dan and Marge Brook**

No. of Rooms: **2**
No. of Private Baths: **2**

Double/pb: **$65–$70**
Open: **All year**
Breakfast: **Full**
Pets: **No**

Children: **Welcome, infants or over 10**
Smoking: **No**
Social Drinking: **Permitted**

This pre-Revolutionary white brick Colonial, situated on 28 acres, is appropriately furnished with Early American antiques. A unique hanging spiral staircase rises from the center hall to the third floor. Each room boasts its own fireplace. Guests rave about Marge's puff pastries, muffins, and coffee cakes. Coffee, tea, and soft drinks are always available. Reserve well in advance for the popular Chestertown Tea Party Festival in May, or the Candlelight Walking Tour of Historic Chestertown in September.

Chevy Chase Bed & Breakfast
6815 CONNECTICUT AVENUE, CHEVY CHASE, MARYLAND 20815

Tel: **(301) 656-5867**
Best Time to Call: **Anytime**
Host: **S. C. Gotbaum**
Location: **1 mi. N of Washington**
No. of Rooms: **2**
No. of Private Baths: **1**
Max. No. Sharing Bath: **3**
Double/pb: **$55**
Single/pb: **$45**

Single/sb: **$45**
Open: **All year**
Reduced Rates: **Weekly; families**
Breakfast: **Continental**
Pets: **No**
Children: **Welcome**
Smoking: **Permitted**
Social Drinking: **Permitted**

Enjoy the convenience of being close to the sights of Washington, D.C., while staying at a relaxing country-style house outside the city. Rooms have beamed ceilings and are filled with rare tapestries, Oriental rugs, baskets, copperware, and native crafts from Mexico to the Mideast. Your host is a sociologist with a private consulting business. For breakfast she offers homemade muffins, jams, pancakes, French toast, and a special blend of Louisiana coffee. When you want to take a break from touring, a quiet backyard and garden will relax you. Tennis courts and a swimming pool are nearby.

The Garden Cottage at Sinking Springs Herb Farm ✪
234 BLAIR SHORE ROAD, ELKTON, MARYLAND 21921

Tel: **(301) 398-5566**
Best Time to Call: **8 AM–8 PM**
Hosts: **Ann and Bill Stubbs**
Location: **4½ mi. from Rte. 40**
No. of Rooms: **1**
No. of Private Baths: **1**
Guest Cottage: **$68; sleeps 3**
Open: **All year**
Reduced Rates: **5%, seniors**

Breakfast: **Continental**
Credit Cards: **MC, VISA**
Other Meals: **Available**
Pets: **Sometimes**
Children: **Welcome**
Smoking: **No**
Social Drinking: **Permitted**
Airport/Station Pickup: **Yes**

Guests frequently comment on the peaceful beauty of this 128-acre historical farm. The garden cottage has a sitting room and fireplace adjoining the bedroom. Breakfast features coffee ground from organically grown beans, herbal teas, homemade buns, fruit, and juice. A full country breakfast prepared with unprocessed food fresh from the farm is available at no extra charge. Lectures on herbs and craft classes are available, and a gift shop is on the premises. Longwood Gardens and the famed Winterthur Museum are close by. Historic Chesapeake City is five minutes away.

Hayland Farm
5000 SHEPPARD LANE, ELLICOTT CITY, MARYLAND 21043

Tel: **(301) 531-5593**	Double/sb: **$35**
Host: **Dorothy Mobley**	Single/sb: **$25**
Location: **Bet. Baltimore and D.C.**	Open: **All year**
No. of Rooms: **3**	Breakfast: **Full**
No. of Private Baths: **1**	Pets: **No**
Max. No. Sharing Bath: **4**	Children: **No**
Double/pb: **$50**	Smoking: **No**
Single/pb: **$40**	Social Drinking: **Permitted**

When you breathe the country-fresh air, it may surprise you that Baltimore and Washington, D.C., are only a short drive away. At Hayland Farm you will find gracious living in a large manor house furnished in a handsome, yet comfortable, style. Dorothy is retired and has traveled extensively. She enjoys sharing conversation with her guests. In warm weather, the 20- by 50-foot swimming pool is a joy.

Lewrene Farm B&B ✪
RD 3, BOX 150, HAGERSTOWN, MARYLAND 21740

Tel: **(301) 582-1735**	Wheelchair Accessible: **Yes**
Hosts: **Lewis and Irene Lehman**	Open: **All year**
Location: **3½ mi. from I-70 and I-81**	Breakfast: **Full**
No. of Rooms: **6**	Pets: **Sometimes**
No. of Private Baths: **3**	Children: **Welcome**
Max. No. Sharing Bath: **4**	Smoking: **No**
Double/pb: **$60–$65**	Social Drinking: **No**
Double/sb: **$45–$50**	Foreign Languages: **Spanish**
Suites: **$75**	

Lewis and Irene will help you discover the peaceful beauty of their 125-acre farm located in a historic area near the Antietam Battlefield. Guests are treated like old friends and are welcome to lounge in front of the fireplace or to play the piano in the colonial-style living room. You're invited to enjoy snacks and a video in the evening. Harpers Ferry, Fort Frederick, the C&O Canal, and Gettysburg are nearby. Irene sells antiques and collectibles on the premises.

Oakwood ✪
4566 SOLOMONS ISLAND ROAD, HARWOOD, MARYLAND 20776

Tel: (301) 261-5338
Hosts: **Dennis and Joan Brezina**
Location: **10 mi. S of Annapolis**
No. of Rooms: **2**
Max. No. Sharing Bath: **4**
Double/sb: **$65**
Single/sb: **$60**

Open: **Mar. 1–Nov. 30**
Breakfast: **Full**
Pets: **No**
Children: **Welcome, over 12**
Smoking: **Permitted**
Social Drinking: **Permitted**

This elegant antebellum manor house, featured on Maryland House Tours, has six fireplaces, 11-foot ceilings, and handmade rugs. Guests are welcome to relax on the veranda or stroll in the terraced gardens. Your hosts serve an English-style breakfast in the open-hearthed kitchen. They are happy to advise on day trips to Washington, D.C., or nearby Chesapeake Bay and Annapolis.

Olde Shade Bed and Breakfast ✪
4137 FOX TRAIL, HAVRE DE GRACE, MARYLAND 21078

Tel: (301) 939-3902
Best Time to Call: **After 5 PM**
Host: **Mrs. Ruth Fender**
Location: **30 mi. N of Baltimore**
No. of Rooms: **2**
Max. No. Sharing Bath: **3**
Double/sb: **$75**

Single/sb: **$40**
Open: **All year**
Breakfast: **Full**
Pets: **No**
Children: **Welcome, over 10**
Smoking: **No**
Social Drinking: **Permitted**

Ruth invites you to her brick colonial home in a restful tree-lined neighborhood three miles outside historic Havre de Grace. In your spare time, admire exhibits at Aberdeen Proving Ground Museum, or take a boat ride in Chesapeake Bay. Then come back and lounge by your hostess's pool. Full breakfasts are highlighted by homemade muffins and blueberry pancakes.

The Mill House B&B ✪
102 MILL LANE, NORTH EAST, MARYLAND 21901

Tel: (301) 287-3532
Best Time to Call: **Before 9 AM; after 4 PM**
Hosts: **Lucia and Nick Demond**
Location: **40 mi. NE of Baltimore**
No. of Rooms: **2**
Max. No. Sharing Bath: **4**
Double/sb: **$55–$65**

Single/sb: **$50–$60**
Open: **Mar. 1–Oct. 31**
Breakfast: **Full**
Credit Cards: **MC, VISA**
Pets: **No**
Children: **Welcome, over 12**
Smoking: **Permitted**
Social Drinking: **Permitted**

A genuine mill house that dates to the early 18th century, this B&B is furnished entirely in antiques. You'll see picturesque mill ruins and wildflowers on the grounds, but you won't see the parlor's original Queen Anne paneling; that was purchased by Henry Francis Du Pont and installed in his Winterthur estate bedroom. The Winterthur Museum and the Brandywine River Museum are less than an hour's drive away, as is Baltimore's Inner Harbor. Sightseers will be sustained with a full breakfast, including homemade breads fresh from the oven.

Red Run Inn ✪
ROUTE 5, BOX 268, OAKLAND, MARYLAND 21550

Tel: **(301) 387-6606**	Open: **All year**
Host: **Ruth Umbel**	Breakfast: **Continental**
Location: **180 mi. W of Baltimore**	Credit Cards: **AMEX, MC, VISA**
No. of Rooms: **5**	Pets: **No**
No. of Private Baths: **5**	Children: **Welcome**
Double/pb: **$65–$85**	Smoking: **Permitted**
Single/pb: **$35**	Social Drinking: **Permitted**
Suites: **$100**	Airport/Station Pickup: **Yes**

Nestled in a wooded setting on 18 acres, Red Run overlooks the expansive blue waters of Deep Creek Lake. The grounds and structures have been carefully planned to preserve the unspoiled atmosphere. The property includes a swimming pool, tennis courts, horseshoe pits, dock facilities, and a cross-country ski trail.

The Thoroughbred Bed & Breakfast
16410 BATCHELLORS FOREST ROAD, OLNEY, MARYLAND 20832

Tel: **(301) 774-7649**	No. of Private Baths: **3**
Host: **Helen Polinger**	Max: No. Sharing Bath: **4**
Location: **12 mi. N of Washington, D.C.**	Double/pb: **$55–$80**
	Double/sb: **$65**
No. of Rooms: **5**	Open: **All year**

Breakfast: **Full**
Credit Cards: **MC, VISA ($5 surcharge)**
Pets: **No**

Children: **Welcome, over 12**
Smoking: **No**
Social Drinking: **Permitted**

This beautiful estate is surrounded by 175 acres of rolling hills, fields, and pastures. Helen is a breeder of some of the finest racehorses in the country. Her modern, country-style home has such amenities as a hot tub and champion-size pool table. Don't worry if you eat like a horse at breakfast, which often features such diet busters as waffles and pancakes. You can work off the calories in the swimming pool or on a brisk walk on the property. It's only 12 miles to the attractions of Washington, D.C., easily reached by Metrorail, only 6 miles away.

Parsonage Inn ○
210 NORTH TALBOT STREET, ST. MICHAELS, MARYLAND 21663

Tel: **(301) 745-5519**
Hosts: **Dave and Sharon Proctor**
Location: **15 mi. off Route 50**
No. of Rooms: **7**
No. of Private Baths: **7**
Double/pb: **$82–$94**
Open: **All year**
Reduced Rates: **10%, seniors; $10 less, midweek, off-season**

Breakfast: **Continental**
Wheelchair Accessible: **Yes**
Credit Cards: **MC, VISA**
Pets: **No**
Children: **Welcome**
Smoking: **Permitted**
Social Drinking: **Permitted**

Built in the 1880s with bricks fired in the St. Michaels brickyard, the Parsonage Inn was completely restored in 1985. This striking Victorian B&B is part of the town's historic district, and it's an easy stroll to shops, restaurants, and the Chesapeake Bay Maritime Museum. More ambitious guests may borrow the inn's 12-speed bicycles and venture farther afield. A continental breakfast of coffee, juice, muffins, breads, and bagels is set out in the dining room; tray service is also available upon request.

St. Michael's Manor B&B ○
ST. MICHAEL'S MANOR, SCOTLAND, MARYLAND 20687

Tel: **(301) 872-4025**
Hosts: **Joe and Nancy Dick**
Location: **9 mi. S of St. Marys City**
No. of Rooms: **3**
Max. No. Sharing Bath: **4**
Double/sb: **$55**
Open: **All year**

Reduced Rates: **10%, after Oct. 1**
Breakfast: **Full**
Pets: **No**
Children: **Welcome (crib, high chair)**
Smoking: **Downstairs only**
Social Drinking: **Permitted**

St. Michael's Manor was built in 1805 on land patented to Leonard Calvert during the 17th century. Today, the white stucco manor home on picturesque Long Neck Creek is included on the state's Pilgrimage Tour. The beautifully handcrafted woodwork has been preserved and is complemented with antiques and handcrafts. Guests are sure to enjoy the added touches, such as fresh fruit and flowers in the rooms. For breakfast, choose from a tasty array of homemade muffins, jellies, and farm-fresh fruit in season. Your hosts offer the use of a boat or canoe on the creek or Chesapeake Bay. The Manor House is near Point Lookout State Park, half a mile from Chespeake Bay, and close to many historic sites.

Inn at Antietam ✪

220 EAST MAIN STREET, P.O. BOX 119, SHARPSBURG, MARYLAND 21782

Tel: **(301) 432-6601**	Open: **Jan. 2–Dec. 23**
Best Time to Call: **Mornings; evenings**	Reduced Rates: **5%, seniors**
Hosts: **Betty and Cal Fairbourn**	Breakfast: **Continental**
Location: **15 mi. SW of Hagerstown**	Credit Cards: **AMEX**
No. of Rooms: **5**	Pets: **No**
No. of Private Baths: **5**	Children: **Welcome, over 6**
Double/pb: **$60–$85**	Smoking: **Permitted**
Suites: **$85–$110**	Social Drinking: **Permitted**

This classic restored Victorian, on eight and a half rolling acres, and located next to the historic Antietam Battlefield, was built in 1908. The wraparound porch, with its rockers and swing, is a great place to relax. The house is decorated in period decor with antique accents. It is close to the C & O Canal, Harpers Ferry, and less than an hour from Gettysburg. Shepherd College in Shepherdstown, West Virginia, is four miles away.

Blue Bear Bed & Breakfast

ROUTE 2, BOX 378, HOLIDAY DRIVE, SMITHSBURG, MARYLAND 21783

Tel: **(301) 824-2292**	Open: **July 1–Aug. 31; weekends,**
Best Time to Call: **After 4 PM**	**Apr.–June, Sept.–Dec.**
Host: **Ellen Panchula**	Breakfast: **Continental**
Location: **6 mi. from I-70, Exit 35**	Pets: **No**
No. of Rooms: **2**	Children: **Welcome, over 12**
Max. No. Sharing Bath: **4**	Smoking: **No**
Double/sb: **$40**	Social Drinking: **Permitted**
Single/sb: **$30**	

Ellen is a full-time schoolteacher from September through June, so she can entertain guests during the week only in July and August; during the school year it's strictly weekends only. Her home is decorated in an informal country mode, with several antiques complementing the decor. Smithsburg is located in apple and peach country. It is convenient to the Antietam Battlefield in Sharpsburg, and to many fine restaurants in Hagerstown. Homemade breads, coffee cakes, quiche, fresh fruit, and beverages constitute the breakfast menu. Snacks, dessert, and wine and cheese are generously offered in the evenings.

"Long Way" Bed & Breakfast ✪
7406 SPRINGFIELD AVENUE, SYKESVILLE, MARYLAND 21784

Tel: **(301) 795-8129**	Double/sb: **$49**
Best Time to Call: **After 7 PM**	Single/sb: **$45**
Host: **Anita-Barbara Huddlestun**	Open: **All year**
Location: **20 mi. W of Baltimore**	Breakfast: **Full (except Saturday,**
No. of Rooms: **3**	**Continental)**
No. of Private Baths: **2**	Pets: **Sometimes**
Max. No. Sharing Bath: **4**	Children: **Welcome**
Double/pb: **$49**	Smoking: **Permitted**
Single/pb: **$45**	Social Drinking: **Permitted**

Anita-Barbara Huddlestun's entire block is listed on the National Register of Historic Places. She welcomes you to her Victorian cottage, set on five and a half landscaped acres. The property includes fruit trees, flowers, woods, and a swimming pool to enjoy in the summer months. The rooms are decorated with charming pieces ranging in period from the 1900s to the 1930s, with lovely wallpapers, wood furnishings, and fine linens. Breakfast specialties such as homemade cinnamon-raisin buns, eggs, and bacon are served in a sunny dining room with floral wallpaper and an old-fashioned curio cabinet. Long Way Hill is located in a rural area, yet is close to fine dining, shopping, and a movie theater. Columbia and Newmarket, the antiques capital of the state, are just a short drive from the house.

Null's Bed & Breakfast ✪
4910 BAPTIST ROAD, TANEYTOWN, MARYLAND 21787

Tel: **(301) 756-6112**	Double/sb: **$50**
Hosts: **Francis and Betty Null**	Single/sb: **$45**
Location: **8 mi. S of Gettysburg, PA**	Open: **All year**
No. of Rooms: **2**	Breakfast: **Full**
No. of Private Baths: **1**	Pets: **No**
Max. No. Sharing Bath: **4**	Children: **Welcome**
Double/pb: **$55**	Smoking: **Permitted**
Single/pb: **$50**	Social Drinking: **Permitted**

Francis Null grew up in this blue farmhouse, which has always been in his family. While it is no longer a working farm, the property's 22 acres invite exploration. Ask your hosts about the furniture; some pieces are genuine antiques, others are artful reproductions Francis created in his woodworking shop. Taneytown is about nine miles from

Gettysburg, and Baltimore, Washington, D.C., and Amish country are all accessible by car. Homemade bread and jam accompany Betty's full breakfasts.

The Tavern House ✪
111 WATER STREET, P.O. BOX 98, VIENNA, MARYLAND 21869

Tel: (301) 376-3347	Reduced Rates: **After 1 night**
Hosts: **Harvey and Elise Altergott**	Breakfast: **Full**
Location: **15 mi. NW of Salisbury**	Credit Cards: **MC, VISA**
No. of Rooms: **4**	Pets: **No**
Max. No. Sharing Bath: **4**	Children: **Welcome, over 12**
Double/sb: **$55–$60**	Smoking: **Permitted**
Single/sb: **$45–$55**	Social Drinking: **Permitted**
Open: **All year**	Foreign Languages: **German, Spanish**

Vienna is a quiet little town on the Nanticoke River, where one can escape the stress of the 20th century. Careful restoration has brought back the simple purity of this Colonial tavern. The stark white "lime, sand, and hair" plaster accents the authentic furnishings. This is a place for those who enjoy looking at the river and marshes, watching an osprey, or taking a leisurely walk. Days begin with fruits of the season and end with complimentary cheese and wine. For the sports minded, there's tennis, boating, and flat roads for bicycling, all within easy reach. This is an excellent base for exploring the Eastern Shore, interesting small towns, and Blackwater National Wildlife Refuge.

Winchester Country Inn ✪
430 SOUTH BISHOP STREET, WESTMINSTER, MARYLAND 21157

Tel: (301) 876-7373	Single/sb: **$55**
Best Time to Call: **8 AM–7 PM**	Open: **All year**
Host: **Estella Williams and Joyce Dell**	Reduced Rates: **10% weekly; 10%,**
Location: **35 mi. NW of Baltimore**	**seniors**
No. of Rooms: **5**	Breakfast: **Full**
No. of Private Baths: **3**	Credit Cards: **MC, VISA**
Max. No. Sharing Bath: **4**	Pets: **No**
Double/pb: **$65**	Children: **Welcome, over 6**
Single/pb: **$60**	Smoking: **Permitted**
Double/sb: **$60**	Social Drinking: **Permitted**

Built in the 1760s, this inn is one of the oldest inns in Carroll County. It is furnished with period antiques that enhance the interior. It is only a quarter of a mile to the historic Carroll County Farm Museum, which is the site of special events such as the Maryland Wine Festival. It is within walking distance of the Farmers Market, where produce, flowers, and crafts may be bought. Breakfast includes farm-fresh eggs and country sausage or ham.

MASSACHUSETTS

Essex
Gloucester
Lowell• •Salem
Sterling Concord• •Marblehead
•Buckland Boston• •Swampscott
Peru • Ashfield Sudbury• •N. Scituate
Scituate•
Lenox •
•Tyringham •Ware South Dennis Provincetown
•Sturbridge Dennis• •Brewster
Yarmouth Port •Eastham
Attleboro • Barnstable •E. Orleans
Rehoboth Sandwich• West Harwich
West Falmouth— Harwich Port
Wareham • Bass River
New Bedford• •Centerville
Woods Hole• •Falmouth Cape Cod
Vineyard Haven •Edgartown
Nantucket
Martha's Vineyard

Pineapple Hospitality, Inc. ✪
P.O. BOX F 821, NEW BEDFORD, MASSACHUSETTS 02740

Tel: **(508) 990-1696; 1798**
Best Time to Call: **Winter: Noon–
7 PM; Summer: 9 AM–7 PM**
Coordinator: **Judy Mulford**
States/Regions Covered: **Connecticut,
Maine, Massachusetts, New
Hampshire, Rhode Island, Vermont**

Descriptive Directory: **$5.95**
Rates (Single/Double):
  Modest: **$50**   **$60**
  Average: **$55**   **$65**
  Luxury: **$75**   **$145**
Credit Cards: **AMEX, MC, VISA**

The pineapple has been the symbol of rare hospitality since early
Colonial days, and the host homes on Judy's roster personify this
spirit. They are located in cities and in the countryside, at beach
resorts and lakeside communities, in historic districts and near hundreds of schools and colleges; you are bound to find just the spot to
call home. There's a $5 processing fee.

Bed & Breakfast Associates—Bay Colony, Ltd. ✪
P.O. BOX 57166, BABSON PARK, BOSTON, MASSACHUSETTS 02157-0166

Tel: (617) 449-5302
Best Time to Call: 10 AM–12:30 PM;
  1:30–5 PM
Coordinators: Arline Kardasis and
  Marilyn Mitchell
States/Regions Covered: Boston,
  Brookline, Cambridge, Cape Cod,
  Concord, Framingham, Gloucester,
  Newton, North Shore, South Shore

Descriptive Directory: $3.75
Rates (Single/Double):
  Modest: $40–$50 $50–$55
  Average: $55–$65 $55–$75
  Luxury: $70–$95 $80–$115
Credit Cards: AMEX, MC, VISA
Minimum Stay: 2 nights

A wide variety of 120 host homes is available in the city, in the country, and at the shore. They range from historic brownstones to contemporary condominiums. Many are convenient to the major colleges and universities. There's a $10 surcharge for one-night stays.

Bed & Breakfast Marblehead & North Shore ✪
P.O. BOX 172, BEVERLY, MASSACHUSETTS 01915

Tel: (508) 921-1336; (617) 964-1606
Best Time to Call: Mon.–Fri. 7:30
  AM–8 PM; Sat. 9 AM–1 PM
Coordinator: Helena Champion
States/Regions Covered: Beverly,
  Cape Ann, Danvers, Gloucester,
  Lexington, Lynn, Manchester,
  Marblehead, Peabody, Rockport,
  Salem, Swampscott; Maine, New
  Hampshire, Vermont

Descriptive Directory: $3.50
Rates (Single/Double):
  Modest: $36–$42 $42–$50
  Average: $45–$55 $55–$70
  Luxury: $60–$120 $75–$125
Credit Cards: AMEX, MC, VISA (5%
  surcharge)

Ranging from the reasonable to the regal, Helena's B&Bs all assure the warm, friendly atmosphere of a private home. This service has many accommodations just thirty minutes from downtown Boston, yet they are in quaint seaside towns, on the ocean, or in ski areas. This is a membership organization with annual dues of $25. Nonmembers are charged $10 to $15 for each booking.

Bed & Breakfast in Minuteman Country
P.O. BOX 665, CAMBRIDGE, MASSACHUSETTS 02140

Tel: (617) 576-2112
Coordinators: Tally and Pamela
  Carruthers
States/Regions Covered: Arlington,
  Bedford, Boston, Brookline,
  Cambridge, Concord, Lexington,
  Sudbury, Waltham, Winchester

Rates (Single/Double):
  Average: $45 $66
  Luxury: $50 $86
Credit Cards: AMEX, MC, VISA
Minimum Stay: 2 nights

Tally and Pamela can place you in host homes convenient to historic Lexington and Concord, downtown Boston, or in Cambridge. Many are close to Harvard and MIT, Lahey Clinic, historic Wright Tavern, Emerson's home, Walden Pond, and the Charles River. Unusual restaurants, specialty shops, and cultural happenings abound. Just tell your host about your interests and you will be assured of excellent advice. There's a $6 surcharge for one-night stays.

Be Our Guest Bed & Breakfast, Ltd. ✪
P.O. BOX 1333, PLYMOUTH, MASSACHUSETTS 02360

Tel: **(617) 837-9867**	Descriptive Directory: **$1**
Coordinators: **Diane Gillis and Mary Gill**	Rates (Single/Double):
	Modest: **$38** **$65**
States/Regions Covered: **Boston, Cohasset, Duxbury, Falmouth, Hanover, Kingston, Marshfield, Plymouth, Sandwich, Scituate, Quincy**	Average: **$50** **$75**
	Luxury: **$110**
	Credit Cards: **AMEX, MC, VISA**

The homes range from historic to traditional New England–style. Some are in private settings; others are surrounded by tourist activities. A few have commanding views of the waterfront. All are hosted by people who are dedicated to making certain that you enjoy your visit. Don't miss Plymouth Rock, the Mayflower, the Wax Museum, and winery tours. If you enjoy the sea, whale watching, deep-sea fishing, and sailing are all available.

BOSTON AREA

Greater Boston Hospitality ✪
P.O. BOX 1142, BROOKLINE, MASSACHUSETTS 02146

Tel: **(617) 277-5430**	Descriptive Directory: **Free**
Coordinator: **Lauren A. Simonelli**	Rates (Single/Double):
States/Regions Covered: **Boston, Brookline, Cambridge, Gloucester, Lexington, Marblehead, Needham, Newton, Wellesley, Winchester**	Modest: **$35** **$45**
	Average: **$45** **$55**
	Luxury: **$55** **$100**
	Credit Cards: **MC, VISA**

Lauren's accommodations are convenient to many of the 75 colleges and universities in the greater Boston area. They're in inns, condos, or self-serve apartments. Many include parking, most are near public transportation. What a boon it is for people applying to school, and to parents visiting undergrads, to have a home-away-from-home nearby. There's a $10 surcharge for one-night stays.

Host Homes of Boston ✪
P.O. BOX 117, WABAN BRANCH, BOSTON, MASSACHUSETTS 02168

Tel: (617) 244-1308
Best Time to Call: **9 AM–12 PM;**
  1:30–4:30 PM weekdays
Coordinator: **Marcia Whittington**
States/Regions Covered: **Boston,**
  Brookline, Cambridge, Concord,
  Marblehead, Needham, Newton,
  Wellesley, Westwood, Weymouth

Descriptive Directory: **Free**
Rates (Single/Double):
  Modest: **$45–$55 $54–$57**
  Average: **$55–$65 $57–$68**
  Luxury: **$68–$95 $68–$125**
Credit Cards: **AMEX, MC, VISA**
Minimum Stay: **2 nights**

Marcia has culled a variety of select private homes in excellent areas convenient to good public transportation. Most hosts prepare a full breakfast, although only Continental breakfast is required. It's their special way of saying welcome to their city of colleges, universities, museums, and cultural life. There's a $10 surcharge for one-night stays if a reservation is made at the last minute.

George Fuller House
148 MAIN STREET, ESSEX, MASSACHUSETTS 01929

Tel: (508) 768-7766
Best Time to Call: **10 AM–10 PM**
Hosts: **Cindy and Bob Cameron**
Location: **3 mi. off Route 128, Exit 15**
No. of Rooms: **5**
No. of Private Baths: **5**
Double/pb: **$70–$78**
Suites: **$98**
Open: **All year**

Reduced Rates: **$10 discount, Nov. 1–**
  May 31
Breakfast: **Full**
Credit Cards: **AMEX, MC, VISA**
Pets: **No**
Children: **Welcome, over 6**
Smoking: **No**
Social Drinking: **Permitted**
Airport/Station Pickup: **Yes**

This handsome Federalist home retains much of its 19th-century panelling and woodwork; two of the guest rooms have working fireplaces. The Camerons have decorated the house with antique beds, handmade quilts, braided rugs, and caned Boston rockers. Three hundred years ago, Essex was a shipbuilding center; today, appropriately enough, Bob—a licensed captain—teaches sailing and takes guests for cruises on his 30-foot yacht. Among landlubbers, Essex's main claim to fame is its antique shops. Whether you venture out on sea or on land, you'll be fortified by Cindy's versions of breakfast classics, such as her French toast drizzled with brandied lemon butter.

Williams Guest House ✪
136 BASS AVENUE, GLOUCESTER, MASSACHUSETTS 01930

Tel: (508) 283-4931
Best Time to Call: **8 AM–9 PM**
Host: **Betty Williams**

Location: **30 mi. N of Boston**
No. of Rooms: **7**
No. of Private Baths: **5**

Max. No. Sharing Bath: **4**
Double/pb: **$50–$55**
Double/sb: **$45–$48**
Guest Cottage: **$450 weekly for 2**
Open: **May 1–Nov. 1**
Reduced Rates: **Off-season, before June 17 and after Labor Day**

Breakfast: **Continental**
Pets: **No**
Children: **Welcome, in cottage**
Smoking: **Permitted**
Social Drinking: **Permitted**

Located five miles from Rockport, and one and a half miles from Rocky Neck, Gloucester is a quaint fishing village on the North Shore. Betty's Colonial Revival house borders the finest beach, Good Harbor. The guest rooms are furnished with comfort in mind, and her homemade breakfast muffins are delicious. Betty will be happy to suggest many interesting things to do, such as boat tours, sport fishing, whale-watching trips, sightseeing cruises around Cape Ann, the Hammond Castle Museum, and the shops and galleries of the artist colony.

Rasberry Ink ✪
748 COUNTRY WAY, NORTH SCITUATE, MASSACHUSETTS 02060

Tel: **(617) 545-6629**
Best Time to Call: **Evenings**
Hosts: **Frances Honkonen and Carol Hoban**
Location: **25 mi. SE of Boston**
No. of Rooms: **2**
No. of Private Baths: **1**
Max. No. Sharing Bath: **4**
Double/pb: **$75**
Double/sb: **$65**

Single/sb: **$60**
Open: **All year**
Breakfast: **Full**
Pets: **Sometimes**
Children: **No**
Smoking: **No**
Social Drinking: **Permitted**
Airport/Station Pickup: **Yes**
Minimum Stay: **2 nights in season**

This 19th-century farmhouse is set in a small seaside town rich in Colonial and Victorian history. Frances and Carol have restored the house and furnished the rooms with antiques and lace. Guest quarters are located on the second floor and feature a private sitting room. Rasberry Ink is five minutes from the beach and is conveniently located on a bus line, midway between Boston and the Cape Cod Canal. In season, fresh raspberries are offered at breakfast.

Five O'Clock Tea at the Allen House ✪
18 ALLEN PLACE, SCITUATE, MASSACHUSETTS 02066

Tel: **(617) 545-8221**
Best Time to Call: **Morning, evening**
Hosts: **Christine and Iain Gilmour**
Location: **32 mi. SE of Boston**
No. of Rooms: **4**
No. of Private Baths: **2**
Max. No. Sharing Bath: **4**

Double/pb: **$85**
Double/sb: **$75**
Open: **All year**
Breakfast: **Full**
Pets: **No**
Children: **Welcome, over 16**
Smoking: **No**

Social Drinking: **Permitted**
Airport/Station Pickup: **Yes**

Foreign Languages: **Limited French,
German, Spanish**

With views of the village center, this white gabled Victorian overlooks the yacht harbor, where Scituate's commercial fishermen unload lobster and cod. When the Gilmours came to the United States in 1976, they brought along the lovely furniture of their native Great Britain. English antiques fill the house. They also imported British rituals: high tea is a frequent celebration. For breakfast, Christine, a professional caterer, offers standards such as waffles, pancakes, and homemade breads as well as gourmet treats. Allen House is distinguished by good music and good food. Iain, an accomplished musician, cheerfully shares the large library of classical music.

Checkerberry Corner
5 CHECKERBERRY CIRCLE, SUDBURY, MASSACHUSETTS 01776

Tel: **(508) 443-8660**
Best Time to Call: **Evenings**
Hosts: **Stuart and Irene MacDonald**
Location: **20 mi. W of Boston**
No. of Rooms: **3**
Max. No. Sharing Bath: **4**
Double/sb: **$55–$65**
Single/sb: **$50–$55**

Open: **All year**
Reduced Rates: **10%, families**
Breakfast: **Full**
Pets: **No**
Children: **Welcome**
Smoking: **No**
Social Drinking: **Permitted**

Checkerberry Corner is a classic Colonial with stained-glass entry windows, red doors, and a large porch. The rooms are tastefully decorated with traditional mahogany furnishings and comfortable Colonial accents. Beverages and snacks are always available. Stuart and Irene serve breakfast on fine china in the dining room. Homemade muffins, jams, and coffee cakes are specialties of the house. This charming Colonial is located in a historic district, close to the Lexington Minuteman Statue, Old North Bridge, the homes of Louisa May Alcott, Hawthorne, and Emerson, and Longfellow's Wayside Inn.

Marshall House ✪
11 EASTERN AVENUE, SWAMPSCOTT, MASSACHUSETTS 01907

Tel: **(617) 595-6544**
Hosts: **Pat and Al Marshall**
Location: **10 mi. N of Boston**
No. of Rooms: **3**
Max. No. Sharing Bath: **4**
Double/sb: **$60–$65**
Single/sb: **$50–$55**
Open: **All year**

Reduced Rates: **10%, seniors**
Breakfast: **Continental**
Credit Cards: **AMEX, MC, VISA**
Pets: **No**
Children: **Welcome, over 6**
Smoking: **No**
Social Drinking: **Permitted**
Airport/Station Pickup: **Yes**

Marshall House, built circa 1900, is located just a short walk from the beaches of the North Shore. The many porches of this spacious home offer salty breezes and an ocean view. Inside, the rooms are decorated with country furnishings, some cherished antiques, and accents of wood and stained glass. The bedrooms have modern amenities such as color televisions and refrigerators. Guests are welcome to relax in the common room and warm up beside the wood stove. This B&B is located ten miles from Logan International Airport. Pat and Al will gladly direct you to nearby restaurants, historic seacoast villages, and popular bicycle touring routes.

Oak Shores ✪
64 FULLER AVENUE, SWAMPSCOTT, MASSACHUSETTS 01907

Tel: **(617) 599-7677**	Single/sb: **$45**
Best Time to Call: **5–8 PM**	Open: **Apr. 1–Dec. 1**
Host: **Marjorie McClung**	Breakfast: **Continental**
Location: **13 mi. N. of Boston**	Pets: **No**
No. of Rooms: **2**	Children: **Welcome, over 9**
Max. No. Sharing Bath: **4**	Smoking: **No**
Double/sb: **$50**	Social Drinking: **Permitted**

This 60-year-old Dutch Colonial is located on Boston's lovely North Shore. Enjoy rooms filled with fine restored furniture, and sleep in the comfort of old brass and iron beds. Relax in the private, shady garden, on the deck, or take a two-block stroll to the beach. Swampscott was the summer White House of Calvin Coolidge. It is a convenient place to begin tours of nearby Marblehead, birthplace of the United States Navy, and Salem, famous for its witch trials. Marjorie is glad to help with travel plans, and has an ample supply of maps and brochures.

CAPE COD/MARTHA'S VINEYARD

Bed & Breakfast—Cape Cod
P.O. BOX 341, WEST HYANNISPORT, MASSACHUSETTS 02672

Tel: **(508) 775-2772**	Rates (Single/Double):	
Best Time to Call: **9:30 AM–7:30 PM**	Modest: **$38**	**$44**
Coordinator: **Clark Diehl**	Average: **$40**	**$58**
States/Regions Covered: **Cape Cod,**	Luxury: **$60**	**$150**
Martha's Vineyard, Nantucket;	Credit Cards: **AMEX, MC, VISA**	
Boston Area—Cape Ann, Gloucester	Minimum Stay: **2 nights**	
Descriptive Directory: **Free**		

It is just a little over an hour's drive from sophisticated Boston to the relaxed, quaint charm of the Cape. Year-round, you can choose from Clark's roster of 65 homes. The B&B you stay in may be a Victorian inn, a sea captain's home, or an oceanfront house. Your hosts will direct you to the restaurants and shops off the tourist trail. There is a $5 surcharge for one-night stays.

House Guests—Cape Cod and the Islands ✪
BOX 1881, ORLEANS, MASSACHUSETTS 02653

Tel: **(508) 896-7053 or (800) 666-HOST**	Rates (Single/Double):
Best Time to Call: **8 AM–7 PM**	Modest: **$40** **$48–$58**
Coordinator: **Richard Griffin**	Average: **$50–$60** **$59–$75**
States/Regions Covered: **Cape Cod, Martha's Vineyard, Nantucket**	Luxury: **$60–$150** **$76–$187**
Descriptive Directory: **$3.95**	Credit Cards: **AMEX, MC, VISA**
	Minimum Stay: **2 nights Memorial Day weekend through Columbus Day**

Richard's accommodations range from a simple single bedroom with shared bath to historic homes furnished with antiques. Some are on the ocean; others are in wooded country areas. There are even a few self-contained guest cottages on private estates. A $15 booking fee is waived for members of Richard's service who pay $25 annual dues.

Orleans Bed & Breakfast Associates ✪
P.O. BOX 1312, ORLEANS, MASSACHUSETTS 02653

Tel: **(508) 255-3824**	Rates (Single/Double):
Best Time to Call: **8 AM–8 PM**	Modest: **N/A** **$50**
Coordinator: **Mary Chapman**	Average: **N/A** **$65**
States/Regions Covered: **Cape Cod— Brewster, Chatham, Harwich, Orleans, Truro, Wellfleet**	Luxury: **N/A** **$90**
	Credit Cards: **AMEX, MC, VISA**
Descriptive Directory: **$1**	Minimum Stay: **2 nights**

Mary offers a variety of accommodations with a diversity of styles, and guests may choose from historic to contemporary houses, all compatible with the atmosphere of the Cape. The fine reputation this service enjoys is largely due to the attitude of the host to the guest. Under Mary's direction, hosts meet regularly to share experiences, role-play B&B situations, and tour member homes. Each host is aware that a guest's experience reflects on the association as a whole. We applaud the professionalism of this organization! A $5 booking fee is charged per reservation.

Bacon Barn Inn

P.O. BOX 621, 3400 MAIN STREET, BARNSTABLE, MASSACHUSETTS 02630

Tel: **(508) 362-5518**	Reduced Rates: **Lower rates, Nov. 15–**
Best Time to Call: **Early morning to**	**May 15**
noon	Breakfast: **Full**
Hosts: **Mary and Robert Guiffreda**	Pets: **No**
Location: **3 mi. off Route 6, Exit 6**	Children: **Welcome, over 14**
No. of Rooms: **3**	Smoking: **No**
No. of Private Baths: **3**	Social Drinking: **Permitted**
Double/pb: **$75–$85**	Minimum Stay: **2 nights during peak**
Single/pb: **$65–$75**	**season**
Open: **All year**	

You can still see the original posts and beams in this beautifully restored barn, which dates to the 1820s. For more examples of early-19th-century architecture (and fine 20th-century dining), stroll over to Barnstable Village. Snacks and afternoon tea are served at Bacon Barn Inn, and there is a refrigerator for guests' use. Full breakfasts feature juice, coffee, muffins, and French toast or pancakes.

Thomas Huckins House ✪

2701 MAIN STREET (ROUTE 6A), P.O. BOX 515, BARNSTABLE, MASSACHUSETTS 02630

Tel: **(508) 362-6379**	Open: **All year**
Hosts: **Burt and Eleanor Eddy**	Breakfast: **Full**
Location: **2 mi. from Rte. 6, Exit 6**	Credit Cards: **MC, VISA**
No. of Rooms: **3**	Pets: **No**
No. of Private Baths: **3**	Children: **Welcome, over 6**
Double/pb: **$75–$95**	Smoking: **Permitted**
Suites: **$85–$115**	Social Drinking: **Permitted**

Located in the historic district, which is less crowded and less commercial than much of the Cape, the house (circa 1705) has all the privacy and charm of a small country inn. Each bedroom has a small sitting area and a four-poster bed with canopy. Two rooms have working fireplaces. The parlor is comfortably furnished with antiques and handmade reproductions. It's a short walk to a small beach, boat ramp, and the inlet that overlooks the dunes of Sandy Neck. Whale watching, the Nantucket ferry, the Sandwich Glass Museum, and Plimoth Plantation are but 15 minutes away. Eleanor loves to garden, and the jam served at breakfast is literally the fruits of her labor. Breakfast is served in the original keeping room in front of the fireplace. Banana pancakes and Cape Cod cranberry muffins are two favorites.

Old Cape House ✪
108 OLD MAIN STREET, BASS RIVER, MASSACHUSETTS 02664

Tel: **(508) 398-1068**
Hosts: **George and Linda Arthur**
Location: **5 mi. E of Hyannis**
No. of Rooms: **4**
No. of Private Baths: **4**
Double/pb: **$55–$65**
Single/sb: **$45–$55**
Open: **May–Oct.**
Reduced Rates: **Off season**

Breakfast: **Continental**
Pets: **No**
Children: **Welcome, over 15**
Smoking: **No**
Social Drinking: **Permitted**
Foreign Languages: **French, Italian**
Minimum Stay: **2 nights July, Aug.,
        holiday weekends**

This fine Greek Revival home was built in 1815 and is convenient to fine beaches, restaurants, and scenic attractions of Cape Cod. You will enjoy home-baked items at breakfast, and the use of a spacious porch and garden. All of the rooms are charmingly decorated in New England style. It's a great place to stay in the fall for visits to antique shops and craft fairs. Linda is from London, and George also lived in Europe for many years, so they know how to bring the bed-and-breakfast tradition here. A playful resident cat is part of the household.

Old Sea Pines Inn ✪
2553 MAIN STREET, BREWSTER, MASSACHUSETTS 02631

Tel: **(508) 896-6114**
Hosts: **Michele and Steve Rowan**
Location: **16 mi. E of Hyannis**
No. of Rooms: **14**
No. of Private Baths: **14**
Double/pb: **$40–$90**
Suites: **$85–$95**
Open: **All year**

Reduced Rates: **Off season**
Breakfast: **Continental**
Credit Cards: **AMEX, DC, MC, VISA**
Pets: **No**
Children: **Welcome, over 8**
Smoking: **Permitted**
Social Drinking: **Permitted**
Foreign Languages: **German, Italian**

Originally a women's finishing school, this sprawling inn has kept many of its turn-of-the-century features, such as brass and iron beds, as well as antique and wicker furniture. A breakfast of homemade specialities is served on the porch or in the sunny dining room. Located on over three acres, the inn is close to beaches, bike paths, shops, and restaurants.

Copper Beech Inn on Cape Cod ✪
497 MAIN STREET, CENTERVILLE, MASSACHUSETTS 02632

Tel: **(508) 771-5488**
Best Time to Call: **8:30 AM–5:30 PM**
Host: **Joyce Diehl**
Location: **4 mi. W of Hyannis**

No. of Rooms: **3**
No. of Private Baths: **3**
Double/pb: **$75**
Open: **All year**

Breakfast: **Full**
Credit Cards: **AMEX, MC, VISA**
Pets: **No**
Children: **Welcome, over 11**

Smoking: **Permitted**
Social Drinking: **Permitted**
Airport/Station Pickup: **Yes**

Home of the largest European beech tree in Cape Cod, the inn, listed on the National Register of Historic Places, is set in the heart of town amid private estates and vintage homes. It features traditional furnishings, formal parlors, well-kept grounds with sunning areas, and a duck pond. Golf, tennis, fishing, sailing, and swimming are available nearby; Craigville Beach is less than a mile away. The Hyannis Ferry to Nantucket and Martha's Vineyard is four miles away.

Isaiah Hall B&B Inn ✪
152 WHIG STREET, DENNIS, MASSACHUSETTS 02638

Tel: **(508) 385-9928**
Best Time to Call: **8 AM–10 PM**
Host: **Marie Brophy**
Location: **7 mi. E of Hyannis**
No. of Rooms: **11**
No. of Private Baths: **10**
Max. No. Sharing Bath: **3**
Double/pb: **$61–$90**
Single/pb: **$50–$80**
Double/sb: **$50**

Single/sb: **$44**
Open: **Mar. 15–Oct. 31**
Breakfast: **Continental**
Credit Cards: **AMEX, MC, VISA**
Pets: **No**
Children: **Welcome, over 7**
Smoking: **Permitted (5 nonsmoking rooms)**
Social Drinking: **Permitted**

This Cape Cod farmhouse built in 1857 offers casual country living on the quiet, historic northside. The house is decorated in true New England style with quilts, antiques, and Oriental rugs. Four rooms have balconies and one has a fireplace. Within walking distance are the beach, good restaurants, the Cape Playhouse, and countless antique and craft shops. It is also close to freshwater swimming, bike paths, and golf.

The Over Look Inn ✪
ROUTE 6, 3085 COUNTY ROAD, P.O. BOX 771, EASTHAM, MASSACHUSETTS 02642

Tel: **(508) 255-1886; (800) 649-5782 in MA**
Hosts: **Ian and Nan Aitchison**
Location: **90 mi. E of Boston**
No. of Rooms: **10**
No. of Private Baths: **10**
Double/pb: **$55–$95**
Open: **All year**
Reduced Rates: **10%, off-season; 10%, seniors**

Breakfast: **Full**
Credit Cards: **AMEX, MC, VISA**
Pets: **No**
Children: **Welcome, over 12**
Smoking: **Permitted**
Social Drinking: **Permitted**
Airport/Station Pickup: **Yes**
Foreign Languages: **French**

From its site opposite the entrance to the Cape Cod National Seashore, Over Look Inn offers immediate access to more than 30 miles of unspoiled beaches. The Aitchisons are happy to arrange such activities as bike tours, hikes, clambakes, and deep-sea fishing expeditions. The inn itself is a grand Queen Anne–style mansion with wraparound porches and landscaped gardens; inside, period furniture complements the rich mahogany woodwork. On the walls you'll see paintings by the innkeepers' younger son. In the evenings guests are welcome to browse in the library or shoot pool in the game room. Breakfasts feature Scottish dishes like kedgeree.

The Penny House
P.O. BOX 238, ROUTE 6, EASTHAM, MASSACHUSETTS 02651

Tel: **(508) 255-6632**
Hosts: **Bill and Margaret Keith**
No. of Rooms: **12**
No. of Private Baths: **6**
Max. No. Sharing Bath: **4**
Double/pb: **$70–$100**
Double/sb: **$70–$90**
Open: **All year**

Reduced Rates: **$55–$80, Sept.–June**
Breakfast: **Full**
Credit Cards: **AMEX, MC, VISA**
Pets: **No**
Children: **No**
Smoking: **Permitted**
Social Drinking: **Permitted**

Back in 1751, Captain Isiah Horton built the Penny House and crowned it with a shipbuilder's bow roof. She has weathered many a storm, but this spacious cape just gets more charming. The rooms have wide-pine floors and are decorated with a blend of antiques and country accents. Your hosts provide special treats in the public room, where beautiful old wooden beams provide a sense of nostalgia. The Penny House is five minutes from National Seashore Park, and is just as convenient to the warm waters off Cape Cod Bay.

The Parsonage
P.O. BOX 1016, 202 MAIN STREET, EAST ORLEANS, MASSACHUSETTS 02643

Tel: **(508) 255-8217**
Best Time to Call: **9 AM–9 PM**
Hosts: **Chris and Lloyd Shand**
Location: **90 mi. SE of Boston**
No. of Rooms: **7**
No. of Private Baths: **7**
Double/pb: **$60–$75**
Single/pb: **$50–$55**
Suites: **$80–$100**

Open: **All year**
Reduced Rates: **20%, Nov.–Apr.**
Breakfast: **Continental**
Credit Cards: **MC, VISA**
Pets: **No**
Children: **Welcome, over 6**
Smoking: **Permitted**
Social Drinking: **Permitted**

The Parsonage is located on the road to Nauset Beach, a street lined with lovely old homes of early settlers and sea captains. This spacious

Cape Cod, circa 1770, has old wavy glass windows, low ceilings, and is decorated with antiques. Enjoy a homemade breakfast on a tray in your room or outside in the sunny courtyard. Cranberry muffins are the specialty of the house. The Parsonage is located between the Atlantic Ocean and Cape Cod Bay. Bike trails, restaurants, sailing, fishing, and swimming are minutes away.

The Arbor ✪
222 UPPER MAIN STREET, P.O. BOX 1628, EDGARTOWN, MARTHA'S VINEYARD, MASSACHUSETTS 02539

Tel: **(508) 627-8137**
Best Time to Call: **8 AM–8PM**
Host: **Peggy Hall**
Location: **7 mi. SE of Woods Hole Ferry**
No. of Rooms: **10**
No. of Private Baths: **8**
Max. No. Sharing Bath: **4**
Double/pb: **$85–$110**
Double/sb: **$75–$85**

Open: **May 1–Oct. 31**
Reduced Rates: **May 1–June 14; Sept. 16–Oct. 30**
Breakfast: **Continental**
Credit Cards: **MC, VISA**
Pets: **No**
Children: **Welcome, over 12**
Smoking: **Permitted**
Social Drinking: **Permitted**

This turn-of-the-century guest house offers island visitors a unique experience in comfort and charm. The house is a short distance from downtown, and at the same time provides the feeling of being away from it all. Relax in a hammock, enjoy tea on the porch, and retire to a cozy room filled with the smell of fresh flowers. Peggy provides setups and mixers at cocktail time, and will gladly direct you to unspoiled beaches, walking trails, sailing, fishing, and the delights of Martha's Vineyard. There's a three-night minimum stay required in season.

Captain Tom Lawrence House—1861 ✪
75 LOCUST STREET, FALMOUTH, MASSACHUSETTS 02540

Tel: **(508) 540-1445; 548-9178**
Best Time to Call: **8 AM till noon**
Host: **Barbara Sabo**
Location: **67 mi. S of Boston**
No. of Rooms: **6**
No. of Private Baths: **6**
Double/pb: **$65–$89**
Open: **All year**

Reduced Rates: **Off season**
Breakfast: **Full**
Credit Cards: **MC, VISA**
Pets: **No**
Children: **Welcome, over 11**
Smoking: **No**
Social Drinking: **Permitted**
Foreign Languages: **German**

Captain Lawrence was a successful whaler in the 1800s. When he retired from the sea, he built himself a town residence on Locust Street. Today, the house remains much as he left it, including the original hardwood floors, circular stairwell, high ceilings, and antique furnishings. In the morning, Barbara serves a hearty breakfast of fruit and creative entrées. Her Black Forest bread and Belgian waffles are truly special. She grinds her own flour from organically grown grain. She will gladly help you get around town—it's half a mile to the beach, a short walk to downtown Falmouth, and four miles to Woods Hole Seaport.

Mostly Hall B&B Inn ✪
27 MAIN STREET, FALMOUTH, MASSACHUSETTS 02540

Tel: **(508) 548-3786**
Best Time to Call: **10 AM–9 PM**
Hosts: **Caroline and Jim Lloyd**
Location: **73 mi. SE of Boston on Rte. 28**
No. of Rooms: **6**
No. of Private Baths: **6**
Double/pb: **$90–$100**
Single/pb: **$80**
Open: **Mid-Feb. through New Year's Day**
Reduced Rates: **20%, Nov. 1–Apr. 30**
Breakfast: **Full**
Pets: **No**
Children: **Welcome, over 16**
Smoking: **No**
Social Drinking: **Permitted**
Minimum Stay: **2 nights, May 1–Oct. 31**
Airport/Station Pickup: **Yes**
Foreign Languages: **German**

This B&B got its name when a young child walked through the front door, surveyed the atrium and staircases, and gasped, "It's mostly hall!" Built in 1849 by a sea captain who wanted to please his New Orleans–born bride, the house has a distinctly southern ambience, with its wide, wraparound porch, high ceilings, and garden gazebo. History buffs should note that the church in the Village Green has a bell cast by Paul Revere. Cyclists will want to borrow the inn's bicycles and follow the Shining Sea Bikeway that connects Falmouth to the Woods Hole ferry docks. Mostly Hall's breakfasts are sure to provide stamina: juice, fruit, and home-baked goods are always served, plus an entrée such as stuffed French toast or cheese blintz muffins.

Palmer House Inn ✪
81 PALMER AVENUE, FALMOUTH, MASSACHUSETTS 02540

Tel: **(508) 548-1230**
Best Time to Call: **After 2 PM**
Hosts: **Bud Peacock and Phyllis Niemi-Peacock**
Location: **1 block from Rte. 28**
No. of Rooms: **8**
No. of Private Baths: **8**
Double/pb: **$80–$95**
Single/pb: **$70–$85**
Open: **All year**
Reduced Rates: **Off season**
Breakfast: **Full**
Credit Cards: **MC, VISA**
Pets: **No**
Children: **Welcome, over 14**
Smoking: **Permitted**
Social Drinking: **Permitted**

Warmth and charm are evident in this turn-of-the-century Victorian home, with its stained-glass windows, soft warm wood, antiques, and collectibles. Centrally located within the Historic District, it is convenient to recreational diversions, miles of sandy beaches, ferries, and Woods Hole. Guests rave about breakfast entrées such as Pain Perdue with orange cream and Vermont maple syrup, Belgian waffles with honey butter, or Finnish pancakes and strawberry soup served in the dining room on fine linen, china, and crystal. Return from your afternoon activities and enjoy a glass of lemonade in a rocker on the front porch. Spend your after-dinner hours relaxing before the fireplace or sampling theater offerings close by.

A bedroom from the Palmer House is shown on the back cover.

Village Green Inn ✪
40 WEST MAIN STREET, FALMOUTH, MASSACHUSETTS 02540

Tel: **(508) 548-5621**
Hosts: **Linda and Don Long**
Location: **15 mi. S of Bourne Bridge**
No. of Rooms: **5**
No. of Private Baths: **5**
Double/pb: **$85**
Suites: **$100**
Open: **All year**

Reduced Rates: **20%, Nov. 1–**
 Memorial Day
Breakfast: **Full**
Pets: **No**
Children: **No**
Smoking: **No**
Social Drinking: **Permitted**
Airport/Station Pickup: **Yes**

This lovely Victorian is located on Falmouth's village green. Feel free to relax on the outdoor porch or in the parlor. Breakfast is a treat that includes hot, spiced fruit, eggs Mornay, homemade breads and muffins, and freshly ground coffee. Linda and Don look forward to pampering you with such delights as sherry, cordials, lemonade, fresh flowers, and sinfully delicious chocolates.

The Coach House ✪
74 SISSON ROAD, HARWICH PORT, MASSACHUSETTS 02646

Tel: (508) 432-9452	Open: May–Oct.
Hosts: Sara and Cal Ayer	Breakfast: Continental
Location: 1 mi. from Rtes. 39 and 124	Credit Cards: AMEX, MC, VISA
No. of Rooms: 2	Pets: No
No. of Private Baths: 2	Children: No
Double/pb: $65–$70	Smoking: Permitted
Single/pb: $65	Social Drinking: Permitted

Built in 1909, the Coach House was the original barn of one of Cape Cod's old estates. In the mid-1950s, the barn was fully converted into a lovely Cape Cod home. The rooms are quiet and elegant, and guests may choose from king- and queen-size beds. A breakfast of fresh fruit compote, home-baked muffins, coffee cake, or croissants is served in the dining room each morning. Enjoy three picturesque harbors, beautiful beaches, sailing, windsurfing, golf, and tennis. A 21-mile hard-surface bike trail will take you through the scenic woods and cranberry bogs to the National Seashore. Your hosts will gladly recommend shops, museums, fine restaurants, and summer theater.

Dunscroft by the Sea
24 PILGRIM ROAD, HARWICH PORT, MASSACHUSETTS 02646

Tel: (508) 432-0810	Open: All year
Best Time to Call: 7 AM–11 PM	Breakfast: Continental
Hosts: Alyce and Wally Cunningham	Credit Cards: AMEX, MC, VISA
Location: 80 mi. SE of Boston	Pets: No
No. of Rooms: 9	Children: Welcome, over 12; no age
No. of Private Baths: 9	restriction in cottage or suite
Double/pb: $80–$110	Smoking: Permitted
Guest Cottage: $90–$150	Social Drinking: Permitted
Suite: $85–$125; sleeps 5	

Its cedar shingles weathered a traditional waterfront grey, this Colonial inn offers everything you'd expect from a Cape Cod B&B: flower gardens, spacious grounds, an enclosed sun porch, a piano in the living room, and a private beach within 300 feet. Harwich Port's shops, galleries, theater, and restaurant are within easy walking distance. You'll awaken to the aroma of freshly ground coffee and home-baked breads, as Alyce prepares a large Continental breakfast.

The Inn on Bank Street ✪
88 BANK STREET, HARWICH PORT, MASSACHUSETTS 02646

Tel: (508) 432-3206	Location: 85 mi. S of Boston
Best Time to Call: 8 AM–10 PM	No. of Rooms: 6
Hosts: Arky and Janet Silverio	No. of Private Baths: 6

Double/pb: **$60–$80**
Single/pb: **$55–$75**
Open: **Apr. 1–Nov. 30**
Reduced Rates: **Available**
Breakfast: **Continental**
Credit Cards: **MC, VISA**

Pets: **No**
Children: **Welcome, over 7**
Smoking: **Permitted**
Social Drinking: **Permitted**
Airport/Station Pickup: **Yes**
Foreign Languages: **Italian, Spanish**

This contemporary, sprawling Cape is set in a quaint old town named after an English village. The main house has a large living room and library, with a fine selection of vacation reading. Guest rooms are decorated with comfortable country-style modern pieces. In the morning, breakfast is served on the sun porch or outdoors on the shady grounds where the roses grow wild. Specialties of the house include cranberry crisp, French toast, and fresh-baked breads. The ocean is a five-minute walk from the inn, and you can bike the paved trails for a closer look at Harwich Port. Restaurants, art galleries, and a movie theater are also within walking distance.

Barclay Inn ✪
40 GROVE STREET, SANDWICH, MASSACHUSETTS 02563

Tel: **(508) 888-5738**
Best Time to Call: **10 AM–8 PM**
Hosts: **Patricia and Gerald Barclay**
Location: **50 mi. S of Boston**
No. of Rooms: **3**
No. of Private Baths: **1**
Max. No. Sharing Bath: **4**
Double/pb: **$75**
Single/pb: **$60**
Double/sb: **$55**

Single/sb: **$45**
Guest Cottage: **$425/week**
Open: **All year**
Breakfast: **Continental**
Pets: **No**
Children: **No**
Smoking: **No**
Social Drinking: **Permitted**
Minimum Stay: **1 week for cottage**
Airport/Station Pickup: **Yes**

Located near the center of Sandwich, Cape Cod's oldest town, this bed-and-breakfast makes an ideal home base whether you plan to hunt for antiques or just work on a tan. Local museums house everything from hand-blown glass to military artifacts, and the beach is only a few minutes away. Barclay Inn has two guest rooms; those desiring extra privacy may prefer to stay at the Kelman House, a one-bedroom cottage overlooking Peter's Pond. Whichever you choose, you'll savor continental breakfasts that include glazed orange rolls, coffee cake, and raspberry cream cheese.

Dillingham House ✪
71 MAIN STREET, SANDWICH, MASSACHUSETTS 02563

Tel: **(508) 833-0065**	Reduced Rates: **$20 less, Nov.–Mar.;**
Best Time to Call: **6–8 PM**	**$10 less, Apr., May, Oct.**
Hosts: **Kathleen Kenney, Ed Mattson**	Breakfast: **Continental**
Location: **60 mi. S of Boston**	Pets: **Sometimes**
No. of Rooms: **3**	Children: **Welcome**
No. of Private Baths: **3**	Smoking: **Permitted**
Double/pb: **$75**	Social Drinking: **Permitted**
Open: **All year**	Minimum Stay: **2 nights in off-season**

Dillingham House is named for its first owner, who helped to found Sandwich, Cape Cod's oldest town. The house has many of the hallmarks of 17th-century construction, such as wide pine floors, exposed beams and rafters, and cozy brick hearths. Kathy is a Cape native and loves to discuss local lore. Your hosts charter sailing trips and lend bicycles to landlubbers. A continental breakfast of juice, fresh fruit, muffins, and coffee or tea will fortify you for your excursions, whether they occur on land or on sea.

Hawthorn Hill ✪
P.O. BOX 777, SANDWICH, MASSACHUSETTS 02563

Tel: **(508) 888-3333 or 888-3336**	Breakfast: **Continental**
Best Time to Call: **Evenings**	Pets: **Sometimes**
Host: **Maxime Caron**	Children: **Sometimes**
Location: **60 mi. S of Boston**	Smoking: **Permitted**
No. of Rooms: **2**	Social Drinking: **Permitted**
No. of Private Baths: **2**	Airport/Station Pickup: **Yes**
Double/pb: **$65–$70**	Foreign Languages: **German**
Open: **May–Nov.**	

This rambling English country house, off Grove Street, is set on a hill surrounded by trees, with both the conveniences of an in-town location and the pleasantness of a country setting. The property has a spring-fed pond for boating and swimming, and there is plenty of space for long walks through the woods. Inside, your hosts welcome you to large, sunny rooms, comfortably furnished. Hawthorn Hill is close to beaches, fishing, museums, and shops, and is adjacent to the Heritage Plantation. Maxime will gladly help plan sightseeing in this historic town or day trips to many nearby points of interest.

Country Pineapple Inn ✪
370 MAIN STREET, SOUTH DENNIS, MASSACHUSETTS 02660

Tel: (508) 760-3211	Reduced Rates: $10 less Nov. 1–Apr.
Host: Barbara Olsen	31; 10%, weekly
Location: 1 mi. off Rte. 6, Exit 9	Breakfast: Continental
No. of Rooms: 4	Pets: No
No. of Private Baths: 2	Children: Welcome, over 10
Max. No. Sharing Bath: 4	Smoking: No
Double/pb: $60–$75	Social Drinking: Permitted
Double/sb: $50–$60	Airport/Station Pickup: Yes
Open: Mar. 1–Dec. 31	

A Greek Revival house dating to the mid-19th century, the Country Pineapple Inn is decorated in period style, from the casual white wicker furniture and floral bed linens of the Ashley room, to the antique Oriental rug and crewel wing chair of the more stately Wedgewood room. This B&B is an ideal home base for vacationers eager to explore the beaches, restaurants, and historic homes of Cape Cod. Breakfasts—consisting of juice, fruit, cold cereal, freshly baked muffins, and coffee or tea—are served in the country keeping room, which has stenciled walls, polished pine floors, lavish woodwork, and exposed beams. Weather permitting, guests may dine on the terrace overlooking the inn's old-fashioned gardens.

Little Harbor Guest House ✪
20 STOCKTON SHORTCUT, WAREHAM, MASSACHUSETTS 02571

Tel: (508) 295-6329	Open: All year
Hosts: Dennis and Ken	Reduced Rates: 20%, Nov. 1–May 1
Location: 20 mi. S of Plymouth	Breakfast: Continental
No. of Rooms: 5	Pets: No
Max. No. Sharing Bath: 4	Children: Welcome
Double/sb: $65	Smoking: Permitted
Single/sb: $65	Social Drinking: Permitted

The Little Harbor Guest House is set on three acres surrounded by a lovely 18-hole golf course. The house is a rambling Cape Cod, dating back to 1703. The large, sunny rooms are comfortable and quiet, furnished in antiques, wicker, and a lot of plants. Dennis and Ken prepare a lovely breakfast, featuring many types of homemade breads. They have bicycles to lend, a pool, and will gladly give directions to local attractions. The beach is less than a half mile away, and it's just 20 minutes to Plymouth and Hyannis.

Mulberry Bed and Breakfast ✪
257 HIGH STREET, WAREHAM, MASSACHUSETTS 02571

Tel: **(508) 295-0684**	Reduced Rates: **15%, weekly**
Host: **Frances Murphy**	Breakfast: **Continental**
Location: **52 mi. S of Boston**	Pets: **No**
No. of Rooms: **3**	Children: **Welcome, over 10**
Max. No. Sharing Bath: **4**	Smoking: **No**
Double/sb: **$42–$50**	Social Drinking: **Permitted**
Open: **All year**	Airport/Station Pickup: **Yes**

Frances Murphy welcomes you to her vintage Cape Cod home, built in 1847. The house is one and a half stories and is painted white with red shutters. It is named for the mulberry tree in the yard that attracts many birds and provides shade from the summer sun. Frances has created a home-away-from-home atmosphere, where guests can relax in a small living room with a piano, or join her in a larger living-dining area with fireplace. Spend the night in an Early American–style bedroom and have breakfast on the spacious private deck. Home-baked breads and muffins, casseroles, and fresh fruit are served with jams and jellies made from Frances's fruit trees. In the afternoon, snacks and cool drinks are served. Mulberry Bed and Breakfast is located in the historic part of town, ten minutes from the beach.

The Marlborough ✪
320 WOODS HOLE ROAD, WOODS HOLE, MASSACHUSETTS 02543

Tel: **(508) 548-6218**	Open: **All year**
Best Time to Call: **3–9 PM**	Reduced Rates: **$65 Nov. 1–Apr. 1**
Host: **Patricia Morris**	Breakfast: **Full**
Location: **2½ mi. from Rte. 28**	Pets: **No**
No. of Rooms: **6**	Children: **Welcome, over 2**
No. of Private Baths: **6**	Smoking: **No**
Double/pb: **$85–$95**	Social Drinking: **Permitted**
Single/pb: **$80–$90**	

This faithful reproduction of a full Cape house is beautifully decorated with antiques, collectibles, fabric wall coverings, and matching bed linens. It is situated on a shaded half-acre with a paddle tennis court, swimming pool, hammock, and swing. It's a short stroll to a private beach, where a lifeguard is on duty. Ferries to Martha's Vineyard and Nantucket are a mile away. Pat serves a full, gourmet breakfast year round. Teatime and hospitality hours, 3–5 PM daily. She is an antiques buff and maintains a lovely shop on the premises. Ask about her Art-Antique Auction winter weekend packages.

Liberty Hill Inn ✪
77 MAIN STREET, YARMOUTH PORT, MASSACHUSETTS 02675

Tel: **(508) 362-3976**	Reduced Rates: **$10 less May 30–June**
Best Time to Call: **8 AM–9 PM**	**29, Sept. 5–Oct. 31; 5-night stays**
Hosts: **Jack and Beth Flanagan**	Breakfast: **Full**
Location: **1 mi. off Rte. 6, Exit 7**	Other Meals: **Available**
No. of Rooms: **5**	Credit Cards: **MC, VISA**
No. of Private Baths: **5**	Pets: **No**
Double/pb: **$85**	Children: **Welcome, over 16**
Single/pb: **$65**	Smoking: **Permitted**
Bridal Suite: **$95**	Social Drinking: **Permitted**
Open: **All year**	Airport/Station Pickup: **Yes**

This gracious house sits on a small knoll just a stone's throw away from historic Old Kings Highway. A Greek Revival mansion built by a whaling tycoon in 1825, the inn is listed on the National Register of Historic Places. The interior is richly furnished in Queen Anne style, and each guest room has its own distinctive ambience. As devotees of local history, your hosts can add extra destinations and activities to your itinerary. Breakfasts begin with juice, fresh fruit, home-baked bread, and cheese, followed by French toast, quiche, or the Flanagan's specialty, Irish apple pastry. While outstanding restaurants are within walking distance, fine dinners are served here, by reservation only.

CENTRAL/WESTERN/SOUTHERN MASSACHUSETTS

Emma C's B&B ✪
18 FRENCH FARM ROAD, ATTLEBORO, MASSACHUSETTS 02703

Tel: **(508) 226-6365**	Single/pb: **$50–$60**
Best Time to Call: **9 AM–9 PM**	Open: **All year**
Hosts: **Caroline and Jim Logie**	Reduced Rates: **7th night free; 10%,**
Location: **10 mi. N of Providence, R.I.**	**families and seniors**
No. of Rooms: **3**	Breakfast: **Full**
No. of Private Baths: **1**	Pets: **Sometimes**
Max. No. Sharing Bath: **4**	Children: **Welcome (crib)**
Double/sb: **$55–$65**	Smoking: **No**
Single/sb: **$45–$55**	Social Drinking: **Permitted**
Double/pb: **$60–$70**	Airport/Station Pickup: **Yes**

Folk art, decorative stencils, antique four-poster beds, and handmade quilts make this country Colonial home a warm and friendly place. Your hosts enjoy discussing their world travels with guests. Caroline's well-balanced breakfasts include her own granola, home-baked muffins, fresh fruit, and freshly ground coffee. It's only 45 minutes to Boston or Cape Cod.

1797 House ✪
1797 UPPER STREET, BUCKLAND, MASSACHUSETTS 01338

Tel: (413) 625-2975; 625-2697	Single/pb: $55
Best Time to Call: Evenings; weekends	Open: Jan. 2–Oct. 31
Host: Janet Turley	Breakfast: Full
Location: 13 mi. from Rte. 91, Exit 26	Pets: No
No. of Rooms: 3	Children: No
No. of Private Baths: 3	Smoking: Permitted
Double/pb: $65	Social Drinking: Permitted

This white, center-hall Colonial (circa 1797) has a lovely screened-in porch for summer enjoyment and four fireplaces and down quilts for cozy winter pleasure. Prestigious Deerfield Academy, Old Deerfield, Sturbridge Village, and the historic sights of Pioneer Valley are all close by. The University of Massachusetts, Smith, Amherst, and Williams are convenient to Janet's home. Sensational breakfast treats include stuffed croissants, mushroom pâté, and special casseroles, along with fresh fruit and breakfast meats.

Garden Gables Inn ✪
141 MAIN STREET, LENOX, MASSACHUSETTS 01240

Tel: (413) 637-0193	Breakfast: Continental
Hosts: Lynn and Mario Mekinda	Credit Cards: MC, VISA
Location: 10 mi. off Mass Pike, Exit 2	Pets: No
No. of Rooms: 11	Children: Welcome, over 12
No. of Private Baths: 11	Smoking: Permitted
Double/pb: $55–$130	Social Drinking: Permitted
Single/pb: $50–$125	Minimum Stay: 3 nights during
Open: All year	weekends in July and Aug., and
Reduced Rates: 10%, weekly;	holidays
midweek; off-season	Airport/Station Pickup: Yes

Built in 1790 and expanded a little more than a century later, this white clapboard house has dark green shutters and, true to its name, a gambrel roof with three gables. Inside, the antique furniture and floral wallpapers are reminiscent of an earlier era, but there is nothing old-fashioned about the inviting 72-foot swimming pool in the backyard. The Berkshires in summertime are rich in cultural activities, with music at Tanglewood, dance at Jacob's Pillow, and at the Williamstown Theatre Festival. Winter visitors can choose between the area's downhill ski slopes and cross-country trails; spring through fall, Lenox's stables cater to the horsey set. Plan your day over a buffet-style continental breakfast of fresh fruit and berries, homemade bran and blueberry muffins, cereals, crumb cakes, and low-fat yogurts.

Chalet d'Alicia ✪
EAST WINDSOR ROAD, PERU, MASSACHUSETTS 01235

Tel: (413) 655-8292	Open: All year
Hosts: Alice and Richard Halvorsen	Breakfast: Full
Location: 15 mi. E of Pittsfield	Pets: Sometimes
No. of Rooms: 3	Children: Welcome
Max. No. Sharing Bath: 4	Smoking: Permitted
Double/sb: $45	Social Drinking: Permitted

Chalet d'Alicia is set high in the Berkshire Mountains overlooking the majestic countryside. This Swiss chalet–style home offers a private, casual atmosphere. The large front deck is a perfect spot for reading, sunning, or chatting. Alice and Richard are proud to make everyone feel at home. For breakfast they serve homemade muffins, and jams made from local wild berries. The property has a pond and plenty of places for cross-country skiing. Tanglewood, Jacob's Pillow, and the Williamstown Theatre Festival are all within easy reach.

Perryville Inn ✪
157 PERRYVILLE ROAD, REHOBOTH, MASSACHUSETTS 02769

Tel: (508) 252-9239	Double/sb: $40–$50
Best Time to Call: 8 AM–10 PM	Open: All year
Hosts: Tom and Betsy Charnecki	Breakfast: Continental
Location: 8 mi. E of Providence, R.I.	Credit Cards: AMEX, MC, VISA
No. of Rooms: 5	Pets: Sometimes
No. of Private Baths: 3	Children: Welcome
Max. No. Sharing Bath: 4	Smoking: Permitted
Double/pb: $55–$75	Social Drinking: Permitted

This 19th-century restored Victorian, listed on the National Register of Historic Places, is located on four and a half acres, featuring a quiet brook, stone walls, and shaded paths. You are welcome to use your hosts' bikes for local touring. There's a public golf course across the road. It's a short drive to antique shops, museums, and fine seafood restaurants. Don't miss a traditional New England clambake. All rooms are furnished with antiques and accented with colorful, hand-made quilts. Brown University, Wheaton College, and the Rhode Island School of Design are within a 10-mile radius of the inn.

Glen Cara—An Irish B&B ✪
P.O. BOX 1112, STERLING, MASSACHUSETTS 01564

Tel: (508) 422-6678	Location: 50 mi. W of Boston
Best Time to Call: 8 AM–Noon	No. of Rooms: 2
Host: Rita O'Brien	Max. No. Sharing Bath: 4

Open: **All year**	Children: **Welcome, over 10**
Breakfast: **Continental**	Smoking: **No**
Pets: **Sometimes**	Social Drinking: **Permitted**
Double/sb: **$65**	Airport/Station Pickup: **Yes**
Single/sb: **$60**	Foreign Languages: **French**

Rita has brought a touch of Erin to her spanking clean B&B. Located on a small, two-acre glen, it is contemporary in style and accented with Irish arts and crafts, lace curtains, and charming prints. Irish soda bread made from an old family recipe is a breakfast treat. A brook for fishing and an above-ground swimming pool are pleasant diversions; fine horseback riding and cross-country ski trails are nearby. It's 10 minutes to the Mt. Wachusett Ski Area and the Wachusett Meadow Bird Sanctuary; Sturbridge Village and the Worcester Centrum are less than an hour's drive. Closer by are 15 antique shops in an 8-mile radius.

Lakeshore Bed and Breakfast ❂
94 SOUTH SHORE DRIVE, STURBRIDGE, MASSACHUSETTS 01566

Tel: **(508) 347-9495**	Open: **May 1–Oct. 31**
Hosts: **Paul and Jeannette Baillargeon**	Breakfast: **Full**
Location: **50 mi. W of Boston**	Pets: **No**
No. of Rooms: **3**	Children: **Welcome**
Max. No. Sharing Bath: **3**	Smoking: **Permitted**
Double/sb: **$50**	Social Drinking: **Permitted**
Single/sb: **$45**	Foreign Languages: **French**

This lakeside contemporary is on one of Massachusetts's cleanest lakes, Quacumquasit. Enjoy fishing, boating, swimming, sunbathing, and beautiful sunsets on a private beach, just steps from your room. A hearty breakfast is served on the terrace each morning. In the evening, you are welcome to use the grill and picnic tables for a barbecue. Lakeshore is four miles from Old Sturbridge Village and shopping areas. Your hosts are happy to help make sightseeing plans for you.

The Golden Goose ❂
MAIN ROAD, BOX 336, TYRINGHAM, MASSACHUSETTS 01264

Tel: **(413) 243-3008**	Double/pb: **$70–$95**
Best Time to Call: **8 AM–8 PM**	Single/pb: **$65–$90**
Hosts: **Lilja and Joseph Rizzo**	Double/sb: **$60–$70**
Location: **4 mi. from Mass. Tpk., Exit 2-Lee**	Single/sb: **$55–$65**
	Suites: **$95–$110**
No. of Rooms: **7**	Open: **All year**
No. of Private Baths: **5**	Reduced Rates: **Available**
Max. No. Sharing Bath: **4**	Breakfast: **Continental**

Pets: **No**
Children: **Welcome in apt. suite**
Smoking: **Permitted**
Social Drinking: **Permitted**

Minimum Stay: **2 nights during Tanglewood season; 3 nights holiday weekends**

The inn lies between Stockbridge and Lenox in the Berkshires. Antique beds with firm new mattresses, and washstands, are in each bedroom. Lilja and Joseph serve hors d'oeuvres and drinks by the fireside in the two common rooms. In warm weather, you may play croquet, volleyball, badminton, hike the Appalachian Trail, or fish for trout in the brook across the street and barbecue it at "home." In summer, the cultural attractions of Tanglewood and Jacob's Pillow are nearby. Skiing is popular in winter. A $5 surcharge is added for one-night stays.

The Wildwood Inn ✪
121 CHURCH STREET, WARE, MASSACHUSETTS 01082

Tel: **(413) 967-7798**
Best Time to Call: **5–8 PM**
Host: **Fraidell Fenster**
Location: **70 mi. W of Boston**
No. of Rooms: **5**
Max. No. Sharing Bath: **3**
Double/sb: **$38–$69**

Open: **All year**
Reduced Rates: **10%, weekly**
Breakfast: **Full**
Pets: **No**
Children: **Welcome, over 6**
Smoking: **No**
Social Drinking: **Permitted**

Everything about this old-fashioned country home, with its rambling two acres, is designed to help you unwind. There's a swing on the porch, a hammock under the firs, a blazing fire in the winter, a Norman Rockwell–esque brook-fed swimming hole in the summer. Your host has furnished her guest rooms with heirloom quilts and American primitive antiques, all of which work to spell welcome. Homemade bread and Wildwood's own peach butter and "country yummies" are included with breakfast. Sturbridge Village, Old Deerfield, and Amherst offer recreational activities that are all close by. You can stroll to the tennis court or borrow the canoe, or visit in the parlor for stimulating conversation. Fraidell does her best to spoil you.

NANTUCKET

Lynda Watts Bed & Breakfast ✪
10 UPPER VESTAL STREET, NANTUCKET, MASSACHUSETTS 02554

Tel: **(617) 228-3828**
Hosts: **Lynda and David Watts**
No. of Rooms: **2**
Max. No. Sharing Bath: **4**
Double/sb: **$60**

Open: **All year**
Reduced Rates: **20%, Jan. 1–Apr. 15**
Breakfast: **Continental**
Pets: **No**
Children: **Welcome**

Smoking: **Permitted**   Minimum Stay: **2 nights**
Social Drinking: **Permitted**

Lynda and David's 12-year-old saltbox house is located on a quiet street in a residential neighborhood, only a seven-minute walk to town. It is simply furnished and guest rooms are equipped with TVs. Weather permitting, breakfast is served on the sunny patio.

Seven Sea Street Inn
7 SEA STREET, NANTUCKET, MASSACHUSETTS 02554

Tel: **(508) 228-3577**
Hosts: **Matthew and Mary Parker**
No. of Rooms: **8**
No. of Private Baths: **8**
Double/pb: **$85–$155**
Handicapped Accessible: **4 rooms**
Open: **All year**
Reduced Rates: **Oct.–June**
Breakfast: **Continental**

Credit Cards: **MC, VISA**
Pets: **No**
Children: **Welcome, over 7**
Smoking: **No**
Social Drinking: **Permitted**
Minimum Stay: **2 nights, weekends, May–Oct.**
Airport/Station Pickup: **Yes**
Foreign Languages: **French**

This romantic red-oak post-and-beam country inn is located on a quiet side street in the town's historic district. Each bedroom is decorated with colonial-style furniture, fishnet canopy beds, handmade quilts, and braided rugs covering wide-plank pine floors. A small refrigerator and cable TV will please those who like to snack and view in private. Don't miss the spectacular sunset from the widow's walk overlooking the harbor and do take some time to relax in the Jacuzzi whirlpool. After a good night's sleep, you may have breakfast served to you in bed.

MICHIGAN

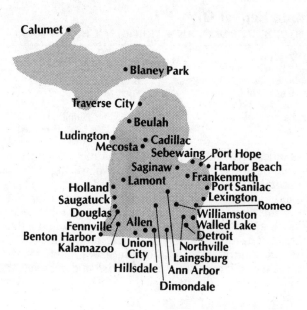

Calumet •

• Blaney Park

Traverse City •

• Beulah

Ludington •
Mecosta • • Cadillac
Sebewaing • Port Hope
Saginaw • • • Harbor Beach
• Lamont • Frankenmuth
Holland • • Port Sanilac
Saugatuck • • Lexington
Douglas • Romeo
Fennville • Allen • Williamston
Benton Harbor • • Walled Lake
Kalamazoo Union • Detroit
City Northville
Laingsburg
Hillsdale | Ann Arbor
Dimondale

The Olde Bricke House ✪
P.O. BOX 211, ALLEN, MICHIGAN 49227

Tel: (517) 869-2349
Hosts: **Erma and Al Jones**
Location: **On Rte. 12**
No. of Rooms: **4**
Max. No. Sharing Bath: **4**
Double/sb: **$50**
Single/sb: **$40**
Open: **Mar. 1–Dec. 15**
Reduced Rates: **10% Sun.–Thurs.**

Breakfast: **Continental**
Credit Cards: **MC, VISA**
Pets: **No**
Children: **Welcome, over 13**
Smoking: **Permitted**
Social Drinking: **Permitted**
Minimum Stay: **2 nights during
Hillsdale College special weekends
(Homecoming, Parents' Weekends,
Graduation)**

This Victorian house, built in 1873, was recently renovated by Erma
and Al, whose humor and eclectic tastes are reflected in its decor. If
you are an antiques buff, spend the day browsing the fabulous shops

(75 at last count) that have made Allen the Antiques Capital of Michigan. Several lakes for boating, swimming, and fishing are nearby, and Hillsdale College is 10 miles away. You are welcome to join your hosts for afternoon refreshments on the porch or in the library or living room.

The Urban Retreat ✪
2759 CANTERBURY ROAD, ANN ARBOR, MICHIGAN 48104

Tel: (313) 971-8110	Single/sb: $40
Best Time to Call: 5–10 PM	Open: All year
Hosts: Andre Rosalik and Gloria Krys	Breakfast: Full
Location: 40 mi. W of Detroit	Pets: No
No. of Rooms: 2	Children: No
Max. No. Sharing Bath: 4	Smoking: Permitted
Double/sb: $50	Social Drinking: Permitted

This 1950s ranch-style house is located on a quiet, tree-lined street, 10 minutes from downtown and the University of Michigan campus. The home is decorated with antiques and collectibles from the early 1900s, with an abundance of birdseye maple furniture. Adjacent to the property is the County Farm Park, 127 acres of meadowland with walking and jogging paths and a 13-box bluebird trail. The Retreat has been designated as a Backyard Wildlife Habitat by the National Wildlife Federation. Andre and Gloria emphasize a quiet, relaxed atmosphere and assure their guests a peaceful visit and personal attention.

Bolins' Bed & Breakfast ✪
576 COLFAX AVENUE, BENTON HARBOR, MICHIGAN 49022

Tel: (616) 925-9068	Single/sb: $20
Hosts: Marilyn and Arnie Bolin	Open: All year
Location: 3 mi. From I-94, Exit 28	Breakfast: Full
No. of Rooms: 4	Pets: Sometimes
No. of Private Baths: 1	Children: Welcome (crib)
Max. No. Sharing Bath: 4	Smoking: No
Double/pb: $30	Social Drinking: No
Single/pb: $27	Airport/Station Pickup: Yes
Double/sb: $25	

Just an hour from Kalamazoo, this English Tudor–style home is conveniently located for the vacationer or business traveler. The atmosphere is relaxed and homey; the cozy living room and spacious backyard are ideal for relaxing while the beaches of southwestern Michigan are close by. Annual events include a Blossom-time Festival, Apple Cider Century Bike Tour, county fairs, and even an International Cherry Pit Spitting Championship! Marilyn and Arnie delight in having guests, and promise a pleasant stay.

Windermere Inn ✪
747 CRYSTAL DRIVE, BEULAH, MICHIGAN, 49617

Tel: **(616) 882-7264**
Best Time to call: **9 AM–6 PM**
Hosts: **Lionel and Josephine Hampton**
Location: **200 mi. NW of Detroit**
No. of Rooms: **4**
No. of Private Baths: **4**
Double/pb: **$70**
Open: **All year**

Reduced Rates: **10%, weekly**
Breakfast: **Continental**
Credit Cards: **MC, VISA**
Pets: **No**
Children: **Sometimes**
Smoking: **No**
Social Drinking: **Permitted**

Set among century-old pine trees, this late 1800s farmhouse is delightfully decorated with a country decor and a collection of dolls and teddy bears. There's a fine view of Crystal Lake, and you're close to Sleeping Bear Dunes National Lakeshore and Interlochen Arts Academy. Recreational activities are plentiful in all seasons. Refreshments are always available.

Celibeth House
ROUTE 1, BOX 58A, M-77 BLANEY PARK ROAD, BLANEY PARK, MICHIGAN 49836

Tel: **(906) 283-3409**
Host: **Elsa Strom**
Location: **60 mi. W of MacKinaw Bridge**
No. of Rooms: **8**
No. of Private Baths: **8**
Double/pb: **$35–$50**
Single/pb: **$35–$40**

Open: **May 1–Dec. 1**
Reduced Rates: **10% less on 3rd night**
Breakfast: **Continental**
Credit Cards: **MC, VISA**
Pets: **No**
Children: **Welcome**
Smoking: **Permitted**
Social Drinking: **No**

Located on Michigan's upper peninsula, this large 20-room mansion, built in 1890, overlooks a lake. Elsa enjoys traveling and collecting antiques. She has done a lovely job of decorating the house with special mementos. A retired personnel manager, she thoroughly enjoys visiting with her guests. Gardening and reading are her pleasures.

Essenmachers Bed & Breakfast ✪
204 LOCUST LANE, CADILLAC, MICHIGAN 49601

Tel: **(616) 775-3828**
Best Time to Call: **Evenings; weekends**
Hosts: **Doug and Vickie Essenmacher**
Location: **1 block from Rte. M55**
No. of Rooms: **2**
No. of Private Baths: **2**
Double/pb: **$55**

Open: **All year**
Breakfast: **Continental**
Credit Cards: **MC, VISA**
Pets: **No**
Children: **Welcome**
Smoking: **No**
Social Drinking: **No**

Large windows of this modern home take in the vista of Lake Mitchell, while the lakeside guest rooms are just steps away from year-round activities. Swim, feed the ducks, fish, boat, and toast marshmallows at an evening bonfire. In winter, enjoy the miles of cross-country and snowmobile trails in nearby Manistee National Forest, or go downhill skiing, just minutes away, then relax with the family in front of a crackling fire on chilly evenings. Coffee and cold drinks are always available.

Calumet House ✪
1159 CALUMET AVENUE, P.O. BOX 126, CALUMET, MICHIGAN 49913

Tel: **(906) 337-1936**	Open: **All year**
Hosts: **George and Rose Chivses**	Breakfast: **Full**
Location: **10 mi. N of Hancock-Houghton**	Pets: **No**
No. of Rooms: **2**	Children: **No**
Max. No. Sharing Bath: **4**	Smoking: **No**
Double/sb: **$25**	Social Drinking: **Permitted**
Single/sb: **$21**	Airport/Station Pickup: **Yes**
	Foreign Languages: **Finnish**

The Calumet House is set in a historic old mining town, known for its clean air and scenic vistas. Built in 1895, the house boasts its original woodwork and is filled with local antique furnishings. In the morning, you're in for a treat with Rose's home cooking. Breakfast specialties include English scones, pancakes, local berries in season, and home-made jam. Calumet House is within walking distance of the village, with its opera house, museum, and antique shops. Your hosts will also direct you to local hunting and fishing, as well as to places that any botanist would call paradise. It's 10 miles north of Michigan Technological University and Suomi College

Bannicks B&B ✪
4608 MICHIGAN ROAD, M99, DIMONDALE, MICHIGAN 48821

Tel: **(517) 646-0224**	Open: **All year**
Hosts: **Pat and Jim Bannick**	Breakfast: **Full**
Location: **5 mi. SW of Lansing**	Pets: **No**
No. of Rooms: **2**	Children: **Welcome**
Max. No. Sharing Bath: **3**	Smoking: **No**
Double/sb: **$30**	Social Drinking: **No**
Single/sb: **$20**	

This large ranch-style home features a stained-glass entry, nautical-style basement, and a Mona Lisa bathroom. Guest accommodations consist of comfortable bedrooms and a den-TV room. Your hosts invite you to share a cup of coffee anytime. They will be happy to advise on the sights of Michigan's capital city, just five minutes away. Michigan State University is eight miles away.

Rosemont Inn

83 LAKESHORE DRIVE, P.O. BOX 857, DOUGLAS, MICHIGAN 49406

Tel: **(616) 857-2637**
Best Time to Call: **8 AM–8 PM**
Hosts: **Mike and Shelly Sajdak**
Location: **10 mi. S of Holland**
No. of Rooms: **14**
No. of Private Baths: **14**
Double/pb: **$85**

Open: **All year**
Breakfast: **Continental**
Credit Cards: **MC, VISA**
Pets: **No**
Children: **Welcome**
Smoking: **Permitted**
Social Drinking: **Permitted**

The Rosemont is a Victorian inn with gingerbread trim. It began receiving guests in 1886, and still maintains a tradition of country living and hospitality. The air-conditioned house is furnished in country prints and antique reproductions, with fireplaces in nine of the guest rooms. On a large porch, enjoy the cool breezes from Lake Michigan, whose beaches are directly across the street. Or swim in the inn's heated pool. Your hosts will gladly supply information on boat trips, golf, and the sights of Saugatuck. Ten of the 14 bedrooms are nonsmoking areas.

Hidden Pond Farm ✪

5975 128TH AVENUE, FENNVILLE, MICHIGAN 49408

Tel: **(616) 561-2491**
Host: **Edward X. Kennedy**
Location: **40 mi. SW of Grand Rapids**
No. of Rooms: **2**
No. of Private Baths: **2**
Double/pb: **$80–$100**
Open: **All year**

Reduced Rates: **Sun.–Thurs.**
Breakfast: **Full**
Pets: **No**
Children: **Welcome, over 12**
Smoking: **Permitted**
Social Drinking: **Permitted**
Airport/Station Pickup: **Yes**

Hidden Pond Farm is set on 28 acres of woods, perfect for birdwatching, hiking, and cross-country skiing. Your host designed the sprawling, 13-room house to provide for the privacy and relaxation of visitors. Seven rooms on the entry level are for the exclusive use of guests, and include the bedrooms and baths, a living room with fireplace, dining room, den, kitchen, and breakfast porch. Edward Kennedy is a retired insurance executive who enjoys pleasing guests and creating an atmosphere of quiet elegance. There are no schedules, and breakfast is served when you wake up. Behind the house is a ravine with a pond, where you might see a deer or two. An outdoor deck and patio are available for relaxing and taking in the sun. This lovely retreat is near the beaches on Lake Michigan, the boutiques of Saugatuck, and the winery and cider mill in Fennville.

The Kingsley House ✪
626 WEST MAIN STREET, FENNVILLE, MICHIGAN 49408

Tel: (616) 561-6425
Hosts: **David and Shirley Witt**
Location: **6 mi. SE of Saugatuck**
No. of Rooms: **5**
No. of Private Baths: **5**
Double/pb: **$65**
Open: **All year**
Reduced Rates: **10% less after 4 nights; 10%, seniors**

Breakfast: **Full**
Pets: **No**
Children: **Welcome, over 3**
Smoking: **No**
Social Drinking: **Permitted**
Airport/Station Pickup: **Yes**
Foreign Languages: **Dutch, Friesian**

Just 10 minutes south of Holland, and surrounded by 90 acres, this 1886 white clapboard house has a red tile roof and 3-story-high turret. A spacious home, it is entirely decorated with Victorian antiques. Breakfast, a bountiful feast, is served in the formal dining room. A backyard picnic area for hotdog and marshmallow roasts, a tree swing, bicycles, and a porch overlooking the Allegan National Forest are all guest favorites. Dutch Village, Tulip Gardens, Windmill Island, marinas, museums, shops, and fine dining are all nearby.

Frankenmuth Bed & Breakfast Reservations ✪
337 TRINKLEIN STREET, FRANKENMUTH, MICHIGAN 48734

Tel: (517) 652-8897
Coordinator: **Beverley J. Bender**
States/Regions Covered: **Bay City, Bridgeport, Frankenmuth, Harbor Beach, Trenton**

Rates (Single/Double);		
Modest:	N/A	$40–$50
Average:	N/A	$45–$59
Luxury:	N/A	$50–$89
Credit Cards: **AMEX, MC, VISA**		

Dating back to the mid-1800s, this area has a distinctive German flavor. There's a Bavarian Festival in June, Volkslaufe races in July, a Polka Festival in August, an Oktoberfest, and a shopping spree in any season at Bronners Christmas Wonderland. To assure that you feel more like a friend than a paying guest, you will receive the name and address of your host after first meeting Beverley. Instead of paying the host, payment is made directly to the reservation service. She usually escorts you to the B&B personally to make the introductions.

Wellock Inn ✪
404 SOUTH HURON AVENUE, HARBOR BEACH, MICHIGAN 48441

Tel: (517) 479-3645
Hosts: **Bill and Lavonne Cloutier**
Location: **125 mi. N of Detroit**
No. of Rooms: **4**
No. of Private Baths: **2**

Max. No. Sharing Bath: **4**
Double/pb: **$45**
Double/sb: **$40**
Open: **All year**
Reduced Rates: **Weekly; seniors**

Credit Cards: **MC, VISA**
Breakfast: **Continental**
Pets: **Welcome**
Children: **Welcome**

Smoking: **Permitted**
Social Drinking: **Permitted**
Airport/Station Pickup: **Local marina**

Beautiful oak woodwork, antique furnishings, and the artful use of beveled glass add to the charm of Lavonne and Bill's gracious home. You may enjoy breakfast in the privacy of your room or with the other guests in the dining room. Afterward, stroll to the nearby beach, browse through local shops or historic sites, fish from the breakwall, launch your boat, or play tennis or have a picnic in the park. Or, just relax at the inn and feel free to use the kitchen, living room, porch, laundry facilities, picnic table, and barbecue.

Shadowlawn Manor ✪
84 UNION STREET, HILLSDALE, MICHIGAN 49242

Tel: **(517) 437-2367**
Hosts: **Art Young and Al Paskevich**
Location: **90 mi. SW of Detroit**
No. of Rooms: **5**
No. of Private Baths: **1**
Max. No. Sharing Bath: **4**
Double/pb: **$60**
Double/sb: **$50**
Single/sb: **$40**
Open: **All year**

Reduced Rates: **10%, Jan., Feb., Dec.;**
 weekly; 10%, seniors
Credit Cards: **MC, VISA**
Breakfast: **Continental**
Pets: **No**
Children: **No**
Smoking: **No**
Social Drinking: **Permitted**
Airport/Station Pickup: **Yes**

Built in 1860, Shadowlawn Manor has been restored and refurbished with your comfort in mind. Art and Al have been collecting furniture, silverware, crystal, and antique accessories for years, and they have used it all to great advantage at Shadowlawn. They will be happy to direct you to the lake, beach, golf course, or Hillsdale College's arboretum. You are welcome to relax on the screened-in porch, where, in springtime, the lilacs perfume the air.

Dutch Colonial Inn ✪
560 CENTRAL AVENUE, HOLLAND, MICHIGAN 49423

Tel: **(616) 396-3664**
Best Time to Call: **After 5 PM**
Hosts: **Bob and Pat Elenbaas**
Location: **30 mi. W of Grand Rapids**
No. of Rooms: **5**
Max. No. Sharing Bath: **5**
Double/sb: **$40–$60**

Open: **All year**
Breakfast: **Full**
Pets: **No**
Children: **Welcome, over 10**
Smoking: **No**
Social Drinking: **No**
Airport/Station Pickup: **Yes**

Bob and Pat Elenbaas invite you to experience Dutch hospitality in their spacious Colonial inn. The house is set in a quiet, residential section, with a large yard and lovely sun porch. Rooms are furnished with traditional family antiques, some dating back to the 1830s. Choose from a bedroom with lovely candlewicking on the drapes, comforters, and pillow shams; a suite with Victorian furnishings and its own sitting area; or the Jenny Lind Room, with its antique beds and dusty rose accents. Breakfast specialties such as quiche, homemade rolls, and muffins are served in the formal dining room. The Elenbaases are centrally located in a beautiful city, famous for its tulip festival, original Dutch windmill, and miles of sandy beaches on Lake Michigan.

The Parsonage 1908 ✪
6 EAST 24TH STREET, HOLLAND, MICHIGAN 49423

Tel: **(616) 396-1316**
Best Time to Call: **9 AM–noon, 5–8 PM**
Hosts: **Bonnie, Kimberly, Heather, and Wendy Verwys**
Location: **4 mi. off I-96, Exit 52**
No. of Rooms: **4**
No. of Private Baths: **2**
Max. No. Sharing Bath: **4**
Double/pb: **$75–$80**
Single/pb: **$60**

Double/sb: **$60–$65**
Single/sb: **$45–$50**
Open: **All year**
Reduced Rates: **Nov. 1–Apr. 30; Mon.–Thurs.; weekly**
Breakfast: **Full**
Pets: **No**
Children: **School-age children welcome**
Smoking: **No**
Social Drinking: **Permitted**

Built in 1908, this church parsonage has leaded-glass windows and rich oak woodwork; depending on the weather, guests can unwind on either the backyard patio or on the enclosed porch. Lake Michigan and Lake Macatawa are nearby for fishing, boating, and swimming, while landlubbers may prefer to take advantage of the local tennis court. You'll be prepared for any sport after a full breakfast of fruit, yogurt, cheese, sausages, muffins, and pancakes.

Seven Oaks Farm
7891 HOLLISTER ROAD, LAINGSBURG, MICHIGAN 48848

Tel: **(517) 651-5598**	Breakfast: **Full**
Hosts: **Terry and Mary Brock**	Other Meals: **Available**
Location: **15 mi. NE of East Lansing**	Pets: **Welcome**
No. of Rooms: **3**	Children: **Welcome (crib)**
Max. No. Sharing Bath: **4**	Smoking: **Permitted**
Double/sb: **$40**	Social Drinking: **Permitted**
Single/sb: **$20**	Airport/Station Pickup: **Yes**
Open: **All year**	

Seven Oaks is a large, comfortable home on a quiet country road. There are 100 acres to roam, a fishing pond, and ample opportunity for bird-watching, snowmobiling, and cross-country skiing. The house dates back 100 years, with spacious, double-bedded rooms now newly remodeled. Guests are invited to browse in the library or relax on the screened-in porch. Nearby are country auctions, bowling, movies, golf, and museums, as well as Michigan State University.

The Stagecoach Stop
0-4819 LEONARD ROAD WEST, P.O. BOX 18, LAMONT, MICHIGAN 49430

Tel: **(616) 677-3940**	Single/sb: **$45**
Host: **Marcia Ashby**	Open: **All year**
Location: **3 mi. from I-96**	Breakfast: **Continental**
No. of Rooms: **3**	Credit Cards: **MC, VISA**
No. of Private Baths: **1**	Pets: **Sometimes**
Max. No. Sharing Bath: **4**	Children: **Welcome (crib)**
Double/pb: **$60**	Smoking: **Permitted**
Single/pb: **$50**	Social Drinking: **No**
Double/sb: **$50**	

Built in 1859, this clapboard house was a thriving stagecoach stop for many years. Its location, midway between Grand Rapids and Grand Haven, made it ideal for the weary traveler. While much has been added over time, the original section of the house remains unchanged. The decor is a blend of Early American furnishings and turn-of-the-century antiques. Guest quarters are extra large and located in a separate wing of the house. This picturesque village overlooking the Grand River has much to offer sightseers. After a day of activity, relax on the front-porch swing or inside an enclosed porch furnished in wicker and warmed by a wood stove.

Governor's Inn ✪
LEXINGTON, MICHIGAN 48450

Tel: (313) 359-5770	Open: **May 25–Sept. 30**
Hosts: **Jane and Bob MacDonald**	Breakfast: **Continental**
Location: **20 mi. N of Port Huron**	Pets: **No**
No. of Rooms: **3**	Children: **Welcome, over 12**
No. of Private Baths: **3**	Smoking: **Permitted**
Double/pb: **$40**	Social Drinking: **Permitted**
Single/pb: **$40**	

A handsome residence built in 1859, it is located near the shore of Lake Huron. It has been refurbished to its original "summer home" style. Wicker furniture, rag rugs, iron beds, and green plants accent the light, airy decor. You can stroll to the nearby beach, browse through interesting shops, fish from the breakwater, or play golf or tennis. Jane and Bob, both educators, look forward to sharing their quaint village surroundings with you.

Vickie Van's Bed and Breakfast ✪
5076 SOUTH LAKESHORE ROAD, LEXINGTON, MICHIGAN 48450

Tel: (313) 359-5533	Double/sb: **$48**
Best Time to Call: **Mornings**	Single/sb: **$43**
Host: **Vickie Van**	Open: **All year**
Location: **80 mi. N of Detroit**	Reduced Rates: **Available**
No. of Rooms: **4**	Breakfast: **Continental**
No. of Private Baths: **2**	Pets: **No**
Max. No. Sharing Bath: **4**	Children: **Welcome, over 11**
Double/pb: **$55**	Smoking: **No**
Single/pb: **$50**	Social Drinking: **Permitted**

Vickie Van's is a big, old, white farmhouse with three porches. The house is situated on five acres right across the street from Lake Huron. The comfortable rooms are furnished with antiques, wicker, and canopy beds. Breakfast is served in the bright, colorful dining room, and includes fresh-picked berries, homemade muffins, hot croissants, served on fine linen and silver. Your host offers lemonade or iced tea in the afternoon. She will gladly direct you to the nearby marina, flea market, orchards, golf course, and much more.

Michigamme Lake Lodge
2403 U.S. 41 WEST, MARQUETTE, MICHIGAN 49855

Tel: (906) 225-1393
Hosts: Linda and Frank Stabile
Location: 30 mi. W of Marquette
No. of Rooms: 12
No. of Private Baths: 3
Max. No. Sharing Bath: 4
Double/pb: $94
Double/sb: $85

Open: Apr.–Jan.
Breakfast: Continental
Credit Cards: MC, VISA
Pets: No
Children: No
Smoking: No
Social Drinking: Permitted

From a bluff surrounded by birch trees, this grand two-story retreat surveys Lake Michigamme. Walkways lead from the secluded, park-like grounds to sandy beaches for swimming, boating, and fishing. Depending on the season, you may enjoy cross-country skiing, snowshoeing, hiking, or biking. Guests interested in wildlife will want to see the McCormick tract, a 17,000-acre federal wilderness area where moose have recently been reintroduced (and motorized vehicles are barred). The historic mining towns of Michigamme and Champion also merit visits.

Blue Lake Lodge
9765 BLUE LAKE LODGE LANE, P.O. BOX 1, MECOSTA, MICHIGAN 49332

Tel: (616) 972-8391
Host: Val Gibson
Location: 65 mi. NE of Grand Rapids
No. of Rooms: 6
Max. No. Sharing Bath: 6
Double/sb: $35
Single/sb: $30
Open: All year

Reduced Rates: 10%, seniors
Breakfast: Continental
Credit Cards: MC, VISA
Pets: Sometimes
Children: Welcome (crib)
Smoking: No
Social Drinking: Permitted
Airport/Station Pickup: Yes

This is a large, informal home built in 1913 and located on the shore of a beautiful lake. All lakeside activities, such as swimming, boating, and fishing, are available. It's close to restaurants, but cooking grills, guest refrigerator, and picnic tables will help you cut down on dining costs.

The Atchison House ✪
501 WEST DUNLAP, NORTHVILLE, MICHIGAN 48167

Tel: (313) 349-3340
Hosts: Don Mroz and Susan Lapine
No. of Rooms: 5
No. of Private Baths: 5
Double/pb: $70–$100
Suite/pb: $100–$125

Open: All year
Reduced Rates: $65 business rate,
    Sun.–Thurs.
Breakfast: Full
Credit Cards: AMEX, MC, VISA
Pets: No

CDunphy

Children: **Welcome, over 5**
Smoking: **No**
Social Drinking: **Permitted**

Airport/Station Pickup: **Yes**
Foreign Languages: **French**

This magnificent 1882 Italianate Victorian home is located in the Historic District. Lovingly and carefully restored to its former splendor, each room is richly furnished and imaginatively decorated with antiques. Your day begins in the handsome dining room with breakfast of granola, home-baked breads, cheese, fruit, yogurt, and freshly ground coffee. Afterward, enjoy a leisurely stroll into another era as you explore street after street of elegant Victorian homes. Nearby points of interest include Greenfield Village, antique shops, golf, tennis, skiing or some excitement at the local race track.

Stafford House ✪
4489 MAIN STREET, PORT HOPE, MICHIGAN 48468

Tel: **(517) 428-4554**
Best Time to Call: **Morning; evening**
Hosts: **Bill and Dolores Grubbs**
Location: **82 mi. N of Port Huron**
No. of Rooms: **3**
No. of Private Baths: **3**
Double/pb: **$45**
Open: **All year**

Reduced Rates: **10% less, Dec.–Mar.**
Breakfast: **Continental**
Credit Cards: **MC, VISA**
Pets: **Sometimes**
Children: **Welcome**
Smoking: **Permitted**
Social Drinking: **Permitted**
Minimum Stay: **Holiday weekends**

Built in 1886 by the town's founder, this classic Victorian, painted three shades of blue, has won a place on the National Historic Register. Antique furnishings, marble fireplaces, and ornate woodwork enhance the décor. Lake Huron is within walking distance for boating, fishing, or just relaxing on the beach. Among the many historic attractions nearby are the Grice Museum and the Huron City museums. Dolores, a retired social service worker, enjoys refinishing antiques and baking breakfast goodies. Bill, semiretired, does woodworking and fishes in his spare time. They look forward to sharing their quiet town with you.

Raymond House Inn ✪
111 SOUTH RIDGE STREET, M-25, PORT SANILAC, MICHIGAN 48469

Tel: **(313) 622-8800**
Host: **Shirley Denison**
Location: **30 mi. N of Port Huron**
No. of Rooms: **7**
No. of Private Baths: **7**
Double/pb: **$45–$55**
Open: **May 1–Oct. 31**

Reduced Rates: **10%, seniors**
Breakfast: **Continental**
Pets: **No**
Children: **Welcome, over 12**
Smoking: **Permitted**
Social Drinking: **Permitted**

Shirley will put you right at ease in her antique-filled inn with the conveniences of today and the ambience of 1895. Each bedroom is furnished with period furniture, brightly colored spreads, and lace curtains. There's an old-fashioned parlor and a dining room where you are served breakfast. Sport fishermen and sailboat enthusiasts will enjoy this area; cultural activities, quilting bees, and the annual summer festival are longtime traditions here. There is a pottery and sculpture gallery in the inn.

Brockway House Bed & Breakfast ✪
1631 BROCKWAY, SAGINAW, MICHIGAN 48602

Tel: **(517) 792-0746**
Best Time to Call: **Morning**
Hosts: **Richard and Danice Zuehlke**
Location: **90 mi. N of Detroit**
No. of Rooms: **4**
No. of Private Baths: **2**
Max. No. Sharing Bath: **4**
Double/pb: **$85**
Double/sb: **$65**

Open: **All year**
Breakfast: **Full**
Credit Cards: **AMEX, MC, VISA**
Pets: **No**
Children: **Welcome**
Smoking: **No**
Social Drinking: **Permitted**
Airport/Station Pickup: **Yes**

This stately home, with huge white pillars, was built in 1864 by a lumber baron for his family. The Zuehlke's have restored it using a charming mix of primitive antiques and Victorian furnishings. Such special touches as sun-dried linens, imaginative window treatments, artfully arranged plants and baskets, and breakfast served on heirloom dishes, are pleasures you'll savor. Tennis, golf, and a visit to the Japanese Gardens are local possibilities. And, given advance notice, Richard will arrange a tour of the General Motors plant in Saginaw.

Twin Gables Country Inn ✪
900 LAKE STREET, P.O. BOX 881, SAUGATUCK, MICHIGAN 49453

Tel: **(616) 857-4346**
Best Time to Call: **Afternoons**
Hosts: **Michael and Denise Simcik**
Location: **9 mi. S of Holland**
No. of Rooms: **14**
No. of Private Baths: **14**
Double/pb: **$49–$89**
Open: **All year**
Reduced Rates: **$34–$68, off season**
Breakfast: **Continental**

Credit Cards: **MC, VISA**
Pets: **No**
Children: **Welcome, over 12**
Smoking: **Permitted**
Social Drinking: **Permitted**
Airport/Station Pickup: **Yes**
Foreign Languages: **French, Italian, Maltese**
Minimum Stay: **2 nights, May 1–Labor Day**

Built in 1865, the inn, a registered State Historic Site, overlooks Lake Kalamazoo. The guest rooms are attractively furnished with wicker, brass, and antiques. The embossed tin ceilings add to the charm. In summer, guests enjoy the outdoor pool; in all seasons, the indoor hot tub is appreciated. It's a short walk to the beach, marinas, museum, and theater. Michael and Denise specialize in old-fashioned hospitality.

Rummel's Tree Haven ✪
41 NORTH BECK STREET, M-25, SEBEWAING, MICHIGAN 48759

Tel: **(517) 883-2450**
Best Time to Call: **Afternoons; evenings**
Hosts: **Carl and Erma Rummel**
Location: **28 mi. NE of Bay City**
No. of Rooms: **2**
Max. No. Sharing Bath: **4**
Double/sb: **$40**

Single/sb: **$30**
Open: **All year**
Breakfast: **Full**
Pets: **Sometimes**
Children: **Welcome (crib)**
Smoking: **Permitted**
Social Drinking: **Permitted**
Airport/Station Pickup: **Yes**

A tree grows right through the porch and roof of this charming old home that was built by the Beck family in 1878. Guests can relax in large, airy rooms furnished with twin beds and comfortable family pieces. City dwellers are sure to enjoy the small-town friendliness and the quiet of the countryside. Saginaw Bay offers fine fishing, hunting, boating, bird-watching, or just plain relaxing. Carl and Erma offer color TV, videocassettes, and the use of the barbecue and refrigerator. They love having company and will do all they can to make you feel welcome and relaxed.

Csatlos' Csarda
P.O. BOX 73, STEPHENSON, MICHIGAN 49887

Tel: **(906) 753-4638 (home); (715) 735-6644 (office)**	Open: **All year**
Host: **Barb Upton**	Breakfast: **Continental**
Location: **70 mi. N of Green Bay, Wisconsin**	Pets: **No**
	Children: **No**
No. of Rooms: **2**	Smoking: **No**
Max. No. Sharing Bath: **4**	Social Drinking: **Permitted**
Double/sb: **$22**	Airport/Station Pickup: **Yes**
Single/sb: **$17**	Foreign Languages: **Hungarian**

Barb offers a touch of things Hungarian to those who wish to sample the charm of a very small town. Two blocks east of the front door and you're downtown; two blocks west and you're in a farmer's field! Lakes and beaches are nearby for summer swimming and boating or winter fishing. Cross-country ski trails are plentiful. It is a perfect spot to stop for the night for those travelers going to Chicago, Milwaukee, Mackinac Island, or Canada. Be sure to stop in at her sister's restaurant, where you'll find fine service and a delicious Hungarian meal.

Linden Lea, A B&B on Long Lake ✪
279 SOUTH LONG LAKE ROAD, TRAVERSE CITY, MICHIGAN 49684

Tel: **(616) 943-9182**	Breakfast: **Full**
Hosts: **Jim and Vicky McDonnell**	Pets: **Sometimes**
Location: **9 mi. W of Traverse City**	Children: **Welcome**
No. of Rooms: **2**	Smoking: **No**
Max. No. Sharing Bath: **4**	Social Drinking: **Permitted**
Double/sb: **$65**	Minimum Stay: **Holiday weekends**
Open: **All year**	Airport/Station Pickup: **Yes**
Reduced Rates: **$55, Nov.–May**	

Linden Lea is an extensively remodeled and expanded 1900 lakeside cottage set on a private sandy beach surrounded by woods. The bedrooms are comfortably furnished in country style, accented with antiques. You are certain to enjoy the window seats and the panoramic views of Long Lake. The area offers the Interlochen Center for the Arts National Music Camp, a PGA golfcourse, and local wineries. Breakfast features local specialties, such as smoked bacon, maple syrup, and berries that make the home-baked muffins so delicious.

The Victorian Villa Guesthouse ✪
601 NORTH BROADWAY STREET, UNION CITY, MICHIGAN 49094

Tel: **(517) 741-7383**	No. of Rooms: **8**
Host: **Ron Gibson**	No. of Private Baths: **6**
Location: **20 mi. S of Battle Creek**	Max. No. Sharing Bath: **4**

Double/pb: **$70–$75**
Single/pb: **$65–$70**
Double/sb: **$60**
Single/sb: **$55**
Open: **All year**
Breakfast: **Full**

Credit Cards: **MC, VISA**
Pets: **No**
Children: **Welcome**
Smoking: **No**
Social Drinking: **Permitted**
Airport/Station Pickup: **Yes**

The Victorian Villa is a 19th-century estate house furnished with antiques. Guests may choose from eight private chambers, all elegantly appointed. Chilled champagne, wine, cheese, and a private "tea for two" can be arranged. Fancy chocolates, a specialty of the house, are placed on the pillows at night. Your host will help make your visit as sparkling as you like, directing you to summer theater, museums, antique shops, and restaurants. Ask Ron about the special "getaway" weekends, including cross-country skiing, Sherlock Holmes mystery themes, a Victorian Christmas, and fun-filled Summer-Daze.

Villa Hammer ✪

3133 LINDA MARIE WAY, WALLED LAKE, MICHIGAN 48088

Tel: **(313) 624-1071**
Best Time to Call: **Evenings**
Hosts: **Veronica and Reinhold Hammer**
Location: **5 mi. N of Novi**
No. of Rooms: **1**
No. of Private Baths: **1**
Double/pb: **$45**
Single/pb: **$35**

Open: **All year**
Reduced Rates: **10%, weekly**
Breakfast: **Full**
Pets: **Sometimes**
Children: **Welcome, over 12**
Smoking: **No**
Social Drinking: **Permitted**

A Tudor house set on three secluded acres on the Huron River, the house is furnished in a contemporary fashion accented with lots of plants. Veronica and Reinhold invite you to relax in the hot tub and sauna. They offer a hearty breakfast; waffles are the house specialty. The Hammers are happy to acquaint you with the delights of the Lake Region and its many recreational activities. The Villa Hammer is 20 miles from Greenfield Village and Ann Arbor.

Williamston Bed and Breakfast ✪

3169 SOUTH WILLIAMSTON ROAD, WILLIAMSTON, MICHIGAN 48895

Tel: **(517) 655-1061**
Best Time to Call: **Mornings; evenings**
Hosts: **Coleen and Bob Stone**
Location: **18 mi. E of Lansing**
No. of Rooms: **3**
No. of Private Baths: **1**
Max. No. Sharing Bath: **4**

Double/pb: **$55**
Double/sb: **$45**
Single/sb: **$38**
Open: **All year**
Breakfast: **Continental**
Other Meals: **Available**
Credit Cards: **MC, VISA**

Pets: **No**
Children: **Welcome**

Smoking: **Permitted**
Social Drinking: **Permitted**

Colleen Stone welcomes you to her 1916 farmhouse located at the edge of historic Williamston. This is a town filled with craftsmen, and your host is no exception. Colleen's basketry and primitive country landscapes accent each room. The bedrooms are decorated with antique beds and matching wood dressers, spanking white quilts and curtains. The breakfast specialties of the house are fresh fruit cup and pastries served with hot beverages. In the afternoon, wine and cheese can be enjoyed by the living room fire or outside on the porch. Antiques dealers, shops, and fine restaurants are within walking distance of the house. Michigan State University and the State Capitol are less than 20 minutes away.

For key to listings, see inside front or back cover.

○ This star means that rates are guaranteed through December 31, 1991, to any guest making a reservation as a result of reading about the B&B in *BED & BREAKFAST U.S.A.*—1991 edition.

Important! To avoid misunderstandings, always ask about cancellation policies when booking.

Please enclose a self-addressed, stamped, business-size envelope when contacting reservation services.

For more details on what you can expect in a B&B, see Chapter 1.

Always mention *Bed & Breakfast U.S.A.* when making reservations!

If no B&B is listed in the area you'll be visiting, use the form on page 675 to order a copy of our "List of New B&Bs."

We want to hear from you! Use the form on page 677.

MINNESOTA

North Branch • Stacy
Dassel • • Minneapolis
St. Paul •
Cannon Falls • • Lake City
Garvin • • Rochester
Spring Valley • Lanesboro

Gabrielson's B&B
RR 1, BOX 269, DASSEL, MINNESOTA 55325

Tel: **(612) 275-3609**
Best Time to Call: **Evenings**
Hosts: **Elaine and Don Gabrielson**
Location: **65 mi. W of Minneapolis**
No. of Rooms: **2**
Max. No. Sharing Bath: **3**
Double/sb: **$42**

Single/sb: **$35**
Open: **All year**
Breakfast: **Continental**
Pets: **Sometimes**
Children: **Welcome, over 9**
Smoking: **No**
Social Drinking: **Permitted**

Perched on a hilltop, this 1910 white clapboard farmhouse, decorated in Early American style, overlooks a private lake. You are welcome to use the paddleboat for getting to the little island, where you can picnic. Or, try your hand at archery, trap shooting, or pond fishing. Elaine and Don are busy raising corn and beans, but they'll happily arrange a farm tour of Meeker County. Wine, cheese, and rolls are stocked in the guest refrigerator. The University of Minnesota is nearby. A hot tub and central air-conditioning add to your comfort.

Red Gables Inn ✪

403 NORTH HIGH STREET, LAKE CITY, MINNESOTA 55041

Tel: **(612) 345-2605**	Open: **All year**
Hosts: **Mary and Douglas De Roos**	Reduced Rates: **Available**
Location: **60 mi. SE of Twin Cities**	Breakfast: **Full**
No. of Rooms: **5**	Other Meals: **Available**
No. of Private Baths: **3**	Credit Cards: **MC, VISA**
Max. No. Sharing Bath: **4**	Pets: **No**
Double/pb: **$68**	Children: **Welcome, over 13**
Single/pb: **$63**	Smoking: **Permitted**
Double/sb: **$48**	Social Drinking: **Permitted**
Single/sb: **$43**	Airport/Station Pickup: **Yes**

Red Gables Inn is located in the Hiawatha Valley on the shore of Lake Pepin. The inn was built in 1865 by a wealthy merchant and is a mixture of Italianate and Greek Revival styles. The original pine floors, white-pine woodwork, and large windows have been carefully restored; and each bedroom has an old-fashioned iron, brass, or walnut bed, antique wood wardrobe, Victorian wall coverings, and ceiling fan. A breakfast buffet of fruit specialties, sticky buns, home-baked breads, eggs, jams, and coffee is served on the screened-in porch or in the fireside dining room, and hors d'oeuvres are served in the parlor. Your hosts are also happy to assist with gourmet picnic lunches, chilled champagne in your room, and reservations for dining. They have bicycles to lend for exploring the nearby marina, antique shops, and nature trails.

Evelo's Bed & Breakfast

2301 BYRANT AVENUE SOUTH, MINNEAPOLIS, MINNESOTA 55405

Tel: **(612) 374-9656**	Open: **All year**
Best Time to Call: **After 4 PM**	Breakfast: **Full**
Hosts: **David and Sheryl Evelo**	Pets: **No**
No. of Rooms: **3**	Children: **Welcome**
Max. No. Sharing Bath: **6**	Smoking: **No**
Double/sb: **$45**	Social Drinking: **Permitted**
Single/sb: **$35**	

Located in the historic Lowry Hill East neighborhood, on the bus line, this 1897 Victorian has one of the best-preserved interiors in the area and is furnished with fine period pieces. David and Sheryl are both school teachers. Breakfast, served in the formal dining room, often features quiche or egg casseroles. The house is within walking distance of the Guthrie Theater, the Walker Art Center, convention center, shops, and restaurants.

Nan's Bed & Breakfast ✪
2304 FREMONT AVENUE SOUTH, MINNEAPOLIS, MINNESOTA 55405

Tel: **(612) 377-5118**
Best Time to Call: **Evenings**
Hosts: **Nan and Jim Zosel**
No. of Rooms: **2**
Max. No. Sharing Bath: **4**
Double/sb: **$45**
Single/sb: **$40**
Open: **All year**

Reduced Rates: **Full week $200**
Breakfast: **Full**
Credit Cards: **AMEX**
Pets: **Yes**
Children: **Welcome (crib)**
Smoking: **Permitted**
Social Drinking: **Permitted**

This charming Victorian B&B makes a great home base for visitors to Minneapolis. The Guthrie Theater, the Minneapolis Institute of Arts, Walker Art Center, and the scenic Lake of the Isle pathway are all within walking distance, and city buses stop one block away. Not sure where to go? Nan and Jim are happy to supply suggestions, directions, and maps.

Red Pine Log B&B ✪
15140 400TH STREET, NORTH BRANCH, MINNESOTA 55056

Tel: **(612) 583-3326**
Best Time to Call:**After 5 PM; weekends**
Hosts: **Lowell and Gloria Olson**
Location: **45 mi. N of St. Paul**
No. of Rooms: **3**
No. of Private Baths: **1**
Max. No. Sharing Bath: **4**
Double/pb: **$95**
Double/sb: **$70–$75**

Single/sb: **$65**
Open: **All year**
Reduced Rates: **10%, weekly; Mar.– Apr. 60 and older all year**
Breakfast: **Full**
Pets: **No**
Children: **Welcome, over 12**
Smoking: **No**
Social Drinking: **Permitted**

If Abe Lincoln had known log homes could look like this, he would have had second thoughts about heading for the White House! Lowell Olson handcrafted this lodge-style home in 1985. His professional training as a log home designer is obvious from the exposed logs and trusses throughout the house. Loft bedrooms are richly paneled and feature country furnishings, skylights, ceiling fans, and a balcony. Your hosts invite you for crassane and cheese in the living room, which boasts a 26-foot-high ceiling and an antique parlor stove. You will find the kitchen an equally cozy place with its antique harvest table and ash cabinets. Here you can relax over Gloria's prize muffins and special fritatas, served with plenty of fresh coffee. The Olsons have 30 acres for you to explore, and they are within easy reach of downhill skiing, Taylors Falls, and Wild River State Park.

Canterbury Inn Bed & Breakfast ✪

723 SECOND STREET SOUTHWEST, ROCHESTER, MINNESOTA 55902

Tel: **(507) 289-5553**
Hosts: **Mary Martin and Jeffrey Van Sant**
Location: **90 mi. SE of Minneapolis**
No. of Rooms: **4**
No. of Private Baths: **4**
Double/pb: **$69**
Single/pb: **$59**
Open: **All year**

Breakfast: **Full**
Credit Cards: **MC, VISA**
Pets: **No**
Children: **Sometimes**
Smoking: **Permitted**
Social Drinking: **Permitted**
Airport/Station Pickup: **Yes**
Foreign Languages: **Italian**

This is a Victorian structure, just three blocks from the Mayo Clinic, with polished hardwood floors, stained-glass windows, and a cozy fireplace complete with carved mantel. Lace curtains and eclectic furnishings give it an air in keeping with its age. Enjoy games, music, and conversation in the parlor. Breakfast is served in the formal dining room and may include such delicious fare as eggs Benedict, pesto omelets, or Swedish pancakes. Afternoon tea, served 5:30–7 except Sunday, features hor d'oeuvres and wine.

The Prairie House on Round Lake ✪

RR 1, BOX 97, ROUND LAKE, MINNESOTA 56167

Tel: **(507) 945-8934**
Hosts: **Ralph and Virginia Schenck**
No. of Rooms: **4**
No. of Private Baths: **1**
Max. No. Sharing Bath: **6**
Double/pb: **$45**
Single/pb: **$42.50**
Double/sb: **$32.50–$35**
Single/sb: **$30**

Open: **All year**
Breakfast: **Full**
Other Meals: **Available**
Pets: **Welcome**
Children: **Welcome**
Smoking: **No**
Social Drinking: **Permitted**
Airport/Station Pickup: **Yes**

Built in 1879 by a prominent Chicago businessman, this 26-room farmhouse is a retreat from the bustle of city life. Ralph and Virginia have restored it by artfully blending modern conveniences with its historic heritage. It's a working horse farm: American paint horses roam the pasture, and three barns house both young stock in training and show horses that are exhibited all over the world. A cupola rising from the central stairway is circled by four dormer bedrooms on the second floor. Antique furniture accented with equine touches reflects the spirit of the farm. Fishing, swimming, boating, and tennis are at the doorstop.

Chatsworth Bed and Breakfast ○
984 ASHLAND AVENUE, ST. PAUL, MINNESOTA 55104

Tel: (612) 227-4288	Single/sb: $45–$50
Best Time to Call: Noon–5 PM	Open: All year
Hosts: Donna and Earl Gustafson	Reduced Rates: Weekly
Location: ½ mi. from I-94	Breakfast: Continental
No. of Rooms: 5	Pets: No
No. of Private Baths: 3	Children: Welcome
Max. No. Sharing Bath: 4	Smoking: No
Double/pb: $75–$90	Social Drinking: Permitted
Single/pb: $65–$80	Airport/Station Pickup: Yes
Double/sb: $55–$60	

This spacious 1902 Victorian is located on a large corner lot surrounded by maple and basswood trees. The setting is quiet and residential, but is just a few blocks from shops, restaurants, and the governor's mansion. Guest rooms are decorated in international motifs and are located on a separate floor from your hosts' quarters. The Victorian Room features a handcarved wood bed, floral rug, lace curtains, and antiques, while the Scandinavian Room uses pine furnishings, white curtains, and matching spread to create a light and airy feeling. Guests may prefer the room with a four-poster bed and private double whirlpool bath, or the one with Afro-Asian furnishings, whirlpool bath, and adjoining porch. The Gustafsons serve breakfast in a beautifully paneled formal dining room. They also invite you to relax in the living room, where you may enjoy the library, the piano, and a roaring fire.

Chase's Bed & Breakfast
508 NORTH HURON, SPRING VALLEY, MINNESOTA 55975

Tel: (507) 346-2850	Double/pb: $60
Hosts: Bob and Jeannine Chase	Single/pb: $60
Location: 26 mi. S of Rochester	Open: Feb.–Dec.
No. of Rooms: 5	Reduced Rates: 15%, weekly
No. of Private Baths: 5	Breakfast: Full

Credit Cards: **MC, VISA**
Pets: **No**
Children: **Sometimes**

Smoking: **No**
Social Drinking: **Permitted**
Airport/Station Pickup: **Yes**

William H. Strong built this Second Empire–style home in 1879 for $8,000. At the time, it was considered to be the most handsome home in the county. Over the years, the house has been an office, motel, and rest home, and is now listed on the National Register of Historic Places. Guests will find elegant rooms furnished in period antiques, many of which are for sale. Bob and Jeannine serve a hearty breakfast and offer snacks and setups in the evening. Nearby activities include swimming, tennis, golf, trout fishing, and hiking. Chase's is 18 miles from the airport, and 28 miles from the Mayo Clinic. The Amish area is nearby.

Kings Oakdale Park Guest House ✪
6933 232 AVENUE NORTHEAST, STACY, MINNESOTA 55079

Tel: **(612) 462-5598**
Hosts: **Donna and Charles Solem**
Location: **38 mi. N of St. Paul**
No. of Rooms: **3**
No. of Private Baths: **2**
Double/pb: **$28**
Single/pb: **$25**
Double/sb: **$26**
Single/sb: **$23**

Suites: **$28**
Open: **All year**
Breakfast: **Continental**
Pets: **Sometimes**
Children: **No**
Smoking: **Permitted**
Social Drinking: **Permitted**
Foreign Languages: **French**

This comfortable home is situated on four landscaped acres on the banks of Typo Creek. The picnic tables, volleyball net, and horseshoe game are sure signs of a hospitable country place. It is a serene retreat for people on business trips to the Twin Cities. The Wisconsin border and the scenic St. Croix River, where boat trips are offered, are minutes from the house. Charles and Donna will direct you to the most reasonable restaurants in town. For late snacks, refrigerators in the bedrooms are provided.

MISSISSIPPI

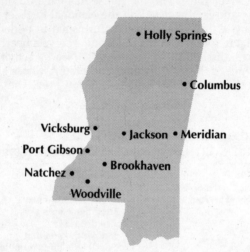

- Holly Springs
- Columbus
- Vicksburg
- Jackson
- Meridian
- Port Gibson
- Natchez
- Brookhaven
- Woodville

Lincoln, Ltd. Bed & Breakfast—Mississippi Reservation Service ✪
P.O. BOX 3479, 2303 23rd AVENUE, MERIDIAN, MISSISSIPPI 39303

Tel: **(601) 482-5483, Resv. only (601) 633-MISS**
Best Time to Call: **9 AM–5 PM**
Coordinator: **Barbara Lincoln Hall**
States/Regions Covered: **Mississippi, statewide**

Descriptive Directory: **$3.50**
Rates (Single/Double):
  Average: **$40–$65 $50–$75**
  Luxury: **$65–$115 $75–$155**
Credit Cards: **MC, VISA**

For the traveling business person or for the vacationer, a stay with one of Barbara's hosts offers a personal taste of the finest Southern hospitality. All rooms have private baths. Mississippi abounds with historic-house tours, called "pilgrimages," in March and April, and Natchez and Vicksburg have similar pilgrimages in autumn. In May, Meridian is host to the Jimmie Rodgers Festival. Accommodations range from a cozy, historic log cabin to an elegant antebellum mansion.

Hamilton Place ✪
105 EAST MASON AVENUE, HOLLY SPRINGS, MISSISSIPPI 38635

Tel. (601) 252-4368	Open: **All year**
Best Time to Call: **After 4:30 PM**	Breakfast: **Full**
Hosts: **Linda and Jack Stubbs**	Credit Cards: **MC, VISA**
Location: **35 mi. SE of Memphis, Tenn.**	Pets: **No**
No. of Rooms: **3**	Children: **Welcome**
No. of Private Baths: **3**	Smoking: **Permitted**
Double/pb: **$65**	Social Drinking: **Permitted**
Single/pb: **$55**	Airport/Station Pickup: **Yes**
Guest Cottage: **$65**	

On the National Historic Register, this antebellum home, circa 1838, is furnished with heirloom antiques. In fact, Linda and Jack have a delightful antique shop on the premises featuring furniture, china, and cut glass. Breakfast can be enjoyed on the veranda or in the garden gazebo. You'll love the taste of the homemade biscuits with strawberry or honey-lemon butter. You are welcome to use the sauna or swimming pool.

Natchez Bed & Breakfast Center
c/o CREATIVE TRAVEL, CANAL STREET DEPOT, NATCHEZ, MISSISSIPPI 39120

Tel: **(800) 824-0355**	Rates (Single/Double):	
Best Time to Call: **9 AM–5 PM**	Average: **$55**	**$65**
Coordinator: **Andrew L. Peabody**	Luxury: **$90**	**$135**
States/Regions Covered: **Natchez**	Credit Cards: **AMEX, MC, VISA**	
Descriptive Directory of B&Bs: **FREE**		

Located on the Mississippi River 80 miles north of Baton Rouge, Natchez exemplifies the 19th-century grandeur of the Old South. More millionaires lived here during the 1850s than anywhere else in the country. Many of their mansions still stand today, and are open to the public. Andrew's service offers comfortable accommodations in contemporary homes as well as historic plantations. This is a delightful place to visit on your way to New Orleans, Louisiana, only 160 miles further south.

Oak Square Plantation ✪
1207 CHURCH STREET, PORT GIBSON, MISSISSIPPI 39150

Tel: **(601) 437-4350; (800) 729-0240**	No. of Private Baths: **8**
Best Time to Call: **Mornings; evenings**	Double/pb: **$65–$85**
Hosts: **Mr. and Mrs. William D. Lum**	Single/pb: **$65–$70**
Location: **On Hwy. 61 between**	Open: **All year**
Natchez and Vicksburg	Breakfast: **Full**
No. of Rooms: **8**	Credit Cards: **AMEX, MC, VISA**

Pets: **No**	Smoking: **No**
Children: **Welcome**	Social Drinking: **Permitted**

Port Gibson is the town that Union General Ulysses S. Grant said was "too beautiful to burn." Oak Square is the largest and most palatial antebellum mansion (circa 1850) in Port Gibson, and is listed on the National Historic Register. The guest rooms are all furnished with family heirlooms, and most have canopied beds. Guests will enjoy the courtyard, gazebo, and beautiful grounds. A chairlift for upstairs rooms is available. You will enjoy the delightful Southern breakfast and tour of the mansion. Your hosts offer complimentary wine, tea, or coffee, and will enlighten you on the many historic attractions in the area. Oak Square has been awarded a four-star rating by AAA.

Square Ten Inn ✪
242 DEPOT STREET, P.O. BOX 371, WOODVILLE, MISSISSIPPI 39669

Tel: **(601) 888-3993**	Open: **All year**
Host: **Elizabeth M. Treppendahl**	Reduced Rates: **25%, 5-day stay**
Location: **35 mi. S of Natchez**	Breakfast: **Continental**
No. of Rooms: **3**	Pets: **No**
No. of Private Baths: **3**	Children: **Welcome, over 6**
Double/pb: **$34**	Smoking: **Permitted**
Suites: **$39.50**	Social Drinking: **Permitted**

This inn is an 1830 town house listed on the National Register of Historic Places. It features a New Orleans–style courtyard and antique furnishings. Other amenities include a stocked breakfast pantry, complimentary wine, and fresh fruit. Woodville was chosen by Harvard University as the city best typifying the Old South in appearance, customs, and traditions. Rosemont, the boyhood home of Jefferson Davis, is nearby.

MISSOURI

Bed & Breakfast Kansas City—Missouri & Kansas ✪
MAILING ADDRESS: P.O. BOX 14781, LENEXA, KANSAS 66215

Tel: **(913) 888-3636**
Coordinator: **Edwina Monroe**
States/Regions Covered: **Kansas—
Lenexa, Overland Park, Wichita;
Missouri—Grandview,
Independence, Kansas City, Lee's
Summit, Parkville, St. Joseph,
Springfield, Warrensburg, Weston**

Directory: **Free**
Rates (Single/Double):
  Average: **$35**   **$35–$50**
  Luxury: **$55**   **$60–$100**
Credit Cards: **No**

You will enjoy visiting such places as the Truman Library and home, Crown Center, Country Club Plaza, Arrowhead Stadium, Royals Stadium, Kemper Arena, the Missouri Repertory Theatre, and the American Heartland Theater. A directory fully describing all of the host homes is available. Please send a self-addressed envelope with 25¢ postage.

Ozark Mountain Country B&B Service ✪
BOX 295, BRANSON, MISSOURI 65616

Tel: **(417) 334-4720; 5077**
Best Time to Call: **5–10 PM**
Coordinators: **Linda Johnson and Kay Cameron**
States/Regions Covered: **Missouri— Branson, Joplin, Hollister, Lee's Summit, Marionville, Rogersville; Arkansas—Eureka Springs, Everton; Oklahoma—Tulsa**

Rates (Single/Double):
  Modest: **$35–$45**
  Average: **$50–$65**
  Luxury: **$70–$95**
Credit Cards: **MC, VISA (5% surcharge)**

Linda and Kay will send you a complimentary copy of their descriptive listing of 50 homes, inns, and guest cottages, so you can select the host of your choice; they'll take care of making your reservation. They would appreciate your sending them a self-addressed, stamped envelope. Discounts are available for groups, honeymooners, and several-night stays.

Borgman's Bed & Breakfast ✪
ARROW ROCK, MISSOURI 65320

Tel: **(816) 837-3350**
Best Time to Call: **7–9 AM**
Hosts: **Helen and Kathy Borgman**
Location: **100 mi. E of Kansas City**
No. of Rooms: **4**
Max. No. Sharing Bath: **4**
Double/sb: **$40–$45**
Single/sb: **$35**

Open: **All year**
Reduced Rates: **10%, 3 nights**
Breakfast: **Continental**
Other Meals: **Dinner (winter only)**
Pets: **Sometimes**
Children: **Welcome**
Smoking: **No**
Social Drinking: **Permitted**

This 1860 home is spacious and comfortable, and it is furnished with cherished family pieces. Helen is a seamstress, artisan, and baker. Wait till you taste her fresh breads! Daughter Kathy is a town tour guide, so you will get firsthand information on this National Historic Landmark town at the beginning of the Santa Fe Trail. A fine repertory theater, the Lyceum, is open in summer. Craft shops, antique stalls, and the old country store are fun places to browse in. Good restaurants are within walking distance.

Country Gardens B&B ✪
LAKESHORE DRIVE, BRANSON, MISSOURI 65616

Tel: **(417) 334-8564**
Hosts: **Bob and Pat Cameron**
Location: **39 mi. from I-44**
No. of Rooms: **3**
No. of Private Baths: **3**

Double/pb: **$50**
Single/pb: **$45**
Guest Cottage: **$60**
Suites: **$90**
Open: **All year**

Reduced Rates: **20%, Nov. 1–Apr. 1**	Children: **Welcome, over 12**
Breakfast: **Full**	Smoking: **Permitted**
Credit Cards: **MC, VISA**	Airport/Station Pickup: **Yes**
Pets: **No**	

A parklike setting of gardens and a waterfall surround this wood-frame-and-rock home, located on beautiful Lake Taneycomo. The Camerons have a variety of accommodations with private entrances. The Rose Suite consists of three rooms and features a large bathroom with spa. The Bittersweet Room is decorated with antiques and has a private deck overlooking the water. Dogwood has a single whirlpool tub and kitchen for those who like to prepare light meals. Breakfast specialties such as waffles with strawberries, and hot biscuits with eggs are served in the garden room overlooking the garden. Bob and Pat invite you to swim in the pool and enjoy a picnic under the trees. They say the best trout fishing around is right on the lake, and they have boats and fishing docks for anglers. Music lovers will be glad to know that there are 22 different country music shows in the area.

Lakeside Guest House ✪
RR 2, BOX 41, NORMAC, CAMDENTON, MISSOURI 65020

Tel: **(314) 346-3767**	Single/pb: **$35**
Best Time to Call: **Evenings**	Open: **May 1–Oct. 31**
Host: **Virginia Dyck**	Breakfast: **Continental**
Location: **170 mi. SE of Kansas City**	Pets: **No**
No. of Rooms: **2**	Children: **No**
No. of Private Baths: **2**	Smoking: **No**
Double/pb: **$40**	Social Drinking: **Permitted**

Virginia's lovely home is a bilevel, modified A-frame just 50 feet from the Lake of the Ozarks, with cathedral ceilings and many glass doors opening onto the patio and deck. You will be lulled to sleep by the sound of lapping water. HaHa Tonka Ruins and Trails, Bridal Cave, country music shows, antique shops, and many fine restaurants are all close by.

Ramblewood Bed and Breakfast ✪
402 PANORAMIC DRIVE, CAMDENTON, MISSOURI 65020

Tel: **(314) 346-3410**	Single/sb: **$35**
Best Time to Call: **After 5 PM**	Open: **All year**
Host: **Mary Massey**	Breakfast: **Full**
Location: **90 mi. S of Columbia**	Pets: **Sometimes**
No. of Rooms: **2**	Children: **No**
Max. No. Sharing Bath: **4**	Smoking: **No**
Double/sb: **$40**	Social Drinking: **Permitted**

Ramblewood is a Pilgrim-red home with white trim. Set on a quiet, wooded lot, it has the feel of an English country cottage. Spend the night in an attractive, comfortable room and awaken to breakfast served on a sunny deck. Ham-and-cheese omelets and homemade breads are specialties of the house. The inn is minutes from Lake of the Ozarks, HaHa Tonka State Park and Castle, and antique shops, malls, and restaurants to suit any taste. After a busy day, enjoy a cool drink on the porch.

Brewer's Maple Lane Farms B&B ✪
RR 1, CARTHAGE, MISSOURI 64836

Tel: **(417) 358-6312**	Open: **All year**
Best Time to Call: **6–10 PM**	Reduced Rates: **15%, weekly**
Hosts: **Arch and Renee Brewer**	Breakfast: **Continental**
Location: **4 mi. from Rte. 96, Exit 10**	Pets: **Sometimes**
No. of Rooms: **4**	Children: **Welcome (crib)**
Max. No. Sharing Bath: **4**	Smoking: **Permitted**
Double/pb: **$50**	Social Drinking: **No**
Guest Cottage: **$60; sleeps 6**	Airport/Station Pickup: **Yes**

Built in 1900, this stone Victorian, with its red tile roof, is situated on farm property encompassing 676 acres. The reception parlor, dining room, and stairway are oak-paneled. Each of the 200 stair rails in the banister was hand turned, and one can see from the main floor up to the third. A climb to the ballroom on the third floor will reward you with views of the 22-acre lake surrounded by trees. The rooms are large and comfortable, furnished with many family heirlooms. Bird's-eye maple was used in the woodwork and Italian marble in the fireplaces. Facilities include fishing ponds, game hunting, farm and exotic animals, a playground, and a picnic area. Carthage hosts a country or craft fair almost every month of the year.

The Fountains ✪
12610 BLUE RIDGE, GRANDVIEW, MISSOURI 64030

Tel: **(816) 763-6260**	Single/sb: **$30**
Best Time to Call: **9 AM–9 PM**	Open: **Jan. 11–Dec. 9**
Host: **Sally J. Stewart**	Breakfast: **Continental**
Location: **1½ mi. W of Rte. 71**	Pets: **Sometimes**
No. of Rooms: **3**	Children: **Welcome, over 9**
Max. No. Sharing Bath: **4**	Smoking: **Permitted**
Double/sb: **$35**	Social Drinking: **Permitted**

Sally's home is convenient to the Truman Library and home, the Nelson-Atkins Art Gallery, Starlight Theatre, Worlds of Fun park, and the famous plaza of Kansas City. The guest quarters has its own private entrance, dining room with fireplace, and kitchen. You are welcome to use the patio, barbecue, and gazebo. Sally enjoys having guests, and her good humor and warm hospitality will make you feel welcome immediately.

Garth Woodside Mansion
NEW LONDON GRAVEL ROAD, RR1, HANNIBAL, MISSOURI 63401

Tel: **(314) 221-2789**	Suite: **$110–$126**
Best Time to Call: **10 AM–4 PM**	Open: **All year**
Hosts: **Irv and Diane Feinberg**	Breakfast: **Full**
Location: **99 mi. N of St. Louis**	Credit Cards: **MC, VISA**
No. of Rooms: **8**	Pets: **No**
No. of Private Baths: **6**	Children: **Welcome, over 12**
Max. No. Sharing Bath: **4**	Smoking: **No**
Double/pb: **$60–$80**	Social Drinking: **Permitted**
Double/sb: **$55–$63**	

A lifetime friend of Mark Twain built this country estate home in 1871. John Garth had someone a bit more sophisticated than Huck Finn in mind when he designed this Second Empire Victorian with its three-story flying staircase, 14-foot-high ceilings, and eight handcarved marble fireplaces. The rooms are furnished with Victorian antiques, many of them dating back to the original owners. Your hosts want you to feel completely at home here, and they offer such touches as nightshirts and turndown service. Breakfast is served in the formal dining room and features French toast, egg casseroles, and quiches. In the afternoon, Irv and Diane serve tea on the veranda. They will help you plan your visit with restaurant, theater, and riverboat ride suggestions. When it's time to relax, there are 39 acres for picnicking and croquet.

Frisco House ✪
P.O. BOX 118, CORNER CHURCH AND ROLLA STREETS, HARTVILLE, MISSOURI 65667

Tel: **(417) 741-7304; 833-0650**	Reduced Rates: **5%, after 2 nights;**
Best Time to Call: **7–9 AM; 6–10 PM**	**5%, seniors**
Hosts: **Betty and Charley Roberts**	Breakfast: **Full**
Location: **50 mi. E of Springfield**	Pets: **No**
No. of Rooms: **3**	Children: **No**
Max. No. Sharing Bath: **4**	Smoking: **No**
Double/sb: **$35**	Social Drinking: **Permitted**
Single/sb: **$30**	Airport/Station Pickup: **Yes**
Open: **Mar.–Dec.**	

Located in the noncommercial historic area of the Missouri Ozarks, this 1890 Victorian, listed on the National Historic Register, has been completely restored, retaining absolute authenticity while being unobtrusively outfitted with central air-conditioning, and up-to-date plumbing and heating systems. Many of the furnishings are third- and fourth-generation family heirlooms, including oil paintings, Oriental rugs, and hanging lamps, as well as china, brass, and wooden artifacts. Most bedrooms have marble-topped sinks. The wainscoted dining room is furnished in oak and decorated with railroad pictures and maps. This is where you'll be served refreshments on arrival, and a bountiful breakfast. The interesting Amish community and the Laura Ingalls Wilder home and museum are close by.

Woodstock Inn ✪
1212 WEST LEXINGTON, INDEPENDENCE, MISSOURI 64050

Tel: **(816) 833-2BED**	Breakfast: **Full**
Hosts: **Lane and Ruth Harold**	Credit Cards: **MC, VISA**
Location: **10 mi. E of Kansas City**	Pets: **No**
No. of Rooms: **11**	Children: **Welcome**
No. of Private Baths: **11**	Smoking: **No**
Double/pb: **$38.50–$42.50**	Social Drinking: **Permitted**
Single/pb: **$33.50–$37.50**	Airport/Station Pickup: **Yes**
Open: **All year**	Foreign Languages: **German**
Reduced Rates: **10% after 2 nights**	

This inn is convenient to all the historic and cultural sites in President Harry Truman's hometown. The guest rooms offer a choice of queen, double, or twin beds; all are tastefully appointed with individual decor and are handicapped accessible. Individual heat and air-conditioning controls add to the comfort. Breakfast is served at a handsome oak table, and special dietary needs can be met. The living room has a TV, a piano, and a variety of reading material. Woodstock Inn is also on the city tourist shuttle bus route.

Visages ✪
327 NORTH JACKSON, JOPLIN, MISSOURI 64801

Tel: **(417) 624-1397**	Double/sb: **$40**
Best Time to Call: **After 4:30 PM**	Single/sb: **$30**
Hosts: **Bill and Marge Meeker**	Open: **All year**
Location: **3 mi. W of Rte. 71**	Breakfast: **Full**
No. of Rooms: **3**	Credit Cards: **MC, VISA**
No. of Private Baths: **2**	Pets: **Yes**
Max. No. Sharing Bath: **4**	Children: **Welcome (crib)**
Double/pb: **$50**	Smoking: **Permitted**
Single/pb: **$45**	Social Drinking: **No**

Visages takes its name from the nineteen sculptured faces imbedded in the masonry walls surrounding the house, a distinctive chocolate-brown colonial that dates to 1898. The Meekers bought the house as an abandoned wreck in 1977 and spent the next ten years refurbishing it; not surprisingly, Bill lists woodworking as one of his hobbies. The breakfast speciality here is whole-wheat pancakes.

Milford House ✪
3605 GILLHAM ROAD, KANSAS CITY, MISSOURI 64111

Tel: **(816) 753-1269**	Breakfast: **Full**
Hosts: **Ian and Pat Mills**	Credit Cards: **MC, VISA**
No. of Rooms: **6**	Pets: **No**
No. of Private Baths: **2**	Children: **Welcome, over 7**
Max. No. Sharing Bath: **4**	Smoking: **No**
Double/pb: **$75**	Social Drinking: **Permitted**
Double/sb: **$65**	Airport/Station Pickup: **Yes**
Open: **All year**	

A striking architectural hybrid, Milford House is a three-story red-brick mansion combining Queen Anne and Dutch colonial elements. Indoors, a dramatic winding staircase leads from the main entrance to a tower on the side; a 70-foot stained-glass window, based on an original Tiffany landscape, dominates the living room. Kansas City's attractions range from museums to theme parks. The athletically inclined can play tennis on courts across the street from Milford House, while more sedentary sorts can exercise their fingers on the Mill's piano. Guests breakfast on dishes like French toast stuffed with cheese, lemon bread, and southern-style grits.

Pridewell ✪
600 WEST 50TH STREET, KANSAS CITY, MISSOURI 64112

Tel: **(816) 931-1642**	Open: **All year**
Best Time to Call: **4–9 PM**	Breakfast: **Full**
Hosts: **Edwin and Louann White**	Pets: **No**
No. of Rooms: **2**	Children: **Welcome**
No. of Private Baths: **1**	Smoking: **No**
Double/pb: **$65**	Social Drinking: **Permitted**
Single/pb: **$58**	

This fine Tudor residence is situated in a wooded residential area on the battlefield of the Civil War's Battle of Westport. The Nelson Art Gallery, the University of Missouri at Kansas City, and the Missouri Repertory Theatre are close by. It is adjacent to the Country Club Plaza shopping district, which includes several four-star restaurants, tennis courts, and a park.

Lakeview Bed and Breakfast ✪
3609 BASSWOOD DRIVE, LEE'S SUMMIT, MISSOURI 64064

Tel: **(816) 478-2154**	Breakfast: **Full Continental**
Hosts: **Delphine and Leon Rice**	Credit Cards: **MC, VISA**
Location: **4 mi. E of Kansas City**	Wheelchair Accessible: **Yes**
No. of Rooms: **3**	Pets: **No**
No. of Private Baths: **3**	Children: **No**
Double/pb: **$55**	Smoking: **No**
Single/pb: **$50**	Social Drinking: **Permitted**
Open: **All year**	Airport/Station Pickup: **Yes**

This spacious three-level brick home is designed for entertaining, with a library, sunroom, and deck at guests' disposal. For boating and fishing, there's a lake across the street; swimmers have their choice of either the lake or three local swimming pools. Sports fans can catch a Kansas city Royals game, while all will enjoy Missouri Pioneer Town and the Truman Library and Home. Generous morning meals may include stratas, quiche, or Delphine's own breakfast lasagna.

Down-to-Earth Lifestyles
ROUTE 22, PARKVILLE, MISSOURI 64152

Tel: **(816) 891-1018**	Reduced Rates: **Families**
Hosts: **Lola and Bill Coons**	Breakfast: **Full**
Location: **15 mi. N of downtown**	Other Meals: **Available**
Kansas City	Pets: **No**
No. of Rooms: **4**	Children: **Welcome**
No. of Private Baths: **4**	Smoking: **Permitted**
Double/pb: **$65**	Social Drinking: **Permitted**
Single/pb: **$55**	Airport/Station Pickup: **Yes**
Open: **All year**	

This spacious new earth-integrated home, with its picture windows and skylights, emphasizes close contact with nature. It's located on an 85-acre ranch, where there are horses and cows, a fishing pond, and lots of space for mind and soul. The furnishings complement the country setting, and the heated indoor pool, exercise room, and jogging and walking trails will keep you in shape. Lola and Bill will be pleased to suggest nearby places of interest if you can bear to tear yourself away from this restorative haven.

Anchor Hill Lodge ✪
ANCHOR HILL RANCH, ROUTE 1, ROGERSVILLE, MISSOURI 65742

Tel: **(417) 753-2930**	No. of Rooms: **3**
Best Time to Call: **After 7 PM**	No. of Private Baths: **3**
Host: **Mrs. T. E. Atkinson**	Double/pb: **$50**
Location: **23 mi. SE of Springfield**	Single/pb: **$40**

Open: **Mar–Dec.**
Breakfast: **Continental**
Pets: **Horses only**
Children: **Welcome (crib)**

Smoking: **Permitted**
Social Drinking: **Permitted**
Airport/Station Pickup: **Yes**

If your horse hasn't taken a vacation in a while, he's most welcome to accompany you to this rural ranch in the foothills of the Ozark Mountains. For $5 he will have a box stall and all he can eat, while you enjoy the comfort of an old-fashioned country home. Your hosts breed and ride Arabian horses and there are miles of trails for you to enjoy. In addition, there's lots to do and see, including an exotic animal farm, theater, museums, water sports, hiking, and craft fairs. Enjoy the relaxing on-premises hot tub as well as the beautiful views.

Boone's Lick Trail Inn ✪
1000 SOUTH MAIN STREET, ST. CHARLES, MISSOURI 63301

Tel: **(314) 947-7000**
Best Time to Call: **7–9 AM; evenings**
Hosts: **V'Anne and Paul Mydler**
Location: **22 mi. W of St. Louis**
No. of Rooms: **6**
No. of Private Baths: **4**
Max. No. Sharing Bath: **4**
Double/pb: **$58**
Single/pb: **$48**
Double/sb: **$55**
Single/sb: **$45**
Suites: **$88 (2-night minimum)**

Open: **All year**
Reduced Rates: **Available**
Breakfast: **Continental**
Credit Cards: **MC, VISA**
Pets: **No**
Children: **Welcome, over 10**
Smoking: **No**
Social Drinking: **Permitted**
Minimum Stay: **2 nights, weekends
(May 1–Oct. 31)**
Airport/Station Pickup: **Yes**

Listed on the National Register of Historic Places, this Greek Revival inn was built 150 years ago. Experience the ambience of 19th-century adventurers who stayed at this last outpost before moving westward. The guest rooms are simply furnished with 19th-century beds adorned with old quilts; lace curtains dress the windows. This B&B is within walking distance of the state's first capitol, the Lewis and Clark Center, and the Missouri River State Trail. Breakfast offerings include fresh fruits, home-baked bread and pastry, homemade jams, and cereal.

B&B Greater St. Louis Reservation Service ✪
P.O. BOX 30069, ST. LOUIS, MISSOURI 63119

Tel: **(314) 961-2252 in Mo.; (800) 666-5656 out of state**	Rates (Single/Double):	
Best Time to Call: **9 AM–9 PM, including weekends**	Modest: **$30**	**$35**
	Average: **$35–$50**	**$45–$60**
	Luxury: **$85**	**$85–$150**
Coordinator: **Janell Tessaro**	Credit Cards: **No**	
States/Regions Covered: **Augusta, Bonne Terre, California, Hannibal, Louisiana, Moberly, New Haven, St. Louis**	Descriptive Directory: **Free**	

By design, Janell has chosen each home on her select roster on the merits of its appearance, location, breakfast menu, and length of host experience. Her homes range from a cozy bungalow hosted by a weaver and a caterer to a renovated 1845 brewery master's mansion furnished with antebellum antiques. She visits each frequently to ensure the superior standards she requires. From the Arch to the Zoo, St. Louis has everything from A to Z to please a visitor.

Caverly Farm and Orchard B&B ✪
389 NORTH MOSLEY ROAD, ST. LOUIS, MISSOURI 63141

Tel: **(314) 432-5074**	Single/sb: **$40**
Hosts: **David and Nancy Caverly**	Open: **All year**
Location: **2 mi. from I-270 and I-40-64**	Reduced Rates: **Weekly; 10%, seniors**
No. of Rooms: **3**	Breakfast: **Full**
No. of Private Baths: **1**	Pets: **No**
Max. No. Sharing Bath: **4**	Children: **Welcome (crib)**
Double/pb: **$50**	Smoking: **Permitted**
Single/pb: **$45**	Social Drinking: **Permitted**
Double/sb: **$45**	Airport/Station Pickup: **Yes**

The farm consists of two large vegetable gardens; the orchard has just a few fruit trees, but the farmhouse, built in the 1880s, makes it all seem more rural than suburban. The harvest is often found on the breakfast table in berry dishes and preserves along with delicious omelets and home-baked yeast breads. Victorian and primitive family antiques enhance the charm of the large and airy bedrooms. David and Nancy enjoy families with children, and have an electric stair chair to make the second-floor bedrooms accessible to those who may have difficulty climbing stairs.

Coachlight Bed & Breakfast ✪
P.O. BOX 8095, ST. LOUIS, MISSOURI 63156

Tel: **(314) 367-5870**	Reduced Rates: **Available**
Best Time to Call: **8 AM–6 PM**	Breakfast: **Continental**
Hosts: **Susan and Chuck Sundermeyer**	Credit Cards: **AMEX, MC, VISA**
No. of Rooms: **3**	Pets: **No**
No. of Private Baths: **3**	Children: **Welcome, over 3**
Double/pb: **$60–$75**	Smoking: **Permitted**
Open: **All year**	Social Drinking: **Permitted**

This 1904 three-story brick home, with twin dormers and bowed windows, is conveniently located to Forest Park, the St. Louis Zoo, City Art Museum, Powell Symphony Hall, and Washington and St. Louis Universities. Susan and Chuck have deftly combined Old World elegance with modern amenities. Laura Ashley fabrics, fine antique furniture, beautiful woodwork, down comforters, ceiling fans, in-room phone and TV, are accented with dried flower arrangements and stained-glass panels created by Susan. The neighborhood is ideal for browsing, shopping, and fine dining. When calling for reservations, be sure to ask for The Coachlight because a reservation service handles all calls.

Lafayette House ✪
2156 LAFAYETTE AVENUE, ST. LOUIS, MISSOURI 63104

Tel: **(314) 772-4429**	Open: **All year**
Hosts: **Sarah and Jack Milligan**	Breakfast: **Full**
No. of Rooms: **5**	Pets: **Sometimes**
No. of Private Baths: **2**	Children: **Welcome (crib)**
Max. No. Sharing Bath: **4**	Smoking: **Permitted**
Double/pb: **$55**	Social Drinking: **Permitted**
Double/sb: **$45**	Airport/Station Pickup: **Yes**
Suite: **$60**	Minimum Stay: **2 nights in suite**

This 1876 Queen Anne mansion is located in the historic district overlooking Lafayette Park. The house is furnished comfortably with some antiques and traditional furniture. The suite on the third floor, accommodating six, has a private bath and kitchen. Your hosts serve a special egg dish and homemade breads each morning, and offer wine,

cheese, and crackers later. They will gladly take you on tour or can direct you to the Botanical Gardens, Convention Center, and other nearby attractions.

Old Convent Guesthouse
2049 SIDNEY, ST. LOUIS, MISSOURI 63104

Tel: **(314) 772-3531**
Best Time to Call: **Before 2 PM**
Hosts: **Paul and Mary La Flam**
Location: **1 mi. from I-44 and I-55**
No. of Rooms: **4**
No. of Private Baths: **2**
Max. No. Sharing Bath: **4**
Double/pb: **$50**
Single/pb: **$45**
Double/sb: **$45**

Single/sb: **$40**
Suites: **$60**
Open: **All year**
Breakfast: **Full**
Other Meals: **Available**
Pets: **No**
Children: **Welcome, over 4**
Smoking: **Yes**
Social Drinking: **Permitted**
Airport/Station Pickup: **Yes**

This three-story brick town house was built in 1881. Its carved marble fireplaces, massive original woodwork, 10-foot pocket doors, and plaster ceiling medallions have all been beautifully restored. The halls have magnificent maple and walnut flooring. This Victorian home is bright and cheery as a result of having 64 windows! Paul is a professional chef, which you'll soon notice from the first breakfast bite, while Mary enjoys collecting art and dictionaries. You are welcome to play their newly acquired baby grand piano. The St. Louis Zoo, the famed Arch, and Busch Stadium are just a 10-minute drive; the Anheuser Busch Brewery is within walking distance.

Stelzer Bed & Breakfast ✪
7106 GENERAL SHERMAN LANE, ST. LOUIS, MISSOURI 63123

Tel: **(314) 843-5757**	Double/sb: **$25**
Best Time to Call: **Mornings; evenings**	Single/sb: **$18**
Hosts: **Pat and Anita Stelzer**	Open: **All year**
Location: **10 mi. W of St. Louis**	Breakfast: **Continental**
No. of Rooms: **2**	Pets: **No**
No. of Private Baths: **1**	Children: **Welcome**
Max. No. Sharing Bath: **4**	Smoking: **No**
Double/pb: **$30**	Social Drinking: **No**
Single/pb: **$20**	Airport/Station Pickup: **Yes**

Pat and Anita Stelzer have a corner house with green siding and window awnings. The lot is quite spacious, with lovely trees and flowers. Inside, you'll find a mixture of Windsor chairs, old-fashioned rockers, books, and family treasures such as the old spoon collection mounted on the wall. Breakfast on fresh fruit, biscuits, cereals, eggs, and bacon. The Stelzers are located 10 miles from the riverfront and within easy reach of the Botanical Garden, fine dining, and shops.

The Winter House B&B ✪
P.O. BOX 922, ST. LOUIS, MISSOURI 63188

Tel: **(314) 664-4399**	Single/sb: **$42**
Best Time to Call: **7–10 PM**	Open: **All year**
Hosts: **Sarah and Kendall Winter**	Reduced Rates: **10% after 2 nights**
Location: **In St. Louis**	Breakfast: **Continental**
No. of Rooms: **2**	Credit Cards: **DC, MC**
No. of Private Baths: **1**	Pets: **No**
Max. No. Sharing Bath: **4**	Children: **Welcome, over 12**
Double/pb: **$48**	Smoking: **No**
Single/pb: **$42**	Social Drinking: **Permitted**
Double/sb: **$48**	Airport/Station Pickup: **Yes**

Built in 1897, this red brick home boasts many original details. Tower Grove Park, just half a block away, offers something for nearly everyone, with fitness trails, illuminated tennis courts, and open-air summer concerts. Missouri Botanical Gardens adjoins the park. St. Louis' myriad attractions—the symphony, the zoo, the Cardinals—are within a radius of several miles. Complimentary beverages are served to guests, and Continental breakfast features fresh fruit, baked goods, and gourmet coffees and teas.

The Schwegmann House B&B Inn ✪
438 WEST FRONT STREET, WASHINGTON, MISSOURI 63090

Tel: **(314) 239-5025**	Location: **50 mi. W of St. Louis**
Host: **Karen**	No. of Rooms: **9**

No. of Private Baths: **7**
Max. No. Sharing Bath: **4**
Double/pb: **$60**
Single/pb: **$50**
Double/sb: **$45**
Single/sb: **$35**
Open: **All year**

Breakfast: **Continental**
Credit Cards: **MC, VISA**
Pets: **No**
Children: **Welcome**
Smoking: **Permitted**
Social Drinking: **Permitted**

A three-story 1861 Georgian brick house included on the National Historic Register, it is located on the Missouri River. It is tastefully furnished with antiques; handmade quilts complement the decor of each guest room. It is close to Daniel Boone's home, Meramec Caverns, Missouri's Rhineland wineries, antiques shops, and fine restaurants. Relax in the graceful parlor by the fireside or stroll the gardens that overlook the river. The innkeeper serves a bountiful breakfast, including fresh-ground coffee, imported cheeses, croissants, and grape juice from Missouri's vineyards.

Washington House B&B Inn ✪
3 LAFAYETTE STREET, WASHINGTON, MISSOURI 63090

Tel: **(314) 239-2417**
Hosts: **Kathy and Chuck Davis**
Location: **50 mi. SW of St. Louis**
No. of Rooms: **3**
No. of Private Baths: **3**
Double/pb: **$55–$65**
Single/pb: **$45–$55**
Open: **All year**
Reduced Rates: **10%, Jan. 2–Mar. 30;
10%, seniors**

Breakfast: **Full**
Pets: **No**
Children: **Welcome**
Smoking: **No**
Social Drinking: **Permitted**
Minimum Stay: **2 nights, weekends in
October**

Facing the Missouri River, this two-story brick Federal-style building was built as an inn during the late 1830s. Located on a quiet corner in the heart of the historic district, avid preservationists Kathy and Chuck have painstakingly restored it, using period antiques and decorations of the era. The rooms are air-conditioned and have canopy beds. This is wine country, and many nearby wineries offer tours and tasting.

Benner House Bed and Breakfast ✪
645 MAIN STREET, WESTON, MISSOURI 64098

Tel: **(816) 386-2616**	Open: **All year**
Hosts: **Ken and Karen West**	Breakfast: **Full**
Location: **30 mi. NW of Kansas City**	Pets: **No**
No. of Rooms: **4**	Children: **Welcome, over 12**
Max. No. Sharing Bath: **4**	Smoking: **No**
Double/sb: **$65**	Social Drinking: **Permitted**
Single/sb: **$58**	Airport/Station Pickup: **Yes**

Listed on the National Register of Historic Places, this fine example of steamboat Gothic architecture is just a short walk from the historic downtown shopping district. Ken and Karen invite you to relax on the charming wraparound porch, tour the hills of Weston in their 1929 automobile, or enjoy the many antebellum homes in their neighborhood. Their beautifully decorated home is accented by a fine collection of antiques. Enjoy relaxed conversation in the main parlor or slip away to the sitting room, where you can curl up in a rocking chair with a book. Karen is likely to spoil you with her delicious brownies at snack time.

MONTANA

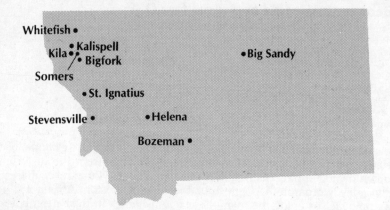

Whitefish •
Kila •• Kalispell
 •• Bigfork
Somers
 • St. Ignatius
Stevensville •   • Helena
           Bozeman •
                          • Big Sandy

Bed and Breakfast Western Adventure
P.O. BOX 20972, BILLINGS, MONTANA 59104

Tel: **(406) 259-7993**
Best Time to Call: **10 AM**
Coordinator: **Paula Deigert**
States/Regions Covered: **Montana—
  Billings, Bozeman, Glacier National
  Park, Kalispell, Missoula;
  Wyoming—Cheyenne, Jackson Hole,
  Yellowstone National Park**

Rates (Single/Double):
  Modest: **$28–$40**
  Average: **$45–$65**
  Luxury: **$65–$175**
Credit Cards: **MC, VISA**

Famous for its national parks, fishing streams, and ski resorts, this
region is perfect for outdoor enthusiasts. Wild-West fans and history
buffs will want to tour forts and battlegrounds, like Little Big Horn,
the site of Custer's Last Stand. For the record, the cost of accommodations has more to do with location than with the relative luxury of
the rooms.

O'Duach'Ain Country Inn ✪
675 FERNDALE DRIVE, BIGFORK, MONTANA 59911

Tel: (406) 837-6851
Best Time to Call: **Before Noon**
Hosts: **Margot and Tom Doohan**
Location: **17 mi. S of Kalispell**
No. of Rooms: **5**
Max. No. Sharing Bath: **4**
Double/sb: **$60**
Single/sb: **$50**
Separate Guest Suites: **$85**
Open: **All year**

Breakfast: **Full**
Other Meals: **Available**
Credit Cards: **AMEX, DISC, MC, VISA**
Pets: **Sometimes**
Children: **Welcome, over 12**
Smoking: **Permitted**
Social Drinking: **Permitted**
Airport/Station Pickup: **Yes**

O'Duach'Ain is a gracious three-level log home set on five beautiful acres. Inside, you'll find a casual atmosphere of open wood logs, stone fireplaces, antiques, and artwork. Guests are welcome to relax on the deck and take in the spectacular view. In the morning, your hosts provide a gourmet breakfast, featuring freshly prepared international dishes. Margot and Tom will gladly take you on a one-day tour of the area in their luxury van; the fee includes an outdoor picnic lunch. Your hosts will also direct you to nearby Glacier National Park, Swan Lake, Big Mountain ski area, and Flatland Lake.

Sky View ✪
BOX 408, BIG SANDY, MONTANA 59520

Tel: (406) 378-2549; 386-2464
Best Time to Call: **Before 11 AM;**
     after 6 PM
Hosts: **Ron and Gay Pearson and**
     family
Location: **75 mi. N of Great Falls**
No. of Rooms: **3**
Max. No. Sharing Bath: **6**
Double/sb: **$35**
Single/sb: **$26**

Guest Cottage: **$35–$60**
Open: **May 1–Dec. 1**
Reduced Rates: **Families**
Breakfast: **Full**
Other Meals: **Available**
Pets: **Sometimes**
Children: **Welcome**
Smoking: **Permitted**
Social Drinking: **Permitted**
Airport/Station Pickup: **Yes**

Sky View is a working ranch located in an area known for its wild and rugged ambience, sparse population, and spectacular scenery. It's in the heart of Lewis and Clark country, just off a major highway to Glacier National Park. The Pearson family enjoys people of all ages and looks forward to sharing its life-style with guests, keeping you informed of local rodeos, Indian powwows, river float trips, tours, and hunting and fishing opportunities. Children enjoy their playground, and baby-sitters are available. A public swimming pool and tennis courts are nearby.

Torch and Toes B&B ✪

309 SOUTH THIRD AVENUE, BOZEMAN, MONTANA 59715

Tel: **(406) 586-7285**
Best Time to Call: **8 AM–noon**
Hosts: **Ronald and Judy Hess**
Location: **100 mi. SE of Helena**
No. of Rooms: **3**
No. of Private Baths: **1**
Max. No. Sharing Bath: **4**
Double/pb: **$45**
Single/pb: **$40**
Double/sb: **$45**

Single/sb: **$40**
Open: **All year**
Reduced Rates: **Government employees**
Breakfast: **Full**
Pets: **No**
Children: **Welcome**
Smoking: **No**
Social Drinking: **Permitted**
Airport/Station Pickup: **Yes**

Set back from the street, this Colonial Revival house is centrally located in the Bon Ton Historic District. Lace curtains, leaded glass windows, and period pieces remind one that this is a house with a past. Ron is a professor of architecture at nearby Montana State University; Judy is a weaver interested in historic preservation. Their home is furnished in a charming blend of nostalgic antiques, humorous collectibles, and fine furnishings. Breakfast always includes a special egg dish, fresh fruit, and muffins. Afterwards, relax on the redwood deck in summer, or by a cozy fire in winter. Nearby attractions include blue-ribbon trout streams, hiking, skiing, and the Museum of the Rockies. Yellowstone National Park is one and a half hours away.

Voss Inn ✪

319 SOUTH WILLSON, BOZEMAN, MONTANA 59715

Tel: **(406) 587-0982**
Best Time to Call: **10 AM–9 PM**
Hosts: **Bruce and Frankee Muller**
Location: **3 mi. from I-90**
No. of Rooms: **6**
No. of Private Baths: **6**
Double/pb: **$55–$65**
Single/pb: **$50–$55**
Open: **All year**

Reduced Rates: **Business travelers, Sun.–Thurs.**
Breakfast: **Full**
Credit Cards: **MC, VISA**
Pets: **No**
Children: **Sometimes**
Smoking: **Permitted**
Social Drinking: **Permitted**

This handsome 100-year-old brick mansion, flanked by Victorian gingerbread porches, is set like a gem on a tree-lined street in historic Bozeman. The bedrooms are elegantly wallpapered and furnished with brass and iron beds, ornate lighting, Oriental throw rugs over polished hardwood floors—a perfect spot for a first or second honeymoon. The parlor has a good selection of books, as well as a chess set for your pleasure. It's north of Yellowstone, on the way to Glacier, with trout fishing, mountain lakes, and skiing within easy reach. Don't miss the Museum of the Rockies on the Montana State University campus 10 blocks away.

Ballymurray B&B
206 FOURTH AVENUE EAST, KALISPELL, MONTANA 59901

Tel: **(406) 755-7080**
Best Time to Call: **9–11 AM; 5–10 PM**
Hosts: **Bryce and Bette Baker**
No. of Rooms: **3**
No. of Private Baths: **1**
Max. No. Sharing Bath: **4**
Double/pb: **$50**
Single/pb: **$35**

Single/sb: **$35**
Open: **All year**
Breakfast: **Full**
Pets: **No**
Children: **Welcome, over 6**
Smoking: **Permitted**
Social Drinking: **Permitted**
Airport/Station Pickup: **Yes**

Bette, the Irish half of the Baker family, is an artist who named their B&B after the village in Ireland where her mother lived. Bryce, who is Irish through inclination, invites you to fish the many lakes, rivers, and streams in Flathead Valley. On mornings when fishing's been good, he's likely to fix you a special fisherman's breakfast, served in the formal dining room or the cheery sun room. You'll enjoy a visit to historic Conrad Mansion or Woodland Park, where you can see exotic birds, swim, or skate. Within a short drive, you can climb the peaks of Glacier National Park, ski the slopes of Big Mountain, waterski on Flathead Lake, try white-water rafting, or play golf on one of five challenging courses. Afterwards, relax in the living room, where the crackling fire takes the chill off cool evenings.

Brick Farmhouse Bed & Breakfast ✪
1946 WHITEFISH STAGE, KALISPELL, MONTANA 59901

Tel: **(406) 756-6230**
Best Time to Call: **After 4 PM**
Hosts: **Don and Carol Young**
Location: **2 mi. from Hwy. 93**
No. of Rooms: **2**
Max. No. Sharing Bath: **4**
Double/sb: **$40–$45**
Single/sb: **$35**

Open: **June 1–Oct. 1**
Breakfast: **Full**
Pets: **No**
Children: **Welcome, over 7**
Smoking: **No**
Social Drinking: **Permitted**
Airport/Station Pickup: **Yes**

This red-brick two-story home in a country setting comes complete with an early rising rooster, milking cow, and assorted barnyard animals. You are certain to enjoy the farm-fresh breakfast of eggs and home-baked breads. Don and Carol will also cater to special requests and diets. Afterwards, walk to the bridge crossing the Whitefish River, or borrow bikes for some cycling. Glacier National Park is 25 miles away, and Flathead Lake offers many recreational activities.

Willows Inn ⊘
224 SOUTH PLATT AVENUE, RED LODGE, MONTANA 59068

Tel: (406) 446-3913
Best Time to Call: **Morning, afternoon**
Hosts: **Elven, Kerry, and Carolyn
  Boggio**
Location: **60 mi. SW of Billings**
No. of Rooms: 5
No. of Private Baths: 3
Max. No. Sharing Bath: 4
Double/pb: **$50–$60**
Double/sb: **$50**
Single/sb: **$45**
Guest Cottage: **$55 for 2**

Open: **All year**
Reduced Rates: **10%, after 4 nights,
  10%, seniors**
Breakfast: **Continental**
Credit Cards: **MC, VISA**
Pets: **No**
Children: **Welcome**
Smoking: **No**
Social Drinking: **Permitted**
Minimum Stay: **2 nights in cottage**
Foreign Languages: **Finnish**

Tucked beneath the majestic Beartooth Mountains in the northern Rockies, the historic town of Red Lodge provides an ideal setting for this charming three story Queen Anne. Flanked by giant evergreens and colorful flower beds, the inn is reminiscent of a bygone age, complete with white picket fence, gingerbread trim, and front porch swing. Overstuffed sofas and wicker pieces complement the warm and cheerful decor. Delicious homebaked pastries are Elven's specialty—she uses her own Finnish recipes for these mouthwatering treats. Championship rodeos, excellent cross-country and downhill skiing, opportunities to hike, golf, and fish abound in this special area, still unspoiled by commercial progress. Yellowstone National Park is only 65 miles away.

Osprey Inn Bed & Breakfast ⊘
5557 HIGHWAY 93 SOUTH, SOMERS, MONTANA 59932

Tel: (406) 857-2042
Best Time to Call: **8 AM–9 PM**
Hosts: **Sharon and Wayne Finney**
Location: **8 mi. S of Kalispell**
No. of Rooms: 5
No. of Private Baths: 3
Max. No. Sharing Bath: 4
Double/pb: **$75**
Single/pb: **$70**
Double/sb: **$65**
Single/sb: **$60**

Guest Cottage: **$75**
Open: **All year**
Reduced Rates: **Sept. 15–Dec. 20,
  Jan. 6–May 15**
Breakfast: **Full**
Credit Cards: **MC, VISA**
Pets: **No**
Children: **Welcome, over 9**
Smoking: **Permitted**
Social Drinking: **Permitted**
Airport/Station Pickup: **Yes**

Yes, you can see osprey—as well as geese, loons, and grebes—from the deck of this rustic lakeshore retreat. In the summer, guests are welcome to bring along a boat or canoe; in the winter, pack your skis. Cameras and binoculars come in handy throughout the year. You'll start the day with fresh seasonal fruit, home-baked cinnamon rolls, and pancakes with homemade fruit syrups.

Country Caboose ✪
852 WILLOUGHBY ROAD, STEVENSVILLE, MONTANA 59870

Tel: **(406) 777-3145**
Host: **Lisa Thompson**
Location: **35 mi. S of Missoula**
No. of Rooms: **1**
No. of Private Baths: **1**
Double/pb: **$40**
Single/pb: **$40**

Open: **May–Sept.**
Breakfast: **Full**
Other Meals: **Available**
Pets: **No**
Children: **Welcome**
Smoking: **No**
Social Drinking: **Permitted**

If you enjoy romantic train rides, why not spend the night in an authentic caboose? This one dates back to 1923, is made of wood, and is painted red, of course. It is set on real rails in the middle of the countryside. The caboose sleeps two and offers a spectacular view of the Bitterroot Mountains, right from your pillow. In the morning, breakfast is served at a table for two. Specialties include huckleberry pancakes, quiche, and strawberries in season. Local activities include touring St. Mary's Mission, hiking the mountain trails, fishing, and hunting.

Duck Inn ✪
1305 COLUMBIA AVENUE, WHITEFISH, MONTANA 59937

Tel: **(406) 862-DUCK**
Hosts: **Ken and Phyllis Adler**
Location: **25 mi. from Glacier Nat'l. Park**
No. of Rooms: **10**
No. of Private Baths: **10**
Double/pb: **$46–$65**
Single/pb: **$46–$65**

Open: **All year**
Reduced Rates: **5%, seniors**
Breakfast: **Continental**
Credit Cards: **AMEX, DC, MC, VISA**
Pets: **No**
Children: **Welcome**
Smoking: **Permitted**
Social Drinking: **Permitted**

The Duck Inn is on the Whitefish River, eight miles from Big Mountain Ski Area. Each guest room features a brass or white iron bed, cozy fireplace, deep soak tub, and a balcony. A large living room with a view of Big Mountain and the river is a relaxing spot. Your hosts offer a different kind of fresh-baked bread each morning, and can provide information on Glacier National Park, wilderness areas, and spots to swim, sail, and fish. A Jacuzzi is available after a heavy day of touring.

For key to listings, see inside front or back cover.

✪ This star means that rates are guaranteed through December 31, 1991, to any guest making a reservation as a result of reading about the B&B in *BED & BREAKFAST U.S.A.*—1991 edition.

Important! To avoid misunderstandings, always ask about cancellation policies when booking.

Please enclose a self-addressed, stamped, business-size envelope when contacting reservation services.

For more details on what you can expect in a B&B, see Chapter 1.

Always mention *Bed & Breakfast U.S.A.* when making reservations!

If no B&B is listed in the area you'll be visiting, use the form on page 675 to order a copy of our "List of New B&Bs."

We want to hear from you! Use the form on page 677.

NEBRASKA

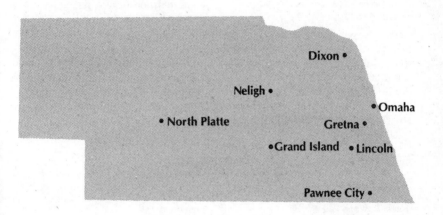

Dixon •

Neligh •

• North Platte

•Omaha

Gretna •

•Grand Island •Lincoln

Pawnee City •

Bed & Breakfast of the Great Plains ✪
P.O. BOX 2333, LINCOLN, NEBRASKA 68502

Tel: **(402) 423-3480**
Coordinator: **Rose Ann Foster**
States/Regions Covered: **Nebraska—**
statewide; Iowa, Kansas, Western
Missouri

Rates (Single/Double):
Modest: **$20–$25 $30**
Average: **$25–$30 $35–$45**
Luxury: **$40–$50 $55–$80**
Credit Cards: **MC, VISA**

Rose Ann's ever-growing roster includes a modest home within blocks of Interstate-80, an air-conditioned farmhouse where the alarm clock is a rooster, and a mansion on the National Register of Historic Places. The friendly hosts will be delighted to direct guests to rodeos, ethnic festivals, museums, state or county fairs, lakeside recreation areas, Indian powwows, concerts, Cornhusker football, and Boys' Town. Tell them your interests and they will custom-tailor an itinerary to suit you.

The Georges ✪
ROUTE 1, BOX 50, DIXON, NEBRASKA 68732

Tel: (402) 584-2625	Open: All year
Best Time to Call: 6:30 AM–6 PM	Breakfast: Full
Hosts: Harold and Marie George	Other Meals: Available
Location: 35 mi. W of Sioux City, Iowa	Pets: Sometimes
	Children: Welcome
No. of Rooms: 3	Smoking: No
Max. No. Sharing Bath: 4	Social Drinking: Permitted
Double/sb: $35	Airport/Station Pickup: Yes
Single/sb: $25	Foreign Languages: Swedish

The Georges have a large, remodeled farmhouse with a spacious backyard. They offer the opportunity to see a farming operation at first hand, right down to the roosters crowing and the birds singing in the morning. Harold and Marie are now full-time farmers after careers in social work and engineering. They prepare a hearty country breakfast featuring homemade jellies and jams. The Georges are close to Wayne State College and Ponca State Park.

Bundy's Bed and Breakfast ✪
16906 SOUTH 255, GRETNA, NEBRASKA 68028

Tel: (402) 332-3616	Single/sb: $15
Best Time to Call: 7 AM–9 PM	Open: All year
Hosts: Bob and Dee Bundy	Breakfast: Full
Location: 30 mi. S of Omaha	Pets: Sometimes
No. of Rooms: 4	Children: No
Max. No. Sharing Bath: 4	Smoking: No
Double/sb: $25	Social Drinking: No

The Bundys have a pretty farmhouse painted white with black trim. Here you can enjoy country living just 30 minutes from downtown Lincoln and Omaha. The rooms are decorated with antiques, attractive wallpapers, and collectibles. In the morning, wake up to farm-fresh eggs and homemade breads. The house is just a short walk from a swimming lake, and is three miles from a ski lodge.

The Rogers House ✪
2145 B STREET, LINCOLN, NEBRASKA 68502

Tel: (402) 476-6961	Reduced Rates: 10% on 3rd and 4th night; 15% thereafter
Best Time to Call: 12–4 PM	
Host: Nora Houtsma	Breakfast: Full
No. of Rooms: 8	Credit Cards: AMEX, MC, VISA
No. of Private Baths: 8	Pets: No
Double/pb: $45–$59	Children: Welcome, over 10
Single/pb: $40–$54	Smoking: Permitted
Open: All year	Social Drinking: Permitted

This Jacobean Revival–style brick mansion was built in 1914 and is a local historic landmark. There are three sun porches, attractively furnished with wicker and plants, and the air-conditioned house is decorated with lovely antiques. Nora will direct you to the diverse cultural attractions available at the nearby University of Nebraska, the surrounding historic district, and antique shops. Don't miss a visit to the Children's Zoo and the beautiful Sunken Gardens. Breakfast is hearty and delicious. A professional staff of five is eager to serve you.

Mary Mahoney's Thissen House
201 MAIN STREET, NELIGH, NEBRASKA 68756

Tel: **(402) 887-4325**	Open: **May 1–Sept. 1**
Best Time to Call: **Afternoons**	Breakfast: **Full**
Host: **Mary Mahoney**	Pets: **No**
Location: **150 mi. W of Omaha**	Children: **Welcome, over 3**
No. of Rooms: **3**	Smoking: **No**
Max. No. Sharing Bath: **5**	Social Drinking: **Permitted**
Double/sb: **$30–$35**	Airport/Station Pickup: **Yes**
Single/sb: **$25**	

Rich in regional significance, this white Victorian housed a number of local entrepreneurs and politicos, not the least of whom was Mary's Dutch-born grandfather—a city councilman, water commissioner, and the mason who set the brick on many of Neligh's public buildings. Tennis courts, a swimming pool, and a nine-hole golf course are nearby. This is a place where you can enjoy small-town pleasures, such as sitting on the glider or strolling in the park. For breakfast, she covers the table with white linen and sets out eggs, bacon, toast, and coffee or tea.

The Offutt House ✪
140 NORTH 39TH STREET, OMAHA, NEBRASKA 68131

Tel: **(402) 553-0951**	Single/sb: **$40**
Host: **Jeannie K. Swoboda**	Suites: **$70–$100**
Location: **1 mi. from I-80**	Open: **All year**
No. of Rooms: **7**	Reduced Rates: **After 5 nights**
No. of Private Baths: **5**	Breakfast: **Continental**
Max. No. Sharing Bath: **4**	Pets: **Sometimes**
Double/pb: **$60–$70**	Children: **Welcome**
Single/pb: **$50**	Smoking: **Permitted**
Double/sb: **$50**	Social Drinking: **Permitted**

This comfortable mansion (circa 1894) is part of the city's Historic Gold Coast, a section of handsome homes built by Omaha's wealthiest residents. Offering peace and quiet, the rooms are air-conditioned, spacious, and furnished with antiques; some have fireplaces. Jeannie will direct you to nearby attractions such as the Joslyn Museum or the Old Market area, which abounds with many beautiful shops and fine restaurants. She graciously offers coffee or wine in late afternoon.

NEVADA

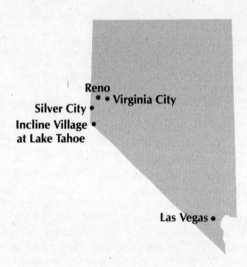

Reno
Silver City • • Virginia City
Incline Village •
at Lake Tahoe

Las Vegas •

Haus Bavaria ⊘

P.O. BOX 3308, 593 NORTH DYER CIRCLE, INCLINE VILLAGE, LAKE
TAHOE, NEVADA 89450

Tel: **(702) 831-6122 or (800) GO-TAHOE**	Single/pb: **$70**
Best Time to Call: **Noon–2 PM**	Open: **All year**
Host: **Bick Hewitt**	Breakfast: **Continental**
Location: **35 mi. SW of Reno**	Pets: **No**
No. of Rooms: **5**	Children: **No**
No. of Private Baths: **5**	Smoking: **No**
Double/pb: **$80**	Social Drinking: **Permitted**
	Minimum Stay: **2 nights**

This Alpine style residence is framed by the mountains and convenient
to the lake. Each guest room opens onto a balcony offering lovely
mountain views. It's close to the gambling casinos and shows, all
water sports, and, in winter, the challenging slopes of Mount Rose
and Heavenly Valley.

Las Vegas B&B
CONTACT: BED AND BREAKFAST INTERNATIONAL, 1181-B SOLANO AVENUE, ALBANY, CALIFORNIA 94706

Tel: **(415) 525-4569**
Best Time to Call: **8:30 AM–5 PM**
Host: **Jean Brown**
No. of Rooms: **2**
No. of Private Baths: **1**
Max. No. Sharing Bath: **3**
Double/pb: **$58**
Single/pb: **$52**

Double/sb: **$50**
Single/sb: **$45**
Open: **All year**
Breakfast: **Full**
Pets: **No**
Children: **Swimmers only**
Smoking: **Permitted**
Social Drinking: **Permitted**

Located a few minutes from the fabled "Strip" of hotels, casinos, and restaurants is this two-story contemporary home. The quiet, residential neighborhood is a welcome respite from the 24-hour hoopla available nearby. You are welcome to use your host's swimming pool.

Bed and Breakfast—South Reno ✪
136 ANDREW LANE, RENO, NEVADA 89511

Tel: **(702) 849-0772**
Best Time to Call: **Mornings**
Hosts: **Caroline Walters and Robert McNeill**
Location: **⅛ mi. from Hwy. 395 South**
No. of Rooms: **3**
No. of Private Baths: **1**
Max. No. Sharing Bath: **4**
Double/pb: **$64**

Double/sb: **$54**
Single/sb: **$44**
Open: **Mar. 15–Nov. 15**
Breakfast: **Full**
Pets: **No**
Children: **Welcome**
Smoking: **Permitted**
Social Drinking: **Permitted**
Minimum Stay: **2 nights**

Situated in Steamboat Valley, and surrounded by unbroken vistas of the 10,000-foot-high Mt. Rose and Slide Mountains, is this rustic home, with its beamed ceilings and Early American decor. The atmosphere is casual and unhurried, and one can really revel in the simple life. Breakfast is ranch-size and always includes one of Caroline's delicious apple–nut creations along with the bacon and eggs. Depending on your mood and the season, you can ski; revisit the gold rush days in Virginia City; gamble, dine, or be entertained at a posh hotel; cruise magnificent Lake Tahoe; or stay "home" and swim in the backyard pool.

Lace and Linen Guest House
4800 KIETZKE LANE, SUITE 114, RENO, NEVADA 89502

Tel: **(702) 826-3547**
Best Time to Call: **10 AM–10 PM**
Host: **Patricia Parks**

Location: **1 mi. from Rte. 395**
No. of Rooms: **3**
No. of Private Baths: **2**

Max. No. Sharing Bath: **4**	Breakfast: **Continental**
Double/pb: **$45**	Pets: **Sometimes**
Single/pb: **$40**	Children: **Sometimes**
Double/sb: **$45**	Smoking: **Permitted**
Single/sb: **$40**	Social Drinking: **Permitted**
Open: **All year**	Airport/Station Pickup: **Yes**

This modern condominium is furnished in a blend of white Victorian wicker and European antiques, but the spectacular view of the Sierra Nevadas is what many guests remember best. You are welcome to relax in the living room, made cozy by its woodburning fireplace, or watch the sun set from the western balcony. There's a heated pool, Jaccuzzi, sauna, and lighted tennis court on premises for your enjoyment. In winter, skiers head for the challenging slopes of Mt. Rose; in all seasons, the casinos, fine restaurants, and Lake Tahoe are easy to reach.

Edith Palmer's Country Inn
SOUTH B STREET, P.O. BOX 756, VIRGINIA CITY, NEVADA 89449

Tel: **(702) 847-0707**	Open: **All year**
Host: **Erlene Brown**	Breakfast: **Full**
Location: **23 mi. S of Reno**	Other Meals: **Available**
No. of Rooms: **5**	Credit Cards: **MC, VISA**
No. of Private Baths: **3**	Pets: **No**
Max. No. Sharing Bath: **4**	Children: **No**
Double/pb: **$60–$75**	Smoking: **No**
Single/pb: **$70**	Social Drinking: **Permitted**
Double/sb: **$70**	Airport/Station Pickup: **Yes**
Single/sb: **$65**	

One of Nevada's first wine merchants built this country Victorian over 100 years ago. What was once a stone wine cellar is now a gourmet restaurant with rock walls and a fireplace crafted from local ores and gemstones. Spend the night in a comfortable bedroom and wake up to a breakfast of freshly ground coffee and a variety of hot breads and egg dishes. Outside, the pretty gardens are often used for wedding receptions. Many celebrities find this inn a wonderful escape spot. Even if you're not a star, you'll be treated like one. Edith Palmer's is within walking distance from the historic sights of Virginia City and close to Lake Tahoe and Reno.

NEW HAMPSHIRE

Colebrook •
Littleton
• • Gorham
Bethlehem Jefferson
•
Sugar Hill • • Franconia
Easton • • N. Woodstock
North Conway • • Intervale
Conway
Plymouth • •
Sunapee Holderness • • Campton
Newport •
Mt. Sunapee • Wolfeboro
E. Andover Laconia • • Strafford
Franklin • Northwood
• Loudon
Marlborough • Concord • • Portsmouth
Jaffrey Suncook • • Greenland
• • Hampton Beach
Rindge

New Hampshire Bed & Breakfast ✪
RFD BOX 88, MEREDITH, NEW HAMPSHIRE 03253

Tel: **(603) 279-8348**
Best Time to Call: **10 AM–5 PM**
Coordinator: **Ernie Taddie**
States/Regions Covered: **Statewide**
Descriptive Directory: **$1**

Rates (Single/Double):
   Modest: **$35–$50**   **$40–$50**
   Average: **$35–$50**   **$40–$60**
   Luxury: **$50–$85**   **$65–$90**
Credit Cards: **MC, VISA**
Minimum Stay: **2 nights, holidays and
   fall foliage**

New Hampshire is a haven for the sports-minded, having facilities for
every type of recreation. Shoppers will find it a bargain haven since
there's no sales tax on merchandise. Ernie's roster ranges from an
18th-century Cape house, where the hostess makes her own cheese,

to a mountainside home, with its own pool and tennis court, overlooking Lake Winnipesaukee, to a contemporary home convenient to the Manchester factory outlets.

The Bells B&B ☉
STRAWBERRY HILL STREET, P.O. BOX 276, BETHLEHEM, NEW HAMPSHIRE 03574

Tel: **(603) 869-2647**
Hosts: **Bill and Louise Sims**
Location: **2½ mi. off I-93, Exit 40**
No. of Rooms: **3**
No. of Private Baths: **3**
Double/pb: **$60**
Single/pb: **$45**
Suites: **$70**
Open: **All year**
Breakfast: **Full**
Pets: **No**
Children: **Welcome, over 12**
Smoking: **Permitted**
Social Drinking: **Permitted**

Named for the more than one hundred tin and wooden bells that dangle from its eaves, this four-story 1892 cottage has been cited by *Victorian Homes* magazine for its pagoda-like architecture. The furnishings—an eclectic mixture of antiques and family heirlooms—are also distinctive. Because Bethlehem is in the heart of the White Mountains, Mt. Washington, Franconia State Park, and excellent ski slopes are a 15-minute drive. Tennis courts and two 18-hole golf courses are within walking distance. Substantial full breakfasts may feature a blintz casserole, eggs Benedict, or baked French toast.

The Mulburn Inn ☉
MAIN STREET, BETHLEHEM, NEW HAMPSHIRE 03574

Tel: **(603) 869-3389**
Best Time to Call: **9 AM–9 PM**
Hosts: **Bob and Cheryl Burns, Moe and Linda Mulkigian**
Location: **20 mi. SE of St. Johnsbury**
No. of Rooms: **7**
No. of Private Baths: **7**
Double/pb: **$50–$70**
Single/pb: **$40**
Open: **All year**

Reduced Rates: **10%, weekly**
Breakfast: **Full**
Other Meals: **Available**
Credit Cards: **AMEX, MC, VISA**
Pets: **No**
Children: **Welcome (crib)**
Smoking: **No**
Social Drinking: **Permitted**
Airport/Station Pickup: **Yes**

Back in the early 1900s, this sprawling Tudor home was known as the Ivie Estate, a family summer retreat. It boasts original oak staircases, stained-glass windows, rounded-corner architecture, three-tile fireplaces, and even has an elevator. There is plenty of room here, with three enclosed wraparound porches for relaxing and a large living room for reading and fireside chats. Breakfast is served by the fire in a sunny dining room. In the afternoon, your hosts offer seasonal snacks such as soup or cider and cheese. If you are visiting in March or April, you'll be treated to fresh syrup right from the family maples. This lively inn is located in the heart of the White Mountains, near Franconia Notch, the Old Man in the Mountain, Mt. Washington, and places to ski, shop, and dine.

Mountain-Fare Inn
BOX 553, CAMPTON, NEW HAMPSHIRE 03223

Tel: **(603) 726-4283**	Open: **All year**
Best Time to Call: **After 5 PM**	Reduced Rates: **15%, Apr.–Aug.;**
Hosts: **Susan and Nick Preston**	**families**
Location: **40 mi. N of Concord**	Breakfast: **Full**
No. of Rooms: **9**	Other Meals: **Dinner available in ski**
No. of Private Baths: **5**	**season**
Max. No. Sharing Bath: **4**	Pets: **No**
Double/pb: **$64**	Children: **Welcome**
Single/pb: **$37**	Smoking: **No**
Double/sb: **$56**	Social Drinking: **Permitted**
Single/sb: **$32**	Minimum Stay: **2 nights, weekends**

Built in the 1800s, this white clapboard farmhouse is located in the foothills of the White Mountains, just minutes away from Franconia Notch and the Waterville Valley Resort. Susan and Nick are professional skiers and into physical fitness. Their enthusiasm is contagious! Generous seasonal snacks are offered. During the ski season, you are invited to have a family-style dinner for $12 per person. Plymouth State College is nearby.

Monadnock B&B ❂
1 MONADNOCK STREET, COLEBROOK, NEW HAMPSHIRE 03576

Tel: **(603) 237-8216**	Open: **All year**
Best Time to Call: **8 AM–9 PM**	Reduced Rates: **15%, weekly**
Hosts: **Barbara and Wendell Woodard**	Breakfast: **Full**
Location: **1 block from the junction of**	Pets: **Sometimes**
Rtes. 3 and 26	Children: **Welcome (crib)**
No. of Rooms: **7**	Smoking: **Permitted**
Max. No. Sharing Bath: **6**	Social Drinking: **Permitted**
Double/sb: **$35**	Airport/Station Pickup: **Yes**
Single/sb: **$25**	

When Wendell was in the Air Force, the Woodards lived all over the world, and their house is decorated with pieces collected in Europe and Asia. Now they have settled in New Hampshire's North Country, within walking distance of Vermont and only a 15-minute drive from Canada. Wendell cheerfully directs skiers, hunters, fishermen, and golfers to all his favorite haunts. But first, Barbara will ply guests with a hearty breakfast, featuring specialties such as sausage quiche, pancakes, and omelets, accompanied by endless supplies of coffee and tea.

The Foothills Farm ✪
P.O. BOX 1368, CONWAY, NEW HAMPSHIRE 03818

Tel: **(207) 935-3799**	Breakfast: **Full**
Best Time to Call: **Early evenings**	Pets: **Welcome**
Hosts: **Kevin Early and Theresa Rovere**	Children: **Welcome**
Location: **40 mi. W of Portland**	Smoking: **Permitted**
No. of Rooms: **4**	Social Drinking: **Permitted**
Max. No. Sharing Bath: **4**	Minimum Stay: **2 nights, weekends,**
Double/sb: **$42–$48**	**during fall foliage, and holidays**
Single/sb: **$32**	Airport/Station Pickup: **Yes**
Open: **All year**	
Reduced Rates: **Available; 10%,**	
seniors	

This restored 1850s clapboard farmhouse is located on a quiet back road in the foothills of the White Mountains. The house is surrounded by flowers, a vegetable garden, and asparagus fields. The well-groomed grounds also include a trout stream and plenty of room to bike or cross-country ski. Bedrooms are furnished in period antiques, and one has a fireplace. Guests are welcome to relax in the den, where they'll find books and a crackling fire. In warmer weather, the screened-in porch overlooking the fields and gardens is a favorite spot. Breakfast specialties such as eggs Benedict with home fries, and blueberry pancakes with sausage are served in a country kitchen, which has an antique stove and pine paneling. Kevin and Theresa have bicycles to lend and are glad to direct you to the sights of this scenic region. Scores of restaurants, factory outlets, and canoeing, hiking, and ski areas are also nearby.

Mountain Valley Manner
P.O. BOX 1649, 148 WASHINGTON STREET, CONWAY, NEW HAMPSHIRE 03818

Tel: **(603) 447-3988**	Location: **125 mi. N of Boston, MA**
Best Time to Call: **9 AM–9 PM**	No. of Rooms: **4**
Hosts: **Bob, Lynn, and Amy Lein**	No. of Private Baths: **2**

Max. No. Sharing Bath: **4**
Double/pb: **$65–$68**
Single/pb: **$45**
Double/sb: **$55–$58**
Single/sb: **$35**
Suites: **$68**
Open: **All year**
Reduced Rates: **10%, after 4 days;
   20%, after 5 days**

Breakfast: **Full**
Credit Cards: **AMEX, MC, VISA**
Pets: **No**
Children: **Welcome; free 2 and under**
Smoking: **Permitted**
Social Drinking: **Permitted**
Airport/Station Pickup: **Yes**
Foreign Languages: **Some French**

Tucked into the White Mountain National Forest, this handsome white Victorian lives up to its name, with its wraparound porch and period and antique furnishings. Hikers, golfers, canoeists, skiers, and skaters will find plenty to do here. If shopping is your sport, there are lots of factory outlets in nearby Conway Village. You'll breakfast on dishes like omelets, pancakes, and French toast accompanied by bacon and sausage.

Patchwork Inn ❂

P.O. BOX 107, MAPLE STREET, EAST ANDOVER, NEW HAMPSHIRE 03231

Tel: **(603) 735-6426**
Best Time to Call: **10 AM–10 PM**
Hosts: **Brad and Ethelyn Sherman**
Location: **23 mi. NW of Concord**
No. of Rooms: **8**
No. of Private Baths: **3**
Max. No. Sharing Bath: **5**
Double/pb: **$60–$65**
Single/pb: **$45–$50**
Double/sb: **$50–$55**
Single/sb: **$40–$45**
Suites: **$85–$98**

Open: **All year**
Reduced Rates: **10%, families,
   seniors; 10%, after 3 days**
Breakfast: **Full**
Credit Cards: **MC, VISA**
Pets: **Sometimes**
Children: **Welcome, over 5**
Smoking: **No**
Social Drinking: **Permitted**
Airport/Station Pickup: **Yes**
Minimum Stay: **During special events**

This colonial inn, built around 1800, has been lovingly restored and furnished with a mixture of antique and country pieces. Guest rooms overlook Highland Lake and Mt. Kearsarge; several other lakes and ski slopes are within an hour's drive. There's cross-country skiing right on the property, and it's an easy walk to the town beach. After the day's adventures, warm up by the living room fireplace, or gather around the piano for an informal singalong. For evening snacking, you'll find fresh fruit and homebaked cookies in your room. House breakfast specialties include cheese strata, baked eggs, French toast, or pancakes bathed in syrup from the Sherman's own maple trees.

Blanche's B&B ✪

EASTON VALLEY ROAD, FRANCONIA, NEW HAMPSHIRE 03580

Tel: **(603) 823-7061**
Best Time to Call: **Evenings, until 10**
Hosts: **Brenda Shannon and John Vail**
Location: **5 mi. SW of Franconia**
No. of Rooms: **5**
Max. No. Sharing Bath: **4**
Double/sb: **$60**
Single/sb: **$40**
Open: **All year**
Reduced Rates: **Weekly**

Breakfast: **Full**
Other Meals: **Available**
Pets: **No**
Children: **Welcome**
Smoking: **No**
Social Drinking: **Permitted**
Minimum Stay: **2 nights, holiday weekends, fall foliage season, winter weekends**
Airport/Station Pickup: **Yes**

Set in a meadow near the Appalachian Trail, this steep-gabled, Victorian farmhouse (circa 1887) is decorated with family pieces and auction finds. Brenda and John provide cotton linens on comfortable beds, a hearty breakfast, and good advice about the nearby hiking and cross-country ski trails. Franconia Notch and Cannon Mountain are a 10-minute drive. Your hosts will be happy to suggest the best spots for antiques, crafts, bird-watching, or help you discover the simple pleasures of life in the White Mountains.

Bungay Jar Bed & Breakfast ✪

15 EASTON VALLEY ROAD, P.O. BOX 15, FRANCONIA, NEW HAMPSHIRE 03580

Tel: **(603) 823-7775**
Hosts: **Kate Kerivan and Lee Strimbeck**

Location: **6 mi. from Rte. I-93, Exit 38**
No. of Rooms: **6**

No. of Private Baths: **4**
Max. No. Sharing Bath: **4**
Double/pb: **$65–$100**
Double/sb: **$60–$65**
Single/sb: **$50–$75**
Open: **All year**
Breakfast: **Full**
Other Meals: **Available**

Credit Cards: **AMEX, MC, VISA**
Pets: **No**
Children: **Welcome, over 6**
Smoking: **No**
Social Drinking: **Permitted**
Minimum Stay: **2 nights, foliage
season; holiday weekends**

Built in 1969 from an 18th-century barn, this post-and-beam house is nestled among eight acres of woodland bounded by a river, forest, and spectacular mountain views. In winter, guests are greeted by a crackling fire and the aroma of mulled cider in the two-story living room reminiscent of a hayloft. Antique country furnishings (many for sale) enhance the decor. Apple pancakes served with local maple syrup are a specialty, as are homemade breads, preserves, fruit compotes, granola, and imaginative egg dishes. Refreshments of cider and cheese are served each afternoon. Your hosts are avid hikers and skiers, so you are sure to benefit from their expert knowledge.

Maria W. Atwood Inn
RFD 2, ROUTE 3A NORTH, FRANKLIN, NEW HAMPSHIRE 03235

Tel: **(603) 934-3666**
Hosts: **Philip and Irene Fournier**
Location: **14 mi. N of Concord**
No. of Rooms: **7**
No. of Private Baths: **7**
Double/pb: **$65–$75**
Single/pb: **$50**
Open: **All year**

Breakfast: **Full**
Credit Cards: **AMEX, DC, MC, VISA**
Pets: **No**
Children: **Welcome, over 11**
Smoking: **Permitted**
Social Drinking: **Permitted**
Airport/Station Pickup: **Yes**

At the turn of the century, Maria Atwood and her husband bought this brick, Federal-style home along with 200 acres. Over the years, the house became known for its quality restorations and impeccable maintenance. The grounds feature formal gardens and acres of fields for walking or cross-country skiing. Today the inn features new plumbing and electrical systems, but restoration has been made according to original designs, and the locks still take an old turnkey. The decor features period antiques, and bedrooms all have old-fashioned beds and fine linens. Your hosts offer complimentary snacks and invite you to BYOB if you like. This lovely inn is within minutes of swimming and boating, and half an hour from the ski slopes.

Webster Lake Inn ✪
WEBSTER AVENUE, FRANKLIN, NEW HAMPSHIRE 03235

Tel: **(603) 934-4050**	Single/sb: **$35**
Hosts: **Shirley and Henry McCue,**	Open: **All year**
Roland and Cheryl Tyner	Breakfast: **Full**
No. of Rooms: **8**	Pets: **No**
No. of Private Baths: **2**	Children: **Welcome**
Max. No. Sharing Bath: **4**	Smoking: **Permitted**
Double/pb: **$55–$65**	Social Drinking: **Permitted**
Double/sb: **$45**	

This country inn, modeled after a Swiss chalet, is set on picturesque Webster Lake. Enjoy a quiet moment in a lovely waterfront gazebo or by the great fireplace in the sitting room. Bedrooms feature panoramic views and original, handcrafted furnishings. Your hosts serve a country-style breakfast in a dining room, with fireplace, overlooking the water. Nearby activities include swimming, fishing, hiking, golf, skiing, and snowmobiling. There are many regional events throughout the year, such as Winter Carnival and an assortment of country fairs. Webster Lake Inn is a short drive from Lake Winnipesaukee, and less than an hour from the White Mountains.

Ayers Homestead Bed & Breakfast ✪
47 PARK AVENUE, GREENLAND, NEW HAMPSHIRE 03840

Tel: **(603) 436-5992**	Single/sb: **$45**
Hosts: **David and Priscilla Engel**	Suites: **$95**
Location: **3 mi. W of Portsmouth**	Open: **All year**
No. of Rooms: **3**	Breakfast: **Full**
No. of Private Baths: **1**	Pets: **Sometimes**
Max. No. Sharing Bath: **4**	Children: **Welcome**
Double/pb: **$55**	Smoking: **No**
Single/pb: **$50**	Social Drinking: **Permitted**
Double/sb: **$50**	Airport/Station Pickup: **Yes**

The Thomas Ayers House, begun in 1737 as a two-room post-and-beam structure, has been enlarged and remodeled many times in its 250-year history. Priscilla and Dave will tell you of the famous people, including Paul Revere, George Washington, and John Adams, who passed by its doors. Set on six acres on the historic village green, its nine rooms have wainscoting, exposed beams, and wide board floors; seven have fireplaces. The bedrooms are made cozy with antiques, braided rugs, afghans, and rockers. Breakfast is served in the dining room on an antique table set in front of a brick fireplace with artfully displayed pewterware and ironware.

Roy Family Bed & Breakfast ✪
473 OCEAN BOULEVARD, HAMPTON BEACH, NEW HAMPSHIRE 03842

Tel: (603) 926-7893; 926-5505
Best Time to Call: After 1 P.M.
Hosts: Debbie and Richard Roy
Location: 50 mi. N of Boston
No. of Rooms: 6
Max. No. Sharing Bath: 4
Double/sb: $45–$65
Open: Jan. 15–Oct. 15

Reduced Rates: Available
Breakfast: Continental
Credit Cards: MC, VISA
Pets: No
Children: Welcome
Smoking: Permitted
Social Drinking: Permitted
Foreign Languages: French

The Atlantic Ocean is right at your feet when you stay at this comfortable, New England–style home. The house is decorated in a mixture of traditional, Victorian, and casual pieces. Bedrooms are immaculate and furnished Colonial-style. Choose from two spacious decks to enjoy the sun and the ocean view. There is a television room furnished in white wicker for rainy days. The beach is one and a half miles long, and includes boardwalk shops, boutiques, and restaurants. A short drive away are many discount shopping areas, Seabrook Raceway, and Portsmouth Harbor.

The Inn on Golden Pond ✪
ROUTE 3, BOX 680, HOLDERNESS, NEW HAMPSHIRE 03245

Tel: (603) 968-7269
Best Time to Call: Evenings
Hosts: Bill and Bonnie Webb
Location: 4 mi. from I-93
No. of Rooms: 9
No. of Private Baths: 7
Max. No. Sharing Bath: 4
Double/pb: $85
Single/pb: $60

Double/sb: $75
Single/sb: $50
Open: All year
Breakfast: Full
Credit Cards: MC, VISA
Pets: No
Children: Welcome, over 12
Smoking: No
Social Drinking: Permitted

If you saw the film *On Golden Pond*, you are familiar with the beauty of the countryside surrounding this inn. Built in 1879 on 55 acres, the house is across the street from Squam Lake, the setting for the movie. The rooms are bright and airy, decorated in a warm, homey style. Breakfast specialties include apple pancakes with local maple syrup, and a sausage, egg, and cheese casserole. Nearby are two golf courses, Waterville Valley, and Loon Mountain.

The Forest—A Country Inn
ROUTE 16A, P.O. BOX 37, INTERVALE, NEW HAMPSHIRE 03845

Tel: (603) 356-9772
Hosts: Rae and Ken Wyman

Location: 50 mi. from Rte. 93
No. of Rooms: 13

No. of Private Baths: **7**
Max. No. Sharing Bath: **4**
Double/pb: **$60–$84**
Double/sb: **$50–$74**
Single/sb: **$40–$52**
Guest Cottage: **$64–$94; sleeps 4**
Open: **May 1–Mar. 31**
Reduced Rates: **May 1–June 30; Oct. 20–Dec. 13**

Breakfast: **Full**
Other Meals: **Available**
Credit Cards: **AMEX, MC, VISA**
Pets: **No**
Children: **Welcome**
Smoking: **No**
Social Drinking: **Permitted**

Located three miles from North Conway, and reigning over 25 wooded acres in the White Mountains, this three-story Victorian inn has been in continuous operation since the late 1800s. Inside, the inn has the feel of a big country home—full of braided rugs, comfortable chairs, antiques, crafts, and country collectibles. The stone cottage has a fireplace and is a favorite of honeymooners. Outside, you're close to all of the wonderful recreational possibilities that the valley has to offer—downhill skiing, hiking, biking, canoeing, kayaking, tennis, golf, and more. In back of the inn is a swimming pool and, in winter, all you have to do is go across the street to the Intervale Nordic Learning Center, where you can use the cross-country ski trails at no extra cost.

The Galway House B&B

247 OLD PETERBOROUGH ROAD, JAFFREY, NEW HAMPSHIRE 03452

Tel: **(603) 532-8083**
Best Time to Call: **Evenings**
Hosts: **Joe and Marie Manning**
Location: **1 mi. from US 202**
No. of Rooms: **2**
Max. No. Sharing Bath: **4**
Double/sb: **$45**
Single/sb: **$35**

Open: **Aug. 15–June 30**
Breakfast: **Full**
Pets: **No**
Children: **Welcome (crib)**
Smoking: **Permitted**
Social Drinking: **Permitted**
Airport/Station Pickup: **Yes**

This new, oversize Cape with a spacious yard and sun deck is situated on a rural road surrounded by acres of woodland. It is located at the foot of 3,165-foot Grand Monadnock, in the center of the Monadnock Region, known as the Currier and Ives corner of the state. Picturesque in every season, the area will make sports enthusiasts revel in the choice of activities. Joe and Marie welcome you to a warm hearth, a suitable beverage, and comfortable accommodations! From June through September they offer B&B on board their sailing sloop.

The Jefferson Inn ○

ROUTE 2, RFD 1, BOX 68A, JEFFERSON, NEW HAMPSHIRE 03583

Tel: **(603) 586-7998**
Hosts: **Greg Brown and Bertie Koelewijn**
Location: **20 mi. from Rte. 93, Exit 35**
No. of Rooms: **10**
No. of Private Baths: **5**
Max. No. Sharing Bath: **4**
Double/pb: **$48**
Double/sb: **$48**
Single/sb: **$42–$46**
Suites: **$80**
Open: **Dec.–Mar.; May–Oct.**

Reduced Rates: **Families; winter weekdays**
Breakfast: **Full**
Credit Cards: **AMEX, MC, VISA**
Pets: **No**
Children: **Welcome**
Smoking: **No**
Social Drinking: **Permitted**
Airport/Station Pickup: **Yes**
Foreign Languages: **Dutch, French, German**

Built in 1896, this B&B is situated in the White Mountain National Forest and boasts beautiful valley and mountain views. Its location is ideal for outdoor activities, including hiking, swimming, canoeing, and golf in summer; downhill and cross-country skiing, skating, and snowshoeing in winter. The village of Jefferson sits within the shadows of Mt. Washington and the Presidential Range, with hiking trails starting near the inn's door. Decorated with period antiques, each impeccably clean room has a distinctive character. Relax on the porch in warm weather and end the day with a soothing cup of tea.

Ferry Point House ○

R-1, BOX 335, LACONIA, NEW HAMPSHIRE 03246

Tel: **(603) 524-0087**
Best Time to Call: **After 6 PM**
Hosts: **Diane and Joe Damato**
Location: **90 mi. N of Boston**
No. of Rooms: **5**
No. of Private Baths: **3**
Max. No. Sharing Bath: **4**
Double/pb: **$70**
Single/pb: **$50–$60**
Double/sb: **$60**

Open: **Memorial Day—Labor Day; weekends during fall foliage**
Reduced Rates: **15%, weekly**
Breakfast: **Full**
Pets: **No**
Children: **Welcome**
Smoking: **Downstairs only**
Social Drinking: **Permitted**
Airport/Station Pickup: **Yes**
Foreign Languages: **French**

New England's past is well preserved in this 150-year-old Victorian located on picturesque Lake Winnisquam. Enjoy breathtaking views of the water and the mountains from a 60-foot veranda. Of course, the view is even more enjoyable when you're sipping lemonade or the house blend of coffee. Guest rooms overlook the lake and are furnished with antiques, collectibles, and fresh flowers. Breakfast is served in a Victorian-style dining room, and your hosts take pride in offering unusual dishes, such as cheese baked apples, crêpes, or Gran Marnier French toast. Ferry Point House is minutes from regional activities such as boating, skiing, dinner cruises, and a large selection of fine restaurants.

The Beal House Inn
247 WEST MAIN STREET, LITTLETON, NEW HAMPSHIRE 03561

Tel: **(603) 444-2661**
Best Time to Call: **10 AM–9 PM**
Hosts: **Jim and Ann Carver**
Location: **1 mi. from I-93**
No. of Rooms: **14**
No. of Private Baths: **10**
Max. No. Sharing Bath: **4**
Double/pb: **$45–$95**
Single/pb: **$40–$75**
Double/sb: **$40–$45**

Suites: **$70–$125**
Open: **All year**
Reduced Rates: **Groups**
Breakfast: **Continental**
Credit Cards: **AMEX, DC, MC, VISA**
Pets: **No**
Children: **Welcome, over 8 years**
Smoking: **Permitted**
Social Drinking: **Permitted**

Jim and Ann have an antiques shop and have furnished their Federal-style home with choice pieces. Breakfast features hot popovers served by the fireside. The inn is conveniently accessible to six great ski areas, Franconia Notch, and the famed Old Man of the Mountain. Popcorn, cheese, and crackers are complimentary. Tea is always available.

The Inn at Loudon Ridge
BOX 195, LOWER RIDGE ROAD, LOUDON, NEW HAMPSHIRE 03301

Tel: **(603) 267-8952**
Best Time to Call: **9 AM–2 PM; 7–10 PM**
Hosts: **Liz and Carol Early**
Location: **8 mi. N of Concord**
No. of Rooms: **5**
No. of Private Baths: **2**
Max. No. Sharing Bath: **4**
Double/pb: **$65**
Single/pb: **$55**

Double/sb: **$50**
Single/sb: **$40**
Open: **All year**
Breakfast: **Full**
Credit Cards: **AMEX, MC, VISA**
Pets: **No**
Children: **Welcome, over 12**
Smoking: **No**
Social Drinking: **Permitted**

A rambling Colonial garrison-style home, situated on 33 acres, the inn's rooms are large, airy, and punctuated with antiques. The cozy sitting room, with its piano and fireplace, invites socializing or quiet relaxation. Your hosts strive to maintain the tradition of hospitality that has been part of their family for years. Browse through dozens of antique and craft shops, sample fresh maple syrup at a nearby sap house, or tour historic Shaker Village. Gunstock Ski Resort and the Lakes Region offer seasonal activities. In warm weather, you are welcome to use the inn's swimming pool and tennis court.

Peep-Willow Farm ✪
BIXBY STREET, MARLBOROUGH, NEW HAMPSHIRE 03455

Tel: **(603) 876-3807**
Best Time to Call: **7:30 AM–8 PM**

Host: **Noel Aderer**
Location: **7 mi. E of Keene**

No. of Rooms: **3**
Max. No. Sharing Bath: **4**
Double/sb: **$40**
Single/sb: **$25**
Open: **All year**
Breakfast: **Full**

Pets: **No**
Children: **Welcome**
Smoking: **No**
Social Drinking: **Permitted**
Airport/Station Pickup: **Yes**

Noel Aderer has a new Colonial farmhouse on a working thorough-bred horse farm. She raises and trains horses for competition, and while there is plenty of room for petting and admiring, guests are not permitted to ride. Peep-Willow is named after horses number one and two, respectively. It is a charming place, with lots of wood accents and antiques. Breakfast specialties include French toast, with local maple syrup, and bacon and eggs. Guests are welcome to watch farm chores, visit the horses, and enjoy a cup of coffee with Noel, who has done everything from working on a kibbutz to training polo ponies for a maharajah.

Blue Goose Inn ✪
ROUTE 103B, P.O. BOX 117, MT. SUNAPEE, NEW HAMPSHIRE 03772

Tel: **(603) 763-5519**
Best Time to Call: **Before noon**
Hosts: **Meryl and Ronald Caldwell**
Location: **10 mi. from I-89**
No. of Rooms: **5**
No. of Private Baths: **4**
Max. No. Sharing Bath: **3**
Double/pb: **$50**
Single/pb: **$45**
Double/sb: **$45**

Single/sb: **$40**
Open: **All year**
Breakfast: **Full**
Credit Cards: **MC, VISA**
Pets: **No**
Children: **Welcome**
Smoking: **Permitted**
Social Drinking: **Permitted**
Airport/Station Pickup: **Yes**

This cozy, early 19th-century Colonial farmhouse is located at the base of Mt. Sunapee on scenic Lake Sunapee. The guest rooms are quiet and spacious, adorned with handmade quilts and attractive antiques. Whether you're coming here for the greening of spring, the long lush summer, the autumn foliage, or the white-blanketed backdrop for skiing or sleighing, you'll be treated to their breakfast specialty: a combination of bacon, eggs, and cheese, baked in a maple flavored biscuit. It is served on the enclosed porch, which is enhanced by skylights and hanging plants. You're invited to join your hosts and other guests for wine, fruit, and cheese served each evening on the porch or by the fireplace in the common room.

The Buttonwood Inn ✪

P.O. BOX 1817, MT. SURPRISE ROAD, NORTH CONWAY, NEW HAMPSHIRE 03860

Tel: **(603) 356-2625**
Hosts: **Hugh and Ann Begley**
Location: **1½ mi. from Rte. 16**
No. of Rooms: **9**
No. of Private Baths: **3**
Max. No. Sharing Bath: **4**
Double/pb: **$50–$80**
Single/pb: **$40–$55**
Double/sb: **$40–$70**
Single/sb: **$35–$50**
Open: **All year**

Reduced Rates: **15%, less than 5 nights July and Aug.; 10%, less than 3 nights**
Breakfast: **Full**
Other Meals: **Available Jan. and Feb.**
Credit Cards: **AMEX, MC, VISA**
Pets: **No**
Children: **Welcome, over 3**
Smoking: **Permitted**
Social Drinking: **Permitted**
Minimum Stay: **2 nights weekends Jan. and Feb.; 3 nights holiday weekends**

The Buttonwood is tucked away on Mt. Surprise, in the heart of the White Mountains. It is secluded and quiet, yet only two miles from excellent town restaurants and factory outlet shopping. This New England-style Cape Cod was built in 1820 and has been enlarged over the years from four to twenty-four rooms. Most guest bedrooms have wide-plank floors and are furnished with antique oak and cottage pine pieces. Hugh loves to fish and ski cross-country; Ann teaches the local schoolchildren downhill skiing.

Wilderness Inn

ROUTES 3 AND 112, RFD 1, BOX 69, NORTH WOODSTOCK, NEW HAMPSHIRE 03262

Tel: **(603) 745-3890**
Best Time to Call: **10 AM–9 PM**
Hosts: **Michael and Rosanna Yarnell**
Location: **120 mi. N of Boston**
No. of Rooms: **7**
No. of Private Baths: **5**
Max. No. Sharing Bath: **4**
Double/pb: **$50–$75**
Single/pb: **$45–$70**
Double/sb: **$40–$60**
Single/sb: **$35–$55**
Suites: **$60–$85**

Open: **All year**
Reduced Rates: **Midweek; off-season**
Breakfast: **Full**
Credit Cards: **AMEX, MC, VISA**
Pets: **No**
Children: **Welcome**
Smoking: **Permitted**
Social Drinking: **Permitted**
Airport/Station Pickup: **Yes**
Foreign Languages: **French, Italian, Bengali, Amharic**

Escape from it all at this mountainside retreat where, depending on the season, you can ski, swim, ride a bike, and hike to your heart's content. Restaurants, craft shops, and a golf course are all nearby. Fresh fruit, café au lait, and cranberry-walnut pancakes will lure you out of bed in the morning, but if you prefer, the Yarnells will bring a continental breakfast to your room.

Meadow Farm
JENNESS POND ROAD, NORTHWOOD, NEW HAMPSHIRE 03261

Tel: **(603) 942-8619**	Open: **All year**
Hosts: **Douglas and Janet Briggs**	Reduced Rates: **Families**
Location: **18 mi. E of Concord**	Breakfast: **Full**
No. of Rooms: **3**	Pets: **Sometimes**
Max. No. Sharing Bath: **3**	Children: **Welcome**
Double/sb: **$45**	Smoking: **Permitted**
Single/sb: **$35**	Social Drinking: **Permitted**

Meadow Farm is set on 50 acres of quiet woods and horse pastures. The house is an authentic New England Colonial dating back to 1770, with wide-pine floors, beamed ceilings, and old fireplaces. In the morning, a country breakfast of homemade breads, seasonal fruit, and local syrup is served in the keeping room. Guests are invited to relax on the private beach on an adjacent lake. The property also has plenty of wooded trails for long walks or cross-country skiing. Meadow Farm is an ideal location for those en route to Concord, the seacoast, or the mountains.

Crab Apple Inn
ROUTE 25, PLYMOUTH, NEW HAMPSHIRE 03264

Tel: **(603) 536-4476**	Open: **All year**
Best Time to Call: **Mornings; evenings**	Breakfast: **Full**
Hosts: **Bill and Carolyn Crenson**	Credit Cards: **MC, VISA**
Location: **4 mi. from Rte. 93**	Pets: **No**
No. of Rooms: **4**	Children: **Welcome, over 8**
No. of Private Baths: **4**	Smoking: **Permitted**
Double/pb: **$70–$75**	Social Drinking: **Permitted**
Suites: **$80–$85**	

Located in the beautiful Baker River Valley at the gateway to the White Mountain region, the inn is an 1835 brick building of Federal design situated beside a small brook at the foot of Tenny Mountain. The bedrooms on the second floor have fireplaces; those on the third floor have a panoramic view of the mountains. All are tastefully furnished. There are several fine restaurants nearby, and the inn is within a 10-minute drive of Plymouth State College. Gift studios and handcraft and antique shops in the area provide treasures for both the discerning and casual buyer.

Leighton Inn ✪
69 RICHARDS AVENUE, PORTSMOUTH, NEW HAMPSHIRE 03801

Tel: **(603) 433-2188**	No. of Rooms: **5**
Host: **Catherine Stone**	No. of Private Baths: **4**
Location: **1 mi. from I-95**	Max. No. Sharing Bath: **4**

Double/pb: **$75**
Single/pb: **$65**
Double/sb: **$65**
Single/sb: **$55**
Open: **All year**
Reduced Rates: **Nov.–Apr.**
Breakfast: **Full**

Credit Cards: **MC, VISA**
Pets: **No**
Children: **Welcome**
Smoking: **Permitted**
Social Drinking: **Permitted**
Airport/Station Pickup: **Yes**
Foreign Languages: **French**

In 1809, cabinetmaker Samuel Wyatt built himself a Federal-style home, sparing no expense. Now named for a prominent Portsmouth family who lived there in the 1800s, the inn is just a short walk from Strawbery Banke, a "living museum" that traces the history of this colorful waterfront city through four centuries. Swimming, boating, and fishing are just a short drive away, and whale-watch cruises can easily be arranged. In summer, guests breakfast on the porch that overlooks the inn's formal gardens; in winter, they sit in front of a fire in the pine-paneled country kitchen. And, if you're musically inclined, Catherine invites you to sit down at the 1913 Steinway concert grand piano in the library and play as long as you'd like.

Grassy Pond House ❂
RINDGE, NEW HAMPSHIRE 03461

Tel: **(603) 899-5166/5167**
Best Time to Call: **Mornings**
Hosts: **Carmen Linares and Robert Multer**
Location: **60 mi. NW of Boston**
No. of Rooms: **3**
No. of Private Baths: **2**
Max. No. Sharing Bath: **4**
Double/pb: **$65**
Double/sb: **$55**

Single/sb: **$45**
Open: **All year**
Breakfast: **Full**
Pets: **No**
Children: **Welcome, over 14**
Smoking: **No**
Social Drinking: **Permitted**
Airport/Station Pickup: **Yes**
Foreign Languages: **Spanish**

This secluded 19th-century farmhouse is set among 150 acres of woods and fields. The house has been restored, enlarged, and decorated in period pieces. Guest quarters, overlooking the gardens and lake, feature a private entrance and a living room with fireplace. Breakfast specialties include pancakes with local maple syrup, fresh eggs and bacon, and plenty of good Colombian coffee. This setting, high in the Monadnock region, is perfect for hiking, skiing, boating, fishing, and swimming.

The Tokfarm ❂
BOX 229, WOOD AVENUE, RINDGE, NEW HAMPSHIRE 03461

Tel: **(603) 899-6646**
Best Time to Call: **Early AM; evenings**

Host: **Mrs. W. B. Nottingham**
Location: **50 mi. NW of Boston**

No. of Rooms: **5**
Max. No. Sharing Bath: **4**
Double/sb: **$35–$45**
Single/sb: **$18**
Open: **Apr. 1–Nov. 14**
Breakfast: **Continental**
Pets: **No**

Children: **No**
Smoking: **No**
Social Drinking: **Permitted**
Airport/Station Pickup: **Yes**
Foreign Languages: **Dutch, French, German**

This 150-year-old farmhouse has a spectacular view of three states from its 1,400-foot hilltop. Mt. Monadnock, the second most climbed peak in the world (Mt. Fuji is first), is practically in its backyard! Mrs. Nottingham raises Christmas trees, is a world traveler, and loves to ski. She'll recommend things to keep you busy. Don't miss the lovely Cathedral of the Pines. Franklin Pierce College is nearby.

Province Inn ✪

P.O. BOX 309, STRAFFORD, NEW HAMPSHIRE 03884

Tel: **(603) 664-2457**
Best Time to Call: **8–10 AM; 7–9 PM**
Hosts: **Steve and Corky Garboski**
Location: **20 mi. W of Portsmouth**
No. of Rooms: **4**
Max. No. Sharing Bath: **4**
Double/sb: **$63**
Open: **All year**
Reduced Rates: **$53, Jan. 1–May 31; weekly**

Breakfast: **Full**
Credit Cards: **MC, VISA**
Pets: **No**
Children: **Welcome**
Smoking: **Permitted**
Social Drinking: **Permitted**
Minimum Stay: **2 nights, Columbus Day weekend**

The ocean and mountains are within easy reach of this classic white 18th-century Colonial, located in an unspoiled country setting. The bedrooms are attractively furnished in maple, and braided rugs highlight polished floors, handmade quilts adorn the beds, and tie-back curtains frame the windows. Breakfast may feature a special sausage and egg casserole, or oven puffed pancakes. You can work off any accumulated calories in the swimming pool or on the inn's tennis court, taking a walk to the nearby waterfall, hiking or bicycling the many country roads, or canoeing on Bow Lake. Corky is a flight attendant and Justice of the Peace, Steve is a pilot and Olympic-class bicyclist; Bethany, age 6, is a minihost.

The Hilltop Inn

MAIN STREET, P.O. BOX 9, SUGAR HILL, NEW HAMPSHIRE 03585

Tel: **(603) 823-5695**
Hosts: **Mike and Meri Hern**
Location: **2½ mi. W of Franconia**

No. of Rooms: **6**
No. of Private Baths: **2**
Max. No. Sharing Bath: **4**

Double/sb: **$50–$60**
Single/sb: **$40**
Double/pb: **$75**
Suites: **$85–$100**
Open: **All year**
Breakfast: **Full**

Pets: **Welcome**
Children: **Welcome (crib)**
Smoking: **Permitted**
Social Drinking: **Permitted**
Airport/Station Pickup: **Yes**

The Hilltop Inn is a sprawling, 19th-century Victorian located in a small, friendly village. Inside, you'll find a warm, cozy atmosphere, comfortable furnishings, and lots of antiques. The kitchen is the heart of the house in more ways than one. In the morning, homemade muffins are served fresh from the old-fashioned Garland stove. In the evening, the sunsets from the deck are breathtaking. Your hosts are professional caterers and are pleased to cater to you. Join them for wine and cheese after a day of activities. Local attractions include Franconia Notch, White Mountain National Forest, North Conway, great skiing, and spectacular foliage.

Suncook House ✪

62 MAIN STREET, SUNCOOK, NEW HAMPSHIRE 03275

Tel: **(603) 485-8141**
Best Time to Call: **Mornings**
Hosts: **Gerry and Evelyn Lavoie**
Location: **6 mi. S of Concord**
No. of Rooms: **4**
No. of Private Baths: **2**
Max. No. Sharing Bath: **3**
Double/pb: **$50**
Single/pb: **$44**
Double/sb: **$42**

Single/sb: **$35**
Open: **All year**
Reduced Rates: **10%, seniors**
Breakfast: **Full**
Pets: **No**
Children: **Welcome, over 12**
Smoking: **No**
Social Drinking: **Permitted**
Airport/Station Pickup: **Yes**

Suncook House is a spacious brick Georgian set on three beautifully maintained acres. The house is newly renovated and its comfortable rooms are furnished with period pieces. A formal living room, sun parlor, den, and an excellent organ are available for your relaxation and pleasure. This country home allows one the benefits of feeling away from it all while still being able to enjoy the convenience of a main road that leads to the mountains and lakes. Walk to village churches, restaurants, and tennis courts. New Hampshire College and Bear Brook State Park are both within a five-mile drive.

NEW JERSEY

Stanhope • • Glenwood
Denville • • Midland Park
Dover • • Lyndhurst
Milford • Madison
Princeton

•Spring Lake

Jobstown •

•Atlantic City
Dennisville • •Ocean City
• North Wildwood
•Cape May

Bed & Breakfast of Princeton—A Reservation Service
P.O. BOX 571, PRINCETON, NEW JERSEY 08450

Tel: **(609) 924-3189**
Coordinator: **John W. Hurley**
States/Regions Covered: **Princeton**

Rates (Single/Double):
Average: **$40–$55** **$50–$65**
Credit Cards: **No**

Princeton is a lovely town; houses are well set back on carefully tended lawns, screened by towering trees. Some of John's hosts live within walking distance of Princeton University. Nassau Hall (circa 1756) is its oldest building; its chapel is the largest of any at an American university. Nearby corporate parks include national companies, such as RCA, Squibb, and the David Sarnoff Research Center. Restaurants feature every imaginable cuisine, and charming shops offer a wide variety of wares. Personal checks are accepted for deposit or total payment in advance; cash or traveler's checks are required for any balance due.

Albert G. Stevens Inn ✪
127 MYRTLE AVENUE, CAPE MAY, NEW JERSEY 08204

Tel: **(609) 884-4717**	Open: **Feb. 1–Dec. 31**
Hosts: **Diane and Curt Rangred**	Breakfast: **Full**
Location: **40 mi. S of Atlantic City**	Credit Cards: **MC, VISA**
No. of Rooms: **7**	Pets: **No**
No. of Private Baths: **7**	Children: **No**
Double/pb: **$85–$95**	Smoking: **No**
Suites: **$105–$145; sleeps 4**	Social Drinking: **Permitted**

This 87-year-old Victorian is located next door to historic Wilbrahan Mansion and three blocks from the beach. The antique decor includes mother-of-pearl inlay in the parlor suite, an oak mantel, and other treasures throughout. The wraparound veranda is a wonderful place for sipping your second cup of coffee or for relaxing later in the day. Breakfast often features ham and cheese quiche, or waffles with whipped cream.

Barnard-Good House ✪
238 PERRY STREET, CAPE MAY, NEW JERSEY 08204

Tel: **(609) 884-5381**	Open: **Apr.–Nov.**
Best Time to Call: **8 AM–9 PM**	Breakfast: **Full**
Hosts: **Nan and Tom Hawkins**	Pets: **No**
No. of Rooms: **5**	Children: **Welcome, over 14**
No. of Private Baths: **5**	Smoking: **No**
Double/pb: **$85–$95**	Social Drinking: **Permitted**
Single/pb: **$76.50–$86.50**	Minimum Stay: **2 nights, spring and**
Suites: **$110**	**fall; 3 nights, summer**

Nan and Tom cordially invite you to their Second Empire Victorian cottage (circa 1869), just two blocks from the "swimming" beach. They love antiques and are continually adding to their collection. They use them generously to create the warm and comfortable atmosphere. Nan's breakfast includes homemade exotic juices, delicious home-baked breads, and unusual preserves. In spring and fall, added gourmet entrées and side dishes make for an epicurean feast. Iced tea and snacks are served evenings.

Colvmns-by-the-Sea ✪
1513 BEACH DRIVE, CAPE MAY, NEW JERSEY 08204

Tel: **(609) 884-2228**	Double/pb: **$95–$145**
Best Time to Call: **11 AM–10 PM**	Single/pb: **$85–$135**
Hosts: **Barry and Cathy Rein**	Open: **Apr.–Dec.**
No. of Rooms: **11**	Reduced Rates: **10%, weekly; 20%,**
No. of Private Baths: **11**	**Mon.–Wed. in June, Sept., Oct.**

Breakfast: **Full**
Credit Cards: **MC, VISA**
Pets: **No**
Children: **Welcome, over 12**
Smoking: **No**

Social Drinking: **Permitted**
Minimum Stay: **3 nights on weekends**
Airport/Station Pickup: **Yes**
Foreign Languages: **German**

Fronted by the ocean and backed by a modern apartment house, this grand Victorian summer "cottage" has 20 rooms, two fireplaces, and handcarved 12-foot ceilings. It combines a whimsical Italian palazzo style with fluted columns on the veranda and Colonial Revival accents. Inside, a three-story staircase leads to large, airy rooms with ocean views. Your hosts have decorated the rooms with Victorian and Chinese pieces collected over years of world travel. Gourmet soufflés and stratas are served in a formal dining room, which has antique wood sideboards and lace curtains. In the afternoon, tea and sherry are offered on the seaside veranda. The Reins have bikes to lend, and they will gladly direct you to charming streets lined with vintage Victorians, shops, and restaurants.

The Mainstay Inn
635 COLUMBIA AVENUE, CAPE MAY, NEW JERSEY 08204

Tel: **(609) 884-8690**
Best Time to Call: **8 AM–10 PM**
Hosts: **Tom and Sue Carroll**
No. of Rooms: **12**
No. of Private Baths: **12**
Double/pb: **$85–$140**
Single/pb: **$75–$130**
Suites: **$95–$140**

Open: **Mar. 15–Dec. 15**
Reduced Rates: **Off season; weekdays**
Breakfast: **Full**
Pets: **No**
Children: **Welcome, over 12**
Smoking: **No**
Social Drinking: **Permitted**
Minimum Stay: **3 nights, in season**

Located in the heart of the historic district, this 116-year-old mansion was originally built as a private gambling club. Except for a few 20th-century concessions, it still looks much as it did when the gamblers were there, with 14-foot ceilings, elaborate chandeliers, and outstanding Victorian antiques. Tom and Sue serve breakfast either in the formal dining room or on the veranda; afternoon tea and homemade snacks are a ritual. Breakfast often features ham and apple pie, or corn quiche with baked ham. Continental breakfast is served in summer. Rock on the wide veranda, enjoy croquet in the garden, or retreat to the cupola. Minimum stay is three nights in season.

The Henry Ludlam Inn ✪
DENNISVILLE, NEW JERSEY (CAPE MAY COUNTY, RD 3, BOX 298, WOODBINE, NEW JERSEY 08270)

Tel: **(609) 861-5847**
Best Time to Call: **After 5 PM**

Hosts: **Ann and Marty Thurlow**
Location: **18 mi. N of Cape May**

No. of Rooms: **5**	Reduced Rates: **Weekly**
No. of Private Baths: **3**	Breakfast: **Full**
Max. No. Sharing Bath: **4**	Pets: **No**
Double/pb: **$75–$95**	Children: **Welcome, over 12**
Double/sb: **$65–$75**	Smoking: **Permitted**
Open: **All year**	Social Drinking: **Permitted**

Built circa 1800, Ann and Marty's home is furnished with antiques, handmade quilts, plump featherbeds, plants, and other nice touches to complete the decor. It's located in Dennisville, on a 55-acre lake that's 20 minutes from the Stone Harbor beaches. During cold months, breakfast is served fireside; in warm months, lakeside. All of the bedrooms have working fireplaces for cozy comfort. Afternoon tea and wine are served.

Lakeside B&B ✪

11 SUNSET TRAIL, DENVILLE, NEW JERSEY 07834

Tel: **(201) 625-5129**	Open: **All year**
Hosts: **Annette and Al Bergins**	Breakfast: **Full**
Location: **35 mi. W of New York City**	Pets: **No**
No. of Rooms: **1**	Children: **No**
No. of Private Baths: **1**	Smoking: **No**
Double/pb: **$50**	Social Drinking: **Permitted**
Single/pb: **$45**	

Just off Route 80, midway between Manhattan and the Pocono Mountains, is this modern, two-story home with private guest quarters on the ground level. There's a lovely view of the bay leading to Indian Lake. Al and Annette will provide you with a rowboat and beach passes, as well as refreshments afterward. Relax on the deck overlooking the bay, or explore the unspoiled towns and points of interest off the tourist trail. Good restaurants of every variety and price range abound.

The Silver Lining Bed & Breakfast ✪

467 ROCKAWAY ROAD, DOVER, NEW JERSEY 07801

Tel: **(201) 361-9245**	Breakfast: **Full**
Hosts: **Joan and Bill Middleton**	Credit Cards: **MC, VISA**
Location: **1 mi. from Rte. I-80**	Pets: **No**
No. of Rooms: **2**	Children: **Welcome, over 12**
Max. No. Sharing Bath: **4**	Smoking: **Permitted**
Double/sb: **$50**	Social Drinking: **Permitted**
Single/sb: **$45**	Airport/Station Pickup: **Yes**
Open: **All year**	Foreign Languages: **Spanish**
Reduced Rates: **Weekly**	

This 85-year-old Dutch Colonial home is set between stately trees in a suburban area within an hour's drive of the Meadowlands Sports Complex, New York City, Waterloo Village, and Action Park. The newly redecorated guest rooms feature wicker and lacquer furniture, and pretty print accessories. Both bedrooms share a sitting room, private kitchen, and separate entrance, making it ideal for two couples to share as an apartment.

Apple Valley Inn ✪

P.O. BOX B, CORNER OF ROUTES 517 AND 565, GLENWOOD, NEW JERSEY 07418

Tel: **(201) 764-3735**	Single/sb: **$50**
Best Time to Call: **5–8 PM**	Grist Mill: **$130; sleeps 6 (available**
Hosts: **Mitzi and John Durham**	**June 1–Sept. 15)**
Location: **45 mi. NW of New York City**	Open: **All year**
No. of Rooms: **5**	Reduced Rates: **10%, seniors**
No. of Private Baths: **2**	Breakfast: **Full**
Max. No. Sharing Bath: **3**	Pets: **No**
Double/pb: **$60**	Children: **Welcome, over 13**
Single/pb: **$50**	Smoking: **Permitted**
Double/sb: **$60**	Social Drinking: **Permitted**

Apple Valley Inn, a rustic 19th-century mansion with exposed beams, red brick chimneys, and hand-painted firescreens, takes its name from the fruit farms that used to dominate the area. Bedrooms are named for apples—Granny Smith, Jonathan, Yellow Delicious—and are furnished in Colonial style. Guests can stroll in an apple orchard, swim in a pool, and fish for river trout without leaving the property. Local recreational options include skiing and horseback riding. Breakfasts feature ham-cheese dandy or Dutch baby pancakes, accompanied by fresh fruit and homemade breads, muffins, and jams.

Belle Springs Farm ✪
RD 1, BOX 420, JOBSTOWN, NEW JERSEY 08041

Tel: **(609) 723-5364**	Open: **All year**
Host: **Lyd Sudler**	Breakfast: **Full**
Location: **5 miles from N.J. Tpke.,**	Other Meals: **Available**
Exit 7	Pets: **No**
No. of Rooms: **3**	Children: **Welcome**
Max. No. Sharing Bath: **4**	Smoking: **Permitted**
Double/sb: **$50**	Social Drinking: **Permitted**
Suites: **$85**	

This spacious, contemporary farmhouse was built in 1961 and is attractively furnished with family heirlooms. The bedrooms are air-conditioned. From the porch, there's a spectacular view of the pastures with the cows grazing, and the deer that come out of the woods at dusk. It's situated in the heart of Burlington County, where every little town, including Burlington, Bordentown, and Mt. Holly, is a pre-Revolutionary gem. It is a half hour to Philadelphia or Princeton. Lyd enjoys music, gardening, and pampering her guests. If you want to bring your horse, there's a $10 charge for the turnout in the pasture.

Jeremiah J. Yereance House ✪
410 RIVERSIDE AVENUE, LYNDHURST, NEW JERSEY 07071

Tel: **(201) 438-9457**	Suites: **$70–$75**
Best Time to Call: **After 6 PM**	Open: **All year**
Hosts: **Evelyn and Frank Pezzolla**	Reduced Rates: **Weekly; 15%, seniors**
Location: **12 mi. W of New York City**	Breakfast: **Continental**
No. of Rooms: **3**	Pets: **No**
No. of Private Baths: **1**	Children: **Welcome, over 12**
Max. No. Sharing Bath: **4**	Smoking: **No**
Double/sb: **$55**	Social Drinking: **Permitted**
Single/sb: **$50**	Airport/Station Pickup: **Yes**

Evelyn and Frank Pezzolla fell in love with this wood-frame Colonial when they first saw it in 1984. After a year of rewiring and replacing the roof and just about everything else, the house began to look like the historical landmark it is. In 1986, the government agreed and placed it on the state and national registers. The house is set in a quiet neighborhood across from a riverside park, with jogging paths, bike trails, and picnic areas. The guest suite occupies the south wing of the house and consists of a small parlor with fireplace and an adjoining bedroom and private bath. In the morning, a help-yourself buffet of hot drinks, homemade breads, muffins, and fresh fruits awaits you. The Jeremiah J. Yereance House is just five minutes from the Meadowlands Sports Complex.

Chestnut Hill on-the-Delaware ✪
63 CHURCH STREET, MILFORD, NEW JERSEY 08848

Tel: **(201) 995-9761**	Single/sb: **$60**
Hosts: **Linda and Rob Castagna**	Open: **All year**
Location: **15 mi. from Rte. 78**	Reduced Rates: **Weekly**
No. of Rooms: **5**	Breakfast: **Full**
No. of Private Baths: **2**	Pets: **No**
Max. No. Sharing Bath: **4**	Children: **Welcome, over 12**
Double/pb: **$80–$90**	Smoking: **No**
Double/sb: **$65**	Social Drinking: **Permitted**

The veranda of this 1860 Neo-Italianate Victorian overlooks the peaceful Delaware River. Linda, Rob, and teenage son Michael have refurbished and restored their home with charm, grace, and beauty. The historic countryside is great for antique hunting, water sports, art shows, and restaurants. It's only minutes to New Hope and Bucks County delights, and to dozens of factory outlets.

Candlelight Inn ✪
2310 CENTRAL AVENUE, NORTH WILDWOOD, NEW JERSEY 08260

Tel: **(609) 522-6200**	Open: **Feb.–Dec.**
Best Time to Call: **8 AM–11 PM**	Reduced Rates: **10%, seniors**
Hosts: **Paul DiFilippo and Diane**	Breakfast: **Full**
Buscham	Credit Cards: **AMEX, MC, VISA**
Location: **40 mi. S of Atlantic City**	Pets: **No**
No. of Rooms: **10**	Children: **No**
No. of Private Baths: **8**	Smoking: **No**
Max. No. Sharing Bath: **4**	Social Drinking: **Permitted**
Double/pb: **$70–$105**	Airport/Station Pickup: **Yes**
Double/sb: **$65–$80**	Foreign Languages: **French**
Suite: **$95–$135**	Minimum Stay: **3 nights, July and Aug.**

Leaming Rice, Sr., built this Queen Anne Victorian at the turn of the century. The house remained in the family until Diane and Paul restored it and created a bed and breakfast. Large oak doors with beveled glass invite you into the main vestibule, which has a fireplace nook. A wide variety of original gas lighting fixtures may be found throughout the house. Guest rooms have fresh flowers and are furnished with period pieces and antiques. Breakfast is served in the dining room with a built-in oak breakfront, and chestnut pocket doors. A hot tub and sun deck are special spots for relaxing. In the afternoon, enjoy tea and cookies on the wide veranda. This elegant inn is convenient to the beaches, boardwalk, and historic Cape May.

Home Suite Home ✪

1410 SURF AVENUE, NORTH WILDWOOD, NEW JERSEY 08260

Tel: **(609) 729-6625**
Hosts: **Jim and Connie Costa**
Location: **40 mi. S of Atlantic City**
No. of Rooms: **4**
No. of Private Baths: **2**
Max. No. Sharing Bath: **4**
Double/pb: **$65–$85**
Single/pb: **$50–$65**
Double/sb: **$60–$75**
Single/sb: **$45–$60**

Open: **Mar. 1–Dec. 31**
Reduced Rates: **10%, seniors; weekly**
Breakfast: **Full**
Credit Cards: **MC, VISA**
Pets: **No**
Children: **Welcome, over 12**
Smoking: **Permitted**
Social Drinking: **Permitted**
Foreign Languages: **Italian, Polish**
Minimum Stay: **3 nights, July and Aug.**

Jim and Connie Costa welcome you to their white marble executive-style home located one block from the beach. The house is decorated in a Grecian motif with comfortable furnishings and family pieces. There is plenty to do in this resort town, and you're just one and a half blocks from the boardwalk when you stay with the Costas. They can suggest bicycle routes, recommend restaurants, and direct you to even more activities in nearby Atlantic City.

BarnaGate Bed & Breakfast ✪

637 WESLEY AVENUE, OCEAN CITY, NEW JERSEY 08226

Tel: **(609) 391-9366**
Hosts: **The Barna family**
Location: **10 mi. S of Atlantic City**
No. of Rooms: **5**
No. of Private Baths: **2**

Max. No. Sharing Bath: **4**
Double/pb: **$60–$75**
Single/pb: **$50–$65**
Double/sb: **$50–$65**
Single/sb: **$40–$55**

Open: **All year**
Breakfast: **Continental**
Credit Cards: **MC, VISA**
Pets: **No**
Children: **Welcome, over 10**

Smoking: **No**
Social Drinking: **Permitted**
Minimum Stay: **Summer holiday
    weekends**
Airport/Station Pickup: **Yes**

This 1895 seashore Victorian, painted a soft peach with mauve and burgundy trim, is only three and a half blocks from the ocean. The attractively furnished bedrooms have paddle fans, antique furnishings, pretty quilts, and wicker accessories. You'll enjoy the homey atmosphere and the sensitive hospitality; if you want privacy, it is respected, if you want company, it is offered. Antique shops, great restaurants, the quaint charm of Cape May and the excitement of Atlantic City are close by.

Ashling Cottage ✪
106 SUSSEX AVENUE, SPRING LAKE, NEW JERSEY 07762

Tel: **(201) 449-3553**
Hosts: **Goodi and Jack Stewart**
Location: **6 mi. from Garden State
    Pky., Exit 98**
No. of Rooms: **10**
No. of Private Baths: **8**
Max. No. Sharing Bath: **4**
Double/pb: **$67–$102**
Single/pb: **$63–$91**
Double/sb: **$58–$75**
Single/sb: **$54–$71**

Open: **Mar.–Dec.**
Reduced Rates: **Sept. 15–May 15**
Breakfast: **Continental**
Pets: **No**
Children: **No**
Smoking: **Permitted**
Social Drinking: **Permitted**
Airport/Station Pickup: **Yes**
Minimum Stay: **2 to 3 nights, May–
    Aug. weekends**

The Jersey shore is a block away from this three-story, mansard-roofed cottage with bay windows, overhangs, nooks, and a small romantic balcony. Each guest room is different, with such features as dormer windows, wainscoting, and individual porches. A buffet breakfast is served in the glass-enclosed solarium with views of the ocean and boardwalk to the east. To the west is the willow-bordered Spring Lake, popular for boaters, with its wooden foot bridges, ducks, and geese.

Whistling Swan Inn ✪
BOX 791, 110 MAIN STREET, STANHOPE, NEW JERSEY 07874

Tel: **(201) 347-6369**
Best Time to Call: **9 AM–6 PM**
Hosts: **Paula Williams and Joe Mulay**
Location: **45 mi. W of New York City**
No. of Rooms: **10**
No. of Private Baths: **10**
Double/pb: **$60–$80**
Open: **All year**

Reduced Rates: **Weekly; 10%, seniors**
Breakfast: **Full**
Credit Cards: **AMEX, MC, VISA**
Pets: **No**
Children: **Welcome, over 12**
Smoking: **No**
Social Drinking: **Permitted**
Airport/Station Pickup: **Yes**

You'll feel like you're back in grandmother's house when you visit this lovely Queen Anne Victorian located in a small, historic village. The massive limestone wraparound porch leads to comfortable rooms filled with family antiques. Your hosts have labored tirelessly to make the ornate woodwork, huge fireplace, old-fashioned fixtures, and even the dumbwaiter look like new. Take a bubble bath in a claw-footed tub and then wrap yourself in a fluffy robe before retiring. Your room will be individually decorated in an Oriental art decor or brass motif. Breakfast includes homemade muffins, breads, and fruit, along with a hot egg, cheese, or fruit dish. Special arrangements are easily made for corporate guests who need to eat early or require the use of a private telephone, copy service, or meeting room. The inn is close to the International Trade Zone, Waterloo Village, Lake Musconetcong, restaurants, and state parks and forests.

For key to listings, see inside front or back cover.

✪ This star means that rates are guaranteed through December 31, 1991, to any guest making a reservation as a result of reading about the B&B in *BED & BREAKFAST U.S.A.*—1991 edition.

Important! To avoid misunderstandings, always ask about cancellation policies when booking.

Please enclose a self-addressed, stamped, business-size envelope when contacting reservation services.

For more details on what you can expect in a B&B, see Chapter 1.

Always mention *Bed & Breakfast U.S.A.* when making reservations!

If no B&B is listed in the area you'll be visiting, use the form on page 675 to order a copy of our "List of New B&Bs."

We want to hear from you! Use the form on page 677.

NEW MEXICO

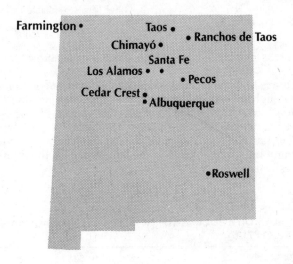

Bed & Breakfast Rocky Mountains—New Mexico ✪
MAILING ADDRESS: P.O. BOX 804, COLORADO SPRINGS, COLORADO 80901

Tel: **(719) 630-3433**
Best Time to Call: **9 AM–5 PM**
Coordinator: **Betty Ann Field**
States/Regions Covered:
  Albuquerque, Santa Fe, Taos

Rates (Single/Double):
  Modest:　**$35**　　**$45**
  Average:　**$60**　　**$65**
  Luxury:　 **$85**　　**$125**
Credit Cards: **MC, VISA**

New Mexico is the Land of Enchantment, where folks are able to maintain their bond with a slower, more relaxed pace. Experience southwestern art galleries, sculptures, ethnic foods, and Indian pueblos. Visit the hot-air balloon festival in Albuquerque, and the Taos Art Festival; go to the Santa Fe opera; ski in winter. B&Bs are in old, thick-walled adobes, lovely suites, modest homes, or unhosted apartments. There is a $4.50 charge for Betty Ann's directory.

The Corner House ✪

9121 JAMES PLACE NORTHEAST, ALBUQUERQUE, NEW MEXICO 87111

Tel: **(505) 298-5800**	Open: **All year**
Host: **Jean Thompson**	Reduced Rates: **10%, families and**
Location: **4 mi. N of I-40**	**seniors**
No. of Rooms: **3**	Breakfast: **Full**
No. of Private Baths: **1**	Other Meals: **Available**
Max. No. Sharing Bath: **3**	Pets: **Sometimes**
Double/pb: **$45**	Children: **Welcome (crib)**
Double/sb: **$35**	Smoking: **No**
Single/sb: **$30**	Social Drinking: **Permitted**

Jean welcomes you to her handsome Southwestern-style home, decorated in a delightful mix of antiques and collectibles. Breakfast specialties include Jean's homemade muffins. The Corner House is located in a quiet residential neighborhood within view of the magnificent Sandia Mountains. It is convenient to Old Town Albuquerque, Santa Fe, and many Indian pueblos, and the launch site for the International Balloon Festival.

Rio Grande House ✪

3100 RIO GRANDE BOULEVARD, NORTHWEST, ALBUQUERQUE, NEW MEXICO 87107

Tel: **(505) 345-0120**	Single/sb: **$35**
Hosts: **Jim Hughes and Dick Gray**	Suites: **$50**
Location: **4 mi. from I-40**	Open: **All year**
No. of Rooms: **3**	Breakfast: **Full**
No. of Private Baths: **2**	Pets: **Sometimes**
Max. No. Sharing Bath: **2**	Children: **No**
Double/pb: **$50**	Smoking: **Permitted**
Single/pb: **$40**	Social Drinking: **Permitted**

This landmark white adobe residence is close to historic Old Town, major museums, and the Rio Grande Nature Center. Southwestern charm is reflected throughout: beamed ceilings, brick floors, and kiva fireplaces. Museum-quality antiques, collectibles from East Africa, Nepal, and Yemen are used to decorate each room. Jim, a college professor, writer, and actor will be happy to relate their history.

Santa Fe Casita

P.O. BOX 287, CEDAR CREST, NEW MEXICO 87008

Tel: **(505) 281-3597**	Guest Cottage: **$65–$95; sleeps 4**
Best Time to Call: **7 AM–10 PM**	Suite: **$45–$65**
Host: **Norma Curry**	Open: **All year**
Location: **12050 Hwy. 14 North**	Reduced Rates: **Weekly in winter**

Breakfast: **Full**
Credit Cards: **AMEX, MC, VISA**
Pets: **Permitted**

Children: **Welcome**
Smoking: **No**
Social Drinking: **Permitted**

The Ambrose family welcomes you to their Santa Fe Territorial-style home. Guests can choose from two accommodations, each with private entrance. You can relax on the patio or next to the kiva fireplace. The private adobe casita features a comfortable bedroom, a kitchen, a wood stove, and a private patio. Your hosts are interior decorators and have created a charming southwestern atmosphere with Santa Fe furnishings, Mexican tile floors, hand-quilted linens, and down pillows. Greet each morning with French-roast coffee and fresh flowers in your room.

La Posada de Chimayó ✪
P.O. BOX 463, CHIMAYÓ, NEW MEXICO 87522

Tel: **(505) 351-4605**
Host: **Sue Farrington**
Location: **30 mi. N of Santa Fe**
No. of Rooms: **2**
No. of Private Baths: **2**
Double/pb: **$85**
Single/pb: **$70**
Open: **All year**

Reduced Rates: **Weekly in winter**
Breakfast: **Full**
Credit Cards: **MC, VISA (for deposits)**
Pets: **Sometimes**
Children: **Welcome, over 12**
Smoking: **Permitted**
Social Drinking: **Permitted**
Foreign Languages: **Spanish**

Chimayó is known for its historic old church and its tradition of fine Spanish weaving. This is a typical adobe home with brick floors and *viga* ceilings. The suite is composed of a small bedroom and sitting room, and is made cozy with Mexican rugs, handwoven fabrics, comfortable furnishings, and traditional corner fireplaces. Sue's breakfasts are not for the fainthearted, and often feature stuffed French toast or chilies rellenos. Wine or sun tea are graciously offered after you return from exploring Bandelier National Monument Park, the Indian pueblos, cliff dwellings, and the "high road" to Taos.

La Casita Guesthouse ✪
P.O. BOX 103, DIXON, NEW MEXICO 87527

Tel: **(505) 579-4297**
Hosts: **Sara Pene and Celeste Miller**
Location: **25 mi. S of Taos**
Guest Cottage: **$60 for 2; $70 for 3; $80 for 4**
Handicapped Accessible: **Yes**
Open: **All year**

Breakfast: **Continental**
Pets: **No**
Children: **Welcome**
Smoking: **No**
Social Drinking: **Permitted**
Foreign Languages: **Spanish**

The rural mountain village of Dixon is home to many artists and craftspeople. La Casita is a traditional New Mexico adobe with vigas, latillas, and Mexican tile floors. Guests enjoy use of the living room, fully equipped kitchen, two bedrooms (each with a double bed), one bath, and a lovely patio. Available only to people traveling together, it is a perfect spot for relaxing and is just minutes from the Rio Grande, river rafting, hiking, and cross-country skiing. Indian Pueblos, ancient Anasazi ruins, museums, art galleries, horseback-riding ranches, and alpine skiing are within an hour's drive. Sara is a horticulturist and weaver; Celeste is a teacher and psychotherapist.

Silver River Inn ❂
3151 WEST MAIN STREET, FARMINGTON, NEW MEXICO 87499

Tel: (505) 325-8219	Breakfast: **Continental**
Best Time to Call: **After 5 PM**	Credit Cards: **MC, VISA**
Hosts: **Diana Ohlson and David Beers**	Wheelchair Accessible: **Yes**
Location: **180 mi. NW of Albuquerque**	Pets: **No**
No. of Rooms: **1**	Children: **Welcome, over 12**
No. of Private Baths: **1**	Smoking: **No**
Suite: **$55–$75**	Social Drinking: **Permitted**
Open: **All year**	Airport/Station Pickup: **Yes**

Silver River Inn is a newly constructed, traditional Mexican home with massive timber beams and exposed adobe. From its cliffside perch, it overlooks the fork of the San Juan and La Plata Rivers. Indian reservations, Aztec ruins, and ski slopes are all within striking distance of this B&B. Private motor tours of the area can be arranged. A highlight of the continental breakfast is green chili corn bread.

Casa del Rey Bed & Breakfast ❂
305 ROVER, LOS ALAMOS, NEW MEXICO 87544

Tel: (505) 672-9401	Open: **All year**
Best Time to Call: **After 5 PM**	Reduced Rates: **Weekly; families**
Host: **Virginia L. King**	Breakfast: **Continental**
No. of Rooms: **2**	Pets: **No**
Max. No. Sharing Bath: **4**	Children: **Welcome, over 5**
Double/sb: **$30**	Smoking: **No**
Single/sb: **$25**	Social Drinking: **Permitted**

This adobe contemporary home is located in the quiet residential area of White Rock, and is situated in the Jémez mountains with a view of Santa Fe across the valley. The surroundings are rich in Spanish and Indian history. Pueblos, museums, Bandelier National Monument, skiing, hiking trails, tennis, and golf are all within easy reach. Virginia is rightfully proud of her beautifully kept house, with its pretty flower gardens. In summer, her breakfast of granola, home-baked rolls and muffins, along with fruits and beverages, is served on the sun porch, where you can enjoy the lovely scenery.

Two Pipe Bed & Breakfast ✪
BOX 52, TALPA ROUTE, RANCHOS DE TAOS, NEW MEXICO 87557

Tel: (505) 758-4770
Hosts: **Dusty and Babs Davis**
Location: **4 mi. SE of Taos**
Guest Cottage: **$75, for 2**
Open: **All year**
Breakfast: **Continental**

Pets: **No**
Children: **Welcome, over 5**
Smoking: **No**
Social Drinking: **Permitted**
Airport/Station Pickup: **Yes**

Beautiful gardens and mountain views surround this 275-year-old adobe hacienda. The house includes many traditional adobe features, such as kiva fireplaces and *viga* ceilings, along with many antiques and family furnishings. Guests are welcome to relax in the hot tub or curl up in front of a cozy fire. Your hosts offer complimentary snacks, wine, and beverages, and will do all they can to make you feel welcome. Five ski areas are located less than an hour from here, and a special hearty skiers' breakfast is served in season. Art galleries, museums, Indian pueblos, and Rio Grande Gorge, as well as great hunting and fishing, can all be enjoyed nearby.

Bed & Breakfast of New Mexico ✪
P.O. BOX 2805, SANTA FE, NEW MEXICO 87504

Tel: (505) 982-3332
Best Time to Call: **9 AM–9 PM**
Coordinator: **Rob Bennett**
States/Regions Covered: **New Mexico, statewide**
Descriptive Directory: **Free**

Rates (Single/Double):
Modest: **$40** **$55**
Average: **$60** **$80**
Luxury: **$85** **$125**
Credit Cards: **AMEX, MC, VISA**

Do come and enjoy the Santa Fe Opera in summer, the vibrant colors of the aspens in autumn, or skiing in winter. Don't miss the Indian pueblos and ancient cliff dwellings, the national forest areas, art colonies, museums, and Taos.

Adobe Abode ✪
202 CHAPELLE, SANTA FE, NEW MEXICO 87501

Tel: (505) 983-3133
Host: **Pat Harbour**
No. of Rooms: **3**
No. of Private Baths: **3**
Double/pb: **$85–$95**
Single/pb: **$80–$85**

Open: **All year**
Breakfast: **Full**
Pets: **No**
Children: **Welcome, over 10**
Smoking: **Permitted**
Social Drinking: **Permitted**

This renovated historic adobe offers all the amenities of a fine country inn just 3 blocks from downtown Santa Fe Plaza. Pat has decorated her house with a discerning eye and a flair for southwestern charm.

The bedrooms feature fine linens, private phones, and handsome antiques. Excellent restaurants, museums, and shops are within walking distance.

Jean's Place ✪

2407 CAMINO CAPITAN, SANTA FE, NEW MEXICO 87505

Tel: (505) 471-4053	Reduced Rates: Weekly; seniors
Host: Jean D. Gosse	Breakfast: Continental
No. of Rooms: 1	Pets: No
No. of Private Baths: 1	Children: Welcome
Double/pb: $40	Smoking: No
Single/pb: $35	Social Drinking: No
Open: All year	

Situated on a quiet residential street, Jean's Place is minutes from downtown and miles from the ordinary. Jean is a certified Crystal Energetics practitioner, medium, spiritual counselor, and teacher of metaphysics. Her home features an extensive collection of crystal that complements the attractive decor. You are welcome to use the tennis, golf, and swimming facilities at the nearby country club.

American Artists Gallery-House ✪

FRONTIER ROAD, P.O. BOX 584, TAOS, NEW MEXICO 87571

Tel: (505) 758-4446	Separate Guest Cottage: $55
Best Time to Call: Mornings; evenings	Open: All year
Hosts: Benjamin and Myra Carp	Breakfast: Full
Location: 3 blocks from Main St.	Pets: No
No. of Rooms: 5	Children: Welcome
No. of Private Baths: 5	Smoking: No
Double/pb: $55–$90	Social Drinking: Permitted
Single/pb: $50–$85	Airport/Station Pickup: Yes

This charming hacienda is filled with artwork, and has a splendid view of Taos Mountain. Your hosts will gladly advise on local craft shops and boutiques. Their home is close to Rio Grande Gorge State Park, 900-year-old Taos Pueblo, and places to go fishing and rafting. Fireplaces, the outdoor hot tub, gardens, and a sculpture courtyard will delight you.

Harrison's B&B ✪

P.O. BOX 242, TAOS, NEW MEXICO 87571

Tel: (505) 758-2630	No. of Rooms: 3
Hosts: Jean and Bob Harrison	No. of Private Baths: 2
Location: 1½ mi. from Rte. 64	Max. No. Sharing Bath: 4

Double/pb: **$50**
Single/pb: **$40**
Double/sb: **$30–$40**
Single/sb: **$20–$30**
Open: **All year**
Reduced Rates: **10% after 4 nights**

Breakfast: **Full**
Pets: **No**
Children: **Welcome (crib)**
Smoking: **No**
Social Drinking: **Permitted**

The Harrisons have lived in this large adobe just outside of Taos for 25 years. The house overlooks town from the foot of the western mesa and, framed by trees and bushes, boasts lovely mountain views. Inside, original works of art enhance the southwestern decor. The Harrisons are just over two miles from the Taos plaza, and are conveniently located near many outdoor pursuits, including skiing, hiking, fishing, and river rafting.

For key to listings, see inside front or back cover.

○ This star means that rates are guaranteed through December 31, 1991, to any guest making a reservation as a result of reading about the B&B in *BED & BREAKFAST U.S.A.—1991* edition.

Important! To avoid misunderstandings, always ask about cancellation policies when booking.

Please enclose a self-addressed, stamped, business-size envelope when contacting reservation services.

For more details on what you can expect in a B&B, see Chapter 1.

Always mention *Bed & Breakfast U.S.A.* when making reservations!

If no B&B is listed in the area you'll be visiting, use the form on page 675 to order a copy of our "List of New B&Bs."

We want to hear from you! Use the form on page 677.

NEW YORK

Thousand
Islands Area

Lake Placid/
Adirondacks Area

Finger Lakes
Area

Niagara/Buffalo/
Rochester Area

Lake George Area

Chautauqua-
Allegheny

Central New York/
Leatherstocking Area

Hudson Valley/Albany/
Kingston Area

Catskills

Long Island

New York City Area

CATSKILLS

Maplewood ✪
PARK ROAD, P.O. BOX 40, CHICHESTER, NEW YORK 12416

Tel: **(914) 688-5433**	Single/sb: **$40**
Best Time to Call: **After 7 PM**	Open: **All year**
Hosts: **Nancy and Albert Parsons**	Breakfast: **Full**
Location: **25 mi. NW of Kingston**	Pets: **No**
No. of Rooms: **4**	Children: **Welcome**
Max. No. Sharing Bath: **4**	Smoking: **No**
Double/sb: **$55**	Social Drinking: **Permitted**

A Colonial manor on a quiet country lane, and nestled among stately
maples, this is a charming B&B. Each spacious bedroom has a view of
the Catskills. In summer, you can swim in the in-ground pool, or play
badminton, croquet, or horseshoes. In winter, ski Belleayre, Hunter,
and Cortina, all only 12 miles away. In any season, enjoy the art

galleries, boutiques, great restaurants, and theater at Woodstock, 20 minutes away. After a great day outdoors, come home to a glass of wine and good conversation. After a good night's sleep, you'll enjoy freshly squeezed orange juice, homemade breads and pastries, and freshly ground coffee.

Timberdoodle Inn ✪
MAIN STREET, FLEISCHMANNS, NEW YORK 12430

Tel: **(914) 254-4884**	Open: **All year**
Hosts: **Peggy and Joe Ruff**	Breakfast: **Full**
Location: **39 mi. W of Kingston**	Credit Cards: **MC, VISA**
No. of Rooms: **7**	Pets: **Sometimes**
No. of Private Baths: **5**	Children: **Welcome**
Max. No. Sharing Bath: **4**	Smoking: **Permitted**
Double/pb: **$65–$80**	Social Drinking: **Permitted**
Single/pb: **$60**	Minimum Stay: **2 nights ski season,**
Double/sb: **$60**	**major holidays**

The inn, a sports enthusiast's paradise, is located in the high peaks of the Catskill Mountains. A spacious late Victorian village "cottage" is attractively furnished with select antiques, wicker, brass, and country chintz. Windows framed in stained glass offer views of the ever-changing seasons. Your host, a licensed New York State Guide, can direct you to world-famous trout streams, well-marked hiking trails, and the Forest Preserve. Belleayre, a popular ski center, is five minutes away. Breakfast often features eggs Florentine, Dutch pancakes, or cinnamon muffins.

The Eggery Inn
COUNTY ROAD 16, TANNERSVILLE, NEW YORK 12485

Tel: **(518) 589-5363**	Reduced Rates: **Families; off season**
Best Time to Call: **10 AM–8 PM**	Breakfast: **Full**
Hosts: **Julie and Abe Abramczyk**	Credit Cards: **AMEX, MC, VISA**
No. of Rooms: **13**	Other Meals: **Available**
No. of Private Baths: **13**	Pets: **No**
Double/pb: **$75–$85**	Children: **Welcome**
Single/pb: **$60**	Smoking: **Permitted**
Suite: **$90 for 2**	Social Drinking: **Permitted**
Open: **May 16–Sept. 7;**	Minimum Stay: **2 nights, weekends; 3**
Sept. 15–Apr. 1	**nights, holiday weekends**

The inn, with its wraparound porch, is nestled amid the majestic ridges of the Catskills at an elevation of 2,200 feet. The sitting room is enhanced by a beautiful oak balustrade leading to cozy guest rooms furnished with antiques, rockers, cable TV, and warm comforters. The player piano, Mission Oak furnishings, and abundance of plants lend a homey atmosphere. It is in the Catskill Game Preserve, and convenient to Hunter, Cortina, and Windham mountains for Alpine skiing, hiking, and seasonal recreational activities. The famous artist colony at Woodstock is nearby. On weekends and holiday periods, rates change because dinner is included.

Sunrise Inn ✪
RD 1, BOX 232B, WALTON, NEW YORK 13856

Tel: **(607) 865-7254**
Best Time to Call: **9 AM–11 PM**
Hosts: **James and Adele Toth**
Location: **135 mi. NW of N.Y.C.; 5 mi. from Rte. 17**
No. of Rooms: **2**
Max. No. Sharing Bath: **4**
Double/sb: **$40**
Single/sb: **$35**

Guest Cottage: **$55 for 2**
Open: **All year**
Reduced Rates: **10%, seniors**
Breakfast: **Continental**
Pets: **No**
Children: **Welcome (crib)**
Smoking: **No**
Social Drinking: **Permitted**

Relax and enjoy the sound of the bubbling brook that borders the landscape of this 19th-century farmhouse. You'll awaken to the aroma of Irish soda bread and other homemade goodies, which you are invited to enjoy in the dining area or, weather permitting, on the wraparound porch. Afterward, browse through the antiques shop adjoining the inn. Area activities include fishing, canoeing, golfing, skiing, country fairs, and fine dining. End the day in quiet and homey comfort around the parlor wood stove.

CENTRAL NEW YORK/LEATHERSTOCKING AREA

Bed & Breakfast—Leatherstocking ✪
389 BROCKWAY ROAD, FRANKFORT, NEW YORK 13340

Tel: **(315) 733-0040**
Best Time to Call: **7 AM–10 PM**
Coordinator: **Floranne McCraith**
States/Regions Covered: **Central N.Y.**
Descriptive Directory: **$2**

Rates (Single/Double):
Average: **$30** **$50**
Luxury: **$55** **$95**
Credit Cards: **MC, VISA**

Leatherstocking country is an 11-county region of New York that extends from the Catskills across the Mohawk Valley to the central Adirondacks. It's a region to be visited in all seasons for all reasons, and its residents warmly welcome visitors. Recreational sports and activities, outlet shopping, antiques, fairs, and fine dining are waiting for you, and your B&B host will tell you where to find the best of everything. There is a $3 reservation charge.

The Inn at Brook Willow Farm ✪
RD 2, BOX 514, COOPERSTOWN, NEW YORK 13326

Tel: **(607) 547-9700**	Open: **All year**
Best Time to Call: **After 6 PM**	Breakfast: **Full**
Hosts: **Joan and Jack Grimes**	Pets: **No**
No. of Rooms: **4**	Children: **Welcome (crib)**
No. of Private Baths: **4**	Smoking: **No**
Double/pb: **$55–$70**	Social Drinking: **Permitted**

Located on 14 acres of meadow and woods, nestled among the pines and willows, this charming Victorian cottage with its restored barn is furnished with lovely antiques, wicker, and plants. Enjoy homemade blueberry muffins at breakfast, and wine, fresh fruit, and fresh flowers in your room. The world-famous Baseball Hall of Fame is here, as well as countless historic and cultural sites to visit. Recreational activities abound on unspoiled Otsego Lake.

Litco Farms Bed and Breakfast ✪
P.O. BOX 1048, COOPERSTOWN, NEW YORK 13326

Tel: **(607) 547-2501**	Reduced Rates: **Dec.–Mar.**
Hosts: **Margaret and Jim Wolff**	Breakfast: **Full**
Location: **2 mi. NW of Cooperstown**	Pets: **No**
No. of Rooms: **4**	Children: **Welcome**
Max. No. Sharing Bath: **4**	Smoking: **Permitted**
Double/sb: **$50–$75**	Social Drinking: **Permitted**
Suites: **$85–$95**	Airport/Station Pickup: **Yes**
Open: **All year**	

Seventy acres of unspoiled meadows and woodlands are yours to explore at Litco Farms. The day begins with fresh-baked breads, fresh eggs, milk, and local bacon, served in the dining room–library. Borrow a canoe to fish on Canadarago Lake, which is stocked with freshwater salmon. There are other places to paddle, including Glimmerglass, the lake made famous by James Fenimore Cooper. After spending a day at the Baseball Hall of Fame, guests may relax and unwind around the large in-ground pool. Heartworks, a charming quilt craft shop, is on premises.

Whisperin Pines Chalet ✪
RD 3, BOX 248, COOPERSTOWN, NEW YORK 13326

Tel: **(607) 547-5640**	Double/pb: **$75**
Best Time to Call: **11 AM**	Single/pb: **$70**
Hosts: **Joyce and Gus Doucas**	Double/sb: **$45–$55**
No. of Rooms: **6**	Suites: **$100**
No. of Private Baths: **5**	Open: **All year**
Max. No. Sharing Bath: **4**	Breakfast: **Full**

Pets: **No**   Social Drinking: **Permitted**
Children: **Welcome**   Airport/Station Pickup: **Yes**
Smoking: **Permitted**   Foreign Languages: **French, Greek**

Guests may choose from a variety of accommodations, including some
with canopy beds, fireplaces, private balconies—even a bubble bath
for two. The country setting offers a private walking trail, waterfalls,
and a brook from which the lucky can catch a trout for breakfast. The
chalet is equipped with a wheelchair ramp and electric chairlift. A
delicious country breakfast is served in the cozy dining room featuring
country-fresh eggs, milk, and butter; homemade sausage and bacon;
and Vermont maple syrup.

Dorchester Farm Bed & Breakfast ✪
RD 1, BOX 6, KEIBEL ROAD, LISLE, NEW YORK 13797

Tel: **(607) 692-4511**   Suites: **$65**
Best Time to Call: **7–9 AM; 6–10 PM**   Open: **All year**
Hosts: **Carolan and Scott Mersereau**   Reduced Rates: **15%, weekly**
Location: **15 mi. N of Binghamton**   Breakfast: **Full**
No. of Rooms: **4**   Pets: **No**
No. of Private Baths: **2**   Children: **Welcome, over 10**
Max. No. Sharing Bath: **4**   Smoking: **Permitted**
Double/pb: **$55**   Social Drinking: **Permitted**
Double/sb: **$45**   Airport/Station Pickup: **Yes**

Enjoy peace and tranquillity at this 100-year-old farmhouse with a
splendid view of rolling hills and a five-mile lake. Carolan and Scott
have created a days-gone-by atmosphere with select antiques, lovely
accessories, attractively updated bathrooms, all in a light and airy
country setting. The area abounds with recreational activities in all
seasons. Cornell University and the State University of New York at
Binghamton are less than a half hour away.

Country Spread Bed & Breakfast ✪
**P.O. BOX 1863, 23 PROSPECT STREET, RICHFIELD SPRINGS, NEW
YORK 13439**

Tel: **(315) 858-1870**   Suites: **$80**
Hosts: **Karen and Bruce Watson**   Open: **All year**
Location: **20 mi. SE of Utica on Rte.**   Breakfast: **Full**
   28   Credit Cards: **MC, VISA**
No. of Rooms: **2**   Pets: **No**
Max. No. Sharing Bath: **4**   Children: **Welcome (crib)**
Double/pb: **$60**   Smoking: **No**
Single/pb: **$45**   Social Drinking: **Permitted**
Double/sb: **$50**   Minimum Stay: **Sometimes**
Single/sb: **$40**   Airport/Station Pickup: **Yes**

Long-time area residents Karen and Bruce have restored their 1893 cozy home into a wonderful retreat, tastefully decorated in country style. Your day will start with warm muffins, homemade preserves, pancakes with pure maple syrup, fresh eggs, granola, and chilled juice. Relax on the deck with the newspaper, and then visit some of the area's attractions, including Cooperstown, museums, summer theater, opera, fine dining, antique and specialty shops, and small-town happenings. Nearby Canadarago and Otsego Lakes offer excellent boating, fishing, and swimming.

Jonathan House ✪
39 EAST MAIN STREET, P.O. BOX 9, RICHFIELD SPRINGS, NEW YORK 13439

Tel: **(315) 858-2870**	Suites: **$70**
Hosts: **Jonathan and Peter Parker**	Open: **All year**
Location: **14 mi. N of Cooperstown**	Reduced Rates: **$10 less, Nov. 1–Apr.**
No. of Rooms: **4**	**30**
No. of Private Baths: **2**	Breakfast: **Full**
Max. No. Sharing Bath: **4**	Credit Cards: **AMEX, MC, VISA**
Double/pb: **$60**	Pets: **Sometimes**
Single/pb: **$60**	Children: **Welcome**
Double/sb: **$50**	Smoking: **No**
Single/sb: **$50**	Social Drinking: **Permitted**

The Parker brothers enjoy cooking and entertaining so, when they were both widowed, their friends suggested that they open a B&B in the house they share with their mother. The 1883 house, a hybrid of the Eastlake and Stick styles, has three full floors and a tower room on a fourth level—a total of 17 rooms. The house is elegantly decorated with antiques (some that belonged to the brothers' great-grandparents and grandparents), fine paintings, and Oriental rugs. Breakfast is served in the dining room—with bone china, damask linen, and English silver.

CHAUTAUQUA/ALLEGHENY AREA

Rainbow Hospitality, Inc.—Chautauqua ✪
466 AMHERST STREET, BUFFALO, NEW YORK 14207

Tel: **(716) 874-8797**	Rates: (Single/Double):	
Best Time to Call: **9 AM–5 PM**	Modest: **$35**	**$45**
Coordinator: **Georgia Brannon**	Average: **$55**	**$65**
States/Regions Covered: **Chautauqua,**	Luxury: **$60**	**$100**
South Dayton, Little Valley	Credit Cards: **MC, VISA**	
Descriptive Directory: **$3**		

This area boasts an infinite variety of cities and farm towns, of colleges and commerce, of skiing and sailing, of attractions both natural and man-made. Chautauqua is famous for the cultural, educational, and religious activities of the summer colony on the lake, as well as for its topnotch recreational diversions.

Wheaten House ✪

RD 2, BOX 404, WEST FIVE MILE ROAD, ALLEGANY, NEW YORK 14706

Tel: **(716) 373-2032**
Hosts: **David and Linda Preston**
Location: **2 mi. N of Route 17, Exit 24**
No. of Rooms: **1**
No. of Private Baths: **1**
Double/pb: **$60**
Single/pb: **$50**
Double/sb: **$50**
Single/sb: **$45**

Open: **All year**
Reduced Rates: **10%, families**
Breakfast: **Full**
Other Meals: **Available**
Pets: **Sometimes**
Children: **Welcome, over 4**
Smoking: **No**
Social Drinking: **Permitted**

A red-brick farmhouse with an Italian accent, Wheaten House is set in the Allegheny Mountains, at the entrance to the Wing Hollow ski area. By car, Allegheny State Park and Holiday Valley's ski slopes are a few minutes away. When summer melts the snow, visitors can cool off in the Prestons' pool. Your hosts are dog fanciers who maintain the Irish Creme Kennel, where they breed the champion soft-coated wheaten terriers that give this B&B its name. For breakfast, Linda serves pancakes, French toast, or Danish on the enclosed rear porch, which enjoys a sweeping view of nearby ski slopes.

Green Acres ✪

ROUTE 474, ASHVILLE, NEW YORK 14710

Tel: **(716) 782-4254**
Best Time to Call: **Mornings**
Hosts: **Lowell and Mary Ann Green**
Location: **8 mi. W of Jamestown**
No. of Rooms: **3**
Max. No. Sharing Bath: **4**
Double/sb: **$55**

Single/sb: **$35**
Open: **All year**
Breakfast: **Full**
Pets: **No**
Children: **Welcome**
Smoking: **No**
Social Drinking: **No**

Lowell and Mary Ann once owned an antique store, and their country Colonial is the perfect setting for their old treasures. The rooms feature hand-hewn beams, paneled walls, and stone fireplaces. Guests are welcome to relax in the comfortable living room or curl up on an old porch rocker. A heated pool is located on the three-acre property, and it is in use from June through September. Just beyond the pool lie the woods, where you can hike, fish in a large stocked pond, and cross-country ski. The breakfast specialty of the house is blueberry pancakes and sausages; the berries are as fresh as you can get, because they grow right out back. Your hosts will gladly direct you to local attractions including skiing, Panama Rocks, and the Chautauqua Institute.

Spindletop ○
POLO DRIVE OFF EAST AVENUE, GREENHURST, NEW YORK 14742

Tel: **(716) 484-2070**	Open: **All year**
Hosts: **Lee and Don Spindler**	Reduced Rates: **Available**
Location: **4 mi. W of Jamestown**	Breakfast: **Continental**
No. of Rooms: **3**	Credit Cards: **MC, VISA**
No. of Private Baths: **1**	Pets: **No**
Max. No. Sharing Bath: **4**	Children: **Welcome (if swimmers)**
Double/pb: **$65**	Smoking: **Permitted**
Double/sb: **$55**	Social Drinking: **Permitted**

Casually elegant and elegantly casual, Oriental carpets and fine furnishings create a lovely background to this air-conditioned home, where all guest rooms overlook Chautauqua Lake. You can relax around the secluded swimming pool, tie your boat at the Spindler's dock, or enjoy such distractions as Amish quilt shops, antique stores, wineries, art galleries, or seasonal sport opportunities. The famed Chautauqua Institute is nearby.

Napoli Stagecoach Inn ○
NAPOLI CORNERS, LITTLE VALLEY, NEW YORK 14755

Tel: **(716) 938-6735; 358-3928**	Breakfast: **Full**
Hosts: **Emmett and Marion Waite**	Credit Cards: **No**
Location: **60 mi. S of Buffalo**	Pets: **No**
No. of Rooms: **3**	Children: **Welcome, over 10**
Max. No. Sharing Bath: **4**	Smoking: **No**
Double/sb: **$35**	Social Drinking: **No**
Single/sb: **$25**	Airport/Station Pickup: **Yes**
Open: **All year**	Foreign Languages: **Spanish**
Reduced Rates: **Weekly**	

Located in the foothills of the Allegheny Mountains, this residence was originally built as a stagecoach inn in 1830. It is now part of a seven-acre fruit and vegetable farm where you can enjoy uncrowded comfort and warm hospitality. Emmett and Marion have many hobbies, such as antique collecting, building grandfather clocks, china painting, doll making, and quilting. The inn is close to Holiday Valley Ski Area, Kinzua Dam and Reservoir, Chautauqua Institute, and the Seneca-Iroquois National Museum. Their 4,000-volume library is a fine place to browse.

Plumbush at Chautauqua ✪
RD 2, BOX 332, MAYVILLE, NEW YORK 14757

Tel: **(716) 789-5309**
Best Time to Call: **Weekdays**
Hosts: **George and Sandy Green**
Location: **90 mi. SW of Buffalo**
No. of Rooms: **4**
No. of Private Baths: **4**
Double/pb: **$55–$85**
Single/pb: **$50–$80**
Open: **All year**

Reduced Rates: **15%, weekly**
Breakfast: **Full**
Credit Cards: **MC, VISA**
Pets: **No**
Children: **Welcome, over 10**
Smoking: **No**
Social Drinking: **Permitted**
Minimum Stay: **Holiday weekends**

Immerse yourself in a bygone era. The intrinsic beauty of this 1865 Italianate villa is situated on 125 acres of meadow and woods. Painted in a monochromatic scheme of pink to mauve to burgundy, a tower offers a commanding view of the countryside. Eleven-foot high ceilings, arched windows, and ceiling fans assure guests an airy, restful night's sleep. Savory baked treats, fruit, fresh coffee, and a variety of teas and homemade granolas start the day. Activities run the gamut from water sports and a musical treat to a visit to the famed Chautauqua Institute, just a mile away.

FINGER LAKES/ROCHESTER AREA

Elaine's B&B and Inn Reservation Service
143 DIDAMA STREET, SYRACUSE, NEW YORK 13224

Tel: **(315) 446-4199**
Best Time to Call: **10 AM–8 PM**
Coordinator: **Elaine Samuels**
States/Regions Covered: **Auburn, Baldwinsville, Cazenovia, Finger Lakes, Oneida Lake, Saranac Lake, Syracuse and suburbs, Vernon**

Descriptive Directory: **$1.25**
Rates (Single/Double):
Modest:	**$35**	**$45**
Average:	**$45**	**$55**
Luxury:	**$55**	**$75**

Credit Cards: **No**

Elaine has many host homes in the vicinity of Syracuse University, theaters, ski areas, the Finger Lakes, lovely old villages, excellent discount shopping centers, and exclusive boutiques. This is her home-town, and if you tell her your interests, she is certain to find you the perfect home-away-from-home.

Bed & Breakfast—Rochester❂
P.O. BOX 444, FAIRPORT, NEW YORK 14450

Tel: **(716) 223-8877**	Rates (Single/Double):
Best Time to Call: **2–5 PM**	Modest: **$40** **$50**
Coordinator: **Beth Kinsman**	Average: **$50** **$55**
States/Regions Covered: **Rochester**	Luxury: **$65** **$65–$135**
area	Credit Cards: **No**
Descriptive Directory: **Free**	

Friendly hosts offer a variety of accommodations, ranging from a contemporary on Lake Ontario to a traditional suburban home. A full breakfast is always included. All will be happy to advise you on the points of interest in their areas. Don't miss the Strong Museum, Eastman International Museum of Photography, and the Science Mu-seum and Planetarium. The University of Rochester and SUNY-Brock-port are local campuses. A nonrefundable $3 fee is charged per booking.

The Country House ❂
37 MILL STREET, CANASERAGA, NEW YORK 14822

Tel: **(607) 545-6439**	Single/sb: **$30**
Best Time to Call: **11 AM–1 PM; 5–7 PM**	Open: **All year**
Hosts: **Robert and Renée Coombs**	Breakfast: **Full**
Location: **50 mi. S of Rochester**	Pets: **Welcome**
No. of Rooms: **6**	Children: **Welcome (crib)**
Max. No. Sharing Bath: **4**	Smoking: **Permitted**
Double/sb: **$45**	Social Drinking: **Permitted**
	Airport/Station Pickup: **Yes**

This 100-year-old Victorian home stands on a quiet street in a charm-ing rural village. Guest rooms are comfortably furnished with an-tiques, and all are for sale. Home-baked pastries and fresh fruit are served each morning in the breakfast room or dining room. Your hosts will happily direct you to the many valleys, forests, and streams nearby for hunting, fishing, hiking, and scenic solitude. Swain Ski Center slopes, Corning Glassworks, and Letchworth State Park are minutes away.

1865 White Birch Bed & Breakfast
69 EAST FIRST STREET, CORNING, NEW YORK 14830

Tel: **(607) 962-6355**	Single/sb: **$45**
Hosts: **Kathy and Joe Donahue**	Open: **All year**
Location: **Off Rte. 17**	Breakfast: **Full**
No. of Rooms: **4**	Credit Cards: **MC, VISA**
No. of Private Baths: **2**	Pets: **No**
Max. No. Sharing Bath: **4**	Children: **Welcome**
Double/pb: **$65**	Smoking: **Downstairs only**
Single/pb: **$55**	Social Drinking: **Permitted**
Double/sb: **$60**	Airport/Station Pickup: **Yes**

The red-carpet treatment awaits you at this spacious 1865 Victorian home that has been restored to show off the beautifully crafted winding staircase and hardwood floors. Guests are welcome to choose a game or enjoy television by the fire in the common room. After a good night's sleep in a comfortable queen-size bed, you'll wake to the smell of homemade breads, muffins, and plenty of hot coffee. The White Birch is located in a residential area just two blocks from restored downtown Corning, and near such attractions as the Corning Glass Center, Rockwell Museum, and many fine wineries.

Rosewood Inn ✪
134 EAST FIRST STREET, CORNING, NEW YORK 14830

Tel: **(607) 962-3253**	Suites: **$100**
Hosts: **Winnie and Dick Peer**	Open: **All year**
Location: **1 block off Rte. 17**	Reduced Rates: **Weekly; families**
No. of Rooms: **6**	Breakfast: **Full**
No. of Private Baths: **4**	Credit Cards: **DC, MC, VISA**
Max. No. Sharing Bath: **4**	Pets: **Sometimes**
Double/pb: **$80**	Children: **Welcome (crib)**
Single/pb: **$70**	Smoking: **Permitted**
Double/sb: **$70**	Social Drinking: **Permitted**
Single/sb: **$60**	Airport/Station Pickup: **Yes**

This two-story stucco English Tudor is decorated with both antiques and originality. Each guest room is named for a famous person, and the accessories echo the personality of that individual's era. It's within walking distance of the Corning Glass Museum and the Rockwell-Corning Museum of Western Art. Winnie taught school, and Dick was the editor of the daily newspaper. Retired, they look forward to your arrival and greet you with refreshments.

Willow Cove ✪

77 SOUTH GLENORA ROAD, RD 1, BOX 87, DUNDEE, NEW YORK 14837

Tel: (607) 243-8482
Best Time to Call: After 4:30 PM
Hosts: George and Joan Van Heusen
Location: 10 mi. N of Watkins Glen
No. of Rooms: 4
Max. No. Sharing Bath: 4
Double/sb: $45

Single/sb: $40
Open: Apr.–Nov.
Breakfast: Continental
Pets: No
Children: Welcome (crib)
Smoking: Permitted
Social Drinking: Permitted

Located on the western side of Seneca Lake, this 200-year old inn is a comfortable home base for the many activities the area offers. Wineries, auctions, country fairs, antique shops, music festivals, and art galleries are but a few of the diversions. George and Joan invite you to enjoy their private beach and picnic area.

The Cobblestones ✪

1160 ROUTES 5 AND 20, GENEVA, NEW YORK 14456

Tel: (315) 789-1896
Best Time to Call: 7–9:30 PM
Hosts: The Lawrence Graceys
Location: 3½ mi. W of Geneva on
    Rtes. 5 and 20, on north side of road
No. of Rooms: 4
Max. No. Sharing Bath: 5
Double/sb: $15 and up

Single/sb: $10
Open: All year
Breakfast: No
Pets: Sometimes
Children: Welcome (crib)
Smoking: Permitted
Social Drinking: Permitted

Located in the heart of the Finger Lakes area, this inspired example of Greek Revival cobblestone architecture was built in 1848 and listed on the state and national registers of historic places. The four, large, fluted columns crowned by Ionic capitals at the front entrance add to its beauty. There are precious antiques and Oriental rugs, which reflect the fine taste of your gracious hosts. Tours are available at nearby wineries. Hobart and William Smith colleges are right in town.

Sandy Creek Manor House

1960 REDMAN ROAD, HAMLIN, NEW YORK 14464

Tel: (716) 964-7528
Best Time to Call: After 5 PM
Hosts: Shirley Hollink and James
    Krempasky
Location: 20 mi. W of Rochester
No. of Rooms: 3
Max. No. Sharing Bath: 4
Double/sb: $45
Single/sb: $40

Open: All year
Reduced Rates: Weekly; fisherman's
    discounts
Breakfast: Full
Pets: Sometimes
Children: Welcome, over 12
Smoking: No
Social Drinking: Permitted

Fishermen's delight! The path behind this 1910 English Tudor home leads through six wooded acres to the shore of Sandy Creek, where you can reel in bullheads, trout, smelt, and salmon. Wading and picnicking is also encouraged. Afterwards, come inside for an old-fashioned sing-along around the antique player piano. Full breakfasts, with fresh fruit and home-baked breads, are served on the spacious fieldstone porch.

Glendale Farm
224 BOSTWICK ROAD, ITHACA, NEW YORK 14850

Tel: **(607) 272-8756**	Suites: **$100**
Best Time to Call: **Evenings**	Separate Guest Cottage: **$75–$100**
Host: **Jeanne Marie Tomlinson**	Open: **All year**
Location: **2 mi. S of Ithaca**	Breakfast: **Full**
No. of Rooms: **6**	Credit Cards: **AMEX, MC, VISA**
No. of Private Baths: **4**	Pets: **Sometimes**
Max. No. Sharing Bath: **4**	Children: **Welcome**
Double/pb: **$75**	Smoking: **No**
Single/pb: **$50**	Social Drinking: **Permitted**
Double/sb: **$65**	Airport/Station Pickup: **Yes**

Glendale Farm is nestled in the heart of the Finger Lakes region on 100 acres of rolling hills, woods, and meadows. Built in 1865, the house is large and comfortable, filled with antiques and Oriental rugs. In winter, a fire always burns in the wood stove; in warmer weather, the large screened-in porch provides a relaxing spot. Your hosts offer popovers hot from the oven, croissants, assorted cheeses, and home-made jams in the morning. They will gladly direct you to nearby wineries, ski areas, lakes, and parks. Rates are higher on special college weekends.

Hanshaw House ✪
15 SAPSUCKER WOODS ROAD, ITHACA, NEW YORK 14850

Tel: **(607) 273-8034**	Reduced Rates: **10–15%, weekly; 10–15%, Jan. 15–Apr. 1**
Best Time to Call: **7–8 AM; 6–10 PM**	
Host: **Helen Scoones**	Breakfast: **Full**
No. of Rooms: **4**	Credit Cards: **MC, VISA**
No. of Private Baths: **4**	Pets: **No**
Double/pb: **$55–$75**	Children: **Welcome**
Single/pb: **$50–$70**	Smoking: **No**
Suites: **$60–$95; sleeps 4**	Social Drinking: **Permitted**
Open: **All year**	Airport/Station Pickup: **Yes**

Not far from downtown Ithaca, this woodframe farmhouse seems light-years away. Built in the 1830s, it has all the comforting country

touches, from its white picket fence and dark blue shutters, to the down-filled quilts and pillows in the bedrooms. Bird-lovers should stroll down the road to Cornell's Laboratory of Ornithology and Sapsucker Woods, a bird sanctuary. Breakfasts include fresh fruit, juice, homemade muffins, and a hot entrée such as pancakes or waffles.

Peregrine House
140 COLLEGE AVENUE, ITHACA, NEW YORK 14850

Tel: **(607) 272-0919**
Hosts: **Nancy Falconer and Susan Vance**
No. of Rooms: **8**
No. of Private Baths: **9**
Double/pb: **$79–$95**
Open: **All year**

Reduced Rates: **Available**
Breakfast: **Full**
Credit Cards: **MC, VISA**
Pets: **No**
Children: **Welcome, over 12**
Smoking: **Permitted**
Social Drinking: **Permitted**

This three-story brick home, with mansard roof, dates back to 1874. Its faux-marble fireplaces and carved-wood ceilings have been beautifully preserved and are accented with Victorian oak furnishings. Pick a good book in the library and relax in a wing chair, or watch some television in your air-conditioned bedroom. At five o'clock your hosts have a sherry hour, and they invite you to plan your evening over a drink. Mexican, Italian, Greek, and Indian food can all be enjoyed within a short walk from here. Peregrine House is two blocks from the Cornell campus and only a few blocks from the Ithaca Commons. Cayuga Lake's wonderful boating and swimming, the wine country, biking, hiking, and cross-country skiing are all close by.

The Iris Farm ✪
162 HOOK ROAD, MACEDON, NEW YORK 14502

Tel: (315) 986-4536
Best Time to Call: **After 9 AM**
Hosts: **JoAnne and Eric Moon**
Location: **10 mi. E of Rochester**
No. of Rooms: **2**
No. of Private Baths: **2**
Double/pb: **$65**
Single/pb: **$55**
Suites: **$110**

Open: **All year**
Reduced Rates: **10%, seniors**
Breakfast: **Full**
Pets: **Sometimes**
Children: **Welcome, over 16**
Smoking: **No**
Social Drinking: **Permitted**
Airport/Station Pickup: **Yes**

Surrounded by rolling farmlands, this 1860 house includes ornate Greek revival plaster work, a magnificent hand-carved stairway, original glass in the windows, and wide plank floors of chestnut, pine, and oak and is framed by lovely flower gardens and mature trees. Refresh yourself by the cool pond in summer, stretch out on the spacious porch and catch up on your reading, or warm yourself by the wood stove on a cold winter's night. Although the house is furnished with artifacts of a simpler time, a cable TV, a VCR, and a music library are also available for your enjoyment. JoAnne dabbles in photography and faux painting; Eric is a disc jockey joining guests for breakfast over the airwaves with light jazz. If your hosts are given a day's notice, they will make every effort to accommodate special dietary needs.

Fawn's Grove
EAST RIVER ROAD, BOX 285, NICHOLS, NEW YORK 13812

Tel: **(607) 699-3222**
Hosts: **Harry and Barbara Hoffman**
Location: **25 mi. W of Binghamton**
No. of Rooms: **3**
No. of Private Baths: **3**
Double/pb: **$40–$45**
Suites: **$65**

Open: **Apr. 1–Nov. 30**
Reduced Rates: **10%, weekly**
Breakfast: **Full**
Pets: **No**
Children: **Welcome, over 10**
Smoking: **No**
Social Drinking: **Permitted**

Once you enter this charming white colonial home, you'll be offered a snack and a seat in your choice of the sitting rooms, back porch, or beautifully landscaped yard. The next morning, you'll awake to the aroma of freshly brewed coffee and breakfast fare like ham-and-egg strata, eggs Benedict, and fruit crêpes. Your hosts are both golfers who can tell you about the local links. Harry's other interests include barbershop quartets, while Barbara likes to garden and cook.

Strawberry Castle Bed & Breakfast ✪
1883 PENFIELD ROAD, PENFIELD, NEW YORK 14526

Tel: (716) 385-3266
Best Time to Call: Evenings
Hosts: Charles and Cynthia Whited
Location: 8 mi. E of Rochester
No. of Rooms: 3
Max. No. Sharing Bath: 4
Double/sb: $60–$75
Single/sb: $50–$60
Suites: $75

Open: All year
Reduced Rates: 15%, weekly
Breakfast: Continental
Credit Cards: AMEX, MC, VISA
Pets: No
Children: Welcome, over 12
Smoking: Permitted
Social Drinking: Permitted
Airport/Station Pickup: Yes

An outstanding example of the Italian villa style of architecture, the Whiteds' home (circa 1878) features columned porches, heavy plaster moldings, high sculptured ceilings, and a white marble fireplace, and is appropriately furnished with antiques and brass beds. Wander the lawns and gardens, sun on the patio, or take a dip in the pool. Charles and Cynthia will direct you to fine restaurants, golf courses, and all of the nearby Rochester attractions.

The Wagener Estate Bed & Breakfast
351 ELM STREET (ROUTE 54-A), PENN YAN, NEW YORK 14527

Tel: (315) 536-4591
Hosts: Norm and Evie Worth
Location: 20 mi. from NYS Thruway,
  Exit 42, Geneva
No. of Rooms: 4
No. of Private Baths: 2
Max. No. Sharing Bath: 3
Double/pb: $65
Single/pb: $55

Double/sb: $55
Single/sb: $45
Open: All year
Breakfast: Full
Credit Cards: AMEX, MC, VISA
Pets: No
Children: Welcome, over 5
Smoking: No
Social Drinking: Permitted

The Worths raised their family in this 16-room historic house, furnished with antiques and country charm, located at the edge of the village on four scenic acres with shaded lawns, apple trees, and gentle breezes. The pillared veranda is a perfect spot for quiet reflection, conversation, and refreshments. Once the home of Abraham Wagener, the founder of Penn Yan, this B&B is perfectly situated for visits to wine country, the Corning Glass Museum, Watkins Glen, and beautiful Keuka Lake. The Worths are retired now and "have always loved to travel. Now we feel we are still traveling, because people from other states and countries bring the world to our door."

Dartmouth House ✪
215 DARTMOUTH STREET, ROCHESTER, NEW YORK 14607

Tel: **(716) 271-7872**
Best Time to Call: **5–7 PM**
Hosts: **Ellie and Bill Klein**
Location: **¹⁄₁₀ mi. from I-490 Exit 18**
No. of Rooms: **2**
No. of Private Baths: **2**
Double/pb: **$65**
Single/pb: **$55**
Open: **All year**

Reduced Rates: **Weekly**
Breakfast: **Full**
Credit Cards: **AMEX**
Pets: **No**
Children: **Welcome, over 10**
Smoking: **No**
Social Drinking: **Permitted**
Minimum Stay: **2 nights some weekends**
Airport/Station Pickup: **Yes**

This 1905 stucco English Tudor is located in the prestigious, quiet, architecturally fascinating Park Avenue neighborhood. A massive fireplace, family antiques, Oriental rugs, padded window seats, box-beamed ceilings, leaded-glass windows, and the great oak kitchen create an elegant atmosphere where visitors find friendliness and warmth in abundance. One guest said, "In this Edwardian gem the king himself would feel at home and even commoners are treated royally!" Bill is a retired Kodak engineer now teaching at R.I.T., and Ellie, a former educator, delights in pampering guests with outstanding breakfasts, served by candlelight, that might include eggs Chardonnay or oatmeal-blueberry pancakes. Guests enjoy being able to walk to the George Eastman Mansion and International Museum of Photography, the Rochester Museum and Science Center, the Planetarium, boutiques, restaurants, and antique shops.

Lake View Farm Bed & Breakfast ✪
4761 ROUTE 364, RUSHVILLE, NEW YORK 14544

Tel: **(716) 554-6973**
Best Time to Call: **After 4 PM**
Hosts: **Betty and Howard Freese**
Location: **15 mi. from NYS Thruway, Exit 44**
No. of Rooms: **2**
Max. No. Sharing Bath: **4**
Double/sb: **$45–$50**

Single/sb: **$35**
Reduced Rates: **10% after 2 nights; weekly**
Breakfast: **Full**
Pets: **No**
Children: **Welcome, over 10**
Smoking: **No**
Social Drinking: **Permitted**

Several rooms have a view of Canandaigua Lake, a Seneca Indian word meaning The Chosen Place. The simple architecture and bright and airy atmosphere create a pleasant background for family antiques and pictures. Stroll the grounds, rest in a hammock, or play horseshoes or badminton. Take the time to explore the 170 acres; in winter, cross-country ski. In summer, restaurants and a public beach are two minutes away.

Sage Cottage ✪

BOX 121, 112 EAST MAIN STREET, TRUMANSBURG, NEW YORK
14886

Tel: **(607) 387-6449**	Open: **All year**
Host: **Dorry Norris**	Breakfast: **Full**
Location: **10 mi. N of Ithaca**	Pets: **No**
No. of Rooms: **4**	Children: **Welcome**
No. of Private Baths: **4**	Smoking: **No**
Double/pb: **$45–$50**	Social Drinking: **Permitted**
Single/pb: **$43–$47**	

This Gothic Revival home built in 1855 has a graceful circular staircase as its focal point. The spacious guest rooms are furnished with period furniture and adorned with treasured family pieces. Greet the morning with a hearty country breakfast on the cheery sun porch. When winter winds blow, relax in front of a cozy fire with a hot cup of tea. The kitchen garden provides the basis for the herb dishes that are so evident in Dorry's delicious cooking. It is convenient to Watkins Glen, Cayuga and Seneca lakes, and fine wineries. A two-night minimum stay is required on Cornell University and Ithaca College "big" weekends and graduation.

HUDSON VALLEY/ALBANY/KINGSTON AREA

The American Country Collection

984 GLOUCESTER PLACE, SCHENECTADY, NEW YORK 12309

Tel: **(518) 370-4948**	Rates (Double):
Best Time to Call: **10 AM–noon; 1–5 PM**	Modest: **$40–$50**
	Average: **$50–$60**
Coordinator: **Beverly K. Walsh**	Luxury: **$60–$120**
States/Regions Covered: **New York— the Adirondacks, Albany, Cooperstown, Saratoga, upper Hudson Valley; Vermont—statewide; Massachusetts—the Berkshires**	Credit Cards: **AMEX, MC, VISA**
	Descriptive Directory: **$4**

The American Country Collection offers comfortable lodging in private homes and small inns. Accommodations range from a 1798 farmhouse, where guests are treated to a pancake breakfast with homemade maple syrup, to a stately Georgian home with canopy beds, fireplaces, and Oriental rugs. Each host offers distinctive touches, such as fresh flowers in the room or breakfast in bed. Many homes have lakefront property, swimming pools, and tennis courts. All are in areas of scenic and cultural interest, convenient to such attractions as the Baseball Hall of Fame, Empire State Plaza, Saratoga Racetrack, and ski areas.

Bed & Breakfast, U.S.A., Ltd. ○
P.O. BOX 606, CROTON-ON-HUDSON, NEW YORK 10520

Tel: (914) 271-6228
Best Time to Call: 10 AM–4 PM
Coordinator: Barbara Notarius
States/Regions Covered: Hudson
Valley, Westchester County, Upstate
New York, NYC, Long Island, Finger
Lakes
Descriptive Directory: $4

Rates (Single/Double):
Modest: $20–$30 $30–$40
Average: $35 $45–$55
Luxury: $50 $60–$200
Credit Cards: MC, VISA
Minimum Stay: 2 nights, weekends;
NYC

Barbara's extensive network includes host homes convenient to colleges, corporate headquarters, historic sites, recreational activities, and cultural events. The ambience ranges from a simple cabin to an elegant mansion, with many choices in between. This is a membership organization; annual dues $35 for entry to B&B's in many states. A surcharge of $15 is imposed for each booking for nonmembers. Sarah Lawrence, Manhattanville, Russell Sage, Vassar, West Point, and Skidmore are but a few of the major colleges nearby.

Riell's Bed and Breakfast ○
40 LOCUST PARK, ALBANY, NEW YORK 12205

Tel: (518) 869-5239
Hosts: James and Dolores Riell
Location: 6 mi. W of Albany
No. of Rooms: 2
No. of Private Baths: 1
Max. No. Sharing Bath: 4
Double/pb: $35
Single/pb: $30

Open: All year
Breakfast: Full
Pets: No
Children: Welcome
Smoking: No
Social Drinking: Permitted
Airport/Station Pickup: Yes

The Riells welcome you to a cozy Cape Cod home in the heart of New York State's capital district. Guests have a separate entrance leading to the second-floor bedrooms. One room features a wicker sitting area and the other a small office area with desk and chair. Both have wall-to-wall carpeting and coordinating linens, and you'll always find a bowl of fresh fruit. Your hosts welcome you to relax on their two-tiered deck. Saratoga Racetrack, Empire State Plaza, and numerous shopping centers and colleges are nearby.

Ananas Hus Bed and Breakfast ○
ROUTE 3, P.O. BOX 301, AVERILL PARK, NEW YORK 12018

Tel: (518) 766-5035
Hosts: Thelma and Clyde Tomlinson
Location: 6 mi. from Rte. 22
No. of Rooms: 3

Max. No. Sharing Bath: 4
Double/sb: $50
Single/sb: $40
Open: All year

Breakfast: **Full**
Pets: **No**
Children: **Welcome, over 12**
Smoking: **No**

Social Drinking: **Permitted**
Foreign Languages: **Norwegian**
Minimum Stay: **2 nights on holiday weekends**

The welcome mat is out at this hillside ranch home on 30 acres, with a panoramic view of the Hudson River Valley. It is informally furnished in the Early American style, accented with mementos from your hosts' international travels and Thelma's lovely needlework. Thelma is a former schoolteacher; Clyde was in the food business. They are serious amateur photographers who compete internationally. It is 15 minutes to Jiminy Peak and Brodie Mountain ski areas; 30 minutes to Tanglewood, Williamstown Theatre Festival, and Clark Art Institute in Massachusetts.

The Gregory House Inn
P.O. BOX 401, ROUTE 43, AVERILL PARK, NEW YORK 12018

Tel: **(518) 674-3774**
Best Time to Call: **5 PM**
Hosts: **Bette and Bob Jewell**
Location: **10 mi. E of Albany**
No. of Rooms: **12**
No. of Private Baths: **12**
Double/pb: **$60–$80**
Single/pb: **$55 and up**
Open: **All year**

Reduced Rates: **Weekly**
Breakfast: **Continental**
Other Meals: **Available**
Credit Cards: **AMEX, DC, MC, VISA**
Pets: **No**
Children: **Welcome, over 6**
Smoking: **Permitted**
Social Drinking: **Permitted**

The Gregory House is a clapboard Colonial dating back to 1830. Your hosts purchased the house in 1964 and opened a small restaurant. Recently, the building was expanded to include beautifully appointed guest rooms and a common room, all in keeping with a relaxed, country style. The house is surrounded by the Catskill, Adirondack, Berkshire, and Green mountains, affording year-round beauty and recreation. The inn is also near the Saratoga Performing Arts Center, Tanglewood, Hancock Shaker Village, and Saratoga Springs. Your hosts invite you to explore their beautifully landscaped property and to join them for fine dining in the restaurant.

Battenkill Bed and Breakfast Barn ✪
ROUTE 313, RD 1, CAMBRIDGE, NEW YORK 12816

Tel: **(518) 677-8868**
Hosts: **Veronica and Walter Piekarz**
Location: **30 mi. E of Saratoga**
No. of Rooms: **2**
Max. No. Sharing Bath: **4**
Double/sb: **$50**
Single/sb: **$40**

Open: **All year**
Breakfast: **Full**
Other Meals: **Available**
Pets: **No**
Children: **Welcome**
Smoking: **Permitted**
Social Drinking: **Permitted**

The post-and-beam structure of this Yankee barn contemporary can be spotted throughout its interior. Guests will enjoy the gourmet meals served by their hosts, who are interested in music and a back-to-basics way of life. Bromley Mountain; Saratoga Performing Arts Center; Manchester, Vermont; and Bennington College in Vermont are close by. Canoe and tube rentals are available for use in the Battenkill River.

The Lace House
ROUTE 22 AT TUNNEL HILL ROAD, CANAAN, NEW YORK 12029

Tel: **(518) 781-4669**	Breakfast: **Full**
Best Time to Call: **After 6 PM**	Credit Cards: **MC, VISA**
Hosts: **John and Sheila Clegg**	Pets: **No**
Location: **1 mi. from I-90**	Children: **Welcome, over 12**
No. of Rooms: **7**	Smoking: **Permitted**
Max. No. Sharing Bath: **4**	Social Drinking: **Permitted**
Double/sb: **$60**	Airport/Station Pickup: **Yes**
Open: **All year**	

The Lace House got its name from the intricately detailed rosettes and oval carvings over the windows and doors. The house was built in 1806 in the Federal style. In 1922, a Victorian section was added. The result is a unique combination of architectural styles that has placed The Lace House in the National Register of Historic Places. The house has been completely restored and furnished with antiques and period pieces. An elegant sitting room with Oriental rug and Victorian furnishings is available for private relaxing. In the morning, fresh-baked muffins and blueberry pancakes are favorites, served in one of three dining areas. The Lace House is minutes from Tanglewood, Jacob's Pillow, Williamstown Theatre Festival, many ski areas, and fine restaurants.

One Market Street ✪
COLD SPRING, NEW YORK 10516

Tel: **(914) 265-3912**	Reduced Rates: **Weekly**
Hosts: **Philip and Esther Baumgarten**	Breakfast: **Continental**
Location: **50 mi. N of New York City**	Credit Cards: **VISA**
No. of Rooms: **1 suite**	Pets: **No**
No. of Private Baths: **1**	Children: **Welcome, over 10**
Suites: **$65**	Smoking: **Permitted**
Open: **All year**	Social Drinking: **Permitted**

This beautiful Federal-style building dates back to the 1800s and looks out on the Hudson, surrounding mountains, and the foliage of the valley. The suite's kitchenette is stocked with rolls, juice, tea, and coffee for a make-it-at-your-leisure breakfast. Don't miss nearby West

Point, Vassar College, and the Vanderbilt Mansion. Philip and Esther will direct you to the fine restaurants and antiques shops in their historic town.

Alexander Hamilton House
49 VAN WYCK STREET, CROTON ON HUDSON, NEW YORK 10520

Tel: **(914) 271-6737**	Suites: **$150**
Best Time to Call: **8–9 AM**	Open: **All year**
Host: **Barbara Notarius**	Breakfast: **Full**
Location: **30 mi. NW of New York City**	Credit Cards: **AMEX, MC, VISA**
No. of Rooms: **5**	Pets: **No**
No. of Private Baths: **2**	Children: **Welcome**
Max. No. Sharing Bath: **4**	Smoking: **No**
Double/pb: **$75–$125**	Social Drinking: **Permitted**
Single/pb: **$50–$100**	Minimum Stay: **2 nights on weekends**
Double/sb: **$55–$65**	Airport/Station Pickup: **Yes**
Single/sb: **$40–$50**	Foreign Languages: **French**

No, Hamilton didn't live here; this beautiful Victorian home was built some eight decades after his death, and one suite is named for the victor in the duel between Hamilton and Aaron Burr. The property, with its 35-foot in-ground swimming pool, small apple orchard, and spectacular Hudson River views, would please even the most patrician lodgers. West Point, Van Cortlandt Manor, Boscobel, and Storm King Art Center are all nearby, and New York City is within striking distance. After sightseeing, relax in the large living room complete with fireplace, piano, and numerous antiques. Baby equipment is available for guests with small children. Paddington, the resident Wheaton terrier, will greet you upon your arrival.

Elaine's Guest House ✪
P.O. BOX 27, JOHNSON, NEW YORK 10933

Tel: **(914) 355-8811**	Double/sb: **$30**
Host: **Elaine Scott**	Single/sb: **$15**
Location: **10 mi. from I-84**	Open: **All year**
No. of Rooms: **2**	Breakfast: **Continental**
No. of Private Baths: **1**	Pets: **Welcome**
Max. No. Sharing Bath: **2**	Children: **Welcome**
Double/pb: **$30**	Smoking: **No**
Single/pb: **$15**	Social Drinking: **Permitted**

Located 10 minutes from Middletown, between Westtown and Slate Hill, Elaine's home features hospitality and comfort. It is furnished with choice items from her on-premises antique and collectibles shop. She will be pleased to direct you to the area's points of special interest, and will suggest good places to dine, suited to your budget.

Sunrise Farm ✪
RD 1, BOX 433A, PINE BUSH, NEW YORK 12566

Tel: (914) 361-3629
Best Time to Call: **Evenings**
Hosts: **Janet and Fred Schmelzer**
Location: **70 mi. N of New York City**
No. of Rooms: **1**
No. of Private Baths: **1**
Double/pb: **$45**
Single/pb: **$30–$35**

Open: **All year**
Reduced Rates: **Families; weekly**
Breakfast: **Full**
Pets: **No**
Children: **Welcome**
Smoking: **No**
Social Drinking: **Permitted**

Scotch Highland cattle are raised on this 30-acre farm just 12 miles from I-84. A restful night is assured in the comfortable second-floor guest room, where, on clear nights, the stars can be seen through the skylight. Breakfast features homemade preserves, honey from the farm's hives, and organically grown fruit. In winter, a wood stove and solar greenhouse keep the house cozy. Cross-country skiing, hiking, canoeing, downhill skiing, horseback riding, golf, house tours, museums, wineries, and antiquing are favorite diversions.

Maggie Towne's B&B ✪
PHILLIPS ROAD, PITTSTOWN, NEW YORK (MAILING ADDRESS: BOX 82, RD 2, VALLEY FALLS, NEW YORK 12185)

Tel: (518) 663-8369; 686-7331
Host: **Maggie Towne**
Location: **14 mi. E of Troy**
No. of Rooms: **3**
Max. No. Sharing Bath: **4**
Double/sb: **$35**
Single/sb: **$25**
Open: **All year**

Reduced Rates: **10%, seniors; families**
Breakfast: **Full**
Other Meals: **Available**
Pets: **Sometimes**
Children: **Welcome (crib)**
Smoking: **No**
Social Drinking: **Permitted**

This lovely old Colonial is located amid beautiful lawns and trees. Enjoy a cup of tea or glass of wine before the huge fireplace in the family room. Use the music room or curl up with a book on the screened-in porch. Mornings, your host serves home-baked goodies. She will gladly prepare a lunch for you to take on tour or enjoy at the house. It's 20 miles to historic Bennington, Vermont, and 30 to Saratoga.

Ridgebury Inn and Hunt Club
RD 1, BOX 342, SLATE HILL, NEW YORK 10973

Tel: (914) 355-HUNT
Hosts: **Bob and Jean Yonelunas**
Location: **60 mi. NW of New York City**
No. of Rooms: **5**

Max. No. Sharing Bath: **4**
Double/sb: **$65–$75**
Single/sb: **$50**
Suites: **$100–$125**

Open: **All year**
Breakfast: **Full**
Credit Cards: **AMEX, MC, VISA**
Pets: **Horses only ($15 per night)**

Children: **Welcome**
Smoking: **Permitted**
Social Drinking: **Permitted**
Airport/Station Pickup: **Yes**

This 1850 farmhouse has been added onto many times over the years, and currently totals 34 rooms. It is furnished in English country decor with a lot of oak and glass, many antiques, equestrian art, and a century-old baby grand piano. It is located on a 90-acre horse farm, with miles of riding trails and a lovely pond that's home to a variety of fish, turtles, and waterfowl. You are invited to bring your horse along; there's a lovely barn to accommodate him, a complete saddle-and-gift shop geared to the English rider, and even a fox hunt! Many guests come to take hot-air balloon rides with the local balloon company—the sight of a dozen balloons drifting over the farm is delightful. Theater, wineries, West Point, Hudson River cruises, and the Goshen Hall of Fame are just a few diversions within a half hour's drive.

Sharon Fern's Bed & Breakfast ✪
8 ETHIER DRIVE, TROY, NEW YORK 12180

Tel: **(518) 279-1966**
Best Time to Call: **Morning**
Hosts: **Bill and Sharon Ernst**
Location: **10 mi. from N.Y. Thruway**
No. of Rooms: **2**
Max. No. Sharing Bath: **3**
Double/sb: **$60**
Single/sb: **$50**

Open: **All year**
Reduced Rates: **10%, seniors**
Breakfast: **Continental**
Pets: **No**
Children: **Welcome (crib)**
Smoking: **No**
Social Drinking: **Permitted**

Bill and Sharon's tri-level contemporary home rests on a quiet street in the country just 20 minutes outside of Albany, New York's capital. Enjoy spacious accommodations plus many extras, including an in-ground pool, a recreation room with a Ping-Pong table, and a beautiful backyard, where badminton and croquet will test your mettle. Skiers and hikers will find mountains in nearly every direction—the Adirondacks, Catskills, and Green Mountains are all a half hour away.

LAKE GEORGE AREA

Hayes's B&B Guest House ✪
P.O. BOX 537, 7161 LAKESHORE DRIVE, BOLTON LANDING, NEW YORK 12814

Tel: **(518) 644-5941**
Best Time to Call: **9 AM–9 PM**

Hosts: **Dick Hayes and Mrs. Martha Hayes**

Location: **250 mi. N of New York City**
No. of Rooms: **2**
No. of Private Baths: **2**
Double/pb: **$75–$80**
Single/pb: **$45**
Suites: **$85–$95**
Open: **All year**

Breakfast: **Continental**
Children: **Welcome, over 12**
Pets: **No**
Smoking: **No**
Social Drinking: **Permitted**
Minimum Stay: **2 nights**

Close to the shores of Lake George, this elegantly appointed 1920s Cape Cod estate is located across from the town beach, picnic area, and public docks. A five-minute walk to town brings you to tennis courts, shops, and fine restaurants. The Hayes family will arrange boat tours and a picnic lunch for a nominal fee in summer and fall. Cable TV and HBO are available. It's only 40 minutes to Saratoga and its famous racetrack. There's a private trout stream on the property, so pack your fishing gear.

Hilltop Cottage ✪
P.O. BOX 186, 6883 LAKESHORE DRIVE, BOLTON LANDING, NEW YORK 12814

Tel: **(518) 644-2492**
Hosts: **Anita and Charlie Richards**
Location: **8 mi. from I-87**
No. of Rooms: **4**
Max. No. Sharing Bath: **4**
Double/pb: **$45**
Open: **All year**

Breakfast: **Full**
Pets: **No**
Children: **Welcome, over 4**
Smoking: **Permitted**
Social Drinking: **Permitted**
Foreign Languages: **German**

Hilltop Cottage is a two-story farmhouse furnished in comfortable, traditional style. The newly decorated guest rooms are located on the second floor, apart from the family living quarters. Breakfast usually includes a German dish and is served on the screened-in porch in the warm weather. Your hosts will gladly help you discover the delights of the Lake George area, including Millionaire's Row, located along Route 9. Beaches, marinas, museums, restaurants, and shops in the town center of Bolton Landing are just a 10-minute walk from the house.

LAKE PLACID/ADIRONDACKS AREA

North Country B&B Reservation Service ✪
BOX 286, LAKE PLACID, NEW YORK 12946

Tel: **(518) 523-9474**
Best Time to Call: **10 AM–10 PM**
Coordinator: **Lyn Witte**
States/Regions Covered: **Adirondack Mountains**

Rates (Single/Double):

Modest:	**$15**	**$30–$40**
Average:	**$20**	**$45–$60**
Luxury:	**$40**	**$65–$100**

Lyn has dozens of hosts waiting to show you Adirondack Mountain hospitality. Your choice may be convenient to Champlain Valley, Revolutionary War forts, John Brown's farm, or Camp Sagamore. Lake Placid, the Olympic Village, and Lake George offer an endless choice of sports in all seasons.

Highland House ✪
3 HIGHLAND PLACE, LAKE PLACID, NEW YORK 12946

Tel: **(518) 523-2377**	Open: **All year**
Best Time to Call: **Mornings**	Reduced Rates: **Apr.–May; Nov.**
Hosts: **Teddy and Cathy Blazer**	Breakfast: **Full**
Location: **25 mi. from Rte. 87, Exit 30**	Pets: **No**
No. of Rooms: **8**	Children: **Welcome**
No. of Private Baths: **8**	Smoking: **Permitted**
Double/pb: **$50–$65**	Social Drinking: **Permitted**
Single/pb: **$50–$65**	Airport/Station Pickup: **Yes**
Guest Cottage: **$70–$155; sleeps 2–6**	

Located on a hill in a lovely section of Lake Placid, Highland House is a five-minute walk from Main Street and the Olympic Center. Cathy and Teddy have created a warm and comfortable atmosphere that guests notice upon entering this 1910 house. Every bedroom is furnished with a large, wooden bunk bed as well as a double bed, each adorned with a bright, fluffy comforter. After a good night's rest, you may look forward to a breakfast of blueberry pancakes or French toast, eggs, and beverages. The cottage is beautifully furnished, and features a wood stove for chilly nights.

LONG ISLAND

A Reasonable Alternative and Hampton B&B ✪
117 SPRING STREET, PORT JEFFERSON, NEW YORK 11777

Tel: **(516) 928-4034**	Rates (Single/Double):		
Best Time to Call: **10 AM–2 PM**	Modest: **$36**	**$48**	
Coordinator: **Kathleen B. Dexter**	Average: **$44**	**$52**	
States/Regions Covered: **Long Island**	Luxury: **$52**	**$60**	**$100 +**
	Credit Cards: **MC, VISA**		
	Minimum Stay: **2 nights in summer at Hamptons; 3 nights, holiday weekends**		

Bounded by Long Island Sound and the Atlantic Ocean, from the New York City border to Montauk 100 miles to the east, the cream of host homes has been culled by Kathleen for you. There's much to see and do, including museums, historic homes, theater, horse racing, and the famous beaches, including Jones Beach, Fire Island, Shelter Island, and the exclusive Hamptons. (The Hamptons require a two-day minimum stay in July and August.) Adelphi College, Hofstra University, C. W. Post, Stony Brook, and St. Joseph's are a few of the nearby schools.

Duvall Bed and Breakfast On-the-Garden City Line ✪
237 CATHEDRAL AVENUE, HEMPSTEAD, NEW YORK 11550

Tel: **(516) 292-9219**	Open: **All year**
Best Time to Call: **6–9 PM**	Breakfast: **Full**
Hosts: **Wendy and Richard Duvall**	Pets: **No**
Location: **20 mi. E of New York City**	Children: **Welcome (crib)**
No. of Rooms: **4**	Smoking: **No**
No. of Private Baths: **3**	Social Drinking: **Permitted**
Double/pb: **$50–$75**	Foreign Languages: **German, Spanish**
Suite: **$120 for 4**	

Guests feel right at home in this charming Dutch Colonial, with four-poster beds and antique reproductions. Wine or soft drinks are served on arrival and breakfast features puff pancakes and French toast. Jones Beach, Fire Island, and New York City are less than an hour away. Guests are welcome to use the patio and garden. Kennedy International Airport and LaGuardia Airport are less than 40 minutes from the door.

Seafield House ✪
2 SEAFIELD LANE, WESTHAMPTON BEACH, NEW YORK 11978

Tel: **(800) 346-3290**	Open: **All year**
Best Time to Call: **9 AM–5 PM**	Reduced Rates: **$95, Oct. 15–May 15**
Host: **Elsie Collins**	Breakfast: **Full**
Location: **90 mi. E of New York City**	Pets: **No**
No. of Rooms: **3 suites**	Children: **No**
No. of Private Baths: **3**	Smoking: **No**
Suites: **$175**	Social Drinking: **Permitted**

This 100-year-old home in posh Westhampton is five blocks from the beach, and boasts its own pool and tennis court. Victorian lounges, a caned rocker, piano, hurricane lamps, Shaker benches, Chinese porcelain all combine to create the casual, country inn atmosphere. When the sea air chills Westhampton Beach, the parlor fire keeps the house toasty warm. The aromas of freshly brewing coffee and Mrs. Collins' breads and rolls baking in the oven are likely to wake you in time for breakfast. You'll leave this hideaway relaxed, carrying one of Mrs. Collins' homemade goodies.

NEW YORK CITY AREA

Abode Bed & Breakfast, Ltd. ✪
P.O. BOX 20022, NEW YORK, NEW YORK 10028

Tel: **(212) 472-2000**
Best Time to Call: **Mon.–Fri., 9 AM–5 PM; Sat., 10 AM–2 PM**
Coordinator: **Shelli Leifer**
States/Regions Covered: **Manhattan, Brooklyn Heights**

Rates (Single/Double):
  Average: **$60–$70** **$75–$85**
  Luxury: **$75–$80** **$85–$100**
Credit Cards: **AMEX**
Minimum Stay: **2 nights**

Shelli is a friendly, savvy New Yorker with sensitive insight as to which guest would be most comfortable with what host. Her roster grows steadily with accommodations in safe neighborhoods that are "East Side, West Side, and all around the town." Unhosted brownstones boasting a country-inn ambience and unhosted luxury apartments are especially attractive for couples traveling together. Prices range from $85 for a studio to $275 for 3 bedroom. Reduced rates are available for extended stays. Theaters, museums, galleries, restaurants, and shopping are within easy reach of all accommodations.

At Home in New York ✪
P.O. BOX 407, NEW YORK, NEW YORK 10185

Tel: **(212) 956-3125; Fax: (212) 247-3294**
Best Time to Call: **9 AM–noon; 2–5 PM, weekdays**
Coordinator: **Lois H. Rooks**
States/Regions Covered: **New York— Brooklyn, Manhattan, Queens, Roosevelt Island, Staten Island**

Rates (Single/Double):
  Modest: **$45** **$55–$60**
  Average: **$55–$60** **$68–$75**
  Luxury: **$65–$75** **$80–$125**
Credit Cards: **No**
Minimum Stay: **2 nights; $10 surcharge for 1-night stays**

Lois offers very personalized service, putting forth her best efforts to place clients in locations ideally suited to their plans in New York City. At Home in New York has more than 200 accommodations—ranging from modest to very luxurious—in prime neighborhoods throughout the city, including spaces in large attended apartment buildings as well as in charming brownstone townhouses. With such a variety of interesting, convenient B&Bs, out-of-towners can be sure their needs and preferences will be satisfied. The hosts are knowledgeable, friendly New Yorkers who are generous with inside info for getting around the city and finding the best restaurants, shopping, and current cultural events. Lois, a former professional actress and singer, often has free and discounted concert, theater, and museum tickets for guests. Early reservations advised.

Bed & Breakfast (& Books)
35 WEST 92ND STREET, NEW YORK, NEW YORK 10025

Tel: **(212) 865-8740**
Coordinator: **Judith Goldberg Lewis**
States/Regions Covered: **Manhattan**

Rates (Single/Double):
  Average: **$65–$70 $75–$80**
Credit Cards: **AMEX**
Minimum Stay: **2 nights**

Accommodations are conveniently located in residential areas near transportation and within walking distance of many cultural attractions. Hosts are photographers, psychologists, lawyers, dancers, teachers, and artists. They are pleased to share their knowledge of fine shops, reasonable restaurants, galleries, theater, and bookstores. There's a $20 surcharge for one-night stays. Unhosted apartments are $90–$150 for two.

Bed & Breakfast Network of New York ☉
134 WEST 32ND STREET, SUITE 602, NEW YORK, NEW YORK 10001

Tel: **(212) 645-8134**
Best Time to Call: **8 AM–noon; 2–6 PM**
Coordinator: **Mr. Leslie Goldberg**
States/Regions Covered: **New York City**

Rates (Single/Double):
  Modest: **$50 $70**
  Average: **$60 $80**
  Luxury: **$70 $90**
Credit Cards: **No**

Accommodations appropriate to your purpose and purse are available, from the chic East Side to the arty West Side; from SoHo to Greenwich Village. They range from a historic brownstone, where the host is an artist, to a terraced apartment near Lincoln Center. Leslie's hosts are enthusiastic about the Big Apple and happy to share their insider information with you. Unhosted apartments range from $80 to $300 in price.

City Lights B&B, Ltd.
P.O. BOX 20355 CHEROKEE STATION, NEW YORK, NEW YORK 10028

Tel: **(212) 737-7049**
Coordinators: **Yedida Mielsen and Dee Staff**
States/Regions Covered: **New York City**

Minimum Stay: **2 nights**
Rates (Single/Double):
  Average: **$60–$95**
Credit Cards: **AMEX, MC, VISA**

From the tony East Side to the West Side; from the downtown New York University and Greenwich Village areas to uptown neighborhoods near Columbia University and the Museum of Natural History, accommodations range from simple to opulent. Many of the hosts are from the theater and the arts; all of them are anxious to make your stay in their town memorable. Unhosted apartments range from $85 to $135 per night, depending upon the location, ambience, and number of people staying. A $10 surcharge is imposed for one-night stays.

Judith Mol Agency ✪
357 WEST 37TH STREET, NEW YORK, NEW YORK 10018

Tel: **(212) 971-9001**
Coordinator: **Judith Mol**
States/Regions Covered: **Manhattan**

Rates (Single/Double):
   Average: **$50**   **$70**
   Luxury: **$75**   **$90–$300**
Credit Cards: **No**
Minimum Stay: **2 nights**

Judith's listings are as diverse as the city. An apartment in the old-world area of Gramercy Park has a queen-size bed and antique decor; one that's close to Columbia University has a loft bed, suitable for one, with a great view of the Hudson River. Another, on the chic East Side, is decorated in contemporary style accented with beautiful art. Some have FAX machines, some have Jacuzzis; all have cable TV. Unhosted apartments range from $80–$300, depending upon size and location. There is a 10% surcharge for one-night stays.

New World Bed & Breakfast ✪
150 FIFTH AVENUE, SUITE 711, NEW YORK, NEW YORK 10011

Tel: **(212) 675-5600 or (800) 443-3800**
Coordinator: **Kathy Kruger**
States/Regions Covered: **Manhattan**

Rates (Single/Double):
   Modest: **$40**   **$60**
   Average: **$65**   **$80**
Credit Cards: **AMEX, MC, VISA**
Minimum Stay: **2 nights**

Offering a unique cross section of accommodations in Manhattan, Kathy's specialties are residential sections such as Greenwich Village, Chelsea, Gramercy Park, the Upper East Side, and the Upper West Side. Business visitors who want to be convenient to Midtown, culture buffs who are happiest near Museum Mile or Lincoln Center, and those who come for theater or shopping, are all accommodated. The toll-free phone allows you the luxury of personally discussing your needs and receiving suggestions and descriptions of places on the phone without waiting to receive a descriptive list. Unhosted accommodations range from $70 to $120.

NIAGARA/BUFFALO AREA

Rainbow Hospitality, Inc.
466 AMHERST STREET, BUFFALO, NEW YORK 14207

Tel: (716) 874-8797
Best Time to Call: 9 AM–5 PM; Sat., 9
  AM–12 PM
Coordinator: **Georgia Brannan**
States/Regions Covered: **Buffalo,
  Chautauqua, Lewiston, Niagara Falls,
  Olcott, Youngstown**

Descriptive Directory: **$3**
Rates (Single/Double):
  Modest: **$35**   **$40**
  Average: **$45**   **$55**
  Luxury: **$60**   **$90**
Credit Cards: **MC, VISA**

The scenic splendor of Niagara Falls is only the beginning of the attractions in this area. Travelers have a wide variety of activities to keep them interested and busy. Lewiston is the home of Artpark, a 200-acre park and open-air theater featuring productions from May through September. Fishing and antiquing are popular pastimes, too. The best things in the area are the hosts, who open their homes to extend the hand of friendship.

The Eastwood House ✪
45 SOUTH MAIN STREET, ROUTE 39, CASTILE, NEW YORK 14427

Tel: (716) 493-2335
Best Time to Call: **Before 8:30 AM;
  after 6 PM**
Host: **Joan Ballinger**
Location: **63 mi. SE of Buffalo on Rte.
  39**
No. of Rooms: **2**
Max. No. Sharing Bath: **4**

Double/sb: **$27**
Single/sb: **$22**
Open: **All year**
Breakfast: **Continental**
Pets: **Sometimes**
Children: **Welcome, over 5**
Smoking: **No**
Social Drinking: **Permitted**

This comfortable older home in a rural area is close to the Genesee Country Museum, Letchworth State Park, which is called the Grand Canyon of the East, Geneseo and Houghton colleges, and Silver Lake, known for fishing and boating. Delicious hot muffins, fresh fruits, and a choice of beverages are typical breakfast fare. Joan will be happy to direct you to local wineries and the Corning Glass factory and museum.

The Fox's Den ✪
88 JAMESTOWN STREET, ROUTE 62, GOWANDA, NEW YORK 14070

Tel: (716) 532-4252
Best Time to Call: **Evenings**
Host: **Janet Fox Mansfield**
Location: **35 mi. SE of Buffalo**
No. of Rooms: **3**

Max. No. Sharing Bath: **6**
Double/sb: **$35**
Single/sb: **$30**
Open: **All year**
Reduced Rates: **10%, seniors; families**

Breakfast: **Continental**
Pets: **No**
Children: **Welcome (crib)**

Smoking: **Permitted**
Social Drinking: **Permitted**

A gracious welcome awaits you at this 100-year-old Gothic Revival home, painted white with green shutters. The large and comfortable rooms are decorated with Early American furnishings. Janet makes her own bran muffins and serves them with fresh fruit for breakfast. On weekends, the meal includes her special recipe for pineapple fritters. In the evening, guests can relax with wine and cheese around the living room fireplace. The Fox's Den is located in a quiet area, close to hiking, boating, skiing, the Seneca Nation of Indians, and the Amish country.

The Teepee ✪
RD 1, BOX 543, ROUTE 438, GOWANDA, NEW YORK 14070

Tel: **(716) 532-2168**
Hosts: **Max and Phyllis Lay**
Location: **30 mi. S of Buffalo**
No. of Rooms: **3**
Max. No. Sharing Bath: **3**
Double/sb: **$40**
Single/sb: **$30**
Open: **All year**

Breakfast: **Full**
Pets: **Sometimes**
Children: **Welcome (crib)**
Smoking: **Permitted**
Social Drinking: **Permitted**
Airport/Station Pickup: **Yes**

Max and Phyllis Lay are Seneca Indians living on the Cattaraugus Indian Reservation. Their airy four-bedroom home is clean, modern, and decorated with family Indian articles, many of them crafted by hand. The reservation offers country living and the opportunity of seeing firsthand the customs of a Native American community. A fall festival with arts, crafts, and exhibition dancing is held in September. Canoeing, fishing, rafting, cross-country and downhill skiing, and a sport called snowsnake are among the local activities. Your hosts will gladly arrange tours of the Amish community, and hot-air balloon rides over the beautiful rolling hills.

The Misserts B&B
66 HIGHLAND AVENUE, HAMBURG, NEW YORK 14075

Tel: **(716) 649-5830**
Hosts: **Tom and Betty Missert**
Location: **14 mi. S of Buffalo**
No. of Rooms: **3**
Max. No. Sharing Bath: **6**
Double/sb: **$35**
Single/sb: **$30**

Open: **All year**
Breakfast: **Full**
Pets: **Sometimes**
Children: **Welcome**
Smoking: **Permitted**
Social Drinking: **Permitted**
Airport/Station Pickup: **Yes**

A three-story wood frame house in a quiet residential neighborhood, the Misserts B&B is designed for company, with its large living room and enclosed front porch. The house is filled with hanging plants and Betty's paintings—she studied art before becoming a professional dressmaker. Lake Erie is 10 minutes away, while Hamburg's large public playground is just around the corner. (Babysitting services are available for an extra fee.) Your host enjoys local acclaim as a baker, and her full breakfasts include apricot muffins and mouthwatering coffee cakes fresh from the oven. Weather permitting, meals are served outside on the deck.

Chestnut Ridge Inn
7205 CHESTNUT RIDGE, LOCKPORT, NEW YORK 14094

Tel: **(716) 439-9124**	Open: **All year**
Hosts: **Frank and Lucy Cervoni**	Breakfast: **Full**
Location: **20 mi. E of Niagara Falls**	Other Meals: **Available**
No. of Rooms: **4**	Pets: **No**
No. of Private Baths: **4**	Children: **Welcome in suite**
Double/pb: **$65–$75**	Smoking: **No**
Single/pb: **$40–$65**	Social Drinking: **Permitted**
Suite: **$75–$95 for 2–6**	Foreign Languages: **Italian**

A white Federal mansion circa 1826, Chestnut Ridge Inn is set on eight acres of lawns and gardens and shaded by century-old trees. The interior is elegant, from the wide central hall, with its rose damask wall covering, Oriental rug, and curving staircase, to the formal living and dining rooms and cherry-paneled library. The large bedrooms have poster beds and fine linens, and there are fireplaces throughout the house, as well as central air conditioning. Want to take some of the period furniture home with you? Browse in the carriage-house antique shop. Lucy and Frank are gracious hosts who will soon make you feel like an honored guest. Afternoon and evening refreshments are served, and holidays are special events.

The William Seward Inn ✪
RD 2, SOUTH PORTAGE ROAD, WESTFIELD, NEW YORK 14787

Tel: **(716) 326-4151**	Breakfast: **Full**
Best Time to Call: **8 AM–9 PM**	Other Meals: **Available**
Hosts: **Peter and Joyce Wood**	Credit Cards: **MC, VISA**
Location: **125 mi. E of Cleveland**	Pets: **No**
No. of Rooms: **10**	Children: **Welcome, over 12**
No. of Private Baths: **10**	Smoking: **No**
Double/pb: **$58–$92**	Social Drinking: **Permitted**
Single/pb: **$48–$82**	Airport/Station Pickup: **Yes**
Open: **All year**	
Reduced Rates: **10%, seniors (Sun.– Thurs.); package rates Nov. 1–May 31**	

Before serving as Abraham Lincoln's Secretary of State, William Seward lived in this Greek revival mansion, which echoes the period of Seward's residence with furnishings from the 1840s and '50s. Pieces from all eras are sold in Westfield's 30 antique shops. Seven wineries ring the town, and the Chautauqua Institute—an educational and cultural center—is just a few miles away. The schedule of weekend workshops and packages includes ski trips, wine tours, stargazing, maple sugaring, and even a seminar on innkeeping as a career. Full breakfasts feature shirred eggs, Monte Cristos, or pancakes.

THOUSAND ISLANDS AREA

Battle Island Inn ✪
BOX 176, RD 1, FULTON, NEW YORK 13069

Tel: **(315) 593-3699**	Open: **All year**
Hosts: **Joyce and Richard Rice**	Breakfast: **Full**
Location: **30 mi. N of Syracuse**	Pets: **No**
No. of Rooms: **6**	Children: **Welcome**
No. of Private Baths: **6**	Smoking: **No**
Double/pb: **$55–$80**	Social Drinking: **Permitted**
Single/pb: **$45–$65**	

The Rice family welcomes you to their pre–Civil War estate, which they restored themselves with lots of love and hard work. The inn is across the street from a golf course and is surrounded by fields and orchards. The rooms feature Victorian antiques and marble fireplaces.

Guest bedrooms are spacious and elegant with imposing high-backed beds. Joyce is a full-time host, who will tempt your palate with homemade rolls, biscuits, and crêpes. Richard is a systems analyst who oversees the challenges of an 1840s house. Whether you're enjoying the privacy of your room or socializing in the formal front parlor, you are sure to appreciate the friendly family atmosphere.

Tug Hill Lodge
8091 SALISBURY STREET, BOX 204, SANDY CREEK, NEW YORK 13145

Tel: **(315) 387-5326**	Single/sb: **$25**
Best Time to Call: **After 3 PM**	Open: **All year**
Host: **Margaret Clerkin**	Breakfast: **Full**
Location: **40 mi. N of Syracuse**	Pets: **Sometimes**
No. of Rooms: **5**	Children: **Sometimes**
Max. No. Sharing Bath: **3**	Smoking: **No**
Double/sb: **$35**	Social Drinking: **Permitted**

Margaret's large Italianate Victorian home, with cupola, was built in 1872. The interior is comfortable, with a two-story sun room and deck. Down quilts on the double or queen-size beds assure a cozy night's sleep. A full English breakfast is the house specialty, but if you prefer vegetarian food or are on a special diet, give Margaret fair notice and she'll accommodate you. Ski, fish, hunt, go to a local concert or theater, shop, or simply curl up with a good book and rest.

NORTH CAROLINA

Boone
Valle Crucis
Spruce Pine
Burnsville
Leicester
Hazelwood
Waynesville
Franklin
Highlands
Glenville
Mountain Home

Mt. Airy
Sparta

Winston-
Salem

Banner
Elk

Black Mountain
Asheville
Hickory

Tryon

Saluda
Brevard

Milton

Durham
Greensboro

Tarboro
Raleigh
Taylorsville
Salisbury

Wilson
Smithfield

Charlotte
Monroe

Hertford

Washington
Bath

New Bern

Swansboro

Wilmington

Applewood Manor ✪
62 CUMBERLAND CIRCLE, ASHEVILLE, NORTH CAROLINA 28801

Tel: (704) 254-2244
Hosts: Jim and Linda LoPresti
Location: ¾ mi. from Rte. 240, Exit 4C
No. of Rooms: 4
No. of Private Baths: 4
Double/pb: $75
Single/pb: $60
Suites: $80
Cottage: $100
Open: All year

Reduced Rates: 10%, Jan.–Mar.; 20%, seniors (Sept. only)
Breakfast: Full
Credit Cards: MC, VISA
Pets: No
Children: Welcome, over 12
Smoking: No
Social Drinking: Permitted
Minimum Stay: Holiday weekends
Foreign Languages: Italian, American sign language

We wish we could share copies of the thank-you notes sent to Linda and Jim from guests who were reluctant to leave the gracious warmth and hospitality that makes this B&B so special. Built in 1906, this Colonial Revival home boasts wide porches, with rockers and a swing, and two manicured acres perfect for a game of badminton or croquet. Fine lace curtains, antique furnishings, heart-pine floors covered with Oriental rugs, and bright and airy rooms, most with fireplaces, are found throughout. Breakfast always includes something special, such

405

as raspberry cream cheese French toast or a delectable soufflé. It's only a mile away from fine restaurants, antique and craft shops, an art museum, theater, and the Thomas Wolfe Memorial.

Cairn Brae

217 PATTON MOUNTAIN ROAD, ASHEVILLE, NORTH CAROLINA 28804

Tel: **(704) 252-9219**
Hosts: **Millicent and Edward Adams**
Location: **5 mi. NE of Asheville**
No. of Rooms: **3**
No. of Private Baths: **3**
Double/pb: **$65**
Suites: **$80**
Open: **May 1–Oct. 31**

Breakfast: **Continental**
Credit Cards: **MC, VISA**
Pets: **No**
Children: **Welcome over 6**
Smoking: **No**
Social Drinking: **Permitted**
Airport/Station Pickup: **Yes**

Cairn Brae, Scottish for "rocky hillside," is a striking circular contemporary home nestled in the Blue Ridge Mountains. It has lavish wood paneling, a stone fireplace, and a dramatic winding staircase connecting upper and lower levels. This wooded 3½-acre property invites exploration. For a taste of urban pleasures, downtown Asheville, with its branch of the University of North Carolina, is just 12 minutes away by car. Continental breakfast consists of fresh fruit, assorted muffins, coffee cake, and corn bread.

Carolina Bed & Breakfast ✪

177 CUMBERLAND AVENUE, ASHEVILLE, NORTH CAROLINA 28801

Tel: **(704) 254-3608**
Best Time to Call: **7 AM–9 PM**
Hosts: **Sam, Karin, and Regina Fain**
Location: **½ mi. N of Asheville**
No. of Rooms: **6**
No. of Private Baths: **6**
Double/pb: **$75**
Single/pb: **$65**
Guest Cottage: **$95**

Open: **All year**
Breakfast: **Full**
Credit Cards: **MC, VISA**
Pets: **No**
Children: **Welcome, over 12**
Smoking: **No**
Social Drinking: **Permitted**
Airport/Station Pickup: **Yes**

This turn-of-the-century Colonial Revival mansion has been painstakingly restored; feel free to relax on the front and back porches, or just take in the view from the bay windows, with their distinctive, twelve-over-one panes. In springtime, the grounds bloom with dogwoods and rhododendrons. On cooler days, you can curl up by a fire in one of the house's seven fireplaces. Your hosts serve a different full breakfast each day; the usual fare includes eggs or quiche and fresh bread and muffins.

Cedar Crest Victorian Inn ✪
674 BILTMORE AVENUE, ASHEVILLE, NORTH CAROLINA 28803

Tel: **(704) 252-1389**
Best Time to Call: **Mornings**
Hosts: **Jack and Barbara McEwan**
Location: **1¼ mi. from I-40**
No. of Rooms: **13**
No. of Private Baths: **9**
Max. No. Sharing Bath: **4**
Double/pb: **$90–$105**
Single/pb: **$84–$99**
Double/sb: **$60–$65**

Single/sb: **$60–$65**
Open: **All year**
Breakfast: **Continental**
Credit Cards: **AMEX, DISC, MC, VISA**
Pets: **No**
Children: **Welcome, over 12**
Smoking: **Permitted**
Social Drinking: **Permitted**

Built in 1891, and listed on the National Register of Historic Places, Cedar Crest is one of the largest and most opulent residences to survive Asheville's boom period. Enter the grand foyer and you'll find the rich warmth of hardwood paneling, lace window treatments, and an intricately carved fireplace. A massive oak staircase leads to the guest rooms, decorated with Victorian antiques and fine linens. Your hosts serve tea or lemonade on the spacious veranda in the summer months. In the cold weather, enjoy hot drinks by the fire. This lovely Queen Anne is located close to the Blue Ridge Parkway, the Biltmore House, and downtown Asheville. Your hosts will be glad to recommend local eateries and invite you back to the inn for hot chocolate and cookies in the evening.

Corner Oak Manor ✪
53 ST. DUNSTANS ROAD, ASHEVILLE, NORTH CAROLINA 28803

Tel: **(704) 253-3525**
Hosts: **Karen and Andy Spradley**
Location: **1¼ mi. from Rte. 40, Exit 50**
No. of Rooms: **4**
No. of Private Baths: **4**
Double/pb: **$80**
Single/pb: **$65**
Open: **All year**
Reduced Rates: **15%, Jan.–Mar.; 15%, seniors; 15%, families**

Breakfast: **Full**
Other Meals: **Available**
Credit Cards: **MC, VISA**
Pets: **No**
Children: **Welcome, over 12**
Smoking: **No**
Social Drinking: **Permitted**
Airport/Station Pickup: **Yes**

Surrounded by maple, oak, and evergreen trees, this lovely English Tudor home is located minutes away from the famed Biltmore Estate and Gardens. The rooms have queen-size beds beautifully covered in fine linen. The window treatments and coordinated wall coverings could easily grace the pages of a decorating magazine. Handmade wreaths, weavings, and stitchery complement the furnishings. Breakfast specialties include orange French toast, blueberry-ricotta pancakes, or four-cheese-herb quiche. A living room fireplace, baby grand piano, outdoor deck, and Jacuzzi are among the gracious amenities.

Cornerstone Inn ✪
230 PEARSON DRIVE, ASHEVILLE, NORTH CAROLINA 28801

Tel: **(704) 253-5644**
Hosts: **Lonnie and Evelyn Wyatt**
No. of Rooms: **3**
No. of Private Baths: **3**
Double/pb: **$55–$65**
Single/pb: **$50**
Open: **All year**

Breakfast: **Full**
Credit Cards: **MC, VISA**
Pets: **No**
Children: **Welcome, over 12**
Smoking: **No**
Social Drinking: **No**

The Dutch Tudor home is surrounded by hemlocks and is located in the heart of the historic area. Lonnie and Evelyn have furnished with family heirlooms, antiques, and treasures collected while living and traveling in Europe. It is a brief walk to the Botanical Garden at the University of North Carolina, and a short distance to shops, restaurants, and cultural events. Depending upon the weather, breakfast may be enjoyed on the covered side porch, in the formal dining room, or in the rock-walled garden amid local wildflowers.

Flint Street Inns ✪
100 & 116 FLINT STREET, ASHEVILLE, NORTH CAROLINA 28801

Tel: **(704) 253-6723**
Hosts: **Rick, Lynne, and Marion Vogel**
Location: **¼ mi. from Rte. 240**
No. of Rooms: **8**
No. of Private Baths: **8**
Double/pb: **$70**
Single/pb: **$55**
Open: **All year**

Breakfast: **Full**
Credit Cards: **AMEX, DISC, MC, VISA**
Pets: **No**
Children: **No**
Smoking: **Permitted**
Social Drinking: **Permitted**

These turn-of-the-century homes on an acre with century-old trees are listed on the National Register of Historic Places. Stained glass, pine floors, and a claw-footed bathtub are part of the Victorian decor. The inns are air-conditioned for summer comfort; some have fireplaces for winter coziness. Guests are served wine, coffee, and soft drinks. The Blue Ridge Parkway is close by.

The Ray House ✪
83 HILLSIDE STREET, ASHEVILLE, NORTH CAROLINA 28801

Tel: **(704) 252-0106**
Best Time to Call: **10 AM–9 PM**
Hosts: **Will and Alice Curtis**
Location: **5 mi. from I-40**
No. of Rooms: **4**
No. of Private Baths: **2**
Max. No. Sharing Bath: **4**
Double/pb: **$57**

Single/pb: **$47**
Double/sb: **$47**
Single/sb: **$37**
Open: **All year**
Reduced Rates: **Weekly**
Breakfast: **Continental**
Pets: **Sometimes**
Children: **Welcome**

Smoking: **Permitted**
Social Drinking: **Permitted**

Airport/Station Pickup: **Yes**
Foreign Languages: **French**

This restored 1908 home sits on an acre of towering trees that provide leafy privacy in a parklike setting. Interior features include windows of unusual design, beamed ceilings, and handsome woodwork. A breakfast of homemade breads, sweet cakes, and jellies is served in the formal dining room or on the shaded wraparound porch.

Bed and Breakfast Over Yonder ✪

269 NORTH FORK ROAD, BLACK MOUNTAIN, NORTH CAROLINA 28711

Tel: **(704) 669-6762**; Nov.–May **(919) 945-9958**
Best Time to Call: **11 AM–2 PM**
Host: **Wilhelmina K. Headley**
Location: **2 mi. N of Black Mountain**
No. of Rooms: **5**
No. of Private Baths: **5**
Double/pb: **$40–$55**

Single/pb: **$35–$50**
Open: **June–Oct.**
Reduced Rates: **5%, after 3 days**
Breakfast: **Full**
Pets: **No**
Children: **Welcome**
Smoking: **Permitted**
Social Drinking: **Permitted**

Spectacular views of the nearby Black Mountain Range make Bed and Breakfast Over Yonder an ideal place to get away from it all. Hikers, tennis players, golfers, and swimmers will find plenty to do within a mile or two, and white-water rafting, gem mining, and rock climbing are all feasible on day trips. For a change of pace, explore the local craft and antique shops. Weather permitting, full breakfasts of fruit, homemade bread, and mountain trout are served on the deck overlooking the wildflower gardens.

The Blackberry Inn ✪

P.O. BOX 965, BLACK MOUNTAIN, NORTH CAROLINA 28711

Tel: **(704) 669-8303**
Best Time to Call: **10 AM–9 PM**
Hosts: **Roy and Barbara DeHaan Miller**
Location: **15 mi. E of Asheville**
No. of Rooms: **6**
No. of Private Baths: **6**
Double/pb: **$45–$65**
Single/pb: **$40**

Open: **All year**
Reduced Rates: **10%, weekly**
Breakfast: **Continental**
Pets: **No**
Children: **Welcome (crib)**
Smoking: **Permitted**
Social Drinking: **Permitted**
Airport/Station Pickup: **Yes**

The Blackberry Inn is a red brick Colonial set on a secluded hilltop surrounded by oaks and evergreens. The house was built in the 1930s, and though it has been renovated, it retains its original charm, with hardwood floors upstairs and polished brass throughout. The rooms have an American country theme and are furnished with antiques of all kinds. The inn is a short drive from the Blue Ridge Parkway and the Biltmore House. Rustic mountain trails, brilliant foliage, and relaxed hospitality are sure to lure you back to this charming inn.

Grandma Jean's Bed and Breakfast ✪
209 MEADOWVIEW DRIVE, BOONE, NORTH CAROLINA 28607

Tel: **(704) 262-3670**
Best Time to Call: **Before 10 AM**
Host: **Dr. Jean Probinsky**
No. of Rooms: **3**
Max. No. Sharing Bath: **4**
Double/sb: **$40**
Single/sb: **$35**
Open: **Apr. 1–Nov. 1**
Breakfast: **Continental**

Pets: **No**
Children: **Welcome, under 2 and over 6**
Smoking: **Permitted**
Social Drinking: **Permitted**
Airport/Station Pickup: **Yes**
Minimum Stay: **Two nights**
Foreign Languages: **Spanish**

Wicker furniture and lots of rocking chairs make this a cozy country home. Boone offers easy access to the Blue Ridge Parkway and Appalachian State University—the summer residence of the North Carolina Symphony—is just one mile away. Grandma Jean prides herself on her southern hospitality. Her continental breakfast includes coffee, tea, seasonal fruit, and croissants with homemade preserves.

Overlook Lodge ✪
P.O. BOX 1327, BOONE, NORTH CAROLINA 28607

Tel: **(704) 963-5785**
Host: **Nancy Garrett**
Location: **4 mi. from Blue Ridge Pkwy.**
No. of Rooms: **5**
No. of Private Baths: **5**
Double/pb: **$55–$70**
Single/pb: **$50–$65**
Suite: **$85–$100; sleeps six**
Open: **All year**

Reduced Rates: **15%, weekly; Nov. 1–Apr. 30**
Breakfast: **Full**
Credit Cards: **MC, VISA**
Pets: **Sometimes**
Children: **Yes (crib)**
Smoking: **Permitted**
Social Drinking: **Permitted**
Airport/Station Pickup: **Yes**

This rustic retreat is perched in the Blue Ridge Mountains and offers intoxicating views from the house's three decks. The secluded setting is ideal for forays into the wilderness. Hikers, canoeists, spelunkers, and fishermen will all find plenty to do here. In cold weather, weary skiers can warm up by the living room's huge stone fireplace. Year round, Nancy serves breakfasts that include home-baked breads and muffins; one of her fortes is cheese soufflé.

The Inn at Brevard ✪
410 EAST MAIN STREET, BREVARD, NORTH CAROLINA 28712

Tel: **(704) 884-2105**
Best Time to Call: **10 AM–8 PM**
Hosts: **Bertrand and Eileen Bourget**
Location: **25 mi. W of Hendersonville**
No. of Rooms: **14**
No. of Private Baths: **14**
Double/pb: **$55–$65**
Single/pb: **$50–$55**
Suite: **$95**

Open: **Mar. 1–Dec. 20**
Reduced Rates: **Weekly**
Breakfast: **Full**
Other Meals: **Available**
Pets: **No**
Children: **Welcome**
Smoking: **No**
Social Drinking: **Permitted**

This white-columned inn is listed on the National Register of Historic Places, and has retained the original brass hardware, carved fireplace mantels, and antique furnishings to recall old-time Southern charm. The bedrooms are comfortable and the clear air and mountain breezes will refresh you. Explore the many splendors of this Land of Water-falls, and return to spend a peaceful evening with other guests on the porch or sitting room.

Hamrick Inn ✪
7787 HIGHWAY 80, BURNSVILLE, NORTH CAROLINA 28714

Tel: **(704) 675-5251**
Best Time to Call: **Mornings**
Hosts: **Neal and June Jerome**
Location: **55 mi. NE of Asheville; 16 mi. from I-40, Exit 72**
No. of Rooms: **4**
No. of Private Baths: **4**
Double/pb: **$50–$60**

Single/pb: **$40–$50**
Open: **Apr. 2–Oct. 31**
Reduced Rates: **Weekly**
Breakfast: **Full**
Pets: **No**
Children: **Welcome**
Smoking: **Permitted**
Social Drinking: **Permitted**

This charming three-story Colonial-style stone inn is nestled at the foot of Mt. Mitchell, the highest mountain east of the Mississippi River. Much of the lovely furniture was built by Neal and June. The den has a fine selection of books as well as a TV set for your enjoyment. There is a private porch off each bedroom, where you may take in the view and the cool mountain breezes. Golfing, hiking, fishing, rock hounding, craft shopping, and fall foliage wandering are local activities. Pisgah National Park, Linville Caverns, Crabtree Mea-dows, and the Parkway Playhouse are area diversions.

The Homeplace ✪
5901 SARDIS ROAD, CHARLOTTE, NORTH CAROLINA 28226

Tel: **(704) 365-1936**
Hosts: **Peggy and Frank Dearien**
Location: **10 mi. from I-77; I-85**
No. of Rooms: **3**

No. of Private Baths: **3**
Double/pb: **$68**
Single/pb: **$63**
Open: **All year**

Breakfast: **Full**
Credit Cards: **AMEX, MC, VISA**
Pets: **No**

Children: **Welcome, over 10**
Smoking: **No**
Social Drinking: **No**

The warm and friendly atmosphere hasn't changed since 1902. The minute you arrive at this country Victorian and walk up to the wraparound porch with its rockers, you'll feel you've "come home." The handcrafted staircase, 10-foot beaded ceilings, and heart-of-pine floors add to the interior's beauty. It's convenient to malls, furniture and textile outlets, and treasure-filled antique shops.

The Inn on Providence
6700 PROVIDENCE ROAD, CHARLOTTE, NORTH CAROLINA 28226

Tel: **(704) 366-6700**
Hosts: **Darlene and Dan McNeill**
No. of Rooms: **5**
No. of Private Baths: **3**
Max. No. Sharing Bath: **4**
Double/pb: **$69–$79**
Double/sb: **$59**
Open: **All year**

Reduced Rates: **Available**
Breakfast: **Full**
Credit Cards: **MC, VISA**
Pets: **No**
Children: **Welcome, over 11**
Smoking: **No**
Social Drinking: **Permitted**

The Inn on Providence is a large, three-story Colonial nestled in South Charlotte, close to many amenities of the Queen City. The walnut-paneled library, sitting room with fireplace, and oak-floored dining room will make both vacationers and business executives feel at home. The bedrooms are decorated with Early American antiques, and each features something special, such as a canopy bed or a sitting room. In warm weather, breakfast is served on the screened veranda, which is decorated with white wicker and paddle fans. The veranda is also a great place to sip afternoon tea while overlooking the gardens and swimming pool.

The Overcarsh House ✪
326 WEST EIGHTH STREET, CHARLOTTE, NORTH CAROLINA 28202

Tel: **(704) 334-8477**
Hosts: **Dennis Cudd and George Brown**
Location: **1 mi. from I-77**
No. of Rooms: **1 suite**
No. of Private Baths: **1**
Suites: **$65–$80 for 2–4**

Open: **All year**
Reduced Rates: **10%, corporate**
Breakfast: **Continental**
Pets: **No**
Children: **Welcome**
Smoking: **Permitted**
Social Drinking: **Permitted**

The Library Suite is a Victorian-style retreat in the luxurious Overcarsh House. The private entrance into the suite leads to a wraparound gallery overlooking Fourth Ward park. The adjoining sleeping quarters feature a draped Savannah plantation bed. Your hosts have stocked the floor-to-ceiling bookcases with plenty of books and periodicals. They also provide wine and a wet bar, fresh flowers, cable TV, and coffeemaker. Overcarsh House is listed on the National Register of Historic Places, and is close to the uptown area, the performing arts center, shopping, and restaurants.

Windsong: A Mountain Inn ✪
120 FERGUSON RIDGE, CLYDE, NORTH CAROLINA 28721

Tel: **(704) 627-6111**	Reduced Rates: **10%, off-season;**
Best Time to Call: **8 AM–9 PM**	**weekly**
Hosts: **Donna and Gale Livengood**	Breakfast: **Full or Continental**
Location: **36 mi. W of Asheville**	Credit Cards: **MC, VISA**
No. of Rooms: **5**	Pets: **No**
No. of Private Baths: **5**	Children: **Welcome, over 12**
Double/pb: **$80–$85**	Smoking: **No**
Single/pb: **$72–$76.50**	Social Drinking: **Permitted**
Open: **All year**	Airport/Station Pickup: **Yes**

From its mountainside perch near Waynesville, this immense contemporary log home affords spectacular views of the surrounding countryside. Inside, the house is bright and airy, thanks to the large windows and skylights and the high exposed-beam ceilings. Each oversized room boasts its own patio, fireplace, and hot tub. There is a tennis court and in-ground pool, plus a billiard table and an extensive video library. Nearby attractions include Cherokee Indian Reservation, Great Smoky National Park, Biltmore House, and the Appalachian Trail. In the morning, you'll relish home-baked goods; if you choose a full breakfast, typical entrées are buckwheat banana pancakes and egg-sausage strata with mushrooms.

Arrowhead Inn ✪
106 MASON ROAD, DURHAM, NORTH CAROLINA 27712

Tel: **(919) 477-8430**	Open: **All year**
Hosts: **Jerry and Barbara Ryan**	Reduced Rates: **10% after 3 nights**
Location: **6.8 mi. from I-85, Exit**	Breakfast: **Full**
Roxboro	Credit Cards: **AMEX, MC, VISA**
No. of Rooms: **8**	Pets: **No**
No. of Private Baths: **4**	Children: **Welcome**
Max. No. Sharing Bath: **4**	Smoking: **Permitted**
Double/pb: **$80–$100**	Social Drinking: **Permitted**
Double/sb: **$55–$65**	Foreign Languages: **French**

Arrowhead Inn is a 200-year-old columned manor house in Durham County's tobacco country. Its rooms reflect various moments in the house's history, from Colonial through Tidewater and Victorian. Stroll the nearly four acres, or visit the historic district, the Museum of Life and Science, Duke University, or famous Research Triangle Park. After dinner at one of the area's fine restaurants, join the other guests for VCR, Scrabble, or conversation.

Buttonwood Inn ✪
190 GEORGIA ROAD, FRANKLIN, NORTH CAROLINA 28734

Tel: (704) 369-8985	Double/sb: $48
Best Time to Call: After 5 PM	Single/sb: $38
Host: Liz Oehser	Suites: $85
Location: 75 mi. SW of Asheville	Open: Apr. 15–Nov. 15
No. of Rooms: 4	Breakfast: Full
No. of Private Baths: 2	Pets: No
Max. No. Sharing Bath: 4	Children: Welcome, over 10
Double/pb: $50–$60	Smoking: Permitted
Single/pb: $40	Social Drinking: Permitted

The Buttonwood is a small country inn surrounded by towering pines, a spacious lawn, and mountain views. The original residence was a small cottage built in the late 1920s adjacent to the greens of the Franklin golf course. Years later, a new wing was added with rustic, charming rooms. Guests may choose from comfortable bedrooms decorated with antiques, cozy quilts, and handcrafts, many of which are offered for sale. Breakfast selections include sausage-apple ring, eggs Benedict, or cheese frittata, with coffee cake and plenty of hot coffee or tea. Golfers will be glad to be so close to the beautiful fairways and Bermuda grass greens right next door. Nearby there are also craft shops, hiking trails, the Blue Ridge Parkway, gem mines, and plenty of places to swim and ride.

Hickory Knoll Lodge ✪
238 EAST HICKORY KNOLL ROAD, FRANKLIN, NORTH CAROLINA 28734

Tel: (704) 524-9666	Breakfast: Full
Best Time to Call: 9 AM–9 PM	Other Meals: Available
Hosts: George and Jean Farrell	Credit Cards: MC, VISA
Location: 70 mi. SW of Asheville	Pets: No
No. of Rooms: 3	Children: Welcome, over 12
No. of Private Baths: 3	Smoking: No
Double/pb: $50–$60	Social Drinking: Permitted
Open: Apr. 1–Nov. 1	

Set in the Smoky Mountains, this rustic lodge makes an ideal home base for anyone who enjoys the great outdoors. White water rafting, hiking, fishing, horseback riding, and golf are just some of your recreational options. At the end of the day, watch the sunset from a hammock on the wide wraparound porch, or take a Jacuzzi bath. George and Jean love to cook, preparing full breakfasts from local produce.

Greenwood ✪
205 NORTH PARK DRIVE, GREENSBORO, NORTH CAROLINA 27401

Tel: **(919) 274-6350**
Best Time to Call: **Mornings**
Host: **Jo Anne Green**
No. of Rooms: **5**
No. of Private Baths: **3**
Max. No. Sharing Bath: **4**
Double/pb: **$55–$80**
Single/pb: **$50**
Double/sb: **$50**

Single/sb: **$40**
Open: **All year**
Breakfast: **Continental**
Credit Cards: **AMEX, MC, VISA**
Pets: **No**
Children: **Welcome, over 5**
Smoking: **Permitted**
Social Drinking: **Permitted**

Located in the historic district, this 1905 house has been lovingly restored and air-conditioned for your comfort. Inside the house, the decor includes wood carvings and art from all over the world. Guests are welcome to relax by the fireside and enjoy wine or soft drinks. Breakfast features fresh fruit, cereals, homemade muffins, and jam. Golf, tennis, boating, and hiking are nearby. There's a swimming pool on the premises.

The Waverly Inn ✪
783 NORTH MAIN STREET, HENDERSONVILLE, NORTH CAROLINA 28792

Tel: **(800) 537-8195; (704) 692-1090**
Best Time to Call: **7:30 AM–11 PM**
Hosts: **John and Diane Sheiry**
Location: **20 mi. S of Asheville**
No. of Rooms: **14**
No. of Private Baths: **14**
Double/pb: **$53–$83**
Single/pb: **$48–$78**
Suites: **$95–$105**

Open: **All year**
Reduced Rates: **Off-season; 15%, weekly**
Breakfast: **Full**
Credit Cards: **AMEX, DISC, MC, VISA**
Pets: **No**
Children: **Welcome**
Smoking: **Permitted**
Social Drinking: **Permitted**

Built as a boardinghouse in 1898, the Waverly is distinguished by its handsome Eastlake staircase—a factor that earned the inn a listing in the National Register of Historic Places. Furnishings like four-poster canopy beds and claw-footed tubs combine Victorian stateliness and Colonial Revival charm. You'll walk away sated from all-you-can-eat breakfasts of pancakes and French toast. Noteworthy local sites include the Biltmore Estate, the Carl Sandburg House, the Blue Ridge Parkway, and the Flatrock Playhouse.

Gingerbread Inn
103 SOUTH CHURCH STREET, HERTFORD, NORTH CAROLINA 27944

Tel: **(919) 426-5809**
Host: **Jenny Harnisch**

Location: **68 mi. SW of Norfolk**
No. of Rooms: **3**

No. of Private Baths: **3**
Double/pb: **$45**
Single/pb: **$35**
Open: **All year**
Breakfast: **Full**
Credit Cards: **MC, VISA**

Pets: **No**
Children: **Welcome**
Smoking: **No**
Social Drinking: **Permitted**
Foreign Languages: **German, Russian**

This beautifully restored turn-of-the-century home is on the local historic tour and boasts a wraparound porch with paired columns. The comfortably furnished rooms are spacious with queen- or king-size beds and plush carpeting. The aroma of freshly baked gingerbread is something you can't miss during your stay. Your hostess even offers a souvenir cookie for the ride home.

Colonial Pines Inn ✪
ROUTE 1, BOX 22B, HICKORY STREET, HIGHLANDS, NORTH CAROLINA 28741

Tel: **(704) 526-2060**
Best Time to Call: **10 AM–10 PM**
Hosts: **Chris and Donna Alley**
Location: **80 mi. SW of Asheville**
No. of Rooms: **7**
No. of Private Baths: **7**
Double/pb: **$65**
Single/pb: **$55**
Suites: **$75**

Guest Cottage: **$75; sleeps 4**
Open: **All year**
Reduced Rates: **Weekly**
Breakfast: **Full**
Credit Cards: **MC, VISA**
Pets: **No**
Children: **Welcome**
Smoking: **No**
Social Drinking: **Permitted**

Located in a charming, uncommercial mountain resort town, this white Colonial is flanked by tall columns and is surrounded by two acres. The scenic view may be enjoyed from comfortable rocking chairs on the wide veranda. Donna, a former interior decorator, has furnished with antiques, art, and interesting accessories. Chris is a classical guitarist, woodworker, and great cook. The hearty breakfast includes a variety of homemade breads.

Lakeside Lodging ✪
ROUTE 1, BOX 189A, HIGHLANDS, NORTH CAROLINA 28741

Tel: **(704) 526-4498**
Best Time to Call: **9 AM–9 PM**
Hosts: **Michael and Eleanor Robel**
Location: **100 mi. N of Atlanta, Georgia**
No. of Rooms: **4**
No. of Private Baths: **4**
Double/pb: **$60**
Single/pb: **$50**
Open: **All year**

Reduced Rates: **10%, weekly**
Breakfast: **Full**
Credit Cards: **MC, VISA**
Pets: **No**
Children: **Welcome**
Smoking: **Permitted**
Social Drinking: **Permitted**
Minimum Stay: **2 nights, holiday weekends**

Located in the Smoky Mountains at an elevation of 4,100 feet, this white Colonial-style home with black shutters overlooks Lake Sequoyah and is bordered by the Nantahala National Forest. It combines a peaceful, scenic ambience with the availability of quaint shops, fine restaurants, mountain trails, and dramatic waterfalls. The immaculate interior is warm and inviting, and attractively furnished with country charm. Entrées of potato quiche, omelets or soufflés, are breakfast treats. Mike and Eleanor will tell you how to get to the nearby facilities for horseback riding, canoeing, golf, gem mining, and rock rapelling. Asheville is 70 miles away.

Ye Olde Stone House ✪
ROUTE 2, BOX 7, HIGHLANDS, NORTH CAROLINA 28741

Tel: **(704) 526-5911**
Best Time to Call: **Afternoons;
  evenings**
Hosts: **Jim and Rene Ramsdell**
Location: **80 mi. SW of Asheville**
No. of Rooms: **4**
No. of Private Baths: **3**
Max. No. Sharing Bath: **3**
Double/pb: **$65–$70**
Single/pb: **$55–$60**
Double/sb: **$45**
Single/sb: **$45**

Open: **All year**
Reduced Rates: **10%, Sun.–Thurs.;
  weekly**
Breakfast: **Full**
Credit Cards: **MC, VISA**
Pets: **No**
Children: **Welcome**
Smoking: **No**
Social Drinking: **Permitted**
Minimum Stay: **2 nights, holiday
  weekends**

Built of stones taken from a local river by mule and wagon, the house is less than a mile from the center of town, where you will find a nature center, museum, galleries, tennis courts, swimming pool, and shops offering antiques or mountain crafts. The rooms are bright, cheerful, and comfortably furnished. The sun room and porch are perfect spots to catch up on that book you've wanted to read. On cool evenings, the Ramsdells invite you to gather round the fireplace for snacks and conversation.

Ye Olde Cherokee Inn Bed & Breakfast ✪
500 NORTH VIRGINIA DARE TRAIL, KILL DEVIL HILLS, NORTH CAROLINA 27948

Tel: **(919) 441-6127**	Reduced Rates: **$5 per night, seniors**
Best Time to Call: **Evenings**	Breakfast: **Continental**
Hosts: **Bob and Phyllis Combs**	Credit Cards: **AMEX, MC, VISA**
Location: **75 mi. S of Norfolk**	Pets: **No**
No. of Rooms: **6**	Children: **No**
No. of Private Baths: **6**	Smoking: **No**
Double/pb: **$55–$75**	Social Drinking: **Permitted**
Open: **Apr. 1–Sept. 30**	Minimum Stay: **3 days July–Aug.; 4 nights holidays**

Only 500 feet from the Atlantic Ocean you'll find this pastel-pink house with wraparound porches, soft cypress interiors, and white ruffled curtains. Cherokee Inn is near the historic Roanoke Island settlement, Cape Hatteras, and the Wright Brothers Memorial at Kitty Hawk. Of course, you may just want to spend the day at the beach. In the evening, curl up with a book or watch TV. You'll start the next day with coffee and pastries.

Greenfield B&B ✪
30 GREENFIELD DRIVE, LEICESTER, NORTH CAROLINA 28748

Tel: **(704) 683-2128**	Double/sb: **$45**
Best Time to Call: **9 AM–5 PM**	Single/sb: **$40**
Hosts: **Mahlon and Janet Green**	Open: **Apr.–Oct.**
Location: **5 mi. NW of Asheville**	Breakfast: **Continental**
No. of Rooms: **3**	Pets: **No**
No. of Private Baths: **1**	Children: **No**
Max. No. Sharing Bath: **4**	Smoking: **No**
Double/pb: **$55**	Social Drinking: **Permitted**
Single/pb: **$50**	

This Southern country estate is set on a hilltop surrounded by lawns and seven acres of pine and hardwood forest. The grounds include over 100 dogwood trees, walking paths, and a pond. The house is a columned Colonial, furnished with a mixture of antiques, traditional furnishings, and artwork. Breakfast is served on the second-story deck, with its 360-degree panorama of the mountains. On colder days home-baked breads, muffins, and coffee cakes are served in the dining room beside the open brick hearth. The Greens are located near the

Great Smoky Mountains National Park and the Blue Ridge Parkway. After a day of touring enjoy a glass of wine or champagne, and a snack on the deck.

Woodside Inn ✪
P.O. BOX 197, NC 57, MILTON, NORTH CAROLINA 28305

Tel: **(919) 234-8646; 694-4450**
Best Time to Call: **After 4 PM**
Hosts: **Tom and Lib McPherson**
Location: **12 mi. E of Danville, Va.; 5 mi. from US 58**
No. of Rooms: **4**
No. of Private Baths: **1 full; 3 half**
Double/pb: **$62**
Single/pb: **$57**

Open: **All year**
Reduced Rates: **15%, weekly**
Breakfast: **Full**
Other Meals: **Available**
Credit Cards: **AMEX, MC, VISA**
Pets: **Small pets welcome**
Children: **Welcome**
Smoking: **Permitted**
Social Drinking: **Permitted**
Airport/Station Pickup: **Yes**

Built on a hill overlooking the rolling countryside, this 1838 Greek Revival manor house is furnished with elegant late Federal and American Empire antiques. The large bedrooms are air-conditioned for summer comfort, and have central heat for chilly winter nights. Breakfast treats are Southern raised biscuits, quick breads, country ham, and pancakes. Complimentary beverages are offered, and laundry facilities are available. Tom is a retired County Supervisor; Lib directs a school nutrition program. They share interests in history, music, travel, golf, reading, and bridge. The on-premises restaurant serves lunch and dinner Thursday through Saturday; other times by appointment.

Buntie's B&B ✪
322 EAST HOUSTON STREET, MONROE, NORTH CAROLINA 28110

Tel: **(704) 289-1155**
Best Time to Call: **7 AM–10 PM**
Host: **Pauline Clair Butler**
Location: **20 mi. SE of Charlotte**
No. of Rooms: **3**
Max. No. Sharing Bath: **3**
Double/sb: **$50**
Single/sb: **$45**
Open: **All year**

Reduced Rates: **15%, weekly, families; 10%, seniors**
Breakfast: **Full**
Pets: **No**
Children: **Welcome, over 4, under 10**
Smoking: **No**
Social Drinking: **Permitted**
Airport/Station Pickup: **Yes**

Located in a lovely, tree-lined neighborhood, this B&B is Monroe's first. Pauline, a New York City native who moved south for a change of pace, has stocked her library with mystery novels and travel books. She has a growing collection of Academy Award–winning films that can be screened on the VCR. Nearby country clubs have facilities for golf, tennis, and swimming. In the morning, enjoy your choice of either Continental or full breakfast; ham and grits, chicken livers with grits, and Jamaican codfish are standard entrées.

Courtland Manor ✪

P.O. BOX 739, 2 COURTLAND BOULEVARD, MOUNTAIN HOME, NORTH CAROLINA 28758

Tel: (704) 692-1133
Hosts: Cy and Mary Ann Miller
Location: 3 mi. N of Hendersonville
No. of Rooms: 5
No. of Private Baths: 3
Max. No. Sharing Bath: 4
Double/pb: $58
Double/sb: $48
Suites: $70

Open: All year
Breakfast: Full
Credit Cards: MC, VISA
Pets: No
Children: Welcome, over 12
Smoking: No
Social Drinking: Permitted
Airport/Station Pickup: Yes

Designed on a generous scale, this granite Colonial has a large front porch, and windows made of hand-poured glass. The ginkgo tree in the front yard—imported from China more than 100 years ago—may be one of the oldest examples of its species in the United States. Nearby woods and caves invite exploration, and the local Folk Art Center merits a visit. Guests wake up to a home-cooked Continental breakfast.

Pine Ridge B&B Inn ✪

2893 WEST PINE STREET, MT. AIRY, NORTH CAROLINA 27030

Tel: (919) 789-5034
Hosts: Ellen and Manford Haxton
Location: 2 mi. from I-77
No. of Rooms: 7
No. of Private Baths: 5
Max. No. Sharing Bath: 4
Double/pb: $75–$85
Double/sb: $40–$50
Open: All year

Reduced Rates: 10%, Jan.–Mar.
Breakfast: Continental
Other Meals: Available
Credit Cards: AMEX, MC, VISA
Pets: No
Children: Welcome (crib)
Smoking: Permitted
Social Drinking: Permitted
Airport/Station Pickup: Yes

Luxury and elegance await you in this 40-year-old mansion set on eight acres in the shadow of the Blue Ridge Mountains. Each guest room is attractively decorated and has a telephone and cable TV. Read in the wood-paneled library, soak in the hot tub, work out on the Nautilus equipment in the exercise room, or swim in the backyard pool. Golf and tennis are available nearby. A few miles away are outlet stores, the world's largest open-face granite quarry, and the famous frescoes of Ashe County.

Harmony House Inn ✪

215 POLLOCK STREET, NEW BERN, NORTH CAROLINA 28560

Tel: (919) 636-3810
Best Time to Call: 9 AM–9 PM

Hosts: A. E. and Diane Hansen
Location: 110 mi. SE of Raleigh

No. of Rooms: **9**
No. of Private Baths: **9**
Double/pb: **$70**
Single/pb: **$49**
Open: **All year**
Breakfast: **Full**

Credit Cards: **AMEX, MC, VISA**
Pets: **No**
Children: **Welcome**
Smoking: **Permitted**
Social Drinking: **Permitted**

Built in 1850, the inn is located in the historic district just four blocks from Tryon Palace and one block from the confluence of the Trent and Neuse rivers. About 7,000 square feet in area, the house is graced with spacious hallways and an aura of elegance. The air-conditioned guest accommodations are furnished with antiques and fine reproductions. You are welcome to help yourself to soft drinks and ice from the well-stocked guest refrigerator. Relax in the parlor, on the front porch with its rockers and swings, or in the pretty backyard.

Kings Arms Inn ✪
212 POLLOCK STREET, NEW BERN, NORTH CAROLINA 28560

Tel: **(919) 638-4409**
Best Time to Call: **8 AM–10 PM**
Hosts: **David and Diana Parks**
No. of Rooms: **9**
No. of Private Baths: **9**
Double/pb: **$75**
Single/pb: **$55**

Open: **All year**
Breakfast: **Continental**
Credit Cards: **AMEX, MC, VISA**
Pets: **Only Seeing-eye dog**
Children: **Welcome (crib)**
Smoking: **Permitted**
Social Drinking: **Permitted**

The Kings Arms is named for an old town tavern said to have hosted members of the First Continental Congress. The inn boasts its own historic significance, as many of its rooms date back to the early 1800s. Today its rooms are available to those seeking superior accommodations in the historic district. The bedrooms have fireplaces, antiques, brass, canopied, or poster beds, and cable TV. Homemade biscuits and breads and beverages are brought to guests each morning. Your hosts will gladly direct you to the waterfront, Tryon Palace, and fine restaurants.

New Berne House Bed and Breakfast Inn ✪
709 BROAD STREET, NEW BERN, NORTH CAROLINA 28560

Tel: **(919) 636-2250 or (800) 842-7688**
Hosts: **Joel and Shan Wilkins**
Location: **1 mi. from Hwy. 70**
No. of Rooms: **6**
No. of Private Baths: **6**
Double/pb: **$75**
Single/pb: **$55**
Suites: **$140**
Open: **All year**
Reduced Rates: **10%, seniors, weekly, families**

Breakfast: **Full**
Credit Cards: **AMEX, DC, DISC, MC, VISA**
Pets: **Sometimes**
Children: **Sometimes**
Smoking: **Permitted**
Social Drinking: **Permitted**
Airport/Station Pickup: **Yes**

Located in the heart of New Bern's historic district, this brick Colonial was home to the Taylor family for generations. Today Joel and Shan Wilkins have furnished the inn in the style of an English country manor with a mixture of antiques, traditional pieces, and attic treasures. Guests are pampered with afternoon tea served in the formal parlor or the library. A sweeping stairway leads upstairs, where you may choose from the romantic Masters Chamber or the whimsical Nursery, with its pink claw-foot tub and a brass bed reportedly rescued in 1897 from a burning brothel. Breakfast specialties such as honey-glazed ham, praline muffins, and homemade breads can be enjoyed downstairs or in your private quarters. New Berne House is within walking distance of Tryon Palace, North Carolina's Colonial Capitol, and the governor's mansion. Ask about their exciting weekend sailing package on an 85-foot luxury yacht.

The Oakwood Inn ✪

411 NORTH BLOODWORTH STREET, RALEIGH, NORTH CAROLINA 27604

Tel: **(919) 832-9712**	Open: **All year**
Best Time to Call: **8 AM–noon; 3–9 PM**	Breakfast: **Full**
Host: **Diana Newton**	Credit Cards: **AMEX, MC, VISA**
No. of Rooms: **6**	Pets: **No**
No. of Private Baths: **6**	Children: **Welcome, over 12**
Double/pb: **$75–$90**	Smoking: **Permitted**
Single/pb: **$65–$80**	Social Drinking: **Permitted**

Built in 1871, the inn is listed on the National Register of Historic Places. Recently restored to their prior elegance, all of the rooms are enhanced by the tasteful use of antique furnishings, appropriate draperies, and accessories. The inn is located within the 20-square-block area of homes built from 1879 to 1920, and visiting it is really like taking a step back in time into an era of horse-drawn carriages and gingerbread architecture. There are six colleges nearby offering cultural opportunities, and a number of museums for history buffs.

The 1868 Stewart-Marsh House ✪

220 SOUTH ELLIS STREET, SALISBURY, NORTH CAROLINA 28144

Tel: **(704) 633-6841**	Breakfast: **Full**
Host: **Gerry Webster**	Pets: **No**
Location: **39 mi. NE of Charlotte**	Children: **Sometimes**
No. of Rooms: **2**	Smoking: **No**
No. of Private Baths: **2**	Social Drinking: **Permitted**
Double/pb: **$45–$50**	Minimum Stay: **Oct., 2 nights during historic homes tour**
Single/pb: **$40–$45**	Airport/Station Pickup: **Yes**
Open: **All year**	
Reduced Rates: **10%, weekly**	

This gracious 1868 Federal-style home is located on a quiet, tree-lined street listed on the National Register of Historic Places. It is furnished with antiques and cherished family pieces reflecting the period immediately following the Civil War. You are welcome to enjoy the cozy library or relax on a wicker chair on the screened-in porch. Gerry is a tour guide and will be happy to conduct a personal tour of interesting local sights and architecture. Shops and restaurants are within walking distance.

Rowan Oak House ✪
208 SOUTH FULTON STREET, SALISBURY, NORTH CAROLINA 28144

Tel: **(704) 633-2086**	Reduced Rates: **10%, seniors**
Hosts: **Bill and Ruth Ann Coffey**	Breakfast: **Full**
Location: **1 mi. from I-85**	Pets: **No**
No. of Rooms: **3**	Children: **Welcome, over 12**
No. of Private Baths: **3**	Smoking: **Permitted**
Double/pb: **$65–$75**	Social Drinking: **Permitted**
Single/pb: **$60–$70**	Airport/Station Pickup: **Yes**
Open: **All year**	Foreign Languages: **Spanish**

Milton Brown built the Rowan Oak House for his bride, Fannie, in 1902. Set in the heart of the West Square historic district, this Queen Anne features a cupola, wraparound porch, and carved oak door. Step through the dark wood entry to see the intricate woodwork and stained glass. The original fixtures are well preserved and complemented by period furnishings and reproductions. Ruth Ann and Bill invite you to choose from three lavishly appointed guest rooms, including the master bedroom, which features a double Jacuzzi and a fireplace in the bathroom. Breakfast is served in your private quarters or downstairs in the formal dining room, beneath the painting of Queen Louise of Prussia. In the afternoon, tea or a glass of wine can be enjoyed in the garden, on the porch, or in the sitting room amid the curios and Victorian knickknacks. Your hosts can guide you to Salisbury's antebellum architecture and an abundance of nearby lakes, parks, and golf courses.

The Oaks
P.O. BOX 1008, SALUDA, NORTH CAROLINA 28773

Tel: **(704) 749-9613**	Breakfast: **Continental**
Hosts: **Ceri and Peggy Dando**	Credit Cards: **MC, VISA**
Location: **12 mi. S of Hendersonville**	Pets: **No**
No. of Rooms: **4**	Children: **No**
No. of Private Baths: **4**	Smoking: **No**
Double/pb: **$53–$57**	Social Drinking: **Permitted**
Open: **All year**	Foreign Languages: **Limited French**

With its distinctive three-story turret, this turn-of-the-century residence is a local landmark. The carved fireplace mantels in the living room and parlor are original, and the Dandos have decorated the house with authentic Victorian color schemes and period furnishings. Saluda, a quiet hilltop village, offers old-fashioned, small-town pleasures. In addition to the antique shops, tennis court, and playground, guests enjoy the slow pace and friendly people. In the morning, Peggy sets out a Continental breakfast that usually features her own banana nut bread.

Eli Olive's ✪
3719 US 70 WEST, SMITHFIELD, NORTH CAROLINA 27577

Tel: **(919) 934-9823; 934-0246**	Breakfast: **Full**
Hosts: **Kay and Taylor Jolliff**	Other Meals: **Available**
Location: **½ mi. W of I-95**	Credit Cards: **MC, VISA**
No. of Rooms: **7**	Pets: **No**
No. of Private Baths: **7**	Children: **Welcome**
Double/pb: **$49**	Smoking: **Permitted**
Single/pb: **$42**	Social Drinking: **Permitted**
Open: **All year**	Airport/Station Pickup: **Yes**
Reduced Rates: **10%, seniors**	

One of Johnston County's most celebrated citizens was Eli Olive, who in his day was famous for riding down the streets scattering silver coins for the children. The inn named in his honor is a restored two-story plantation home with fireplaces, handcrafts, and antebellum charm. Each guest room is named for a celebrated local and features North Carolina furnishings, linens, candles, and soaps. In the dining room, menu selections highlight specialties such as Smithfield ham, corn pudding, beer-battered Vidalia onions, fresh seafood, and peaches-and-cream pie. Your hosts will direct you to local sights, such as the Ava Gardner Museum, Southland Winery, and Bentonville Battleground.

Turby Villa B&B ✪
EAST WHITEHEAD STREET, SPARTA, NORTH CAROLINA 28675

Tel: **(919) 372-8490**	Open: **All year**
Hosts: **Mr. and Mrs. R. E. Turbiville**	Breakfast: **Full**
No. of Rooms: **3**	Pets: **No**
No. of Private Baths: **3**	Children: **Welcome**
Double/pb: **$50**	Smoking: **Permitted**
Single/pb: **$35**	Social Drinking: **Permitted**

At an altitude of 3,000 feet, this contemporary two-story brick home is the centerpiece of a 20-acre farm. The house is surrounded by an acre of trees and manicured lawns, and the lovely views are of the scenic Blue Ridge Mountains. Breakfast is served either on the enclosed porch with its white wicker furnishings or in the more formal dining room with its Early American–style furnishings. The Turbivilles take justifiable pride in their attractive, well-maintained B&B.

The Richmond Inn
101 PINE AVENUE, SPRUCE PINE, NORTH CAROLINA 28777

Tel: **(704) 765-6993**
Best Time to Call: **7 AM–11 PM**
Hosts: **Lenore Boucher and Bill Ansley**
Location: **4 mi. from Blue Ridge Pkwy., Exit 331**
No. of Rooms: **7**
No. of Private Baths: **7**
Double/pb: **$55–$75**

Single/pb: **$45–$65**
Open: **All year**
Breakfast: **Full**
Credit Cards: **MC, VISA**
Pets: **No**
Children: **Welcome**
Smoking: **No**
Social Drinking: **Permitted**

Surrounded by towering pines, this white wooden house trimmed with black window shutters has a stone terrace and rock walls. It is furnished in a comfortable blend of antiques and family treasures. Most mornings, Lenore fixes a Southern repast with bacon, eggs, and grits. Spruce Pine is the mineral capital of the world, and panning for gemstones such as garnets and amethysts is a popular pastime. Hiking the Appalachian Trail, playing golf, or working out at your hosts' community spa will keep you in shape. Internationally known artists schedule shows throughout the year.

Scott's Keep ✪
308 WALNUT STREET, P.O. BOX 1425, SWANSBORO, NORTH CAROLINA 28584

Tel: **(919) 326-1257**
Best Time to Call: **After 3:30 PM**
Hosts: **Frank and Norma Scott**
Location: **150 mi. SE of Raleigh**
No. of Rooms: **3**
No. of Private Baths: **3**
Double/pb: **$45**
Open: **All year**

Reduced Rates: **15%, weekly**
Breakfast: **Full**
Credit Cards: **MC, VISA**
Pets: **No**
Children: **Welcome, over 6**
Smoking: **Permitted**
Social Drinking: **Permitted**

This simple contemporary is located on a quiet street two blocks from the waterfront. Your hosts want you to feel right at home in the bright, spacious living room and comfortable guest rooms. The larger bedroom is decorated with wicker and features an antique trunk, a queen-size bed, and a colorful quilt. The smaller bedroom is furnished in classic maple with a double bed and grandmother's quilt. For breakfast, Norma serves blueberry or apple spice muffins with fruit and homemade jellies. This historic seaside village is filled with inviting shops and waterside seafood restaurants. Your hosts will point the way to beautiful beaches, waterskiing, sailing, and windsurfing.

Little Warren ✪
304 EAST PARK AVENUE, TARBORO, NORTH CAROLINA 27886

Tel: **(919) 823-1314**	Breakfast: **Full**
Hosts: **Patsy and Tom Miller**	Credit Cards: **AMEX, MC, VISA**
Location: **20 mi. E of Rocky Mount**	Pets: **No**
No. of Rooms: **3**	Children: **Welcome, over 4**
No. of Private Baths: **3**	Smoking: **Permitted**
Double/pb: **$58–$65**	Social Drinking: **Permitted**
Single/pb: **$48–$58**	Airport/Station Pickup: **Yes**
Open: **All year**	Foreign Languages: **Spanish**

Little Warren is actually a large and gracious family home built in 1913. It is located along the Albemarle Trail in Tarboro's Historic District. The deeply set, wraparound porch overlooks one of the last originally chartered town commons still in existence. Inside, you'll find rooms of beautiful antiques from England and America, many of which can be purchased. In the morning, choose from a full English, Southern, or Continental breakfast.

Barkley House Bed & Breakfast ✪
ROUTE 6, BOX 12, TAYLORSVILLE, NORTH CAROLINA 28681

Tel: **(704) 632-9060**	Breakfast: **Full**
Best Time to Call: **Mornings**	Credit Cards: **AMEX**
Host: **Phyllis Barkley**	Wheelchair-Accessible: **Yes**
Location: **60 mi. E of Charlotte**	Pets: **Sometimes**
No. of Rooms: **2**	Children: **Welcome**
No. of Private Baths: **2**	Smoking: **Permitted**
Double/pb: **$49**	Social Drinking: **Permitted**
Single/pb: **$38**	Airport/Station Pickup: **Yes**
Open: **All year**	
Reduced Rates: **10%, families, seniors; 15%, weekly**	

After staying in European B&Bs, Phyllis opened the first one in Taylorsville, a small town surrounded by mountains. Barkley House is a white colonial with yellow shutters and a gracious front porch with four columns. The furnishings are homey, combining antiques and pieces from the '50s. Haystack eggs and fruity banana splits are two of Phyllis's breakfast specialties; she'll be happy to cater to guests on restricted diets.

Mill Farm Inn ✪
P.O. BOX 1251, TRYON, NORTH CAROLINA 28782

Tel: **(704) 859-6992 or (800) 545-6992**	Location: **45 mi. SE of Asheville**
Best Time to Call: **Mornings**	No. of Rooms: **8**
Hosts: **Chip and Penny Kessler**	No. of Private Baths: **8**

Double/pb: **$48**
Single/pb: **$40**
Suites: **$70–$90**
Open: **All year**
Reduced Rates: **10%, seniors**
Breakfast: **Continental**

Pets: **No**
Children: **Welcome**
Smoking: **No**
Social Drinking: **Permitted**
Foreign Languages: **French, Spanish, German**

The Pacolet River flows past the edge of this three-and-one-half-acre property in the foothills of the Blue Ridge Mountains. Sitting porches and the living room with fireplace are fine spots to relax. A hearty breakfast of fresh fruit, cereal, English muffins, preserves, and coffee is served. Craft shops, galleries, and antiquing will keep you busy.

Bluestone Lodge
SR 1112, P.O. BOX 736, VALLE CRUCIS, NORTH CAROLINA 28691

Tel: **(704) 963-5177**
Best Time to Call: **9 AM–5 PM**
Hosts: **Merry Lee Mears and Sally and Jim**
Location: **70 mi. NW of Charlotte**
No. of Rooms: **4**
No. of Private Baths: **4**
Double/pb: **$45–$75**
Suites: **$110–$120**

Open: **All year**
Reduced Rates: **Available**
Breakfast: **Full**
Credit Cards: **MC, VISA**
Pets: **No**
Children: **Welcome**
Smoking: **Permitted**
Social Drinking: **Permitted**
Minimum Stay: **2 nights weekends**

Nestled 3,000 feet atop Bluestone Hollow, this rustic cedar lodge is surrounded by trees, blackberry bushes, and wild flowers. The lodge rooms, both with kitchenettes, feature sliding glass doors opening onto the deck, where you can enjoy breathtaking mountain views. The spacious third-floor suite has vaulted ceilings, skylights, a fireplace, a whirlpool bath and a kitchen with a Jenn-Air range. The cozy loft room has a double bed. All rooms are highlighted by family quilts and antiques. Guests are invited to gather around the fireplace in the living room or relax in the hammock, sauna, or hot tub. The outdoor pool, rec room, and barbecue will make it tough to leave this mountain hideaway. Your hosts will start your day off with a breakfast buffet and will be happy to offer you afternoon iced tea or hot seasonal drinks. Trout-filled streams, gourmet restaurants, craft shops, ski areas, and scenic vistas are all nearby.

Pamlico House ✪
400 EAST MAIN STREET, WASHINGTON, NORTH CAROLINA 27889

Tel: **(919) 946-7184**
Best Time to Call: **9 AM–8 PM**
Hosts: **Lawrence and Jeanne Hervey**
Location: **20 mi. E of Greenville**

No. of Rooms: **4**
No. of Private Baths: **4**
Double/pb: **$55–$65**
Single/pb: **$45–$55**

Open: **All year**	Children: **Welcome**
Reduced Rates: **10%, weekly**	Smoking: **Permitted**
Breakfast: **Full**	Social Drinking: **Permitted**
Credit Cards: **MC, VISA**	Airport/Station Pickup: **Yes**
Pets: **No**	

Located in the center of a small, historic town, this stately Colonial Revival home's large rooms are a perfect foil for the carefully chosen antique furnishings. Guests are drawn to the classic Victorian parlor or to the spacious wraparound porch for relaxing conversation. Take a self-guided walking tour of the historic district or a stroll along the quaint waterfront. Recreational pleasures abound. Nature enthusiasts enjoy the wildlife and exotic plants in nearby Goose Creek State Park. Should you get homesick for your favorite pet, Lawrence and Jeanne will share theirs.

Belle Meade Inn ✪

804 BALSAM ROAD, HAZELWOOD, NORTH CAROLINA 28738 (MAILING ADDRESS: P.O. BOX 1319, WAYNESVILLE, NORTH CAROLINA 28786)

Tel: **(704) 456-3234**	Open: **All year**
Hosts: **Larry Hanson and William Shaw**	Reduced Rates: **10% AARP; weekly**
Location: **27 mi. W of Asheville**	Breakfast: **Full**
No. of Rooms: **4**	Credit Cards: **MC, VISA**
No. of Private Baths: **4**	Pets: **No**
Double/pb: **$50–$55**	Children: **Welcome, over 6**
Single/pb: **$45–$50**	Smoking: **No**
	Social Drinking: **Permitted**

Nestled in the mountains, and within easy reach of the Great Smoky National Park, this elegant home is a frame dwelling built in the craftsman style popular in the early 1900s. The warm richness of the chestnut woodwork in the formal rooms and the large stone fireplace in the living room complement the appealing blend of antique and traditional furnishings. The friendly attention to guests' needs are exemplified in such thoughtful touches as "earlybird" coffee brought to your door, complimentary refreshments on the veranda, and fresh flowers and mints in your room. Nearby attractions include Biltmore House, Catalooche Ski Slope, mountain art and craft festivals, and white water rafting and tubing.

Anderson Guest House ✪
520 ORANGE STREET, WILMINGTON, NORTH CAROLINA 28401

Tel: **(919) 343-8128**	Open: **All year**
Best Time to Call: **8 AM–5 PM**	Breakfast: **Full**
Hosts: **Landon and Connie Anderson**	Pets: **Sometimes**
No. of Rooms: 2	Children: **Welcome**
No. of Private Baths: 2	Smoking: **No**
Double/pb: **$65**	Social Drinking: **Permitted**
Single/pb: **$50**	Airport/Station Pickup: **Yes**

This 19th-century town house has a private guest house overlooking a garden. The bedrooms have ceiling fans, fireplaces, and air-conditioning. Enjoy cool drinks upon arrival and a liqueur before bed. Breakfast specialties are eggs Mornay, blueberry cobbler, and crêpes. Your host can point out the sights of this historic town and direct you to the beaches.

Catherine's Inn on Orange ✪
410 ORANGE STREET, WILMINGTON, NORTH CAROLINA 28401

Tel: **(919) 251-0863** or **(800) 476-0723**	Open: **All year**
Best Time to Call: **8 AM–10 PM**	Reduced Rates: **Available**
Host: **Catherine Walter Ackiss**	Breakfast: **Full**
Location: **In Wilmington Historical District**	Credit Cards: **MC, VISA, AMEX**
	Pets: **No**
No. of Rooms: 3	Children: **Welcome**
No. of Private Baths: 3	Smoking: **Permitted**
Double/pb: **$60**	Social Drinking: **Permitted**
Single/pb: **$50**	Airport/Station Pickup: **Yes**

An Italianate residence built by a merchant and Civil War veteran in 1875, this B&B has blue clapboard, white trim, and a white picket fence. All bedrooms have fireplaces. The grounds include a spacious garden and a small swimming pool. Guests are within walking distance of museums, historic buildings, and antique shops; beaches and golf courses are minutes away by car. Morning coffee is served in the library, followed by breakfast in the dining room.

Murchison House B&B Inn
305 SOUTH 3RD STREET, WILMINGTON, NORTH CAROLINA 28401

Tel: **(919) 343-8580**
Best Time to Call: **Before 5 PM**
Hosts: **Mr. and Mrs. Joseph Curry**
No. of Rooms: **3**
No. of Private Baths: **3**
Double/pb: **$60**
Single/pb: **$55**
Open: **All year**

Breakfast: **Full**
Credit Cards: **AMEX, MC, VISA**
Pets: **No**
Children: **Welcome**
Smoking: **Permitted**
Social Drinking: **Permitted**
Airport/Station Pickup: **Yes**

Built in 1876, Murchison House is an example of modified Victorian Gothic architecture. The back of the house faces a formal garden and courtyard. The Chippendale influence is reflected in all the interior woodwork and trim. Antiques and reproductions, along with the elegant parquet floors and the many unusual fireplaces throughout, lend charm and warmth. Feel welcome to curl up with a book in the Mission oak–paneled library. Located in the heart of the Wilmington historic district, it is within easy walking distance of shops, restaurants, churches, and the Cape Fear River.

Miss Betty's Bed & Breakfast Inn ✪
600 WEST NASH STREET, WILSON, NORTH CAROLINA 27893

Tel: **(919) 243-4447**
Hosts: **Elizabeth A. and Fred Spitz**
Location: **50 mi. E of Raleigh**
No. of Rooms: **4**
No. of Private Baths: **2**
Max. No. Sharing Bath: **4**
Double/pb: **$55**
Single/pb: **$55**
Double/sb: **$45**
Single/sb: **$45**

Suite: **$65**
Open: **All year**
Breakfast: **Continental**
Credit Cards: **MC, VISA**
Pets: **Sometimes**
Children: **Welcome**
Smoking: **Permitted**
Social Drinking: **Permitted**
Airport/Station Pickup: **Yes**

Miss Betty's bathes the business traveler and vacationer in Victorian elegance, beauty, and comfort, to offer peace and tranquillity in a warm, friendly setting. Guests in the Davis-Whitehead-Harris house (circa 1858), which is listed in the National Registry of Historic Properties, will be staying in one of Wilson's oldest homes. The Bruce W. Riley house (circa 1910), just moved to the premises, offers additional lodging. Both houses feature cable TV, phones, and central heating and air conditioning. Collectors take note: its numerous local antique shops earn Wilson the title of "antique capital of North Carolina."

Lowe-Alston House ✪

204 CASCADE AVENUE, WINSTON-SALEM, NORTH CAROLINA 27127

Tel: **(919) 727-1211**
Best Time to Call: **Afternoon**
Hosts: **Susan and Wyatt Alston**
Location: **1 mi. from Rte. 40, Exit: Broad St.**
No. of Rooms: **3**
No. of Private Baths: **1**
Max. No. Sharing Bath: **4**
Double/pb: **$60**
Single/pb: **$55**

Double/sb: **$45**
Single/sb: **$40**
Open: **All year**
Reduced Rates: **20%, weekly**
Breakfast: **Continental**
Credit Cards: **MC, VISA**
Pets: **No**
Children: **Welcome (crib)**
Smoking: **No**
Social Drinking: **Permitted**

This glistening 1911 Colonial Revival house with wraparound porch
has earned a place on the National Register of Historic Places. Oak
flooring with exquisite inlays, walnut wainscoting, fireplaces in the
bedrooms, fine quilts, and regional antiques make it special. Susan
and Wyatt are a young couple who love and appreciate old houses.
They graciously serve wine and cheese in the evening. The Old Salem
Historic District, Salem College, and the North Carolina School of the
Arts are a half mile away.

Wachovia B&B, Inc. ✪
513 WACHOVIA STREET, WINSTON-SALEM, NORTH CAROLINA 27101

Tel: **(919) 777-0332**	Single/sb: **$35**
Best Time to Call: **9 AM–5 PM**	Open: **All year**
Host: **Carol Royals**	Reduced Rates: **10%, seniors; 50%,**
Location: **½ mi. S of Winston-Salem**	**children under 12**
No. of Rooms: **5**	Breakfast: **Continental**
No. of Private Baths: **2**	Pets: **No**
Max. No. Sharing Bath: **4**	Children: **Welcome (crib)**
Double/pb: **$55**	Smoking: **No**
Single/pb: **$45**	Social Drinking: **Permitted**
Double/sb: **$45**	

This white and rose Victorian cottage, with its appealing wraparound porch, is just outside the Old Salem historic district, and antique shops, excellent restaurants, and a scenic strollway are within a one-block radius. Noted institutions like North Carolina School of the Arts and Wake Forest University are only a few miles away. This is a good area for cycling, and guests may borrow the house bicycles. Carol serves breakfasts of juice, fruit, yogurt, muesli, and baked goods she learned to make while traveling in Europe. Later in the day, she offers complimentary tea, wine, and cheese.

NORTH DAKOTA

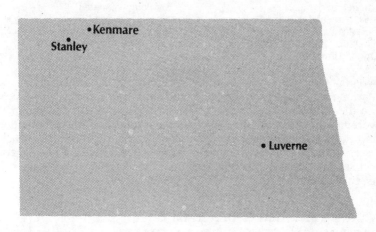

Kirkland Bed and Breakfast
RR2, BOX 18, CARRINGTON, NORTH DAKOTA 58421

Tel: **(701) 652-2775**
Hosts: **James and Maria Harmon**
Location: **3 mi. N of Carrington**
No. of Rooms: **2**
Max. No. Sharing Bath: **4**
Double/sb: **$45–$50**
Single/sb: **$40**
Suites: **$80**

Open: **All year**
Breakfast: **Full**
Other Meals: **Available**
Pets: **No**
Children: **No**
Smoking: **No**
Social Drinking: **Permitted**

Welcome to the Harmon family's farm, established in 1886 by the proprietors' great-grandparents. Enrolled in the National Register of Historic Places, Kirkland remains a working farm, producing wheat, corn, beans, and sunflowers. The Colonial Plantation–style home, which dates to 1910, has a wraparound veranda with stately columns, a large open stairway, oak woodwork, and windows of stained and leaded glass. In addition to books of collector quality, the library contains Indian artifacts accumulated by the farm founder, who found time to serve as a territorial sheriff, Indian agent, and legislator. Breakfast specialties include blueberry pancakes, deer sausage, and muffins, accompanied by real maple syrup and homemade jams.

Farm Comfort—Nelson's Bed & Breakfast
RR2, BOX 71, KENMARE, NORTH DAKOTA 58746

Tel: **(701) 848-2433**	Breakfast: **Continental**
Hosts: **Marion and Delmer Nelson**	Pets: **Yes, outside**
Location: **55 mi. NW of Minot**	Children: **Welcome**
No. of Rooms: **2**	Smoking: **Permitted**
Max. No. Sharing Bath: **4**	Social Drinking: **Permitted**
Double/sb: **$25**	Foreign Languages: **Limited Swedish**
Single/sb: **$20**	Airport/Station Pickup: **Yes**
Open: **All year**	

When not tending to guests in their spacious ranch home, Delmer and Marion raise durum and spring wheat, sunflowers, and barley. Ask to see the antique thresher and old-fashioned tractor they maintain in working order. Kenmare is just 30 miles from the Canadian border, and the woods are filled with hunters' quarry, such as goose, duck, deer, and antelope. If you prefer tamer game, there's a nearby golf course. Continental breakfasts feature homemade pastries, rolls, coffee cake, and muffins.

Volden Farm Bed & Breakfast ✪
RR 2, BOX 50, LUVERNE, NORTH DAKOTA 58056

Tel: **(701) 769-2275**	Breakfast: **Full**
Hosts: **Jim and Joanne Wold**	Other Meals: **Available**
Location: **80 mi. NW of Fargo**	Pets: **Yes (outdoors)**
No. of Rooms: **2**	Children: **Welcome**
Max. No. Sharing Bath: **4**	Smoking: **No**
Double/sb: **$40**	Social Drinking: **Permitted**
Single/sb: **$35**	Airport/Station Pickup: **Yes**
Suites: **$50**	Foreign Languages: **Russian**
Open: **All year**	
Reduced Rates: **Families taking both bedrooms**	

Jim and Joanne's weathered redwood home was built in 1926, and expanded in 1978, and is surrounded by rock gardens and plantings of every hue. One bedroom has a lace canopied bed, the other is of white iron; the bath has a view of the pasture and orchard from the old-fashioned footed tub. Attractive and comfortable, you're welcome to relax with a drink on one of the porches or in the living room conversation pit warmed by a fire on chilly nights. Browse in the library, play the piano in the music room, or play pool in the rec room. Your children will enjoy the small playhouse and yard swing. Breakfast reflects your hosts' Scandinavian heritage with Swedish pancakes or Danish ableskivers served with fresh berry syrup, Norwegian cheeses and flatbread, freshly squeezed fruit juice, and freshly ground coffee or special teas. Outdoor pleasures include hiking, bird-watching, berry picking, fishing or canoeing on the Sheyenne River, cross-country skiing, or a visit with the farm animals.

The Triple T Ranch
ROUTE 1, BOX 93, STANLEY, NORTH DAKOTA 58784

Tel: **(701) 628-2418**	Open: **All year**
Best Time to Call: **8 AM–noon**	Reduced Rates: **Available**
Hosts: **Joyce and Fred Evans**	Breakfast: **Full**
Location: **60 mi. W of Minot**	Pets: **Sometimes**
No. of Rooms: **2**	Children: **Welcome (crib)**
Max. No. Sharing Bath: **4**	Smoking: **No**
Double/sb: **$30**	Social Drinking: **No**
Single/sb: **$25**	

You're warmly invited to come to Joyce and Fred's rustic ranch home, where you're welcome to take a seat in front of the stone fireplace, put your feet up, and relax. There's a lovely view of the hills and the valley, and their herd of cattle is an impressive sight. Lake Sakakawea, for seasonal recreation such as fishing and swimming, is 11 miles away. Indian powwows, area rodeos, and hunting for Indian artifacts are fun. The State Fair is held every July.

OHIO

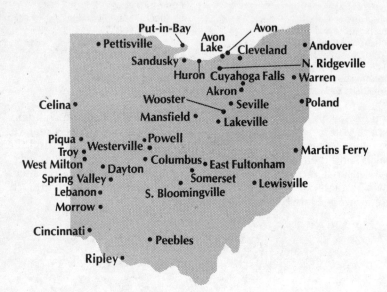

Put-in-Bay
Avon
Avon
• Pettisville
Lake
• Cleveland
• Andover
Sandusky •
N. Ridgeville
Huron Cuyahoga Falls • Warren
Akron •
Celina •
Wooster
• Seville
• Poland
Mansfield •
• Lakeville
Piqua • Powell
Troy • Westerville •
• Martins Ferry
West Milton •
• Dayton
• Columbus • East Fultonham
Spring Valley •
Somerset
Lebanon •
S. Bloomingville
• Lewisville
Morrow •
Cincinnati •
• Peebles
Ripley •

Ohio Valley Bed & Breakfast ✪
6876 TAYLOR MILL ROAD, INDEPENDENCE, KENTUCKY 41051

Tel: **(606) 356-7865**
Best Time to Call: **9 AM–6 PM,**
  Mon.–Thurs.
Coordinator: **Nancy Cully**
States/Regions Covered: **Northern**
  Kentucky; Southern Ohio,
  Cincinnati, Ohio; Southeastern
  Indiana

Rates (Single/Double):
  Modest: **$30**   **$35**
  Average: **$40**   **$50**
  Luxury: **$60**   **$110**
Credit Cards: **DISC, MC, VISA**

Convenient to the attractions of Cincinnati and Dayton, Ohio, which
include professional football and baseball, cultural activities, the Uni-

versity of Cincinnati, Xavier University, and Northern Kentucky University. Regattas and paddleboat cruises are delightful Ohio River pastimes. B&B host homes are also available in rural settings and in Metamora, Indiana, a historic town well known for its antique shops.

Helen's Hospitality House ✪
1096 PALMETTO, AKRON, OHIO 44306

Tel: (216) 724-7151; 3034	Single/sb: $25
Best Time to Call: 8 AM–8 PM	Open: All year
Host: Helen Claytor	Reduced Rates: Weekly
Location: 1 mi. from I-77 S, Exit 123B	Breakfast: Full
No. of Rooms: 2	Pets: No
No. of Private Baths: 1	Children: Welcome, over 10
Max. No. Sharing Bath: 4	Smoking: No
Double/pb: $30	Social Drinking: Permitted
Single/pb: $25	Airport/Station Pickup: Yes
Double/sb: $30	

Located in a quiet neighborhood on a dead-end street, Helen's centrally air-conditioned house is a bit of country in the city. It is a renovated old farmhouse furnished with antiques and reproductions. On warm days, breakfast is served on the screened, glass-enclosed porch. Quaker Square, Akron University, the Firestone PGA, and Portage Lakes are just a few of the local attractions. Helen is a retired teacher who enjoys being a B&B hostess.

Portage House ✪
601 COPLEY ROAD, STATE ROUTE 162, AKRON, OHIO 44320

Tel: (216) 535-1952	Single/sb: $24
Best Time to Call: 8 AM–11 PM	Open: Feb. 1–Nov. 30
Hosts: Jeanne and Harry Pinnick	Reduced Rates: $3 off after 1st night
Location: 2 mi. from I-77	Breakfast: Full
No. of Rooms: 5	Pets: Yes
No. of Private Baths: 1	Children: Welcome (crib)
Max. No. Sharing Bath: 5	Smoking: Permitted
Double/pb: $30	Social Drinking: Permitted
Single/pb: $24	Foreign Languages: French, Spanish
Double/sb: $30	

Steeped in history, nestled in a parklike setting, this gracious Tudor home dates back to 1917. There is a stone wall down the street that was the western boundary of the United States in 1785. Harry is a physics professor at the university, and Jeanne is a gracious hostess. The coffeepot is always on, refreshments are available, and if bread is being baked, you'll be given some with butter. It's close to Akron University.

Vickery's Bed & Breakfast ✪
4942 STATE ROUTE 7 NORTH, ANDOVER, OHIO 44003

Tel: **(216) 293-6875**	Open: **All year**
Hosts: **Robert and Ruth Vickery**	Breakfast: **Full**
Location: **60 mi. E of Cleveland**	Pets: **Sometimes**
No. of Rooms: **3**	Children: **Welcome**
Max. No. Sharing Bath: **4**	Smoking: **Permitted**
Double/sb: **$30**	Social Drinking: **Permitted**
Single/sb: **$25**	

Painted yellow and trimmed with white shutters, this 100-year-old home is set on 100 acres where there's something for everyone. You may play volleyball or horseshoes or take a ride on the pond in a paddleboat. If you prefer, just walk the land and breathe deeply of fresh air. The bedrooms have floral wallpaper, tie-back curtains, and antique dressers. Breakfast specialties, such as blueberry pancakes and bacon, are served in the cozy dining room. It is five minutes from Pymatuning Lake, where a spectacular spillway of fish and ducks attracts many visitors. You are welcome to use the kitchen for light snacks and the laundry to freshen your travel wardrobe.

Williams House ✪
249 VINEWOOD, AVON LAKE, OHIO 44012

Tel: **(216) 933-5089**	Open: **Closed Christmas**
Best Time to Call: **4–9 PM**	Reduced Rates: **20%, seniors**
Host: **Margaret Williams**	Breakfast: **Full**
Location: **20 mi. W of Cleveland**	Pets: **No**
No. of Rooms: **1**	Children: **No**
No. of Private Baths: **1**	Smoking: **No**
Double/pb: **$40**	Social Drinking: **Permitted**
Single/pb: **$25**	Airport/Station Pickup: **Yes**

Located a mile from the Lake Erie public beach, Margaret lives in a quiet residential neighborhood. The house is comfortably decorated in a harmonious blend of styles. She serves beverages and snacks upon your arrival, and will help you plan a pleasant visit. Breakfast is a dandy, from juice to cereal to eggs to bacon to coffee or tea.

The Frederick Fitting House ✪
72 FITTING AVENUE, BELLVILLE, OHIO 44813

Tel: **(419) 886-2863**	Double/pb: **$60**
Hosts: **Ramon and Suzanne Wilson**	Single/pb: **$50**
Location: **50 mi. N of Columbus**	Double/sb: **$50**
No. of Rooms: **3**	Single/sb: **$40**
No. of Private Baths: **1**	Open: **All year**
Max. No. Sharing Bath: **4**	Breakfast: **Full**

Other Meals: **Available**
Pets: **No**
Children: **Welcome, over 8**

Smoking: **Permitted**
Social Drinking: **No**
Airport/Station Pickup: **Yes**

Named for the prominent Bellville citizen who built it in 1863, the Frederick Fitting House is a restored Italianate home with a hand-stenciled dining room and a garden gazebo. Ramon and Suzanne are avid music buffs; you are welcome to play selections from their jazz and classical collection as you lounge by the sitting-room fire. Nearby, Mohican and Malabar Farm State Parks offer a variety of activities, from cross-country skiing to canoeing. Kingwood Garden, Amish country, and Kenyon, Wooster, and Ashland Colleges are a short drive away.

The Old McDill-Anderson Place ✪
3656 POLK HOLLOW ROAD, CHILLICOTHE, OHIO 45601

Tel: **(614) 774-1770**
Hosts: **Ruth and Del Meyer**
Location: **45 mi. S of Columbus**
No. of Rooms: **4**
No. of Private Baths: **3**
Max. No. Sharing Bath: **4**
Double/pb: **$60**
Single/pb: **$50**
Double/sb: **$50**

Single/sb: **$40**
Open: **All year**
Reduced Rates: **20%, weekly; 10%, after 3 nights**
Breakfast: **Full**
Pets: **No**
Children: **Sometimes**
Smoking: **No**
Social Drinking: **No**

This two-story 1864 brick Italianate residence was homesteaded in 1798. Your hosts pursue a variety of interests, including fine wood-working and historic preservation. They cater to their guests' needs by combining some of the bedrooms to make suites—a boon to visitors with children. Some rooms have working fireplaces or woodstoves, especially nice on chilly nights. Breakfast and snacks feature seasonal food and "from scratch" preparation. Chillicothe was Ohio's first capital. You will enjoy the early architecture and fine museums.

Berry Hill House ✪
9694 BERRY HILL DRIVE, CINCINNATI, OHIO 45241

Tel: **(513) 777-4613; 528-6751**
Best Time to Call: **9 AM–5 PM**
Hosts: **Ed and Inge Roll**
Location: **3 mi. from I-75 or I-71**
No. of Rooms: **1**
No. of Private Baths: **1**
Double/pb: **$40**
Single/pb: **$35**

Open: **All year**
Breakfast: **Full**
Pets: **Sometimes**
Children: **Welcome**
Smoking: **Permitted**
Social Drinking: **Permitted**
Airport/Station Pickup: **Yes**
Foreign Languages: **German**

When you arrive at this lovely red-brick house, be prepared for an abundance of hospitality. Ed and Inge have travelled extensively and know exactly how to make a guest's stay special. It is a short drive to the city's historic areas, cultural activities, sports attractions, and excellent dining possibilities. Kings Island, a famous golf center, is nearby.

Private Lodgings, Inc. ✪
P.O. BOX 18590, CLEVELAND, OHIO 44118

Tel: (216) 321-3213
Best Time to Call: **Weekdays 9 AM— noon; 3–5 PM**
Coordinators: **Elaine Phillips and Roberta Cahen**
States/Regions Covered: **Cleveland**

Rates (Single/Double):
   Modest: **$32**   **$40**
   Average: **$45**   **$60**
   Luxury: **$65**   **$90**
Credit Cards: **No**

This is a city with world-renowned cultural and biomedical resources, as well as major corporations and recreational areas. Special attention is given to the needs of relocating and visiting professionals, out-patients, and relatives of hospital in-patients, as well as vacationers. Every effort is made to accommodate persons with physical handicaps. Discounted rates are provided for extended stays. Case Western Reserve, John Carroll, and Cleveland State universities are convenient to the B&Bs. A $5 surcharge is made for one-night stays. Office is closed on Wednesday and Saturday.

Columbus Bed & Breakfast ✪
763 S. THIRD STREET, GERMAN VILLAGE, COLUMBUS, OHIO 43206

Tel: **(614) 443-3680; 444-8888**
Coordinator: **Howard Burns**
States/Regions Covered: **Columbus**

Rates (Single/Double):
   Average: **$45**   **$55**
Credit Cards: **No**

Historic German Village is a registered National Historic Area. It's close to downtown Columbus but a century away in character. Small brick houses, brick sidewalks and streets, and wrought-iron fences combine to create an Old World atmosphere. Charming shops and restaurants are within easy walking distance.

Studio 12 Bed and Breakfast ✪
2850 BAILEY ROAD, CUYAHOGA FALLS, OHIO 44221

Tel: **(216) 928-5843**
Host: **Edith L. Stinaff**
Location: **6 mi. N of Akron; 7 mi. from I-80**
No. of Rooms: **2**
Max. No. Sharing Bath: **4**
Double/sb: **$33**
Single/sb: **$25**

Open: **All year**
Reduced Rates: **10%, seniors; after 1 night**
Breakfast: **Full**
Pets: **Sometimes**
Children: **Welcome (crib)**
Smoking: **No**
Social Drinking: **Permitted**

Edith Stinaff offers attractive accommodations for guests in the new addition to her home, a 1930s brick bungalow. Guest quarters consist of two bedrooms on the second floor with a studio living room and bath. In the morning your host serves a hearty breakfast of scrambled eggs, fresh fruit, bacon, and warm muffins or toast. Studio 12 is convenient to the University of Akron, Kent State University, Blossom Music Center, and Hale Farm.

Prices' Steamboat House B&B ✪
6 JOSIE STREET, DAYTON, OHIO 45403

Tel: **(513) 223-2444**	Open: **All year**
Best Time to Call: **4–12 PM**	Reduced Rates: **10% after 5 nights**
Hosts: **Ron and Ruth Price**	Breakfast: **Full**
Location: **On edge of downtown Dayton**	Pets: **No**
	Children: **Welcome, over 12**
No. of Rooms: **3**	Smoking: **No**
No. of Private Baths: **3**	Social Drinking: **Permitted**
Double/pb: **$65**	Airport/Station Pickup: **Yes**
Single/pb: **$55**	

Built in 1852, this grand 22-room mansion is listed on the National Register of Historic Homes. The house is furnished with period antiques and Oriental rugs. Guests can play the piano, browse in the library, or survey Dayton's skyline from rocking chairs on the first and second-floor porches. Tours, by reservation only, cover the entire residence, ending in a formal tea. The Dayton Art Institute, the U.S. Air Force Museum, and two universities are a few minutes away. Full breakfasts feature home-baked sourdough bread or sour cream coffee cake.

Hill View Acres ✪
7320 OLD TOWN ROAD, EAST FULTONHAM, OHIO 43735

Tel: **(614) 849-2728**	Open: **All year**
Hosts: **Jim and Dawn Graham**	Breakfast: **Full**
Location: **10 mi. SW of Zanesville**	Other Meals: **Available**
No. of Rooms: **2**	Pets: **No**
Max. No. Sharing Bath: **4**	Children: **Welcome**
Double/sb: **$32**	Smoking: **Permitted**
Single/sb: **$27**	Social Drinking: **Permitted**

Hill View is a comfortable, large white house situated on 21 acres with a fishing pond. Homemade breads and delicious gourmet specialties are breakfast fare. You are welcome to relax on the deck, play the piano, or watch TV. Antique shops, potteries, the famous Y Bridge, and the *Lorena* sternwheeler are some of the area's attractions. An on-premises pool and spa add to your summer enjoyment.

Candle Wick ✪
245 E. MAIN STREET, HILLSBORO, OHIO 45133

Tel: **(513) 393-2743**	Open: **All year**
Best Time to Call: **After 6 PM**	Reduced Rates: **5%, seniors**
Hosts: **Mark and Melody Johnson**	Breakfast: **Full**
Location: **50 mi. E of Cincinnati**	Pets: **No**
No. of Rooms: **2**	Children: **Welcome**
Max. No. Sharing Bath: **4**	Smoking: **Permitted**
Double/sb: **$45**	Social Drinking: **Permitted**
Single/sb: **$40**	

Melody and Mark Johnson make this bed-and-breakfast a treat you won't want to miss. Candle Wick is a lovely Victorian home built in the Eastlake style of the 1880s. It boasts a magnificent walnut stairway and stained-glass windows. Fireplaces and functional antiques make each room cozy. Breakfast is your choice of full or continental, served with homemade breads and spreads, muffins, and fresh (seasonal) fruit. Located in the heart of historic Hillsboro, Candle Wick is within an hour's drive of Cincinnati, Columbus, Dayton, and the scenic Ohio River. You can explore quaint antique shops, play at the lakes, enjoy a quiet drive in the country, or a hike through one of the three State Parks nearby.

Captain Montague's Guest House ✪
229 CENTER STREET, HURON, OHIO 44839

Tel: **(419) 433-4756**	Breakfast: **Continental**
Hosts: **Shirley and Bob Reynolds**	Pets: **No**
Location: **54 mi. W of Cleveland**	Children: **No**
No. of Rooms: **6**	Smoking: **No**
No. of Private Baths: **6**	Social Drinking: **Permitted**
Double/pb: **$75**	Minimum Stay: **2 nights, weekends,**
Open: **Feb. 1–Dec. 15**	**Apr. 16–Sept. 30**
Reduced Rates: **$16 less, Oct. 1–Apr. 15**	Airport/Station Pickup: **Yes**

Just two blocks from the beach at Lake Erie, Shirley and Bob have turned their 1876 Southern Colonial into a lavishly appointed accommodation for travelers. The beautiful grounds boast a lattice enclosed garden with a fountain, a gazebo furnished with wicker, and an in-ground swimming pool. The interior has been comfortably furnished and decorated with Victorian accents. A vintage player piano sets the tone for relaxation while you visit in front of the living room fireplace. Take a walk on the mile-long pier, dine at a nearby restaurant, browse in local shops, or enjoy a play at Ohio's oldest summer theater.

White Tor ✪
1620 OREGONIA ROAD, LEBANON, OHIO 45036

Tel: **(513) 932-5892**	Open: **All year**
Best Time to Call: **Before 9 AM; after**	Breakfast: **Full**
6 PM	Pets: **No**
Hosts: **Eric and Margaret Johnson**	Children: **Welcome (crib)**
Location: **25 mi. N of Cincinnati**	Smoking: **No**
No. of Rooms: **1 Suite**	Social Drinking: **Permitted**
No. of Private Baths: **1**	Foreign Languages: **French**
Double/pb: **$50**	

Just a half hour's drive from both Cincinnati and Dayton, this handsome farmhouse, built in 1862, crowns a hilltop on seven wooded acres. Margaret's full English breakfast will give you stamina for a day of antique shopping or viewing artful stitchery at local quilt shows. Area attractions range from Kings Island and the Beach Waterpark to the Honey and Sauerkraut Festivals. Or, simply relax on the porch in view of the pretty Miami Valley, with a good book and cold drink.

Happy Hill ✪
1 LEXINGTON-ONTARIO ROAD, ROUTE 8, MANSFIELD, OHIO 44904

Tel: **(419) 884-3916**	Double/sb: **$55**
Host: **Sam Masur**	Single/sb: **$40**
Location: **4 mi. from I-71, Exit Rte. 13**	Open: **All year**
No. of Rooms: **3**	Breakfast: **Continental**
No. of Private Baths: **2**	Pets: **Sometimes**
Max. No. Sharing Bath: **4**	Children: **Welcome (crib)**
Double/pb: **$60**	Smoking: **Permitted**
Single/pb: **$45**	Social Drinking: **Permitted**

This sprawling brick ranch home is set on six acres in the picturesque village of Lexington. The rooms are elegantly appointed with antiques. After a day at the local racetrack, come home for a swim in a huge private swimming pool. In winter, enjoy a hot drink in front of the fire after a day on the ski slopes. Your host grows berries on the grounds, and you can taste them in the Blueberry Buckel, the breakfast specialty of the house.

Mulberry Inn ✪
53 NORTH FOURTH STREET, MARTINS FERRY, OHIO 43935

Tel: **(614) 633-6058**	Reduced Rates: **Jan.–Mar.; after 4**
Host: **Shirley Probst**	**nights; 5%, seniors**
Location: **5 mi. W of Wheeling, W.Va.**	Breakfast: **Full**
No. of Rooms: **3**	Pets: **No**
Max. No. Sharing Bath: **5**	Children: **Welcome, over 12**
Double/sb: **$35**	Smoking: **Permitted**
Single/sb: **$25**	Social Drinking: **Permitted**
Open: **All year**	

Built in 1868, this frame Victorian is on a tree-lined street within walking distance of a Civil War cemetery and the Sedgwick Museum. (Martins Ferry is the oldest settlement in Ohio.) Beautiful woodwork, antiques, and mantels grace the large rooms, and air-conditioning cools the house in summer. A retired medical secretary, Shirley devotes her time to making her guests feel comfortable and welcome, tempting them with her unusual French toast recipe. Dog races, recreational activities, the Fostoria Glass Outlet, the Jamboree-in-the-Hills, Ohio University, and Bethany College are less than 10 miles away.

Country Manor ✪
6315 ZOAR ROAD, MORROW, OHIO 45152

Tel: **(513) 899-2440**	Single/sb: **$35**
Host: **Rhea Hughes**	Open: **All year**
Location: **33 mi. NE of Cincinnati**	Reduced Rates: **10%, after 2 nights**
No. of Rooms: **3**	Breakfast: **Full**
No. of Private Baths: **1**	Pets: **Sometimes**
Max. No. Sharing Bath: **4**	Children: **Welcome, over 12**
Double/pb: **$55**	Smoking: **No**
Single/pb: **$45**	Social Drinking: **Permitted**
Double/sb: **$45**	Airport/Station Pickup: **Yes**

This beautifully restored 1868 home is nestled on 55 acres of rolling hills that overlook the Little Miami River Valley. Centrally air-conditioned, each large cheery bedroom includes a color TV for your private enjoyment. You'll awaken to the aroma of freshly brewed coffee, the preamble to fresh fruits, breads warm from the oven, and delightful breakfast entrées. Afterwards, walk in the woods, fish in the pond, or help feed the horses down at the barn. When the temperature soars, swing on the front porch and sip a cold lemonade. On cool evenings, a crackling fire awaits in the family room. Nearby attractions include Kings Island Amusement Park, antique shops, canoeing, and hiking the 13 miles of wildlife trails.

St. George House ✪
33941 LORAIN ROAD, NORTH RIDGEVILLE, OHIO 44039

Tel: **(216) 327-9354**	Double/sb: **$35**
Best Time to Call: **Early morning; evenings until 9 PM**	Single/sb: **$30**
	Open: **All year**
Hosts: **Helen Bernardine and Muriel Dodd**	Reduced Rates: **Weekly**
	Breakfast: **Continental**
Location: **30 mi. W of Cleveland**	Pets: **Sometimes**
No. of Rooms: **4**	Children: **Welcome, over 12**
No. of Private Baths: **1**	Smoking: **Permitted**
Max. No. Sharing Bath: **5**	Social Drinking: **Permitted**
Double/pb: **$40**	Airport/Station Pickup: **Yes**
Single/pb: **$37**	Minimum stay: **2 nights**

This Colonial gray house, with its bright red shutters, is decorated with furnishings artfully restored by Helen and Muriel. The surrounding property includes barns, a bird sanctuary, and a pond that is home to a variety of wild ducks and frogs. The game room is the evening gathering place and your hosts will gladly join in the fun. Within 35 miles are Case Western Reserve and John Carroll universities, and the famed Cleveland Clinic. Oberlin College is 10 miles away. Closer by are the clean beaches of Lake Erie, a zoo, and a variety of theaters.

The Bayberry Inn ✪
25675 STATE ROUTE 41 NORTH, PEEBLES, OHIO 45660

Tel: (513) 587-2221	Open: May 15–Oct. 15
Hosts: Marilyn and Larry Bagford	Breakfast: Full
Location: 75 mi. E of Cincinnati	Pets: No
No. of Rooms: 3	Children: Welcome
Max. No. Sharing Bath: 5	Smoking: No
Double/sb: $35	Social Drinking: No
Single/sb: $25	

If you expect to find warm hospitality, cozy accommodations with comfortable appointments, and a front porch on which to relax after a hearty old-fashioned breakfast, you won't be disappointed in Marilyn and Larry's Victorian farmhouse. It's located in Adams County, the hub for those with geological, historical, recreational, and agricultural interests. You are certain to enjoy visiting Serpent Mound, museums, natural wildlife areas, and herb gardens.

Tudor Country Inn ✪
BOX 113, PETTISVILLE, OHIO 43553

Tel: (419) 445-2531	Single/sb: $40
Best Time to Call: 8:30 AM–9 PM	Open: All year
Hosts: LeAnna and Dale Gautsche	Breakfast: Full
Location: 30 mi. W of Toledo; 5 mi. from Ohio Tpk.	Pets: No
	Children: Welcome
No. of Rooms: 2	Smoking: No
Max. No. Sharing Bath: 4	Social Drinking: No
Double/sb: $45	

LeAnna and Dale were restaurant owners until they opened this English Tudor inn. It is set on the edge of a small village, surrounded by farmland in the heart of the Mennonite community. Besides soaking in the hot tub, you may lounge in the great room, where snacks are served in the evenings and a fire burns in winter. Breakfast often includes "Belly Stickers," a creamy-bottom tart, and homemade raised donuts. Local attractions include a farm and craft village, a country store, and an ice-cream parlor and restaurant, all in the Pennsylvania Dutch style.

The Pickwinn ✪
707 NORTH DOWNING STREET, PIQUA, OHIO 45356

Tel: **(513) 773-8877**	Single/sb: **$40**
Hosts: **Rosemary and Paul Gutmann**	Open: **Mar. 1–Oct. 31; other times by**
Location: **25 mi. N of Dayton**	**arrangement**
No. of Rooms: **4**	Breakfast: **Full**
No. of Private Baths: **1**	Pets: **Sometimes**
Max. No. Sharing Bath: **4**	Children: **Welcome**
Double/pb: **$60**	Smoking: **Permitted**
Single/pb: **$50**	Social Drinking: **Permitted**
Double/sb: **$50**	

A brick Second Empire house built in 1883 and lovingly restored 105 years later, this B&B is listed on the National Register of Historic Places. The Pickwinn is beautifully furnished with antique English pine and wicker, and Oriental rugs. North Downing Street is in the middle of the Caldwell Historic District; another local landmark is the Johnston Farm and Indian Museum, which operates a canal boat along part of the Miami and Erie Canal route. You'll have plenty of energy for sightseeing. Your hosts, who live in the house next door, prepare full breakfasts of juice, fruit, eggs, meat, toast, pastry, and coffee.

Inn at the Green ✪
500 SOUTH MAIN STREET, POLAND, OHIO 44514

Tel: **(216) 757-4688**	Single/sb: **$35**
Best Time to Call: **After 12 PM**	Open: **All year**
Hosts: **Ginny and Steve Meloy**	Breakfast: **Continental**
Location: **7 mi. SE of Youngstown**	Other Meals: **No**
No. of Rooms: **4**	Credit Cards: **MC, VISA**
No. of Private Baths: **2**	Pets: **No**
Max. No. Sharing Bath: **4**	Children: **Welcome, over 10**
Double/pb: **$50**	Smoking: **Permitted**
Single/pb: **$45**	Social Drinking: **Permitted**
Double/sb: **$40**	

The Inn at the Green is an 1876 Victorian town house located on the south end of the village green. The rooms have the grandeur of bygone days, with original moldings, 12-foot-high ceilings, and original poplar floors. There are five Italian marble fireplaces and extensive public rooms furnished with gracious antiques. Guests are welcome to relax in the parlor, sitting room, and library. Sleeping quarters are air-conditioned, and are furnished with poster beds, Sealy Posturepedic mattresses, and antiques. Coffee, croissants, muffins, and French jam are served in the greeting room in winter and on the wicker-furnished porch during moderate weather. Enjoy a glass of sherry on the porch overlooking the garden before dinner. Your hosts will gladly direct you to gourmet dining as well as cross-country ski trails, golf, tennis, and the Butler Institute, home of one of the nation's finest American art collections.

Riverlea
10474 RIVERSIDE DRIVE, POWELL, OHIO 43065

Tel: **(614) 889-0472**	Suites: **$65**
Best Time to Call: **9 AM–6 PM**	Open: **All year**
Hosts: **Nancy and Bud Savage**	Breakfast: **Full**
Location: **16 mi. NW of Columbus**	Pets: **No**
No. of Rooms: **2**	Children: **Welcome, under 1 year;**
No. of Private Baths: **2**	**over 16**
Double/pb: **$50**	Smoking: **Permitted**
Single/pb: **$45**	Social Drinking: **Permitted**

This rustic hillside ranch-style house commands a panoramic view of the Scioto River, where beauty abounds in all seasons. The light, airy rooms are furnished with a decorator's eye for color, comfort, and harmony. The bountiful breakfast features home-baked breads, home-made jams, fresh fruit, and treats such as waffles or pancakes. Nancy and Bud generously offer the use of their fishing dock, refrigerator, gas grill, picnic table, and washer and dryer. The Columbus Zoo, the Muirfield Golf Course, and Ohio State and Ohio Wesleyan Universities are all nearby.

The Vineyard ✪
BOX 283, PUT-IN-BAY, OHIO 43456

Tel: **(419) 285-6181**	Single/sb: **$60**
Hosts: **Barbi and Mark Barnhill**	Open: **All year**
Location: **An island 35 mi. E of Toledo**	Breakfast: **Full**
No. of Rooms: **3**	Pets: **Sometimes**
No. of Private Baths: **1**	Children: **No**
Max. No. Sharing Bath: **4**	Smoking: **No**
Double/pb: **$75**	Social Drinking: **Permitted**
Double/sb: **$60**	Airport/Station Pickup: **Yes**

This 130-year-old wood frame house is set on 20 acres of island seclusion. Your hosts grow Catawba grapes for the local winery, which is part of the region's famous wine industry. Guests are greeted with wine and cheese and shown to newly renovated bedrooms furnished with family antiques. You are invited to sun and swim on a private beach after a day of touring. Local attractions include a picturesque harbor, a monument offering a view of Lake Erie's islands, and a unique Victorian village featuring excellent restaurants.

The Signal House ✪
234 NORTH FRONT STREET, RIPLEY, OHIO 45167

Tel: **(513) 392-1640**
Best Time to Call: **Mornings**
Hosts: **Vic and Betsy Billingsley**
Location: **55 mi. E of Cincinnati**
No. of Rooms: **2**
Max. No. Sharing Bath: **4**
Double/sb: **$58–$68**

Open: **All year**
Breakfast: **Continental**
Pets: **No**
Children: **No**
Smoking: **Permitted**
Social Drinking: **Permitted**
Airport/Station Pickup: **Yes**

Before the Civil War, the abolitionist who lived in Signal House hung a lantern from an attic window to tell runaway slaves that the coast was clear. Today this Greek Italianate house is one of the notable sights in Ripley's 55-acre historical district. From the building's three porches, you can watch paddlewheel boats steam up the Ohio River. Ripley boasts several excellent antique shops; in August, the town holds an old-fashioned tobacco festival complete with beauty pageants, a husband-calling competition, and an ugliest-dog contest. Thirteen miles east, Moyer's Winery pleases palates with inexpensive vintages and excellent meals. You'll also savor Betsy's breakfasts of egg-and-cheese strata and homemade breads and jams.

The Big Oak ✪
2501 SOUTH CAMPBELL STREET, SANDUSKY, OHIO 44870

Tel: **(419) 627-0329, 626-6821**
Hosts: **Jim and Jeanne Ryan**
Location: **60 mi. W of Cleveland**
No. of Rooms: **3**
Max. No. Sharing Bath: **3**
Double/sb: **$40–$50**
Single/sb: **$35–$40**

Open: **All year**
Breakfast: **Full**
Credit Cards: **MC, VISA**
Pets: **No**
Children: **Welcome**
Smoking: **No**
Social Drinking: **Permitted**

An 1879 Victorian farmhouse painstakingly restored in 1962, the Big Oak is furnished with antiques and family heirlooms. Extras include a beverage upon arrival—savor it, weather permitting, on the large patio—and a great family room, where you can read and relax by the warmth of the Franklin stove. Jim manufactures concrete lawn statuary while Jeanne owns a craft store. They will happily provide you with tips on the best dining and entertainment Sandusky has to offer.

Pipe Creek Bed and Breakfast ✪
2719 COLUMBUS AVENUE, SANDUSKY, OHIO 44870

Tel: **(419) 626-2067**
Hosts: **Beryl and Carl Dureck**
No. of Rooms: **3**
Max. No. Sharing Bath: **4**

Double/sb: **$40**
Single/sb: **$35**
Open: **All year**
Breakfast: **Full**

Pets: **No**
Children: **Welcome**

Smoking: **No**
Social Drinking: **Permitted**

Set far back from the street, on a tree-shaded acre, this Queen Anne–style home hasn't changed much since it was built in the 1880s. A private entrance leads to the guest rooms, which are decorated with period antiques. To see more old-fashioned buildings and furniture, take the twenty-minute drive to Milan, which has charming shops and museums. Cedar Point Amusement Park and Lake Erie Vacationland are even closer.

Wagner's 1844 Inn ✪
230 EAST WASHINGTON STREET, SANDUSKY, OHIO 44870

Tel: **(419) 626-1726**	Reduced Rates: **Oct.–Apr.**
Hosts: **Walt and Barb Wagner**	Breakfast: **Continental**
Location: **8 mi. from Ohio Tpke, Exit 7**	Credit Cards: **MC, VISA**
No. of Rooms: **3**	Pets: **Sometimes**
No. of Private Baths: **3**	Children: **No**
Double/pb: **$65**	Smoking: **Permitted**
Single/pb: **$50**	Social Drinking: **Permitted**
Open: **All year**	Airport/Station Pickup: **Yes**

This elegantly restored Italianate home, built in 1844, is listed on the National Register of Historic Places. The warm interior features old-fashioned amenities like a billiard room, an antique piano, and a woodburning fireplace. The screened porch and enclosed courtyard provide tranquil settings for conversation with your hosts Walt, an attorney, and Barb, a registered nurse. Within easy walking distance are parks, tennis courts, antique shops, art galleries, and ferries to Cedar Point Amusement Park and the Lake Erie Islands.

Colonial Manor ✪
6075 BUFFHAM ROAD, SEVILLE, OHIO 44273

Tel: **(216) 769-3464**	Single/sb: **$30**
Best Time to Call: **8 AM; after 5 PM**	Open: **May–Nov. 1**
Hosts: **Jane and Herman Perry**	Breakfast: **Full**
Location: **15 mi. W of Akron**	Pets: **Welcome**
No. of Rooms: **2**	Children: **Welcome**
Max. No. Sharing Bath: **4**	Smoking: **Permitted**
Double/sb: **$35**	Social Drinking: **Permitted**

Spend the night in a comfortable room away from noisy highways. There are 63 acres of farmland to wander and an endless amount of fresh air to breathe. Your hosts enjoy entertaining in their 100-year-old Colonial, and serve specialties of the house for breakfast each morning. The manor is close to the Amish country, several historical sights, and small towns.

Somer Tea B&B ✪
200 SOUTH COLUMBUS STREET, BOX 308, SOMERSET, OHIO 43783

Tel: **(614) 743-2909**	Open: **All year**
Hosts: **Richard and Mary Lou Murray**	Breakfast: **Full**
Location: **40 mi. SE of Columbus**	Pets: **Welcome**
No. of Rooms: **2**	Children: **Welcome**
Max. No. Sharing Bath: **4**	Smoking: **Permitted**
Double/sb: **$30**	Social Drinking: **Permitted**
Single/sb: **$25**	

Somerset was the boyhood home of the Civil War general Phil Sheridan. Two of his nieces lived in the Somer Tea, a stately brick residence listed on the National Register of Historic Places. And yes, tea is always available here; guests are encouraged to sit with a cup on the porch swing. Ask Mary Lou to show you her collection of more than 225 teapots. If you'd like to do some collecting yourself, she'll direct you to the region's numerous antique shops and craft stores. Full country breakfasts, with an egg casserole, a fruit dish, home fries, and raisin bran muffins, are served in the elegant dining room.

Deep Woods ✪
24830 STATE ROUTE 56, SOUTH BLOOMINGVILLE, OHIO 43152

Tel: **(614) 332-6084**	Open: **All year**
Best Time to Call: **Evenings**	Reduced Rates: **15%, weekly**
Hosts: **John and Barbara Holt**	Breakfast: **Full**
Location: **60 mi. SE of Columbus**	Pets: **No**
No. of Rooms: **2**	Children: **Welcome**
Max. No. Sharing Bath: **4**	Smoking: **Permitted**
Double/sb: **$35**	Social Drinking: **Permitted**
Single/sb: **$30**	

Set on a hillside and surrounded by trees, this log house is a rustic retreat, with simple but comfortable furnishings. Spelunkers take note: Ash Cave is only two miles away. A typical morning meal at Deep Woods may include fresh local fruit, French breakfast puffs, and yogurt muffins.

3 B's Bed 'n' Breakfast ✪
103 RACE STREET, SPRING VALLEY, OHIO 45370

Tel: **(513) 862-4241; 862-4278**	Double/sb: **$38–$42**
Best Time to Call: **Noon; after 5 PM**	Single/sb: **$30–$35**
Hosts: **Pat and Herb Boettcher**	Open: **All year**
Location: **16 mi. SE of Dayton**	Reduced Rates: **15%, weekly**
No. of Rooms: **5**	Breakfast: **Full**
Max. No. Sharing Bath: **4**	Other Meals: **Available**

Pets: **Sometimes**
Children: **Welcome, over 4**
Smoking: **Permitted**

Social Drinking: **Permitted**
Airport/Station Pickup: **Yes**

This restored 19th-century farmhouse and adjacent Victorian home are combined to make one very special B&B. The rooms are spacious and airy, and abound with family heirlooms and homemade crafts. The quilts on the beds are handmade. Nearby attractions include historic Lebanon, Kings Island, Dayton's Air Force Museum, and the antique shops at Waynesville. Pat and Herb are retired from the Air Force and look forward to visiting with you. Wright State University, Antioch, and Cedarville colleges are nearby.

Allen Villa B&B ✪
434 SOUTH MARKET STREET, TROY, OHIO 45373

Tel: **(513) 335-1181**
Best Time to Call: **9 AM–9 PM**
Hosts: **Robert and June Smith**
Location: **20 mi. N of Dayton**
No. of Rooms: **4**
No. of Private Baths: **4**
Double/pb: **$60**
Single/pb: **$40**
Open: **All year**

Reduced Rates: **After 3 nights**
Breakfast: **Full**
Credit Cards: **AMEX, MC, VISA**
Pets: **No**
Children: **Welcome, over 12**
Smoking: **Permitted**
Social Drinking: **Permitted**
Airport/Station Pickup: **Yes**

After painstakingly restoring this Victorian mansion, built in 1874, the Smiths furnished it with the antiques they collect as a hobby. The wooden Venetian blinds, walnut trim, and decorative stencils are all original to the house. This is a good neighborhood for strolling. Other local attractions include a public golf course, Stillwater Vineyards, and Brukner Nature Center. Full breakfasts feature such specialties as vegetable omeletts and French toast. You are welcome to use the snack bar with its refrigerator, ice maker, and microwave.

Shirlee's Chambers ✪
535 ADELAIDE NORTH EAST, WARREN, OHIO 44483

Tel: **(216) 372-1118**	Open: **All year**
Hosts: **Shirlee and Wayne Chambers**	Breakfast: **Full**
Location: **7 mi. from I-80**	Pets: **No**
No. of Rooms: **3**	Children: **Welcome, over 10**
Max. No. Sharing Bath: **3**	Smoking: **Permitted**
Double/sb: **$37**	Social Drinking: **Permitted**
Single/sb: **$30**	Airport/Station Pickup: **Yes**

Shirlee welcomes you to her Colonial home with wine, cheese, or tea and cookies. Her guest rooms are comfortably furnished. Start the day with a French mushroom omelet, the specialty of the house. Your hosts can direct you to the many nearby antique shops. Local attractions include summer theater and fine dining. Lake Erie is an hour's drive.

Locust Lane Farm ✪
5590 KESSLER COWLESVILLE ROAD, WEST MILTON, OHIO 45383

Tel: **(513) 698-4743**	Single/pb: **$40**
Best Time to Call: **Early morning; late evening**	Double/sb: **$40**
	Single/sb: **$35**
Host: **Ruth Shoup**	Open: **All year**
Location: **7 mi. SW of Troy**	Breakfast: **Full**
No. of Rooms: **2**	Pets: **No**
No. of Private Baths: **1**	Children: **Welcome (high chair)**
Max. No. Sharing Bath: **4**	Smoking: **No**
Double/pb: **$45**	Social Drinking: **Permitted**

Enjoy a peaceful night in a big old farmhouse, tucked away in a locust grove, set on 58 acres in the country. This air-conditioned house is tastefully decorated with family antiques. Your host offers fluffy bath towels, extra pillows, and goodies such as hot spiced cider, quick breads, and iced tea in the afternoon. Ruth loves entertaining and serves a farm-style breakfast of fresh fruit, muffins, eggs, homemade breads, and sweet rolls. In the warmer weather, breakfast is served on a lovely screened-in porch. Locust Lane is convenient to Milton and Troy, and four restaurants are located within two miles.

Priscilla's Bed & Breakfast ✪
5 SOUTH WEST STREET, WESTERVILLE, OHIO 43081

Tel: **(614) 882-3910**	Max. No. Sharing Bath: **3**
Best Time to Call: **10 AM–5 PM**	Double/sb: **$40**
Host: **Priscilla H. Curtis**	Single/sb: **$35**
Location: **2 mi. N of Columbus**	Open: **All year**
No. of Rooms: **2**	Breakfast: **Continental**

Pets: **No**
Children: **Welcome**
Smoking: **Permitted**

Social Drinking: **Permitted**
Airport/Station Pickup: **Yes**

Located in a historic area adjacent to Otterbein Campus, this 1854 home, surrounded by a white picket fence, abounds with antiques and collectibles. Guests are welcome to borrow bicycles, use the patio, enjoy concerts in the adjoining park, walk to the Benjamin Hanby Museum or the quaint shops, or just stay "home" and relax. Priscilla is an authority on miniatures and dollhouse construction. Everyone enjoys browsing through her on-premises shop.

The Howey House
340 NORTH BEVER STREET, WOOSTER, OHIO 44691

Tel: **(216) 264-8231**
Hosts: **James and Jo Howey**
Location: **60 mi. S of Cleveland**
No. of Rooms: **4**
No. of Private Baths: **1**
Max. No. Sharing Bath: **6**
Double/sb: **$34**
Single/sb: **$24**

Suites: **$45**
Open: **All year**
Breakfast: **Continental**
Pets: **No**
Children: **Welcome, over 12**
Smoking: **No**
Social Drinking: **Permitted**

This 139-year-old Victorian Gothic Revival home is located on Route 30 between Canton and Mansfield. The house has been recently restored, and each room is furnished with comfortable family pieces. Your hosts offer an assortment of pastries, fruit juice, fresh fruit, and freshly brewed coffee for breakfast. Howey House is located near the College of Wooster, the Ohio Agricultural Research and Development Center, and the Amish Country. Several fine restaurants and downtown Wooster are within walking distance.

OKLAHOMA

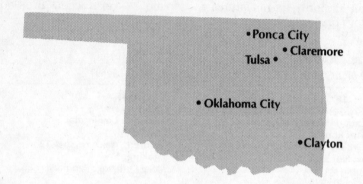

- •Ponca City
- • Claremore
- Tulsa •
- • Oklahoma City
- •Clayton

Country Inn ✪
ROUTE 3, BOX 1925, CLAREMORE, OKLAHOMA 74017

Tel: **(918) 342-1894**
Best Time to Call: **2–10 PM**
Hosts: **Leland and Kay Jenkins**
Location: **25 mi. NE of Tulsa**
No. of Rooms: **2**
No. of Private Baths: **2**
Double/pb: **$35**
Single/pb: **$30**

Open: **All year**
Reduced Rates: **15%, seniors**
Breakfast: **Continental**
Pets: **Sometimes**
Children: **No**
Smoking: **No**
Social Drinking: **Permitted**

Leland and Kay look forward to making you feel right at home in the charming barn-style guest quarters, separate from the main house. They invite you to enjoy the swimming pool, improve your suntan, or just sit back in the shade and enjoy a cool drink. A gift shop featuring handcrafted quilts is on premises. The Will Rogers Memorial, the J. M. Davis Gun Museum, the 29,500-acre Oologah Lake, and Oral Roberts University are close by. Horse racing buffs will enjoy parimutuel betting at Will Rogers Downs during August and September.

Clayton Country Inn ✪
ROUTE 1, BOX 8, HIGHWAY 271, CLAYTON, OKLAHOMA 74536

Tel: **(918) 569-4165; 627-1956**	Guest Cottage: **$32–$50; sleeps 5**
Best Time to Call: **7 AM–10 PM**	Open: **All year**
Hosts: **Betty Lundgren and Melody**	Breakfast: **Continental**
and Paul Payne	Other Meals: **Available**
Location: **140 mi. SE of Tulsa**	Credit Cards: **MC, VISA**
No. of Rooms: **11**	Pets: **No**
No. of Private Baths: **11**	Children: **Welcome**
Double/pb: **$35**	Smoking: **Permitted**
Single/pb: **$29**	Social Drinking: **Permitted**

Perched on a hill amid 140 acres and surrounded by the Kiamichi Mountains is this 42-year-old, two-story, stone and wood inn. It's furnished in a simple, traditional style with a beamed ceiling and fireplace. The restaurant on-premises is noted for its fine cooking. Bass fishing at Lake Sardis is two miles away, and an 18,000-acre game preserve is just across the highway. Feel free to bring your horse and enjoy trail rides under the vast western skies.

The Grandison ✪
1841 NORTHWEST FIFTEENTH STREET, OKLAHOMA CITY, OKLAHOMA 73106

Tel: **(405) 521-0011**	Breakfast: **Continental**
Hosts: **Claudia and Bob Wright**	Other Meals: **Available**
Location: **2 mi. off I-44, Tenth St. exit**	Credit Cards: **VISA**
No. of Rooms: **5**	Pets: **Sometimes**
No. of Private Baths: **5**	Children: **Welcome, over 12**
Double/pb: **$40–$65**	Smoking: **Permitted**
Suites: **$90**	Social Drinking: **Permitted**
Open: **All year**	Airport/Station Pickup: **Yes**

Named for its first owner and resident, Grandison Crawford, this turn-of-the-century brick Colonial was expanded in 1919, and again in the 1930s. It is furnished with antiques from many eras, so each bedroom has a distinctive look. The closest attractions—Civic Center Music Hall, the Convention Center, and Oklahoma City's fairgrounds—are just five minutes away. Breakfast consists of coffee, juice, fresh fruit, and home-baked muffins, biscuits, or pastries. For snacking, you'll find fruit, nuts, cookies, and mints in your bedroom.

Davarnathey Inn ✪
1001 WEST GRAND, PONCA CITY, OKLAHOMA 74601

Tel: **(405) 765-9922**
Hosts: **David and Shirley Zimmerman**
Location: **80 mi. S of Witchita, Kansas**
No. of Rooms: **3**
No. of Private Baths: **3**
Double/pb: **$55**
Single/pb: **$45**
Open: **All year**

Breakfast: **Full**
Credit Cards: **MC, VISA**
Pets: **No**
Children: **Welcome**
Smoking: **No**
Social Drinking: **Permitted**
Airport/Station Pickup: **Yes**

Built in 1906 by an Oklahoma oilman, Davernathey Inn has its original fretwork stairway, ornate mirrored mantel, and stained-glass windows. Period furnishings and floral wallpapers sustain the Victorian mood. Guests are encouraged to browse in the library; the musically inclined have both a piano and an organ to play. Other amenities include a hot tub and a pool. Snacks are served, but after a full breakfast of fresh baked Scandinavian breads, fruit crêpes, soufflés, and quiche, it may be a while before you're hungry again.

Robin's Nest Bed & Breakfast ✪
1700A UTICA SQUARE, SUITE 250, TULSA, OKLAHOMA 74114

Tel: **(918) 446-8700**
Hosts: **Dale and Robin Pressnall**
No. of Rooms: **2**
No. of Private Baths: **2**
Suites: **$65–$90**
Open: **All year**
Reduced Rates: **10%, seniors**

Breakfast: **Full**
Pets: **Sometimes**
Children: **Welcome, over 12**
Smoking: **No**
Social Drinking: **Permitted**
Airport/Station Pickup: **Yes**

Built in 1987, this five-level hillside home is located on a woodsy cul-de-sac overlooking a 600-acre forest. Furnished in Queen Anne style, it features 10-foot-high ceilings with crown moldings, a fireplace, and a grand piano in the living room. Both the guest rooms have sitting areas, cable TV, private telephones, and a fine view of the Tulsa skyline. Chocolates, fresh flowers, and homemade dessert highlight each evening.

Sunrise Bed and Breakfast ✪
4510 EAST 32ND PLACE, TULSA, OKLAHOMA 74135

Tel: **(918) 743-4234**
Best Time to Call: **Before 8 AM; after 5 PM**
Host: **Sue Sark**
Location: **4 mi. from I-244**
No. of Rooms: **1**
No. of Private Baths: **1**
Double/pb: **$35**

Single/pb: **$25**
Open: **Jan. 15–Nov. 15**
Breakfast: **Continental**
Pets: **No**
Children: **No**
Smoking: **Permitted**
Social Drinking: **Permitted**

Sunrise Bed and Breakfast is a comfortable ranch-style home, minutes from downtown Tulsa. The atmosphere is clean, homey, and relaxed. In the morning, enjoy Sue's coffee and homemade cinnamon rolls. The Sarks will gladly direct you to the nearby Philbrook and Gilcrease museums and Oral Roberts University, as well as to places to shop and dine.

OREGON

Seaside •
Portland
Newberg • • Oregon City   La Grande •
Coburg •   • Welches
Corvallis •   • Stayton
Junction City • •   Leaburg
Elmira • • Eugene   • Bend
North Bend •
Coos Bay •   • Oakland

Port Orford •

Gold Beach • • Rogue River
                      • Ashland
Brookings •
          Grants Pass

Northwest Bed and Breakfast Travel Unlimited
610 SW BROADWAY, SUITE 606, PORTLAND, OREGON 97205

Tel: (503) 243-7616
Coordinators: **Laine Friedman and Gloria Shaich**
States/Regions Covered: **California, Hawaii, Idaho, Oregon, Washington; Canada—British Columbia**

Rates (Single/Double):
Modest: **$30–$35 $35–$40**
Average: **$40–$45 $45–$50**
Luxury: **$50–$85 $60–$96**
Credit Cards: **No**
Descriptive Directory: **$9.50**

Laine and Gloria have a network established in 1979 of hundreds of host homes throughout the Pacific Northwest and Canada. They charge an annual membership fee of $25. Upon joining, you will receive a directory of all the lodgings, which range from city to suburban to rural to coast, mountains, and desert. There is just a $10 processing fee for those who will only use the service once; no fee to members.

458

Chanticleer
120 GRESHAM STREET, ASHLAND, OREGON 97520

Tel: (503) 482-1919
Hosts: Jim and Nancy Beaver
Location: 2 mi. from I-5, Exit 14
No. of Rooms: 7
No. of Private Baths: 7
Double/pb: $75–$110
Suites: $125–$140

Open: All year
Breakfast: Full
Pets: No
Children: Welcome, over 12
Smoking: No
Social Drinking: Permitted
Airport/Station Pickup: Yes

The Chanticleer overlooks Bear Creek Valley and the Cascade foothills. A large living room with a stone fireplace, a sunny patio, and French country furnishings create a comfortable atmosphere. Guests are welcome to juices, coffee, and sherry. Some of the specialty breakfast items include Italian-roast coffee, blintzes, and cheese-baked eggs. Shops, restaurants, and the site of the Shakespeare Festival are a short walk away. Mount Ashland ski area and the Rogue River are a 30-minute drive from the house. Southern Oregon State College is nearby.

Mt. Ashland Inn ✪
550 MT. ASHLAND ROAD, P.O. BOX 944, ASHLAND, OREGON 97520

Tel: (503) 482-8707
Best Time to Call: 11 AM–7 PM
Hosts: Elaine and Jerry Shanafelt
Location: 6 mi. from I-5, Exit 5
No. of Rooms: 5
No. of Private Baths: 5
Double/pb: $60–$85
Single/pb: $55–$75

Open: All year
Breakfast: Full
Other Meals: Dinner available Nov.–
    Apr. Only
Pets: No
Children: Welcome, over 10
Smoking: No
Social Drinking: Permitted

Nestled among tall evergreens, this beautifully handcrafted log structure is situated on a mountain ridge with views of the Cascade Mountains, including majestic Mt. Shasta. Inside, handcarvings, Oriental rugs, homemade quilts, antiques, and finely crafted furniture provide an atmosphere of comfort and elegance. Breakfasts are hearty to satisfy the appetites of skiers and hikers who take advantage of nearby trails. For quiet relaxation, you are welcome to enjoy the sunny deck or curl up with a book by the large stone fireplace.

Neil Creek House ✪
341 MOWETZA DRIVE, ASHLAND, OREGON 97520

Tel: (503) 482-1334, Fax (503) 482-
    4253
Best Time to Call: After 10 AM
Hosts: Edith and Thomas Heumann

No. of Rooms: 2
No. of Private Baths: 2
Double/pb: $90
Single/pb: $85

Open: **All year**
Reduced Rates: **10%, weekly; $10
    less, Nov.–Feb.**
Breakfast: **Full**
Pets: **No**

Children: **No**
Smoking: **No**
Social Drinking: **Permitted**
Foreign Languages: **French, German**

This country house is set on five wooded acres with a duck pond and creek for boating. Guests are welcome to relax by the swimming pool or on the decks. Breakfast treats may include homemade jams and syrups, ranch eggs, sausage, bacon, or ebelskivers. The guest rooms overlook the creek or mountains, and are furnished with antiques and 19th-century art. Skiing, sailing, river rafting, and Shakespeare performances are nearby.

Royal Carter House ✪
514 SISKIYOU BOULEVARD, ASHLAND, OREGON 97520

Tel: **(503) 482-5623**
Best Time to Call: **Mornings**
Hosts: **Alyce and Roy Levy**
No. of Rooms: **4**
No. of Private Baths: **4**
Double/pb: **$52–$70**
Suites: **$70**

Open: **All Year**
Breakfast: **Full**
Pets: **No**
Children: **Welcome, over 7**
Smoking: **No**
Social Drinking: **Permitted**
Airport/Station Pickup: **Yes**

This beautiful 1909 Craftsman home is listed on the National Historic Register. Located four blocks from Ashland's famous Shakespeare Theatre, it is surrounded by lovely old trees in a parklike setting. It is suitably modernized but retains the original room structure. Alyce has added decorator touches of vintage hats and old periodicals to the antique furnishings. The Levys have traveled extensively abroad and will share stories of their experiences with you. Southern Oregon State College is six blocks away.

Lighthouse Bed & Breakfast ✪
650 JETTY ROAD, P.O. BOX 24, BANDON, OREGON 97411

Tel: **(503) 347-9316**	Breakfast: **Full**
Best Time to Call: **3–6 PM**	Credit Cards: **MC, VISA**
Hosts: **Bruce and Linda Sisson**	Pets: **No**
Location: **26 mi. S of Coos Bay**	Children: **Welcome, over 12**
No. of Rooms: **4**	Smoking: **No**
No. of Private Baths: **4**	Social Drinking: **Permitted**
Double/pb: **$65–$75**	Airport/Station Pickup: **Yes**
Open: **All year**	

Located on the beach across from the historic Bandon Lighthouse, Bruce and Linda's contemporary home is light and airy, with an ocean-view deck. The guestrooms are bright and comfortable and have pretty plants. All have river or ocean views. "Old Town" and many of Bandon's finest seafood restaurants are within easy walking distance. A short stroll along the beach will give you a glimpse of the ancient sea stacks jutting from the water just off shore. This is a wonderful environment for those who like to beachcomb, birdwatch, or photograph spectacular sunsets.

Cedar Crest Inn
64169 HIGHWAY 20, BEND, OREGON 97701

Tel: **(503) 382-5052**	Open: **All year**
Best Time to Call: **8 AM–1 PM; after 6 PM**	Reduced Rates: **Available**
	Breakfast: **Full**
Hosts: **Kaye and Dean Kine**	Pets: **No**
Location: **165 mi. SE of Portland**	Children: **Welcome, over 14**
No. of Rooms: **5**	Smoking: **Permitted**
No. of Private Baths: **5**	Social Drinking: **Permitted**
Double/pb: **$55–$70**	Airport/Station Pickup: **Yes**

The Cedar Crest Inn is set on a tree-covered ridge overlooking the Cascade Mountains and the Deschutes River. The house is a sprawling Tudor, designed especially for bed-and-breakfasting. Hosts Dean and Kaye have decorated each bedroom in a different theme and color, created with wicker, brass, and Victorian and traditional furnishings.

Early morning coffee is followed by a full country breakfast featuring freshly baked biscuits and a variety of other dishes prepared according to your preferences. The inn is located in an area known for its beautiful scenery and recreational activities, such as hunting, fishing, river rafting, and skiing at the Mt. Bachelor resort.

Mirror Pond House ☉
1054 N.W. HARMON, BEND, OREGON 97701

Tel: **(503) 389-1680**	Suites: **$80**
Best Time to Call: **Mornings**	Open: **All year**
Host: **Beryl Kellum**	Breakfast: **Full**
No. of Rooms: **2**	Pets: **No**
No. of Private Baths: **2**	Children: **Welcome, over 12**
Double/pb: **$60**	Smoking: **Permitted**
Single/pb: **$55**	Social Drinking: **Permitted**

Mirror Pond House overlooks a wildlife sanctuary where wild ducks and geese glide ashore. A quiet residential area close to downtown and right at the water's edge, the location is both serene and convenient. Beryl Kellum's Cape Cod house has a high-ceilinged living room with mahogany moldings, flowered chintz chairs, and a curved sofa overlooking the pond. The downstairs bedroom has hardwood floors, and Early American furnishings. Breakfast specialties such as champagne mimosas, creamy scrambled eggs, and breakfast steaks with mushrooms are served in a sunny dining room with cloth napkins and fine silver. Beryl will even cook fresh trout if you wake up early enough to catch it. Fish right off the bank or borrow the house canoe. Later, you can laze on the deck or just curl up by the living room fire with a complimentary glass of wine.

Wheeler's Bed & Breakfast ☉
BOX 8201, COBURG, OREGON 97401

Tel: **(503) 344-1366**	Open: **Mar. 1–Dec. 1**
Hosts: **Joe and Isabel Wheeler**	Breakfast: **Full**
Location: **7 mi. N of Eugene; ½ mi.**	Pets: **Sometimes**
from I-5, Exit 199	Children: **Welcome, over 10**
No. of Rooms: **2**	Smoking: **Permitted**
Max. No. Sharing Bath: **4**	Social Drinking: **Permitted**
Double/sb: **$39**	Airport/Station Pickup: **Yes**
Single/sb: **$34**	Foreign Languages: **Spanish**

Joe and Isabel welcome you to their historic town, which offers a unique atmosphere of antiques shops and century-old homes. The guest quarters are separate from the rest of the house, offering complete privacy. Visit in the living room, use the washer-dryer, and make yourselves "at home." The University of Oregon and downtown Eugene are minutes away.

Captain's Quarters Bed & Breakfast ✪
P.O. BOX 3231, 265 SOUTH EMPIRE BOULEVARD, COOS BAY,
OREGON 97420

Tel: **(503) 888-6895**	Open: **All year**
Best Time to Call: **8 AM–8 PM**	Breakfast: **Full**
Hosts: **John and Jean Griswold**	Pets: **No**
Location: **3 mi. W of Coos Bay**	Children: **Welcome, over 10**
No. of Rooms: **2**	Smoking: **No**
Max. No. Sharing Bath: **4**	Social Drinking: **Permitted**
Double/sb: **$45**	Airport/Station Pickup: **Yes**

Captain's Quarters is an 1890 Victorian painted gray with white trim. It was the home of Captain Thomas McGenn, chief of the steamship *Breakwater*. John and Jean have lovingly restored the house to its original beauty and created a homey atmosphere with antiques and even some of the old captain's memorabilia. Bedrooms face the beautiful bay and the North Spit, where you can watch the ships come in. Homemade hotcakes with berries, fresh-baked breads, and local cheeses are just some of the breakfast treats served in the dining room or sun parlor. Later, your hosts invite you to have a snack or a cup of coffee in the parlor. A vast selection of activities can be enjoyed nearby, including beachcombing, boat charters, crabbing, and clamming. You can take a trip to the botanical gardens, or just take a break at one of the restaurants tucked along the shores.

This Olde House B&B ✪
202 ALDER STREET, CORNER 2ND AVENUE, COOS BAY,
OREGON 97420

Tel: **(503) 267-5224**	Open: **All year**
Hosts: **Ed and Jean Mosieur**	Reduced Rates: **10%, seniors**
Location: **½ block from Hwy. 101**	Breakfast: **Full**
No. of Rooms: **4**	Pets: **No**
No. of Private Baths: **1**	Children: **Welcome, over 12**
Max. No. Sharing Bath: **4**	Smoking: **Permitted**
Double/sb: **$50**	Social Drinking: **Permitted**
Single/sb: **$40**	Airport/Station Pickup: **Yes**
Suite: **$60**	

Situated with a view of the bay, this stately Victorian beauty is located only one half block from Highway 101. Guests can catch a glimpse of ships on the bay just before they head downstairs to a breakfast of fresh fruit, eggs, muffins, coffee or tea, served in the dining room. Downtown Coos Bay is only two blocks away from the house, and after a short drive, guests will find a lovely state park, a small boat basin, beaches, South Slough Sanctuary, and the beautiful gardens of Shore Acres.

Huntington Manor

3555 N.W. HARRISON BOULEVARD, CORVALLIS, OREGON 97330

Tel: **(503) 753-3735**
Best Time to Call: **8 AM–8 PM**
Host: **Ann Sink**
Location: **84 mi. S of Portland**
No. of Rooms: **3**
No. of Private Baths: **3**
Double/pb: **$48**

Open: **All year**
Reduced Rates: **10%, weekly**
Breakfast: **Full**
Pets: **No**
Children: **Welcome, over 12**
Smoking: **No**
Social Drinking: **Permitted**

Huntington Manor is a 64-year-old Williamsburg-style Colonial, set beneath towering trees and surrounded by gardens. The house has been completely refurbished and furnished with a mixture of American and European antiques. Guest rooms feature queen or double beds, color TV, down comforters, fine imported linens, and special touches such as a decanter of wine and fresh fruit. Your host has 20 years of experience in interior design, and she loves caring for her home and catering to guests. Breakfast specialties include ham-and-cheese-filled crêpes, egg strata, and homemade muffins; tea and scones are served in the afternoon. Huntington Manor is four blocks from Oregon State University and within walking distance of parks, churches, and the countryside.

McGillivray's Log Home and Bed and Breakfast ✪

88680 EVERS ROAD, ELMIRA, OREGON 97437

Tel: **(503) 935-3564**
Best Time to Call: **8 AM–8 PM**
Host: **Evelyn McGillivray**
Location: **14 mi. W of Eugene**
No. of Rooms: **2**
No. of Private Baths: **2**
Double/pb: **$40–$60**
Single/pb: **$35–$50**

Open: **All year**
Breakfast: **Full**
Credit Cards: **MC, VISA**
Pets: **No**
Children: **Welcome**
Smoking: **No**
Social Drinking: **Permitted**
Airport/Station Pickup: **Yes**

This massive home is situated on five acres covered with pines and firs. The air-conditioned structure is designed with six types of wood, and features a split-log staircase. Guests may choose from a spacious, wheelchair-accessible bedroom, or an upstairs room that can accommodate a family. All are beautifully decorated in a classic Americana motif. Evelyn usually prepares buttermilk pancakes using an antique griddle her mother used to use. She also offers fresh-squeezed juice from farm-grown apples and grapes, fresh bread, eggs, and all the trimmings. It's just three miles to a local vineyard; country roads for bicycling and a reservoir for fishing and boating are close by.

The House in the Woods ○
814 LORANE HIGHWAY, EUGENE, OREGON 97405

Tel: **(503) 343-3234**	Open: **All year**
Best Time to Call: **Mornings; evenings**	Reduced Rates: **Available**
Hosts: **Eunice and George Kjaer**	Breakfast: **Full**
Location: **3 mi. from I-5**	Pets: **No**
No. of Rooms: **2**	Children: **Welcome, under 1 or over**
No. of Private Baths: **1**	**14**
Max. No. Sharing Bath: **2**	Smoking: **No**
Double/pb: **$60**	Social Drinking: **Permitted**
Single/pb: **$42**	Airport/Station Pickup: **Yes**
Double/sb: **$55**	Foreign Languages: **German**
Single/sb: **$40**	

This turn-of-the-century home is situated in a wooded glen surrounded by fir trees, rhododendrons, and azaleas. Inside, you'll find Oriental rugs on the original hardwood floors, a cozy fireplace, antiques, and a square grand piano. Guest rooms always have fresh flowers. Breakfast is served in the formal dining room or beside the warmth of the Franklin stove. Specialties of the house include homemade jams and breads, fruit soups, and a variety of egg dishes. The neighborhood is full of wildlife and bicycle and jogging trails, yet is close to shops, art galleries, museums, wineries, and restaurants.

Maryellen's Guest House
1583 FIRCREST, EUGENE, OREGON 97403

Tel: **(503) 342-7375**	Breakfast: **Full**
Best Time to Call: **9 AM–9 PM**	Other Meals: **Available**
Hosts: **Maryellen and Bob Larson**	Credit Cards: **MC, VISA**
Location: **1 mi. off I-5, Exit 191**	Pets: **No**
No. of Rooms: **2**	Children: **Welcome, over 12**
No. of Private Baths: **2**	Smoking: **No**
Double/pb: **$72**	Social Drinking: **Permitted**
Single/pb: **$62**	Airport/Station Pickup: **Yes**
Open: **All year**	
Reduced Rates: **10%, weekly**	

Maryellen's Guest House is one and a half blocks from beautiful Hendricks Park, and just a few minutes away from the University of Oregon campus. In Maryellen's own backyard you'll find a swimming pool and a hot tub. You can also luxuriate in the master suite bathroom, with its double shower and deep Roman tub. In the morning, enjoy Continental breakfast in your room, or come to the dining room for fresh fruit followed by your choice of eggs, cereal, waffles, and muffins. When weather permits, meals can be served on the deck overlooking the pool.

Endicott Gardens ✪
95768 JERRY'S FLAT ROAD, GOLD BEACH, OREGON 97444

Tel: **(503) 247-6513**
Best Time to Call: **10 AM–noon**
Hosts: **Stewart and Mary Endicott**
No. of Rooms: **4**
No. of Private Baths: **4**
Double/pb: **$45**
Single/pb: **$35**

Open: **All year**
Breakfast: **Full**
Pets: **Sometimes**
Children: **Welcome**
Smoking: **Permitted**
Social Drinking: **Permitted**
Airport/Station Pickup: **Yes**

This classic contemporary B&B is across the road from Rogue River, famous for fishing and riverboat trips to white water. The guest rooms are located in a private wing of the house with decks overlooking the forest, mountains, and beautiful grounds. Homegrown strawberries, blueberries, apples, and plums are often featured in delicious breakfast treats served on the deck or in the dining room. In cool weather, the living room with its cozy fireplace is a favorite gathering spot. Mary and Stewart will be happy to share their collection of restaurant menus from nearby eating establishments with you.

Ahlf House Bed & Breakfast ✪
762 N.W. 6TH STREET, GRANTS PASS, OREGON 97526

Tel: **(503) 474-1374**
Hosts: **Herbert and Betty Buskirk; and Rosemary Althaus**
Location: **2 blocks from downtown Grants Pass**
No. of Rooms: **2**
Max. No. Sharing Bath: **4**
Double/sb: **$65**
Single/sb: **$55**

Open: **All year**
Breakfast: **Full**
Pets: **No**
Children: **No**
Smoking: **No**
Social Drinking: **Permitted**
Airport/Station Pickup: **Yes**

Ahlf House is located on a main street on a hill overlooking the surrounding mountains. The house dates back to 1902, and is listed on the National Register of Historic Places. The rooms are beautifully appointed and furnished in fine antiques. Guest rooms feature fluffy comforters, down pillows, fresh flowers, and candles. Enjoy a cup of fresh coffee first thing in the morning in the quiet of your room or on the sunny front porch. Your coffee is followed by a full gourmet breakfast including fruit, fresh-baked muffins, and homemade jams and jellies. There is much to explore in Grants Pass, which is set on the Rogue River and is surrounded by the beautiful Cascade Mountains. Your hosts can direct you to guided fishing, raft trips, and jet boats. In the evening, return to this lovely Victorian for parlor music, complimentary wine, and a light snack.

The Handmaiden's Inn ✪
230 RED SPUR DRIVE, GRANTS PASS, OREGON 97527

Tel: **(503) 476-2932**
Hosts: **Bette and Jody Hammer**
Location: **3 mi. S of Grants Pass**
No. of Rooms: **3**
No. of Private Baths: **1**
Max. No. Sharing Bath: **4**
Double/pb: **$80**
Double/sb: **$60–$70**
Single/sb: **$45**
Open: **All year**

Reduced Rates: **15%, families**
Breakfast: **Full**
Other Meals: **Available**
Credit Cards: **AMEX, MC, VISA**
Pets: **No**
Children: **Welcome, over 11**
Smoking: **No**
Social Drinking: **No**
Airport/Station Pickup: **Yes**

The Handmaiden's Inn is a newly built three-story cedar home surrounded by beautifully landscaped greenery and gardens. The inside is filled with elegant country oak furnishings. Guests are welcome to sun themselves on the spacious deck furnished with comfortable chairs and lounges or relax under the stars in the hot tub. Bette and Jody are professional cooks who used to have a catering business in Southern California. They lovingly prepare hearty breakfasts featuring sausage and egg dishes, homemade breads and jams, fresh fruit, and plenty of coffee. They also invite you to join them for complimentary wine and cheese. The inn is located 5 minutes from white-water rafting and salmon fishing, and is 45 minutes from the Ashland Shakespeare Festival.

The Washington Inn Bed & Breakfast ✪
1002 NORTHWEST WASHINGTON BOULEVARD, GRANTS PASS, OREGON 97526

Tel: **(503) 476-1131**
Hosts: **Maryan and Bill Thompson**
Location: **½ mi. from I-5**
No. of Rooms: **3**
No. of Private Baths: **2**
Max. No. Sharing Bath: **2**
Double/pb: **$50–$65**
Single/pb: **$40–$55**
Double/sb: **$40–$55**
Single/sb: **$30–$45**

Open: **All year**
Reduced Rates: **Available**
Breakfast: **Continental**
Credit Cards: **MC, VISA**
Pets: **No**
Children: **Welcome, over 14**
Smoking: **No**
Social Drinking: **Permitted**
Airport/Station Pickup: **Yes**

The Washington Inn is a charming Victorian listed on the National Register of Historic Places. Each guest room is named for one of the Thompsons' three children and offers individual charms. Linda's is a large suite with fireplace, queen-size bed, private bath, and balcony overlooking the mountains; Pattie's Parlor is a spacious red room with fireplace and large private bath with claw-footed tub; Sally's Sunny View overlooks the mountains, has a canopied bed, and is decorated in delicate pink. Your hosts offer bicycles for exploring the area, and many interesting shops and restaurants are within easy walking distance. Fishing, rafting, and jet-boat rides can be enjoyed on the Rogue River. If you prefer, spend the afternoon relaxing on the porch swing, taking in the view.

The Wilson House Inn ✪
746 NORTHWEST SIXTH STREET, GRANTS PASS, OREGON 97526

Tel: **(503) 479-4754**
Best Time to Call: **3:30–8:30 PM**
Hosts: **Jacqueline and Jack Hanson**
No. of Rooms: **4**
No. of Private Baths: **4**
Double/pb: **$65**
Single/pb: **$55**
Open: **All year**
Reduced Rates: **10%, families,
    seniors: $10/night, Nov. 1–Apr. 30**

Breakfast: **Full**
Credit Cards: **MC, VISA**
Pets: **No**
Children: **Welcome, over 10**
Smoking: **No**
Social Drinking: **Permitted**
Airport/Station Pickup: **Yes**

Jacqueline and Jack are only the fifth owners of this Colonial Revival home, a local landmark built in 1908. Inside, antique Victorian furniture complements the house's original hardwood floors. A mile away, the Rogue River is the main source of recreation; options include salmon fishing, white-water rafting, jet boat rides, and hiking. For indoor sports, there are plenty of appealing shops, starting with the Hansons' own gift shop on the B&B premises. The morning menu features freshly ground coffee, granola, homemade jams, and mouthwatering breakfast desserts.

Black Bart Bed & Breakfast ✪
94125 LOVE LAKE ROAD, JUNCTION CITY, OREGON 97448

Tel: **(503) 998-1904**
Hosts: **Don and Irma Mode**
Location: **14 mi. N of Eugene**
No. of Rooms: **2**
No. of Private Baths: **2**
Double/pb: **$45–$60**
Single/pb: **$35–$50**
Open: **All year**

Breakfast: **Full**
Credit Cards: **MC, VISA**
Pets: **No**
Children: **No**
Smoking: **No**
Social Drinking: **Permitted**
Airport/Station Pickup: **Yes**

Don and Irma named this B&B for their National Grand Champion mammoth donkey, who strutted his stuff in a parade of equines at the 1984 Olympics; time and weather permitting, Black Bart will oblige guests by pulling them around in an antique shay. The other resident equines, the Belgian mules Nip and Tuck, can be called on for wagon rides. The B&B itself is a remodeled 1880s farmhouse, filled with antiques and—surprise!—lots of donkey collectibles. Nearby, you'll find lots of wineries and farmers' markets, plus golf courses and antique shops. Ableskivers, eggs, bacon, or sausage, fruit, and juice constitute the hearty farm breakfasts.

Marjon Bed and Breakfast Inn ✪
44975 LEABURG DAM ROAD, LEABURG, OREGON 97489

Tel: **(503) 896-3145**	Breakfast: **Full**
Host: **Marguerite Haas**	Credit Cards: **MC, VISA**
Location: **24 mi. E of Eugene**	Pets: **No**
No. of Rooms: **2**	Children: **No**
No. of Private Baths: **2**	Smoking: **Permitted**
Double/pb: **$80**	Social Drinking: **Permitted**
Suites: **$100**	Airport/Station Pickup: **Yes**
Open: **All year**	

This cedar chalet is located on the banks of the McKenzie River. The suite overlooks the river and a secluded Japanese garden, and features a sunken bath. The other has a fish bowl shower and a view of a 100-year-old apple tree. Relax in the living room with its wraparound seating and massive stone fireplace. One of the walls is made entirely of glass with sliding doors that lead to a terrace that faces the river. A multicourse breakfast is served there on balmy days. Waterfalls, trout fishing, white-water rafting, and skiing are all nearby.

Secluded B&B ✪
19719 NORTHEAST WILLIAMSON ROAD, NEWBERG, OREGON 97132

Tel: **(503) 538-2635**	Hosts: **Del and Durell Belanger**
Best Time to Call: **8 AM**	Location: **27 mi. SW of Portland**

No. of Rooms: **2**	Breakfast: **Full**
No. of Private Baths: **1**	Pets: **No**
Max. No. Sharing Bath: **4**	Children: **Welcome, under 1 and over 6**
Double/pb: **$50**	
Double/sb: **$35**	Smoking: **No**
Single/sb: **$30**	Social Drinking: **No**
Open: **Mar. 1–Dec. 15**	

A rustic home with a gambrel roof and sunny decks, this B&B is secluded, but not isolated. Set on 10 wooded acres, it is near several notable wineries. George Fox College is also in the area. Your hosts' hobbies include gardening, cooking, and carpentry; Durell made the stained-glass windows that accent the house. The mouthwatering breakfasts might include fresh shrimp omelets, Grand Marnier French toast, or Dutch babies swathed in apple-huckleberry sauce and whipped cream, accompanied by juice, fruit, and coffee or tea.

The Highlands Bed and Breakfast ✪
608 RIDGE ROAD, NORTH BEND, OREGON 97459

Tel: **(503) 756-0300**	Breakfast: **Full**
Hosts: **Jim and Marilyn Dow**	Credit Cards: **MC, VISA**
Location: **4 mi. from Hwy. 101**	Pets: **No**
No. of Rooms: **2**	Children: **Welcome, over 10**
No. of Private Baths: **2**	Smoking: **No**
Double/pb: **$55**	Social Drinking: **Permitted**
Single/pb: **$50**	Airport/Station Pickup: **Yes**
Open: **All year**	

This uniquely designed contemporary cedar home, with its wide expanses of glass and wraparound deck, has a spectacular view of the valley, inlet, and bay. From the floor-to-ceiling windows of the family room you'll be able to watch unforgettable sunrises and sunsets. Dark oak-pegged flooring, beamed vaulted ceilings, and cedar paneling make a perfect setting for the Dows' antiques. A separate entrance for guests assures privacy, and separate heat controls assure comfort. Breakfast includes fresh-squeezed juice, fruit compote with special sauce, baked eggs on rice with cheese, ham or bacon, and freshly baked muffins or popovers. A short drive away are Oregon's beaches, sand dunes, and many fine restaurants. The Dows are retired and like to fly, sail, and garden.

The Pringle House ✪
P.O. BOX 578, OAKLAND, OREGON 97462

Tel: **(503) 459-5038**	No. of Rooms: **2**
Best Time to Call: **9 AM–10 PM**	No. of Private Baths: **2**
Hosts: **Jim and Demay Pringle**	Double/pb: **$45–$55**
Location: **1½ mi. from I-5, Exit 138**	Single/pb: **$35–$40**

Open: **All year**	Children: **Welcome, over 12**
Breakfast: **Full**	Smoking: **No**
Pets: **No**	Social Drinking: **Permitted**

Built in 1893, Pringle House stands on a rise overlooking historic downtown Oakland. Returned to its original Victorian beauty by Jim and Demay, it is listed on the National Register of Historic Places. Breakfast features a variety of entrees and is served in the dining room. Special attention is given to those on diets. You will enjoy seeing Demay's doll collection.

Inn of the Oregon Trail ✪
416 SOUTH MCLOUGHLIN, OREGON CITY, OREGON 97045

Tel: **(503) 656-2089**	Suites: **$77.50**
Best Time to Call: **7–5 PM**	Open: **All year**
Hosts: **Mary and Tom Dehaven**	Breakfast: **Full**
Location: **13 mi. SE of Portland**	Credit Cards: **MC, VISA**
No. of Rooms: **3**	Pets: **No**
Max. No. Sharing Bath: **4**	Children: **Welcome, over 12**
Double/sb: **$57.50**	Smoking: **No**
Single/sb: **$42.50**	Social Drinking: **Permitted**

A superb Gothic Revival home built in 1867 by a Willamette River captain, Inn of the Oregon Trail is listed on the National Registry of Historic Places. In fact, this Oregon City neighborhood is filled with distinctive buildings and museums—ask your hosts to recommend walking and driving tours. You'll have plenty of energy for sightseeing after one of Tom's ample breakfasts of juice, coffee, eggs, pancakes, and French toast.

Hartman's Hearth
2937 NORTHEAST 20TH AVENUE, PORTLAND, OREGON 97212

Tel: **(503) 281-2210**	Open: **All year**
Hosts: **Christopher and Katie Hartman**	Breakfast: **Full**
Location: **1 mi. off I-5, Exit 302-A**	Credit Cards: **MC, VISA**
No. of Rooms: **3**	Pets: **No**
No. of Private Baths: **1**	Children: **No**
Max. No. Sharing Bath: **4**	Smoking: **Permitted**
Double/sb: **$50**	Social Drinking: **Permitted**
Single/sb: **$45**	Airport/Station Pickup: **Yes**
Suites: **$70**	

Just 10 minutes from downtown Portland, Hartman's Hearth is near the Memorial Coliseum, the Lloyd Center, and the new Convention Center. A white gabled example of the Arts and Crafts style, this turn-of-the-century house is equally distinctive inside, with decorative moldings and stained-glass windows. Antique furnishings are paired with contemporary art. Your hosts enjoy sailing, skiing, bridge, music, and the culinary arts; their breakfast specialties range from egg dishes to gingerbread waffles. At the end of a long day, guests can unwind in the spa or the sauna.

John Palmer House ✪
4314 NORTH MISSISSIPPI AVENUE, PORTLAND, OREGON 97217

Tel: (503) 284-5893
Best Time to Call: 7 AM–8 PM
Hosts: Mary and Richard Sauter
Location: 3½ mi. N of Portland
No. of Rooms: 6
No. of Private Baths: 3
Max. No. Sharing Bath: 4
Double/sb: $45–$55
Single/sb: $30
Guest Cottage: $120; sleeps 5
Suites: $75–$105

Open: All year
Reduced Rates: $10 less, Sun.–Thurs., Jan.–Apr.
Breakfast: Full
Other Meals: Available
Credit Cards: MC, VISA
Pets: No
Children: Welcome in cottage
Smoking: No
Social Drinking: Permitted
Airport/Station Pickup: Yes

John Palmer built this ornate Victorian in 1890, and today it is a nationally registered landmark home. Hundred-year-old gaslight fixtures, gleaming woodwork, and hand-screened wallpapers have been beautifully preserved and are complemented by plush carpets, lace, and velvet accents. Your hosts cater to the romantic in everyone with afternoon tea, chilled champagne, and an occasional recital from the resident pianist. Guest quarters range from the main house's bridal suite with canopy bed and balcony to one of grandma's cottage rooms with its pretty wallpapers and brass beds. Breakfast choices such as blueberry crêpes and mushroom omelets are served in the formal dining room and enhanced by fresh roses and candlelight. This sprawling house has two parlors, a veranda, and a Jacuzzi on the porch. The Sauters will arrange a horse-and-carriage ride to your favorite restaurant or, if you like, can prepare a gourmet dinner at the house.

Home by the Sea B&B ✪
444 JACKSON STREET, PORT ORFORD, OREGON 97465

Tel: (503) 332-2855
Hosts: Brenda and Alan Mitchell
Location: 54 mi. N of California border
No. of Rooms: 2
No. of Private Baths: 2
Double/pb: $70
Single/pb: $60

Open: All year
Breakfast: Full
Credit Cards: MC, VISA
Pets: No
Children: No
Smoking: No
Social Drinking: Permitted

Alan and Brenda built their contemporary wood home on a spit of land overlooking the Oregon coast. The breathtaking view can be enjoyed from both lovely bedrooms and from the sunspace lounge where the Mitchells serve breakfast and get to know their guests. Port Orford is a quiet fishing village, a favorite of bird, storm, and whale watchers (whale-watching season runs from October to May). It's a short walk to restaurants, public beaches, historic Battle Rock Park, and the town harbor, the home port of Oregon's only crane-launched commercial fishing fleet. The Oregon Islands National Wildlife Refuge is just offshore, and Jedediah Smith Redwood National Park is nearby. Amenities include direct beach access, Jacuzzi, queen-size beds, laundry privileges, cable TV, and phone jacks in rooms.

The Boarding House Bed & Breakfast
208 NORTH HOLLADAY DRIVE, SEASIDE, OREGON 97138

Tel: **(503) 738-9055**	Open: **All year**
Hosts: **Dick and Barb Edwards**	Reduced Rates: **Available**
Location: **½ mi. from Rte. 101**	Breakfast: **Full**
No. of Rooms: **6**	Credit Cards: **MC, VISA**
No. of Private Baths: **6**	Pets: **No**
Double/pb: **$55–$65**	Children: **Welcome**
Single/pb: **$50–$60**	Smoking: **No**
Separate Guest Cottage: **$85**	Social Drinking: **Permitted**
for 2; sleeps 6	Airport/Station Pickup: **Yes**

Located on the banks of the Necanicum River, this rustic Victorian was built as a private residence in 1898. During World War I, the house became a boarding home. After an extensive renovation, the wood walls and beamed ceilings have been restored to their original charm. Guest rooms feature brass or white iron beds, down quilts, family heirlooms, wicker, and wood. Claw-footed tubs, window seats, antiques, and a picture of grandma make you feel as if this house is your own. A fire is often burning in the fir-paneled parlor, and an old melody sounds just right on the old-fashioned victrola. A 100-year-old guest cottage with wood paneling, country furnishings, bedroom, loft, and river view is also available. Breakfast specialties such as cheese-and-egg strata, orange French toast, and blueberry scones are served in the dining room or outside on the wraparound porch. The house is just four blocks from the ocean and two blocks from downtown.

Horncroft ✪
42156 KINGSTON LYONS DRIVE, STAYTON, OREGON 97383

Tel: **(503) 769-6287**	No. of Rooms: **3**
Hosts: **Dorothea and Kenneth Horn**	No. of Private Baths: **1**
Location: **17 mi. E of Salem**	Max. No. Sharing Bath: **4**

Double/pb: **$45**
Single/pb: **$35**
Double/sb: **$35**
Single/sb: **$30**
Open: **All year**

Breakfast: **Full**
Pets: **No**
Children: **Sometimes**
Smoking: **No**
Social Drinking: **Permitted**

This lovely home is situated in the foothills of the Cascade Mountains on the edge of Willamette Valley. In summer, swim in the heated pool or hike on one of the scenic nature paths. The area is dotted with farms, and the valley is abundant in fruits, berries, and vegetables. Willamette and Oregon State universities are nearby. The Mount Jefferson Wilderness hiking area is an hour away. A guest comments, "The hospitality and breakfasts were topnotch!"

Old Welches Inn ✪
26401 EAST WELCHES ROAD, WELCHES, OREGON 97067

Tel: **(503) 622-3754**
Best Time to Call: **After 6 PM**
Hosts: **Judith and Ted Mondun**
Location: **50 mi. E of Portland**
No. of Rooms: **3**
Max. No. Sharing Bath: **3**
Double/sb: **$50–$65**
Single/sb: **$40**

Open: **All year**
Breakfast: **Full**
Credit Cards: **AMEX, MC, VISA**
Pets: **Dogs welcome**
Children: **Welcome, over 12**
Smoking: **No**
Social Drinking: **Permitted**
Minimum Stay: **2 nights, holidays**

Built as a resort in the late 19th century, the Old Welches Inn is a large white Colonial with blue shutters. The house stands on the edge of the Mt. Hood wilderness area, crisscrossed by miles of hiking and ski trails. Fishermen may carry poles to the back of the B&B property, where they can drop lines in the Salmon River. And just across the road, golfers will find that 27 holes await. You'll be ready for action after a full, Southern-style breakfast, highlighted by home-baked muffins, biscuits, and breads.

The Carriage House ✪
515 SOUTH PACIFIC HIGHWAY, WOODBURN, OREGON 97071

Tel: **(503) 982-6321**
Best Time to Call: **Before 9 AM; after 6 PM**
Hosts: **Lawrence and Marilyn Paradis**
Location: **30 mi. S of Portland**
No. of Rooms: **2**
Max. No. Sharing Bath: **4**
Double/sb: **$50**
Single/sb: **$45**

Open: **All year**
Breakfast: **Full**
Credit Cards: **MC, VISA**
Pets: **Sometimes**
Children: **Welcome**
Smoking: **No**
Social Drinking: **Permitted**
Airport/Station Pickup: **Yes**
Foreign Languages: **French**

The Carriage House is a 1906 Victorian known for its peaceful country elegance. Completely restored, it is furnished with family treasures and heirloom quilts. Lawrence and Marilyn keep horses and an antique buggy in a carriage house next to the inn. This is an excellent location for visiting the Enchanted Forest, the Oregon State Fair, the Octoberfest in Mt. Angel, the Bach Festival, historic Champoeg, and numerous antique shops and wineries.

For key to listings, see inside front or back cover.

✪ This star means that rates are guaranteed through December 31, 1991, to any guest making a reservation as a result of reading about the B&B in *BED & BREAKFAST U.S.A.*—1991 edition.

Important! To avoid misunderstandings, always ask about cancellation policies when booking.

Please enclose a self-addressed, stamped, business-size envelope when contacting reservation services.

For more details on what you can expect in a B&B, see Chapter 1.

Always mention *Bed & Breakfast U.S.A.* when making reservations!

If no B&B is listed in the area you'll be visiting, use the form on page 675 to order a copy of our "List of New B&Bs."

We want to hear from you! Use the form on page 677.

PENNSYLVANIA

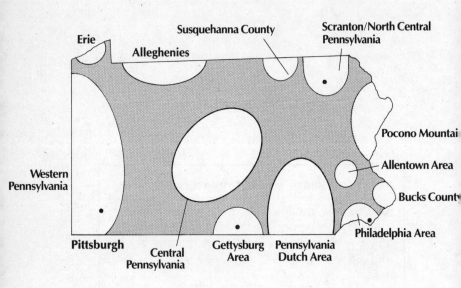

Erie

Alleghenies

Susquehanna County

Scranton/North Central Pennsylvania

Pocono Mountai

Allentown Area

Western Pennsylvania

Bucks Count

Philadelphia Area

Pittsburgh

Central Pennsylvania

Gettysburg Area

Pennsylvania Dutch Area

Bed & Breakfast in Pennsylvania ✪
P.O. BOX 169, PINE GROVE MILLS, PENNSYLVANIA 16868

Tel: **(814) 238-1484**
Best Time to Call: **Mon.–Fri., 9 AM–Noon, Sat.; 9 AM–Noon (closed Thur.)**
Coordinator: **Linda Feltman**

States/Regions Covered: **Statewide**
Rates (Single/Double):
  Average: **$20–$60 $25–$125**
Credit Cards: **Varies with each B&B**
Descriptive Directory: **$11.50**

Call Linda for the name and phone number of a B&B in the area you want to visit anywhere in the state. You can then call the host directly. Accommodations range from a clean, simple mountain lodge to a comfortable suburban split-level to a pre-Revolutionary manor house. There is no charge for this service. If you haven't decided where in the state you'd like to go, Linda's 200-page loose-leaf directory includes all her inspected member homes.

ALLEGHENIES AREA

Allegheny Bed & Breakfast Association ✪
BOX 95, TURTLE POINT, PENNSYLVANIA 16750

Tel: **(814) 642-2334**
Coordinator: **Peter Meissner**
States/Regions Covered:
  Alleghenies—Potter County, McKean County, Warren County

Rates (Single/Double):
  Average: **$30–$35 $40–$50**
Credit Cards: **MC, VISA**

One can find peace and tranquillity at an unrushed pace in this rural pocket in the mountains. Horseback riding, hiking on mountain trails, cross-country skiing, the Kinzua Reservoir for boating and swimming, the Allegheny National Forest, summer fairs, and year-round antiquing are some of the local diversions. Truly off the beaten path, the area hosts genuinely appreciate the "excitement" of having visitors and go out of their way to please them.

BUCKS COUNTY

Maplewood Farm ✪
5090 DURHAM ROAD, P.O. BOX 239, GARDENVILLE, PENNSYLVANIA 18926

Tel: **(215) 766-0477**
Best Time to Call: **8 AM–10 PM**
Hosts: **Linda and Ray Psulkowski**
Location: **30 mi. NW of Philadelphia**
No. of Rooms: **5**
No. of Private Baths: **5**
Double/pb: **$75**
Single/pb: **$70**
Suites: **$100**
Open: **All year**

Reduced Rates: **Mon.–Thur.; 10%, weekly; 10%, seniors**
Breakfast: **Full**
Credit Cards: **AMEX, MC, VISA**
Pets: **No**
Children: **Sometimes**
Smoking: **No**
Social Drinking: **Permitted**
Minimum Stay: **2 nights, weekends**
Airport/Station Pickup: **Yes**

Hundred-year-old maple trees shelter this fieldstone farmhouse built in 1826. The house is set on five acres, including a tranquil stream and a barn; you can gather your eggs fresh from the source each morning and have them turned into fluffy breakfast omelets. Fresh-baked breads, local fruits, and waffles or pancakes complete the meal, served in a romantic dining room with random-width wood floors and an exposed stone wall. Morning coffee can also be enjoyed at an intimate table for two on the sun porch. Guest rooms feature Linda's hand-stenciled walls, cozy comforters, or handmade quilts. Choose the Homestead Room, with four-poster bed and ceiling fan, or the two-story loft suite, with exposed beams and sitting room. Linda and Ray invite you for afternoon and evening snacks in the antique summer kitchen, with its two walk-in fireplaces. They will direct you to nearby lakes, covered bridges, and the shops of New Hope.

CENTRAL PENNSYLVANIA

Rest & Repast Bed & Breakfast Service ✪
P.O. BOX 126, PINE GROVE MILLS, PENNSYLVANIA 16868

Tel: **(814) 238-1484**
Coordinators: **Linda and Brent Peters**
States/Regions Covered: **Aaronsburg, Bellefonte, Boalsburg, Huntington, Phillipsburg, Potters Mills, Spruce Creek, State College, Tyrone**

Rates (Single/Double):
Modest:	**$28–$30**	**$30–$40**
Average:	**$29–$35**	**$35–$45**
Luxury:	**N/A**	**$50–$70**

Credit Cards: **No**

You will enjoy touring historic mansions, Penns Cave, Woodward Cave, and several Civil War museums in this lovely area. A two-day minimum stay is required for the second week in July, the time of the annual Central Pennsylvania Festival of the Arts, and for the Penn State University Homecoming Football game in autumn. Rates are increased during peak weekends to a maximum of $65 per night double. (No single rates on football weekends.) Pennsylvania State University is close by.

The Garmanhaus ✪
BOX 307, BOILING SPRINGS, PENNSYLVANIA 17009

Tel: **(717) 258-3980**
Hosts: **John and Molly Garman**
Location: **5 mi. from Rtes. 76 and 81**
No. of Rooms: **4**
Max. No. Sharing Bath: **4**
Double/sb: **$50**

Open: **All year**
Breakfast: **Continental**
Pets: **No**
Children: **Welcome, over 12**
Smoking: **No**
Social Drinking: **Permitted**

The Garmans' elegant Victorian is on Front Street, by the lake. John, an insurance agent, and Molly, a realtor, will help you feel at home. Snacks, beverages, wine, and beer are always on hand for your enjoyment. Feel free to use the grill, TV, and laundry facilities. Bicycles and a canoe may be rented. Dickinson College and Law School is nearby.

Yoders ✪
RD 1, BOX 312, HUNTINGDON, PENNSYLVANIA 16652

Tel: **(814) 643-3221**
Best Time to Call: **After 4 PM**
Hosts: **Randy and Peggy Yoder**
Location: **On Rte. 22**
No. of Rooms: **3**
No. of Private Baths: **2**
Double/pb: **$40**
Single/pb: **$30**
Open: **All year**

Reduced Rates: **10%, seniors**
Breakfast: **Continental**
Other Meals: **Available**
Pets: **Sometimes**
Children: **No**
Smoking: **No**
Social Drinking: **No**
Airport/Station Pickup: **Yes**

After you've visited the Swigart Museum of antique American automobiles, explored the caves of Lincoln Caverns, or taken advantage of Lake Raystown with its recreational diversions, come home to Randy and Peggy's. The house, fronted with a huge picture window and native stone, is located at the edge of a 200-acre forest where you may feel free to hike. Breakfast often features croissants, waffles, pancakes, or special omelets. Fresh fruit and cheese snacks are complimentary.

Sommerville Farms ✪
RD 4, BOX 22, JERSEY SHORE, PENNSYLVANIA 17740

Tel: **(717) 398-2368**	Breakfast: **Full**
Best Time to Call: **Noon–11 PM**	Pets: **No**
Hosts: **Bill and Jane Williams**	Children: **Welcome**
Location: **12 mi. W of Williamsport**	Smoking: **No**
No. of Rooms: **6**	Social Drinking: **Permitted**
Max. No. Sharing Bath: **4**	Airport/Station Pickup: **Yes**
Double/sb: **$40**	Minimum Stay: **2 nights**, Oct.
Single/sb: **$25**	**weekends**
Open: **Mar.–Nov.**	

As part of a 200-acre working farm, this large white 19th-century farmhouse looks the way it's supposed to, from the gabled roof to the side porch. The living room fireplace has an imposing, hand-rubbed cherry mantel, and hand-painted scenes decorate the ceiling. Jane, a former antiques dealer, has furnished the house in period style. This area draws hunters, fishermen, skiers, canoeists, and shoppers— Woolrich Woolen Mills Outlet Store is a notable attraction. You'll be ready for any activity after breakfasting on a variety of muffins, breads, and coffee cake.

Mrs. G's Bed & Breakfast ✪
256 WEST RIDGE AVENUE, STATE COLLEGE, PENNSYLVANIA 16803

Tel: **(814) 238-0733**	Reduced Rates: **Weekly**
Best Time to Call: **Evenings**	Breakfast: **Continental**
Host: **Ursula A. Gusse**	Pets: **No**
Location: **90 mi. NE of Pittsburgh**	Children: **Welcome, over 6**
No. of Rooms: **2**	Smoking: **Permitted**
Max. No. Sharing Bath: **4**	Social Drinking: **Permitted**
Double/sb: **$30–$50**	Airport/Station Pickup: **Yes**
Single/sb: **$25–$35**	Foreign Languages: **German, some**
Open: **All year**	**French**

Simply but comfortably furnished, Mrs. G's B&B offers visitors the best of both worlds: the college town pleasures of Penn State University and the rural charm of the surrounding communities. Attend performances by internationally celebrated musicians and actors on the Penn State campus, then go hiking or skiing in the area's many parks. Continental breakfasts feature fresh fruit, sweet rolls and Danish, specialty breads, and muesli.

GETTYSBURG AREA

Goose Chase ✪

200 BLUEBERRY ROAD, GARDNERS, PENNSYLVANIA 17324

Tel: **(717) 528-8877**	Open: **All year**
Best Time to Call: **Evening**	Breakfast: **Full**
Hosts: **Marsha and Rich Lucidi**	Credit Cards: **MC, VISA**
Location: **12 mi. N of Gettysburg**	Pets: **No**
No. of Rooms: **5**	Children: **Welcome, over 12**
No. of Private Baths: **3**	Smoking: **No**
Max. No. Sharing Bath: **4**	Social Drinking: **Permitted**
Double/pb: **$69–$89**	Airport/Station Pickup: **Yes**
Double/sb: **$59**	

This restored 18th-century stone house on a 25-acre farm is located in apple orchard country. Air conditioned for summer comfort, it is handsomely furnished with handmade quilts, folk art, and carefully chosen American antiques. Wide-plank floors, Oriental rugs, stenciled walls, and deep-silled windows add to the charming atmosphere. Breakfast always features a delicious main dish and is served by Marsha in authentic Colonial garb. Fresh flowers, terry cloth robes, beds turned down with chocolate treats on the pillow are a few of the Lucidis' thoughtful touches. Wine or tea are graciously offered and, in winter, hot mulled cider is served by a crackling fire. Gettysburg Battlefield is within easy reach. Summer swimming pool and walking trails are on the property. Inquire about the package featuring weekday cooking school classes. Antiqueing, skiing, fishing, and golf are nearby.

The Brafferton Inn ✪

44–46 YORK STREET, GETTYSBURG, PENNSYLVANIA 17325

Tel: **(717) 337-3423**	Double/sb: **$65**
Hosts: **Mimi and Jim Agard**	Open: **All year**
Location: **90 mi. N of D.C.; 2 mi. from**	Breakfast: **Full**
Rte. 15, York Exit	Credit Cards: **MC, VISA**
No. of Rooms: **10**	Pets: **No**
No. of Private Baths: **6**	Children: **Welcome, over 7**
Max. No. Sharing Bath: **4**	Smoking: **No**
Double/pb: **$80**	Social Drinking: **Permitted**

This Early American stone structure is listed on the National Register of Historic Places. The clapboard addition dates back to pre–Civil War days. Four of the guest rooms, decorated with hand-painted stencils, are separated from the main house by an atrium where one may sit and enjoy the pretty plantings during the warm months. The sumptuous breakfast is served in the dining room on antique tables. There are hosts of activities to whet the appetite of the history buff, sportsman, antique collector, or nature lover.

Keystone Inn ✪
231 HANOVER STREET, GETTYSBURG, PENNSYLVANIA 17325

Tel: (717) 337-3888	Open: **All year**
Best Time to Call: **7 AM–10 PM**	Reduced Rates: **Available**
Hosts: **Wilmer and Doris Martin**	Breakfast: **Full**
Location: **35 mi. S of Harrisburg**	Other Meals: **Available**
No. of Rooms: **4**	Credit Cards: **MC, VISA**
No. of Private Baths: **2**	Pets: **No**
Max. No. Sharing Bath: **4**	Children: **Welcome**
Double/pb: **$70**	Smoking: **No**
Double/sb: **$60**	Social Drinking: **No**

Keystone Inn is a large Victorian built in 1913 by Clayton Reaser, a local furniture maker. His talents as a craftsman are evident in the natural oak and chestnut found throughout the house. The beautiful woodwork is complemented with lace, ruffles, and floral designs favored by the Martin family. The guest rooms are decorated with brass or antique wood beds and soft pastel wallpapers, and each bedroom has a reading nook and windowside writing table overlooking historic Gettysburg. A full breakfast features such specialties as cinnamon-apple or blueberry pancakes, waffles, eggs, and fruits. Afternoon lemonade is served on the front porch in summer; in winter guests can enjoy a hot drink by the fireplace. The inn is close to historic sites and Civil War battlefields, antiques shops, state parks, and is nine miles from the Liberty ski area.

The Old Appleford Inn ✪
218 CARLISLE STREET, GETTYSBURG, PENNSYLVANIA 17325

Tel: (717) 337-1711	Breakfast: **Full**
Hosts: **Frank and Maribeth Skradski**	Credit Cards: **AMEX, MC, VISA**
No. of Rooms: **12**	Pets: **No**
No. of Private Baths: **12**	Children: **Welcome, over 14**
Double/pb: **$78–$108**	Smoking: **No**
Open: **All year**	Social Drinking: **Permitted**

This is a beautiful brick mansion built in 1867 and decorated with Victorian antique furnishings dating back to the Civil War. After your tour of the battlefield, Frank and Maribeth invite you to enjoy the warmth of several fireplaces, sip a complimentary sherry, and bask in the mellifluous strains of the baby grand piano in the parlor. There are ski slopes nearby for winter sports enthusiasts, spring apple blossoms, and fall foliage to enjoy. All rooms are air-conditioned for summer comfort. You are certain to awaken each morning to the scent of homemade breads, muffins, or to other olfactory indications of the gourmet breakfast to come.

The Tannery B&B ✪
449 BALTIMORE STREET, GETTYSBURG, PENNSYLVANIA 17325

Tel: (717) 334-2454
Best Time to Call: **9 AM–9 PM**
Hosts: **Charlotte and Jule Swope**
No. of Rooms: **5**
No. of Private Baths: **5**
Double/pb: **$75–$95**
Open: **Daily, May 1–Sept. 30; weekends, Oct. 1–May 1**

Breakfast: **Continental**
Credit Cards: **MC, VISA**
Pets: **No**
Children: **Welcome, over 12**
Smoking: **No**
Social Drinking: **Permitted**

To stay in this large Gothic home is to rub shoulders with history. During the third day of the Battle of Gettysburg, Union soldiers took over the front porch, Rebels occupied the building's rear, and the owner—a tanner named John Rupp—dodged bullets by hiding in the cellar. Civil War buffs can walk to most of Gettysburg's museums and landmarks. Those who would rather dwell in the present can take advantage of several local golf courses. At the end of the day you can relax with complimentary wine and cheese, or a glass of iced tea. Continental breakfast consists of juice, fresh fruit, cereal, baked goods, and coffee.

The Doubleday Inn ✪
104 DOUBLEDAY AVENUE, GETTYSBURG BATTLEFIELD, PENNSYLVANIA 17325

Tel: (717) 334-9119
Hosts: **Joan and Sal Chandon, and Olga Krossick**
No. of Rooms: **11**
No. of Private Baths: **6**
Max. No. Sharing Bath: **4**
Double/pb: **$75–$90**
Double/sb: **$65**

Open: **All year**
Breakfast: **Full**
Credit Cards: **MC, VISA**
Pets: **No**
Children: **Welcome, over 7**
Smoking: **No**
Social Drinking: **Permitted**

The only B&B located on the battlefield, this beautifully restored Colonial recalls past-century charms with Civil War furnishings and antique accessories. Afternoon tea is served with country-style drinks and hors d'oeuvres on the outdoor patio, or by the fireplace in the main parlor. One of the largest known library collections devoted exclusively to the Battle of Gettysburg is available to you. On selected evenings, you are welcome to participate in a discussion with a Civil War historian who brings the battle alive with accurate accounts and displays of authentic memorabilia and weaponry.

Beechmont Inn ✪
315 BROADWAY, HANOVER, PENNSYLVANIA 17331

Tel: **(717) 632-3013**
Best Time to Call: **9 AM–9 PM**
Hosts: **Terry and Monna Hormel, and Glenn and Maggie Hormel**
Location: **13 mi. E of Gettysburg**
No. of Rooms: **7**
No. of Private Baths: **7**
Double/pb: **$70–$75**
Single/pb: **$64–$69**

Suites: **$75–$90**
Open: **All year**
Breakfast: **Full**
Credit Cards: **AMEX, MC, VISA**
Pets: **No**
Children: **Welcome, over 12**
Smoking: **Permitted**
Social Drinking: **Permitted**

This Georgian house, restored to its Federal-period elegance, offers the visitor a bridge across time. Climb the winding staircase to freshly decorated rooms named in honor of the gallant heroes of the Civil War. At breakfast time, enjoy homemade granola, baked goods, a hot entrée, and fruit. Join the other guests in the dining room, or take a tray to your room for breakfast in bed. Visit nearby Gettysburg, the Eisenhower Farm, Hanover Shoe Farms, Codorus State Park for boating and fishing, or go antique hunting in New Oxford. Upon your return, you may relax in the quiet comfort of the parlor. The Hormels look forward to pampering you.

Country View Acres ✪
676 BEAVER CREEK ROAD, HANOVER, PENNSYLVANIA 17331

Tel: **(717) 637-8992**
Best Time to Call: **Evenings**
Hosts: **Alan and Teena Smith**
Location: **13 mi. E. of Gettysburg**
No. of Rooms: **2**
No. of Private Baths: **1**
Double/pb: **$42**

Single/pb: **$34**
Open: **All year**
Breakfast: **Full**
Pets: **Sometimes**
Children: **Welcome**
Smoking: **No**
Social Drinking: **Permitted**

This spacious Colonial-style home is on several acres within view of the mountains and valley. The interior features Early American furnishings and a player piano in the living room. Guests may stroll the grounds and use the outdoor whirlpool spa. Attractions such as the Hanover and Lana Lobell Standardbred horse farms and Gettysburg National Military Park are nearby. Boating and sailing are minutes away at Codorus State Park.

The Forge Bed & Breakfast Inn ✪
RD1, BOX 438, PINE GROVE, PENNSYLVANIA 17963

Tel: **(717) 345-8349**
Best Time to Call: **8 AM–9 PM**
Host: **Lucille Valibus**

Location: **34 mi. NE of Harrisburg**
No. of Rooms: **6**
No. of Private Baths: **2**

Max. No. Sharing Bath: **4**
Double/pb: **$65**
Single/pb: **$60**
Double/sb: **$55**
Single/sb: **$50**
Open: **All year**
Breakfast: **Full**

Credit Cards: **MC, VISA**
Pets: **No**
Children: **Welcome, over 14**
Smoking: **No**
Social Drinking: **Permitted**
Airport/Station Pickup: **Yes**

This magnificent three-story fieldstone mansion dates to 1830, and has been in Lucille's family since 1860. Many of the antique furnishings are treasured heirlooms. Picturesque hiking paths crisscross the 250-acre property, and fishermen are welcome to try their luck in the stream in front of the house. Visitors can also avail themselves of the swimming pool and the piano. Home-baked goods, like sticky buns and blueberry muffins, highlight breakfast.

PENNSYLVANIA DUTCH AREA

Adamstown Inn ✪

62 WEST MAIN STREET, ADAMSTOWN, PENNSYLVANIA 19501

Tel: **(215) 484-0800**
Hosts: **Tom and Wanda Berman**
Location: **10 mi. SW of Reading**
No. of Rooms: **4**
No. of Private Baths: **2**
Max. No. Sharing Bath: **4**
Double/pb: **$70–$85**
Double/sb: **$50–$55**
Open: **All year**

Reduced Rates: **10%, seniors; 10%,**
   after 4 nights
Breakfast: **Continental**
Credit Cards: **MC, VISA**
Pets: **No**
Children: **Welcome, over 12**
Smoking: **Permitted**
Social Drinking: **Permitted**

In the heart of Adamstown's antique district, and just a short drive from Pennsylvania Dutch Country and Reading's factory outlets, you'll find this handsome brick Victorian. Inside, lace and balloon curtains and Oriental rugs complement the chestnut woodwork and leaded-glass windows. Your hosts are avid antiquers and will gladly direct you to their favorite haunts. Coffee or tea will be brought to your door in the morning; refills, as well as juice, fresh fruit, cheese, and home-baked goodies are served during a continental breakfast.

Umble Rest ✪

RD 1, BOX 79, ATGLEN, PENNSYLVANIA 19310

Tel: **(215) 593-2274**
Best Time to Call: **7–10 AM; 3–7 PM**
Hosts: **Ken and Marilyn Umble**
Location: **15 mi. E of Lancaster**
No. of Rooms: **3**
Max. No. Sharing Bath: **6**
Double/sb: **$25–$30**

Open: **May 15–Oct. 15**
Breakfast: **No**
Pets: **No**
Children: **Welcome**
Smoking: **No**
Social Drinking: **No**
Minimum Stay: **Holiday weekends**

Ken and Marilyn are busy Mennonite farmers with interests in crafts, quilting, and restoring their 1800 farmhouse. You are invited to watch the milking of their 50 cows, stroll a country lane to their pond, and to participate in the simple life-style. Bring your children to play with their boys, ages five and eight. All the popular tourist attractions are nearby.

Sunday's Mill Farm B&B ✪
RD 2, BOX 419, BERNVILLE, PENNSYLVANIA 19506

Tel: **(215) 488-7821**
Hosts: **Sally and Len Blumberg**
Location: **11 mi. N of Reading**
No. of Rooms: **2**
Max. No. Sharing Bath: **4**
Double/sb: **$45–$55**
Single/sb: **$35–$45**
Open: **All year**

Reduced Rates: **10% after 1 night; families**
Breakfast: **Full**
Pets: **Horses, welcome**
Children: **Welcome**
Smoking: **Permitted**
Social Drinking: **Permitted**
Airport/Station Pickup: **Yes**

With a grist mill dating to 1820 and main buildings that are thirty years younger, this pastoral property is part of a National Historic District. Sunday's Mill Farm looks like a farmhouse should: exposed beams, rich woodwork, a brick dining room fireplace, quilts on the beds. Bring your fishing pole—Len stocks the pond. This is the rare B&B that accommodates both horseback riders and their mounts. Guests who prefer to use their own legs can explore the area's antique shops and factory outlets; Sally is active in historic preservation and can tell you a lot about the region over a breakfast of deep dish apple pancakes and sausage.

Greystone Manor B&B ✪
2658 OLD PHILADELPHIA PIKE, P. O. BOX 270, BIRD-IN-HAND, PENNSYLVANIA 17505

Tel: **(717) 393-4233**
Hosts: **Sally and Ed Davis**
No. of Rooms: **13**
No. of Private Baths: **13**
Double/pb: **$54**
Single/pb: **$51**
Suites: **$60–$82**
Open: **All year**

Reduced Rates: **Available**
Breakfast: **Continental**
Credit Cards: **MC, VISA**
Pets: **No**
Children: **Welcome**
Smoking: **Permitted in Carriage House**
Social Drinking: **Permitted**

Situated on two acres of lush lawn and trees, the lodge was built in 1883. Back then, this French Victorian mansion and carriage house did not boast of air-conditioning, TV, and suites as it does today. Though a great deal of renovation has taken place, the antique features and charm of the mansion are intact. Good restaurants are nearby.

Cottage at the Quiltery ✪
RD 4, BOX 337, BENFIELD ROAD, BOYERTOWN, PENNSYLVANIA
19512

Tel: **(215) 845-8845**	Reduced Rates: **$5 less after 2 nights**
Hosts: **Peg and Richard Groff**	Breakfast: **Full**
Location: **16 mi. S of Allentown**	Pets: **No**
No. of Private Baths: **1**	Children: **Welcome, over 12**
Guest Cottage: **$60–$70**	Smoking: **Permitted**
Open: **All year**	Social Drinking: **Permitted**

Complete privacy awaits you in this cozy cottage nestled in a clearing in the woods. Downstairs, the exposed beams, woodburning fireplace, quilts, and antique furniture lend themselves to quiet, romantic evenings. On the second floor you'll find an air-conditioned double bedroom and a Laura Ashley bathroom. Gourmet breakfasts are served in the main house in front of either the garden or a cheerful fire, depending on the season. While the cottage is a destination in itself, you'll have easy access to the Pennsylvania Dutch area, the Reading factory outlets, antique shops, historic sites, and country auctions. An excellent restaurant is within walking distance.

Twin Turrets Inn ✪
11 EAST PHILADELPHIA AVENUE, BOYERTOWN, PENNSYLVANIA
19512

Tel: **(215) 367-4513**	Reduced Rates: **Corp. rate: $60**
Best Time to Call: **9 AM–5 PM**	**single; 15%, seniors**
Host: **Gary Slade**	Breakfast: **Continental**
Location: **40 mi. NW of Philadelphia**	Credit Cards: **AMEX, MC, VISA**
No. of Rooms: **10**	Pets: **No**
No. of Private Baths: **10**	Children: **Welcome, over 12**
Double/pb: **$80**	Smoking: **No**
Single/pb: **$70**	Social Drinking: **Permitted**
Open: **All year**	Airport/Station Pickup: **Yes**

The Twin Turrets is a wonderful Victorian mansion in all its restored glory: stained-glass windows, chandeliers, elegant wallpaper, period furniture, and drapery. If this whets your appetite, an antique shop on the first floor sells sterling silver, glass, china, and furniture. Guests have use of the parlor piano. Each bedroom has a newfangled amenity—remote-controlled TV.

Churchtown Inn B&B ✪
ROUTE 23 W, CHURCHTOWN, PENNSYLVANIA 17555

Tel: **(215) 445-7794**	Hosts: **Jim Kent, and Hermine and**
Best Time to Call: **9 AM–9 PM**	**Stuart Smith**

Location: **4 mi. off Pennsylvania Turnpike, Exit 22**
No. of Rooms: **8**
No. of Private Baths: **6**
Max. No. Sharing Bath: **4**
Double/pb: **$75–$95**
Single/pb: **$65–$85**
Double/sb: **$49–$55**
Open: **All year**

Reduced Rates: **Weekly**
Breakfast: **Full**
Other Meals: **Available**
Credit Cards: **MC, VISA**
Pets: **No**
Children: **Welcome, over 12**
Smoking: **No**
Social Drinking: **Permitted**
Foreign Languages: **German**

Churchtown Inn is a lovely fieldstone Federal Colonial mansion built in 1735. Located in the heart of Pennsylvania Dutch country, this B&B is close to Amish attractions, antique markets, and manufacturers' outlets. Rooms are decorated with the hosts' personal treasures: antique furniture, original art, and music boxes. Stuart (a former music director) and Jim (a former accountant who moonlighted as a ballroom dance instructor) stage events throughout the year. The schedule includes concerts, costume balls, carriage rides, walks, and holiday celebrations. Every Saturday, guests have the opportunity of joining Amish or Mennonite families for dinner at an additional fee. Of course, after a Churchtown Inn breakfast, you may not have room for any more meals; the table groans with English oatmeal custard, apple pancakes, Grand Marnier French toast, homemade coffee cake, and other delectables.

The Foreman House B&B ✪
2129 MAIN STREET, CHURCHTOWN, PENNSYLVANIA 17555

Tel: **(215) 445-6713**
Best Time to Call: **Morning, Evening**
Hosts: **Stephen and Jacqueline Mitrani**
Location: **19 mi. E of Lancaster**
No. of Rooms: **2**
Max. No. Sharing Bath: **4**
Double/sb: **$50**
Single/sb: **$40**
Open: **All year**

Breakfast: **Full (weekends); continental (weekdays)**
Pets: **No**
Children: **Welcome, over 10**
Smoking: **No**
Social Drinking: **Permitted**
Minimum Stay: **Holiday weekends**
Foreign Languages: **Spanish**

An elaborate leaded-glass front door adorns the entrance to the Foreman House, a Georgian Revival building constructed in 1919. The interior is decorated with family heirlooms, Oriental rugs, and locally handmade quilts, some of which are for sale. Crafts made by local artisans are displayed in the dining room and may be purchased by guests. Churchtown, founded in 1722, is a residential area surrounded by Amish farmland. From the porch and guestroom windows, you can watch the Amish and Mennonite horse-drawn carriages pass by. Outlet shopping and a variety of entertainment are within reasonable driving distances.

The Columbian

360 CHESTNUT STREET, COLUMBIA, PENNSYLVANIA 17512

Tel: (717) 684-5869; 800-422-5869
Hosts: Linda and John Straitiff
Location: 8 mi. W of Lancaster
No. of Rooms: 5
No. of Private Baths: 5
Double/pb: $60–$65
Suites: $70
Open: All year

Reduced Rates: $10 less per day after 3 nights
Breakfast: Full
Credit Cards: MC, VISA
Pets: No
Children: Welcome, over 12
Smoking: No
Social Drinking: Permitted
Airport/Station Pickup: Yes

The Columbian is a restored turn-of-the-century brick mansion, a fine example of Colonial Revival architecture with unique wrap-around porches, stained-glass windows, and a majestic tiered staircase. The air-conditioned rooms are decorated with antiques in Victorian and simple country style. Breakfast is a hearty buffet offering a chef's choice of such morsels as Quiche Lorraine, Peaches and Cream French Toast, or Belgian Waffles along with fresh fruit and homemade breads. A brief stroll takes you to antique shops, art galleries, the Wright's Ferry Mansion, the Bank Museum, the National Watch and Clock Museum, and the Susquehanna Glass Factory.

Bechtel Mansion Inn ✪

400 WEST KING STREET, EAST BERLIN, PENNSYLVANIA 17316

Tel: (717) 259-7760
Hosts: Marian and Charles Bechtel, and Ruth Spangler
Location: 18 mi. E of Gettysburg
No. of Rooms: 8
No. of Private Baths: 8
Double/pb: $77–$110
Single/pb: $45–$85
Suites: $120–$135

Open: All year
Reduced Rates: 10%, seniors
Breakfast: Continental
Credit Cards: AMEX, DISC, MC, VISA
Pets: No
Children: Welcome
Smoking: No
Social Drinking: Permitted

A romantic getaway, this sprawling mansion was designed for the William Leas family in 1897. It is listed on the National Register of Historic Places, and located in the historic district. The rooms have been beautifully restored and feature original brass chandeliers. Air-conditioned sleeping quarters are elegantly appointed with handmade quilts and antique furnishings. Choose from the Sara Leas Room, with its turret-shaped bay window, or the Downstairs Suite, with its hand-made walnut furniture and folding oak interior shutters. Guests are welcome to relax in the living room with an oak-and-mahogany secretary and red Bokhara rug. Fresh muffins, juice, fruit ambrosia, coffee cake, and coffee are served in the dining room, which has a

large window seat, etched-glass windows, and antique rug. There is a large front-and-side porch for sipping a glass of wine or just relaxing and watching the village activity.

Red Door Studio B&B ✪

6485 LEMON STREET, EAST PETERSBURG, PENNSYLVANIA 17520

Tel: **(717) 569-2909**
Best Time to Call: **8–9 AM**
Host: **Mary Elizabeth Patton**
Location: **1½ mi. N of Lancaster**
No. of Rooms: **3**
Max. No. Sharing Bath: **5**
Double/sb: **$30–$40**
Single/sb: **$20**

Open: **All year**
Breakfast: **Continental**
Pets: **Sometimes**
Children: **Welcome (crib)**
Smoking: **No**
Social Drinking: **Permitted**
Airport/Station Pickup: **Yes**

Open the red door and you instantly know you're in an artist's home. A former teacher of art history, Mary Elizabeth is now a full-time artist and portrait painter. Her B&B is warm, bright, and inviting, with many souvenirs and pictures of her world travels. Of special interest is her collection of Indian and African works. Breakfast is an inviting spread of fresh fruit, yogurt, granola, Danish pastry, coffee, or herb tea. You are welcome to relax in the backyard, use the barbecue, or watch TV.

Elm Country Inn Bed & Breakfast ✪
P.O. BOX 37, ELM AND NEWPORT ROADS, ELM, PENNSYLVANIA 17521

Tel: **(717) 664-3623**	Reduced Rates: **10%, Jan. 2–Mar. 31;**
Best Time to Call: **After 4:30 PM**	**10%, seniors**
Hosts: **Betty and Melvin Meck**	Breakfast: **Full**
Location: **12 mi. N of Lancaster**	Credit Cards: **MC, VISA**
No. of Rooms: **2**	Pets: **No**
Max. No. Sharing Bath: **4**	Children: **Welcome**
Double/sb: **$40–$45**	Smoking: **No**
Single/sb: **$25–$30**	Social Drinking: **Permitted**
Open: **All year**	Airport/Station Pickup: **Yes**

Located in a small country village, this 1860 brick farmhouse overlooks beautiful farmland. The large, sunny rooms feature original wood trim and are furnished with a pleasing blend of antiques and collectibles. Antique shops, craft shops, and opportunities to fish or canoe are available. Betty and Melvin thoroughly enjoy having visitors and do their best to have them feel instantly at home.

Rocky-Side Farm ✪
RD 1, ELVERSON, PENNSYLVANIA 19520

Tel: **(215) 286-5362**	Open: **All year**
Best Time to Call: **Before 5 PM**	Breakfast: **Full**
Host: **Reba Yoder**	Other Meals: **Available**
Location: **18 mi. S of Reading**	Pets: **No**
No. of Rooms: **2**	Children: **Welcome (crib)**
Max. No. Sharing Bath: **4**	Smoking: **No**
Double/sb: **$35**	Social Drinking: **No**
Single/sb: **$25**	

You will be warmly welcomed by the Yoders to their farm, where they raise dairy cows, corn, wheat, soybeans, and hay. The stone farmhouse dates back to 1919 and has a wraparound columned porch for lazying away an afternoon. The rooms are furnished country style, complemented by handmade braided-wool rugs and pretty quilts. Light breakfasts are Reba's style, so you're certain to be on your diet during your stay. Hopewell Village and the Amish country-side are pleasant destinations.

Clearview Farm Bed & Breakfast ✪
355 CLEARVIEW ROAD, EPHRATA, PENNSYLVANIA 17522

Tel: **(717) 733-6333**	Location: **9 mi. N of Lancaster**
Best Time to Call: **Evenings**	No. of Rooms: **3**
Hosts: **Glenn and Mildred Wissler**	No. of Private Baths: **1**

Max. No. Sharing Bath: **4**	Credit Cards: **MC, VISA**
Double/pb: **$69**	Pets: **No**
Double/sb: **$55**	Children: **Welcome**
Open: **All year**	Smoking: **No**
Breakfast: **Full**	Social Drinking: **Permitted**

A lovely rural retreat, this limestone farmhouse surveys a 200-acre working farm. As you watch swans drift around the pond, you'll find it hard to believe that major highways are only a mile away. The antique beds, graceful chandeliers, and elegant wallpapers allow guests to relax in style. The convenient location offers easy access to five antique malls, Hershey Park, and other area attractions. Ham-and-cheese soufflés, French cinnamon toast, eggs Benedict, and waffles are a few of the highlights of the Wissler's breakfasts.

Gerhart House B&B ✪
287 DUKE STREET, EPHRATA, PENNSYLVANIA 17522

Tel: **(717) 733-0263**	Double/sb: **$45–$50**
Best Time to Call: **9 AM–10 PM**	Single/sb: **$40–$45**
Hosts: **Judith and Richard Lawson**	Open: **All year**
Location: **13 mi. N of Lancaster**	Reduced Rates: **$10, senior citizens**
No. of Rooms: **5**	Breakfast: **Full**
No. of Private Baths: **3**	Pets: **No**
Max. No. Sharing Bath: **4**	Children: **Sometimes**
Double/pb: **$65–$80**	Smoking: **Permitted**
Single/pb: **$60–$75**	Social Drinking: **Permitted**

Gerhart House was built in 1926 by one of Ephrata's most prominent designers. Alexander Gerhart saw to it that his spacious brick home reflected the rich woods and elegant fixtures of the period. The front parlor has oak flooring with walnut inlays, chestnut woodwork, and comfortable furnishing. Bedrooms are decorated in warm Williamsburg colors and have large, sunny windows, fresh flowers, and vintage carpets. In summer, enjoy a glass of lemonade on the porch or large veranda; in winter, afternoon tea is served. House specialties such as extra-thick French toast and quiche are served in a quiet breakfast room with small tables. Gerhart House is a short walk from the Ephrata Cloister, close to the Amish country, outlet shopping, and antiques markets.

Historic Smithton Country Inn ✪
900 WEST MAIN STREET, EPHRATA, PENNSYLVANIA 17522

Tel: **(717) 733-6094**	Location: **12 mi. NE of Lancaster**
Best Time to Call: **8 AM–10 PM**	No. of Rooms: **7**
Host: **Dorothy Graybill**	No. of Private Baths: **7**

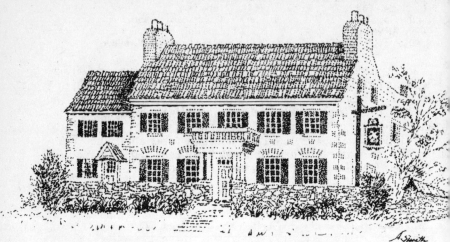

Double/pb: **$65–$115**
Single/pb: **$55–$105**
Suites: **$140–$170**
Open: **All year**
Breakfast: **Full**
Other Meals: **Available**
Credit Cards: **AMEX, MC, VISA**

Pets: **Sometimes**
Children: **Welcome**
Smoking: **No**
Social Drinking: **Permitted**
Minimum Stay: **2 nights on weekends**
Airport/Station Pickup: **Yes**

The inn has been serving guests since 1763. Picture yourself returning "home" after seeing the Pennsylvania Dutch sights and trudging wearily to your bedroom. Waiting for you are candle sconces, canopy beds, Amish quilts, down pillows, and on cool nights, a cozy fire. There's even a flannel nightshirt to snuggle in. And after a restful sleep, come down to an all-you-can-eat breakfast that often features blueberry waffles.

Hershey Bed & Breakfast Reservation Service
P.O. BOX 208, HERSHEY, PENNSYLVANIA 17033

Tel: **(717) 533-2928**
Best Time to Call: **10 AM–4 PM**
Coordinator: **Renee Deutel**
States/Regions Covered: **Hanover, Harrisburg, Hershey, Lancaster, Palmyra**

Rates (Single/Double):

Modest:	**$45**	**$50**
Average:	**$55**	**$60**
Luxury:	**$70**	**$90**

Credit Cards: **MC, VISA**

Renee has a small roster of lovely homes close to main thoroughfares. Hosts come from a variety of interesting backgrounds, and all share a common enthusiasm to share their homes and communities. You may choose a cozy farmhouse, a large older home with beautiful furnishings, or a country inn. Whatever your wishes, the town that chocolate made famous will welcome you.

Gibson's Bed & Breakfast ❂
141 WEST CARACAS AVENUE, HERSHEY, PENNSYLVANIA 17033

Tel: **(717) 534-1305**	Breakfast: **Full**
Hosts: **Frances and Bob Gibson**	Pets: **No**
Location: **One block off Rte. 422**	Children: **Welcome, over 5**
No. of Rooms: **3**	Smoking: **Permitted**
Max. No. Sharing Bath: **3**	Social Drinking: **Permitted**
Double/sb: **$45**	Airport/Station Pickup: **Yes**
Single/sb: **$35**	Foreign Languages: **Italian**
Open: **All year**	

Bob and Frances Gibson have a 50-year-old Cape Cod, located in the center of Hershey, walking distance from many local attractions. The house has been recently renovated to enhance the charm of the hardwood floors, wood trim, and original windows. The atmosphere is friendly and informal, and your hosts are glad to offer complimentary nibbles such as wine and cheese. Gourmet specialties such as Scotch eggs, scones, homemade breads, jams, and cinnamon buns are served each morning in a cozy breakfast room. The Gibsons will gladly help you find local sights such as Hershey Park, Chocolate World, Founders Hall, and the Amish country.

Bed & Breakfast—The Manor ❂
830 VILLAGE ROAD, P.O. BOX 416, LAMPETER, PENNSYLVANIA 17537

Tel: **(717) 464-9564**	Single/sb: **$50**
Best Time to Call: **9 AM–9 PM**	Open: **All year**
Hosts: **Mary Lou Paolini and Jackie Curtis**	Reduced Rates: **25%, seniors Oct.– Mar.**
Location: **3 mi. SE of Lancaster**	Breakfast: **Full**
No. of Rooms: **3**	Credit Cards: **MC, VISA**
No. of Private Baths: **1**	Pets: **No**
Max. No. Sharing Bath: **4**	Children: **Welcome**
Double/pb: **$60**	Smoking: **No**
Single/pb: **$55**	Social Drinking: **No**
Double/sb: **$55**	Airport/Station Pickup: **Yes**

Set on 4½ acres of lush Amish farmland, this cozy farmhouse is just minutes away from Lancaster's historical sights and attractions. Dutch Wonderland, the Strasburg Railroad, Amish farms, and Hershey are but a few of the don't-miss sights nearby. Guests delight in Mary Lou's delicious breakfasts, which often feature gourmet treats such as Eggs Mornay, crêpes or strata, apple cobbler, and her homemade jams and breads. In summer, a swim in the pool or a nap under one of the many shade trees is the perfect way to cap a day of touring.

Walkabout Inn ✪
837 VILLAGE ROAD, LAMPETER, PENNSYLVANIA 17537

Tel: (717) 464-0707
Hosts: **Richard and Maggie Mason**
Location: **3 mi. S of Lancaster**
No. of Rooms: **4**
No. of Private Baths: **2**
Max. No. Sharing Bath: **4**
Double/pb: **$65**
Single/pb: **$50**
Double/sb: **$45**
Single/sb: **$35**
Guest Cottage: **$125; sleeps 6**

Suites: **$100**
Open: **All year**
Reduced Rates: **Available**
Breakfast: **Full**
Other Meals: **Available**
Credit Cards: **AMEX, MC, VISA**
Pets: **No**
Children: **Welcome (crib)**
Smoking: **No**
Social Drinking: **Permitted**
Airport/Station Pickup: **Yes**

The Walkabout Inn takes its name from the Australian word, which means to go out and discover new places. Australian-born host Richard Mason and his wife, Maggie, will help you explore the Amish country that surrounds their brick Mennonite farmhouse. The twenty-two-room house was built in 1925 and features wraparound porches, balconies, and chestnut woodwork. Guest rooms feature Maggie's hand stenciling and are decorated with antiques, Oriental rugs, and Pennsylvania Dutch quilts. When it's time to say "good-day," a candlelight gourmet breakfast is served on silver and crystal in the dining room. Homemade Australian bread, pastries, and tea imported from down under are always on the menu. Your hosts invite you to visit their country craft shop and can direct you to numerous other shops, restaurants, and historic sites. The inn is AAA rated.

Buona Notte B&B ✪
2020 MARIETTA AVENUE, LANCASTER, PENNSYLVANIA 17603

Tel: (717) 295-2597
Best Time to Call: **Evenings**
Hosts: **Joe and Anna Kuhns Predoti**
Location: **1 mi. off Route 30,**
   Rohrerstown exit
No. of Rooms: **3**
No. of Private Baths: **1**
Max. No. Sharing Bath: **4**
Double/pb: **$50**
Double/sb: **$45**

Open: **All year**
Breakfast: **Continental**
Pets: **No**
Children: **Welcome, over 2**
Smoking: **No**
Social Drinking: **No**
Foreign Languages: **French, Italian**
Minimum Stay: **2 nights, holiday**
   weekends

This spacious, turn-of-the-century home is within striking distance of Hershey Park and Gettysburg, while Pennsylvania Dutch country is only 10 minutes away. Franklin and Marshall College and Millersville University are also in the area. For breakfast, you'll enjoy a variety of homemade muffins, breads, and jams, accompanied by all the coffee or tea you can drink.

O'Flaherty's Dingeldein House ✪
1105 EAST KING STREET, LANCASTER, PENNSYLVANIA 17602

Tel: **(717) 293-1723**	Reduced Rates: **Weekly**
Best Time to Call: **8 AM–9 PM**	Breakfast: **Full**
Hosts: **Jack and Sue Flatley**	Credit Cards: **MC, VISA**
No. of Rooms: **4**	Pets: **Sometimes**
No. of Private Baths: **2**	Children: **Welcome**
Max. No. Sharing Bath: **4**	Smoking: **No**
Double/pb: **$65**	Social Drinking: **No**
Double/sb: **$55**	Airport/Station Pickup: **Yes**
Open: **All year**	

This 1912 Dutch Colonial home, surrounded by a lovely landscaped garden, offers traditional furnishings. The delicious country breakfast features Sue's freshly baked muffins. The table is set with a variety of herb teas and fresh fruits of the season from local farms. The menu may include a variety of pancakes or Jack's special omelets.

Hollinger House ✪
2336 HOLLINGER ROAD, LANCASTER, PENNSYLVANIA 17602

Tel: **(717) 464-3050**	Reduced Rates: **Dec.–May; families**
Best Time to Call: **Mornings**	Breakfast: **Full**
Host: **Jean Thomas**	Pets: **No**
No. of Rooms: **4**	Children: **Welcome**
Max. No. Sharing Bath: **4**	Smoking: **No**
Double/sb: **$45–$55**	Social Drinking: **Permitted**
Single/sb: **$35–$40**	Airport/Station Pickup: **Yes**
Open: **All year**	Foreign Languages: **German**

While this house, built in 1870, is undeniably grand in style, it is also homey. Jean invites you to relax on the wide porch, or stroll about the five acres of land crossed by a woodland stream. Although it is convenient to all the area's attractions, it is peacefully away from the tourist traffic. Jean has led tours throughout the Lancaster area and will be happy to answer your questions and give expert advice.

Meadowview Guest House ✪
2169 NEW HOLLAND PIKE, LANCASTER, PENNSYLVANIA 17601

Tel: **(717) 299-4017**	Reduced Rates: **$3 less on 3rd night;**
Best Time to Call: **Before 10:30 PM**	**off season**
Hosts: **Edward and Sheila Christie**	Open: **Mar. 1–Nov. 30**
No. of Rooms: **3**	Breakfast: **Continental**
No. of Private Baths: **1**	Pets: **No**
Max. No. Sharing Bath: **4**	Children: **Welcome, over 7**
Double/pb: **$40**	Smoking: **No**
Single/pb: **$40**	Social Drinking: **Permitted**
Double/sb: **$25–$30**	Airport/Station Pickup: **Yes**

Situated in the heart of Pennsylvania Dutch country, the house has a pleasant blend of modern and traditional furnishings. Your hosts offer a fully equipped guest kitchen where you can store and prepare your own light meals. Ed and Sheila supply coffee and tea. The area is known for great farmers' markets, antique shops, craft shops, country auctions, and wonderful restaurants.

Patchwork Inn Bed & Breakfast ✪
2319 OLD PHILADELPHIA PIKE, LANCASTER, PENNSYLVANIA 17602

Tel: **(717) 293-9078**	Open: **All year**
Best Time to Call: **Morning**	Breakfast: **Continental**
Host: **Lee Martin**	Credit Cards: **MC, VISA**
No. of Rooms: **4**	Pets: **No**
No. of Private Baths: **2**	Children: **Welcome, over 10**
Max. No. Sharing Bath: **4**	Smoking: **No**
Double/pb: **$65**	Social Drinking: **Permitted**
Double/sb: **$55**	Airport/Station Pickup: **Yes**
Suites: **$75**	

Upon entering this lovely 19th-century farmhouse, you won't be surprised to discover that quilts are the innkeeper's hobby. Gorgeous quilts cover the queen-size beds, art and posters feature quilts, and several adorn the walls as hangings. Lee will be happy to direct you to special shops where quilting material or completed quilts are sold. The inn features a handsome collection of fine, oak furniture including an oak phone booth where Lee displays a collection of interesting antique telephones. Breakfast, served in the dining room decorated with Holland Delft, is a generous repast.

The Loom Room
RD 1, BOX 1420, LEESPORT, PENNSYLVANIA 19533

Tel: **(215) 926-3217**	Single/sb: **$40**
Hosts: **Mary and Gene Smith**	Open: **All year**
Location: **4 mi. N of Reading**	Breakfast: **Full**
No. of Rooms: **3**	Reduced Rates: **Weekly**
No. of Private Baths: **1**	Pets: **No**
Max. No. Sharing Bath: **4**	Children: **Welcome (crib)**
Double/pb: **$45**	Smoking: **Permitted**
Single/pb: **$45**	Social Drinking: **Permitted**
Double/sb: **$40**	Airport/Station Pickup: **Yes**

The Loom Room is a stucco-covered stone farmhouse dating back more than 175 years. It is located in the countryside surrounded by shade trees, flowers, and herb gardens. Inside, the spacious rooms feature country antiques, open beams, fireplaces, and handwoven accessories. Mary invites you to her studio, where her work is on display. Her talents also extend to the kitchen, where she helps Gene cook up eggnog French toast, homemade jams, muffins, and chipped beef. Breakfast may be served in the sunny kitchen or outside in the gazebo. This lovely farm is near Reading's outlet complexes, Blue Marsh Lake Recreation Area, antique shops, and many historic sights.

The Sleepy Fir Bed & Breakfast ✪
RD 2, BOX 2802, ZIEGLER NURSERY ROAD, LEESPORT, PENNSYLVANIA 19533

Tel: **(215) 926-1014**	Single/sb: **$35**
Best Time to Call: **3–9 PM**	Open: **All year**
Hosts: **Phil and Judy Whitmoyer**	Reduced Rates: **After 2nd night**
Location: **7 mi. NW of Reading**	Breakfast: **Full**
No. of Rooms: **2**	Pets: **No**
No. of Private Baths: **1**	Children: **Welcome, over 6**
Max. No. Sharing Bath: **4**	Smoking: **No**
Double/pb: **$45**	Social Drinking: **Permitted**
Single/pb: **$40**	Airport/Station Pickup: **Yes**
Double/sb: **$40**	

A brick Cape Cod with black shutters, this house offers rural privacy on three and a half acres of landscaped and wooded countryside. The guest rooms have double beds and share a luxury bath with a whirlpool and sauna. Your hosts, Phil and Judy Whitmoyer, tour guides at the Berk County Heritage Center, are natives of the area, and they will be happy to direct you to outlet shopping, public golf courses, and the sights of Pennsylvania Dutch Country. The Whitmoyers have bicycles and a 17-foot canoe to lend for exploring the nearby Blue Marsh Lake Recreation Area. After a busy day they invite you to unwind with a game of pool or a stroll through the wooded property.

Alden House ✪
62 EAST MAIN STREET, LITITZ, PENNSYLVANIA 17545

Tel: **(717) 627-3363**	Open: **All year**
Best Time to Call: **1–9 PM**	Reduced Rates: **10%, after 2 nights**
Host: **Gloria Adams**	**from Nov. 1–Apr. 30**
Location: **7 mi. N of Lancaster**	Breakfast: **Continental**
No. of Rooms: **7**	Credit Cards: **MC, VISA**
No. of Private Baths: **5**	Pets: **No**
Max. No. Sharing Bath: **4**	Children: **Welcome, over 6**
Double/pb: **$75**	Smoking: **Permitted**
Double/sb: **$65**	Social Drinking: **Permitted**
Suites: **$90–$95**	

Built in 1850 and fully restored, this brick townhouse has lots of old-fashioned appeal. At the end of the day, grab a chair on one of the three porches and savor the chocolate aroma wafting over from the local candy factory. The farmers' markets and craft shops of Amish country are a short drive away, and numerous restaurants are within walking distance. Breakfast includes juice, coffee or tea, cereal, fresh seasonal fruit, and baked goods.

Country Spun Farm B&B ✪
BOX 117, SOUTH MAIN STREET, LOGANVILLE, PENNSYLVANIA 17342

Tel: **(717) 428-1162**
Best Time to Call: **10 AM–8 PM**
Hosts: **Greg and Martha Lau**
Location: **1 mi. off I-83, Exit 3**
No. of Rooms: **2**
No. of Private Baths: **2**
Double/pb: **$65**
Single/pb: **$55**

Open: **All year**
Breakfast: **Full**
Credit Cards: **DISC, MC, VISA**
Pets: **No**
Children: **Welcome, over 12**
Smoking: **No**
Social Drinking: **Permitted**

Visitors to this red brick farmhouse get to see modern shepherds in action. The Laus raise pedigreed English Oxford sheep. A high school history teacher, Greg doubles as resident sheep shearer; Martha sells the processed, machine washable wool—as well as sweaters, knitting patterns and knick-knacks—at her Country Spun shop. Feel free to ramble around the farm's 23 acres. Tennis courts are nearby, and it's an easy drive to York County's parks, wineries, antique shops, and historic homes. Breakfasts, served in either the kitchen or the patio, include fresh fruit, juice, cheese, hot muffins, and Martha's specialties, perhaps skillet quiche or cheddar creamed eggs on toast.

Market Sleigh Bed & Breakfast ✪
BOX 99, WALNUT VALLEY FARM, LOGANVILLE, PENNSYLVANIA 17342-0099

Tel: **(717) 428-1440**
Best Time to Call: **3–6 PM**
Hosts: **Judy and Jerry Dietz**
Location: **7 mi. S of York**
No. of Rooms: **1**
No. of Private Baths: **1**
Suite: **$55–$100**
Open: **All year**
Reduced Rates: **Corporate travelers, Mon.–Thurs.**

Breakfast: **Full**
Wheelchair-Accessible: **Yes**
Credit Cards: **MC, VISA**
Pets: **No**
Children: **Welcome, over 12**
Smoking: **No**
Social Drinking: **Permitted**
Minimum Stay: **2 nights convention weekends**

This bed-and-breakfast takes its name from the large 19th-century sleigh parked by the main entrance, as if stranded when the snow melted. Guests are encouraged to wander around the 22-acre property, or just sit with a book in the back porch swing. The many local attractions range from parks and wineries to museums and malls. Judy dishes out a hearty farmer's breakfast of fruit, homemade breads, eggs, cheese, bacon, and French toast or pancakes.

Herr Farmhouse Inn ✪
2256 HUBER DRIVE, MANHEIM, PENNSYLVANIA 17545

Tel: **(717) 653-9852**
Best Time to Call: **After 4 PM**
Host: **Barry A. Herr**
Location: **9 mi. W of Lancaster; ¼ mi. from Rte. 283**
No. of Rooms: **4**
No. of Private Baths: **2**
Max. No. Sharing Bath: **4**
Double/pb: **$75**

Double/sb: **$65**
Suites: **$85**
Open: **All year**
Breakfast: **Continental**
Credit Cards: **MC, VISA**
Pets: **No**
Children: **Welcome, over 6**
Smoking: **Permitted**
Social Drinking: **Permitted**

Nestled on more than 11 acres of rolling farmland, this farmhouse, dating back to 1738, has been restored with the greatest of care and attention to detail. Fanlights adorn the main entrance, there are six working fireplaces, and it has the original pine floors. Whether spending a winter's night by a cozy fire, or a bright summer morning sipping tea in the sun room, it is the perfect retreat. It is less than 20 minutes to the sights, shops, and restaurants of Amish country.

Maple Lane Guest House ✪
505 PARADISE LANE, PARADISE, PENNSYLVANIA 17562

Tel: **(717) 687-7479**
Hosts: **Marion and Edwin Rohrer**
Location: **10 mi. E of Lancaster**
No. of Rooms: **4**
No. of Private Baths: **1**
Max. No. Sharing Bath: **4**
Double/pb: **$45–$55**
Single/pb: **$40–$45**
Double/sb: **$40–$50**

Single/sb: **$38–$42**
Open: **All year**
Breakfast: **Continental**
Pets: **No**
Children: **Welcome (crib)**
Smoking: **No**
Social Drinking: **No**
Minimum Stay: **2 nights, weekends**

From the hill nearby you can see for 40 miles. Stroll the 200 acres of this working farm, with its stream and woodland. Your hosts welcome you to rooms decorated with homemade quilts, needlework, and antiques. The sights of the Amish country, such as the farmers' market, antique shops, flea markets, and restaurants, are within easy reach.

Frogtown Acres Bed and Breakfast Inn ✪
44 FROGTOWN ROAD, PARADISE, PENNSYLVANIA 17562

Tel: **(717) 768-7684**
Hosts: **Lieke and Bryan Byler-van Huystee**
Location: **10 mi. E of Lancaster**
No. of Rooms: **4**
Max. No. Sharing Bath: **4**
Double/sb: **$50–$60**

Open: **All year**
Breakfast: **Full**
Pets: **No**
Children: **Welcome, over 10**
Smoking: **No**
Social Drinking: **Permitted**

Set amid the rolling pastures of the Pennsylvania Dutch farmlands, this was once the home of a country squire. The house was built circa 1850, and its large rooms have been fully restored and decorated with comfortable, informal furnishings. Each bedroom features a queen-size bed and can accommodate a family of four. Breakfast specialties such as French toast and Pennsylvania scrapple are served in your room or on the sun porch. The Rose and Crown is near canoeing and hiking at Pinnacle Point, Lake Eldred Recreational Area, and the attractions of the Pennsylvania Dutch countryside.

The Inn at Mundis Mills ✪
586 MUNDIS RACE ROAD, YORK, PENNSYLVANIA 17402

Tel: **(717) 755-2002**
Best Time to call: **Afternoons**
Hosts: **Joseph and Marilyn Korsak**
Location: **2½ mi. from Rte. 30**
No. of Rooms: **2**
No. of Private Baths: **2**
Double/pb: **$60**

Single/pb: **$45**
Open: **All year**
Breakfast: **Full**
Pets: **No**
Children: **Welcome**
Smoking: **No**
Social Drinking: **Permitted**

This quiet country inn is surrounded by York County farmland. The wide front porch welcomes guests to sit and spend some time listening to the chatter of the birds. The pre–Civil War Dutch farmhouse is restored and warmly furnished with antiques. Homemade muffins and jams, fruits, cereals, eggs, and meats will start your day. And, you can walk off the calories as you tour the nearby museums, battlegrounds, and wineries.

PHILADELPHIA AREA

Bed & Breakfast of Chester County
P.O. BOX 825, KENNETT SQUARE, PENNSYLVANIA 19348

Tel: **(215) 444-1367**
Coordinator: **Doris Passante**
States/Regions Covered: **Chester County, Chadds Ford, Valley Forge**

Rates (Single/Double):
Modest:	**$40**	**$45–$55**
Average:	**$45**	**$55–$65**
Luxury:	**$50**	**$70 and up**

Credit Cards: **No**

Doris has a wide selection of homes located in the beautiful and historic Brandywine Valley, which is known for the River Museum, Longwood Gardens, Winterthur, Brandywine Battlefield, and Valley Forge. The area is convenient to the Pennsylvania Dutch country. Send for her brochure, which fully describes each B&B. The University of Delaware, Lincoln University, and West Chester University are close by. There's a $5 surcharge for one-night stays.

Bed & Breakfast of Philadelphia ✪
P.O. BOX 252, GRADYVILLE, PENNSYLVANIA 19039

Tel: **(215) 358-4747 or (800) 733-4747**	Rates (Single/Double):
Best Time to Call: **9 AM–7 PM**	Modest: **$35** **$45**
Coordinator: **Joan Ralston**	Average: **$50** **$60**
States/Regions Covered: **Philadelphia**	Luxury: **$95** **$95 and up**
and surrounding counties	Credit Cards: **AMEX, MC, VISA**
Descriptive Directory: **$3**	

Joan represents over 100 host homes in Center City, the Main Line suburbs, Valley Forge, Chester County, the Brandywine Valley, and New Hope. The accommodations vary from city town houses to country manors or farms to suburban mansions. Several historic properties are available, including several listed on the National Register of Historic Places. There is a $5 surcharge for one-night stays.

All About Town B&B ✪
P.O. BOX 562, VALLEY FORGE, PENNSYLVANIA 19481-0562

Tel: **(215) 783-7838**	Rates (Single/Double):
Best Time to Call: **9 AM–9 PM daily**	Average: **$40–$65** **$45–$150**
Coordinator: **Carolyn J. Williams**	Credit Cards: **AMEX, MC, VISA**
States/Regions Covered: **Brandywine**	
Valley, Bucks County, King of	
Prussia, Lancaster County,	
Philadelphia, Pocono Mtns., Valley	
Forge	

Carolyn's roster includes town houses, historic homes, farmhouses, inns, estates, and ski locations. Some have multilingual hosts, handicapped facilities, honeymoon cottages, jacuzzi, pool, and tennis courts.

Guesthouses ✪
BOX 2137, WEST CHESTER, PENNSYLVANIA 19380

Tel: **(215) 692-4575**	States/Regions Covered: **Main Line**
Best Time to Call: **Noon–4 PM**	**Philadelphia, Brandywine Valley,**
Coordinator: **Joyce K. Archbold**	**Chesapeake Bay; Delaware,**
	Maryland, New Jersey

Rates (Single/Double): Credit Cards: **AMEX, MC, VISA**
   Modest: **$40–$45**   **$50–$55**
   Average: **$60–$65**   **$80–$85**
   Luxury: **$90–$95**   **$150**

Most of the homes on Joyce's roster are architecturally or historically significant. Choose from an 18th-century home with a swimming pool and surrounded by gardens, or an authentic log house on a large estate adjacent to the Brandywine River. Some hosts are professional chefs, interior designers, or teachers who enjoy sharing cultural and scenic surroundings. Many homes are listed on the National Register of Historic Places. Some are on yachts. All are comfortable and friendly, serving the high-tech corridor, local prep schools and universities, and much more.

Steele Away Bed and Breakfast
7151 BOYER STREET, PHILADELPHIA, PENNSYLVANIA 19119

Tel: **(215) 242-0722**
Best Time to Call: **9 AM–9 PM**
Host: **Diane Robertson-Steele**
No. of Rooms: **2**
Max. No. Sharing Bath: **4**
Double/sb: **$55–$60**
Single/sb: **$50**
Open: **All year**

Reduced Rates: **10%, after 1 week; 15%, after 1 month**
Breakfast: **Continental**
Pets: **No**
Children: **Welcome, over 6**
Smoking: **No**
Social Drinking: **Permitted**
Airport/Station Pickup: **Yes**

Trees shade this stone turn-of-the-century home in Philadelphia's historic Mt. Airy neighborhood, well served by train and bus lines. Your host is a weaver who has decorated the house with her own handiwork, including hand-stenciled wall borders. Cat-lovers will feel right at home: four felines are in residence. For an extra fee, guests have a private kitchen all to themselves. There is no lack of things to do here: Fairmount Park, the Morris Arboretum, Woodmere Art Museum, the Philadelphia Zoo, and the Philadelphia Museum of Art are among the nearby points of interest. Breakfasts are highlighted by peach soup, fresh fruit cobblers, and rum-raisin French toast.

The Barn ✪
1131 GROVE ROAD, WEST CHESTER, PENNSYLVANIA 19380

Tel: **(215) 436-4544**
Hosts: **Susan Hager and son, Ted**
Location: **30 mi. SW of Philadelphia; 16 mi. from Penn. Tpke.**
No. of Rooms: **2**
No. of Private Baths: **1**
Max. No. Sharing Bath: **4**
Double/pb: **$60**
Double/sb: **$55**

Suites: **$90 (2 bedrooms)**
Open: **All year**
Reduced Rates: **Available**
Breakfast: **Full**
Pets: **Welcome**
Children: **Welcome**
Smoking: **Permitted**
Social Drinking: **Permitted**

Dating back to the 1800s, the Barn has been beautifully restored without sacrificing its original identity. Old beams, random-width pine floors, and stone walls are enhanced by simple furnishings and special antiques. Susan's pewter collection, old earthenware, and dried flowers are artfully arranged to add a nice touch. Children love the third-floor "open room," with its double bed, cots, and TV. It's 15 minutes away from Longwood Gardens, Winterthur, and Brandywine Valley attractions. Breakfast often features scrambled eggs in crêpes with Hollandaise sauce, Philadelphia scrapple, popovers, and fresh fruit. Wine and cheese are graciously served in the evening.

POCONO MOUNTAINS

Toby Valley Lodge ✪
P.O. BOX 431, ROUTE 940, BLAKESLEE, PENNSYLVANIA 18610

Tel: **(717) 646-4893**
Best Time to Call: **9 AM–9 PM**
Host: **Marion Whitner**
Location: **1½ mi. from Rte. 80**
No. of Rooms: **7**
No. of Private Baths: **7**
Double/pb: **$40–$50**
Open: **All year**

Reduced Rates: **Weekly**
Breakfast: **Continental**
Credit Cards: **MC, VISA**
Pets: **Sometimes**
Children: **Welcome**
Smoking: **Permitted**
Social Drinking: **Permitted**

If you've ever longed for your own mountain retreat, you'll feel as if your dream came true at this B&B. It faces the woods and Tobyhanna Creek, an excellent trout stream. In chilly weather, the huge fireplace serves as a cheery backdrop to the breakfast area. The comfortable furnishings are accented with antiques, good prints, and western art. Marion provides a guest refrigerator, and you may stock it with drinks and snacks. Activities for the sportsminded abound in the area. Jack Frost Ski Area and Pocono International Raceway are nearby attractions.

Nearbrook ✪
ROUTE 447, CANADENSIS, PENNSYLVANIA 18325

Tel: **(717) 595-3152**
Best Time to Call: **Mornings; evenings**
Location: **20 mi. N of I-80 and I-84**
Hosts: **Barb and Dick Robinson**
No. of Rooms: **3**
No. of Private Baths: **1½**
Max. No. Sharing Bath: **4**
Double/sb: **$40–$50**
Double/pb: **$45–$55**

Single/pb: **$30**
Open: **All year**
Breakfast: **Full**
Pets: **Sometimes**
Children: **Welcome, over 6**
Smoking: **No**
Social Drinking: **Permitted**
Airport/Bus Pickup: **Yes**

Enjoy the Poconos while making Barb and Dick's charming, informal home your base. Meander through winding rock garden paths, and over a tiny arched bridge. Artists and musicians are especially welcome. An upright piano, games, and puzzles are here for your entertainment. Opportunities for hiking, golf, skating, skiing, horseback riding, swimming, and fine dining are nearby. Bedrooms feature such amenities as a sink and a desk.

La Anna Guest House ✪
RD 2, BOX 1051, CRESCO, PENNSYLVANIA 18326

Tel: **(717) 676-4225**
Hosts: **Kay Swingle and Julie Wilson**
Location: **9 mi. from I-80 and I-84**
No. of Rooms: **2**
Max. No. Sharing Bath: **4**
Double/sb: **$30**
Single/sb: **$25**

Open: **All year**
Breakfast: **Continental**
Pets: **No**
Children: **Welcome (crib)**
Smoking: **Permitted**
Social Drinking: **Permitted**

This Victorian home has large rooms furnished with antiques; it is nestled on 25 acres of lush, wooded land, and has its own pond. Kay will happily direct you to fine dining spots that are kind to your wallet. Enjoy scenic walks, waterfalls, mountain vistas, Tobyhanna and Promised Land state parks; there's cross-country skiing right on the property. Lake Wallenpaupack is only 15 minutes away.

Academy Street Bed & Breakfast ✪
528 ACADEMY STREET, HAWLEY, PENNSYLVANIA 18428

Tel: **(717) 226-3430**
Hosts: **Judith and Sheldon Lazan**
Location: **100 mi. NW of New York City**
No. of Rooms: **7**
No. of Private Baths: **4**
Max. No. Sharing Bath: **3**
Double/pb: **$75**
Single/pb: **$40**

Double/sb: **$65**
Single/sb: **$35**
Open: **May–Oct.**
Breakfast: **Full**
Credit Cards: **MC, VISA**
Pets: **No**
Children: **Welcome, over 12**
Smoking: **Permitted**
Social Drinking: **Permitted**

This Italian-style Victorian (circa 1865) is situated on a rise near the Lackawaxen River. Judith and Sheldon have done a marvelous job of restoring the rare and beautiful woodwork, paneling, and inlay to make a fitting background for their lovely antiques and furnishings. You'd better diet before you arrive because you won't be able to resist the culinary delights at breakfast or the complimentary high tea. It's only minutes away from famed Lake Wallenpaupack.

The Vines ✪
107 EAST ANN STREET, MILFORD, PENNSYLVANIA 18337

Tel: (717) 296-6775	Open: All year
Hosts: Joan and Don Voce	Reduced Rates: 20%, seniors
Location: 1 mi. from I-84	Breakfast: Full
No. of Rooms: 4	Pets: No
Max. No. Sharing Bath: 3	Children: Welcome
Double/sb: $50–$60	Smoking: No
Single/sb: $25–$30	Social Drinking: Permitted

The Vines is a Queen Anne Victorian, built in 1864, and has been completely restored. There are parks, flea markets, canoeing, antiquing, historical sites, skiing, fishing, and many charming restaurants within a short distance. Coffee and tea are available in the guest rooms; Saturday nights often have the added attraction of wine and cheese. It is a mile from Grey Towers, Apple Valley with its quaint little shops, and the Milford Theatre.

Bonny Bank ✪
P.O. BOX 481, MILLRIFT, PENNSYLVANIA 18340

Tel: (717) 491-2250	Open: May 15–Oct. 15
Best Time to Call: 9 AM–10 PM	Reduced Rates: 15%, weekly; seniors
Hosts: Doug and Linda Hay	Breakfast: Full
Location: 5 mi. from I-84	Pets: No
No. of Rooms: 1	Children: No
No. of Private Baths: 1	Smoking: No
Double/pb: $35	Social Drinking: Permitted
Single/pb: $25	

Stay in a picture-book small town on a dead-end road. The sound of the rapids will lull you to sleep in this charming bungalow perched on the banks of the Delaware River. Doug and Linda invite you to use their private swimming area and will lend you inner-tubes for float trips. Nearby attractions include the Zane Grey house, Minisink Battlefield, Grey Towers Historical Site, the Victorian village of Milford, and all the sports and variety of restaurants the Poconos are known for.

Elvern Country Lodge ✪
P.O. BOX 177, STONE CHURCH–FIVE POINTS ROAD, MOUNT BETHEL, PENNSYLVANIA 18343

Tel: (215) 588-7922	Max. No. Sharing Bath: 4
Best Time to Call: After 4 PM	Double/pb: $60
Hosts: Dos and Herb Deen	Single/pb: $35
Location: 16 mi. N of Easton	Double/sb: $50
No. of Rooms: 4	Single/sb: $30
No. of Private Baths: 2	Suite: $70

Open: **All year**
Reduced Rates: **10%, seniors; weekly;**
   Former guests; Mon.–Thurs.
Breakfast: **Full**
Other Meals: **Available**
Pets: **Sometimes**

Children: **Welcome (crib)**
Smoking: **Permitted**
Social Drinking: **Permitted**
Airport/Station Pickup: **Yes**
Minimum Stay: **2 nights, some**
   weekends

This is a working farm in the foothills of the Pocono Mountains. The house dates back to the Victorian period and includes a sun deck and patio. Guest quarters have cool summer breezes, individual thermostats, and wall-to-wall carpeting. Your hosts raise their own beef, vegetables, and fruit. They prepare a breakfast of country bacon, fresh eggs, and homemade jams. Fishing, boating, and swimming can be enjoyed in the two-acre lake on the farm. The Delaware Water Gap Recreation Area, Appalachian Trail, and Pocono Recreation Area are nearby.

The Lampost Bed & Breakfast ✪
HCR BOX 154, ROUTE 507, PAUPACK, PENNSYLVANIA 18451

Tel: **(717) 857-1738**
Best Time to Call: **7 AM–10 PM**
Hosts: **Lily, Karen, and David Seagaard**
Location: **9 mi. S of Hawley**
No. of Rooms: **3**
No. of Private Baths: **2**
Max. No. Sharing Bath: **4**
Double/pb: **$70**
Double/sb: **$60**
Single/sb: **$50**

Open: **Apr.–Oct.**
Reduced Rates: **10%, Mon.–Thurs.**
Breakfast: **Continental**
Credit Cards: **MC, VISA**
Pets: **Sometimes**
Children: **Welcome, over 10**
Smoking: **No**
Social Drinking: **Permitted**

An assortment of lampposts line the driveway leading to this white colonial home on two acres overlooking Lake Wallenpaupack. This is an ideal stopover for those who love waterfront activities—swimming, boating, fishing, and waterskiing. If you'd rather stay high and dry, there are facilities for golfing, tennis, and horseback riding nearby. Other recreational options include scenic train excursions and balloon rides.

High Hollow ✪
STAR ROUTE, BOX 9-A1, SOUTH STERLING, PENNSYLVANIA 18460

Tel: **(717) 676-4275**
Best Time to Call: **10 AM–9 PM**
Hosts: **Tex and Robbie Taylor**
Location: **12 mi. N of Mt. Pocono**
   from I-80, 5.4 mi. S of I-84
No. of Rooms: **1 suite**
No. of Private Baths: **1**
Suite: **$35–$40**

Open: **Apr. 1–Nov. 30**
Breakfast: **Continental**
Pets: **Sometimes**
Children: **No**
Smoking: **No**
Social Drinking: **Permitted**
Minimum Stay: **2 nights weekends; 3**
   nights holiday weekends

Built of stone and rough-hewn wood, with a pond in front and a stream in back, this handsome retreat fits right into the countryside. Lake Wallenpaupack and Tobyhanna and Gouldsboro State Parks are nearby; Tex, an avid hunter and fisherman, will direct guests to other recreational areas. Weather permitting, the Continental breakfast of juice, homemade muffins, fruit, cheese, and coffee and tea is served on the terrace overlooking the pond.

The Redwood House ✪
BOX 9B, EAST SIDE BORO, WHITE HAVEN, PENNSYLVANIA 18661

Tel: **(717) 443-7186; (215) 355-1754**	Suites: **$60**
Hosts: **John and Emma Moore**	Open: **All year**
No. of Rooms: **4**	Reduced Rates: **5%, seniors**
No. of Private Baths: **2**	Breakfast: **Continental**
Max. No. Sharing Bath: **4**	Pets: **No**
Double/pb: **$35**	Children: **Welcome**
Single/pb: **$25**	Smoking: **Permitted**
Double/sb: **$30**	Social Drinking: **Permitted**
Single/sb: **$20**	

This frame chalet is minutes from the slopes at Big Boulder and Jack Frost. In summer enjoy sunning and swimming at Hickory Run State Park. Nearby Lehigh River offers fishing and rafting. Your hosts recommend a visit to Eckley, where the movie *The Molly Maguires* was filmed—a true example of what life was like in a 19th-century mining community. After a day of touring, come and relax on the large, comfortable porch.

SCRANTON/NORTH-CENTRAL PENNSYLVANIA

Hill Top Haven ✪
RD 1, BOX 5C, LIBERTY, PENNSYLVANIA 16930

Tel: **(717) 324-2608**	Open: **All year**
Hosts: **Richard and Betty Landis**	Breakfast: **Full**
Location: **29 mi. N of Williamsport**	Pets: **No**
No. of Rooms: **2**	Children: **Welcome**
Max. No. Sharing Bath: **4**	Smoking: **No**
Double/sb: **$35**	Social Drinking: **No**
Single/sb: **$30**	

This sprawling ranch home is in a rural mountain area surrounded by fields, flower beds, and woods. The house is furnished with many antiques and offers beautiful views of the surrounding countryside. A 10-acre lake is available for fishing and snowmobiling, and biking trails abound. The kids will want to visit the ducks, geese, and dairy cows. State parks and a ski resort are close by, but if all you desire is fresh air and quiet, you'll find plenty of both at Hill Top Haven.

The Carriage House at Stonegate ✪
RD 1, BOX 23, MONTOURSVILLE, PENNSYLVANIA 17754

Tel: (717) 433-4340
Best Time to Call: 5:30 PM–9:30 PM
Hosts: Harold and Dena Mesaris
Location: 6 mi. E of Williamsport
No. of Rooms: 2
No. of Private Baths: 1
Guest Cottage: $50 for 2; $70 for 4

Open: All year
Breakfast: Continental
Pets: Welcome
Children: Welcome
Smoking: Permitted
Social Drinking: Permitted
Airport/Station Pickup: Yes

This self-contained facility was converted from the original carriage house of an 1830 farmhouse. Perfect for a family, there are two bedrooms, a bathroom, a living room with cable television, a dining area, and a kitchen stocked with all your breakfast needs. Decorated in country fashion, with some antiques, it offers complete privacy just 30 yards from your host's home. You'll have access to a creek, a barn complete with a variety of animals, and 30 acres on which to roam. It's close to the Little League Museum and Loyalsock Creek for swimming, canoeing, tubing, and fishing.

The Bodine House ✪
307 SOUTH MAIN STREET, MUNCY, PENNSYLVANIA 17756

Tel: (717) 546-8949
Best Time to Call: Evenings
Hosts: David and Marie Louise Smith
Location: 15 mi. S of Williamsport; 10 mi. from I-80, Exit 31B
No. of Rooms: 4
No. of Private Baths: 3
Max. No. Sharing Bath: 3
Double/pb: $50–$60
Single/pb: $45–$50

Double/sb: $45
Single/sb: $30
Open: All year
Credit Cards: AMEX, MC, VISA
Breakfast: Full
Pets: No
Children: Welcome, over 6
Smoking: No
Social Drinking: Permitted

This restored town house dates back to 1805. A baby grand piano, four fireplaces, and a candlelit living room add to its old-fashioned appeal. A full country breakfast and wine and cheese are on the house. Local attractions include the Susquehanna River, the Endless Mountains, and the fall foliage.

Collomsville Inn ✪
RD #3, WILLIAMSPORT, PENNSYLVANIA 17701

Tel: (717) 745-3608
Best Time to Call: 9 AM–5 PM
Host: Betty Callahan
Location: 13 mi. W of Williamsport
No. of Rooms: 5

Max. No. Sharing Bath: 5
Double/sb: $40
Single/sb: $35
Open: All year
Breakfast: Continental

Credit Cards: **MC, VISA**
Pets: **Sometimes**
Children: **Welcome, over 12**

Smoking: **No**
Social Drinking: **Permitted**
Airport/Station Pickup: **Yes**

A distinctive four-story wooden building with many balconies, this B&B is located on Route 44 in the lush green countryside just west of Williamsport. During the early 19th century, Collomsville served as a stagecoach stop. Today, the five guest rooms retain a rustic charm, and the dining and kitchen areas are filled with antiques suggestive of the inn's rich heritage. Williamsport, the county seat, is best known as the home of the Little League Hall of Fame and Museum. Bargain hunters are sure to score a hit with accessories from Woolrich Woolen Mills, just a short drive away. And sport of another kind waits nearby at Pine Creek, a paradise for anglers, hunters, hikers, cross-country skiers, and snowmobilers.

SOUTHEASTERN PENNSYLVANIA

Brennans B&B ✪
3827 LINDEN STREET, ALLENTOWN, PENNSYLVANIA 18104

Tel: **(215) 395-0869**
Best Time to Call: **11:30AM–11:30 PM**
Hosts: **Lois and Edward Brennan**
Location: **1 mi. from 78 & 22**
No. of Rooms: **2**
No. of Private Baths: **1**
Max. No. Sharing Bath: **2**
Double/pb: **$40**
Single/pb: **$35**

Double/sb: **$30**
Single/sb: **$25**
Open: **Apr.–Dec.**
Breakfast: **Full**
Pets: **Sometimes**
Children: **Welcome**
Smoking: **Permitted**
Social Drinking: **Permitted**
Airport/Station Pickup: **Yes**

Furnished in Early American fashion, accented with lush plants and family treasures, this comfortable brick ranch-style house can be your home away from home. The Brennans are history buffs who, now that they're retired, enjoy traveling and entertaining travelers. Breakfast features bacon and eggs with home fries, or sausages and pancakes, or delicious muffins to go with the homemade jam. You can walk off the calories on your way to the Haines Mill, Dorney Park, or one of the area's many museums.

Longswamp Bed and Breakfast ✪
RD 2, BOX 26, MERTZTOWN, PENNSYLVANIA 19539

Tel: **(215) 682-6197**
Hosts: **Elsa Dimick and Dr. Dean Dimick**
Location: **12 mi. SW of Allenton**
No. of Rooms: **9**
No. of Private Baths: **5**

Max. No. Sharing Bath: **4**
Double/pb: **$60–$65**
Single/pb: **$50**
Double/sb: **$60–$65**
Single/sb: **$50**
Open: **All year**

Breakfast: **Full**	Smoking: **Permitted**
Credit Cards: **MC, VISA**	Social Drinking: **Permitted**
Pets: **No**	Airport/Station Pickup: **Yes**
Children: **Welcome**	Foreign Languages: **French**

This guest house was originally built around 1750 and served as the first post office in town. The main house, completed in 1863, was a stop on the underground railroad. Today, Longswamp is a comfortable place with high ceilings, antiques, large fireplaces, plants, and bookcases full of reading pleasure. Breakfast specialties include home-dried fruits, *pain perdu*, quiche, and homemade breads. Your host offers wine, cheese, and coffee anytime. She will gladly direct you to antiques shops, auction houses, Reading, and the Amish country.

SUSQUEHANNA COUNTY

Linger Longer at Quaker Lake ✪
RD 1, BOX 44, BRACKNEY, PENNSYLVANIA 18812

Tel: **(717) 663-2844**	Open: **All year, Thurs.–Sun.**
Best Time to Call: **7 AM–7 PM**	Breakfast: **Continental**
Hosts: **Dan and Nancy Strnatka**	Pets: **Sometimes**
Location: **10 mi. S of Binghamton, N.Y.**	Children: **No**
No. of Rooms: **4**	Smoking: **No**
Max. No. Sharing Bath: **4**	Social Drinking: **Permitted**
Double/sb: **$60–$75**	Airport/Station Pickup: **Yes**
Single/sb: **$55–$65**	

Linger Longer is a quiet retreat on the shore of Quaker Lake in the Endless Mountains. In the summer, you may catch cool breezes on the front porch, or relax in the hot tub on the patio; come winter, the living room's old stone fireplace wards off any hint of chill. The house is decorated with pottery and art crafted by local artists. Similar pieces, and gifts ranging from jewelry to imported Aran Island sweaters, are sold in the Linger Longer shop. Breakfast features croissants, imported preserves, and imported coffees. Guests are welcome to use the Strnatka's gas grill and picnic area.

WESTERN PENNSYLVANIA

Pittsburgh Bed & Breakfast ✪
785 STONEGATE DRIVE, WEXFORD, PENNSYLVANIA 15090

Tel: **(412) 934-1212**	Rates (Single/Double):	
Coordinator: **Judy Antico**	Average: **$30**	**$48**
States/Regions Covered: **Pittsburgh**	Luxury: **$58**	**$115**
and western Pennsylvania	Credit Cards: **MC, VISA**	
Descriptive Directory: **Free**	Descriptive Directory: **Free**	

Judy has many comfortable accommodations within a 100-mile radius, as well as in Pittsburgh's metropolitan area. Many homes are convenient to Carnegie-Mellon University, Duquesne, the University of Pittsburgh, ski resorts, historic Bedford, and Lake Erie. This is a great place to stop off en route to Cleveland (80 miles), Chicago (400 miles), and West Virginia (60 miles).

Bluebird Hollow Bed & Breakfast
BLUEBIRD HOLLOW, RD4, BOX 217, BROOKVILLE, PENNSYLVANIA 15825

Tel: **(814) 856-2858**
Best Time to Call: **Before 8 AM, after 6 PM**
Hosts: **Ned and Joan Swigart**
Location: **75 mi. NE of Pittsburgh**
No. of Rooms: **4**
No. of Private Baths: **1**
Max. No. Sharing Bath: **4**
Double/pb: **$47–$51**
Single/pb: **$42–$46**
Double/sb: **$40–$44**

Single/sb: **$35–$39**
Open: **All year**
Reduced Rates: **15%, weekly**
Breakfast: **Full**
Pets: **Yes**
Children: **Welcome, infants free (crib)**
Smoking: **Permitted**
Social Drinking: **Permitted**
Airport/Station Pickup: **Yes**

A white farmhouse built in 1894, Bluebird Hollow is filled with cherished family antiques, restored "finds," and lovely old quilts. There's something for everyone here, from trout fishing in nearby Redbank Creek to workshops and demonstrations at Cook Forest Sawmill Center for the Arts. It's always fun to stroll the Swigarts' 17-acre property, where you're likely to see deer and other wildlife. To start you off properly, Joan serves up a big country breakfast of berries from her own garden, homemade muffins, stuffed pancakes, and locally cured ham.

Garrott's Bed & Breakfast ✪
RD 1, BOX 73, COWANSVILLE, PENNSYLVANIA 16218

Tel: **(412) 545-2432**
Best Time to Call: **Evenings, weekends**
Host: **Denise Garrott**
Location: **50 mi. NE of Pittsburgh**
No. of Rooms: **3**
Max. No. Sharing Bath: **3**
Double/sb: **$60**

Single/sb: **$50**
Open: **All year**
Breakfast: **Full**
Pets: **Sometimes**
Children: **Welcome, over 8**
Smoking: **Permitted**
Social Drinking: **Permitted**

Experience comfortable elegance in this 100-year-old restored farmhouse set on 40 acres. This is a nature lover's paradise, with rolling fields, groves of trees, and a fishing pond. Sled riding, ice skating, or cross-country skiing can be enjoyed on the grounds. If you're an amateur astronomer, Garrott's is an ideal spot for serious star watching because of the altitude and absence of pollution. Denise offers comfortable rooms decorated in antiques, collectibles, and colorful rugs. A cozy TV room and a sunny sitting area are available for relaxing. Breakfast includes eggs, preserves, and freshly baked treats.

Mountain View Bed and Breakfast ✪
MOUNTAIN VIEW ROAD, DONEGAL, PENNSYLVANIA 15628

Tel: **(412) 593-6349**
Hosts: **Lesley and Jerry O'Leary**
Location: **1 mi. E from Penn. Tpke., Exit 9**
No. of Rooms: **6**
No. of Private Baths: **2**
Max. No. Sharing Bath: **4**
Double/pb: **$75**
Double/sb: **$65**

Suites: **$75**
Reduced Rates: **Sun.–Thurs.**
Open: **All year**
Breakfast: **Full**
Credit Cards: **AMEX, DC, MC, VISA**
Pets: **No**
Children: **Welcome, over 6**
Smoking: **No**
Social Drinking: **Permitted**

Every window of this 1865 farmhouse has a beautiful view of the surrounding Laurel Mountains. The house is a county landmark set on six acres. Hosts Lesley and Jerry are antique dealers and have decorated the rooms with period furnishings from their shop, located in the adjacent barn. They offer fresh fruit and homemade bread and muffins for breakfast. Mountain View is near hiking, ski resorts, white-water rafting, and several historic sites. Your hosts will gladly guide you to recreational activities or invite you to simply relax on the porch and enjoy the view.

Blueberry Acres ✪
3925 McCREARY ROAD, ERIE, PENNSYLVANIA 16506

Tel: **(814) 833-6833**
Hosts: **Nan and Don Fabian**
Location: **100 mi. W of Buffalo**
No. of Rooms: **1 suite**
No. of Private Baths: **1**
Suites: **$40**

Open: **All year**
Breakfast: **Full**
Pets: **No**
Children: **Welcome**
Smoking: **No**
Social Drinking: **Permitted**

This quaint red house is set on a country lane, surrounded by nine acres of wooded land and blueberry bushes. The house was originally built as a summer retreat and has been remodeled for year-round use. The Fabians offer a second-floor suite with private entrance and separate patio for guests. The suite includes a living room, small kitchen, and a bedroom decorated with maple furnishings and ruffled curtains. Breakfast is served in the downstairs dining room and features homemade blueberry muffins and blueberry pancakes served with plenty of bacon or sausage. In summer, when the bushes are bearing luscious fruit, the grounds are perfect for hiking and picnicking. Presque Isle State Park on the shores of Lake Erie offers year-round recreational activities and is located just two miles away.

Gillray Inn ✪
NORTH MAIN STREET, P.O. BOX 493, HARRISVILLE, PENNSYLVANIA 16030

Tel: **(412) 735-2274**
Best Time to Call: **Afternoon; evening**
Hosts: **Dick and Wendy Christner**
Location: **60 mi. N of Pittsburgh**
No. of Rooms: **3**
No. of Private Baths: **3**
Double/pb: **$45**
Single/pb: **$35**
Open: **All year**

Reduced Rates: **10%, seniors, families; weekly**
Breakfast: **Full**
Pets: **No**
Children: **Welcome, over 12**
Smoking: **Permitted**
Social Drinking: **Permitted**
Airport/Station Pickup: **Yes**

Old-fashioned hospitality is the hallmark of this restored home, built during the Civil War. Comfortably furnished, the decor is enhanced by the tall arched windows, five fireplaces, and the original staircase. You are welcome to relax in the living room or watch TV in the library. Freshly brewed coffee, tea, and snacks are available, and breakfast features a generous sampling of country ham, a local specialty. Slippery Rock University and Grove City College are nearby.

Shady Elms Farm B&B ✪
P. O. BOX 188, RD 1, HICKORY, PENNSYLVANIA 15340

Tel: **(412) 356-7755**
Hosts: **Marjorie and Connie Curran**
Location: **7 mi. from I-70**
No. of Rooms: **3**
No. of Private Baths: **1**
Max. No. Sharing Bath: **4**
Double/pb: **$50**
Single/pb: **$45**
Double/sb: **$50**
Single/sb: **$45**

Suites: **$50**
Open: **All year**
Reduced Rates: **15%, weekly**
Breakfast: **Full**
Pets: **Sometimes**
Children: **Welcome**
Smoking: **Permitted**
Social Drinking: **Permitted**
Airport/Station Pickup: **Yes**

Built in 1840, this Colonial mansion is set on 140 acres in the rolling hills of Pennsylvania farm country. Sixteen rooms, many with fireplaces, have been refurbished and decorated with floral wallpapers, dark wood antiques, and an array of brass and canopy beds, quilts, plants, pictures, and curios. Marjorie and Connie Curran serve a hearty breakfast featuring home-baked rolls, muffins, and coffee cake. They invite you to get up early to watch the farm activities and visit with the horses and cattle. Swimming, fishing, and ice skating can be enjoyed right on the Currans' pond. For water sports of all kinds,

Cross Creek Park is just three miles away. After a busy day, the Currans invite you to share a glass of wine and perhaps an impromptu concert in the music room.

The Stranahan House ✪
117 EAST MARKET STREET, MERCER, PENNSYLVANIA 16137

Tel: **(412) 662-4516**	Open: **All year**
Hosts: **Jim and Ann Stranahan**	Reduced Rates: **15%, weekly**
Location: **60 mi. N of Pittsburgh**	Breakfast: **Full**
No. of Rooms: **2**	Pets: **No**
No. of Private Baths: **2**	Children: **Welcome**
Double/pb: **$50**	Smoking: **No**
Single/pb: **$45**	Social Drinking: **Permitted**

Jim and Ann welcome you to share their 150-year-old Colonial Empire decorated with local antiques and cherished family heirlooms. After a delicious breakfast of quiche Lorraine, German apple pancakes, or ham and country eggs, Ann will be pleased to arrange a tour of the area based upon your interests. It may include Indian artifacts, a pioneer display, the historical museum, observing the Old Order Amish, visiting local artisans, with a stop at the corner drugstore with its old-fashioned soda fountain. Wine and snacks are offered while you sit around the fireplace or on the back porch.

Beighley Flower Cottage ✪
515 WEST SIXTH STREET, OIL CITY, PENNSYLVANIA 16301

Tel: **(814) 677-3786**	Breakfast: **Full**
Hosts: **Martha and Jack Beighley**	Pets: **No**
Location: **60 mi. S of Erie**	Children: **Welcome, over 10**
No. of Rooms: **2**	Smoking: **No**
Max. No. Sharing Bath: **4**	Social Drinking: **Permitted**
Double/sb: **$45**	Airport/Station Pickup: **Yes**
Open: **All year**	
Reduced Rates: **Long stays, families with children**	

Welcome to Pennsylvania's oil country, where you can see some of the world's oldest producing oil wells. The Beighleys are avid gardeners, which accounts for the name of this B&B. For the best view of the flowers, your hosts will pour you a beverage and settle you on the back porch of their white ranch house. Full breakfasts are served in the country-style kitchen, with its exposed beams and hanging wicker baskets. While the menu varies, you can expect to sample homemade bran-raisin muffins and peach honey.

Applebutter Inn ✪
152 APPLEWOOD LANE, SLIPPERY ROCK, PENNSYLVANIA 16057

Tel: **(412) 794-1844**
Best Time to Call: **9 AM–9 PM**
Hosts: **Gary and Sandra McKnight**
Location: **60 mi. N of Pittsburgh**
No. of Rooms: **11**
No. of Private Baths: **11**
Double/pb: **$85–$115**
Single/pb: **$60–$81**
Handicapped Accessible: **Yes**
Open: **All year**

Reduced Rates: **10%, seniors; 15%, weekly**
Breakfast: **Full**
Credit Cards: **MC, VISA**
Pets: **No**
Children: **Welcome**
Smoking: **No**
Social Drinking: **Permitted**
Airport/Station Pickup: **Yes**

Applebutter Inn offers a window to the past. A six-room farmhouse built in 1844, it has been expanded, retaining the fine original mill-work, flooring, and brick fireplaces. It is furnished with antiques and canopy beds, combining today's comforts and yesterday's charm. Slippery Rock University, Grove City College, two state parks, Amish country, and Wendall August Forge are local points of interest. A variety of sporting activities abound close by. Full country breakfasts feature rolled omelets, specialty pancakes, and home-baked muffins and breads. Evening refreshments are served in the keeping room. Guests celebrating a special occasion receive complimentary champagne or wine or a pint of homemade apple butter.

Heart of Somerset ✪
130 WEST UNION STREET, SOMERSET, PENNSYLVANIA 15501

Tel: **(814) 445-6782**
Best Time to Call: **8 AM–10 PM**
Hosts: **Ken and Rita Halverson**
Location: **67 mi. SE of Pittsburgh**
No. of Rooms: **4**
No. of Private Baths: **2**
Max. No. Sharing Bath: **4**
Double/pb: **$60–$85**
Single/pb: **$45–$75**
Double/sb: **$50–$75**

Single/sb: **$40–$65**
Open: **All year**
Reduced Rates: **$10 less, Sun.–Thurs.**
Breakfast: **Continental**
Credit Cards: **AMEX, MC, VISA**
Pets: **No**
Children: **Sometimes**
Smoking: **No**
Social Drinking: **Permitted**
Airport/Station Pickup: **Yes**

Located in the historic section of town, one can see the ridges of the Laurel Highlands from the front porch. This 1839 Federal-style clap-board home has been restored, and furnished with suitable antiques and collectibles. Guests comment on the comfortable beds, original pine floorboards, and the freshly baked muffins at breakfast. You can take a walking tour, climb mountains, ski at Seven Springs or Hidden Valley, hunt, fish, golf, or shoot the rapids. Some folk just enjoy relaxing at this quiet, spacious house.

RHODE ISLAND

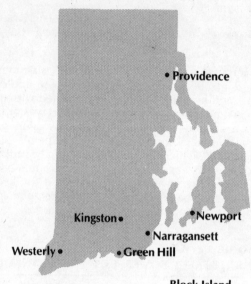

Providence

Kingston • •Newport
• Narragansett
Westerly • •Green Hill

Block Island

Bed & Breakfast of Rhode Island ✪
P. O. BOX 3291, 38 BELLEVUE AVENUE, NEWPORT, RHODE ISLAND 02840

Tel: **(401) 849-1298**
Best Time to Call: **9 AM–5:00 PM; summer: until 8 PM**
Coordinators: **Joy Meiser and Ken Mendis**
States/Regions Covered: **Rhode Island—statewide; Massachusetts**
Descriptive Directory: **$3**

Rates (Single/Double)
   Modest: **$40–$50** **$45–$55**
   Average: **$50–$65** **$65–$75**
   Luxury: **$65–$80** **$75–$120**
Credit Cards: **AMEX, MC, VISA**
Minimum stay: **3 nights, holiday weekends; 2 nights, summer weekends**

Joy will share her interest in local history with you from the time she confirms your reservation. Many B&Bs are listed on the National Register of Historic Places; some are near the shore, and several are located in or near Newport. Send $3 for a descriptive host directory or phone with details of your needs and she will place you in a comfortable lodging that suits your taste and purse. Joy has several B&Bs close to hiking trails or bicycle routes.

Hedgerow Bed & Breakfast ✪

1747 MOORESFIELD ROAD (ROUTE 138), P.O. BOX 1586, KINGSTON, RHODE ISLAND 02881

Tel: **(401) 783-2671**	Open: **All year**
Hosts: **Ann and Jim Ross**	Breakfast: **Full**
Location: **11 mi. from I-95, Exit 3A**	Pets: **No**
No. of Rooms: **4**	Children: **Welcome (crib)**
Max. No. Sharing Bath: **4**	Smoking: **Permitted**
Double/sb: **$60**	Social Drinking: **Permitted**
Single/sb: **$55**	Airport/Station Pickup: **Yes**

Built in 1933, this white, shingled Colonial with its Wedgewood blue shutters is just half a mile from the University of Rhode Island. The grounds are maintained in accordance with the original horticultural blueprints and include hedgerows, gardens, a fish pond, and a gazebo. The tennis court in no way distracts from the landscaping. The dining room, with its pink marble fireplace and corner cabinets housing a lovely china collection, is the setting for a bountiful breakfast. Providence, Newport, Block Island, and Rhode Island beaches are nearby, but be sure to return at 5 P.M. for the wine-and-cheese hour.

The House of Snee ✪

191 OCEAN ROAD, NARRAGANSETT, RHODE ISLAND 02882

Tel: **(401) 783-9494**	Open: **All year**
Best Time to Call: **After 6 PM**	Breakfast: **Full**
Host: **Mildred Snee**	Pets: **No**
Location: **15 mi. SW of Newport**	Children: **Welcome, over 2**
No. of Rooms: **3**	Smoking: **Permitted**
Max. No. Sharing Bath: **4**	Social Drinking: **Permitted**
Double/sb: **$45–$50**	Airport/Station Pickup: **Yes**
Single/sb: **$35**	

This century-old Dutch Colonial overlooks the waters of Rhode Island Sound. It's just across the street from the fishing pier where you can buy tackle and everything you need to hook a big one. It's a mile to the beach and just minutes from the Block Island ferry. Mildred's kitchen is her kingdom and her breakfast often features delicious

specialties such as crêpes, egg and meat combinations, homemade scones, and plenty of freshly brewed coffee. Winery tours are a fun diversion in the area. The University of Rhode Island is nearby.

La Forge Cottage ✪
96 PELHAM STREET, NEWPORT, RHODE ISLAND 02840

Tel: **(401) 847-4400**
Hosts: **Margot and Louis Droual**
No. of Rooms: **12**
No. of Private Baths: **10**
Max. No. Sharing Bath: **4**
Double/pb: **$55–$85**
Double/sb: **$45–$60**
Suites: **$95–$125**

Open: **All year**
Breakfast: **Full**
Credit Cards: **MC, VISA**
Pets: **No**
Children: **Welcome**
Smoking: **Permitted**
Social Drinking: **Permitted**
Foreign Languages: **French, German**

A large white Victorian with dark green awnings, La Forge Cottage has been a Newport fixture for more than 100 years. Beaches and downtown areas are just a stone's throw away. The spacious guest rooms are equipped with phones, color TVs, and refrigerators. In the morning, have your choice of full or Continental breakfast served in your room.

The Melville House ✪
39 CLARKE STREET, NEWPORT, RHODE ISLAND 02840

Tel: **(401) 847-0640**
Hosts: **Rita and Sam Rogers**
Location: **35 mi. from I-95, Exit 3**
No. of Rooms: **7**
No. of Private Baths: **5**
Max. No. Sharing Bath: **4**
Double/pb: **$85–$95**
Double/sb: **$75–$85**
Open: **Mar. 1–Jan. 1**

Reduced Rates: **Off season**
Breakfast: **Continental**
Credit Cards: **AMEX, MC, VISA**
Pets: **No**
Children: **Welcome, over 12**
Smoking: **Permitted**
Social Drinking: **Permitted**
Minimum Stay: **2 nights, weekends**

The Melville House is a 1750s shingled home set in Newport's historic hill section. This quiet street is just one block from the Brick Market and wharfs, and around the corner from Touro Synagogue and Trinity Church. Rita and Sam welcome you to guest rooms decorated with oak furnishings, braided rugs, and lace curtains, with special touches such as fresh flowers and a bowl of fruit. Rita will start your day off with homemade muffins and granola served at polished wood tables in her sunny breakfast room. When you want to relax, the country parlor with its collection of old grinders and gadgets and comfortable wing chairs awaits. Rita will be glad to provide sightseeing advice, and when the day is at a close, enjoy a 5 o'clock sherry at the house.

The Pilgrim House
123 SPRING STREET, NEWPORT, RHODE ISLAND 02846

Tel: **(401) 846-0040**	Double/sb: **$45–$85**
Best Time to Call: **Early mornings; evenings**	Open: **Feb. 1–Dec. 31**
Hosts: **Bruce and Pam Bayuk**	Breakfast: **Continental**
Location: **10 mi. from I-95, Exit 3**	Credit Cards: **MC, VISA**
No. of Rooms: **10**	Pets: **No**
No. of Private Baths: **8**	Children: **Welcome, over 14**
Max. No. Sharing Bath: **4**	Smoking: **No**
Double/pb: **$55–$125**	Social Drinking: **Permitted**

Centrally located, Pilgrim House (circa 1872) sits on a historic hill next to Trinity Church. It is an easy walk to shops, restaurants, the wharf area, the spectacular mansions, and the beaches. In summer, the third-floor deck is often the site for breakfast, when one may enjoy gourmet coffee and fresh fruit while watching the boats in the harbor. It is served fireside in cooler months. The rooms are immaculate, decorated with period furnishings and appropriate wallpapers.

Woody Hill Guest House ✪
330 WOODY HILL ROAD, WESTERLY, RHODE ISLAND 02891

Tel: **(401) 322-0452**	Single/sb: **$46**
Best Time to Call: **After 5 PM, during school year**	Open: **All year**
	Reduced Rates: **Off season**
Host: **Ellen L. Madison**	Breakfast: **Full**
Location: **¾ mi. from Rte. 1**	Pets: **No**
No. of Rooms: **3**	Children: **Welcome**
Max. No. Sharing Bath: **4**	Smoking: **No**
Double/sb: **$60**	Social Drinking: **Permitted**

This Colonial reproduction is set on a hilltop among informal gardens and fields. Antiques, wide-board floors, and handmade quilts create an Early American atmosphere. Your hostess may serve homemade jams, muffins, and fresh raspberries in the morning. She can direct you to Mystic Seaport, Block Island, and historic areas. Watch Hill and Westerly beaches are two miles away.

SOUTH CAROLINA

Camden

Myrtle Beach •

Beech Island •

Summerville •   • Georgetown

Charleston • Mt. Pleasant

Dale •   • Isle of Palms

• Beaufort

Hilton Head Island

The Rhett House Inn ✪
1009 CRAVEN STREET, BEAUFORT, SOUTH CAROLINA 29902

Tel: **(803) 524-9030**
Hosts: **Steve and Marianne Harrison**
Location: **69 mi. S of Charleston**
No. of Rooms: **8**
No. of Private Baths: **8**
Double/pb: **$70–$100**
Single/pb: **$60–$90**

Open: **All year**
Breakfast: **Full**
Credit Cards: **MC, VISA**
Pets: **No**
Children: **Welcome, over 5**
Smoking: **No**
Social Drinking: **Permitted**

If you ever wondered what the South was like before the Civil War, come visit this inn located in the historic district. Two of the bedrooms have fireplaces; all have homespun quilts and pretty touches such as freshly cut flowers. After breakfast, stroll in the lovely gardens or take a bicycle ride around town. The restored waterfront on the Intracoastal Waterway, with its shops and restaurants, is within walking distance. If you ask, your hosts will pack a picnic lunch and direct you to the beach. Hilton Head Island is 35 miles away.

The Cedars ✪

1325 WILLISTON ROAD, P.O. BOX 117, BEECH ISLAND, SOUTH CAROLINA 29841

Tel: **(803) 827-0248**
Hosts: **Ralph and Maggie Zieger**
Location: **6 mi. E of Augusta, Ga.**
No. of Rooms: **4**
No. of Private Baths: **3**
Double/pb: **$50**
Single/pb: **$44**
Suites: **$70 and up**
Open: **All year**
Reduced Rates: **10%, weekly; 10%, seniors**

Breakfast: **Continental**
Credit Cards: **MC, VISA**
Pets: **No**
Children: **Welcome, over 10**
Smoking: **Permitted**
Social Drinking: **Permitted**
Airport/Station Pickup: **Yes**
Foreign Languages: **German**

Beautifully set in 12 parklike acres, surrounded by dogwood and wisteria, this elegant manor (circa 1827) has been completely renovated. The gracious guest rooms feature queen-size poster beds, ceiling fans, fireplaces, and traditional furniture with antique accents. It is easily accessible to the Masters Golf Tournament, fine restaurants, antique shops, and Aiken, South Carolina, famed for its thoroughbred horse farms. Redcliffe Plantation State Park is nearby.

The Carriage House ✪

1413 LYTTLETON STREET, CAMDEN, SOUTH CAROLINA 29020

Tel: **(803) 432-2430**
Best Time to Call: **After 10 AM**
Hosts: **Appie and Bob Watkins**
Location: **30 mi. N of Columbia**
No. of Rooms: **2**
No. of Private Baths: **1½**
Double/pb: **$50**

Open: **All year**
Breakfast: **Full**
Pets: **No**
Children: **Welcome, over 6**
Smoking: **Permitted**
Social Drinking: **Permitted**

The Carriage House is an antebellum cottage with window boxes and a picket fence. Located in the center of historic Camden, it is within walking distance of tennis, parks, and shops. The guest rooms have twin or queen-size beds and are decorated with colorful fabrics and lovely antiques. Visitors are welcomed to their quarters with complimentary sherry and fruit. Your hosts serve a Southern-style breakfast.

Charleston East Bed & Breakfast ✪

1031 TALL PINE ROAD, MOUNT PLEASANT, SOUTH CAROLINA 29464

Tel: **(803) 884-8208**
Best Time to Call: **9 AM–4 PM**
Coordinator: **Bobbie Auld**

States/Regions Covered: **East Cooper, Isle of Palms, McClellanville, Mount Pleasant, Sullivans Island**

Rates (Single/Double):
   Modest: **$20**   **$40**
   Average: **$35**   **$50**
   Luxury: **$50**   **$60**

East Cooper is an historic area dating back to 1767. Fort Moultrie, on Sullivan's Island stands guard over quiet beaches. Bobbie's hosts are convenient to the historic district of Charleston and close to the sights that have made this city famous. The B&Bs range from quiet village homes near the harbor to modern suburban homes.

Historic Charleston Bed & Breakfast ✪
43 LEGARE STREET, CHARLESTON, SOUTH CAROLINA 29401

Tel: **(803) 722-6606**
Best Time to Call: **Noon–6 PM**
Coordinator: **Charlotte Fairey**
States/Regions Covered: **Charleston;**
  Georgia—Savannah
Descriptive Directory: **Free**

Rates (Single/Double):
  Modest: **$60**   **$70**
  Average: **$75**   **$90**
  Luxury: **$95**   **$130**
Credit Cards: **AMEX, MC, VISA**
Minimum Stay: **2 nights, Mar. 15–**
  June 15, Oct.

This port city is one of the most historic in the United States. Through the auspices of Charlotte, you will enjoy your stay in a private home, carriage house, or mansion in a neighborhood of enchanting walled gardens, cobblestoned streets, and moss-draped oak trees. Each home is unique, yet each has a warm and friendly atmosphere provided by a host who sincerely enjoys making guests welcome. All are historic properties dating from 1720 to 1890, yet all are up to date with air-conditioning, phones, and television. Reduced rates are available for weekly stays but there is a $5 surcharge for one-night stays.

Almost Home ✪
1236 OCEAN VIEW ROAD, CHARLESTON, SOUTH CAROLINA 29412

Tel: **(803) 795-8705**
Hosts: **Randy and Leita Harrison**
Location: **7 mi. SW of Charleston**
No. of Rooms: **3**
No. of Private Baths: **1**
Max. No. Sharing Bath: **4**
Double/sb: **$50**
Guest Cottage: **$60**

Open: **All year**
Reduced Rates: **Weekly**
Breakfast: **Full or continental**
Pets: **No**
Children: **Welcome**
Smoking: **Permitted**
Social Drinking: **Permitted**

You'll wish this big white house with its red shutters and roof were your home. The location is ideal, seven miles from downtown Charleston and five miles to the nearest beach. The city's charms include landmark buildings and excellent restaurants. Each room at Almost

Home has its own TV. In the morning, choose between a full meal or a light breakfast of fresh fruit and home-baked breads.

Ann Harper's Bed & Breakfast
56 SMITH STREET, CHARLESTON, SOUTH CAROLINA 29401

Tel: **(803) 723-3947**
Best Time to Call: **Before 10 AM;
  after 6 PM**
Host: **Ann D. Harper**
Location: **1 mi. from I-26**
No. of Rooms: **2**
Max. No. Sharing Bath: **3**
Double/sb: **$55**

Single/sb: **$45**
Open: **All year**
Breakfast: **Full**
Pets: **No**
Children: **Welcome, over 10**
Smoking: **Permitted**
Social Drinking: **Permitted**

This attractive home (circa 1870) is located in Charleston's historic district. The rooms, ideally suited for two friends traveling together, are decorated with wicker pieces and family treasures. Take a moment to relax on the porch or in the intimate walled garden out back. Ann serves a hot, Southern-style breakfast each morning featuring home-made bread and hominy grits. She will gladly direct you to the interesting sights of this historic area. There is a $5 surcharge for one-night stays; no single rates March 15–June 15.

Villa de la Fontaine
138 WENTWORTH STREET, CHARLESTON, SOUTH CAROLINA 29401

Tel: **(803) 577-7709**
Best Time to Call: **8 AM–6 PM**
Hosts: **Aubrey W. Hancock and Bill
  Fontaine**
No. of Rooms: **4**
No. of Private Baths: **4**
Double/pb: **$85–$90**
Single/pb: **$85–$90**
Suites: **$85–$135**

Open: **All year**
Reduced Rates: **Available**
Breakfast: **Full**
Credit Cards: **AMEX, MC, VISA**
Pets: **No**
Children: **No**
Smoking: **No**
Social Drinking: **Permitted**

Villa de la Fontaine is an enormous four-columned Greek Revival home in the heart of the historic district. The house was built in 1838, and boasts a half-acre garden complete with fountain and terraces. Inside, the rooms have been restored to mint condition, and Aubrey, a retired interior designer, has decorated them with 18th-century American antiques and reproductions. Several of the guest rooms feature canopy beds. Breakfast is prepared by a master chef who prides himself on serving something different every day. Guests staying in the cottage gazebo are provided with Continental fare.

Coosaw Plantation ✪
DALE, SOUTH CAROLINA 29914

Tel: **(803) 846-6555**
Best Time to Call: **After 6 PM**
Hosts: **Joan and Ken Kraft**
Location: **50 mi. S of Charleston; 15 mi. from I-95**
Guest Cottage: **$45 for 2; $55 for 4**

Open: **Mar.–Dec.**
Breakfast: **Continental**
Pets: **Welcome**
Children: **Welcome**
Smoking: **Permitted**
Social Drinking: **Permitted**

This sprawling plantation offers a relaxed setting on the Coosaw River. The guest cottage has a living room with fireplace, a full kitchen, and a bath. Your hosts will prepare a breakfast of muffins or casseroles, or will leave the fixings for you. Boating, fishing, or a visit to Beaufort and Savannah are just a few of the local possibilities. Or, stay "home" and use the pool and tennis court on premises.

Shaw House ✪
8 CYPRESS COURT, GEORGETOWN, SOUTH CAROLINA 29440

Tel: **(803) 546-9663**
Best Time to Call: **Early AM**
Host: **Mary Shaw**
Location: **1 block off Hwy. 17**
No. of Rooms: **3**
No. of Private Baths: **3**
Double/pb: **$45**
Single/pb: **$45**

Open: **All year**
Reduced Rates: **10% after 4 nights**
Breakfast: **Full**
Pets: **No**
Children: **Welcome**
Smoking: **Permitted**
Social Drinking: **Permitted**
Airport/Station Pickup: **Yes**

Shaw House is a two-story Colonial with a beautiful view of the Willowbank Marsh. Your host is knowledgeable about antiques and has filled the rooms with them. The rocking chairs and cool breeze will tempt you to the porch. Each morning a pot of coffee and Southern-style casserole await you. Fresh fruit and homemade snacks are available all day. The house is within walking distance of the historic district and is near Myrtle Beach, Pawleys Island, golf, tennis, and restaurants.

Ambiance Bed & Breakfast ✪
8 WREN DRIVE, HILTON HEAD ISLAND, SOUTH CAROLINA 29928

Tel: **(803) 671-4981**
Best Time to Call: **Evenings**
Host: **Marny Kridel Daubenspeck**
Location: **40 mi. from I-95, Exit 28**
No. of Rooms: **2**
No. of Private Baths: **2**
Double/pb: **$55–$65**

Single/pb: **$50–$60**
Open: **All year**
Breakfast: **Continental**
Pets: **No**
Children: **Welcome, over 12**
Smoking: **Permitted**
Social Drinking: **Permitted**

This contemporary cypress home is located in the area of Sea Pines Plantation. Floor-length windows afford beautiful views of the sub-tropical surroundings. Marny runs an interior decorating firm, so it's no surprise that everything is in excellent taste. The beach and the Atlantic Ocean are immediately accessible, and sports facilities are readily available.

The Cain House ✪
206 29TH AVENUE SOUTH, MYRTLE BEACH, SOUTH CAROLINA 29577

Tel: **(803) 448-3063**
Best Time to Call: **9 AM–5 PM**
Hosts: **Emily and Wilson Cain**
Location: **100 mi. N of Charleston**
No. of Rooms: **3**
No. of Private Baths: **3**
Double/pb: **$65–$125**

Open: **All year**
Breakfast: **Continental**
Pets: **No**
Children: **Sometimes**
Smoking: **Permitted**
Social Drinking: **Permitted**

The Cain House is a Low Country cypress home centrally located along South Carolina's famous Grand Strand. You can see the ocean and a par 3 golf course from the large front porch. The spacious rooms are attractively furnished and accessorized with antiques, beautiful linens, interesting clocks, artwork, plants and flower arrangements. Your hosts sincerely enjoy making their guests feel welcome. Beaches, golf, tennis, fishing, fine restaurants, and shops are nearby attrac-tions.

Serendipity, an Inn ✪
407 71ST AVENUE NORTH, MYRTLE BEACH, SOUTH CAROLINA 29577

Tel: **(803) 449-5268**
Best Time to Call: **8 AM–11 PM**
Hosts: **Cos and Ellen Ficarra**
Location: **60 mi. from Rte. 95**
No. of Rooms: **15**
No. of Private Baths: **15**
Double/pb: **$47–$65**
Suites: **$68–$90**

Open: **Feb.–Nov.**
Breakfast: **Continental**
Credit Cards: **AMEX, MC, VISA**
Pets: **No**
Children: **Welcome**
Smoking: **Permitted**
Social Drinking: **Permitted**
Foreign Languages: **Italian, Spanish**

Serendipity is a Spanish Mission-style inn surrounded by lush tropical plants and flowers. The setting is peaceful, the street is quiet, and the ocean is less than 300 yards away. Bedrooms are highlighted with antiques drawing from Art Deco, Oriental, wicker, and pine motifs. The Garden Room is the place for a generous breakfast of homemade breads, fresh fruit, eggs, and cereal. Guests also gather here for afternoon drinks and conversation. Your hosts invite you to use the heated pool and spa, play shuffleboard, Ping-Pong, or just share a quiet moment beside the patio fountain. Myrtle Beach is known for its fine restaurants, but the Ficarras have a gas grill if you want to do your own cooking. Cos and Ellen will gladly direct you to nearby shops, fishing villages, golf courses, and miles of beaches.

Gadsden Manor Inn ✪

329 OLD POSTERN ROAD, SUMMERVILLE, SOUTH CAROLINA 29483

Tel: **(803) 875-2333**	Breakfast: **Continental**
Best Time to Call: **9 AM–6 PM**	Credit Cards: **AMEX, MC, VISA**
Hosts: **Franklin Ellis and Martin Verson**	Pets: **No**
Location: **20 mi. NW of Charleston**	Children: **No**
No. of Rooms: **14**	Smoking: **Permitted**
No. of Private Baths: **14**	Social Drinking: **Permitted**
Double/pb: **$85**	Airport/Station Pickup: **Yes**
Suites: **$110**	Foreign Languages: **French**
Open: **All year**	

Gadsden Manor Inn is a Georgian Revival surrounded by lush foliage and gardens. The house dates back to 1906 and is furnished with four-poster beds and claw-footed tubs. Traditions such as live parlor music and leisurely afternoon refreshments also recall a more elegant past. Breakfast specialties include blueberry muffins, croissants, and fresh fruit.

SOUTH DAKOTA

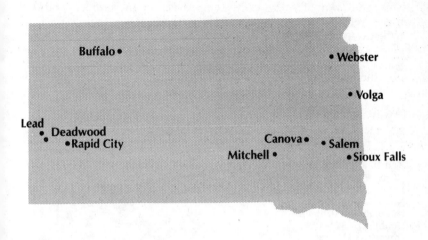

South Dakota Bed and Breakfast ✪
903 NORTH DAKOTA STREET, CANTON, SOUTH DAKOTA 57013

Tel: **(605) 987-2834**
Best Time to Call: **After 6 PM**
Coordinator: **Irene Koob**
States/Regions Covered: **South Dakota, statewide**

Rates (Single/Double):
  Average: **$25**   **$35**
  Luxury: **$45**   **$75**
Credit Cards: **No**

From the majestic Black Hills across rolling prairie to the city and to awesome Mt. Rushmore, you will be treated to midwestern hospitality at its best. Whether traveling through the state, skiing, hunting, or on business, you will enjoy staying in a private home of a host who is sincerely pleased to welcome you.

Skoglund Farm ✪
CANOVA, SOUTH DAKOTA 57321

Tel: **(605) 247-3445**
Best Time to Call: **Early AM; evenings**
Hosts: **Alden and Delores Skoglund**
Location: **12 miles from I-90**

No. of Rooms: **5**
Max. No. Sharing Bath: **3**
Double/sb: **$50**
Single/sb: **$30**

Open: **All year**	Children: **Welcome (crib)**
Reduced Rates: **Under 18**	Smoking: **Permitted**
Breakfast: **Full**	Social Drinking: **Permitted**
Other Meals: **Dinner included**	Airport/Station Pickup: **Yes**
Pets: **Welcome**	

This is a working farm where the emphasis is on the simple, good life. It is a welcome escape from urban living. You may, if you wish, help with the farm chores, or just watch everyone else work; the family raises cattle, fowl, and peacocks. You may ride the horses over the wide, open spaces. You are welcome to use the laundry facilities or play the piano. The coffeepot is always on.

Adams House ✪
22 VAN BUREN, DEADWOOD, SOUTH DAKOTA 57732

Tel: **(605) 578-3877**
Best Time to Call: **10 AM–6 PM**
Hosts: **Bruce and Rebecca Crosswait**
Location: **40 mi. NW of Rapid City**
No. of Rooms: **4**
No. of Private Baths: **4**
Double/pb: **$49–$85**
Single/pb: **$44–$80**
Open: **All year**
Breakfast: **Full**
Credit Cards: **MC, VISA**
Pets: **No**
Children: **Welcome, over 12**
Smoking: **No**
Social Drinking: **Permitted**

Deadwood has retained the flavor of the Old West and the gold strikes of the 1870s. Listed on the National Register of Historic Places, this 1892 Queen Anne Victorian mansion was unoccupied for more than 50 years. Periodic, careful maintenance preserved the elegant furnishings, and they are today still in their original condition. Three presidents—Taft, Teddy Roosevelt, and Coolidge—were once houseguests here. You'll awaken to the fragrance of freshly ground coffee and homemade specialties. It's a short walk to Mt. Moriah, the burial place of Wild Bill Hickock and Calamity Jane. Back "home" you are welcome to play the parlor piano or play tennis not two blocks away. Bruce, a former college professor, and Rebecca, a registered nurse, invite you to afternoon tea.

Cheyenne Crossing B&B ✪
HC 37, BOX 1220, LEAD, SOUTH DAKOTA 57754

Tel: **(605) 584-3510**	Reduced Rates: **Families; groups**
Hosts: **Jim and Bonnie LeMar**	Breakfast: **Continental**
Location: **Junction Hwys. 85 and 14A**	Other Meals: **Available**
No. of Rooms: **3**	Credit Cards: **MC, VISA**
Max. No. Sharing Bath: **4**	Pets: **No**
Double/sb: **$59**	Children: **Welcome, over 6**
Single/sb: **$45**	Smoking: **No**
Open: **All year**	Social Drinking: **Permitted**

This two-story frame building with its facade of rough-sawed pine is situated in the heart of Spearfish Canyon. The main floor houses a typical country general store and café; the guest quarters are upstairs. From 1876 to 1885 the original building was a stop for the Deadwood–Cheyenne stagecoach. After it burned down in 1960, the present building was built to replace it. Jim and Bonnie will be delighted to map out special trips tailored to your interests. Spend the day visiting Mt. Rushmore and Crazy Horse Monument, pan for gold, hike, or fish for trout on Spearfish Creek, which flows behind the store. It's also close to the Black Hills Passion Play. Sourdough pancakes are a frequent breakfast treat.

Audrie's Cranbury Corner B&B ✪
RR 8, BOX 2400, RAPID CITY, SOUTH DAKOTA 57702

Tel: **(605) 342-7788**	Open: **All year**
Hosts: **Hank and Audry Kuhnhauser**	Breakfast: **Full**
Location: **¼ mi. from Hwy. 44**	Pets: **No**
No. of Rooms: **3**	Children: **No**
No. of Private Baths: **3**	Smoking: **No**
Double/pb: **$65**	Social Drinking: **Permitted**
Single/pb: **$60**	

Located in the beautiful Black Hills, just 30 miles from Mt. Rushmore, Audry's country home is the epitome of Old World hospitality. The fireplaced guest rooms have private entrances, private patios, hot tubs, and are furnished with lovely antiques. She will be happy to lend you a fishing pole so you can try your hand at trout fishing at nearby Rapid Creek. Complimentary wine, assorted beverages, and tempting appetizers are offered.

Bed and Breakfast Domivara ✪
HC33, BOX 3004, RAPID CITY, SOUTH DAKOTA 57702

Tel: **(605) 574-4207**	Host: **Betty Blount**
Best Time to Call: **Mornings; 6–8 PM**	Location: **26 mi. SW of Rapid City**

No. of Rooms: **2**
No. of Private Baths: **2**
Double/pb: **$65–$70**
Single/pb: **$55**
Open: **All year**
Breakfast: **Full**
Other Meals: **Available**

Pets: **Sometimes**
Children: **Welcome**
Smoking: **Permitted**
Social Drinking: **Permitted**
Airport/Station Pickup: **Yes**
Minimum Stay: **2 nights**

Enjoy Western hospitality in a unique log home located in the pictur-esque Black Hills of South Dakota. The homey wood interior is decorated with comfortable antiques and accents of stained glass. A large picture window overlooks the countryside where you may see an occasional wild turkey or deer. Betty Blount offers complimentary snacks served with wine or coffee. She prepares a variety of special breakfast dishes including sourdough pancakes, egg soufflés, fresh trout, and homemade blueberry muffins. There are good restaurants nearby, or if you prefer home cooking, your host will be glad to prepare dinner for you. Domivara is conveniently located just 20 minutes from Mt. Rushmore and the Crazy Horse Memorial.

Willow Springs Cabin ✪
HCR 39, BOX 108, RAPID CITY, SOUTH DAKOTA 57702

Tel: **(605) 342-3665**
Hosts: **Joyce and Russell Payton**
Location: **15 mi. off I-90, Exit 57**
Guest Cottage: **$60, for 2**
Open: **All year**

Breakfast: **Full**
Pets: **Sometimes**
Children: **Welcome (crib)**
Smoking: **No**
Social Drinking: **Permitted**

Willow Springs is a one-room rustic log cabin nestled in the native pines just inside the Black Hills National Forest. The cabin is cozily decorated with family heirlooms. Guests begin each day with freshly ground coffee, seasonal fruits, and warm-from-the-oven breads. After-ward, diversions include hiking, swimming or fishing in a private mountain stream, or just relaxing on the front porch while admiring the breathtaking view. In winter, ice skating and cross-country skiing are popular. Centrally located in the Black Hills, it's just minutes away from the Mt. Rushmore National Monument.

Lakeside Farm ✪
RR 2, BOX 52, WEBSTER, SOUTH DAKOTA 57274

Tel: **(605) 486-4430**
Hosts: **Joy and Glenn Hagen**
Location: **60 mi. E of Aberdeen on Hwy. 12**
No. of Rooms: **2**
Maximum No. Sharing Bath: **4**
Double/sb: **$30**

Single/sb: **$20**
Open: **All year**
Breakfast: **Full**
Pets: **No**
Children: **Welcome**
Smoking: **No**
Social Drinking: **No**

This 750-acre farm where Joy and Glenn raise oats, corn, and Holstein dairy cows, is located in the Lake Region where recreational activities abound. You are certain to be comfortable in their farmhouse, built in 1970 and furnished in a simple, informal style. You will awaken to the delicious aroma of Joy's heavenly cinnamon rolls or bread and enjoy breakfast served on the enclosed porch. Nearby attractions include Fort Sisseton and the June festival that recounts Sam Brown's historic ride. You will also enjoy the Blue Dog fish hatchery, and the Game Reserve. Dakotah, Inc., manufacturers of linens and wall hangings, is located in Webster. They have an outlet shop where great buys may be found.

For key to listings, see inside front or back cover.

✪ This star means that rates are guaranteed through December 31, 1991, to any guest making a reservation as a result of reading about the B&B in *BED & BREAKFAST U.S.A.*—1991 edition.

Important! To avoid misunderstandings, always ask about cancellation policies when booking.

Please enclose a self-addressed, stamped, business-size envelope when contacting reservation services.

For more details on what you can expect in a B&B, see Chapter 1.

Always mention *Bed & Breakfast U.S.A.* when making reservations!

If no B&B is listed in the area you'll be visiting, use the form on page 675 to order a copy of our "List of New B&Bs."

We want to hear from you! Use the form on page 677.

TENNESSEE

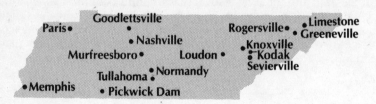

Paris •   Goodlettsville •   Rogersville • • Limestone   Greeneville
• Nashville   • Knoxville
Murfreesboro •   Loudon •   • Kodak
Tullahoma • • Normandy   Sevierville
• Memphis   • Pickwick Dam

Bed & Breakfast Hospitality—Tennessee ✪
P.O. BOX 110227, NASHVILLE, TENNESSEE 37222-0227

Tel: (615) 331-5244 for information;
  Fax (615) 833-7701; (800) 458-2421
  for reservations
Coordinator: **Fredda Odom**
States/Regions Covered:
  Chattanooga, Columbia, Franklin,
  Gatlinburg, Greeneville, Knoxville,
  Memphis, Nashville, Shelbyville

Rates (Single/Double):
  Modest: **$35**   **$45**
  Average: **$40–$50**   **$65**
  Luxury: **$80–$100 $80–$120**
Credit Cards: **AMEX, MC, VISA**

From the Great Smoky Mountains to the Mississippi, here is a diversity of attractions that includes fabulous scenery, Tennessee's Grand Ole Opry and Opryland, universities, Civil War sites, horse farms, and much more. Fredda will arrange sightseeing tours, car rentals, tickets to events, and everything she can to assure you a pleasant stay. There is a $5 booking fee; $3 for the descriptive directory.

Woodshire B&B ✪
600 WOODSHIRE DRIVE, GOODLETTSVILLE, TENNESSEE 37072

Tel: (615) 859-7369
Best Time to Call: **Before 9 AM, after**
  9 PM
Hosts: **Beverly and John Grayson**
Location: **11 mi. N of Nashville**
No. of Rooms: **2**
No. of Private Baths: **2**
Double/pb: **$45**

Single/pb: **$40**
Open: **Mar. 15–Oct. 31**
Breakfast: **Continental**
Pets: **No**
Children: **Welcome**
Smoking: **No**
Social Drinking: **No**
Airport/Station Pickup: **Yes**

A blue clapboard house inspired by New England saltboxes, Wood-shire B&B is 20 minutes from downtown Nashville and its attrac-tions—Opryland Park, Andrew Jackson's Hermitage, and the homes and museums of country music stars. Beverly will gladly tell you the stories behind the antique family furniture. She's a retired art teacher, and as you look around you'll see her paintings and weavings, and John's woodcrafts. Continental breakfast features homemade pre-serves. In the afternoon, the Graysons like to serve tea in their Japanese garden.

Big Spring Inn ✪
315 NORTH MAIN STREET, GREENEVILLE, TENNESSEE 37743

Tel: **(615) 638-2917**	Open: **All year**
Hosts: **Jeanne Driese and Cheryl Van Dyck**	Reduced Rates: **Available**
	Breakfast: **Full**
Location: **70 mi. NE of Knoxville**	Other Meals: **Available**
No. of Rooms: **5**	Credit Cards: **AMEX, MC, VISA**
No. of Private Baths: **4**	Pets: **Sometimes**
Max. No. Sharing Bath: **2**	Children: **Welcome, over 12**
Double/pb: **$75**	Smoking: **Permitted**
Single/pb: **$70**	Social Drinking: **Permitted**
Double/sb: **$55**	Airport/Station Pickup: **Yes**
Single/sb: **$50**	

Big Spring Inn is a three-story manor house located in Greeneville's historic district, an area that includes President Andrew Johnson's home and tailor shop. The inn has a grand entrance hall, leaded and stained-glass windows, and many fireplaces. The rooms are spacious, with high ceilings, and are decorated with a comfortable mix of antiques and reproductions. The bedrooms have special touches, such as fresh flowers, snacks, baskets of toiletries, and even terry cloth robes. Jeanne and Cheryl serve homemade breads and pastries, with a variety of egg dishes for breakfast; gourmet dinners are also avail-able. Big Spring is within an hour of Smoky Mountain National Park and the Blue Ridge Parkway.

Compton Manor
3747 KINGSTON PIKE, KNOXVILLE, TENNESSEE 37919

Tel: **(615) 523-1204**	Breakfast: **Continental**
Hosts: **Brian and Hala Hunt**	Credit Cards: **MC, VISA**
Location: **2 mi. off I-40 East, Exit 383**	Pets: **No**
No. of Rooms: **3**	Children: **Welcome, over 12**
No. of Private Baths: **3**	Smoking: **No**
Double/pb: **$75**	Social Drinking: **Permitted**
Single/pb: **$70**	Airport/Station Pickup: **Yes**
Open: **All year**	Foreign Languages: **Arabic**

A Tudor-style house made of stone, slate, and leaded glass, Compton Manor looks like a contemporary castle for some latter-day knight. Oaks, walnut trees, and dogwoods shade the three-acre grounds, which encompass a pool and a tennis court. Other recreational options include croquet and horseshoes. The main draw in Knoxville is the University of Tennessee, but the city also boasts lots of antique shops. Nashville and Dollywood are within driving distance. Continental breakfast is served in the solarium, or on the terrace in good weather.

The Graustein Inn ✪
8300 NUBBIN RIDGE ROAD, KNOXVILLE, TENNESSEE 37923

Tel: **(615) 690-7007**
Best Time to Call: **8 AM–9 PM**
Hosts: **Darlene and Jim Lara**
Location: **10 mi. W of Knoxville**
No. of Rooms: **5**
No. of Private Baths: **3**
Max. No. Sharing Bath: **4**
Double/pb: **$75–$98**
Single/pb: **$69–$89**
Double/sb: **$55–$65**
Single/sb: **$49–$59**

Suites: **$84–$98**
Open: **All year**
Breakfast: **Full**
Other Meals: **Available**
Credit Cards: **AMEX, MC, VISA**
Pets: **No**
Children: **No**
Smoking: **No**
Social Drinking: **Permitted**
Airport/Station Pickup: **Yes**

Constructed of cedar and limestone and set on 20 acres, the Graustein Inn resembles a European château. Hosts Darlene and Jim Lara have furnished the guest rooms with 17th- and 18th-century antiques, highlighted by Darlene's needlepoint, homemade candy, and fresh flowers. Some rooms have private balconies, and the suite features a canopy bed, fireplace, and marble bath. Breakfast is served on the porch or in the family kitchen. Among their specialties are homemade pastry, granola, and Austrian quark. The inn has a mile-long nature trail with dogwood and wildflowers, and you might even see an owl, quail, or fox.

Windy Hill B&B ✪
1031 WEST PARK DRIVE, KNOXVILLE, TENNESSEE 37909

Tel: **(615) 690-1488**
Host: **Mary M. Mitchell**
Location: **1.6 mi. from I-75-40, Exit 380**
No. of Rooms: **1**
No. of Private Baths: **1**
Double/pb: **$40**
Single/pb: **$35**

Open: **All year**
Breakfast: **Continental**
Pets: **Sometimes**
Children: **Welcome**
Smoking: **Permitted**
Social Drinking: **Permitted**
Airport/Station Pickup: **Yes**

Located in a pleasant, quiet neighborhood with numerous shade trees, Mary's B&B is air-conditioned and has a private entrance with no steps to climb. There's a double bed and a rollaway is available. Breakfast features homemade muffins or cinnamon rolls with coffee. Windy Hill is convenient to the University of Tennessee; Oakridge is only a 15-minute drive while Smoky Mountain National Park is an hour away.

Grandma's House ✪
734 POLLARD ROAD, KODAK, TENNESSEE 37764

Tel: **(615) 933-3512**	Open: **All year**
Best Time to Call: **8 AM–5 PM**	Breakfast: **Full**
Hosts: **Charlie and Hilda Hickman**	Credit Cards: **MC, VISA**
Location: **8 mi. N of Sevierville**	Pets: **No**
No. of Rooms: **3**	Children: **Welcome, over 15**
No. of Private Baths: **3**	Smoking: **No**
Double/pb: **$55**	Social Drinking: **No**
Suites: **$75**	Airport/Station Pickup: **Yes**

Your hosts at this big country farmhouse are native Tennesseans who pride themselves on offering Southern hospitality. When you return from exploring Mountains National Park, Oak Ridge, and Dollywood Theme Park, Charlie and Hilda will meet you with refreshments in hand. Then you can spend the evening playing games, watching movies on the VCR, or reading books and magazines. A typical breakfast, served either on the porch or in the dining room, features apple stack cake, buttermilk biscuits, homemade jams and jellies, and hominy grits and sausage gravy.

Snapp Inn B&B
ROUTE 3, BOX 102, LIMESTONE, TENNESSEE 37681

Tel: **(615) 257-2482**	Single/sb: **$40**
Best Time to Call: **Before 10 AM;**	Open: **All year**
after 7 PM	Breakfast: **Full**
Hosts: **Dan and Ruth Dorgan**	Pets: **Welcome**
Location: **4 mi. from Rte. 11 E**	Children: **Welcome (one at a time)**
No. of Rooms: **2**	Smoking: **No**
Max. No. Sharing Bath: **4**	Social Drinking: **Permitted**
Double/sb: **$50**	Airport/Station Pickup: **Yes**

Built in 1815 and situated in farm country, this Federal brick home has lovely mountain views. The house is decorated with antiques, including a Victorian reed organ. Now retired, Ruth and Dan have the time to pursue their interests in antiques restoration, history, needlework, and bluegrass music. It is an easy walk to Davy Crockett Birthplace State Park, and 15 minutes to historic Jonesboro or the Andrew Johnson Home in Greeneville. A swimming pool, golf, and fishing are close by. You are welcome to use the laundry facilities, television and pool table. The Blue Room is pictured on our back cover.

River Road Inn ✪
ROUTE 1, BOX 372, RIVER ROAD, LOUDON, TENNESSEE 37774

Tel: (615) 458-4861
Best Time to Call: **Before 7 PM**
Hosts: **Pamela and Kent Foster**
Location: **30 mi. SW of Knoxville; 1½ mi. from I-75, Exit 72**
No. of Rooms: **5**
No. of Private Baths: **5**
Double/pb: **$65–$90**
Single/pb: **$65–$90**

Open: **All year**
Breakfast: **Full**
Other Meals: **Available (picnics)**
Pets: **No**
Children: **Welcome**
Smoking: **No**
Social Drinking: **Permitted**
Airport/Station Pickup: **Yes**

Nestled in the foothills of the Smoky Mountains stands the antebellum mansion, built in 1857, of the late Albert Lenoir. Rich in Civil War history, it is restored and has earned a place on the National Register of Historic Places. Bedrooms are furnished with beautiful antiques and other period pieces. Guests are invited to relax by the pool or take advantage of the pastoral river location with boating, fishing, or hiking.

Lowenstein-Long House ✪
217 NORTH WALDRAN, MEMPHIS, TENNESSEE 38105

Tel: (901) 527-7174; 526-4931
Hosts: **Walter and Samantha Long**
No. of Rooms: **4**
No. of Private Baths: **4**
Double/pb: **$50–$55**
Open: **All year**

Breakfast: **Continental**
Credit Cards: **AMEX, MC, VISA**
Pets: **Sometimes**
Children: **Welcome**
Smoking: **Permitted**
Social Drinking: **Permitted**

Listed on the National Register of Historic Places, Lowenstein-Long House has been fully restored to its original grandeur. It is located half a mile from a Victorian village, and close to Mud Island, the DeSoto Bridge, and Beale Street. Elvis fans will note that the route to Graceland is nearby.

Clardy's Guest House ✪
435 EAST MAIN STREET, MURFREESBORO, TENNESSEE 37130

Tel: (615) 893-6030
Best Time to Call: **After 4 PM**
Hosts: **Robert and Barbara Deaton**
Location: **2 mi. from I-24**
No. of Rooms: **4**
No. of Private Baths: **3**
Max. No. Sharing Bath: **4**
Double/pb: **$38**
Single/pb: **$30**

Double/sb: **$30**
Single/sb: **$25**
Open: **All year**
Breakfast: **Continental**
Pets: **Sometimes**
Children: **Welcome (crib)**
Smoking: **Permitted**
Social Drinking: **Permitted**

This Romanesque-style Victorian dates back to 1898. The 20 rooms are filled with antiques; with 40 antiques dealers in town, you can guess what Murfreesboro is best known for. The world championship horse show at Shelbyville is 30 minutes away. Your hosts will be glad to advise on local tours and can direct you to the home of Grand Ole Opry, one hour away in Nashville, and fine eating places. Middle Tennessee State University is close by.

Quilts and Croissants
2231 RILEY ROAD, MURFREESBORO, TENNESSEE 37130

Tel: **(615) 893-2933**
Hosts: **Robert and Mary Jane Roose**
Location: **28 mi. S of Nashville**
No. of Rooms: **1**
No. of Private Baths: **1**
Double/pb: **$35**
Single/pb: **$30**

Open: **All year**
Reduced Rates: **Seniors**
Breakfast: **Continental**
Pets: **No**
Smoking: **No**
Social Drinking: **Permitted**

This unusual home, constructed out of logs hewn in 1834, combines old-fashioned country charm and modern efficiency. Stencils and folk art ornament the walls of the guest room, and patchwork quilts drape the twin beds. Don't be fooled by the kitchenette's quaint ice-box appearance—it's really a refrigerator stocked with juice, breakfast foods, and soda. Quilts and Croissants is less than an hour's drive from Nashville, but your hosts can steer you to the notable sights of Murfreesboro, such as Oaklands Mansion (a mid-19th century land-mark) and Canonsburgh (a restored Civil War–era village). Breakfast here is a do-it-yourself affair; take whatever you want from the refrigerator.

New World Bed & Breakfast ✪
P.O. BOX 29241, NASHVILLE, TENNESSEE 37229

Tel: **(615) 228-7851**
Best Time to Call: **Mon.–Fri., 8 AM–5 PM**
Coordinator: **Barbara Garrish**
States/Regions Covered: **Nashville, midwestern Tennessee**

Rates (Single/Double):
Modest: **$40–$50**
Average: **$50–$75**
Luxury: **$65–$80**
Credit Cards: **AMEX, MC, VISA**
Minimum Stay: **2 nights**

Whether you're traveling for business or pleasure, Barbara, a Nashville native, can find something to suit you. A wide selection of hosted homes and private apartments are available in locations close to Opryland, Music Row, downtown Nashville, hospitals, universities, and other sites of interest.

Virginia's Homestead House Inn ✪
P.O. BOX 76, HIGHWAY 57, PICKWICK DAM, TENNESSEE 38365

Tel: **(901) 689-5500**
Best Time to Call: **9 AM–9 PM**
Hosts: **Stephen and Mary Lee Virginia**
Location: **100 mi. E of Memphis**
No. of Rooms: **3**
No. of Private Baths: **3**
Double/pb: **$55**
Single/pb: **$40**

Open: **All year, except Jan. and Feb.**
Breakfast: **Continental**
Credit Cards: **MC, VISA**
Pets: **No**
Children: **Welcome, over 12**
Smoking: **Permitted**
Social Drinking: **Permitted**

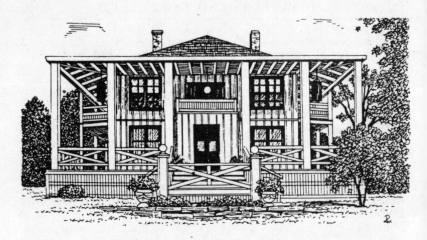

The Homestead House Inn was built in 1843 as the Red Sulphur Springs Hotel. In its glory days, people came to soak in the sulphur springs and attend annual fox hunts. Today the house sits on 14 wooded acres and offers beautifully restored rooms decorated with antiques. Your hosts love catering to their guests and serve a selection of Danish pastries, seasonal fruit, and the house special strawberry bread for breakfast. You are sure to enjoy the colorful past of the inn, where it is said Jesse and Frank James hid out between raids. Your hosts will do all they can to ensure you a pleasant stay and will direct you to such historic sights as Shiloh National Park and Battlefield.

Blue Mountain Mist Country Inn ✪
ROUTE 3, BOX 490, SEVIERVILLE, TENNESSEE 37862

Tel: **(615) 428-2335**
Best Time to Call: **10 AM–4 PM**
Hosts: **Norman and Sarah Ball**
Location: **4 mi. E of Pigeon Forge**
No. of Rooms: **12**

No. of Private Baths: **12**
Double/pb: **$69**
Suites: **$80–$98**
Open: **All year**
Breakfast: **Full**

Pets: **No**
Children: **Welcome**
Smoking: **No**

Social Drinking: **Permitted**
Minimum Stay: **2–3 nights, holiday weekends**

This Victorian-style inn is remote from congestion and noise, yet has easy access to Pigeon Forge, Dollywood Theme Park, factory outlets, and the crafts community. A view of rolling meadows framed by the Great Smoky Mountains can be enjoyed from rocking chairs on the huge front porch or from the backyard hot tub and patio. Country antiques, claw-foot tubs, handmade quilts and accessories, all make for a homey atmosphere. Two suites have in-room Jacuzzis. The large, fireplaced living room is the gathering spot on cool evenings. The Southern breakfast often features fresh fruit, sausages and eggs, grits and gravy, and homemade biscuits.

Milk & Honey Country Hideaway ✪
P.O. BOX 4972, SEVIERVILLE, TENNESSEE 37864

Tel: **(615) 428-4858**
Best Time to Call: **4 PM–10 PM**
Hosts: **Fern Miller, and Ray and Linda Barnhart**
Location: **5 mi. W of Pigeon Forge**
No. of Rooms: **6**
No. of Private Baths: **2**
Max. No. Sharing Bath: **4**
Double/pb: **$60–$100**
Single/pb: **$50–$90**
Double/sb: **$45–$65**

Single/sb: **$35–$60**
Open: **All year**
Reduced Rates: **After 3 nights**
Breakfast: **Full**
Credit Cards: **MC, VISA**
Pets: **No**
Children: **Welcome, over 14**
Smoking: **No**
Social Drinking: **No**
Minimum Stay: **2 nights, October; holiday weekends**

Rustic charm awaits you at this peaceful mountain retreat with its large wraparound front porch. Guest rooms are furnished with antiques and quilts in a decor that combines Victorian, Amish, and country styles. Often, the aroma of sumptuous home-baked goodies will draw you into the parlor. Ray is responsible for much of the woodwork in the house, and Linda and Fern are accomplished cooks. To test their talents, sample the full breakfasts, which consist of seasonal fruit, biscuits and gravy, fried apples, and surprise oven omelets. If you care to venture out into civilization, Pigeon Forge, Gatlinburg, and Dollywood are nearby.

The Tullahoma B&B ✪
308 NORTH ATLANTIC STREET, TULLAHOMA, TENNESSEE 37388

Tel: **(615) 455-8876**
Hosts: **Mike and Deanna Farley**
Location: **65 mi. SE of Nashville**
No. of Rooms: **3**

No. of Private Baths: **1**
Max. No. Sharing Bath: **4**
Double/pb: **$45–$50**
Double/sb: **$40–$45**

Open: **All year**	Pets: **No**
Reduced Rates: **Weekly**	Children: **Welcome, over 10**
Breakfast: **Continental**	Smoking: **No**
Credit Cards: **MC, VISA**	Social Drinking: **Permitted**

From the exterior gingerbread trim to the lavish ornamental woodwork in the entrance hall, this home testifies to the elegance of a bygone era. Guests interested in historic preservation are welcome to look at the Farley's photo album, which documents the building's continuing restoration. To see the neighborhood's other impressive homes, take a walking tour of Tullahoma's historic Depot District. Cool off afterward at Woods Reservoir, Normandy Lake, or Tims Ford Lake—these man-made lakes have boating, fishing, and water skiing facilities. For a different form of refreshment, visit the Jack Daniels distillery, the nation's oldest distillery, in nearby Lynchburg.

For key to listings, see inside front or back cover.

✪ This star means that rates are guaranteed through December 31, 1991, to any guest making a reservation as a result of reading about the B&B in *BED & BREAKFAST U.S.A.*—1991 edition.

Important! To avoid misunderstandings, always ask about cancellation policies when booking.

Please enclose a self-addressed, stamped, business-size envelope when contacting reservation services.

For more details on what you can expect in a B&B, see Chapter 1.

Always mention *Bed & Breakfast U.S.A.* when making reservations!

If no B&B is listed in the area you'll be visiting, use the form on page 675 to order a copy of our "List of New B&Bs."

We want to hear from you! Use the form on page 677.

TEXAS

Amarillo •
•Canyon

Garland   Lone Star
Dallas •   • Jefferson
Tyler •   •Marshall
Marble Falls •
• .Georgetown
Granite Shoals • • Austin   • Huntsville
Fredericksburg   Columbus • • Houston
San Antonio• • Shiner
New Braunfels
Victoria •
•Ingleside

The Bed & Breakfast Society of Texas ✪
8880-B2, BELLAIRE BOULEVARD, SUITE #284, HOUSTON, TEXAS 77036-4900

	Rates (Single/Double):		
Tel: **(713) 771-3919**	Modest:	**$30**	**$40**
Best Time to Call: **9 AM–5 PM**	Average:	**$35**	**$55**
Coordinator: **Pat Thomas**	Luxury:	**$50**	**$85**
States/Regions Covered: **Texas, statewide**			

Whether you're traveling for business or pleasure, Pat's hosts offer the kind of friendliness and individualized care that will make your stay pleasant. The area is known for the Astrodome, Galveston Bay, NASA, and the Texas Medical Center. There are wonderful restaurants, shops, museums, and historic sights, and Baylor, Rice, and the University of Houston are nearby. Many are conveniently located urban homes, serene country houses, historic inns, waterfront cottages, and one is a 42-foot yacht.

Bed & Breakfast Texas Style ✪
4224 WEST RED BIRD LANE, DALLAS, TEXAS 75237

Tel: **(214) 298-8586**
Best Time to Call: **9 AM–5 PM**
Coordinator: **Ruth Wilson**
States/Regions Covered: **Arlington, Austin, Dallas, El Paso, Fort Worth, Houston, Santa Fe**

Descriptive Directory: **$3.50**
Rates (Single/Double):
   Modest: **$25**   **$39**
   Average: **$30**   **$45**
   Luxury: **$60**   **$100**
Credit Cards: **MC, VISA**

The above cities are only a small sample of the locations of hosts waiting to give you plenty of warm hospitality. Ruth's register includes comfortable accommodations in condos, restored Victorians, lakeside cottages, and ranches. Texas University, Southern Methodist University, Baylor University, Rice University, and Texas Christian University are convenient to many B&Bs.

Parkview House
1311 SOUTH JEFFERSON, AMARILLO, TEXAS 79101

Tel: **(806) 373-9464**
Best Time to Call: **Before 10 AM; after 5 PM**
Hosts: **Nabil and Carol Dia**
Location: **½ mi. from I-40**
No. of Rooms: **5**
No. of Private Baths: **1**
Max. No. Sharing Bath: **4**
Double/pb: **$60**
Double/sb: **$50**

Suite: **$75**
Open: **All year**
Breakfast: **Continental**
Credit Cards: **MC, VISA**
Pets: **No**
Children: **No**
Smoking: **No**
Social Drinking: **Permitted**
Foreign Languages: **Arabic**
Airport/Station Pickup: **Yes**

Carol is a full-time host; Nabil a civil engineer. Both share interests in restoration and antiques, which is evident in their charming Prairie Victorian located in the historic district. The guest rooms are furnished with selected antiques, lace, and luxurious linens. The large columned porch is a fine place to start the day with breakfast or to relax. Carol will lend you a bike and be glad to prepare a picnic basket to take to nearby Palo Duro Canyon State Park or Lake Meredith. West Texas State University is nearby. They enjoy having guests join them for a "social hour" before dinner.

The McCallum House ✪
613 WEST 32ND, AUSTIN, TEXAS 78705

Tel: **(512) 451-6744**
Hosts: **Roger and Nancy Danley**
Location: **2 mi. from I-35**
No. of Rooms: **5**

No. of Private Baths: **5**
Double/pb: **$75**
Single/pb: **$65**
Suites: **$85**

Open: **All year**
Reduced Rates: **10%, 2 nights or
more**
Breakfast: **Full**
Credit Cards: **MC, VISA**

Pets: **No**
Children: **Welcome, over 8**
Smoking: **No**
Social Drinking: **Permitted**

This late Victorian home is just 10 blocks north of the University of Texas and 20 blocks from the capitol and downtown. Air-conditioned and furnished with antiques, the house has one guest room with a large screened-in porch with wicker furniture; all have kitchen facilities ideal for longer stays. Roger and Nancy will be happy to share the interesting history of their house, built by a former Texas secretary of state and her husband. Fruit cups, quiches, and muffins are breakfast delights.

Southard House ✪
908 BLANCO, AUSTIN, TEXAS 78703

Tel: **(512) 474-4731**
Hosts: **Jerry and Rejina Southard**
No. of Rooms: **6**
No. of Private Baths: **6**
Double/pb: **$49**
Single/pb: **$39**
Suites: **$89**
Open: **All year**

Reduced Rates: **15%, weekly**
Breakfast: **Continental (weekdays)**
Credit Cards: **AMEX, DC, MC, VISA**
Pets: **No**
Children: **Welcome, over 12**
Smoking: **Permitted**
Social Drinking: **Permitted**
Airport/Station Pickup: **Yes**

Conveniently located 12 blocks from the capitol, this 1890 Greek Revival home is furnished with antiques and original art. White cutwork lace coverlets are on the queen-size beds, and breakfast is served on a 19th-century English refectory table. On weekends, the breakfast is expanded to include such delicious fare as apple pancakes, eggs-and-cheese casserole, and a variety of meats and berries. Complimentary drinks and snacks are always offered. You are welcome to use their extensive library and to relax on the deck, porch, or in the gazebo.

Hudspeth House ✪
1905 4TH AVENUE, CANYON, TEXAS 79015

Tel: **(806) 655-9800**
Hosts: **Sally and David Haynie**
Location: **14 mi. S of Amarillo**
No. of Rooms: **8**
No. of Private Baths: **6**
Max. No. Sharing Bath: **4**
Double/pb: **$50–$70**
Double/sb: **$40–$45**
Suites: **$90**
Open: **All year**

Reduced Rates: **15%, Jan. 1–Apr. 30;
20%, weekly**
Breakfast: **Full**
Other Meals: **Available**
Credit Cards: **MC, VISA**
Pets: **No**
Children: **Welcome (crib)**
Smoking: **Permitted**
Social Drinking: **Permitted**
Airport/Station Pickup: **Yes**

Named for Mary E. Hudspeth, a leading Texas educator, this landmark home is rich in local history. Restored several times, the house was bought by Sally and Dave in 1987, and they have again refurbished it while retaining much of the original stained glass and chandeliers. In keeping with the elegant tone, breakfast features such delights as eggs Benedict. Sally, a former manager of the chic Zodiac Dining Room at Neiman-Marcus in Dallas, knows all about elegance with comfort. Within walking distance are Canyon Square, West Texas State University, and the Panhandle Plains Museum.

Be My Guest ✪

402 WEST MAIN, FREDERICKSBURG, TEXAS 78624

Tel: **(512) 997-7227**
Best Time to Call: **9 AM–9 PM**
Coordinator: **Helen K. Taylor**
States/Regions Covered:
  Fredericksburg, Hill County
Descriptive Directory: **Free**

Rates (Double):
  Modest: **$55**
  Average: **$65**
  Luxury: **$76–$85**
Credit Cards: **MC, VISA**

Helen's hosts pride themselves on providing more than just lodging. They extend a warm "Willkommen," for some of them speak fluent German. You may choose an 1848 pioneer home in the historic district, a newly decorated Victorian close to downtown, a farmhouse backed by the Pedernales River, or a restored log cabin on 10 acres. Discounts are offered on two-night stays or longer, weekdays.

Catnap Creek Bed & Breakfast ✪

417 GLEN CANYON DRIVE, GARLAND, TEXAS 75040

Tel: **(214) 530-0819**
Best Time to Call: **9 PM**
Hosts: **Gene and Nancy Cushion**
Location: **15 mi. NE of Dallas**
No. of Rooms: **1**
No. of Private Baths: **1**
Double/pb: **$45**
Single/pb: **$35**
Open: **All year**

Breakfast: **Full on weekends;**
  continental on weekdays
Wheelchair-Accessible: **Yes**
Credit Cards: **MC, VISA**
Pets: **No**
Children: **No**
Smoking: **No**
Social Drinking: **Permitted**
Airport/Station Pickup: **Yes**

Here is a bed-and-breakfast for cat-lovers: the Cushions have two cats, and throughout this spacious brick ranch, the dishes, towels, pillows, and pictures have a kitty motif. Catnap Creek has a covered patio for outdoor dining and, in the back of the house, a wide deck with a hot tub. (Terry robes are provided.) On weekdays, breakfasts feature breads, fruit, yogurt, and granola. On weekends, morning meals are more elaborate, and the menu is apt to include quiche, pancakes, or waffles.

Claibourne House ✪
912 FOREST STREET, GEORGETOWN, TEXAS 78626

Tel: **(512) 863-2761**
Host: **Clare Easley**
Location: **30 mi. N of Austin**
No. of Rooms: **4**
No. of Private Baths: **4**
Double/pb: **$55–$75**
Guest Cottage: **$150; sleeps 3**

Open: **All year**
Breakfast: **Continental**
Credit Cards: **AMEX, MC, VISA**
Pets: **Sometimes**
Children: **Welcome, over 6**
Smoking: **No**
Social Drinking: **Permitted**

Six blocks from cafés and boutiques of Georgetown's historic square, this 1896 Victorian was recently restored by Clare, a preservation enthusiast. You'll marvel at the elegance she recreated: rooms with oak over pine floors, 12-foot ceilings, walkthrough windows, five fireplaces, all furnished in an eclectic mix of abstract art and antiques. Enjoy morning coffee or afternoon wine on the big front porch, play the piano in the entrance hall, bike country lanes, or tour the surrounding countryside.

The Lovett Inn ✪
501 LOVETT BOULEVARD, HOUSTON, TEXAS 77006

Tel: **(713) 522-5224**
Best Time to Call: **After 5 PM**
Host: **Tom Fricke**
Location: **In Houston**
No. of Rooms: **4**
No. of Private Baths: **3**
Max. No. Sharing Bath: **2**
Double/pb: **$35–$75**
Single/pb: **$30–$70**
Double/sb: **$35–$65**
Single/sb: **$30–$60**

Suites: **$50–$85**
Open: **All year**
Reduced Rates: **Mon.–Thurs.; weekly discounts**
Breakfast: **Continental**
Credit Cards: **MC, VISA**
Pets: **Sometimes**
Children: **No**
Smoking: **Permitted**
Social Drinking: **Permitted**

It's easy to be fooled by the Lovett Inn: although it looks far older, this stately Federalist-style mansion, attractively furnished with 19th-century reproductions, was actually built in 1924. Its convenient museum-district location puts visitors within easy striking distance of downtown Houston, the Galleria, and the Houston Medical Center. After spending the day in the city, guests are sure to appreciate a dip in the pool. Each room has a color TV.

Sara's Bed & Breakfast Inn ✪
941 HEIGHTS BOULEVARD, HOUSTON, TEXAS 77008

Tel: **(713) 868-1130**
Best Time to Call: **After 11 AM**
Hosts: **Donna and Tillman Arledge**

Location: **6 blocks from I-10**
No. of Rooms: **12**
No. of Private Baths: **3**

Max. No. Sharing Bath: **4**
Double/pb: **$52**
Double/sb: **$46–$58**
Suites: **$96 for 4**
Open: **All year**
Breakfast: **Continental**

Credit Cards: **AMEX, CB, DC, MC, VISA**
Pets: **No**
Children: **Welcome**
Smoking: **No**
Social Drinking: **Permitted**

This Queen Anne Victorian, with its turret and widow's walk, is located in Houston Heights, a neighborhood of historic homes, many of which are on the National Historic Register. Each bedroom is uniquely furnished, having either single, double, queen- or king-size beds. The Balcony Suite consists of two bedrooms, two baths, full kitchen, living area, and a fine view overlooking the deck and spa. Cool drinks or hot coffee are graciously offered in the afternoon. The sights and sounds of downtown Houston are four miles away.

Blue Bonnet ✪
ROUTE 2, BOX 68, HUNTSVILLE, TEXAS 77340

Tel: **(409) 291-5833**
Hosts: **John and Bette Nelson**
Location: **70 mi. N of Houston**
No. of Rooms: **4**
No. of Private Baths: **3**
Max. No. Sharing Bath: **4**
Double/sb: **$38**
Single/sb: **$35**

Suites: **$48**
Open: **All year**
Breakfast: **Continental**
Pets: **Sometimes**
Children: **Welcome**
Smoking: **No**
Social Drinking: **Permitted**

Seven tree-shaded acres frame this appealing blue Victorian-style house, with its white trim and wraparound porch. Try your luck fishing in the pond, sit on the porch, or play horseshoes and croquet on the lawn. The house is less than five minutes from Sam Houston State University and the adjacent Sam Houston Grave and Museum complex. Antique lovers will find plenty of shops in the neighborhood; Bette, who manages two antique malls, can give you some good suggestions. Continental breakfast may include apple fritters, poppy seed muffins, filled croissants, and fruit compote.

Sunset Retreat Bed & Breakfast ✪
ROUTE 1, BOX 282, 38 BAYSHORE DRIVE, INGLESIDE, TEXAS 78362

Tel: **(512) 776-2534**
Hosts: **Betty and Jim Barnes**
Location: **15 mi. NE of Corpus Christi**
No. of Rooms: **3**
No. of Private Baths: **1**
Max. No. Sharing Bath: **4**
Double/sb: **$60**
Suites: **$75**
Open: **All year**

Reduced Rates: **1 free night for a 7-day stay**
Breakfast: **Continental**
Wheelchair-Accessible: **Yes**
Pets: **Sometimes**
Children: **Welcome, over 12**
Smoking: **Permitted**
Social Drinking: **Permitted**
Airport/Station Pickup: **Yes**

Located on the Texas Coast, with beautiful views of Ingleside Cove and Corpus Christi Bay, Sunset Retreat lives up to its name. The house commands 135 feet of waterfront; guests can fish from the Barneses' dock, watch porpoises, and swim to their hearts' content. Boats can be chartered for voyages to nearby islands. Enjoy a breakfast of fresh fruit, homemade breads, cinnamon rolls, and quiche in your room, on the patio, or in the sunroom.

McKay House ✪
306 EAST DELTA, JEFFERSON, TEXAS 75657

Tel: **(214) 665-7322**
Hosts: **Peggy and Tom Taylor**
No. of Rooms: **6**
No. of Private Baths: **4**
Max. No. Sharing Bath: **4**
Double/pb: **$80–$95**
Double/sb: **$80–$95**
Suite: **$125–$145**

Separate Cottage: **$80–$85**
Open: **All year**
Breakfast: **Full**
Credit Cards: **MC, VISA**
Pets: **No**
Children: **Welcome**
Smoking: **No**
Social Drinking: **Permitted**

The McKay House is listed on the National Register of Historic Places. It dates back to 1851 and is within walking distance of more than 200 homes and commercial buildings in the historic district. This Greek Revival house has 14-foot-high ceilings and nine-foot windows. Each room has been restored and features a fireplace and antique furnishings. Your host wears a long period dress when she serves breakfast. Enjoy country ham and biscuits with the sun streaming through the lace curtains of the morning room. After you've had a gentleman's breakfast, you're ready to explore the delights of this riverboat town. Guests are provided with Victorian gowns and sleepshirts to better enjoy an old-fashioned night's sleep.

Three Oaks
609 NORTH WASHINGTON AVENUE, MARSHALL, TEXAS 75670

Tel: **(214) 938-6123**
Hosts: **Sandra and Bob McCoy**
Location: **2½ hrs. E of Dallas on I-20**
No. of Rooms: **1 suite**
No. of Private Baths: **1½**
Suites: **$65–$115; sleeps 2–4**
Open: **Thurs., Fri., and Sat. nights only**
Closed: **Jan.–March**

Reduced Rates: **After 2 nights**
Breakfast: **Full**
Pets: **No**
Children: **No**
Smoking: **No**
Social Drinking: **Permitted**
Airport/Station Pickup: **Yes**

Towering oak trees shelter this lovely 1893 Victorian home, located in a National Historic District. Original leaded-glass transoms, seven hand-carved fireplaces, beamed ceilings, and polished oak floors will take you back to an earlier era. If you like, breakfast is wheeled into your bedroom on a tea cart adorned with antique linens, silver, and fine china. Your hosts invite you to browse through their vintage newspaper collection, watch TV, or use the porch swing. They will gladly direct you to the many quaint shops and Victorian restaurant within walking distance.

The White House ✪
217 MITTMAN CIRCLE, NEW BRAUNFELS, TEXAS 78130

Tel: **(512) 629-9354**
Best Time to Call: **9 AM–9 PM**
Hosts: **Beverly and Jerry White**
Location: **25 mi. N of San Antonio**
No. of Rooms: **2**
Max. No. Sharing Bath: **4**
Double/sb: **$35–$40**
Single/sb: **$30–$35**

Open: **All year**
Breakfast: **Full**
Other Meals: **Available**
Pets: **Sometimes**
Children: **Welcome (crib)**
Smoking: **No**
Social Drinking: **Permitted**

This Spanish-style white-brick ranch home is nestled among cedar and oaks in Texas hill country. Guests are welcomed here with tea and pastries and shown to comfortable rooms with antique iron beds and oak dressers. A large fishing pond is located on the premises, and a few miles away you may enjoy a refreshing tube or raft ride down the Guadalupe River. Your hosts have giant inner tubes to lend. Other attractions include the Alamo, the Riverwalk, and the many old missions located in nearby San Antonio.

Bed & Breakfast Hosts of San Antonio ✪
166 ROCKHILL, SAN ANTONIO, TEXAS 78209

Tel: **(512) 824-8036**
Best Time to Call: **9 AM–5 PM**
Coordinator: **Lavern Campbell**
States/Regions Covered: **Bandera, Boerne, Comfort, New Braunfels, San Antonio, Schertz**

Descriptive Directory: **Free**
Rates (Single/Double):

Modest:	**$29**	**$42.50**
Average:	**$40.50**	**$59**
Luxury:	**$51.50**	**$90.40**

Credit Cards: **MC, VISA**

You'll find hospitable hosts waiting to welcome you and to suggest how best to enjoy this beautiful and historic city. Don't miss the Paseo del Rio (a bustling river walk), the Alamo, the Arneson River Theatre showplace, El Mercado (which is a restored Mexican and Farmers Market), the Southwest Craft Center, wonderful restaurants, marvelous shops, and delightful, friendly folks. The University of Texas, Trinity University, and St. Mary's University are nearby. There is a booking fee of $7.50 per person; the descriptive directory is free.

The Belle of Monte Vista ✪
505 BELKNAP PLACE, SAN ANTONIO, TEXAS 78212

Tel: **(512) 732-4006**
Hosts: **Mary Lou and Jim Davis**
No. of Rooms: **5**
No. of Private Baths: **3**
Max. No. Sharing Bath: **4**
Double/pb: **$50**
Single/pb: **$40**
Double/sb: **$50**

Single/sb: **$40**
Open: **All year**
Breakfast: **Full**
Pets: **No**
Children: **Welcome**
Smoking: **No**
Social Drinking: **Permitted**
Airport/Station Pickup: **Yes**

J. Riely Gordon designed this Queen Anne Victorian as a model house for a local developer. Built in 1890 with limestone that was quarried less than half a mile away, the house has been beautifully restored and is located in the elegant Monte Vista historic district. Inside, you'll find eight fireplaces, stained-glass windows, a hand-carved oak staircase, and Victorian furnishings. Mary Lou and Jim serve a Southern breakfast with homemade muffins and jellies each morning. They are happy to help you plan your day and will direct you to nearby attractions such as Alamo Plaza, the River Walk, and El Mercado Market Place.

Falling Pines B&B ✪
300 WEST FRENCH PLACE, SAN ANTONIO, TEXAS 78212

Tel: **(512) 733-1998**
Best Time to Call: **9 AM–Noon**
Hosts: **Grace and Bob Daubert**
No. of Rooms: **5**
No. of Private Baths: **5**
Double/pb: **$65**
Single/pb: **$65**
Open: **All year**

Reduced Rates: **15%, families, weekly**
Breakfast: **Continental**
Pets: **No**
Children: **Welcome, over 10**
Smoking: **No**
Social Drinking: **Permitted**
Airport/Station Pickup: **Yes**
Minimum Stay: **2 nights**

When you enter Falling Pines through the magnificent front archway, you realize that they don't make estates like this anymore. Pines, oaks, and pecan trees shade the one-acre property. Inside, the brick-and-limestone mansion is sumptuously decorated with oak paneling, Oriental rugs, and antique furnishings. Tennis courts, a swimming pool, and a zoo are all a short walk away, or you can ride over on the bikes Grace and Bob will lend you. A continental breakfast of fresh fruit, pastries, and hot and cold cereals is served in the tiled solarium.

Rosevine Inn ✪

415 SOUTH VINE AVENUE, TYLER, TEXAS 75702

Tel: (903) 592-2221	Breakfast: **Full**
Hosts: **Bert and Rebecca Powell**	Pets: **No**
Location: **10 mi. from I-20**	Children: **Welcome, over 12**
No. of Rooms: **5**	Smoking: **No**
No. of Private Baths: **5**	Social Drinking: **Permitted**
Double/pb: **$55–$65**	Airport/Station Pickup: **Yes**
Open: **All year**	

Dr. Irwin Pope, Jr., made his home here on a quaint brick street back in the 1930s. Years later a devastating fire burned all but the foundation and beautiful grounds. Your hosts bought the property in 1986 and built the Rosevine Inn, a Federal-style red-brick home. They have furnished the house with antiques and country collectibles. In the morning, wake-up coffee is provided in the central hallway. When you come downstairs, hot muffins, baked breads, fresh fruit, and quiches are served. Your hosts will help you discover the charms of Tyler, known as the Rose Capital of the World. Antique shops are nearby, and the Rosevine makes an excellent base for discovering the many parks and lakes in the area. After a busy day, return to the inn, where you can sip a hot chocolate by the fire or relax in a quiet courtyard.

Bellsen Bed & Breakfast ✪

401 NORTH CRAIG, VICTORIA, TEXAS 77901

Tel: (512) 573-4980	Reduced Rates: **10%, seniors**
Best Time to Call: **Evenings**	Breakfast: **Continental**
Hosts: **Lynette and Amy Dugat**	Pets: **No**
Location: **125 mi. SW of Houston**	Children: **Welcome, over 12**
No. of Rooms: **1 suite**	Smoking: **No**
No. of Private Baths: **1**	Social Drinking: **Permitted**
Suites: **$35–$45**	Airport/Station Pickup: **Yes**
Open: **All year**	

Built nearly 90 years ago, this two-story white Victorian home with dark green shutters is located in a beautiful, tree-shaded neighborhood in the old section of the city. The guest suite is furnished with family treasures and antiques. The suite leads onto a large private wraparound porch with antique rockers, perfect for relaxing among the treetops. You are also welcome to swim in the pool or to enjoy the player piano. Victoria has several festivals throughout the year, as well as a variety of cultural choices.

UTAH

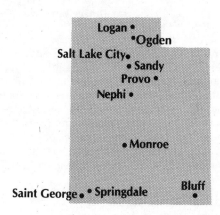

Logan •
•Ogden
Salt Lake City•
• Sandy
Provo •
Nephi •

• Monroe

Saint George • • Springdale   Bluff
•

Bed and Breakfast Rocky Mountains—Utah ✪
P.O. BOX 804, COLORADO SPRINGS, COLORADO 80901

Tel: **(719) 630-3433**	Rates (Single/Double):
Best Time to Call: **9 AM–5 PM**	Modest: **$25** **$35**
Coordinator: **Betty Ann Fields**	Average: **$30** **$45**
States/Regions Covered: **Statewide**	Luxury: **$65** **$95–$140**
Descriptive Directory: **$4.50**	Credit Cards: **MC, VISA**

Don't miss Salt Lake City and the Mormon Tabernacle, especially the Sunday morning Free Mormon Tabernacle Choir Broadcast. The B&Bs range from a modest inn to an elegant mansion. In winter, ski Park City, Alta, Snowbird, Brighton, or Solitude! Canyon lands, Bryce and Zion National Park are within easy reach.

Bluff Bed and Breakfast ✪
BOX 158, BLUFF, UTAH 84512

Tel: (801) 672-2220	Breakfast: **Full**
Host: **Rosalie Goldman**	Other Meals: **Available**
Location: **On Rtes. 163 and 191**	Pets: **No**
No. of Rooms: 2	Children: **Welcome**
No. of Private Baths: 2	Smoking: **No**
Double/pb: $59	Social Drinking: **Permitted**
Single/pb: $53.75	Airport/Station Pickup: **Yes**
Open: **All year**	Foreign Languages: **French**
Reduced Rates: **10% after 2 nights**	

Close to the Four Corners (the junction of Colorado, New Mexico, Arizona, and Utah), this air-conditioned Frank Lloyd Wright–style home is nestled among huge boulders at the foot of redrock cliffs, beside the San Juan River. On the main highway between Grand Canyon and Mesa Verde, it is secluded on seventeen desert acres. Across the river is the Navaho Reservation, and prehistoric ruins have been discovered nearby. Simply furnished, it is bright, clean, and tidy; large picture windows frame four different spectacular views. Rosalie prepares your breakfast of choice, from oatmeal to steak.

Peterson's Bed and Breakfast
95 NORTH 300 WEST, MONROE, UTAH 84754

Tel: (801) 527-4830	Suite: $55
Host: **Mary Ann Peterson**	Open: **All year**
Location: **8 mi. SW of Richfield**	Breakfast: **Full**
No. of Rooms: 3	Pets: **No**
No. of Private Baths: 2	Children: **Welcome**
Double/pb: $40	Smoking: **No**
Single/pb: $30	Social Drinking: **No**

Halfway between Los Angeles and Denver, this immaculate farmhouse, casual and comfortable, is surrounded by 10,000-foot mountains in the heart of hunting and fishing country. Mary Ann has written a marvelous cookbook called *Country Cooking,* containing rural Mormon recipes. Hot Springs is seven blocks away. It's a 2½-hour drive to Provo. A swimming pool, tennis, golf, and historic sites are nearby.

The Whitmore Mansion ✪
110 SOUTH MAIN STREET, NEPHI, UTAH 84648

Tel: (801) 623-2047	No. of Rooms: 6
Best Time to Call: **Evening**	No. of Private Baths: 6
Hosts: **Bob and Dorothy Gliske**	Double/pb: $45–$65
Location: **85 mi. S of Salt Lake City**	Suites: $75

Open: **All year**	Pets: **Sometimes**
Reduced Rates: **10%, seniors**	Children: **Welcome, over 5**
Breakfast: **Full**	Smoking: **No**
Other Meals: **Available**	Social Drinking: **Permitted**
Credit Cards: **MC, VISA**	Airport/Station Pickup: **Yes**

Located in a small farming community, this 1898 Victorian brick and sandstone mansion, listed on the National Register of Historic Places, has leaded glass windows, a huge front porch, and is topped by a turret that encases a sitting room of the third-floor suite. The interior has imported oak woodwork, a magnificent staircase, and high ceilings. Hand-crocheted afghans and handcrafted rugs complement the antique furnishings. The hearty breakfast often includes such delights as fresh apple muffins or German pancakes. In warm weather, lemonade is graciously served; during the cooler months, hot cider.

Rogers Rest
914 29TH STREET, OGDEN, UTAH 84403

Tel: **(801) 393-5824**	Reduced Rates: **10%, seniors**
Best Time to Call: **9 AM–9 PM**	Breakfast: **Continental**
Hosts: **Frank and Connie Rogers**	Pets: **No**
Location: **3 mi. E of I-15**	Children: **No**
No. of Rooms: **1**	Smoking: **No**
Max. No. Sharing Bath: **4**	Social Drinking: **Permitted**
Double/sb: **$35**	Airport/Station Pickup: **Yes**
Single/sb: **$30**	Foreign Languages: **French**
Open: **All year**	

This contemporary ranch-style home surrounded by decks rests on a small lot overlooking Mt. Benlomond, which is used in the logo for Paramount Pictures. The guest room is an eclectic meld of antique French Provincial and modern. Everything is nonallergenic with central air conditioning, humidity control, and electronic air cleaning. Connie has cooked both as a profession and avocation, so her breakfast treats are home-baked and mouth-watering. Fruit is fresh; the coffee's plentiful. You are welcome to use the kitchen for snack preparation and storage. Salt Lake City, the Mormon Temple, Hill Air Force Base, and Weber State College are within easy reach. The Golden Spike Monument is a perfect setting for a picnic.

Seven Wives Inn ✪
217 NORTH 100 WEST, ST. GEORGE, UTAH 84770

Tel: **(801) 628-3737**	Open: **All year**
Best Time to Call: **After 9 AM**	Breakfast: **Full**
Hosts: **Jay and Donna Curtis, and Alison and Jon Bowcutt**	Credit Cards: **MC, VISA**
	Pets: **Welcome**
Location: **125 mi. NE of Las Vegas**	Children: **Welcome (crib)**
No. of Rooms: **13**	Smoking: **No**
No. of Private Baths: **13**	Social Drinking: **Permitted**
Double/pb: **$35–$75**	Airport/Station Pickup: **Yes**
Single/pb: **$25–$75**	

This delightful inn is featured on the walking tour of St. George; it is just across from the Brigham Young home and two blocks from the historic Washington County Court House. Your hosts offer traditional Western hospitality. Their home is decorated with antiques collected in America and Europe. Some bedrooms are named after one of the seven wives of Donna's polygamous great-grandfather. A gourmet breakfast is served in the elegant dining room that will give you a hint of the past. St. George is located near Zion and Bryce National Parks, boasts eight golf courses, and is noted for its mild winters. Dixie College is nearby. There's a swimming pool for your pleasure.

Anton Boxrud House ✪
57 SOUTH 600 EAST, SALT LAKE CITY, UTAH, 84102

Tel: **(801) 363-8035**	Single/sb: **$45**
Best Time to Call: **9 AM–9 PM**	Open: **All year**
Hosts: **Ray and Margaret Fuller**	Reduced Rates: **10% weekly, families**
Location: **5 blocks from downtown**	Breakfast: **Full**
No. of Rooms: **4**	Credit Cards: **MC, VISA**
No. of Private Baths: **2**	Pets: **No**
Max. No. Sharing Bath: **4**	Children: **Welcome (crib)**
Double/pb: **$59**	Smoking: **Permitted**
Single/pb: **$55**	Social Drinking: **Permitted**
Double/sb: **$49**	Airport/Station Pickup: **Yes**

Located in the downtown historic district, the Anton Boxrud House is one of Salt Lake City's grand old homes. The beveled-glass windows and beautiful woodwork have been carefully restored according to the original 1899 plans. Rooms are furnished with antiques, including a handcarved German dining room table where breakfast is served. Guests are invited to meet one another at five o'clock, when wine and cheese are served to the tunes of the old player piano. This Victorian inn is close to the governor's mansion, Temple Square, and two major shopping malls. Ray and Margaret can guide you to the sights and can arrange to have a horse-drawn carriage take you on a tour.

Dave's Cozy Cabin Inn B&B ✪
2293 EAST 6200 SOUTH, SALT LAKE CITY, UTAH 84121

Tel: **(801) 278-6136**	Open: **All year**
Best Time to Call: **10 AM–6 PM**	Reduced Rates: **5% seniors, families,**
Hosts: **David and Dorothy Moore**	**after 5 nights**
No. of Rooms: **3**	Breakfast: **Full**
No. of Private Baths: **1**	Pets: **No**
Max. No. Sharing Bath: **4**	Children: **Welcome, over 12**
Double/pb: **$45**	Smoking: **No**
Single/pb: **$35**	Social Drinking: **Permitted**
Double/sb: **$40**	Minimum Stay: **2 nights**
Single/sb: **$30**	

This log cabin at the base of the Wasatch Mountains is a handsome retreat, with its knotty pine paneling, large fireplace, and lovely garden patio. For that extra bit of relaxation, hop into the redwood hot tub. Between the nearby ski slopes and the sights of Salt Lake City, visitors will find plenty to do. You'll start the day off right with a full breakfast highlighted by oven-fresh muffins with homemade jams and jellies.

The National Historic Bed & Breakfast ✪
936 EAST 1700 SOUTH, SALT LAKE CITY, UTAH 84105

Tel: **(801) 485-3535**	Suites: **$77**
Host: **Lance Davis**	Open: **All year**
Location: **6 blocks from I-80**	Reduced Rates: **Weekly**
No. of Rooms: **5**	Breakfast: **Full**
No. of Private Baths: **3**	Credit Cards: **AMEX, MC, VISA**
Max. No. Sharing Bath: **4**	Pets: **No**
Double/pb: **$67**	Children: **Welcome, over 3**
Single/pb: **$57**	Smoking: **No**
Double/sb: **$47**	Social Drinking: **Permitted**
Single/sb: **$47**	

The ornate facade of this house combines brick, wood, and stained glass to achieve its handsome Victorian style. Located in the historic

Sugarhouse section, its 19th-century pieces meld attractively with Art Deco and contemporary furnishings. The bedrooms have down comforters and freshly cut flowers; the bathrooms boast plush towels and fine soaps. Conveniently located, it's just 2 blocks from Westminster College, 5 minutes to the Mormon Temple and downtown, and only 20 minutes away from the famed ski slopes of Snowbird, Alta, and Solitude.

Under the Eaves Guest House ✪

P.O. BOX 29, 980 ZION PARK BOULEVARD, SPRINGDALE, UTAH 84767

Tel: (801) 772-3457	Single/sb: $35
Hosts: Kathleen Brown-Wilkerson, John O'Shea, Dale Wilkerson	Suites: $65
	Open: All year
Location: 45 mi. E of St. George	Reduced Rates: Available
No. of Rooms: 5	Breakfast: Full
No. of Private Baths: 3	Credit Cards: MC, VISA
Max. No. Sharing Bath: 4	Pets: Sometimes
Double/pb: $45–$65	Children: Welcome
Single/pb: $40–$55	Smoking: No
Double/sb: $45	Social Drinking: Permitted

Under the Eaves is a historic stone-and-stucco cottage located at the gate of Zion National Park. Constructed of massive sandstone blocks from the canyon, the guest house has served as a landmark for visitors to Zion for more than 50 years. Choose from two antique-filled bedrooms or a luxurious suite. Your hosts provide turndown service at night. The garden cottage dates from the 1920s and has two nonconnecting private bedrooms and baths.

VERMONT

Montgomery Center North Troy
North Hero • • • Morgan
Jeffersonville • • East Burke
Burlington • • Jericho Craftsbury Common
Waterbury • • Stowe • Plainfield
Warren • • Barre
Middlebury Brookfield Chelsea
Bethel • • South Strafford
• Gaysville
Cuttingsville Rutland • Reading
Fair Haven • • Wallingford
Danby • • Belmont
Dorset • • Weston Ludlow
Manchester •
Manchester Center • Chester Townshend
East Dorset • West Dover
• Bennington

American Country Collection–Bed & Breakfast Vermont

984 GLOUCESTER PLACE, SCHENECTADY, NEW YORK 12309

Tel: **(518) 370-4948**
Best Time to Call: **10 AM–noon; 1–5 PM, Mon.–Fri.**
Coordinator: **Beverly Walsh**
States/Regions Covered: **Vermont— Bennington, Burlington, Ludlow, Middlebury, Manchester, Rutland, Stowe**

Descriptive Directory of B&Bs: **$4**
Rates (Single/Double):
  Modest: **$30–$40** **$40–$50**
  Average: **$45–$50** **$55–$70**
  Luxury: **$55 up** **$75 up**
Credit Cards: **AMEX, MC, VISA**

Beverly's ambition is to have a B&B in every town and hamlet, statewide. Her roster of special hosts is steadily increasing in number and professionalism since she practices, "Give the guests their money's worth." Her listings range from an 1850 Colonial on eight acres in South Stratford with a full breakfast, to a tranquil home bordered by a brook in Manchester, to a romantic "couples only" retreat in Ludlow. She can also take care of reservations in the Massachusetts Berkshires and areas of northeastern New York.

Woodruff House ✪

13 EAST STREET, BARRE, VERMONT 05641

Tel: **(802) 476-7745**	Reduced Rates: **Weekly**
Best Time to Call: **Evenings**	Open: **All year**
Hosts: **Robert and Terry Somaini**	Breakfast: **Full**
Location: **130 mi. SE of Montreal**	Pets: **No**
No. of Rooms: **2**	Children: **Welcome, over 12**
Max. No. Sharing Bath: **4**	Smoking: **No**
Double/sb: **$65**	Social Drinking: **No**
Single/sb: **$55**	

Woodruff House is located in a quiet park in the heart of town. Guest rooms are furnished in antiques and decorated with flair. Guests are welcome to relax in the two living rooms and use the TV and piano. Breakfast specialties include homemade breads and eggs prepared with Vermont cheddar. Your host will point the way to the state capital, five ski areas, museums, and some of the greatest fall foliage in the state.

The Parmenter House ✪

BOX 106, BELMONT, VERMONT 05730

Tel: **(802) 259-2009**	Open: **June 15–Oct. 15**
Best Time to Call: **8–10 AM; evenings**	Reduced Rates: **Available**
Hosts: **Lester and Cynthia Firschein**	Breakfast: **Continental**
Location: **25 mi. SE of Rutland; 2 mi.**	Credit Cards: **MC, VISA**
from Rte. 155	Pets: **No**
No. of Rooms: **5**	Children: **Welcome, over 7**
No. of Private Baths: **5**	Smoking: **No**
Double/pb: **$65–$90**	Social Drinking: **Permitted**
Single/pb: **$55**	Airport/Station Pickup: **Yes**

You are certain to benefit from the clear mountain air of this idyllic lakeside village. In summer, swim or canoe on Star Lake by day, stargaze from the large deck by night. Explore a country lane on a crisp autumn morning or rent an all-terrain bike for an excursion followed with mulled cider from the wood stove. Cynthia and Lester invite you to relax in the serene atmosphere of their parlor. Retire to your bedroom furnished with Victorian antiques, handmade quilts, and herbal wreaths. The bountiful breakfast buffet of fruit, local cheeses, homemade granola, and freshly baked breads is a gastronomic treat.

Greenhurst Inn
RIVER STREET, BETHEL, VERMONT 05032

Tel: **(802) 234-9474**	Single/sb: **$40–$55**
Hosts: **Lyle and Claire Wolf**	Open: **All year**
Location: **30 mi. E of Rutland**	Breakfast: **Continental**
No. of Rooms: **13**	Credit Cards: **Discover, MC, VISA**
No. of Private Baths: **7**	Pets: **Welcome (no cats)**
Max. No. Sharing Bath: **5**	Children: **Welcome (crib)**
Double/pb: **$75–$95**	Smoking: **Permitted**
Single/pb: **$65–$85**	Social Drinking: **Permitted**
Double/sb: **$50–$65**	

Located 100 yards from the White River, this elegant Queen Anne mansion is listed on the National Register of Historic Places. Built in 1890, the heavy brass hinges, embossed floral brass doorknobs, and etched windows at the entry have withstood the test of time. The cut-crystal collection is magnificent, and the stereoscope and old Victrola add to the old-fashioned atmosphere. It's close to many points of historic interest, and seasonal recreational activities are abundant. There's tennis and croquet on the premises. Vermont Law School is close by.

Poplar Manor
RD 2, ROUTES 12 AND 107, BETHEL, VERMONT 05032

Tel: **(802) 234-5426**	Reduced Rates: **10%, weekly**
Hosts: **Carmen and Bob Jaynes**	Breakfast: **Continental**
Location: **16 mi. N of Woodstock**	Pets: **Sometimes**
No. of Rooms: **4**	Children: **Welcome**
Max. No. Sharing Bath: **4**	Smoking: **Permitted**
Double/sb: **$34**	Social Drinking: **Permitted**
Single/sb: **$26**	Foreign Languages: **Spanish**
Suites: **$36**	Minimum Stay: **2 nights, foliage**
Open: **All year**	**season and holiday weekends**

This early 19th-century Colonial is surrounded by green meadows and cornfields. The rooms are large and bright, with exposed-beam ceilings, collectibles, and plants. Your hosts offer wine and mulled cider, served spiked if you wish. The fields back up to the White River and a swimming hole. Other area attractions include the National Fish Hatchery, Silver Lake, seasonal sports and the shops of Woodstock. Vermont Law School is nearby.

Green Trails Country Inn ✪
POND VILLAGE, BROOKFIELD, VERMONT 05036

Tel: **(802) 276-3412**	Location: **8 mi. from I-89, Exit 4**
Hosts: **Peter and Pat Simpson**	No. of Rooms: **15**

No. of Private Baths: **9**	Breakfast: **Full**
Max. No. Sharing Bath: **4**	Other Meals: **Available**
Double/pb: **$77–$90**	Pets: **No**
Single/pb: **$56–$66**	Children: **Welcome (crib)**
Double/sb: **$69–$80**	Smoking: **No**
Single/sb: **$50–$56**	Social Drinking: **Permitted**
Open: **May–Mar.**	Airport/Station Pickup: **Yes**
Reduced Rates: **Groups**	

The inn consists of two buildings. One is an 1840 farmhouse; the other was built in the late 1700s and has pumpkin pine floorboards. They are located across from the famous Floating Bridge and Sunset Lake. Furnished in antiques and "early nostalgia," the rooms have stenciling (circa 1800), handmade quilts, and fresh flowers. The historic village is a perfect base for seasonal excursions to the Shelburne Museum or Woodstock. Cross-country skiers can start at the doorstep, while downhill enthusiasts can try Sugarbush and Killington.

Shire Inn
MAIN STREET, CHELSEA, VERMONT 05038

Tel: **(802) 685-3031**	Breakfast: **Full**
Hosts: **James and Mary Lee Papa**	Other Meals: **Available**
Location: **20 mi. from I-89**	Credit Cards: **MC, VISA**
No. of Rooms: **6**	Pets: **No**
No. of Private Baths: **6**	Children: **Welcome, over 6**
Double/pb: **$65–$95**	Smoking: **No**
Open: **All year**	Social Drinking: **Permitted**

In 1832 a successful Chelsea businessman built this stately home entirely of Vermont brick. The Federal-style house was made to last, from the unusually high ceilings above to the pine floors below, now carefully restored and gleaming under coats of varnish. Enter through the granite front archway and step into the parlor, where a crackling fire and a warm welcome awaits. Your hosts are transplanted New York professionals who have left the city life for a white picket fence and a river flowing out back. They invite you to antique-filled bedrooms, several with fireplaces, and modern baths with fluffy, oversize towels and English soaps. A typical Shire breakfast features German pancakes served with apricot sauce. Home cooking can also be enjoyed in the evening, when a five-course meal is served in the dining room. The inn is set on 17 acres in a quiet country village that is said to have the state's oldest general store.

Stone Hearth Inn ✪
ROUTE 11, CHESTER, VERMONT 05143

Tel: **(802) 875-2525**	Location: **10 mi. from I-91, Exit 6**
Hosts: **Janet and Don Strohmeyer**	No. of Rooms: **10**

No. of Private Baths: **8**
Max. No. Sharing Bath: **4**
Double/pb: **$60–$80**
Single/pb: **$40–$60**
Double/sb: **$50–$70**
Single/sb: **$40–$60**
Open: **All year**
Reduced Rates: **Available**

Breakfast: **Full**
Pets: **Sometimes**
Children: **Welcome (crib)**
Smoking: **Permitted**
Social Drinking: **Licensed pub**
Airport/Station Pickup: **Yes**
Foreign Languages: **Dutch, French, German**

This white 19th-century Colonial is set on seven acres of fields and wooded land. The rooms have been lovingly restored and feature wide-board pine floors and open beams, floral wallpapers, antiques, quilts, and a player piano. A fire-warmed living room and library are available. After a busy day, relax in the licensed pub and recreation room, or enjoy the whirlpool spa. Horseback riding, downhill and cross-country skiing, and swimming in the river across the road are but a handful of the local pleasures. Your hosts offer fresh-baked breads, pancakes, and French toast for breakfast. The dining room and licensed pub are open to the public.

Craftsbury Bed & Breakfast on Wylie Hill ✪
CRAFTSBURY COMMON, VERMONT 05827

Tel: **(802) 586-2206**
Best Time to Call: **Morning or evening**
Host: **Margaret Ramsdell**
Location: **40 mi. N of Montpelier**
No. of Rooms: **4**
Max. No. Sharing Bath: **4**
Double/sb: **$50–$60**
Single/sb: **$35**

Open: **All year**
Breakfast: **Full**
Pets: **No**
Children: **Welcome (crib)**
Smoking: **No**
Social Drinking: **Permitted**
Foreign Languages: **French**

This 1860 Georgian hilltop farmhouse has beautiful views. The homey guest rooms adjoin the living room with its wood stove, where you are welcome to relax and visit. You may use Margaret's kitchen, barbecue, and picnic table should the crisp mountain air stoke your appetite. You're sure to enjoy the bountiful breakfast that often features apple pancakes with fresh maple syrup. Dinner is served only by prior arrangement. The ski slopes of Stowe are 30 miles away, and lakes and rivers are within a two-mile radius. Cross-country skiing starts at the door.

Buckmaster Inn ✪
LINCOLN HILL ROAD, CUTTINGSVILLE, VERMONT 05738

Tel: **(802) 492-3485**
Best Time to Call: **8 AM–8 PM**
Hosts: **Sam and Grace Husselman**

Location: **8 mi. SE of Rutland**
No. of Rooms: **4**
No. of Private Baths: **1**

Max. No. Sharing Bath: **4**	Breakfast: **Full**
Double/pb: **$50–$65**	Pets: **No**
Single/pb: **$50–$65**	Children: **Welcome, over 8**
Double/sb: **$40–$50**	Smoking: **No**
Single/sb: **$35–$50**	Social Drinking: **Permitted**
Open: **All year**	Airport/Station Pickup: **Yes**
Reduced Rates: **Weekly**	Foreign Languages: **Dutch**

The Buckmaster Inn, located near Cuttingsville in the Green Mountains, is a Federal clapboard Colonial overlooking a picturesque valley. Its center hall, grand staircase, and wide pine floors are typical of 19th-century style. This is New England relaxation at its best: fireplaces, wood-burning stove, library, and two porches. Homemade muffins, casseroles, and jams are among the specialties served in the country kitchen each morning. A pond for skating and fishing is within walking distance, and ski slopes, hiking trails, and craft shops are nearby.

The Quail's Nest Bed and Breakfast ✪
P.O. BOX 221, MAIN STREET, DANBY, VERMONT 05739

Tel: **(802) 293-5099**	Single/sb: **$35**
Hosts: **Chip and Anharad Edson**	Open: **All year**
Location: **13 mi. N of Manchester**	Breakfast: **Full**
No. of Rooms: **5**	Credit Cards: **MC, VISA**
No. of Private Baths: **3**	Pets: **No**
Double/pb: **$65**	Children: **Welcome, over 6**
Single/pb: **$50**	Smoking: **Permitted**
Double/sb: **$50**	Social Drinking: **Permitted**

The Quail's Nest is a Greek Revival–style inn circa 1835. The guest rooms are furnished with antiques and handmade country quilts. Your host loves entertaining and offers such homemade breakfast specialties as apple-puff pancakes, muffins, and quiches. Danby is a quiet village close to five major ski areas. The Green Mountains are just east of here, offering some of the finest swimming, fishing, hiking, and downhill and cross-country skiing in the state.

The Little Lodge at Dorset ✪
ROUTE 30, BOX 673, DORSET, VERMONT 05251

Tel: **(802) 867-4040**	Open: **All year**
Hosts: **Allan and Nancy Norris**	Breakfast: **Continental**
Location: **6 mi. N of Manchester**	Credit Cards: **AMEX**
No. of Rooms: **5**	Pets: **No**
No. of Private Baths: **5**	Children: **Welcome (crib)**
Double/pb: **$80–$100**	Smoking: **No**
Single/pb: **$70–$90**	Social Drinking: **Permitted**

Situated in one of the prettiest little towns in Vermont, this delightful 1820 Colonial house, on the Historic Register, is perched on a hillside way back from the road, overlooking the mountains and its own trout pond that's used for skating in winter or swimming in summer. The original paneling and wide floorboards set off the splendid antiques. After skiing at nearby Stratton or Bromley, toast your feet by the fireplace while sipping hot chocolate. If you prefer, bring your own liquor, and Nancy and Allan will provide Vermont cheese and crackers.

Maplewood Colonial Inn ✪
BOX 1019, ROUTE 30, DORSET, VERMONT 05251

Tel: **(802) 867-4470**	Single/sb: **$55**
Best Time to Call: **After 5 PM**	Open: **All year**
Hosts: **Marge and Leon Edgerton**	Breakfast: **Continental**
No. of Rooms: **5**	Pets: **Sometimes**
No. of Private Baths: **3**	Children: **Welcome, over 12**
Max. No. Sharing Bath: **4**	Smoking: **No**
Double/pb: **$70**	Social Drinking: **Permitted**
Single/pb: **$55**	Minimum Stay: **3 nights, holiday**
Double/sb: **$70**	**weekends**

This large, 20-room white Colonial with green shutters is in a lovely setting. The five corner bedrooms are airy, comfortably furnished with antiques; the dining table is pre–Civil War vintage. You are welcome to wander the acreage, canoe on the pond, bicycle, or browse in Marge and Leon's library. In winter, skiing at Bromley or Stratton is convenient. The fall foliage is fabulous. Credit cards may be used to secure a reservation.

Christmas Tree Bed & Breakfast
BENEDICT ROAD, EAST DORSET, VERMONT 05253

Tel: **(802) 362-4889**	Single/sb: **$25**
Hosts: **Dennis and Catherine Conroy**	Open: **All year**
Location: **4.5 mi. N of Manchester**	Breakfast: **Continental**
No. of Rooms: **4**	Pets: **Sometimes**
Max. No. Sharing Bath: **4**	Children: **Welcome**
Double/pb: **$50–$55**	Smoking: **No**
Single/pb: **$30–$35**	Social Drinking: **Permitted**
Double/sb: **$45**	

Dennis and Catherine invite you to share their contemporary wood-paneled home where you are welcome to relax on the deck or in front of the wood stove, depending upon the season. There's a pond and a stream for fishing, and it is located close to Emerald Lake State Park. It is 15 minutes from the slopes at Bromley; 30 minutes to Stratton.

The coffeepot is always on, and pretzels and chips are complimentary. The generous breakfast may let you skip lunch.

Maplewood Inn ✪
ROUTE 22A SOUTH, FAIR HAVEN, VERMONT 05743

Tel: **(802) 265-8039**
Best Time to Call: **2 PM–9 PM**
Hosts: **Cindy and Paul Soder**
Location: **18 mi. W of Rutland**
No. of Rooms: **5**
No. of Private Baths: **5**
Double/pb: **$65–$70**
Suites: **$95**
Open: **All year**

Reduced Rates: **After 5 nights**
Breakfast: **Full**
Credit Cards: **MC, VISA**
Pets: **No**
Children: **Welcome, over 12**
Smoking: **Permitted**
Social Drinking: **Permitted**
Minimum Stay: **Parents college weekends, holidays**
Airport/Station Pickup: **No**

The inn is a beautifully restored Greek Revival–style home, built in 1850, with lovely country views from every window. Chippendale furnishings, original pine floors polished to a warm glow, four-poster or brass beds, wingback chairs, and carefully chosen accessories provide a soothing backdrop for a relaxing visit. After a multicourse breakfast, enjoy a walk in the historic village or participate in the recreational activities at nearby Lakes Bomoseen and St. Catherine, or take a short drive to ski the slopes of Killington or Pico. Linger on the porch, play croquet on the lawn, enjoy a board game or a book in the parlor. The gourmet restaurants and shops of Rutland are close by. Reserve early for the fall foliage season.

Silver Maple Lodge and Cottages ✪
SOUTH MAIN STREET, RR1, BOX 8, FAIRLEE, VERMONT 05045

Tel: **(802) 333-4326**
Hosts: **Scott and Sharon Wright**
Location: **20 mi. N of White River Junction**
No. of Rooms: **14**
No. of Private Baths: **12**

Max. No. Sharing Bath: **4**
Double/pb: **$48–$58**
Single/pb: **$46–$56**
Double/sb: **$42**
Single/sb: **$38**
Open: **All year**

Reduced Rates: **10%, seniors**
Breakfast: **Continental**
Credit Cards: **AMEX, MC, VISA**
Pets: **Sometimes**

Children: **Welcome**
Smoking: **Prmitted**
Social Drinking: **Permitted**
Airport/Station Pickup: **Yes**

Built as a farmhouse in 1855, Silver Maple Lodge became an inn some seventy years later. To accommodate extra guests, several cottages were added, constructed from lumber cut on the property. It's easy to see why this B&B remains popular. There's swimming, boating, and fishing at two local lakes. Other outdoor activities in the area include golf, tennis, horseback riding, canoeing, hiking, and skiing. If you're tired of feeling earthbound, Post Mills Airport, seven miles away, offers flights in a hot-air balloon and gliding rides. (Special packages, combining a flight in a hot-air balloon and other activities of your choice, can be arranged.) And for concerts, theater, and art exhibits, it's an easy drive to Dartmouth College, in Hanover, New Hampshire.

Cobble House Inn
P.O. BOX 49, GAYSVILLE, VERMONT 05746

Tel: **(802) 234-5458**
Best Time to Call: **8 AM–9 PM**
Hosts: **Philip and Beau Benson**
Location: **Off Rte. 107**
No. of Rooms: **6**
No. of Private Baths: **6**
Double/pb: **$65–$95**
Open: **All year**

Breakfast: **Full**
Other Meals: **Available**
Credit Cards: **MC, VISA**
Pets: **No**
Children: **Welcome, over 6**
Smoking: **No**
Social Drinking: **Permitted**

A grand 1860s mansion awaits you on a hilltop overlooking the beautiful Green Mountains. Each guest room is decorated with antiques and accented with country furnishings. Ornate carved beds, colorful quilts, and flannel sheets are sure to offer a peaceful night's rest. Breakfast specialties such as French apple pancakes, homemade coffee cakes, peach fritters, or eggs Benedict are served each morning. Just outside the door is the White River, with its clear waters for fishing, canoeing, tubing, and swimming. Skiing, golf, tennis, and horseback riding are all within easy reach. In the evening, the inn offers Italian and French cuisine served in the country dining room.

Mannsview Inn ✪
RD1, BOX 431, ROUTE 108 SOUTH, JEFFERSONVILLE, VERMONT 05464

Tel: **(802) 644-8321**
Best Time to Call: **Mon.–Sat., 9 AM–6 PM**
Hosts: **Bette and Kelley Mann**

Location: **22 mi. E of Burlington**
No. of Rooms: **6**
No. of Private Baths: **2**
Max. No. Sharing Bath: **4**

Double/pb: **$60**
Single/pb: **$50**
Double/sb: **$50**
Single/sb: **$45**
Suite: **$70**
Open: **All year**
Reduced Ratse: **10%, seniors**
Breakfast: **Full**

Credit Cards: **MC, VISA**
Pets: **Sometimes**
Children: **Welcome, over 12**
Smoking: **No**
Social Drinking: **Permitted**
Airport/Station Pickup: **Yes**
Minimum Stay: **2 nights**

On a plateau at the base of Mt. Mansfield, this sprawling white colonial inn is surrounded by pastures, woods, and trout streams. Activities—from warm-weather hiking and water sports to fall foliage tours—depend on the season. During the winter, of course, there is downhill and cross-country skiing, sleigh rides, and skating. Mannsview's guest rooms are furnished with queen-size beds; cable TV is available on request. In the evening, complimentary drinks are served by the large stone fireplace. Quiche Lorraine and Belgian waffles are typical breakfast entrées.

The Spirited Dove Bed & Breakfast ✪
P.O. BOX 459, JEFFERSONVILLE, VERMONT 05464

Tel: **(802) 644-5450**
Best Time to Call: **Evening**
Hosts: **Joan and Jim Foltz**
Location: **35 mi. NE of Burlington**
No. of Rooms: **3**
Max. No. Sharing Bath: **4**
Double/sb: **$52.50**
Single/sb: **$49.50**

Open: **All year**
Breakfast: **Full**
Credit Cards: **MC, VISA**
Pets: **No**
Children: **Welcome, over 12**
Smoking: **Permitted**
Social Drinking: **Permitted**

Joan and Jim have created a cozy, family-oriented atmosphere at their historic colonial "three-brick-thick" farmhouse (circa 1815). Guests will find rooms filled with primitive antiques and collectibles, and can expect special touches such as homemade fudge at bedside upon retiring. Delicious breakfasts include breads and spreads, fresh fruit of the season, and a chef's specialty such as cheese strata or egg puff. Located just 10 miles from Smuggler's Notch Ski Resort and Mt. Mansfield State Park, you'll find a wide range of recreational activities. Joan is interested in fashion and interior design; Jim operates an antique shop on the premises.

Henry M. Field House Bed & Breakfast
ROUTE 15, RR2, BOX 395, JERICHO, VERMONT 05452

Tel: **(802) 899-3984**
Best Time to Call: **After 5 PM**
Hosts: **Mary Beth Perilli and Terrence L. Horan**

Location: **10 mi. E of Burlington**
No. of Rooms: **3**
No. of Private Baths: **1**
Max. No. Sharing Bath: **4**

Double/pb: **$65**	Pets: **No**
Double/sb: **$55**	Children: **Welcome, over 8**
Open: **All year**	Smoking: **No**
Breakfast: **Continental**	Social Drinking: **Permitted**
Credit Cards: **MC, VISA**	

This is an opulent, Italian-style Victorian with all the trimmings: high ceilings, ornamental plaster, etched glass, and butternut and mahogany woodwork. Guests may relax on one of three porches or stroll along the Browns River, which borders the lovely 1½-acre property. Jericho is convenient to skiing at Bolton Valley or Smuggler's Notch; hiking, biking, golf, and water sports are all within a 30-minute drive. The Henry M. Field House also offers easy access to Burlington, home of the University of Vermont and many fine shops and restaurants.

Milliken's ✪
RD 2, BOX 397, JERICHO, VERMONT 05465

Tel: **(802) 899-3993**	Suites: **$60**
Best Time to Call: **Mornings; evenings**	Open: **All Year**
Hosts: **Rick and Jean Milliken**	Breakfast: **Full**
Location: **12 mi. E of Burlington**	Pets: **No**
No. of Rooms: **3**	Children: **Welcome**
Max. No. Sharing Bath: **4**	Smoking: **No**
Double/sb: **$40**	Social Drinking: **Permitted**
Single/sb: **$30**	Airport/Station Pickup: **Yes**

This Second Empire early Victorian was built in 1867 by a lumber magnate. The house has a graceful mansard roof, original woodwork, and floors of alternating cherry and white maple. The spaciousness of the rooms is enhanced by high ceilings, large windows, and gracious decor. Rick is a hotel manager and Jean is a choreographer and host. She prepares such breakfast specialties as French toast with maple syrup and hot mulled cider. In the evening, a good-night brandy and snack is offered. Your family is sure to enjoy its stay with the Millikens, their two children, and a friendly dog named Bailey. Nearby attractions are hiking trails on Mt. Mansfield, skiing, and fabulous fall foliage.

Brook 'n' Hearth
STATE ROAD 11/30, BOX 508, MANCHESTER CENTER, VERMONT 05255

Tel: **(802) 362-3604**	Double/pb: **$60**
Best Time to Call: **2–10 PM**	Single/pb: **$40**
Hosts: **Larry and Terry Greene**	Suites: **$70 for 2**
Location: **1 mi. E of US 7**	Open: **June 1–Oct. 28; Nov. 24–Apr. 30**
No. of Rooms: **3**	
No. of Private Baths: **3**	Reduced Rates: **Available**

Breakfast: **Full**
Credit Cards: **AMEX, MC, VISA**
Pets: **No**

Children: **Welcome (crib)**
Smoking: **Permitted**
Social Drinking: **Permitted**

True to its name, a brook runs through the property and a fire warms the living room of this country home. Terry and Larry offer setups and happy-hour snacks for your self-supplied cocktails. You're within five miles of the ski slopes at Bromley and Stratton; it is also convenient to art centers, summer theater, restaurants, and a score of sports that include hiking on the Long Trail. Air-conditioned in summer, enjoy the pool, lawn games, and barbecue. The game room, with its VCR, pocket billiards, and Ping-Pong, is always available.

Brookside Meadows ✪
RD 3, BOX 2460, MIDDLEBURY, VERMONT 05753-8751

Tel: **(802) 388-6429**
Location: **2½ mi. from Rte. 7**
Hosts: **Linda and Roger Cole**
No. of Rooms: **5**
No. of Private Baths: **5**
Double/pb: **$65–$90**
Suites: **$85–$125**
Open: **All year**

Breakfast: **Full**
Pets: **No**
Children: **Welcome, over 5**
Smoking: **No**
Social Drinking: **Permitted**
Airport/Station Pickup: **Yes**
Minimum Stay: **2 nights, weekends and peak times**

This attractive farmhouse was built in 1979, based on a 19th-century design. The house is on a country road, on 20 acres of meadowland. The property borders on a brook. It is also home to geese and two dogs. The two-bedroom suite has a wood stove in the living room as well as a private entrance. Relax and enjoy a view of the Green Mountains. Area attractions include excellent downhill and cross-country skiing, hiking, maple syrup operations, Middlebury College, and the University of Vermont Morgan Horse Farm.

Phineas Swann ✪
P.O. BOX 344, MONTGOMERY, VERMONT 05471

Tel: **(802) 326-4306**
Best Time to Call: **8 AM–9 PM**
Hosts: **Frank and Maureen Kane**
Location: **56 mi. NE of Burlington**
No. of Rooms: **4**
No. of Private Baths: **2**
Max. No. Sharing Bath: **4**
Double/pb: **$70**
Single/pb: **$50**
Double/sb: **$60**

Single/sb: **$45**
Open: **All year**
Reduced Rates: **15%, weekly**
Breakfast: **Full**
Credit Cards: **MC, VISA**
Pets: **No**
Children: **Welcome, over 6**
Smoking: **No**
Social Drinking: **Permitted**
Airport/Station Pickup: **Yes**

A Victorian house with a country flavor, Phineas Swann has an enclosed porch and lots of gingerbread trim. Inside, the house is decorated in pastels, with overstuffed chairs and sofas and period-style furniture. Because of its Green Mountain setting, this B&B draws hikers, skiers, and cyclists. If you didn't bring your own bicycle, you can rent both road and mountain bikes from your hosts, who also can arrange tours. More sedentary types will want to visit the many area antique shops and restaurants. Full breakfasts, served by candlelight, consist of homebaked breads and muffins and an entrée like French toast or apple pancakes.

Hunt's Hideaway
RR 1, BOX 570, WEST CHARLESTON, MORGAN, VERMONT 05872

Tel: **(802) 895-4432; 334-8322**	Open: **All year**
Best Time to Call: **7 AM–11 PM**	Reduced Rates: **Available**
Host: **Pat Hunt**	Breakfast: **Full**
Location: **6 mi. from I-91**	Pets: **Sometimes**
No. of Rooms: **3**	Children: **Welcome**
Max. No. Sharing Bath: **4**	Smoking: **Permitted**
Double/sb: **$35**	Social Drinking: **Permitted**
Single/sb: **$25**	

This modern, split-level home is located on 100 acres of woods and fields, with a brook, pond, and large swimming pool. Pancakes with Vermont maple syrup are featured at breakfast. Ski Jay Peak and Burke, or fish and boat on Lake Seymour, two miles away. Visiting antique shops or taking a trip to nearby Canada are other local possibilities.

Charlie's Northland Lodge ✪
BOX 88, NORTH HERO, VERMONT 05474

Tel: **(802) 372-8822**	Guest Cottage: **$350–$550 weekly;**
Best Time to Call: **Before 8 PM**	**sleeps 6**
Hosts: **Charles and Dorice Clark**	Open: **All year**
Location: **60 mi. S of Montreal,**	Breakfast: **Continental**
Canada	Pets: **No**
No. of Rooms: **3**	Children: **Welcome, over 5**
Max. No. Sharing Bath: **5**	Smoking: **Permitted**
Double/sb: **$40**	Social Drinking: **Permitted**
Single/sb: **$38**	

The lodge is a restored Colonial (circa 1850) located on Lake Champlain, where bass and walleye abound. A sport and tackle shop is on the premises. Fall and winter fishing should appeal to all anglers. In summer, tennis, hiking, or relaxing in the reading room are pleasant activities.

Rose Apple Acres Farm ✪
RR 1, BOX 300, EAST HILL ROAD, NORTH TROY, VERMONT 05859

Tel: **(802) 988-4300**
Best Time to Call: **Evenings**
Hosts: **Jay and Camilla Mead**
Location: **60 mi. N of St. Johnsbury**
No. of Rooms: **3**
No. of Private Baths: **1**
Max. No. Sharing Bath: **4**
Double/pb: **$48**
Double/sb: **$38**

Single/sb: **$28**
Open: **All year**
Breakfast: **Full**
Pets: **No**
Children: **Welcome, over 6**
Smoking: **No**
Social Drinking: **Permitted**
Airport/Station Pickup: **Yes**

Located 2 miles from the Canadian border and 2 hours from Montreal or Burlington, the farm is situated on 52 acres of fields, woods, and streams. The farmhouse has a bright and friendly atmosphere, enhanced by panoramic mountain views. Hiking, cross-country skiing, and snowshoeing may be enjoyed on-premises. Horse-drawn carriage and sleigh rides are offered. It is only 10 miles to Jay Peak for skiing. Camilla and Jay are interested in classical music and gardening.

Yankees' Northview Bed & Breakfast ✪
RD 2, PLAINFIELD, VERMONT 05667

Tel: **(802) 454-7191**
Best Time to Call: **Evenings**
Hosts: **Joani and Glenn Yankee**
Location: **9 mi. NE of Montpelier**
No. of Rooms: **3**
Max. No. Sharing Bath: **5**
Double/sb: **$40–$50**
Single/sb: **$35–$45**

Open: **All year**
Reduced Rates: **Available**
Breakfast: **Full**
Pets: **Sometimes**
Children: **Welcome**
Smoking: **No**
Social Drinking: **Permitted**

Although it has a Plainfield mailing address, this roomy Colonial is located on a quiet country lane in the picturesque town of Calais. The house is surrounded by stone walls and white fences. Fresh flowers and after-dinner mints are just a few of the special touches you will find in your antique-filled bedroom. A delightful breakfast is served on the garden patio overlooking the mountains and the meadows. In cold weather, specialties such as homemade Swedish coffee ring, French toast, pancakes, and eggs are offered in the stenciled dining room or beside the pot-belly stove in the country kitchen. Your hosts invite you to relax with a cup of coffee by the fire, or stroll down to the unique quaking bog, just a five-minute walk from the house. Yankees' Northview is minutes from seasonal recreation and historic Kent's Corner.

Hillcrest Guest House ✪
RR 1, BOX 4459, RUTLAND, VERMONT 05701

Tel: **(802) 775-1670**	Open: **All year**
Hosts: **Bob and Peg Dombro**	Breakfast: **Continental**
Location: **³⁄₁₀ mi. from Rte. 7**	Pets: **No**
No. of Rooms: **3**	Children: **Welcome (crib)**
Max. No. Sharing Bath: **5**	Smoking: **No**
Double/sb: **$40**	Social Drinking: **Permitted**
Single/sb: **$35**	Airport/Station Pickup: **Yes**

This 150-year-old farmhouse, with a comfortable screened porch for warm-weather relaxing, is furnished with country antiques. Pico and Killington ski areas are 7 and 16 miles away. Summer brings the opportunity to explore charming villages, covered bridges, and antiques and craft centers. Country auctions, marble quarries, trout streams, and Sunday-evening band concerts are pleasant pastimes. Bob and Peg always offer something in the way of between-meal refreshments.

Watercourse Way ✪
ROUTE 132, SOUTH STRAFFORD, VERMONT 05070

Tel: **(802) 765-4314**	Open: **All year**
Hosts: **Lincoln and Anna Alden**	Breakfast: **Full**
Location: **10 mi. from I-91**	Pets: **Sometimes**
No. of Rooms: **3**	Children: **Welcome**
Max. No. Sharing Bath: **3**	Smoking: **Permitted**
Double/sb: **$60**	Social Drinking: **Permitted**
Single/sb: **$40**	

Watercourse Way, surrounded by towering evergreens and fragrant herb gardens, is situated on the Ompompanoosuc River. It is an 1850 farmhouse cape with wide pine floors and original Shaker-style doors. There's a place for everyone beside the giant fieldstone fireplace, and plenty of books to borrow. Freshly ground gourmet coffee and herbal teas from the garden are part of a large country breakfast. Lake Fairlee is nearby, and fishing, kayaking, and wading can be enjoyed a few steps from the front door. Dartmouth College in Hanover, New Hampshire, is close by.

Bittersweet Inn
RR 2, BOX 2900, ROUTE 100, STOWE, VERMONT 05672

Tel: **(802) 253-7787**	Location: **36 mi. E of Burlington**
Best Time to Call: **7 AM–11 PM**	No. of Rooms: **8**
Hosts: **Barbara and Paul Hansel**	No. of Private Baths: **5**

Max. No. Sharing Bath: **4**
Double/pb: **$60–$76**
Double/sb: **$54–$68**
Suites: **$125–$157**
Open: **All year**
Reduced Rates: **5-day stays**
Breakfast: **Continental**

Credit Cards: **AMEX, MC, VISA**
Pets: **Yes, small ones**
Children: **Welcome (play area)**
Smoking: **Permitted**
Social Drinking: **Permitted**
Airport/Station Pickup: **Yes**

Bittersweet Inn is a brick cape with converted clapboard carriage house, dating back to 1835. The house is set on nine and a half acres, overlooking Camel's Hump Mountain. Inside you'll find comfortable rooms decorated with a combination of antiques and family pieces. It's just a half mile to the center of town and minutes to ski lifts and a cross-country touring center. A good-size swimming pool is located out back with plenty of room for laps or just taking it easy. In the winter season, hot soup and the indoor hydro-spa will be waiting after your last ski run. Your hosts, Barbara and Paul, invite you to relax in the game room with BYOB bar and will help you plan your evening.

The Inn at the Brass Lantern ✪
ROUTE 100 NORTH, RR2, BOX 2610, STOWE, VERMONT 05672

Tel: **(802) 253-2229**
Best Time to Call: **7:30 AM–9:30 PM**
Hosts: **Mindy and Andy Aldrich**
Location: **10 mi. from I-89, Exit 10**
No. of Rooms: **9**
No. of Private Baths: **9**
Double/pb: **$70–$110**
Single/pb: **$56–$88**
Open: **All year**

Reduced Rates: **Available**
Breakfast: **Full**
Credit Cards: **AMEX, MC, VISA**
Pets: **No**
Children: **Welcome**
Smoking: **No**
Social Drinking: **Permitted**
Minimum Stay: **2-night weekends in ski season**

The inn was originally built as a farmhouse and carriage barn around 1800. Andy and Mindy won an award for their efforts in its restoration by maintaining its character with the artful use of period antiques, handmade quilts, and handmade accessories. Its setting provides panoramic views of Mt. Mansfield and the valley. A 15% gratuity is added to all rates. You are invited to join your hosts for wine, tea, and dessert while watching the sun set over the Green Mountains.

Ski Inn ✪
ROUTE 108, STOWE, VERMONT 05672

Tel: **(802) 253-4050**
Best Time to Call: **9–11 AM; evenings**
Hosts: **Larry and Harriet Heyer**
Location: **47 mi. NE of Burlington**
No. of Rooms: **10**
No. of Private Baths: **5**

Max. No. Sharing Bath: **5**
Double/pb: **$40–$95**
Double/sb: **$35–$70**
Single/sb: **$25–$45**
Open: **All year**
Reduced Rates: **Off-season**

Breakfast: **Continental**
Other Meals: **Full breakfast and
  dinner included in winter**
Pets: **Sometimes**

Children: **Welcome**
Smoking: **Permitted**
Social Drinking: **Permitted**

This traditional New England inn, set back from the highway among evergreens on a gentle sloping hillside, is a quiet place to relax and sleep soundly. In winter, it's a skier's delight, close to Mt. Mansfield's downhill and cross-country trails. In summer, the rates drop and include just Continental breakfast. Larry and Harriet offer warm hospitality in all seasons.

Boardman House Bed & Breakfast ✪
P.O. BOX 112, TOWNSEND, VERMONT 05353

Tel: **(802) 365-4086**
Hosts: **Sarah Messenger and Paul
  Weber**
Location: **125 mi. N of Boston**
No. of Rooms: **6**
No. of Private Baths: **5**
Max. No. Sharing Bath: **4**
Double/pb: **$70–$80**
Single/pb: **$65–$75**
Suites: **$90–$100**

Open: **All year**
Reduced Rates: **10–15%, seniors, off-
  season, week**
Breakfast: **Full**
Pets: **Sometimes**
Children: **Welcome**
Smoking: **Permitted**
Social Drinking: **Permitted**
Airport/Station Pickup: **Yes**

If you tried to imagine an idealized New England home, it would resemble this white 19th-century farmhouse set on Townsend's Village Green. This is a prime foliage and antiquing area. Direct access to State Routes 30 and 35 allows you to pursue other interests, from skiing at Stratton to canoeing on the West River. Gourmet breakfasts feature pear pancakes, individual soufflés, hot fruit compotes, and more.

Newton's 1824 House Inn
ROUTE 100, BOX 159, WAITSFIELD, VERMONT 05673

Tel: **(802) 496-7555**
Best Time to Call: **9:30 AM**
Hosts: **Nick and Joyce Newton**
Location: **18 mi. SE of Montpelier**
No. of Rooms: **6**
No. of Private Baths: **6**
Double/pb: **$75–$95**
Single/pb: **$65–$85**
Guest Cottage: **$135; sleeps 4**
Open: **All year**
Breakfast: **Full**

Credit Cards: **AMEX, MC, VISA**
Pets: **Sometimes**
Children: **Infants welcome; children
  over 12**
Smoking: **No**
Social Drinking: **Permitted**
Minimum Stay: **2 nights Aug. 30–Oct.
  13**
Airport/Station Pickup: **Yes**
Foreign Languages: **Spanish**

Surrounded by original art, Oriental rugs, select antiques, and period furniture, guests enjoy a relaxed elegance at this two-story clapboard farmhouse crowned with ten gables. Built in 1824, it was recently recommended for National Register status. The farm's 52 acres include scenic hills, pastures, stands of pines and sugarbush. The Mad River runs through the property and feeds a great private swimming hole. It's only minutes from Sugarbush Resort and Mad River Glen ski areas. After a good night's sleep in one of the cozy bedrooms, one can look forward to such breakfast treats as baked stuffed pears with nuts and currants, oatmeal soufflé, or apple muffins.

White Rocks Inn ☉

RR 1, BOX 297, ROUTE 7, WALLINGFORD, VERMONT 05773

Tel: (802) 446-2077	Breakfast: **Full**
Best Time to Call: **Mornings; evenings**	Credit Cards: **MC, VISA**
Hosts: **June and Alfred Matthews**	Pets: **No**
Location: **20 mi. N of Manchester**	Children: **Welcome, over 10**
No. of Rooms: **5**	Smoking: **No**
No. of Private Baths: **5**	Social Drinking: **Permitted**
Double/pb: **$65–$90**	Minimum Stay: **2 nights, holidays, fall**
Single/pb: **$55–$80**	**foliage season**
Open: **Dec. 1–Oct. 31**	Foreign Languages: **French, Spanish**

If your idea of paradise is a pasture, a creek stocked with trout, an old-fashioned swimming hole, and a peaceful valley surrounded by mountains, then reserve a room here. June and Alfred have renovated their vintage 1800 farmhouse with care, preserving the charm of wide-board floors, wainscoting, ornate moldings, and high ceilings, while enhancing it with antiques, Oriental rugs, and canopied beds. In summer, such breakfast delights as banana pancakes or raisin bread French toast is served on the large veranda overlooking the meadows. In cooler weather, this feast is presented in the dining room. Five downhill ski areas are a short drive away, and miles of cross-country ski trails are adjacent to the inn.

West Hill House ☉

RR 1, BOX 292, WEST HILL ROAD, WARREN, VERMONT 05674

Tel: (802) 496-7162	Open: **All year**
Best Time to Call: **2–9 PM**	Reduced Rates: **10%, seniors; 5-night**
Hosts: **Nina and Bob Heyd**	**midweek discount**
Location: **25 mi. SW of Montpelier**	Breakfast: **Full**
No. of Rooms: **4**	Credit Cards: **MC, VISA**
No. of Private Baths: **2**	Pets: **No**
Max. No. Sharing Bath: **4**	Children: **Welcome, over 10**
Double/pb: **$75–$80**	Smoking: **No**
Single/pb: **$65–$70**	Social Drinking: **Permitted**
Double/sb: **$65–$70**	Minimum Stay: **2 nights on weekends**
Single/sb: **$55–$60**	**in ski season**

Enjoy casual country lodging at Bob and Nina's charming Vermont farmhouse located a mile from the famed Sugarbush Ski Resort and adjacent to its golf course. Each guest room is attractively decorated with handmade quilts and curtains, and country crafts accented with lovely antiques. Begin your day with homemade treats such as crêpes, quiche, muffins, or coffee cake and burn off the calories by skiing, horseback riding, canoeing, river bathing, ballooning, or golfing. In winter, après-ski treats are served near the fireplace in the living room; on summer afternoons, tea and pastries are proffered on the porch.

Grünberg Haus ✪
RR2, BOX 1595, WATERBURY, VERMONT 05676

Tel: (802) 244-7726	Breakfast: **Full**
Hosts: **Christopher Sellers and Mark Frohman**	Other Meals: **Available**
	Credit Cards: **AMEX, MC, VISA**
Location: **25 mi. E of Burlington**	Pets: **No**
No. of Rooms: **10**	Children: **Welcome, over 6**
Max. No. Sharing Bath: **4**	Smoking: **No**
Double/sb: **$60**	Social Drinking: **Permitted**
Single/sb: **$45**	Minimum Stay: **2 nights Sept. 15–Oct.**
Open: **All year**	**15 and some winter weekends**
Reduced Rates: **10%, after 4 days;**	
10%, Nov., Apr., May	

You'll think you're in the Alps when you see this hand-built Tyrolean chalet perched on a secluded hillside. The living room features an eight-foot grand piano, a massive fieldstone fireplace, and a long breakfast table overlooking the valley and distant forest. All ten guest rooms open onto the quaint balcony that surrounds the chalet. The BYOB rathskeller features hand-stenciled booths; the formal dining room is furnished with antiques. Outside, cleared logging trails provide cross-country skiing and hiking access to hundreds of acres of meadows and woodlands. And Waterbury's central location makes it easy to get to ski resorts like Stowe and Sugarbush. Whatever you plan to do, bring an appetite; Grünberg Haus serves memorable gourmet breakfasts, and other meals can be arranged.

Inn at Blush Hill ✪
BOX 1266, BLUSH HILL ROAD, WATERBURY, VERMONT 05676

Tel: (802) 244-7529	Reduced Rates: **Available**
Hosts: **Gary and Pam Gosselin**	Breakfast: **Full**
Location: **22 mi. E. of Burlington**	Credit Cards: **MC, VISA**
No. of Rooms: **6**	Pets: **No**
No. of Private Baths: **2**	Children: **Welcome**
Max. No. Sharing Bath: **4**	Smoking: **Permitted**
Double/pb: **$75–$100**	Social Drinking: **Permitted**
Double/sb: **$65–$90**	Airport/Station Pickup: **Yes**
Open: **All year**	

This 1790 brick farmhouse is located halfway between the Stowe and Sugarbush ski areas. The atmosphere is warm and homey, with antiques, old-time rockers, books, and lots of fireplaces. Your host is a gourmet cook and enjoys making her own bread and muffins each morning. A huge lake with boating, swimming, and fishing is located just one and a half miles from the house, and a nine-hole golf course is located directly across the street. At the end of the day, sit back and enjoy the surroundings, relaxing on the large, old-fashioned porch.

The Weathervane ✪
DORR FITCH ROAD, BOX 57, WEST DOVER, VERMONT 05356

Tel: **(802) 464-5426**
Hosts: **Liz and Ernie Chabot**
Location: **1 mi. from Rte. 100**
No. of Rooms: **10**
No. of Private Baths: **2**
Max. No. Sharing Bath: **5**
Double/pb: **$64–$72**
Double/sb: **$42–$56**
Single/sb: **$39–$42**

Suites: **$88**
Open: **All year**
Reduced Rates: **Ski weeks; off season**
Breakfast: **Full**
Pets: **No**
Children: **Welcome (crib)**
Smoking: **Permitted**
Social Drinking: **Permitted**

Only four miles from Haystack, Mount Snow, and Corinthia, this Tyrolean-style ski lodge is decorated with authentic antiques and Colonial charm. The lounge and recreation room have fireplaces and a bring-your-own bar. Winter rates include cross-country ski equipment, sleds, and snowshoes, so that you may explore the lovely marked trails. Summer brings lakeshore swimming, boating, fishing, tennis, riding, museums, and the Marlboro Music Festival.

VIRGINIA

Gore
Woodstock
Mt. Jackson • Flint Hill Waterford
New Market • • Culpeper Springfield
Luray Washington • Manassas
Gordonsville • Montross
Swoope • Fredericksburg • Bowling Green
Raphine Staunton Charlottesville Orange • Mollusk
Amherst Scottsville • Mathews
Newport • • Lexington Richmond • Williamsburg • Cape
Draper Roanoke • • Glasgow Smithfield • • Norfolk Charles
Abingdon • Hillsville • • Mountain Lake Capron • • Virginia Beach
Floyd Smith

Bed & Breakfast of Tidewater Virginia ✪
P.O. BOX 3343, NORFOLK, VIRGINIA 23514

Tel: (804) 627-1983; 627-9409	Rates (Single/Double):	
Coordinators: **Ashby Willcox** and	Modest: **$30**	**$35**
Susan Hubbard	Average: **$35**	**$45**
States/Regions Covered: **Chesapeake,**	Luxury: **$55**	**$75**
Eastern Shore of Virginia, Norfolk,	Credit Cards: **No**	
Northern Neck, Virginia Beach,		
Williamsburg		

The world's largest naval base is in Norfolk, as are the famed Chrysler Museum and MacArthur Memorial. It is also a cultural hub in which top-rated opera, symphony, and stage productions abound. There are miles of scenic beaches to explore on Chesapeake Bay and the Atlantic Ocean. Old Dominion University, Eastern Virginia Medical School, and Virginia Wesleyan College are conveniently located.

577

Blue Ridge Bed & Breakfast ✪
ROUTE 2, ROCKS & RILLS, BOX 3895, BERRYVILLE, VIRGINIA 22611

Tel: (703) 955-1246
Best Time to Call: **Tues.–Fri., 9 AM–3 PM; Sat., 9 AM–12 PM**
Coordinator: **Rita Z. Duncan**
States/Regions Covered: **Virginia— Amissville, Berryville, Flint Hill, Hamilton, Luray, Winchester; West Virginia—Charlestown, Middleway; Pennsylvania; Maryland**

Rates (Double):
  Modest: **$45**
  Average: **$50**
  Luxury: **$150**
Credit Cards: **MC, VISA**

Rita's hosts are within 50 to 200 miles of the Capitol, perfect for those wishing to visit rural areas near Washington, D.C. The variety includes houses on the Historic Register, mountain retreats, quaint inns, and traditional private homes in small towns. This beautiful area is known for its part in American history, horses, and farming.

Summerfield Inn ✪
101 WEST VALLEY STREET, ABINGDON, VIRGINIA 24210

Tel: (703) 628-5905
Best Time to Call: **Mornings; after 3 PM**
Hosts: **Champe and Don Hyatt**
Location: **15 mi. NE of Bristol**
No. of Rooms: **4**
No. of Private Baths: **4**
Double/pb: **$60–$70**
Single/pb: **$55**
Suites: **$110**

Open: **Apr. 1–Nov. 1**
Reduced Rates: **15%, 3-night stays; off season**
Breakfast: **Continental**
Credit Cards: **MC, VISA**
Pets: **No**
Children: **Welcome, over 12**
Smoking: **Permitted**
Social Drinking: **Permitted**
Airport/Station Pickup: **Yes**

A large covered porch with comfortable rockers graces the front and side of this meticulously restored Victorian residence. Guests are welcome to share the large living room, handsomely appointed morning room, and a sunroom. Your hosts will gladly pack picnic lunches for trips to the mountain trails or for a fishing trip to one of the nearby lakes or rivers. A guests' pantry is also available for preparing light snacks. Summerfield Inn is a short walk from Barter Theatre, Old Abingdon, and fine dining. Set at 2,300 feet and surrounded by mountains, this was one of the first communities formed in western Virginia.

Dulwich Manor B&B Inn ✪
ROUTE 5, BOX 173A, AMHERST, VIRGINIA 24521

Tel: (804) 946-7207
Hosts: **Robert and Judith Reilly**

Location: **14 mi. N of Lynchburg**
No. of Rooms: **5**

No. of Private Baths: **3**
Max. No. Sharing Bath: **4**
Double/pb: **$75–$85**
Single/pb: **$70–$80**
Double/sb: **$65**
Single/sb: **$60**
Open: **All year**
Reduced Rates: **10%, Mon.–Thurs.**
　and **weekly**

Breakfast: **Full**
Pets: **No**
Children: **Welcome**
Smoking: **Permitted**
Social Drinking: **Permitted**
Airport/Station Pickup: **Yes**

A stately English country house built at the turn of the century, Dulwich Manor sits on five secluded acres surrounded by the Blue Ridge Mountains. The scenic Blue Ridge Parkway and the Washington and Jefferson National Forests are among the area's major attractions. Points of historic interest include Appomattox Courthouse and Monticello. Guests start off the day with a full country breakfast either in the formal dining room or on the veranda. In the evening, your hosts will offer you wine and cheese. Outdoor hot tub for guest enjoyment. Guest rooms have fireplaces or whirlpool baths.

Nottingham Ridge
P.O. BOX 97-B, CAPE CHARLES, VIRGINIA 23310

Tel: **(804) 331-1010**
Best Time to Call: **Evenings**
Host: **Bonnie Nottingham**
Location: **20 mi. N of Norfolk**
No. of Rooms: **3**
No. of Private Baths: **2**
Max. No. Sharing Bath: **3**
Double/pb: **$70**
Double/sb: **$65**

Single/sb: **$50**
Open: **All year**
Breakfast: **Full**
Other Meals: **Available**
Pets: **No**
Children: **Welcome, over 10**
Smoking: **Permitted**
Social Drinking: **Permitted**
Airport/Station Pickup: **Available**

Nottingham Ridge is a picturesque country retreat high atop the sand dunes of Virginia's eastern shore. Guests can spend hours on a private beach, or charter a fishing boat for the day. Bonnie offers comfortable rooms furnished with antiques and reproductions. She loves entertaining and offers homemade biscuits, Virginia ham, and quiche for breakfast. Later in the day, enjoy wine, cheese, and a breathtaking view of the sun setting over the water. This lovely home is just three and a half miles north of the Chesapeake Bay Bridge Tunnel, and 25 minutes from the Norfolk and Virginia Beach areas. Bonnie will gladly direct you to historic sights, the Nature Conservancy, and the U.S. Fish and Wildlife Refuge.

Picketts Harbor
BOX 97AA, CAPE CHARLES, VIRGINIA 23310

Tel: **(804) 331-2212**
Best Time to Call: **After 5 PM, 5–7:30 AM**
Hosts: **Sara and Cooke Goffigon**
Location: **21 mi. N of Norfolk**
No. of Rooms: **6**
Max. No. Sharing Bath: **4**
Double/pb: **$75**
Single/pb: **$60**
Double/sb: **$65**

Single/sb: **$50**
Open: **All year**
Breakfast: **Full**
Other Meals: **Available**
Pets: **No**
Children: **Welcome**
Smoking: **No**
Social Drinking: **Permitted**
Airport/Station Pickup: **Yes**

Picketts Harbor is set in a rural, wooded section of Virginia's Eastern Shore. The house is decorated country-style, with antiques, reproductions, plants, and collectibles. Outside, the property spans 17 acres including a large private beach. Breakfast is served overlooking Chesapeake Bay. There are many local opportunities for fishermen and hunters, and your hosts will gladly provide a picnic lunch. Williamsburg, Yorktown, and many historic sights are within an hour's drive.

Sandy Hill Farm B&B ✪
ROUTE 1, BOX 55, CAPRON, VIRGINIA 23829

Tel: **(804) 658-4381**
Best Time to Call: **6:30–8 AM; 7:30–11:30 PM**
Hosts: **Anne Kitchen**
Location: **11 mi. from I-95**
No. of Rooms: **2**
Max. No. Sharing Bath: **3**
Double/sb: **$30**
Single/sb: **$25**

Open: **Mar. 20–Dec.**
Reduced Rates: **Families; 5 nights**
Breakfast: **Continental**
Other Meals: **Available**
Pets: **Welcome**
Children: **Welcome**
Smoking: **Permitted**
Social Drinking: **Permitted**

Experience the pleasures of an unspoiled rural setting at this ranch-style farmhouse. There are animals to visit, quiet places to stroll, and a lighted tennis court on the grounds. This is an ideal hub from which to tour southeastern and central Virginia. Day trips to Williamsburg, Norfolk, and Richmond are possibilities. Fresh fruits and homemade breads are served at breakfast.

Guesthouses Reservation Service ✪
P.O. BOX 5737, CHARLOTTESVILLE, VIRGINIA 22905

Tel: **(804) 979-7264**
Best Time to Call: **12–5 PM, Mon.– Fri.**
Coordinator: **Mary Hill Caperton**
States/Regions Covered: **Albemarle County, Charlottesville, Luray**
Descriptive Directory: **$1**

Rates (Single/Double):
  Modest: **$48**   **$52**
  Average: **$56**   **$60**
  Luxury: **$68**   **$160**
  Estate Cottages: **$80 up**
Credit Cards: **AMEX, MC, VISA**

Charlottesville is a gracious town. The hosts in Mary's hospitality file offer you a genuine taste of Southern hospitality. All places are close to Thomas Jefferson's Monticello and James Madison's Ash Lawn, as well as the University of Virginia. Unusual local activities include ballooning, steeplechasing, and wine festivals. Please note that the office is closed from Christmas through New Year's Day. Reduced rates are available for extended stays, and most hosts offer a full breakfast.

Miss Molly's Inn
113 NORTH MAIN STREET, CHINCOTEAGUE ISLAND, VIRGINIA 23336

Tel: **(804) 336-6686**
Hosts: **Dr. and Mrs. James Stam**
Location: **45 mi. S of Salisbury, Md.**
No. of Rooms: **7**
No. of Private Baths: **1**
Max. No. Sharing Bath: **4**
Double/pb: **$85–$105**
Single/pb: **$75–$95**
Double/sb: **$59–$95**
Single/sb: **$49–$85**

Open: **Apr. 1–Dec. 1**
Reduced Rates: **Before Memorial Day; after Labor Day**
Breakfast: **Full**
Pets: **No**
Children: **Welcome, over 12**
Smoking: **Permitted**
Social Drinking: **Permitted**
Minimum Stay: **2 nights weekends**

The 22 rooms of this seaside Victorian have been lovingly restored to their 19th-century charm. Relax in an ambience of lace curtains, stained-glass windows, and period pieces. While writing her book *Misty*, Marguerite Henry stayed here. The ponies made famous by that story roam wild at the nearby National Wildlife Refuge. You too may find "Miss Molly's" cool breezes, five porches, and afternoon

teas worth writing about. Chincoteague has beaches, gourmet restaurants, and the NASA museum. Your hosts will gladly direct you to these sights, beginning with the bay, which is 150 feet from the front door.

The Oaks Bed & Breakfast Country Inn
311 EAST MAIN STREET, CHRISTIANSBURG, VIRGINIA 24073

Tel: **(703) 381-1500**	Reduced Rates: **Available**
Best Time to Call: **Evening**	Breakfast: **Full**
Hosts: **Margaret and Tom Ray**	Other Meals: **Available**
Location: **22 mi. S of Roanoke**	Credit Cards: **MC, VISA**
No. of Rooms: **5**	Pets: **No**
No. of Private Baths: **3**	Children: **Welcome, over 12**
Max. No. Sharing Bath: **4**	Smoking: **No**
Double/pb: **$75–$95**	Social Drinking: **Permitted**
Double/sb: **$65–$85**	Airport/Station Pickup: **Yes**
Open: **All year**	

Step into the wide entry hall of this Queen Anne/Victorian and you'll experience the graciousness of the 19th century. With its grand staircase, stained-glass windows, turrets, window nooks, and elaborate fireplaces, the Oaks delights the eye and the spirit. Visitors are pampered with lavish breakfasts, complimentary fresh fruit, fluffy terry robes, and luxurious linens. A spa, sauna, and small kitchen are at your disposal. Assuming you can tear yourself away, the Blue Ridge Parkway, Virginia Tech, Radford University, and the Shenandoah Valley are within an easy drive.

Fountain Hall ✪
609 SOUTH EAST STREET, CULPEPER, VIRGINIA 22701-3222

Tel: (703) 825-8200	Open: **All year**
Best Time to Call: **8 AM–8 PM**	Reduced Rates: **10%, seniors; after 3**
Hosts: **Steve and Kathi Walker**	**nights; business travelers**
Location: **1 mi. from Va. Rte. 29/522**	Breakfast: **Continental**
No. of Rooms: **5**	Credit Cards: **AMEX, MC, VISA**
No. of Private Baths: **5**	Pets: **No**
Double/pb: **$70**	Children: **Welcome (crib)**
Single/pb: **$60**	Smoking: **Permitted**
Suites: **$85**	Social Drinking: **Permitted**

The first county surveyor of Culpeper was a teenaged George Washington, who called it "a high and pleasant situation." Indeed it still is, with many unspoiled historic and natural treasures for you to enjoy. Fountain Hall is furnished with antiques, comfortable beds, and an old-fashioned flavor. It is a fine home base from which to explore north-central Virginia. Some local points of interest include the Cavalry Museum, the Civil War reenactment of the Battle of Cedar Mountain, Little Fork Church, Commonwealth Park horse shows, wineries, antiquing, and some fine restaurants. Steve and Kathi serve tea, coffee, or lemonade upon your return from touring.

Claytor Lake Homestead Inn ✪
P.O. BOX 7, DRAPER, VIRGINIA 24324

Tel: (703) 980-6777 (800) 676-Lake	Reduced Rates: **Corporate discounts**
Hosts: **Betsey and Bob Thomas**	Breakfast: **Full**
Location: **60 mi. S of Roanoke**	Credit Cards: **MC, VISA**
No. of Rooms: **5**	Pets: **No**
Max. No. Sharing Bath: **4**	Children: **Welcome, over 12**
Double/sb: **$50–$65**	Smoking: **No**
Open: **All year**	Social Drinking: **No**

From its humble origins as a log cabin, Homestead Inn grew to include a brick-and-stone wraparound front porch and Victorian-style bay windows. The original floors and doors are still in use. Claytor Lake, created by the construction of Claytor Dam, is stocked with walleye and striped bass, and other types of sport fish are plentiful. In the summer, a lifeguard is on duty for swimmers. When you emerge from the water, hike along the lake's 101-mile shoreline. You'll need a full breakfast before all this activity, and the Thomases oblige, setting out homemade muffins, Virginia ham, and Bob's own sausage.

Caledonia Farm ✪
ROUTE 1, BOX 2080, FLINT HILL, VIRGINIA 22627

Tel: (703) 675-3693
Best Time to Call: **Weekdays**
Host: **Phil Irwin**
Location: **68 mi. SW of Washington, D.C.; 4 mi. N of Washington, Va.**
No. of Rooms: **3**
Max. No. Sharing Bath: **4**
Suite: **$100**

Double/sb: **$70**
Open: **All year**
Breakfast: **Full**
Credit Cards: **MC, VISA**
Pets: **No**
Children: **Welcome, over 12**
Smoking: **No**
Social Drinking: **Permitted**

This charming 1812 stone manor house and its companion "summer kitchen" are located on a working beef cattle farm adjacent to Shenandoah National Park. Each accommodation has a fireplace, period furnishings, individual temperature controls for heat or air-conditioning, and spectacular views of the Blue Ridge Mountains. A candlelight breakfast is served from a menu that offers a choice of omelet, smoked salmon, or eggs Benedict. The Skyline Drive, fine dining, caves, wineries, hayrides, antiquing, historic sites, and sporting activities are a few of the possible diversions. Afterward, join Phil for the evening social hour.

La Vista Plantation ✪
4420 GUINEA STATION ROAD, FREDERICKSBURG, VIRGINIA 22401

Tel: (703) 898-8444
Best Time to Call: **Before 9:30 AM**
Hosts: **Michele and Edward Schiesser**
Location: **60 mi. S of D.C.; 4.5 mi. from I-95**
No. of Rooms: **1**
No. of Private Baths: **1**
Double/pb: **$70**
Single/pb: **$55**
Suites: **$70; sleeps 6**

Open: **All year**
Reduced Rates: **7th night free; families**
Breakfast: **Full**
Credit Cards: **MC, VISA**
Pets: **No**
Children: **Welcome**
Smoking: **Permitted**
Social Drinking: **Permitted**
Airport/Station Pickup: **Yes**

Guest lodgings at La Vista are located in an English basement blessed with a sunny exposure and featuring a private entrance. The spacious, air-conditioned suite has a large living room with fireplace, full kitchen, sitting room, and bath. Ten acres surround the manor house (circa 1838), and you are welcome to stroll, bird-watch, or fish in a pond stocked with bass and sunfish.

Chester House Inn ✪
43 CHESTER STREET, FRONT ROYAL, VIRGINIA 22630

Tel: (703) 635-3937
Best Time to Call: **9 AM–5 PM**

Hosts: **Bill and Ann Wilson**
Location: **70 mi. W of Wash., D.C.**

No. of Rooms: **6**
No. of Private Baths: **1**
Max. No. Sharing Bath: **4**
Double/pb: **$95**
Double/sb: **$55–$80**
Open: **All year**

Breakfast: **Continental**
Credit Cards: **MC, VISA**
Pets: **No**
Children: **Welcome, over 12**
Smoking: **Permitted**
Social Drinking: **Permitted**

This stately Georgian mansion with extensive formal gardens rests on two acres in Front Royal's historic district. This is the perfect spot to experience elegance as it existed in bygone days. It's an easy walk to antique and gift shops, and a short drive to Skyline Caverns, Skyline Drive, Shenandoah River, golf and tennis, fine wineries, and excellent restaurants. Bill and Ann take pleasure in making arrangements to help guests get the most out of their visit. They invite you to relax in the living room, enjoy the lovely gardens, and partake of their snacks.

Balcony Downs Plantation B&B Inn ✪
P.O. BOX 563, HIGHWAY 501, GLASGOW, VIRGINIA 24555

Tel: **(703) 258-2100 or (800) 359-3616**
Best Time to Call: **8–9 AM**
Hosts: **Philip and Catherine Clayton**
Location: **15 mi. SE of Lexington**
No. of Rooms: **4**
No. of Private Baths: **1**
Max. No. Sharing Bath: **4**
Double/pb: **$60**
Single/pb: **$50**

Double/sb: **$50**
Single/sb: **$40**
Open: **Jan. 16–Dec. 14**
Reduced Rates: **20% after 5 days**
Breakfast: **Continental**
Pets: **Sometimes**
Children: **Welcome**
Smoking: **Permitted**
Social Drinking: **Permitted**

By prior arrangement, you can fly to this B&B and land on the grass airstrip. Or you can arrive by horseback and stable your mount on the premises. No matter how you get to this early 19th-century estate, you won't want to leave, thanks to the swimming pool, well-stocked fishing pond, and hiking trails that crisscross the 50-acre property and lead into George Washington National Forest. Continental breakfast, highlighted by your host's own lemon curd spread, is served in the oak-paneled dining room.

Sleepy Hollow Farm Bed & Breakfast ✪
ROUTE 231 N., GORDONSVILLE, VIRGINIA 22942 (MAILING ADDRESS: RD 3, BOX 43)

Tel: **(703) 832-5555**
Best Time to Call: **8 AM–noon; 5–10 PM**
Host: **Beverley Allison**
Location: **25 mi. N of Charlottesville**
No. of Rooms: **6**
No. of Private Baths: **6**

Double/pb: **$55–$85**
Single/pb: **$40–$50**
Guest Cottage: **$100–$210; sleeps 4–8**
Suites: **$75–$85**
Open: **All year**
Reduced Rates: **Weekly**

Breakfast: **Full**
Credit Cards: **MC, VISA**
Pets: **Sometimes**
Children: **Welcome**

Smoking: **Permitted**
Social Drinking: **Permitted**
Minimum Stay: **2 nights, weekends,**
    Sept.–Nov.

Sleepy Hollow Farm lies in the heartland of American history, where evidence of Indians, the Revolutionary and Civil War periods still exist. The air-conditioned brick farmhouse evolved from an 18th-century structure, and today boasts terraces, porches, gazebo, pond, a croquet lawn and rooms with fireplaces. Furnished with antiques and carefully chosen accessories, the decor is picture pretty. Beverley, a retired missionary and journalist, is a fine cook as evidenced by breakfast treats such as sausage pie, fried apples, apple cake, and fruit compote. While in the area, you may want to visit Montpelier, home of James and Dolley Madison, local wineries, a church dating back to 1769, or fish at Lake Orange.

Rainbow's End B&B
ROUTE 1, BOX 335, GORE, VIRGINIA 22637

Tel: **(703) 858-2808**
Best Time to Call: **10 AM–8 PM**
Hosts: **Eleanor and Thom McKay**
Location: **20 mi. W of Winchester**
No. of Rooms: **2**
Max. No. Sharing Bath: **3**
Double/sb: **$40**

Single/sb: **$35**
Open: **All year**
Breakfast: **Continental**
Pets: **No**
Children: **No**
Smoking: **No**
Social Drinking: **Permitted**

Rainbow's End is a brick and wood ranch situated on Timber Ridge in the Blue Ridge Mountains. The McKays offer cozy rooms filled with comfortable family furnishings. Eleanor serves a tasty breakfast of homemade breads, muffins, cakes, and coffee. Later in the day, join your hosts for wine and cheese. Guests can experience rural life in the heart of apple country. You may see a deer, a fox, or any one of a number of colorful birds that frequent the pond nestled among the pines. Nearby attractions include George Washington's Office, Ole Towne Winchester with its quaint stores, several famous caverns, and Civil War battlefields.

Fassifern Bed & Breakfast ✪
POSTAL ROUTE 5, BOX 87, LEXINGTON, VIRGINIA 24450

Tel: **(703) 463-1013**
Best Time to Call: **1 PM–8 PM**
Hosts: **Ann Carol and Arthur Perry**
Location: **50 mi. N of Roanoke**
No. of Rooms: **5**
No. of Private Baths: **5**

Double/pb: **$65–$70**
Single/pb: **$60**
Open: **All year**
Breakfast: **Continental**
Credit Cards: **AMEX, MC, VISA**
Pets: **No**

Children: **Welcome, over 16**	Social Drinking: **Permitted**
Smoking: **No**	Airport/Station Pickup: **Yes**

Fassifern is a 19th-century manor home, located on three and a half acres with a pond and stately trees. Over the years, the house has been rebuilt, authentically restored, and furnished with antiques. When you relax on the porch, patio, or in the conservatory, your hosts will gladly supply reading or writing materials. They offer such breakfast specialties as homemade breads, seasonal fruit, freshly ground coffee, and gourmet teas. Fassifern is adjacent to the Virginia Horse Center, near Lexington, and 20 minutes away from the Blue Ridge Parkway and the Natural Bridge.

Llewellyn Lodge at Lexington ✪
603 SOUTH MAIN STREET, LEXINGTON, VIRGINIA 24450

Tel: **(703) 463-3235**	Open: **All year**
Best Time to Call: **8 AM–1 PM**	Breakfast: **Full**
Host: **Ellen and John Roberts**	Credit Cards: **AMEX, MC, VISA**
Location: **50 mi. N of Roanoke**	Pets: **No**
No. of Rooms: **6**	Children: **Welcome, over 5**
No. of Private Baths: **6**	Smoking: **Permitted**
Double/pb: **$55–$65**	Social Drinking: **Permitted**
Single/pb: **$45–$60**	Airport/Station Pickup: **Yes**
Suite: **$70**	

Guests are welcomed to this lovely brick Colonial with seasonal refreshments. Your host has 20 years of experience in the travel and hospitality business, and guarantees to make you feel at home. The decor combines traditional and antique furnishings. Homemade coffee cake, biscuits, and omelets are favorites at the breakfast table. Llewellyn is close to local attractions such as the homes of Robert E. Lee, Stonewall Jackson, and the Natural Bridge.

Sunrise Hill Farm ✪
5513 SUDLEY ROAD, MANASSAS, VIRGINIA 22110

Tel: (703) 754-8309
Hosts: **Frank and Sue Boberek**
Location: **29 mi. W of Washington, D.C.**
No. of Rooms: **2**
No. of Private Baths: **2**
Double/sb: **$60–$65**
Open: **All year**

Reduced Rates: **15%, families using both rooms**
Breakfast: **Full**
Credit Cards: **MC, VISA**
Pets: **Horses boarded**
Children: **Welcome, over 10**
Smoking: **Permitted**
Social Drinking: **Permitted**

This Civil War treasure is located within the heart of the 6,000-acre Manassas National Battlefields Park. Sunrise Hill Farm is an uncommonly charming Federal-period country home overlooking Bull Run Creek. Situated within the famous Virginia hunt country, it's close to many small towns known for their antique shops, wineries, and historic sites. Furnished in period style, it is a haven for Civil War buffs and artists. Frank and Sue spoil everyone with their delightful breakfast menu.

Greenvale Manor
P.O. BOX 174, MOLLUSK, VIRGINIA 22517

Tel: (804) 462-5995
Hosts: **Pam and Walt Smith**
Location: **70 mi. NE of Richmond**
No. of Rooms: **9**
No. of Private Baths: **7**
Max. No. Sharing Bath: **4**
Double/pb: **$70–$85**
Single/pb: **$50**
Double/sb: **$65–$70**
Single/sb: **$45**

Suites: **$105**
Open: **All year**
Breakfast: **Full**
Pets: **No**
Children: **Over 14**
Smoking: **Permitted**
Social Drinking: **Permitted**
Minimum Stay: **Holiday weekends**
Airport/Station Pickup: **Yes**

Greenvale Manor is an 1840 Colonial set on the Rappahannock River and Greenvale Creek. It is located in an area known for its historic waterfront homes. The house has been owned by several prominent Virginia families and has been beautifully restored and maintained. The 13-acre estate includes a sandy beach, pool, and private dock. The house is furnished in period antiques and reproductions and its large windows make the most of its best feature—the waterfront. Breakfast is served on a large screened veranda in summer, and in winter the day begins beside a crackling fire in the Federal Room. The manor offers many diversions, such as croquet, badminton, boating with a licensed captain, fishing, and crabbing right off the dock. Pam and Walt invite you to share a glass of wine and will gladly suggest nearby restaurants and historic sites.

The Inn at Montross ☉
COURTHOUSE SQUARE, MONTROSS, VIRGINIA 22520

Tel: **(804) 493-9097**
Hosts: **Eileen and Michael Longman**
Location: **46 mi. E of Fredericksburg**
No. of Rooms: **6**
No. of Private Baths: **6**
Double/pb: **$65**
Single/pb: **$55**
Open: **All year**
Reduced Rates: **10%, seniors;
   corporations**

Breakfast: **Continental**
Other Meals: **Available**
Credit Cards: **DISC, MC, VISA**
Pets: **Sometimes**
Children: **Welcome**
Smoking: **Permitted**
Social Drinking: **Permitted**

The original sections of the Inn at Montross date back over 300 years. Your hosts have decorated the rooms with a mixture of primitive and modern art, porcelains, antiques, and reproductions. Each guest room is furnished with four-poster beds, with extras such as bedside brandy and chocolates. The main floor boasts a magnificent grand piano, which guests are welcome to use. A small lounge with television and a spacious living room are available for relaxing. Your hosts serve home-baked croissants, fresh fruit, muffins, or Danish for breakfast. Bountiful meals at affordable prices are served in the Colonial dining rooms, which are open to the public. The Longmans will be glad to direct you to Stratford Hall, Ingleside Winery, and Westmoreland State Park. Golf and fishing can be enjoyed nearby, and there are tennis courts on the grounds.

Holly Point ☉
P.O. BOX 64, MORATTICO, VIRGINIA 22523

Tel: **(804) 462-7759**
Host: **Mary Chilton Graham**
Location: **60 mi. N of Williamsburg**
No. of Rooms: **3**
No. of Private Baths: **1**
Max. No. Sharing Bath: **5**
Double/pb: **$40**
Single/pb: **$35**
Double/sb: **$35**

Single/sb: **$30**
Wheelchair-Accessible: **Yes**
Open: **May 1–Nov. 1**
Breakfast: **Continental**
Pets: **Welcome**
Children: **Welcome**
Smoking: **No**
Social Drinking: **Permitted**
Airport/Station Pickup: **Yes**

George Washington never slept here, but his aunt was Mary Graham's direct ancestor. Situated halfway between Williamsburg and Fredericksburg, her immaculate farmhouse offers breathtaking views of the Rappahannock River and the surrounding countryside. There are plenty of opportunities for land or water sports, including hiking, boating, and swimming. Weather permitting, breakfast is served on the wraparound porch featuring jams made from property trees and home-baked breads from George's favorite recipe.

The Widow Kip's Shenandoah Inn ✪
ROUTE 1, BOX 117, MT. JACKSON, VIRGINIA 22842

Tel: **(703) 477-2400**	Suites: **$70–$80**
Best Time to Call: **Before noon; after 3 PM**	Open: **All year**
	Reduced Rates: **10%, seniors**
Host: **Rosemary Kip**	Breakfast: **Full**
Location: **1 mi. from I-81, Exit 69**	Other Meals: **Available**
No. of Rooms: **7**	Pets: **Sometimes**
No. of Private Baths: **7**	Children: **Welcome**
Double/pb: **$65**	Smoking: **Permitted**
Single/pb: **$55**	Social Drinking: **Permitted**

This Colonial homestead, built in 1830, is nestled on seven acres in the Shenandoah Valley. After a breakfast of sausage patties, biscuits with homemade apple butter, and plum gumbo (or other specialties), you may hike, canoe, play tennis, fish, ski, or visit a cavern. Bikes are provided and Rosemary will pack a picnic lunch for your day's jaunt. If you'd rather "stay home," you may enjoy a dip in the 32-foot pool on warm days, sip sherry or tea in front of your bedroom's fireplace in cool weather, or wander through the rooms where all the furnishings are priced for sale. A gift shop is on the premises.

A Touch of Country Bed & Breakfast ✪
9329 CONGRESS STREET, NEW MARKET, VIRGINIA 22844

Tel: **(703) 740-8030**	Open: **All year**
Hosts: **Jean Schoellig and Dawn Kasow**	Breakfast: **Full**
Location: **18 mi. N of Harrisonburg**	Credit Cards: **MC, VISA**
No. of Rooms: **6**	Pets: **No**
No. of Private Baths: **6**	Children: **Welcome, over 12**
Double/pb: **$65**	Smoking: **Permitted**
Single/pb: **$55**	Social Drinking: **Permitted**

This restored 1870s home is located in a historic town in the beautiful Shenandoah Valley. It displays the original hardwood floors and is decorated with antiques and collectibles in a country motif. You'll start your day with a hearty breakfast of pancakes, meats, gravy and biscuits. Daydream on the porch swings or stroll through town with its charming shops, dine at a variety of restaurants, or visit the legendary New Market Battlefield and Park. Close by are Skyline Drive, George Washington National Forest, caverns, and vineyards.

Mayhurst Inn
ROUTE 15 SOUTH, P.O. BOX 707, ORANGE, VIRGINIA 22960

Tel: **(703) 672-5597**	Open: **All year**
Best Time to Call: **9 AM–9 PM**	Reduced Rates: **Available**
Hosts: **Stephen and Shirley Ramsey**	Breakfast: **Full**
Location: **27 mi. N of Charlottesville**	Pets: **No**
No. of Rooms: **7**	Children: **Welcome, over 12**
No. of Private Baths: **7**	Smoking: **No**
Double/pb: **$95–$135**	Social Drinking: **Permitted**
Guest Cottage: **$135**	

The Mayhurst is an early Victorian mansion noted for its fanciful architecture and oval spiral staircase ascending four stories to the rooftop gazebo. The rooms are large and sunny, with original floor-to-ceiling windows made of handblown glass. Bedrooms are elegantly furnished with 18th- and 19th-century beds, chests, and tables. Each room is named for someone who spent the night at the inn or is associated with it in some way. The Stonewall Jackson Room was offered to the Confederate general the night before the Battle of Cedar Mountain. Four rooms in the main house have working fireplaces, and the guest cottage features a fireplace, exposed beams, and pine floors. Guests are welcome to congregate in the main hall for afternoon tea or port. In the dining room, the full country breakfast includes Virginia ham or sausage, eggs, baked apples, pumpkin muffins, and homemade marmalade. The Mayhurst is situated on 36 acres, with a fishing pond, fields, and magnolias, and is listed on the National Register of Historic Places.

Oak Spring Farm and Vineyard ✪
ROUTE 1, BOX 356, RAPHINE, VIRGINIA 24472

Tel: **(703) 377-2398**	Breakfast: **Continental**
Best Time to Call: **9 AM–5 PM**	Credit Cards: **MC, VISA**
Hosts: **Jim and Pat Tichenor**	Pets: **No**
Location: **55 mi. S of Charlottesville**	Children: **Welcome, over 16**
No. of Rooms: **3**	Smoking: **No**
No. of Private Baths: **3**	Social Drinking: **Permitted**
Double/pb: **$55–$65**	Minimum Stay: **May graduation**
Single/pb: **$35–$50**	**weekends**
Open: **All year**	Airport/Station Pickup: **Yes**

This is a 40-acre working farm and vineyard. There are wonderful views of the Blue Ridge Mountains, an orchard, gardens, lawns, and a pasture with a herd of friendly burros. Located halfway between historic Lexington and Staunton, there are historical sites and antique shops to visit, and opportunities to ski or swim. The plantation house was built in 1826 and has been completely restored and renovated—including air conditioning. It is filled with family heirlooms and treasures collected during Jim's 26 years of worldwide military service. Virginia Military Institute and Washington and Lee University are nearby. The Tichenors invite you to join them for complimentary wine and appetizers before dinner; port and sherry afterward.

Abbie Hill Bed & Breakfast

P.O. BOX 4503, RICHMOND, VIRGINIA 23220

Tel: **(804) 355-5855; 353-4656**	Open: **All year**
Best Time to Call: **9 AM–5 PM**	Breakfast: **Full**
Hosts: **Barbara and Bill Fleming**	Credit Cards: **MC, VISA ($150**
Location: **2½ mi. from I-95**	**minimum)**
No. of Rooms: **2**	Pets: **No**
No. of Private Baths: **2**	Children: **No**
Double/pb: **$65–$85**	Smoking: **No**
Single/pb: **$50**	Social Drinking: **Permitted**
Suites: **$85**	Airport/Station Pickup: **Yes**

This elegant Federal-style townhouse is located within Richmond's most prestigious urban historic district, close to museums, fine restaurants, sightseeing tours, historic sites, and shops. The ambience of the old South awaits as you come from the broad front porch into the elegantly appointed entrance hall of this mansion, built in 1910. It is appropriately furnished with antiques and decoratored with special handcrafts. Your hosts, house restorers by second occupation, will proudly give you a detailed tour. Tea and cookies are served when you arrive; hot beverages are available anytime.

The Mary Bladon House ✪

381 WASHINGTON AVENUE SOUTH WEST, ROANOKE, VIRGINIA 24016

Tel: **(703) 344-5361**	Reduced Rates: **Available**
Hosts: **Bill and Sheri Bestpitch**	Breakfast: **Full**
Location: **220 mi. S of Washington,**	Credit Cards: **MC, VISA**
D.C.	Pets: **No**
No. of Rooms: **4**	Children: **Welcome**
No. of Private Baths: **4**	Smoking: **No**
Double/pb: **$70**	Social Drinking: **Permitted**
Single/pb: **$50**	Airport/Station Pickup: **Yes**
Suites: **$95**	Foreign Languages: **German**
Open: **All year**	

The Mary Bladon House is located in the old southwest neighborhood, just five minutes away from the Blue Ridge Parkway. This Victorian dates back to the late 1800s and has four porches. Although the original brass light fixtures are still in place, the decor in the public rooms is constantly changing, with works by local artists and craftsmen. All the rooms are elegantly appointed with antiques, and guest rooms feature fresh flowers in season. Breakfast is served by candle-light in the dining room or on the porch in summer months.

High Meadows—Virginia's Vineyard Inn ✪
ROUTE 4, BOX 6, ROUTE 20 SOUTH, SCOTTSVILLE, VIRGINIA 24590

Tel: (804) 286-2218
Hosts: Peter and Jae Abbitt Sushka
Location: 17 mi. S of Charlottesville
No. of Rooms: 6
No. of Private Baths: 6
Double/pb: $95
Single/pb: $75
Suites: $120
Open: All year

Breakfast: Full
Other Meals: Available
Pets: Sometimes
Children: Welcome, over 8
Smoking: No
Social Drinking: Permitted
Foreign Languages: French
Minimum Stay: Weekends, Apr., May,
    Sept., Oct., and all holidays

This Virginia Historic Landmark is situated on 23 acres, and comprises dwellings built in 1832 and 1882 that are joined by a longitudinal "grand" hall. Recently restored, it is furnished with carefully chosen period antiques. You will enjoy the many fireplaces and whirlpool bath, the lovely flower gardens, the Pinot Noir vineyard, the ponds, and the gazebo. Bicycles are available for local touring. Jefferson's Monticello, Monroe's Ash Lawn, the University of Virginia, and James River tubing, fishing, and canoeing are nearby. Peter is a retired naval submariner; Jae's a financial analyst with the Securities Exchange Commission; son Peter plays classical guitar. Virginia wine with hors d'oeuvres is an evening tradition.

Isle of Wight Inn ✪
1607 SOUTH CHURCH STREET, SMITHFIELD, VIRGINIA 23430

Tel: (804) 357-3176
Best Time to Call: 9 AM–5 PM
Hosts: Bob Hart, Sam Earl, and
    Marcella Hoffman
Location: 27 mi. W of Norfolk
No. of Rooms: 12
No. of Private Baths: 12
Double/pb: $59
Single/pb: $49

Suites: $79–$99
Open: All year
Breakfast: Full
Credit Cards: AMEX, MC, VISA
Pets: No
Children: Welcome
Smoking: Permitted
Social Drinking: Permitted

The Isle of Wight Inn is a sprawling brick Colonial, one mile from downtown Smithfield. Inside you will find antiques, reproductions, motifs of glass, wood, and wicker, and an old player piano. Wake up to fresh coffee and Smithfield's own ham rolls. This riverport town has numerous historic homes that will surely delight you. Williams-burg, Norfolk, and Virginia Beach are less than an hour's drive from the house. An antiques shop is on the premises.

The Manor at Taylor's Store ✪
ROUTE 1, BOX 533, SMITH MOUNTAIN LAKE, VIRGINIA 24184

Tel: (703) 721-3951
Hosts: **Lee and Mary Lynn Tucker**
Location: **20 mi. E of Roanoke**
No. of Rooms: **6**
No. of Private Baths: **4**
Double/pb: **$60–$85**
Guest Cottage: **$85–$175; sleeps 2–8**
Open: **All year**
Reduced Rates: **$340–$700 week for cottage**

Breakfast: **Full**
Other Meals: **Available**
Credit Cards: **MC, VISA**
Pets: **No**
Children: **Welcome in cottage**
Smoking: **No**
Social Drinking: **Permitted**
Airport/Station Pickup: **Yes**

Situated on 100 acres in the foothills of the Blue Ridge Mountains, this elegant manor house (circa 1799) was the focus of a prosperous tobacco plantation. It has been restored and refurbished, and you'll experience the elegance of the past combined with the comfort of tasteful modernization. The estate invites hiking, swimming, and fishing. The sun room, parlor, and hot tub are special spots for relaxing. Smith Mountain Lake, with its seasonal sporting activity, is five miles away. Breakfast, designed for the health-conscious, features a variety of fresh gourmet selections.

Bonniemill B&B ✪
7305 BONNIEMILL LANE, SPRINGFIELD, VIRGINIA 22150

Tel: (703) 569-9295
Best Time to Call: **Early evening**
Hosts: **Lynn and David Tikkala**
Location: **10 mi. S of Washington, D.C.**
No. of Rooms: **2**
No. of Private Baths: **2**
Double/pb: **$45–$60**

Open: **All year**
Reduced Rates: **10%, seniors**
Breakfast: **Full**
Pets: **No**
Children: **No**
Smoking: **Permitted**
Social Drinking: **Permitted**

Stay in a quiet residential neighborhood convenient to the nation's capital. The Jacuzzi suite has a four-poster queen-size bed, TV, VCR, and double whirlpool bath; the Victorian suite has an antique bed and armoire, floral wallpaper, and rich draperies. Lynn runs her interior decorating business from her home, and her touch is evident throughout. Feel free to use the bicycles, Lifecycle, and gas grill. Want to go sightseeing in Washington? David, an accountant who commutes downtown, will give you a lift after you've tucked away a breakfast omelet with homemade fruit bread.

Kenwood ✪
235 EAST BEVERLEY STREET, STAUNTON, VIRGINIA 24401

Tel: (703) 886-0524	Single/sb: $40
Hosts: Liz and Ed Kennedy	Open: All year
Location: 30 mi. W of Charlottesville	Breakfast: Full
No. of Rooms: 4	Credit Cards: MC, VISA
No. of Private Baths: 2	Pets: No
Max. No. Sharing Bath: 4	Children: Welcome
Double/pb: $60	Smoking: Permitted
Single/pb: $50	Social Drinking: Permitted
Double/sb: $50	Airport/Station Pickup: Yes

Kenwood, a stately brick colonial revival home built in 1910, has been restored and decorated with floral wallpapers and antique furniture. The Woodrow Wilson Birthplace—and its museum and research library—are next door. Staunton boasts several other museums and numerous antique shops, and it's only a half-hour drive to attractions like Monticello and the Virginia Horse Center. Select your destinations over such breakfast fare as fresh seasonal fruit and homemade baked goods.

Thornrose House at Gypsy Hill ✪
531 THORNROSE AVENUE, STAUNTON, VIRGINIA 24401

Tel: (703) 885-7026	Double/pb: $45–$55
Best Time to Call: 8 AM–10 PM	Single/pb: $35–$45
Hosts: Carolyn and Ray Hoaster	Open: All year
Location: I-81 Shenandoah Valley, Exit 57	Breakfast: Full
	Pets: No
No. of Rooms: 3	Children: Infants and ages 10 and up
No. of Private Baths: 3	Smoking: No
	Social Drinking: Permitted
	Airport/Station Pickup: Yes

A wraparound veranda and Greek colonnades distinguish the entrance of this turn-of-the-century Georgian residence. Inside, family antiques, a grand piano, and fireplaces create a formal but comfortable atmosphere. An unusual winding staircase leads to restful, attractive rooms. The house specialty, Birchermuesli, a Swiss concoction made from oats, fresh fruits, nuts, and whipped cream, is just part of the hearty breakfast. Your hosts also offer afternoon tea and conversation. They are located adjacent to a 300-acre city park with tennis, golf, walks, and ponds. Other nearby attractions include Blue Ridge National Park, Natural Chimneys, Skyline Drive, the birthplace of Woodrow Wilson, and the Museum of American Frontier Culture.

Lambsgate Bed and Breakfast ✪
ROUTE 1, BOX 63, SWOOPE, VIRGINIA 24479

Tel: (703) 337-6929	Open: **All year**
Hosts: **Daniel and Elizabeth Fannon**	Reduced Rates: **10%, weekly**
Location: **6 mi. W of Staunton; 10 mi. from I-81**	Breakfast: **Full**
	Pets: **No**
No. of Rooms: **3**	Children: **Welcome**
Max. No. Sharing Bath: **6**	Smoking: **No**
Double/sb: **$35**	Social Drinking: **Permitted**
Single/sb: **$30**	

Lambsgate is a restored vernacular farmhouse on seven acres in the Shenandoah Valley. The house dates back to 1816 and though it has been added to and modernized, the bedrooms have retained their original woodwork and floors. The Fannons offer a breakfast of home-made muffins, bacon, eggs, grits, and jellies each morning. They will provide information on such local sights as George Washington National Forest, Shenandoah National Park, and Luray Caverns. There is also plenty to see on the farm. Guests are invited to visit the lambs or relax and enjoy the view from the wraparound veranda.

The Duck Farm Inn
P.O. BOX 787, RTES. 227 AND 639, URBANNA, VIRGINIA 23175

Tel: (804) 758-5685	Guest Cottage: **$150; sleeps 6**
Host: **Fleming Godden**	Open: **All year**
Location: **55 mi. E of Richmond**	Reduced Rates: **After first visit**
No. of Rooms: **6**	Breakfast: **Full**
No. of Private Baths: **2**	Pets: **No**
Max. No. Sharing Bath: **4**	Children: **Welcome, over 12**
Double/pb: **$75**	Smoking: **No**
Single/pb: **$60**	Social Drinking: **Permitted**
Double/sb: **$65**	Airport/Station Pickup: **Yes**
Single/sb: **$50**	

This elegant, contemporary inn is situated on Virginia's middle peninsula, surrounded by 800 secluded acres and bordered by the Rappahannock River. Guests are welcome to hike along the shore or through the woods, fish in the river, sunbathe on the private beach, lounge on the deck, or retire to the cozy library with a good book. Fleming has traveled all over the world and thoroughly enjoys her role as full-time innkeeper. One of her breakfast menus consists of seasonal fresh fruit, jumbo blueberry muffins, cheese-and-egg scramble served with spiced sausage, and a variety of hot beverages.

Angie's Guest Cottage ✪
302 24TH STREET, VIRGINIA BEACH, VIRGINIA 23451

Tel: **(804) 428-4690**	Guest Cottage: **$375–$500 weekly;**
Best Time to Call: **10 AM–10 PM**	**sleeps 2–6**
Host: **Barbara G. Yates**	Open: **Apr. 1–Oct. 1**
Location: **20 mi. E of Norfolk**	Reduced Rates: **Off-season**
No. of Rooms: **6**	Breakfast: **Continental**
No. of Private Baths: **1**	Pets: **Sometimes**
Max. No. Sharing Bath: **4**	Children: **Welcome (crib)**
Double/pb: **$60**	Smoking: **No**
Single/pb: **$50**	Social Drinking: **Permitted**
Double/sb: **$40–$56**	Minimum Stay: **2 nights**
Single/sb: **$34–$48**	

Just a block from the beach, shops, and restaurants is this bright and comfortable beach house. Former guests describe it as: "cozy, cute, and clean." Deep-sea fishing, nature trails, and harbor tours are but a few things to keep you busy. Freshly baked croissants in various flavors are a breakfast delight. You are welcome to use the sundeck, barbecue, and picnic tables.

The Picket Fence ✪
209 43RD STREET, VIRGINIA BEACH, VIRGINIA 23451

Tel: **(804) 428-8861**	Open: **All year**
Host: **Kathleen Hall**	Breakfast: **Full**
Location: **20 mi. E of Norfolk**	Pets: **No**
No. of Rooms: **2**	Children: **No**
No. of Private Baths: **2**	Smoking: **No**
Double/pb: **$50–$75**	Social Drinking: **Permitted**
Single/pb: **$40–$55**	Minimum Stay: **2 nights**
Guest Cottage: **$75**	

The furnishings in Kathy's comfortable Colonial home glow with the patina of loving care. She thoroughly enjoys her hobbies of fishing and cooking and often incorporates the two into special breakfasts for her guests. The beach is just a block away and beach chairs and umbrellas are provided for your comfort. Complimentary wine and cheese are graciously served before you go out to dinner. Don't leave the area without visiting the new Marine Science Museum.

The Foster-Harris House
P.O. BOX 333, WASHINGTON, VIRGINIA 22747

Tel: **(703) 675-3757**	Location: **65 mi. W of Washington,**
Hosts: **Patrick Foster and Camille**	**D.C.**
Harris	No. of Rooms: **3**

No. of Private Baths: **3**
Double/pb: **$85**
Single/pb: **$75**
Suites: **$105**
Open: **All year**
Reduced Rates: **3 nights or more**

Breakfast: **Full**
Pets: **Sometimes**
Children: **Welcome, over 10**
Smoking: **Permitted**
Social Drinking: **Permitted**

This pastoral Victorian is surrounded by the Blue Ridge Mountains. The rooms are furnished with many antiques and the guest quarters are newly renovated. There is much to see in this historic village, which was surveyed by George Washington and was the first place in the country to be named for him. Your hosts serve freshly baked treats each morning and offer wine and cheese or coffee and cookies in the afternoon. They recommend five-star dining at a nearby inn and will gladly direct you to Skyline Drive, antique shops, horseback riding, and hiking trails.

The Travel Tree ✪
P.O. BOX 838, WILLIAMSBURG, VIRGINIA 23185

Tel: **(804) 253-1571**
Best Time to Call: **6–9 PM, weekdays**
Coordinators: **Joann Proper and Sheila Zubkoff**
States/Regions Covered: **Williamsburg, Jamestown, Yorktown**

Rates (Single/Double):
    Modest: **$50–$60**
    Average: **$65–$80**
    Luxury: **$85–$100**
Credit Cards: **No**

You will thoroughly enjoy Colonial Williamsburg, historic Jamestown and Yorktown, Busch Gardens, and Carter's Grove Plantation. Your bedroom might be furnished with four-poster beds and antiques, or be tucked under the eaves in a wooded setting, or be a two-room suite with a private entrance. Other choices are, of course, available.

Blue Bird Haven B&B ✪
8691 BARHAMSVILLE ROAD, WILLIAMSBURG-TOANO, VIRGINIA 23168

Tel: **(804) 566-0177**
Best Time to Call: **Early AM**
Hosts: **June and Ed Cottle**
Location: **9 mi. N of Williamsburg**
No. of Rooms: **3**
No. of Private Baths: **2**
Max. No. Sharing Bath: **4**
Double/pb: **$48**
Double/sb: **$38**

Suites: **$58**
Open: **All year**
Breakfast: **Full**
Other Meals: **Available**
Pets: **Sometimes**
Children: **Welcome**
Smoking: **Permitted**
Social Drinking: **Permitted**

June and Ed welcome you to their ranch-style home, located 20 minutes from Colonial Williamsburg. Guest accommodations, located in a private wing, feature traditional furnishings. June is interested in many kinds of handcrafts and has decorated the rooms with one-of-a-kind quilts, spreads, rugs, and pictures. Breakfast includes a southern-style assortment of Virginia ham, spoonbread, red-eye gravy, blueberry pancakes, fresh fruits, home-baked biscuits, and granola. Blue Bird Haven is convenient to Busch Gardens, James River Plantations, and Civil War battlefields. After a full day of seeing the sights, you are welcome to enjoy some of June's evening desserts.

Colonial Capital Bed & Breakfast ✪
501 RICHMOND ROAD, WILLIAMSBURG, VIRGINIA 23185

Tel: **(800) 776-0570**	Open: **All year**
Hosts: **Barbara and Phil Craig**	Reduced Rates: **10%, Jan. 1–Mar. 31**
Location: **2.5 mi. from I-64, Exit 56**	Breakfast: **Full**
No. of Rooms: **5**	Pets: **Sometimes**
No. of Private Baths: **5**	Children: **Welcome, over 6**
Double/pb: **$80**	Smoking: **Permitted**
Single/pb: **$60**	Social Drinking: **Permitted**
Suites: **$124; sleeps 4**	Airport/Station Pickup: **Yes**

Four blocks from the historic area, Barbara and Phil offer a warm welcome to guests in their Colonial Revival three-story home. Decorated with period antiques, Oriental rugs, and most of the original lighting and plumbing fixtures (c. 1926), rooms are furnished with four-poster beds, many crowned with charming canopies. In the morning you can look forward to such treats as a soufflé, French toast, or fluffy omelet, served either in the sunny solarium or in the formal dining room. After a full day that might include a visit to Jamestown, Yorktown, and some of the state's finest plantations, you can enjoy complimentary snacks and visit in the parlor. Games, books, and puzzles are provided for your pleasure.

For Cant Hill Guest Home
4 CANTERBURY LANE, WILLIAMSBURG, VIRGINIA 23185

Tel: **(804) 229-6623**	Open: **All year**
Best Time to Call: **After 5 PM;**	Breakfast: **Continental**
weekends	Pets: **No**
Hosts: **Martha and Hugh Easler**	Children: **Welcome, over 8**
No. of Rooms: **2**	Smoking: **No**
No. of Private Baths: **2**	Social Drinking: **Permitted**
Double/pb: **$55**	

Martha and Hugh's home is in a secluded, wooded setting overlooking a lake, which is part of the campus of William and Mary. It is a short walk to the restored district. The guest rooms are attractively decorated, accented with homemade quilts in winter. Restaurants to suit every budget are nearby. Your hosts will be happy to make dinner reservations for you and provide helpful information on the area's attractions.

Fox Grape of Williamsburg ✪
701 MONUMENTAL AVENUE, WILLIAMSBURG, VIRGINIA 23185

Tel: **(804) 229-6914**	Single/sb: **$40**
Hosts: **Pat and Bob Orendorff**	Open: **All year**
Location: **2 mi. from I-64, Exit 56**	Reduced Rates: **10%, seniors**
No. of Rooms: **4**	Breakfast: **Continental**
No. of Private Baths: **1**	Pets: **No**
Max. No. Sharing Bath: **4**	Children: **Welcome**
Double/pb: **$55**	Smoking: **Permitted**
Single/pb: **$45**	Social Drinking: **Permitted**
Double/sb: **$45**	Airport/Station Pickup: **Yes**

This brick Cape Cod, a 10-minute walk to the restored area, is furnished with stained glass, antiques, needlepoint, and a decoy collection. The Orendorffs offer fresh muffins, fruit, and cereal in the morning, served in the dining room. They will advise on nearby tourist attractions and restaurants. William and Mary College is nearby. Pat enjoys counted cross-stitch; Bob carves duck head walking sticks.

Himmelbed Inn ✪
706 RICHMOND ROAD, WILLIAMSBURG, VIRGINIA 23185

Tel: **(804) 229-6421**	Open: **All year**
Hosts: **Bernie and Mary Peters**	Breakfast: **Full**
Location: **45 mi. E of Richmond**	Pets: **No**
No. of Rooms: **3**	Children: **Welcome, over 10**
No. of Private Baths: **3**	Smoking: **No**
Double/pb: **$70–$85**	Social Drinking: **Permitted**
Single/pb: **$65**	Airport/Station Pickup: **Yes**

This air-conditioned, Cape Cod–style house, with its stencilled walls, is attractively furnished in Pennsylvania antiques. It is within walking distance of the historic area and William and Mary College. Comfortable canopy beds provide a good night's rest. In the morning you'll awaken to the aroma of bread and muffins baking.

Liberty Rose Colonial B&B
1022 JAMESTOWN ROAD, WILLIAMSBURG, VIRGINIA 23185

Tel: **(804) 253-1260**	Hosts: **Brad and Sandi Hirz**
Best Time to Call: **9 AM–9 PM**	No. of Rooms: **4**

No. of Private Baths: **4**
Double/pb: **$80–$125**
Suites: **$135–$175**
Open: **All year**
Reduced Rates: **10%, Feb.1–Mar.31**
Breakfast: **Full**
Credit Cards: **MC, VISA**

Pets: **No**
Children: **Welcome, over 7**
Smoking: **No**
Social Drinking: **Permitted**
Airport/Station Pickup: **Yes**
Minimum Stay: **Weekends**

A farmer and interior designer turned home renovators, Brad and Sandi have redone this slate-roofed, two-story clapboard house themselves. Borrowing freely from Colonial, French, English, and Victorian styles, they have created a warm romantic look; you'll find unusual floral wallpapers and charming collectibles at every turn. Breakfast specialties such as French toast made from home-baked cinnamon bread will bolster tourists walking to the Williamsburg historic district one mile away.

Newport House ✪
710 SOUTH HENRY STREET, WILLIAMSBURG, VIRGINIA 23185

Tel: **(804) 229-1775**
Best Time to Call: **8–10 AM**
Hosts: **John and Cathy Millar**
No. of Rooms: **2**
No. of Private Baths: **2**
Double/pb: **$80–$95**
Open: **All year**

Breakfast: **Full**
Pets: **No**
Children: **Welcome**
Smoking: **No**
Social Drinking: **Permitted**
Airport/Station Pickup: **Yes**
Foreign Languages: **French**

Constructed in 1988, this house is based on blueprints drawn in 1756. In an unusual touch, the wood siding is cut to resemble stone. John, a former museum director, has furnished the house with period antiques and top-quality reproductions; many of the pieces are for sale. On Tuesday nights, the past really comes alive, as your hosts sponsor Colonial-style country dancing. Guests are welcome to participate, and no experience is necessary. Waffles, eggs, baked apples, and other breakfast favorites are served in the morning.

War Hill ✪
4560 LONG HILL ROAD, WILLIAMSBURG, VIRGINIA 23188

Tel: **(804) 565-0248**
Best Time to Call: **9 AM–9 PM**
Hosts: **Shirley and Bill Lee**
Location: **2 mi. from Rte. 60**
No. of Rooms: **5**
No. of Private Baths: **5**
Double/pb: **$55–$65**
Suite: **$70–$100; sleeps 5**

Cottage: **$90–$120; sleeps 5**
Open: **All year**
Breakfast: **Full**
Credit Cards: **AMEX, MC, VISA**
Pets: **No**
Children: **Welcome**
Smoking: **No**
Social Drinking: **Permitted**

War Hill is situated in the center of a 32-acre working farm, just three miles from the tourist attractions. Built in 1968, this Colonial replica couples the charm of yesteryear with today's contemporary conveniences. The suite is composed of two bedrooms and a bath. The wide heart-pine floors came from an old school, the stairs from a church, the overhead beams from a barn; the oak mantel is over 200 years old. Fruits from a variety of trees in the orchard are yours to pick in season. In autumn, Shirley and Bill serve delicious homemade applesauce and cider. Angus show cattle graze in the pasture, and the sounds you'll hear are crickets, frogs, owls, and the morning crowing of the rooster.

The Legacy of Williamsburg Tavern
930 JAMESTOWN ROAD, WILLIAMSBURG, VIRGINIA 23185

Tel: **(804) 220-0524 or (800) WMB-GSBB**	Open: **All year**
Hosts: **Ed and Mary Ann Lucas**	Breakfast: **Full**
Location: **2 mi. from Rte. 64, Exit 59**	Credit Cards: **MC, VISA**
No. of Rooms: **4**	Pets: **No**
No. of Private Baths: **4**	Children: **No**
Double/pb: **$70**	Smoking: **No**
Suite: **$120**	Social Drinking: **Permitted**
	Airport/Station Pickup: **Yes**

Ed and Mary have furnished their 18th-century-style home with lovely antiques from that era. The suite is the ultimate in privacy, and features a canopy bed in the bedroom and a comfortable sofa facing a fireplace in the living room. Flowers, fruit, wine, and candy will make you feel welcome. You'll awaken to the aroma of freshly baked breads, just the beginning of a hearty breakfast. Afterward, stroll across the street to the campus of William and Mary College, walk to the restored area, or drive to Busch Gardens nearby.

Williamsburg Sampler Bed & Breakfast ✪
922 JAMESTOWN ROAD, WILLIAMSBURG, VIRGINIA 23185

Tel: **(804) 253-0398**	Open: **All year**
Hosts: **Helen and Ike Sisane**	Breakfast: **Full**
Location: **Heart of Williamsburg**	Pets: **No**
No. of Rooms: **3**	Children: **Welcome**
No. of Private Baths: **3**	Smoking: **No**
Double/pb: **$75**	Social Drinking: **Permitted**
Suite: **$110**	Airport/Station Pickup: **Yes**

This stately brick Colonial parallels the College of William and Mary, and is within walking distance of historic Colonial Williamsburg. Embroidered and cross-stitched American samplers accent the Colonial-style furnishings. Waffles or French toast are often featured at breakfast. It is only a short drive to the Yorktown Battlefields, Jamestown Island, James River plantations, and Busch Gardens.

Azalea House ✪
551 SOUTH MAIN STREET, WOODSTOCK, VIRGINIA 22664

Tel: **(703) 459-3500**
Hosts: **Margaret and Price McDonald**
Location: **35 mi. N of Harris**
No. of Rooms: **3**
Max. No. Sharing Bath: **3**
Double/sb: **$45–$50**
Single/sb: **$35**
Open: **Mar. 1–Jan. 31**

Reduced Rates: **20%, after 3 nights**
Breakfast: **Full**
Credit Cards: **MC, VISA**
Pets: **Sometimes**
Children: **Welcome, over 12**
Smoking: **No**
Social Drinking: **Permitted**

This spacious home, built in the early 1890s, served as a parsonage for 70 years. It has been restored following its Victorian tradition and has porches, bay windows, and a white picket fence—in spring, one hundred blooming azaleas enhance its beauty. The interior is made particularly lovely with family heirlooms and pretty color schemes. Azalea House is within walking distance of fine restaurants, antique shops, and an art gallery. It is convenient to local wineries, orchards, and good fishing on the Shenandoah River. Air conditioning assures your summer comfort, and the backyard swimming pool is a real treat after a day of touring.

The Country Fare ✪
402 NORTH MAIN STREET, WOODSTOCK, VIRGINIA 22664

Tel: **(703) 459-4828**
Best Time to Call: **7–11 AM; 6–10 PM**
Host: **Bette Hallgren**
Location: **35 mi. S of Winchester**
No. of Rooms: **3**
No. of Private Baths: **1**
Max. No. Sharing Bath: **3**
Double/pb: **$55**

Double/sb: **$45**
Single/sb: **$40**
Open: **All year**
Breakfast: **Continental**
Pets: **No**
Children: **Welcome, by arrangement**
Smoking: **No**
Social Drinking: **Permitted**

This is a small cozy inn, circa 1772, within walking distance of the village. The rooms are decorated with hand stenciling and a mixture of grandmother's antiques and country collectibles. Choose from the master bedroom with private shower, an ample guest room with twin beds, and another room with a fireplace all its own. Guests may enjoy homemade breads and biscuits by the dining room wood stove when the air turns colder. An inviting brick patio overlooks the grounds. Your host will gladly help you get to know this historic Shenandoah Valley town, and can suggest many restaurants, shops, and interesting sights.

For key to listings, see inside front or back cover.

✪ This star means that rates are guaranteed through December 31, 1991, to any guest making a reservation as a result of reading about the B&B in *BED & BREAKFAST U.S.A.—1991* edition.

Important! To avoid misunderstandings, always ask about cancellation policies when booking.

Please enclose a self-addressed, stamped, business-size envelope when contacting reservation services.

For more details on what you can expect in a B&B, see Chapter 1.

Always mention *Bed & Breakfast U.S.A.* when making reservations!

If no B&B is listed in the area you'll be visiting, use the form on page 675 to order a copy of our "List of New B&Bs."

We want to hear from you! Use the form on page 677.

WASHINGTON

Lummi Island
Eastsound • Orcas • Ferndale
Deer Harbor • • Anacortes
• La Conner
Bellevue • Langley • Mt. Vernon • Pateros
Port Angeles • • Edmonds
Port Orchard • • Redmond
Gig Harbor • • Seattle • Leavenworth • Spokane
Tacoma • • Maple Valley
Olympia • Seabeck
• Ashford
• Little Cape Horn
Cathlamet
• White Salmon

Pacific Bed & Breakfast Agency ✪
701 NORTHWEST 60TH STREET, SEATTLE, WASHINGTON 98107

Tel: **(206) 784-0539**; Fax **(206) 782-4036**
Best Time to Call: **9 AM–5 PM**
Coordinator: **Irmgard Castleberry**
States/Regions Covered: **Statewide; Canada—Vancouver, Victoria, British Columbia**

Rates (Single/Double):
Modest: **$35** **$45**
Average: **$45** **$55**
Luxury: **$85** **$145**
Credit Cards: **AMEX, MC, VISA**
Minimum Stay: **2 nights in Seattle**
Descriptive Directory: **$5**

Victorians, contemporaries, island cottages, waterfront houses, and private suites with full kitchens are available. Most are close to downtown areas, near bus lines, in fine residential neighborhoods, or within walking distance of a beach. Many extras are included, such as pickup service, free use of laundry facilities, guided tours and more. The University of Washington and the University of Puget Sound are nearby. There is a $5 surcharge for one-night stays.

A Burrow's Bay B&B
4911 MACBETH DRIVE, ANACORTES, WASHINGTON 98221

Tel: **(206) 293-4792**
Hosts: **Beverly and Winfred Stocker**
Location: **92 mi. N of Seattle**
Suites: **$85; sleeps 2–6**
Open: **All year**
Breakfast: **Full**

Credit Cards: **MC, VISA**
Pets: **Sometimes**
Children: **Welcome**
Smoking: **No**
Social Drinking: **Permitted**
Airport/Station Pickup: **Yes**

Enjoy sweeping views of the San Juan Islands from this lovely contemporary Northwest home. The guest suite consists of a large sitting room with a view and a comfortable bedroom with a blue-and-tan motif and wall-to-wall carpeting. You are sure to enjoy the privacy and relaxation of having your own private deck, fireplace, TV, and a separate entrance. Beverly and Winfred offer an extensive menu from which you may select breakfast. They are located within walking distance of Washington Park, restaurants, and ferry rides to the nearby islands. Your hosts will be glad to provide touring advice for day trips to Victoria, B.C., Deception Pass, and Port Townsend.

The Channel House ✪
2902 OAKES AVENUE, ANACORTES, WASHINGTON 98221

Tel: **(206) 293-9382**
Hosts: **Dennis and Patricia McIntyre**

Location: **65 mi. N of Seattle; 18 mi. W of I-5, Exit 230**

No. of Rooms: **6**
No. of Private Baths: **4**
Max. No. Sharing Bath: **4**
Double/pb: **$65–$85**
Double/sb: **$65**
Single/sb: **$55**
Open: **All year**
Reduced Rates: **$10 less, Oct. 1–Apr. 30**

Breakfast: **Full**
Credit Cards: **MC, VISA**
Pets: **No**
Children: **Welcome, over 12**
Smoking: **No**
Social Drinking: **Permitted**
Airport/Station Pickup: **Yes**

Built in 1902 by an Italian count, this three-story Victorian house has stained-glass windows, rare antiques, gracious ambience, and is in mint condition. The guest rooms have beautiful views of Puget Sound and the San Juan Islands. It's an ideal getaway for relaxing in the "cleanest corner of the country." Your hosts serve gourmet breakfasts in front of the fireplace. The communal hot tub is a treat after salmon fishing, tennis, or golf. And it's only minutes from the ferry for visiting Victoria, British Columbia.

Mountain Meadows Inn ✪
28912 STATE ROUTE 706 E, ASHFORD, WASHINGTON 98304

Tel: **(206) 569-2788**
Best Time to Call: **After 6 PM**
Host: **Tanna Barney**
Location: **6 mi. from Mt. Rainier National Park**
No. of Rooms: **3**
No. of Private Baths: **3**
Double/pb: **$70**
Single/pb: **$60**
Suites: **$70**

Open: **All year**
Reduced Rates: **$10 less, weekdays, Nov.–Apr.**
Breakfast: **Full**
Credit Cards: **MC, VISA**
Pets: **No**
Children: **Welcome, over 12**
Smoking: **Permitted**
Social Drinking: **Permitted**
Minimum Stay: **2 nights, holidays**

Tanna Barney welcomes you to her historic home, set on a picture-perfect pond. The water attracts a wide variety of wildlife, and you'll find it a fine spot for fishing and evening campfires. Inside, gracious, comfortable rooms are decorated in Early American antique furnishings. French omelets, pancakes, and homemade muffins are lovingly prepared each morning. Guests are invited to relax on the expansive veranda overlooking the pond or visit with the pet llama. Tanna is a Northwest tour specialist well-versed in the area's recreational activities. She can direct you to nearby Mt. Rainier National Park, beautiful scenic spots, waterfalls, skiing, and much more.

The Country Keeper Bed & Breakfast Inn ✪
61 MAIN STREET, CATHLAMET, WASHINGTON 98612

Tel: **(206) 795-3030**
Hosts: **Terry and Meredith Beaston**

Location: **70 mi. NW of Portland**
No. of Rooms: **5**

No. of Private Baths: **2**
Max. No. Sharing Bath: **3**
Double/pb: **$65**
Single/pb: **$40**
Double/sb: **$40–$60**
Single/sb: **$35–$55**
Guest Cottage: **$80; sleeps 4**
Open: **All year**
Reduced Rates: **Weekly; 10%, Sun.–
    Thurs. Nov.–Mar.**

Breakfast: **Full**
Credit Cards: **MC, VISA**
Pets: **No**
Children: **Welcome**
Smoking: **No**
Social Drinking: **Permitted**
Airport/Station Pickup: **Yes**

Cathlamet is a scenic, quiet place on the Columbia River, within an easy drive of the Mount St. Helens National Monument. It is a fishing and farming community with a strong sense of history. The inn was built in 1907 from local timber; the fine work of craftsmen is seen in the inlaid floors and stained-glass windows. Meredith and Terry, both art teachers who moved here from Australia, have named and decorated each charming bedroom after an Impressionist artist. Breakfast is a romantic affair served by candlelight in the handsome dining room. Afterward, cycle the game refuge on a borrowed bike, play a round of golf or a set of tennis, fish, sail, or windsurf.

Palmer's Chart House ✪
P.O. BOX 51, ORCAS ISLAND, DEER HARBOR, WASHINGTON 98243

Tel: **(206) 376-4231**
Hosts: **Majean and Don Palmer**
Location: **50 mi. N of Seattle**
No. of Rooms: **2**
No. of Private Baths: **2**
Double/pb: **$60–$70**
Single/pb: **$45**
Open: **All year**

Breakfast: **Full**
Other Meals: **Dinner: $7.50**
Pets: **No**
Children: **Welcome, over 10**
Smoking: **No**
Social Drinking: **Permitted**
Foreign Languages: **Spanish**

It's just an hour's ride on the Washington State ferry from Anacortes to Orcas Island. Seasoned travelers, Majean and Don know how to make your stay special. Each guest room has a private deck from which to view the harbor scene. Blueberry pancakes are a breakfast specialty. *Amante*, the 33-foot sloop, is available for sailing with Don, the skipper.

Turtleback Farm Inn
ROUTE 1, BOX 650, EASTSOUND, ORCAS ISLAND, WASHINGTON 98245

Tel: **(206) 376-4914**
Best Time to Call: **9 AM–9 PM**
Hosts: **William and Susan Fletcher**
Location: **60 mi. NW of Seattle**

No. of Rooms: **7**
No. of Private Baths: **7**
Double/pb: **$65–$130**
Single/pb: **$55–$120**

Open: **All year**
Reduced Rates: **Available off season**
Breakfast: **Full**
Other Meals: **Available**
Credit Cards: **MC, VISA**

Pets: **No**
Children: **Welcome, over 8**
Smoking: **No**
Social Drinking: **Permitted**
Airport/Station Pickup: **Yes**

This peaceful retreat is situated on 80 acres of meadow, pasture, ponds, and woods overlooking lovely Crow Valley. The farmhouse dates back to the early 1900s. Each bedroom is furnished with antiques and each bed boasts an unusual cotton-covered wool comforter. Breakfast might consist of strawberry crêpes, corn waffles, or a delectable quiche, served on Aynsley china with pretty crystal. Guests enjoy leisurely walks, bird-watching, the music of Mozart, relaxing on the expansive deck, and the pleasant peace of being pampered.

The Harrison House ✪
210 SUNSET AVENUE, EDMONDS, WASHINGTON 98020

Tel: **(206) 776-4748**
Hosts: **Jody and Harve Harrison**
Location: **15 mi. N of Seattle**
No. of Rooms: **2**
No. of Private Baths: **2**
Double/pb: **$40–$50**
Single/pb: **$30–$40**

Open: **All year**
Breakfast: **Continental**
Pets: **No**
Children: **No**
Smoking: **No**
Social Drinking: **Permitted**

This new, informal, waterfront home has a sweeping view of Puget Sound and the Olympic Mountains. It is a block north of the ferry dock and two blocks from the center of this historic town. Many fine restaurants are within walking distance. Your spacious room has a private deck, TV, wet bar, telephone, and king-size bed. The University of Washington is nearby.

Heather House ✪
1011 "B" AVENUE, EDMONDS, WASHINGTON 98020

Tel: **(206) 778-7233**
Best Time to Call: **5–6:30 PM**
Hosts: **Harry and Joy Whitcutt**
Location: **15 mi. N of Seattle**
No. of Rooms: **1**
No. of Private Baths: **1**
Double/pb: **$48.50**

Single/pb: **$38**
Open: **All year**
Breakfast: **Continental**
Pets: **No**
Children: **No**
Smoking: **No**
Social Drinking: **Permitted**

This contemporary home has a spectacular view of Puget Sound and the Olympic Mountains. The guest room has a comfortable king-size bed and opens onto a private deck. Joy and Harry are world travelers and enjoy their guests. The homemade jams, jellies, and marmalades are delicious. You can work off breakfast by walking a mile to the shops, beaches, and fishing pier.

Hudgens Haven ✪

9313 190 SOUTH WEST, EDMONDS, WASHINGTON 98020

Tel: **(206) 776-2202**
Best Time to Call: **4–8 PM**
Hosts: **Lorna and Edward Hudgens**
No. of Rooms: **1**
No. of Private Baths: **1**
Double/pb: **$40**
Single/pb: **$35**

Open: **Mar. 1–Nov. 30**
Breakfast: **Continental**
Pets: **No**
Children: **Welcome, over 10**
Smoking: **No**
Social Drinking: **Permitted**

Hudgens Haven is located in a picture postcard town on the shores of Puget Sound. The house overlooks the water as well as the Olympic Mountain Range. The rooms are decorated in early-American style and the guest room has a queen-size bed, a desk, an easy chair, and plenty of drawer space. Your hosts will gladly help plan daytrips and can suggest waterfront restaurants, fine shopping, and a score of recreational activities.

The Maple Tree ✪

18313 OLYMPIC VIEW DRIVE, EDMONDS, WASHINGTON 98020

Tel: **(206) 774-8420**
Hosts: **Marion and Hellon Wilkerson**
Location: **15 mi. N of Seattle**
No. of Rooms: **1**
No. of Private Baths: **1**
Double/pb: **$40**
Single/pb: **$35**

Open: **All year**
Breakfast: **Continental**
Pets: **No**
Children: **Welcome, over 5**
Smoking: **No**
Social Drinking: **Permitted**

The Maple Tree is a beautifully restored older home with landscaped grounds. Located across the street from Puget Sound, it commands a stunning view of the Olympic Mountains. You're welcome to watch the activity on Puget Sound through the telescope in the solarium. Lounge on the brick patio or watch the sun set over the snowcapped mountains as you sip a glass of Washington State wine. Hellon and Marion enjoy having guests and exchanging travel experiences with them. Hellon loves to cook; both like to work in their rose garden.

Anderson House ✪

P.O. BOX 1547, 2140 MAIN STREET, FERNDALE, WASHINGTON 98248

Tel: **(206) 384-3450**
Hosts: **Dave and Kelly Anderson**

Location: **8 mi. N of Bellingham**
No. of Rooms: **5**

No. of Private Baths: **2**
Max. No. Sharing Bath: **4**
Double/pb: **$45**
Double/sb: **$35–$40**
Suites: **$65**
Open: **All year**
Breakfast: **Full**
Credit Cards: **MC, VISA**

Pets: **No**
Children: **Welcome, over 8**
Smoking: **No**
Social Drinking: **Permitted**
Minimum Stay: **2 nights, holiday
weekends**

Anderson House is a slice of America as it was a hundred years ago. The authenticity of the period is evident in the carefully selected furnishings; the Bavarian crystal swan chandelier is frequently photographed by guests. It hangs over the dining room table, where freshly baked scones and muffins are served with homemade jams, fruit, and freshly ground Kona coffee. It is minutes away from the Strait of Georgia waterfront, 16 miles to Canada, and a one-hour drive to Mt. Baker.

Hill Top Bed and Breakfast
5832 CHURCH STREET, FERNDALE, WASHINGTON 98248

Tel: **(206) 384-3619**
Best Time to Call: **Mornings; evenings**
Hosts: **Paul and Doris Matz**
Location: **12 mi. S of Canadian border**
No. of Rooms: **3**
No. of Private Baths: **2**
Double/pb: **$49**
Double/sb: **$44**
Single/sb: **$39**

Open: **Apr. 1–Nov. 1**
Reduced Rates: **Available**
Breakfast: **Full**
Credit Cards: **MC, VISA**
Pets: **No**
Children: **Welcome (crib)**
Smoking: **No**
Social Drinking: **Permitted**
Airport/Station Pickup: **Yes**

Hill Top Bed and Breakfast is located in the Puget Sound area close to several beautiful state and local parks. The house overlooks Mt. Baker and the Cascade Mountain Range, and the view is especially nice from the patio. The house is decorated with Early American charm and the rooms have four-poster beds and homemade quilts to snuggle up in. The suite has a fireplace. Homemade breakfast specialties include coffee cakes, muffins, jams, and applesauce. This is a perfect spot for families and is convenient to Birch Bay, local islands, and Vancouver, Canada.

The Parsonage

4107 BURNHAM DRIVE, GIG HARBOR, WASHINGTON 98335

Tel: **(206) 851-8654**	Single/sb: **$35**
Best Time to Call: **10 AM–10 PM**	Open: **All year**
Hosts: **Edward and Sheila Koscik**	Breakfast: **Full**
Location: **9 mi. W of Tacoma**	Pets: **Sometimes**
No. of Rooms: **2**	Children: **Sometimes**
Max. No. Sharing Bath: **4**	Smoking: **No**
Double/sb: **$45**	Social Drinking: **Permitted**

The Parsonage is a 1901 Victorian surrounded by towering pines and strawberry fields. This was Gig Harbor's first Methodist parsonage, until 1984 when the Kosciks purchased the house. They added modern touches, such as a new guest bath, but were careful to retain the old-fashioned charm of the rooms. Breakfast features fresh seasonal berries, homemade muffins, and applesauce. The Parsonage is just a short walk from the picturesque harbor, with a variety of restaurants, shops, galleries, and marinas. In the evening, you are welcome to enjoy a classic movie from the 1940s or '50s.

Lake Stevens Peony House ✪

1602 EAST LAKESHORE DRIVE, LAKE STEVENS, WASHINGTON 98258

Tel: **(206) 334-1046**	Open: **All year**
Host: **(Mrs.) Halo Thompson**	Breakfast: **Full**
Location: **25 mi. outside Seattle**	Pets: **Sometimes**
No. of Rooms: **1**	Children: **Welcome**
No. of Private Baths: **1**	Smoking: **No**
Double/pb: **$55**	Social Drinking: **Permitted**
Single/pb: **$45**	

This enchanting home—which, true to its name, is filled with floral paintings—rests on a beautifully landscaped lot adjacent to Lake Stevens. Avid anglers can catch trout, bass, and catfish, then put aside their rod and reel to enjoy other waterfront sports. In the morning, homegrown raspberries and blueberries accompany your host's fabulous French toast.

Log Castle Bed & Breakfast ✪
3273 EAST SARATOGA ROAD, LANGLEY, WASHINGTON 98260

Tel: **(206) 321-5483**	Breakfast: **Full**
Best Time to Call: **8 AM–9 PM**	Credit Cards: **MC, VISA**
Hosts: **Jack and Norma Metcalf**	Pets: **No**
Location: **40 mi. N of Seattle**	Children: **Welcome, over 11**
No. of Rooms: **4**	Smoking: **No**
No. of Private Baths: **4**	Social Drinking: **No**
Double/pb: **$60–$90**	Airport/Station Pickup: **Yes**
Open: **All year**	

You don't have to build your castle on the sand on Whidbey Island, because one already awaits you. The imaginative design of this log lodge includes an eight-sided tower where any modern-day princess would feel at home. Taredo wood stairways, leaded and stained-glass motifs, and comfortable furnishings create a rustic yet sophisticated atmosphere. The four guest rooms all offer beautiful views of the surrounding mountains and water. Relax beside a large stone fireplace, take a rowboat ride, or a long walk on the beach. Your host offers breads and cinnamon rolls right from the oven as part of a hearty breakfast served on a big, round, log table. Host Jack Metcalf is a state senator and also loves to entertain when he is not working at the legislature.

Run of the River ✪
P.O. BOX 448, 9308 EAST LEAVENWORTH ROAD, LEAVENWORTH, WASHINGTON 98826

Tel: **(509) 548-7171**	Open: **All year**
Hosts: **Monty and Karen Turner**	Reduced Rates: **10%, seniors; 10%,**
Location: **110 mi. E of Seattle**	**Sun.–Thurs.**
No. of Rooms: **6**	Breakfast: **Full**
No. of Private Baths: **2**	Pets: **No**
Max. No. Sharing Bath: **4**	Children: **No**
Double/pb: **$79**	Smoking: **No**
Double/sb: **$69**	Social Drinking: **Permitted**
Suites: **$95**	Foreign Languages: **Spanish**

As its name suggests, this large log home is set in splendid seclusion. While you soak in the hot tub on the deck, watch ducks, geese, eagles, herons, and pheasant from the area's bird refuge flock to the Icicle River. Wood-burning stoves in two bedrooms add to the rustic ambience. Nonetheless, the shops of downtown Leavenworth are merely a mile away. The Turners pamper guests with enormous breakfasts that start with juice, fruit, muffins, yogurt, and freshly ground coffee, followed by platters of French toast and ham and eggs.

West Shore Farm B&B ✪
2781 WEST SHORE DRIVE, LUMMI ISLAND, WASHINGTON 98262

Tel: **(206) 758-2600**
Best Time to Call: **8 AM–9 PM**
Hosts: **Polly and Carl Hanson**
Location: **10 mi. from I-5, Exit 260**
No. of Rooms: **2**
No. of Private Baths: **2**
Double/pb: **$70**
Single/pb: **$60**
Open: **All year**

Breakfast: **Full**
Other Meals: **Available**
Credit Cards: **MC, VISA**
Pets: **No**
Children: **Welcome (crib)**
Smoking: **No**
Social Drinking: **Permitted**
Airport/Station Pickup: **Yes**

Architects are intrigued by the Hansons' self-built home, marveling at the design and innovative solution to common storage problems. Large windows overlook the Puget Sound islands and Canadian mountains. Sunsets are stunning. You can sit on the beach and watch bald eagles fly by, seals sunning on the offshore rocks, and boats on course to Alaska and Canada. Polly is a librarian and Carl is an aeronautical engineer who built and flies his own plane. They both enjoy having guests and often treat them to homemade ice cream topped with just-picked local fruit.

Maple Valley Bed & Breakfast ✪
20020 SOUTHEAST 228, MAPLE VALLEY, WASHINGTON 98038

Tel: **(206) 432-1409**
Hosts: **Clarke and Jayne Hurlbut**
Location: **26 mi. SE of Seattle**
No. of Rooms: **2**
Max. No. Sharing Bath: **4**
Double/sb: **$50**
Single/sb: **$40**

Open: **All year**
Breakfast: **Full**
Pets: **No**
Children: **Welcome**
Smoking: **No**
Social Drinking: **Permitted**
Airport/Station Pickup: **Yes**

After a good night's sleep in either of the B&B's guest rooms—one with a four-poster log bed and the other complete with a pink rosebud tea set, you'll come down to breakfast at a table that overlooks the lawn, the Hurlbuts' resident peacocks, and a wildlife pond teeming with a variety of northwestern birds. If the morning is cool, you'll be warmed by a stone fireplace and you won't go away hungry after orange juice, lemon-blueberry muffins, a plate-size hootenanny pancake (served with whipped cream, strawberries, slivered almonds, and syrup), ham, sausage or bacon, fresh-ground coffee, tea, or hot chocolate.

The White Swan Guest House
1388 MOORE ROAD, MT. VERNON, WASHINGTON 98273

Tel: **(206) 445-6805**
Best Time to Call: **Morning; evening**
Host: **Peter Gold**
Location: **60 mi. N of Seattle**
No. of Rooms: **4**
Max. No. Sharing Bath: **3**
Double/sb: **$65**
Single/sb: **$55**
Guest Cottage: **$95–$145; sleeps 4**

Open: **All year**
Reduced Rates: **Weekly in cottage**
Breakfast: **Continental**
Credit Cards: **MC, VISA**
Pets: **Sometimes**
Children: **Welcome (in cottage)**
Smoking: **No**
Social Drinking: **Permitted**

Surrounded by farmland and country roads, this storybook Victorian farmhouse, built in 1898, is painted crayon yellow and framed by English-style gardens. There's a woodstove in the parlor, wicker chairs on the porch, books for browsing, and a unique collection of old samplers. A platter of homemade chocolate-chip cookies is waiting for you on the sideboard. It's only 6 miles to LaConner, a delightful fishing village brim-full of interesting art galleries, shops, waterfront restaurants, and antique stores. The San Juan ferries are a half hour away.

Chy-An-Dour ✪
6210 BOARDMAN ROAD NORTHWEST, OLYMPIA, WASHINGTON 98502

Tel: **(206) 866-8422**
Best Time to Call: **8 AM–9 PM**
Hosts: **Barbara and Bill Painter**
Location: **15 mi. W of Olympia**
No. of Rooms: **2**
Max. No. Sharing Bath: **3**
Double/sb: **$50**
Single/sb: **$38**

Open: **All year**
Breakfast: **Continental**
Pets: **No**
Children: **Welcome, over 12**
Smoking: **No**
Social Drinking: **Permitted**
Airport/Station Pickup: **Yes**

True to its name—Cornish for "view of the water"—this B&B is a spacious contemporary home overlooking Eld Inlet, in lower Puget Sound, an ideal destination for people who like to fish, swim, and sail. The area is woodsy and secluded, but conveniently near major highways. Your English-born host will be only too happy to show off her English flower garden. Have your choice of complimentary tea, coffee, or wine in the evening. Breakfasts consist of fresh fruit, cereal, and freshly baked muffins and rolls.

Puget View Guesthouse ✪
7924 61ST NORTHEAST, OLYMPIA, WASHINGTON 98506

Tel: **(206) 459-1676**
Best Time to Call: **Evenings**
Hosts: **Dick and Barbara Yunker**
Location: **4½ mi. from I-5, Exit 111**
No. of Rooms: **1 cottage**
No. of Private Baths: **1**
Guest Cottage: **$55–$102; sleeps 4**
Open: **All year**

Reduced Rates: **Families; weekly; off season**
Breakfast: **Continental**
Credit Cards: **MC, VISA**
Pets: **Sometimes**
Children: **Welcome**
Smoking: **Permitted**
Social Drinking: **Permitted**

This charming waterfront guest cottage is located next to Tolmie State Park and adjacent to Dick and Barbara's log home. The panoramic Puget Sound setting makes it a popular, romantic getaway. You are apt to discover simple pleasures such as beachcombing or bird-watching and activities such as kayaking or scuba diving. Barbara and Dick are likely to invite you on a boat picnic or an oystering excursion. Your breakfast tray, a lavish and elegant repast, is brought to the cottage. You are welcome to use the beachside campfire for an evening cookout or to barbecue on your deck.

Orcas Hotel ☯
P.O. BOX 155, ORCAS, WASHINGTON 98280

Tel: **(206) 376-4300**	Reduced Rates: **Mid-week off season**
Hosts: **Barbara and John Jamieson**	Breakfast: **Continental**
Location: **90 mi. NW of Seattle**	Other Meals: **Available**
No. of Rooms: **12**	Credit Cards: **AMEX, MC, VISA**
No. of Private Baths: **5**	Pets: **No**
Max. No. Sharing Bath: **4**	Children: **No**
Double/pb: **$90–$150**	Smoking: **Permitted**
Single/pb: **$80–$140**	Social Drinking: **Permitted**
Double/sb: **$55–$75**	Airport/Station Pickup: **Yes**
Single/sb: **$45–$65**	Foreign Languages: **French, German,**
Open: **All year**	**Spanish**

The Orcas Hotel is a Victorian seaside inn overlooking Harney Channel and the ferry landing. The hotel has been lovingly restored and is listed on the National Register of Historic Places. The rooms feature antiques and modern, queen-size beds, with quilts custom stitched by island quilters. A fully stocked cocktail lounge with a bar menu and fine wine list is available for your relaxing pleasure. A wide range of homemade pastries, fruit-filled pancakes, sticky buns, omelets, and meats are served for breakfast. Your hosts will gladly direct you to Moran State Park, Cascade Lake, hiking and mo-ped trails, and a score of other activities in the San Juan Islands. The dining room, open to the public, serves three meals a day, and is noted for its fine cuisine at reasonable prices.

Ogle's Bed and Breakfast
1307 DOGWOOD HILL S.W., PORT ORCHARD, WASHINGTON 98366

Tel:**(206) 876-9170**	Handicapped Accessible:
Hosts: **Quentin and Louise Ogle**	Open: **All year**
Location: **25 mi N of Tacoma**	Breakfast: **Full**
No. of Rooms: **2**	Pets: **No**
Max. No. Sharing Bath: **4**	Children: **Welcome, over 8**
Double/sb: **$45**	Smoking: **No**
Single/sb: **$35**	Social Drinking: **Permitted**

Guests write to us constantly praising the hospitality and comfort they encounter at the Ogle's single level hillside home bounded by gardens and overlooking Puget Sound's Sinclair Inlet. The rooms are comfortably furnished with special touches like Louise's hand braided wool rugs, brass-bound chests, Oriental screens and oil paintings. Each morning, the tasty breakfast may be enjoyed on the sunny deck or at a table set before picture windows. Port Orchard is known for its marinas, marquee-covered downtown sidewalks, antique shops, art galleries, and appealing restaurants.

Cedarym—A Colonial Bed & Breakfast ✪
1011 240TH AVENUE NORTHEAST, REDMOND, WASHINGTON 98053

Tel: **(206) 868-4159**	Breakfast: **Full**
Hosts: **Mary Ellen and Walt Brown**	Credit Cards: **MC, VISA**
Location: **15 mi. E of Seattle**	Pets: **No**
No. of Rooms: **2**	Children: **No**
Max. No. Sharing Bath: **4**	Smoking: **No**
Double/sb: **$45**	Social Drinking: **Permitted**
Open: **All year**	

Cedarym is a spacious Colonial reproduction located on the Sammamish Plateau. The house has Cape Cod–style pine floors, wrought-iron door latches, and a large cooking-style fireplace in the keeping room. Guest rooms feature antique brass beds and comfortable sitting areas for reading or watching television, and each has old-fashioned wall stenciling. The breakfast table glows with hand-dipped candles and is covered with specialties such as Dutch Babies, muffins, and a variety of egg dishes. Guests are welcome to stroll the spacious grounds and visit the rose garden and the cottage garden, with its flowers and herbs. A gazebo-sheltered spa is guaranteed to relax you. This lovely Colonial is a short drive from historic Marymoor Park, Ste. Michelle Winery, and the sights of Seattle.

Summer Song B&B ✪
P.O. BOX 82, SEABECK, WASHINGTON 98380

Tel: **(206) 830-5089**	Open: **All year**
Best Time to Call: **After 2 PM**	Breakfast: **Continental**
Hosts: **Ron and Sharon Barney**	Credit Cards: **MC, VISA**
Location: **9 mi. SW of Silverdale**	Pets: **No**
No. of Rooms: **1**	Children: **Sometimes**
No. of Private Baths: **1**	Smoking: **Permitted**
Double/pb: **$55**	Social Drinking: **Permitted**

Enjoy your own private cottage on the shores of Hood Canal when you visit Summer Song. The cabin sleeps four, and features a bedroom, living and dining room, full kitchen, and bath. A cozy fireplace, old-fashioned wainscoting, and private decks with fire pit, barbecue, and mountain view complete this cozy retreat. Your hosts serve breakfast at the cottage or on the beach. Ron and Sharon provide all the comforts of home, such as beach towels and robes. Their beach is perfect for swimming and a public boat launch is just one mile away. Beautiful nature trails at Scenic Beach State Park are just a short walk away. Carriage rides and charter boats for fishing or sailing are available.

Galer Place B&B ✪

318 WEST GALER, SEATTLE, WASHINGTON 98119

Tel: **(206) 282-5339**	Open: **All year**
Hosts: **Chris and Terry Giles**	Breakfast: **Full**
Location: **2 mi. from I-5, Mercer St. exit**	Credit Cards: **AMEX, DC, MC, VISA**
	Pets: **Welcome**
No. of Rooms: **4**	Children: **Welcome, over 12**
No. of Private Baths: **4**	Smoking: **Permitted**
Double/pb: **$85–$100**	Social Drinking: **Permitted**
Single/pb: **$80–$95**	

A south Queen Anne Hill location sets this early-1900s home within walking distance of Seattle Center. A trolley line provides front-door service to the downtown area. The hallmarks of the generous breakfast are its fresh-baked breads, homemade preserves, and just-ground coffee. Several parks and scenic viewpoints are within strolling distance, as are an indoor swimming pool and running track. You are invited to join your British host for tea and homemade cookies.

Hainsworth House

2657 37TH SOUTH WEST, P.O. BOX 16438, SEATTLE, WASHINGTON 98126

Tel: **(206) 938-1020; 932-0654**	Reduced Rates: **Weekly**
Hosts: **Carl and Charlotte Muia**	Breakfast: **Full**
Location: **3 mi. W of Seattle**	Pets: **No**
No. of Rooms: **2**	Children: **No**
No. of Private Baths: **2**	Smoking: **No**
Double/pb: **$75–$85**	Social Drinking: **Permitted**
Open: **All year**	

The Hainsworth House is an English Tudor mansion overlooking Seattle. It is surrounded by beautiful lawns and is across the street from a park donated to the city by the Hainsworth family. The present owners, Carl and Charlotte Muia, have done extensive restoration work to the interior, following the original drawings down to the last ceiling beam. Guests will find the antique-filled rooms and gourmet breakfasts in keeping with the elegant traditions of the house. Eggs Benedict, salmon strata, German pancakes, and omelets are a few of the favorites.

Prince of Wales ✪

133 THIRTEENTH AVENUE EAST, SEATTLE, WASHINGTON 98102

Tel: **(206) 325-9692**	Location: **In heart of Seattle**
Best Time to Call: **10 AM–9 PM**	No. of Rooms: **4**
Hosts: **Naomi Reed and Bert Brun**	No. of Private Baths: **2**

Max. No. Sharing Bath: **4**
Double/sb: **$55–60**
Suites: **$70–$80**
Open: **All year**
Reduced Rates: **10%, weekly**
Breakfast: **Full**
Credit Cards: **MC, VISA**

Pets: **No**
Children: **Welcome**
Smoking: **No**
Social Drinking: **Permitted**
Foreign Languages: **French,
  Norwegian, Spanish**

From this convenient address, it's just a brief walk to the Convention Center and a short bus ride to the Space Needle, Pikes Place Market, and downtown Seattle's many other attractions. In the evening, you're sure to be tempted by the menus of neighborhood restaurants. Wake up to coffee in your bedroom, then come down to the dining room for a delicious breakfast. The guest rooms have great views; the suite has a queen-size bed, sitting room, and private bath.

Roberta's Bed and Breakfast
1147 SIXTEENTH AVENUE EAST, SEATTLE, WASHINGTON 98112

Tel: **(206) 329-3326**
Host: **Roberta Barry**
No. of Rooms: **5**
No. of Private Baths: **4**
Max. No. Sharing Bath: **3**
Double/pb: **$74–$82**
Single/pb: **$64–$75**
Double/sb: **$63–$68**

Single/sb: **$54–$60**
Open: **All year**
Breakfast: **Full**
Credit Cards: **AMEX, DC, MC, VISA**
Pets: **No**
Children: **Sometimes**
Smoking: **No**
Social Drinking: **Permitted**

Roberta's is a 1904 frame Victorian with a large, old-fashioned front porch. The house is located in a quiet, historic neighborhood near the heart of the city. Cheerful rooms filled with antiques await you: the

Peach Room has a brass bed, bay windows, and grandma's fancy desk; the Plum Room has a queen-size bed and a loft that can sleep an extra person. In the morning you'll smell a pot of coffee right beside your door. That's just a warmup for the large breakfast to come. The specialty of the house is Dutch Babies, a local dish, served with powdered sugar or fresh berries.

Salisbury House ✪
750 16TH AVENUE EAST, SEATTLE, WASHINGTON 98112

Tel: **(206) 328-8682**	Reduced Rates: **10%, weekly**
Hosts: **Mary and Catherine Wiese**	Breakfast: **Full**
Location: **1 mi. from I-5**	Credit Cards: **AMEX, DC, MC, VISA**
No. of Rooms: **4**	Pets: **No**
Max. No. Sharing Bath: **4**	Children: **Welcome, over 12**
Double/sb: **$60–$70**	Smoking: **No**
Single/sb: **$55–$65**	Social Drinking: **Permitted**
Open: **All year**	Foreign Languages: **Spanish**

This elegant family home, built in 1904, has been lovingly restored by your hosts, a mother-daughter team. It is located in a quiet neighborhood within walking distance of parks, restaurants, shops, and the Seattle Art Museum. Two of the guest rooms are small and cozy; the other two face the front of the house with window seats providing an attractive accent. A renovated Victorian-style bathroom features a six-foot clawfoot tub. You are invited to enjoy your morning coffee on the sun porch.

Seattle Bed & Breakfast ✪
2442 N.W. MARKET # 300, SEATTLE, WASHINGTON 98107

Tel: **(206) 783-2169**	Breakfast: **Continental**
Host: **Inge Pokrandt**	Credit Cards: **AMEX, MC, VISA**
Location: **1 mi. from I-5**	Pets: **No**
No. of Rooms: **4**	Children: **Welcome (crib)**
No. of Private Baths: **2**	Smoking: **No**
Suites: **$40–$45**	Social Drinking: **Permitted**
Guest Cottage: **$75 for 2**	Foreign Languages: **German**
Open: **All year**	

Built in 1925, this charming two-bedroom cottage is close to downtown, the University of Washington, fine beaches and all sightseeing. Enjoy the privacy, the fine oak furniture, the fireplace, and all the little touches that make you feel welcome. The private suite in Inge's home has a full kitchen, and some breakfast food is provided. Fresh flowers, fruits, and candy all spell out a warm welcome. The cedar deck in the sunny backyard is most enjoyable.

Hillside House ✪

E 1729 18TH AVENUE, SPOKANE, WASHINGTON 99203

Tel: (509) 534-1426, 7 AM–9 PM; 535-1893, evenings and weekends	Reduced Rates: Weekly
	Breakfast: Full
Best Time to Call: 7 AM–9 PM	Credit Cards: MC, VISA
Hosts: Jo Ann and Bud	Pets: Sometimes
Location: 2 mi. from US 90	Children: Sometimes
No. of Rooms: 2	Smoking: No
Max. No. Sharing Bath: 4	Social Drinking: Permitted
Double/sb: $48	Minimum Stay: 2 nights
Single/sb: $43	Airport/Station Pickup: Yes
Open: All year	

Hillside House has a spectacular view of Spokane and the nearby mountains. A cozy home, furnished in the country manner with antiques, its quiet, residential setting is within walking distance of lovely parks. Jo Ann is a third generation B&B hostess—her mother helped Grandma Jenny host guests in Minnesota over 70 years ago. Exotic egg dishes, unusual breakfast meats, and crêpes are often choices at breakfast. Pampering guests and guiding them to exciting events, places, and personalities are your hosts' pleasures.

Luckey's Residence ✪

WEST 828 28TH AVENUE, SPOKANE, WASHINGTON 99203

Tel: (509) 747-5774	Double/sb: $35
Best Time to Call: 6–8 AM; 3–5 PM	Single/sb: $25
Hosts: Robert, Patricia, and Royden Luckey	Open: All year
	Breakfast: Continental
Location: 2 mi. from I-90	Pets: No
No. of Rooms: 4	Children: Welcome
No. of Private Baths: 2	Smoking: No
Max. No. Sharing Bath: 4	Social Drinking: No

Luckey's has been described as a Hansel and Gretel house. It was built in the 1930s to look like an English cottage. The house is set in the South Hill section, a neighborhood set on a hillside covered with pine trees and volcanic rock. Your hosts offer a choice of twin- or queen-size beds. They serve a breakfast of homemade breads, cheeses, fruits, assorted juices, and plenty of coffee or tea. Luckey's is two blocks from High Drive, a scenic parkway along the hillside overlooking the canyon. A park with a large public swimming pool, children's wading pool, tennis court, and play area is a short walk from the house.

Marianna Stoltz House ✪
427 EAST INDIANA, SPOKANE, WASHINGTON 99207

Tel: **(509) 483-4316**	Breakfast: **Full**
Hosts: **James and Phyllis Maguire**	Credit Cards: **MC, VISA**
No. of Rooms: **4**	Pets: **No**
No. of Private Baths: **3**	Children: **Welcome, over 12**
Max. No. Sharing Bath: **4**	Smoking: **No**
Double/pb: **$50**	Social Drinking: **Permitted**
Single/pb: **$45**	Airport/Station Pickup: **Yes**
Open: **All year**	

The Marianna Stoltz House, a Spokane landmark, is a classic American foursquare home built in 1908. Period furnishings complement the house's woodwork, tile fireplace, and leaded glass bookshelves and cupboards. The bedroom quilts are heirlooms from Phyllis' mother, the B&B's namesake. The Maguires are Spokane natives—Phyllis grew up in this very house—and can tell you about local theaters, museums, and parks. Full breakfasts consist of juice, fruit, muffins, and main dishes such as sausage-cheese strata and puffy Dutch pancakes with homemade syrup.

Inge's Place ✪
6809 LAKE GROVE S.W., TACOMA, WASHINGTON 98499

Tel: **(206) 584-4514**	Suites: **$60**
Host: **Ingeborg Deatherage**	Open: **All year**
Location: **3 mi. from I-5**	Reduced Rates: **Available**
No. of Rooms: **3**	Breakfast: **Full**
No. of Private Baths: **1**	Pets: **No**
Max. No. Sharing Bath: **4**	Children: **Welcome**
Double/pb: **$45**	Smoking: **Permitted**
Single/pb: **$35**	Social Drinking: **Permitted**
Double/sb: **$40**	Airport/Station Pickup: **Yes**
Single/sb: **$30**	Foreign Languages: **German**

This spic-and-span home is in a lovely Tacoma suburb called Lakewood. Feel welcome to use the hot tub, large backyard, and patio. There are many restaurants and shopping centers within walking distance, and several nearby lakes where fishing is excellent. Tacoma is the gateway to Mount Rainier. Inge is a world traveler, teacher, and enthusiast about B&Bs.

Keenan House ✪
2610 NORTH WARNER, TACOMA, WASHINGTON 98407

Tel: **(206) 752-0702**	Location: **2½ mi. from I-5**
Best Time to Call: **Evenings**	No. of Rooms: **8**
Host: **Lenore Keenan**	No. of Private Baths: **1**

Max. No. Sharing Bath: **4**	Reduced Rates: **Weekly; 15%, families**
Double/pb: **$55**	Breakfast: **Full**
Single/pb: **$45**	Pets: **No**
Double/sb: **$45**	Children: **Welcome**
Single/sb: **$35**	Smoking: **No**
Open: **All year**	Social Drinking: **Permitted**

This spacious Victorian house is located in the historic district near Puget Sound. It is furnished in antiques and period pieces. Afternoon tea is served, and ice is available for cocktails; fruit and croissants are served with breakfast. Local possibilities include Puget Sound, Vashon Island, the state park, zoo, and ferry. It's only five blocks to the University of Puget Sound.

Traudel's Haus
15313 17TH AVENUE COURT EAST, TACOMA, WASHINGTON 98445

Tel: **(206) 535-4422**	Open: **All year**
Host: **Gertraude M. Taut**	Reduced Rates: **Available**
Location: **5 mi. from I-5**	Breakfast: **Full**
No. of Rooms: **3**	Pets: **No**
Max. No. Sharing Bath: **4**	Children:
Double/sb: **$40**	Smoking: **Permitted**
Single/sb: **$30**	Social Drinking: **Permitted**
Suites: **$45–$60**	Airport/Station Pickup: **Yes**
Handicapped Accessible:	Foreign Languages: **German**

Mrs. Taut offers a guest-oriented haven located in a quiet neighborhood only minutes from Pacific Lutheran University, Spanaway Park, and Sprinker Recreation Center. It is an easy springboard to other explorations, including the Tacoma Dam, Mt. Ranier National Park, and Mount St. Helens. The German-born Mrs. Taut collects antiques and clocks and enjoys making lace.

Llama Ranch Bed & Breakfast ○
1980 HIGHWAY 141, WHITE SALMON, WASHINGTON 98672

Tel: **(509) 395-2786**	Reduced Rates: **$5 less, Dec. –Mar.;**
Hosts: **Jerry and Rebeka Stone**	**15%, weekly**
Location: **50 mi. E of Portland, Ore.**	Breakfast: **Continental**
No. of Rooms: **5**	Credit Cards: **DISC, MC, VISA**
Max. No. Sharing Bath: **4**	Pets: **Sometimes**
Double/sb: **$45**	Children: **Welcome**
Single/sb: **$35**	Smoking: **No**
Open: **All year**	Social Drinking: **Permitted**

Jerry and Rebeka enjoy sharing their love of llamas with their guests, and it is a rare person who can resist a llama's charm. Their B&B commands stunning views of Mt. Adams and Mt. Hood. The guest rooms are unpretentious and comfortable. Llama Ranch is located on 97 acres at the base of the Mt. Adams Wilderness Area. Nearby activities include horseback riding, white-water rafting, plane trips over Mount Saint Helens, water sports, and cave exploration. The less adventurous are certain to enjoy learning about the ranch's serene animals.

For key to listings, see inside front or back cover.

✪ This star means that rates are guaranteed through December 31, 1991, to any guest making a reservation as a result of reading about the B&B in *BED & BREAKFAST U.S.A.*—1991 edition.

Important! To avoid misunderstandings, always ask about cancellation policies when booking.

Please enclose a self-addressed, stamped, business-size envelope when contacting reservation services.

For more details on what you can expect in a B&B, see Chapter 1.

Always mention *Bed & Breakfast U.S.A.* when making reservations!

If no B&B is listed in the area you'll be visiting, use the form on page 675 to order a copy of our "List of New B&Bs."

We want to hear from you! Use the form on page 677.

WEST VIRGINIA

Wheeling •

Morgantown • Shepherdstown • • Gerrardstown
Summit Point •

Elkins •
Huttonsville • • Moorefield

• Mathias

• Marlinton

Prospect Hill
BOX 135, GERRARDSTOWN, WEST VIRGINIA 25420

Tel: **(304) 229-3346**
Best Time to Call: **Evenings**
Hosts: **Hazel and Charles Hudock**
Location: **4 mi. from Rte. 81**
No. of Rooms: **3**
No. of Private Baths: **3**
Double/pb: **$75–85**
Single/pb: **$65–$75**

Separate Guest Cottage: **$85 for 2;
$125 for 4**
Open: **All year**
Breakfast: **Full**
Pets: **No**
Children: **Welcome in cottage**
Smoking: **Permitted**
Social Drinking: **Permitted**

Prospect Hill is a Georgian mansion set on 225 acres. The house dates back to the 1790s, and is listed on the National Register of Historic Places. One can see that this was a well-to-do gentleman's home, with permanent Franklin fireplaces, antiques, and a hall mural depicting life in the days of the early Republic. Guests may choose one of the beautifully appointed rooms in the main house or the former servants' quarters, complete with country kitchen and a fireplace in the living room. There is much to do on this working farm, including visiting the antebellum outbuildings, fishing, biking, and exploring the vast grounds. Near historic Harpers Ferry, Martinsburg, and Winchester, the area offers fine sightseeing and splendid restaurants.

The Hutton House ✪
ROUTES 219 AND 250, HUTTONSVILLE, WEST VIRGINIA 26273

Tel: (304) 335-6701	Suites: $85
Best Time to Call: 8 AM–9 PM	Open: All year
Hosts: Dean and Loretta Murray	Reduced Rates: Available
Location: 17 mi. S of Elkins	Breakfast: Full
No. of Rooms: 7	Other Meals: Available
No. of Private Baths: 3	Credit Cards: MC, VISA
Max. No. Sharing Bath: 4	Pets: No
Double/pb: $65	Children: Welcome
Single/pb: $58	Smoking: No
Double/sb: $55	Social Drinking: Permitted
Single/sb: $48	Airport/Station Pickup: Yes

Built in 1899 by a scion of Huttonsville's founder, Hutton House commands a broad view of the Tygart Valley and Laurel Mountain ridges. This ornate Queen Anne mansion, with its extraordinary woodwork and windows, is listed on the National Register of Historic Places. Travelers come here to ski at Snowshoe, visit Cass Railroad, and hike in the Monongahela National Forest. Civil War buffs will find plenty of battle sites to study, and the Augusta Heritage Arts Festival, in nearby Elkins, also merits a detour. For breakfast, your hosts dish out cantaloupe sorbet and whole-wheat pancakes drizzled with maple syrup made from their own trees.

Valley View Farm ✪
ROUTE 1, BOX 467, MATHIAS, WEST VIRGINIA 26812

Tel: (304) 897-5229	Reduced Rates: Weekly
Best Time to Call: Evenings after 7 PM	Breakfast: Full
Host: Edna Shipe	Other Meals: Available
Location: 130 mi. SW of D.C.	Pets: Welcome
No. of Rooms: 4	Children: Welcome (crib)
Max. No. Sharing Bath: 6	Smoking: Permitted
Double/sb: $30	Social Drinking: Permitted
Single/sb: $15	Airport/Station Pickup: Yes
Open: All year	

Edna and Ernest raise cattle and sheep on their 250-acre farm. The 1920s farmhouse is decorated with comfortable Early American–style furniture and family mementos, and there's a nice porch for relaxed visiting. This is no place to diet because Edna is a good cook. Seasonal recreational activities are available in nearby Lost River State Park and on Rock Cliff Lake. You are certain to enjoy the local festivals, house tours, and interesting craft shops. Bryces Ski Resort is less than an hour away.

McMechen House Inn
109 NORTH MAIN STREET, MOOREFIELD, WEST VIRGINIA 26836

Tel: **(304) 538-2417**	Single/pb: **$35**
Best Time to Call: **8 AM–noon;**	Open: **Jan. 15–Dec. 15**
4–10 PM	Breakfast: **Full**
Hosts: **Art and Evelyn Valotto**	Credit Cards: **AMEX, MC, VISA**
Location: **At junction of Rtes. 55 and**	Pets: **No**
220	Children: **Welcome**
Suites: **4**	Smoking: **Permitted**
No. of Private Baths: **3**	Social Drinking: **Permitted**
Double/pb: **$50**	

Cradled in the historic South Branch Valley and surrounded by the majestic mountains of the Potomac Highlands, the inn, built in 1853, is a three-story brick Federal-style house. During the Civil War it served as headquarters for both North and South as the region changed hands. Breakfast is served family-style in the dining room. When calling, please allow 10 rings.

Chestnut Ridge School ✪
1000 STEWARTSTOWN ROAD, MORGANTOWN, WEST VIRGINIA 26505

Tel: **(304) 598-2262**	Single/pb: **$48**
Hosts: **Sam and Nancy Bonasso**	Open: **All year**
Location: **70 mi. S. of Pittsburgh,**	Breakfast: **Continental**
Penn.	Pets: **No**
No. of Rooms: **4**	Children: **Welcome (crib)**
No. of Private Baths: **4**	Smoking: **No**
Double/pb: **$54**	Social Drinking: **Permitted**

A yellow brick and stucco building erected in the 1920s, Chestnut Ridge retains the oversize windows, beadboard trim, and broad staircase that mark its past as an elementary school. Situated on the outskirts of Morgantown, this B&B is just minutes from the West Virginia University campus and medical center. A state park, a large lake, a golf course and tennis courts are all within easy reach. Continental breakfast features fresh, multigrain muffins. Guests can take this morning meal in their rooms, in the kitchen, in the parlor, or on the deck.

Hampshire House 1884 ✪

165 NORTH GRAFTON STREET, ROMNEY, WEST VIRGINIA 26757

Tel: **(304) 822-7171**
Hosts: **Jane and Scott Simmons**
Location: **35 mi. W of Winchester, Va.**
No. of Rooms: **4**
No. of Private Baths: **4**
Double/pb: **$60–$70**
Single/pb: **$50–$60**
Open: **All year**
Reduced Rates: **Available**

Breakfast: **Full**
Other Meals: **Available**
Credit Cards: **AMEX, DC, MC, VISA**
Pets: **No**
Children: **Welcome**
Smoking: **No**
Social Drinking: **Permitted**
Airport/Station Pickup: **Yes**

Only 2½ hours west of Washington, D.C., via Route 50 lies Romney, the oldest town in West Virginia. Surrounded by beautiful rolling hills, Hampshire House is conveniently located to the downtown area. Bicycles are ready for touring the town, with its quaint shops and historic buildings. Trail rides and hayrides are available at the local equestrian center, and winery tours are nearby. The bedrooms are attractively furnished with old-fashioned furniture and wallpapers and kept comfortable with central heating and air conditioning. Jane and Scott graciously offer complimentary snacks and invite you to enjoy the old pump organ, television, VCR, or a variety of games.

Countryside ✪

P.O. BOX 57, SUMMIT POINT, WEST VIRGINIA 25446

Tel: **(304) 725-2614**
Best Time to Call: **8–10 AM; 8–10 PM**

Hosts: **Lisa and Daniel Hileman**
Location: **6 mi. from Rtes. 7 and 340**

No. of Rooms: **2**
No. of Private Baths: **2**
Double/pb: **$50–$70**
Single/pb: **$50–$60**
Open: **All year**

Breakfast: **Continental**
Pets: **No**
Children: **Welcome, over 12**
Smoking: **No**
Social Drinking: **Permitted**

In the Shenandoah Valley of the Eastern Panhandle, only 20 minutes from Harpers Ferry, this cheerful country home with white shutters, large yard, and patio is on a quiet street in a charming old village. It is attractively furnished with country oak furniture, antique quilts, original art, pretty baskets, and collectibles. Breakfast trays are brought to each guest room. Afternoon tea is served; snacks and beverages are always available. Guests always remark on the cleanliness and hospitality Lisa and Daniel provide.

The James Wylie House ✪
208 EAST MAIN STREET, WHITE SULPHUR SPRINGS, WEST VIRGINIA 24986

Tel: **(304) 536-9444**
Hosts: **Cheryl and Joe Griffith**
Location: **100 mi. SE of Charleston**
No. of Rooms: **5**
No. of Private Baths: **3**
Max. No. Sharing Bath: **4**
Double/pb: **$45**
Single/pb: **$40**
Double/sb: **$45**
Guest Cottage: **$100; sleeps 4**

Open: **All year**
Reduced Rates: **10%, after 3 nights**
Breakfast: **Full**
Other Meals: **Available**
Credit Cards: **MC, VISA**
Pets: **No**
Children: **Welcome**
Smoking: **No**
Social Drinking: **Permitted**
Airport/Station Pickup: **Yes**

This three-story Georgian Colonial-style dwelling dating back to 1819 features large, airy rooms that are comfortably furnished and accented with antiques. Pretty quilts, iron beds, old toys, and select period pieces enhance the bedrooms' decor. Specialties such as apple pudding, homemade coffee cake, and a delicious egg-and-sausage casserole are often part of the breakfast fare. The world-famous Greenbrier Resort and historic Lewisburg are less than a mile away. Recreational opportunities abound in the nearby state parks and ski resorts.

WISCONSIN

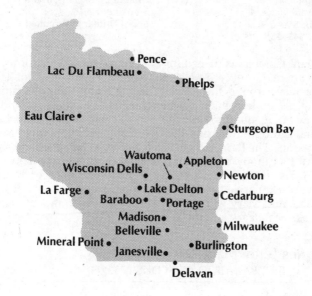

Pence
Lac Du Flambeau
Phelps
Eau Claire
Sturgeon Bay
Wautoma
Appleton
Wisconsin Dells
Newton
La Farge
Lake Delton
Baraboo
Portage
Cedarburg
Madison
Belleville
Milwaukee
Mineral Point
Janesville
Burlington
Delavan

Bed & Breakfast Guest-Homes
ROUTE 2, ALGOMA, WISCONSIN 54201

Tel: **(414) 743-9742**	Rates (Single/Double):
Best Time to Call: **7 AM–9 PM**	Average: **$35–$45** **$40–$55**
Coordinator: **Eileen Wood**	Luxury: **$45–$80** **$55–$90**
States/Regions Covered: **Statewide**	Credit Cards: **MC, VISA**
Descriptive Directory: **$5.95**	

This reservation service offers you local color and relaxing surroundings, with many accommodations in popular Door County. Eileen carefully selects the accommodations to assure each guest of a hospitable host in clean, comfortable homes. Most serve full breakfasts. Homes on the waterfront are slightly more expensive from July to early September. There is a 10-percent discount for week-long stays.

The Barrister's House
226 9TH AVENUE, BARABOO, WISCONSIN 53913

Tel: **(608) 356-3344**	Open: **All year**
Hosts: **Glen and Mary Schulz**	Breakfast: **Continental**
Location: **45 mi. NW of Madison**	Pets: **No**
No. of Rooms: **4**	Children: **Welcome, over 6**
No. of Private Baths: **4**	Smoking: **No**
Double/pb: **$50–$60**	Social Drinking: **Permitted**
Single/pb: **$45–$55**	

This elegant Colonial is named for the prominent town attorney who once lived here. Guests are welcome to settle down with a book in the library or relax around the fireplace in the living room. In summer, enjoy a glass of lemonade on the screened-in porch, veranda, or terrace. Sleeping quarters include the Garden Room, furnished in wicker and wrought iron, and the Colonial Room, appointed in 18th-century pieces. The Barrister's Room is a favorite for special occasions, because of its canopy bed, natural cherry wood, and cranberry-glass appointments. Juice, sweet rolls, fresh fruit, and cheese are served beside the black marble fireplace in the dining room, or outside, if you prefer. Glen and Mary will gladly direct you to such nearby sights as Devil's Lake State Park and the Wisconsin Dells.

Frantiques Showplace ✪
704 ASH STREET, BARABOO, WISCONSIN 53913

Tel: **(608) 356-5273**	Breakfast: **Full**
Hosts: **Fran and Bud Kelly**	Pets: **No**
Location: **13 mi. from I-90**	Children: **Welcome**
No. of Rooms: **2**	Smoking: **No**
No. of Private Baths: **2**	Social Drinking: **Permitted**
Double/pb: **$50–$55**	Airport/Station Pickup: **Yes**
Open: **All year**	

Fran Kelly has turned her three-story 125-year-old house into a Baraboo tourist attraction. She conducts tours through her house, showing off her antique dishes, children's toys, turn-of-the-century clothing, cameras, 1918 fireless cook stove, and more. The Cinema Suite has movie posters on the walls and comes with an antique brass bed, a refrigerator, stove, microwave oven, private bath, and private entrance. Baraboo is the Circus City of the World, and Fran seems to have more than just a bit of the showman in her, too. Nearby you'll find the Circus World Museum, the Al Ringling Theater, Devil's Lake State Park, the International Crane Foundation, and, 10 miles away, Wisconsin Dells.

The House of Seven Gables ✪
215 6TH STREET, BARABOO, WISCONSIN 53913
(MAILING ADDRESS: P.O. BOX 204)

Tel: **(608) 356-8387**	Open: **All year**
Best Time to Call: **8 AM–10 PM**	Breakfast: **Full**
Hosts: **Ralph and Pamela W. Krainik**	Credit Cards: **MC, VISA**
Location: **13 mi. from I-90**	Pets: **No**
No. of Rooms: **2**	Children: **Welcome, over 5**
No. of Private Baths: **2**	Smoking: **No**
Double/pb: **$60**	Social Drinking: **Permitted**
Single/pb: **$53**	

Seven Gables is a restored 1860 Gothic Revival home. It is on the National Register of Historic Places as one of the best examples of this architecture. The 17 rooms are furnished entirely in the Civil War period. Circus World Museum, Wisconsin Dells, and Devils Head, and Cascade ski resorts are close by.

Abendruh Bed and Breakfast Swiss Style
7019 GEHIN ROAD, BELLEVILLE, WISCONSIN 53508

Tel: **(608) 424-3808**	Single/sb: **$40**
Best Time to Call: **7 AM–9 PM**	Open: **All year**
Hosts: **Mathilde and Franz Jaggi**	Reduced Rates: **Available**
Location: **13 mi. SW of Madison**	Breakfast: **Full**
No. of Rooms: **3**	Pets: **No**
No. of Private Baths: **2**	Children: **No**
Max. No. Sharing Bath: **3**	Smoking: **No**
Double/pb: **$55**	Social Drinking: **Permitted**
Single/pb: **$45**	Foreign Languages: **French, German,**
Double/sb: **$45**	**Swiss**

Abendruh is a stucco-and-stone ranch designed and built by the Jaggi family. The house is filled with homemade items ranging from the furniture to the afghans. Your host, Franz, is a master brick-and-stone mason. Mathilde is certified as a French chef, and in hotel and restaurant management. Together they provide a Swiss atmosphere and the utmost in international service. The breakfast menu changes daily according to guest preference. Specialties include homemade muffins, croissants, and a variety of egg dishes. Guests are welcome to explore the spacious grounds or relax in front of a crackling fire at one of the four fireplaces. Abendruh is 30 minutes from downtown Madison, and is close to such attractions as New Glarus, America's Little Switzerland, Mt. Horeb, Cave of the Mounds, skiing, and biking.

Hillcrest ❍
540 STORLE AVENUE, BURLINGTON, WISCONSIN 53105

Tel: **(414) 763-4706**	Double/sb: **$50**
Best Time to Call: **After 3 PM,**	Open: **All year**
weekdays; weekends	Breakfast: **Full**
Hosts: **Dick and Karen Granholm**	Credit Cards: **MC, VISA**
Location: **30 mi. SW of Milwaukee**	Pets: **No**
No. of Rooms: **3**	Children: **Welcome, over 12**
No. of Private Baths: **1**	Smoking: **No**
Max. No. Sharing Bath: **4**	Social Drinking: **Permitted**
Double/pb: **$65**	

The Granholms welcome you to their 100-year-old home with a snack of locally prepared cheese and sausage. Hillcrest is a historic estate set on four wooded acres, just a short walk from downtown. The house is peaceful and quiet, with a spectacular view of Echo Lake. It has several leaded and beveled-glass windows and doors, mahogany woodwork, beamed ceilings, and a huge staircase dominating the first and second floors. Each guest room is decorated with antiques, lace curtains, and brass accents. Two large porches furnished with wicker chairs, love seats, and rockers will tempt you to doze away the afternoon. Breakfast dishes include fresh fruit and homemade muffins, served with omelets and plenty of hot coffee. Your hosts will gladly direct you to nearby craft and antique shops, golf courses, and lakes.

Stagecoach Inn Bed & Breakfast ❍
W61 N520 WASHINGTON AVENUE, CEDARBURG, WISCONSIN 53012

Tel: **(414) 375-0208**	Open: **All year**
Hosts: **Brook and Liz Brown**	Breakfast: **Continental**
Location: **17 mi. N of Milwaukee**	Credit Cards: **AMEX, DISC, MC, VISA**
No. of Rooms: **12**	Pets: **No**
No. of Private Baths: **12**	Children: **Welcome**
Double/pb: **$55**	Smoking: **No**
Single/pb: **$45**	Social Drinking: **Permitted**
Suites: **$85**	

The inn, listed on the National Register of Historic Places, is housed in a completely restored 1853 stone building in downtown, historic Cedarburg. The rooms, air-conditioned for summer comfort, combine antique charm with modern conveniences. Each bedroom is decorated with Laura Ashley linens and trimmed with wall stenciling. A bookstore, candy shop, and a pub that is a popular gathering place for guests, occupy the first floor. Specialty stores, antique shops, a winery, a woolen mill, and a variety of fine restaurants are within walking distance.

Allyn House Inn ✪
511 EAST WALWORTH, DELAVAN, WISCONSIN 53115

Tel: (414) 728-9090
Best Time to Call: Weekends; after 4 PM
Hosts: Joe Johnson and Ron Markwell
Location: 2 mi. from Rte. 43
No. of Rooms: 8
Max. No. Sharing Bath: 4
Double/sb: $40–$75
Open: All year

Reduced Rates: Corporate, Mon.– Thurs.
Breakfast: Full
Pets: No
Children: Welcome, over 12
Smoking: No
Social Drinking: Permitted
Airport/Station Pickup: Yes
Foreign Languages: French

This 22-room Victorian mansion will transport you to an era of elegant marble fireplaces, gleaming chandeliers, stained glass, and parquet floors. The rooms are furnished with Oriental rugs, antiques, and period pieces, some of which are for sale. Enjoy wine and Wisconsin cheese in front of the parlor fireplace. The hearty breakfast includes home-baked breads, rolls, and preserves in the formal dining room. In the 19th century, Delavan was home to many circus shows, and many of the past entertainers are buried in nearby Spring Grove Cemetery. Only five minutes away is Delavan Lake, where you may go horseback riding or play golf. Some of the best skiing in the state is just 10 miles from the house, and greyhound racing is available nearby.

Jackson Street Inn ✪
210 SOUTH JACKSON STREET, JANESVILLE, WISCONSIN 53545

Tel: (608) 754-7250
Hosts: Ilah and Bob Sessler
Location: 1.9 mi. from I-90, on Hwy. 11
No. of Rooms: 4
No. of Private Baths: 2
Max. No. Sharing Bath: 4
Double/pb: $60
Single/pb: $50
Double/sb: $50
Single/sb: $35

Suites: $55
Open: All year
Reduced Rates: Available
Breakfast: Full
Credit Cards: MC, VISA
Pets: No
Children: Welcome
Smoking: Permitted
Social Drinking: Permitted
Airport/Station Pickup: Yes

This turn-of-the-century home is finely appointed, with brass fixtures, leaded beveled-glass windows, and Italian fireplace mantels. The air-conditioned rooms are in soft colors with Colonial-period English wallpaper, fancy pillows, dust ruffles, and cozy quilts. The guest sitting room has books and a refrigerator with ice. Your hosts serve breakfast on the screened-in porch or in the fireplaced dining room overlooking the grounds. A four-hole putting green, shuffleboard, and a horseshoe court are part of their landscaping. Local attractions include the beach, Old Town restorations, hiking trails, golf, and museums.

Ty Bach B&B ✪
3104 SIMPSON LANE, LAC DU FLAMBEAU, WISCONSIN 54538

Tel: **(715) 588-7851**	Single/pb: **$40–$45**
Best Time to Call: **8 AM–10 PM**	Open: **All year**
Hosts: **Janet and Kermit Bekkum**	Breakfast: **Full**
Location: **70 mi. N of Wausau**	Pets: **Sometimes**
No. of Rooms: **2**	Children: **No**
No. of Private Baths: **2**	Smoking: **No**
Double/pb: **$45–$50**	Social Drinking: **Permitted**

In Welsh, *ty-bach* means "little house." Located on an Indian reservation in Lac Du Flambeau, this modern little house overlooks a small, picturesque Northwoods lake. Sit back on the deck and enjoy the beautiful fall colors, the call of the loons, and the tranquillity of this out-of-the-way spot. Choose from two comfortable rooms: one features a brass bed, the other opens onto a private deck. Your hosts offer oven-fresh coffee cakes, homemade jams, and plenty of fresh coffee along with hearty main entrées.

Trillium ✪
ROUTE 2, BOX 121, LA FARGE, WISCONSIN 54639

Tel: **(608) 625-4492**	Reduced Rates: **Single guest; weekly; winter**
Best Time to Call: **Mornings; evenings**	
Hosts: **Joe Swanson and Rosanne Boyett**	Pets: **No**
	Children: **Welcome (crib)**
Location: **40 mi. SE of LaCrosse**	Smoking: **Permitted**
Guest Cottage: **$63 for 2**	Social Drinking: **Permitted**
Open: **All year**	Airport/Station Pickup: **Yes**
Breakfast: **Full**	

This private cottage is on a working farm located in the heart of a thriving Amish community. It has a large porch and is surrounded by an orchard, garden, and a lovely tree-shaded yard. There's a path beside the stream that winds through woods and fields. The cottage is light and airy, with comfortable wicker furniture. Nearby attractions include the Elroy-Sparta Bike Trail, Mississippi River, trout streams, and cheese factories.

O. J.'s Victorian Village Guest House ✪
220 WISCONSIN DELLS PARKWAY SOUTH, LAKE DELTON, WISCONSIN 53940

Tel: **(608) 254-6568**	No. of Rooms: **4**
Best Time to Call: **Evenings**	No. of Private Baths: **4**
Hosts: **O.J. and Lois Thompto**	Double/pb: **$40–$55**
Location: **50 mi. N of Madison; 1 mi. from I-94, Exit 92**	Single/pb: **$30**
	Guest Cottage: **$65 for 4**

Open: **All year**	Children: **Sometimes**
Reduced Rates: **10%, Nov. 1–May 31**	Smoking: **No**
Breakfast: **Continental**	Social Drinking: **Permitted**
Pets: **Sometimes**	Airport/Station Pickup: **Yes**

Located at Wisconsin Dells, midway between Chicago and the Twin Cities, this brand-new house was built especially for B&B. It is situated on a major waterway; there's access to an enchanting creek and lake for fishing, swimming, and boating. It's five miles from the International Crane Foundation, where you can watch cranes from Africa, Asia, and America. O.J. and Lois look forward to greeting you, and will arrange for discounts in many restaurants and shops. The University of Wisconsin at Baraboo is nearby.

Annie's Bed & Breakfast
2117 SHERIDAN DRIVE, MADISON, WISCONSIN 53704

Tel: **(608) 244-2224**	Open: **All year**
Hosts: **Annie and Larry Stuart**	Reduced Rates: **Weekdays, Nov.–Mar.**
No. of Rooms: **3**	Breakfast: **Full**
No. of Private Baths: **2**	Credit Cards: **AMEX, MC, VISA**
Max. No. Sharing Bath: **4**	Pets: **No**
Double/pb: **$65–$85**	Children: **Sometimes**
Double/sb: **$60–$80**	Smoking: **No**
Single/sb: **$60–$80**	Social Drinking: **Permitted**
Suite: **$95–$115**	Airport/Station Pickup: **Yes**

This hand-cut cedar shake home overlooks a large park and is one block from Lake Mendota's eastern shore. It's 10 minutes from the Capitol and the university campus, and one minute from a lovely natural setting of meadows, water, and oak woods. Tennis courts and an exercise course, swimming beach, and boating are available nearby for summer fun; cross-country skiing, skating, and a sledding hill will add to your winter enjoyment. The morning starts with coffee in the gazebo, followed by a robust breakfast in the great hall dining room.

Bed & Breakfast of Milwaukee, Inc.
1916 W. DONGES BAY ROAD, MEQUON, WISCONSIN 53092

Tel: **(414) 242-9680**	Rates (Single/Double):	
Coordinator: **Suzanne Zabransky**	Modest: **$30**	**$35**
States/Regions Covered: **Milwaukee**	Average: **$40**	**$55**
and southeastern Wisconsin	Luxury: **$55–$70**	**$65–$125**
	Credit Cards: **AMEX, MC, VISA**	

Choose from a variety of homes in the city, suburbs, or countryside, on lakes, or near marinas. There is no shortage of fine restaurants; your host will be happy to make suitable recommendations to suit your taste and purse. There is a fine zoo, museums, and renowned cultural attractions. Major league sports and miles of Lake Michigan offer diversion and fun. The University of Wisconsin and Marquette University are convenient to many B&Bs. Ask Suzanne about corporate rates, group facilities, and discounts.

Marie's Bed & Breakfast ✪
346 EAST WILSON STREET, MILWAUKEE, WISCONSIN 53207

Tel: **(414) 483-1512**
Best Time to Call: **8 AM–8 PM**
Host: **Marie M. Mahan**
No. of Rooms: **2**
Max. No. Sharing Bath: **4**
Double/sb: **$45–$55**
Open: **All year**

Breakfast: **Full**
Pets: **No**
Children: **Welcome (crib)**
Smoking: **No**
Social Drinking: **Permitted**
Airport/Station Pickup: **Yes**

Your hostess has decorated this turn-of-the-century Victorian with an eclectic mixture of antiques, collectibles, and her own original artwork. Give yourself time to walk around the historic Bay View neighborhood, with its many architectural styles. Downtown Milwaukee is just six minutes away. Breakfast, served in the garden when weather permits, is highlighted by homemade breads, pastries, and a variety of locally prepared sausages.

Ogden House ✪
2237 NORTH LAKE DRIVE, MILWAUKEE, WISCONSIN 53202

Tel: **(414) 272-2740**
Hosts: **Mary Jane and John Moss**
No. of Rooms: **2**
No. of Private Baths: **2**
Double/pb: **$65**
Single/pb: **$65**
Suites: **$75**

Open: **All year**
Breakfast: **Continental**
Pets: **No**
Children: **Welcome**
Smoking: **Permitted**
Social Drinking: **Permitted**

The Ogden House is a white-brick Federal-style home listed on the National Register of Historic Places. It is located in the North Point–South district, a neighborhood shared by historic mansions overlooking Lake Michigan. Miss Ogden herself would feel at home here having homemade butterhorns for breakfast in the sun room overlooking the garden. You are sure to feel at home, too, whether you're relaxing on the sun deck, sitting by the fire, or retiring to your four-poster bed. Ogden House is convenient to theaters, the botanical garden, the Brewers' Stadium, the breweries, and many fine restaurants.

The Wilson House Inn ✪
110 DODGE STREET, MINERAL POINT, WISCONSIN 53565

Tel: **(608) 987-3600**	Double/sb: **$50**
Best Time to Call: **Evenings**	Single/sb: **$45**
Hosts: **Bev and Jim Harris**	Open: **All year**
Location: **50 mi. SW of Madison**	Breakfast: **Full**
No. of Rooms: **4**	Credit Cards: **MC, VISA**
No. of Private Baths: **2**	Pets: **Sometimes**
Max. No. Sharing Bath: **4**	Children: **Welcome (crib)**
Double/pb: **$55**	Smoking: **Permitted**
Single/pb: **$50**	Social Drinking: **Permitted**

The Wilson House Inn is located in the heart of the beautiful uplands area. This red-brick Federal mansion was built in 1853 by Alexander Wilson, who became one of the state's first attorneys general. A veranda was added later, and it is where guests are welcomed with lemonade. The rooms are airy, comfortable, and furnished in antiques. Mineral Point was a mining and political center in the 1880s, and it is filled with many historic sites. Fishing, golfing, swimming, skiing, and the House on the Rock are all nearby.

Rambling Hills Tree Farm ✪
8825 WILLEVER LANE, NEWTON, WISCONSIN 53063

Tel: **(414) 726-4388**	Hosts: **Pete and Judie Stuntz**
Best Time to Call: **Evenings**	Location: **18 mi. N of Sheboygan**

No. of Rooms: **3**	Open: **All year**
No. of Private Baths: **2**	Breakfast: **Full**
Max. No. Sharing Bath: **5**	Pets: **Sometimes**
Double/pb: **$40**	Children: **Welcome**
Single/pb: **$30**	Smoking: **Permitted**
Double/sb: **$40**	Social Drinking: **Permitted**
Single/sb: **$30**	Airport/Station Pickup: **Yes**

Enjoy the serenity of country living in a comfortable modern home set on 50 acres. The house overlooks the beautiful hills and a private fishing lake. Guests are welcome to make themselves at home, enjoy the screened-in porch, or curl up with a book before the fire. Outside there are hiking trails, boats, a swimming pond with a beach, and a play area for the children. When the snow falls, the trails are suitable for cross-country skiing and the pond freezes for skating. Your hosts recommend several nearby supper clubs, and can direct you to the attractions of Lake Michigan and the city of Manitowoc.

Northland House
609 HIGHWAY 77, PENCE, WISCONSIN 54550

Tel: **(715) 561-3120**	Reduced Rates: **After 2 nights**
Host: **Roger Margason**	Breakfast: **Full**
Location: **120 mi. W of Duluth,**	Credit Cards: **MC, VISA**
Minnesota	Pets: **Sometimes**
No. of Rooms: **4**	Children: **Welcome**
Max. No. Sharing Bath: **4**	Smoking: **Permitted**
Double/sb: **$40**	Social Drinking: **Permitted**
Single/sb: **$27**	Airport/Station Pickup: **Yes**
Open: **All year**	

Located in the heart of the north woods, Northland House is surrounded by miles of forest, with secluded lakes, streams, and waterfalls just waiting to be explored. Depending on the season, you'll enjoy hiking, biking, fishing, canoeing, and downhill or cross-country skiing. The bedrooms here are comfortable but not in the least fussy. Full breakfasts give guests the stamina for outdoor adventure.

The Limberlost Inn
HIGHWAY 17, #2483, PHELPS, WISCONSIN 54554

Tel: **(715) 545-2685**	Reduced Rates: **10%, weekly**
Hosts: **Bill and Phoebe McElroy**	Breakfast: **Full**
No. of Rooms: **2**	Pets: **No**
Max. No. Sharing Bath: **4**	Children: **Welcome, over 10**
Double/sb: **$47**	Smoking: **No**
Open: **All year**	Social Drinking: **Permitted**

The inn was designed and constructed by Bill and Phoebe McElroy. They picked a fine spot for their log home, just a minute from one of the best fishing lakes and largest national forests in the state. Each guest room is decorated with antiques, and the beds all have cozy down pillows and hand-stitched coverlets. Breakfast is served on the screened porch, by the fieldstone fireplace, in the dining room, or in your room. Stroll through the garden, rock on the porch swing, or take a picnic lunch and explore the streams and hiking trails. When you return, a Finnish sauna and a glass of wine or a mug of beer awaits.

Breese Waye Bed & Breakfast ✪

816 MacFARLANE ROAD, PORTAGE, WISCONSIN 53901

Tel: **(608) 742-5281**	Open: **All year**
Hosts: **Keith and Gretchen Sprecher**	Breakfast: **Full**
Location: **35 mi. N of Madison**	Pets: **Welcome**
No. of Rooms: **3**	Children: **Welcome (crib)**
No. of Private Baths: **3**	Smoking: **Permitted**
Double/pb: **$55**	Social Drinking: **Permitted**
Single/pb: **$45**	Airport/Station Pickup: **Yes**

Located across the street from a public indoor pool, this century-old Victorian mansion has three original fireplaces. It is comfortably furnished with lovely antiques. Portage is a historic city, so don't miss the Old Indian Agency House and the famed Portage Canal. Wisconsin Dells is 16 miles away.

Country Aire

N4452 COUNTY U, BOX 175, PORTAGE, WISCONSIN 53901

Tel: **(608) 742-5716**	Suites: **$60**
Best Time to Call: **Evenings**	Open: **All year**
Hosts: **Bob and Rita Reif**	Breakfast: **Continental**
Location: **37 mi. N of Madison**	Pets: **No**
No. of Rooms: **3**	Children: **Welcome**
No. of Private Baths: **2**	Smoking: **No**
Double/pb: **$45**	Social Drinking: **Permitted**
Single/pb: **$35**	

Forty acres of woods and meadows surround this spacious country home, built into a hillside overlooking the Wisconsin River. The house has open cathedral ceilings and a beautiful view from every room. Choose from comfortable bedrooms with queen-size or twin beds; the kids will enjoy the room with bunk beds. Guests are welcome to use the tennis court or go canoeing on the river. In the winter, skating can be enjoyed on the pond, and the area is perfect for cross-country skiing. Devil's Head and Cascade Mountain are close by for downhill skiing. Bob and Rita are minutes away from the Wisconsin Dells, Baraboo, and Devil's Lake State Park. At the end of the day, relax with wine and cheese, and enjoy a beautiful sunset.

Inn at Cedar Crossing
336 LOUISIANA STREET, STURGEON BAY, WISCONSIN 54235

Tel: (414) 743-4200
Host: **Terry Wulf**
Location: **45 mi. NE of Green Bay**
No. of Rooms: **9**
No. of Private Baths: **9**
Double/pb: **$65–$109**
Single/pb: **$58–$78**
Suites: **$85–$109**
Open: **All year**

Reduced Rates: **Available**
Breakfast: **Continental**
Other Meals: **Available**
Credit Cards: **DISC, MC, VISA**
Pets: **No**
Children: **Welcome, over 5**
Smoking: **Permitted**
Social Drinking: **Permitted**
Airport/Station Pickup: **Yes**

The inn, located in Door County, was built in 1884 as a two-story hotel and enjoys a place on the National Register of Historic Places. The interior features the original 13-foot-high tin ceilings, and a sweeping banistered staircase. The rooms are decorated in country antiques and primitives, with handwoven rag rugs, fine wallpapers, and beautiful knotty pine woodwork. Double whirlpools are featured in three. Enjoy a restful night in a canopy bed and wake up to homemade muffins, coffee cakes, juice, and coffee. Moravian sugar cake, a traditional breakfast bread handed down by the area's original settlers, is the house specialty. Terry invites you for evening popcorn by the fire, or you may retire to the privacy of your room. The inn is within walking distance of shops and the waterfront. A full-service gourmet restaurant open to the public is on the premises.

White Lace Inn—A Victorian Guest House
16 NORTH FIFTH AVENUE, STURGEON BAY, WISCONSIN 54235

Tel: (414) 743-1105
Hosts: **Dennis and Bonnie Statz**
Location: **150 mi. N of Milwaukee**
No. of Rooms: **15**
No. of Private Baths: **15**
Double/pb: **$60–$95**
Single/pb: **$43–$88**
Suites: **$110–$135**
Open: **All year**

Reduced Rates: **Nov.–May**
Breakfast: **Continental**
Credit Cards: **MC, VISA**
Pets: **No**
Children: **Welcome, over 12**
Smoking: **Permitted**
Social Drinking: **Permitted**
Airport/Station Pickup: **Yes**

This elegant Victorian guest house is beautifully furnished with quality antiques, down pillows, cozy comforters, brass canopy beds, lace curtains, and fine rugs. Seven rooms have fireplaces. Located in a residential area close to the bay, it is near shops and historic sites.

Winter features great cross-country skiing, snow sports, and hot chocolate in front of the fireplace. Summer offers boating, tennis, and swimming, with iced tea served on the front porch.

Kristine Ann's Inn ✪

303 EAST MAIN STREET, WAUTOMA, WISCONSIN 54982

Tel: **(414) 787-4901**
Best Time to Call: **7 AM–8 PM**
Hosts: **Kristine and Jim Wisnefske**
Location: **100 mi. NNW of Milwaukee**
No. of Rooms: **4**
No. of Private Baths: **4**
Double/pb: **$49–$125**
Single/pb: **$42–$125**
Open: **All year**
Reduced Rates: **Business, Sun.–Thurs.; winter; extended stays; ski and snowmobile packages**

Breakfast: **Continental**
Credit Cards: **MC, VISA**
Pets: **No**
Children: **Welcome, over 3**
Smoking: **Permitted**
Social Drinking: **Permitted**
Airport/Station Pickup: **Yes**

A white frame house with an enclosed porch, this inn is furnished with antiques, which is not surprising, since Kristine operates an antique shop on the first floor. Other antique shops, as well as galleries and specialty stores, are within walking distance. Duffers will be challenged by the local 18-hole golf course, and skiers can schuss down the slopes of Fantastic Nordic Mountain nearby. Breakfast features home-baked muffins, coffee cakes, soufflés, and pies.

WYOMING

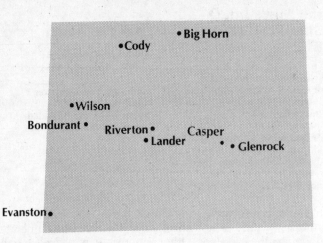

- •Big Horn
- •Cody
- •Wilson
- Bondurant •
- Riverton•
- •Lander
- Casper
- • •Glenrock
- Evanston•

Spahn's Big Horn Mountain Bed and Breakfast ✪
P.O. BOX 579, BIG HORN, WYOMING 82833

Tel: **(307) 674-8150**
Hosts: **Ron and Bobbie Spahn**
Location: **15 mi. SW of Sheridan**
No. of Rooms: **3**
No. of Private Baths: **3**
Double/pb: **$45–$60**
Open: **All year**
Cabins: **$65–$80**

Reduced Rates: **Families**
Breakfast: **Full**
Pets: **Sometimes**
Children: **Welcome (baby-sitter)**
Smoking: **No**
Social Drinking: **Permitted**
Airport/Station Pickup: **Yes**

Ron and Bobbie Spahn and their two children built their home and this authentic log cabin. The house is set on 40 acres of whispering pines, and borders the Big Horn Mountain forestland, which stretches for over a million acres. The main house has two guest bedrooms with private baths, a three-story living room, and an outside deck. The cabin is secluded from the main house and features a bedroom, large sleeping loft, bath, kitchen facilities, and front porch. You are invited to relax in the hot tub, sip a drink beside the wood stove, or take in the 100-mile view from an old porch rocker. Ron Spahn is a geologist and former Yellowstone Ranger. He can direct you to nearby fishing and hunting and can also tell you where to find the best walking and cross-country skiing trails.

Bessemer Bend Bed & Breakfast ✪
5120 ALCOVA ROUTE, BOX 40, CASPER, WYOMING 82604

Tel: **(307) 265-6819**
Hosts: **Opal and Stan McInroy**
Location: **10 mi. SW of Casper**
No. of Rooms: **3**
Max. No. Sharing Bath: **4**
Double/sb: **$45**
Single/sb: **$35**
Open: **All year**

Reduced Rates: **$5 less after 1 night**
Breakfast: **Full**
Pets: **Sometimes**
Children: **Welcome**
Smoking: **No**
Social Drinking: **Permitted**
Airport/Station Pickup: **Yes**

This two-level ranch house offers great views of the North Platte River and Bessemer Mountain; the McInroys' property was once part of the Goose Egg Ranch, as commemorated in Owen Wistern's *The Virginian*. Western history buffs will want to visit other points of interest, such as the site of the Red Butte Pony Express Station. In Casper you'll find a wealth of museums, parks, and restaurants. The sports-minded will be challenged by local options ranging from rock climbing and hang gliding to fishing and skiing. For indoor diversions, the McInroys' recreation room is equipped with a Ping-Pong table, an exercise bike, and plenty of books and games. Breakfasts feature coffee, fresh fruit or juice, toast, and an egg casserole.

Hotel Higgins ✪
416 WEST BIRCH, GLENROCK, WYOMING 82637

Tel: **(307) 436-9212**
Best Time to Call: **9 AM–3 PM**
Hosts: **Jack and Margaret Doll**
Location: **18 mi. E of Casper**
No. of Rooms: **8**
No. of Private Baths: **8**
Double/pb: **$52**
Single/pb: **$38**
Suites: **$60**

Open: **All year**
Breakfast: **Full**
Other Meals: **Available**
Credit Cards: **AMEX, MC, VISA**
Pets: **No**
Children: **Welcome**
Smoking: **Permitted**
Social Drinking: **Permitted**

This fascinating hotel was built in the early 1900s, and is today a Designated Historic Site. Filled with many of the original furnishings, beveled-glass doors, and terrazzo tile floors, it currently boasts the award-winning Paisley Shawl restaurant. Located on the historic Oregon Trail, it is minutes from Deer Creek, the home station of the Pony Express. An exquisite variety of quiches or omelets, champagne and orange juice, fresh fruits, and breakfast meats are offered at breakfast. Complimentary hors d'oeuvres are served in the lounge from 4 to 6 P.M.

Black Mountain Ranch ✪
ROUTE 63, 548 NORTH FORK ROAD, LANDER, WYOMING 82520

Tel: **(307) 332-6442**
Hosts: **Dan and Rosie Ratigan**
Location: **5.3 mi. from Hwy. 287**
No. of Rooms: **6**
No. of Private Baths: **4**
Double/pb: **$56**
Single/pb: **$33**
Open: **May 1–Oct. 1**

Reduced Rates: **Available**
Breakfast: **Full**
Other Meals: **Available**
Credit Cards: **MC, VISA**
Pets: **No**
Children: **Welcome (crib)**
Smoking: **No**
Social Drinking: **Permitted**

The ranch is nestled among the foothills of the Wind River Mountain Range on the way to Yellowstone National Park, which is only 2½ hours away. It offers all the peace and quiet you can handle and all the outdoor activities you can imagine. The rooms are decorated with a country flair and offer homey comfort. The tasty breakfast features whole wheat blueberry pancakes with choke cherry syrup as well as homemade granola. Trout fishing, hiking, hayrides, and bird-watching are just a few of the on-premises recreations. Within an hour's drive are a restored 1870 gold mining town and the Wind River Indian Reservation, where powwows are scheduled throughout the summer.

Cottonwood Ranch
951 MISSOURI VALLEY ROAD, RIVERTON, WYOMING 82501

Tel: **(307) 856-3064**
Best Time to Call: **After 7 PM**
Hosts: **Earl and Judie Anglen**
Location: **13 mi. N of Riverton**
No. of Rooms: **3**
Max. No. Sharing Bath: **6**
Double/sb: **$35**
Single/sb: **$30**
Open: **All year**

Reduced Rates: **10%, seniors; $5 less,**
  Oct. –May
Breakfast: **Full**
Other Meals: **Available**
Pets: **Sometimes**
Children: **Welcome**
Smoking: **Permitted**
Social Drinking: **No**
Airport/Station Pickup: **Yes**

Cottonwood is a working farm where you can observe firsthand the cattle being rounded up by men on horseback and getting branded in the old corral. Earl and Judie offer warm western hospitality, home cooking with homegrown produce and beef, and wide open spaces to enjoy and explore. Judie's "ranch" breakfast includes homemade breads, jams and salsa, biscuits and gravy, eggs, and "whatever you like." The guest quarters include a family room with a pool table and TV set. This is the West made familiar by old John Wayne movies, with spectacular mountain scenery, horseback riding, a historic gold mine, buffalo herds, a nearby Indian reservation, and friendly folks to show you around.

Fish Creek Bed & Breakfast ✪
2455 FISH CREEK ROAD, P.O. BOX 366, WILSON, WYOMING 83014

Tel: **(307) 733-2586**	Breakfast: **Full**
Best Time to Call: **Early morning, evening**	Credit Cards: **MC, VISA**
	Pets: **No**
Hosts: **Putzi and John Harrington**	Children: **Welcome, over 8**
Location: **6 mi. W of Jackson**	Smoking: **No**
No. of Rooms: **3**	Social Drinking: **Permitted**
No. of Private Baths: **3**	Airport/Station Pickup: **Yes**
Double/pb: **$75**	Minimum Stay: **2 days**
Open: **All year**	Foreign Languages: **German, French**

From the doorsteps of Putzi and John's rustic log cabin home, summertime guests can go fly fishing in complete privacy. Other warm-weather activities include bird watching, exploring Yellowstone and Grand Teton National Parks, and relaxing in the hot tub. In the winter, the Harringtons will be glad to guide you to both downhill and cross-country skiing. Whatever the season, you'll savor homemade breakfast specialties like fruit quiche, egg-and-vegetable ramekins, and coffee cakes, breads, and muffins.

Teton Tree House ✪
P.O. BOX 550, WILSON, WYOMING 83014

Tel: **(307) 733-3233**	Reduced Rates: **Available**
Hosts: **Chris and Denny Becker**	Breakfast: **Full**
Location: **8 mi. W of Jackson**	Credit Cards: **MC, VISA**
No. of Rooms: **5**	Pets: **No**
No. of Private Baths: **5**	Children: **Welcome**
Double/pb: **$85–$95**	Smoking: **No**
Single/pb: **$80–$90**	Social Drinking: **Permitted**
Open: **All year**	

This is an impressive house of rustic open-beam construction, where guests are entertained in the large living room. The bedroom windows and decks overlook a private, forested mountainside. Wildflowers and berry bushes cover the land in summer; in winter it's a pristine, snowy wonderland. Breakfast is a low-cholesterol feast featuring huckleberry pancakes, zucchini breads, and other homemade treats. It is only eight miles from Grand Teton National Park, ski areas, a mountain climbing school, and a rodeo.

5

CANADA

ALBERTA

Note: All prices listed in this section are quoted in Canadian dollars.

Alberta Bed & Breakfast ✪
P.O. BOX 15477, M.P.O., VANCOUVER, BRITISH COLUMBIA, CANADA V6B 5B2 (FORMERLY EDMONTON, ALBERTA)

Tel: **(604) 944-1793**
Best Time to Call: **8 AM–2 PM**
Coordinator: **June Brown**
States/Regions Covered: **Alberta—
Banff, Calgary, Canmore, Edmonton,
Jasper; British Columbia—Kamloops,
Vancouver, Victoria, Whistler**

Rates (Single/Double):
  Modest: **$30**   **$40**
  Average: **$35**   **$45**
  Luxury: **$45–$90** **$50–$95**
Credit Cards: **No**

Try a bit of Canadian western hospitality by choosing from June's variety of lovely homes in Alberta and British Columbia. Make a circle tour of Calgary, Banff, Lake Louise, the Columbia Icefields, Jasper, and Edmonton, and stay in B&Bs all the way. Send one dollar for a descriptive list of the cordial hosts on her roster, make your selections, and June will do the rest. The agency is closed on Canadian holidays and October through March. There's a $5 surcharge for each Banff, Jasper, and Victoria reservation.

BRITISH COLUMBIA

Note: All prices listed in this section are quoted in Canadian dollars.

Canada-West Accommodations ☉
P.O. BOX 86607, NORTH VANCOUVER, BRITISH COLUMBIA,
CANADA V7L 4L2

Tel: **(604) 987-9338**
Best Time to Call: **Evenings; weekends**
Coordinator: **Ellison Massey**
States/Regions Covered: **Greater
  Vancouver, Victoria, Kelowna,
  Whistler**

Rates (Single/Double):
  Average: **$35–$40 $60–$81**
Credit Cards: **AMEX, MC, VISA**

This registry has over 100 hosts with comfortable bed-and-breakfast accommodations. All serve a full breakfast, and most have a private bath for guest use. When traveling through British Columbia, visitors should note that B&Bs are available within a day's drive of one another. Canada-West features friendly host families eager to share their knowledge of cultural and scenic attractions. A ski package is available at Whistler.

Weston Lake Inn ☉
813 BEAVER POINT ROAD RR1, FULFORD HARBOUR, BRITISH
COLUMBIA, CANADA V0S 1C0

Tel: **(604) 653-4311**
Hosts: **Susan Evans and Ted Harrison**
Location: **30 mi. N of Victoria**
No. of Rooms: **3**
No. of Private Baths: **3**
Double/pb: **$70–$90**
Single/pb: **$55–$70**
Open: **All year**
Reduced Rates: **10%, weekly; winter
  rates, Nov.–Mar.**

Breakfast: **Full**
Credit Cards: **MC, VISA**
Pets: **Sometimes**
Children: **Welcome, over 14**
Smoking: **No**
Social Drinking: **Permitted**
Foreign Languages: **French**

Nestled on a knoll of flowering trees and shrubs overlooking Weston Lake, the Inn offers Old World charm in a comfortable new home. The house is on a 10-acre farm on Salt Spring Island, the largest of British

Columbia's Gulf Islands. Each guest room overlooks the countryside and has a down comforter. The rooms all have different finishing touches such as a brass bed, Chilean folk art, or Eskimo prints. Throughout the house there are a number of original Canadian art pieces and intricate petitpoint needlework crafted by your host, Ted. Breakfast is a full-course meal served to the sounds of classical music in the antique-filled dining room. Eggs Benedict, quiche, homemade muffins, and jams are specialties of the house. Guests can relax in the hot tub, on the garden terrace, or enjoy a book in the lounge beside a wood-burning stove. It's just a few steps to swimming, boating, and fishing. You can also follow forest trails or take to a bicycle and explore this quaint country island with its country roads, pastoral beauty, and talented artisans.

Cassidy's Bed & Breakfast ✪
2010 CASSIDY ROAD, S43 C23 RR2, GIBSON, BRITISH COLUMBIA, CANADA V0N 1V0

Tel: **(604) 886-7222**	Reduced Rates: **10%, Feb., Mar.,**
Best Time to Call: **6–8 PM**	**Nov., Dec.**
Hosts: **Bill and Rita Clark**	Breakfast: **Full**
Location: **10 mi. NW of Vancouver**	Pets: **Sometimes**
No. of Rooms: **2**	Children: **No**
Max. No. Sharing Bath: **4**	Smoking: **Permitted**
Double/sb: **$55**	Social Drinking: **Permitted**
Single/sb: **$40**	Airport/Station Pickup: **Yes**
Open: **Feb.–Dec.**	Foreign Languages: **German**

If you need to get away from it all, this is the place. Cassidy's B&B is on the Sunshine Coast, a 52-mile Pacific peninsula accessible only by the ferry that sails from Vancouver eight times daily. Bill and Rita will be happy to meet you at the dock and show you around. As you relax on the sun deck of their ranch house, you can watch Alaska Cruise ships pass by on their way up north. Fishing charters are a big attraction here, but there are also golf and tennis facilities nearby. Afternoon tea and hors d'oeuvres are served, as well as full breakfasts that have gotten rave reviews from past guests.

Grouse Mountain Bed and Breakfast ✪
900 CLEMENTS AVENUE, NORTH VANCOUVER, BRITISH COLUMBIA, CANADA V7R 2K7

Tel: **(604) 986-9630**	No. of Private Baths: **1**
Best Time to Call: **Early morning;**	Max. No. Sharing Bath: **2**
evening	Double/pb: **$65**
Hosts: **Lyne and John Armstrong**	Double/sb: **$65**
Location: **10 min. from city core**	Open: **All year**
No. of Rooms: **2**	Breakfast: **Full**

Pets: **Welcome**
Children: **Welcome (crib)**

Smoking: **No**
Social Drinking: **Permitted**

Your hosts welcome you to a comfortable, clean, modern home in the foothills of Grouse Mountain. Enjoy views of Vancouver Island from two sun decks overlooking the secluded grounds, with close proximity to Stanley Park, the beaches, and downtown. Large rooms await you, one with cedar-paneled bath, the other with flagstone fireplace. Both have ample sitting room. Breakfast features something different each day, such as berry pancakes, waffles, and scones with homemade jam. Skiing is only five minutes away.

Town & Country Bed & Breakfast in B.C. ✪
P.O. BOX 46544, STATION G, VANCOUVER, BRITISH COLUMBIA V6R 4G6

Tel: **(604) 731-5942**
Coordinator: **Helen Burich**
States/Regions Covered: **Vancouver, Vancouver Island, Victoria**

Rates (Single/Double):
  Modest: **$35–$45** **$45–$55**
  Average: **$40–$50** **$55–$65**
  Luxury: **$55–$90** **$65–$160**
  Minimum Stay: **2 nights**

Helen has the oldest reservation service in British Columbia. She has dozens of host homes, many of which have been accommodating guests for eight years. Ranging from a simple bungalow to a grand waterfront home, they are located near Stanley Park, excellent beaches, convenient to the ferry to Vancouver Island, the Grouse Mountain Sky Ride, Capilano Canyon, museums, art galleries, and restaurants. There is a $5 surcharge for Victoria and Vancouver Island reservations. In addition to normal business hours, Helen is often available evenings and weekends.

Kenya Court Guest House At-the-Beach ✪
2230 CORNWALL AVENUE, VANCOUVER, BRITISH COLUMBIA, CANADA V6K 1B5

Tel: **(604) 738-7085**
Host: **Dorothy-Mae Williams**
Location: **20 mi. from the U.S. border**
No. of Rooms: **5**
No. of Private Baths: **5**
Double/pb: **$85**
Single/pb: **$70–$85**
Suites: **$80 up**

Open: **All year**
Breakfast: **Full**
Pets: **No**
Children: **Welcome, over 8**
Smoking: **No**
Social Drinking: **Permitted**
Foreign Languages: **French, German, Italian**

There is an unobstructed view of the park, ocean, mountains, and downtown Vancouver from this heritage building on the waterfront. Across the street are tennis courts, a large heated outdoor saltwater pool, and walking and jogging paths along the water's edge. Just minutes from downtown, it's an easy walk to Granville Market, the Planetarium, and interesting shops and restaurants. All the rooms are large and tastefully furnished. Breakfast is served in a glass solarium with a spectacular view of English Bay.

Sunnymeade House Inn
1002 FENN AVENUE, VICTORIA, BRITISH COLUMBIA, CANADA V8Y 1P3

Tel: **(604) 658-1414**	Suites: **$79–$89; sleeps 3–4**
Best Time to Call: **Mid-morning; evenings**	Open: **All year**
Hosts: **Jack and Nancy Thompson**	Breakfast: **Full**
Location: **1½ mi. from Rte. 17**	Other Meals: **Available**
No. of Rooms: **5**	Pets: **No**
Max. No. Sharing Bath: **4**	Children: **No**
Double/sb: **$65–$75**	Smoking: **No**
Single/sb: **$40–$45**	Social Drinking: **Permitted**

Take the scenic route into Victoria and discover this inn on a winding country road by the sea. The Thompsons designed, built, decorated, and custom furnished the English-style house. Nancy, a former professional cook, will prepare your choice of breakfast from a choice of seven. You'll be steps away from the beach and within walking distance of tennis courts and restaurants. All bedrooms have vanity sinks and mirrors for makeup and shaving.

Beachside Bed and Breakfast ✪
4208 EVERGREEN AVENUE, WEST VANCOUVER, BRITISH COLUMBIA, CANADA V7V 1H1

Tel: **(604) 922-7773**	Credit Cards: **MC, VISA**
Hosts: **Gordon and Joan Gibbs**	Pets: **Sometimes**
Location: **4 mi. W of Vancouver**	Children: **Welcome**
No. of Rooms: **3**	Smoking: **No**
No. of Private Baths: **3**	Social Drinking: **Permitted**
Double/pb: **$85–$95**	Airport/Station Pickup: **Yes**
Open: **All year**	Foreign Languages: **French**
Breakfast: **Full**	

Guests are welcomed to this beautiful waterfront home with a fruit basket and fresh flowers. The house is a Spanish-style structure, with stained-glass windows, located at the end of a quiet cul-de-sac. Its southern exposure affords a panoramic view of Vancouver. A sandy beach is just steps from the door. You can watch the waves from the patio or spend the afternoon fishing or sailing. The hearty breakfast features homemade muffins, French toast, and Canadian maple syrup. Gordon and Joan are knowledgeable about local history, and can gladly direct you to Stanley Park, the site of Expo 86, hiking, skiing, and much more.

NEW BRUNSWICK

Note: All prices listed in this section are quoted in Canadian dollars.

Oakley House ✪
LOWER JEMSEG, NEW BRUNSWICK, CANADA E0E 1S0

Tel: **(506) 488-3113**
  FAX: **488-2785**
Hosts: **Max and Willi Evans Wolfe**
Location: **33 mi. E of Fredericton; 3
  mi. from Trans-Can. Hwy.**
No. of Rooms: **3**
Max. No. Sharing Bath: **6**
Double/sb: **$45**
Single/sb: **$35**
Open: **All year**

Breakfast: **Full**
Other Meals: **Available**
Credit Cards: **VISA**
Pets: **Sometimes**
Children: **Sometimes**
Smoking: **No**
Social Drinking: **Permitted**
Airport/Station Pickup: **Yes**
Foreign Languages: **French, Spanish**

Max and Willi's home is set right in the heart of strawberry country; their 20-acre property borders the Jemseg River, the waterway that connects Saint John River and Grand Lake. The 150-year-old house is surrounded by lilacs, acacias, and old apple trees. Whatever the season, there's plenty to do nearby—swimming and sailing in summer, and cross-country skiing and ice skating in winter. Bird-watching is excellent, especially in migratory season—loons, osprey, and eagles nest nearby. Thanks to a Jersey cow and a large organic garden, your hosts produce most of their own food. Breakfasts are bountiful—fresh fruit salad, granola, hot muffins, and more. Gagetown—just a short ferry ride away—is a favorite, with its craft shops, restaurants, marina, and historic sites.

ONTARIO

Note: All prices listed in this section are quoted in Canadian dollars.

Bed & Breakfast—Kingston ✪
10 WESTVIEW ROAD, KINGSTON, ONTARIO, CANADA K7M 2C3

Tel: **(613) 542-0214**
Coordinator: **Ruth MacLachlan**
Best Time to Call: **8 AM–10 PM, Mon.–Sat.**
States/Regions Covered: **Ontario— Bath, Gananoque, Harrowsmith, Kingston, Morrisburg, Napanee, Seeley's Bay, Sydenham, Westport**

Descriptive Directory: **$1**
Rates (Single/Double):
    Average: **$38**   **$49–$54**
    Luxury: **$43**   **$54–$60**
Credit Cards: **No**

Situated at the eastern end of Lake Ontario, at the head of the St. Lawrence River, Kingston has much to offer besides gorgeous scenery. There's Old Fort Henry, boat cruises through the Thousand Islands, historic sites, museums, and sports activities of every sort; the Rideau Nature Trail starts here and heads northeast toward Ottawa.

Bed and Breakfast Homes of Toronto ✪
P.O. BOX 46093, COLLEGE PARK POST OFFICE, 444 YOUNG STREET, TORONTO, ONTARIO, CANADA M4R 1C2

Tel: **(416) 363-6362**
Coordinator: **Arleen Baldwin**
States/Regions Covered: **Toronto, Mississauga**

Rates (Single/Double):
    Modest: **$30–$40**
    Average: **$45–$55**
    Luxury: **$70–$85**

Bed and Breakfast Homes of Toronto is a group of independent, quality B&Bs located in many prime locations spread over the city, near Toronto's excellent public transit. Accommodations range from downtown locations to suburban settings.

Windmere Bed & Breakfast ✪
SELWYN, RR 3, LAKEFIELD, ONTARIO, CANADA K0L 2H0

Tel: **(705) 652-6290**
Hosts: **Joan and Wally Wilkins**
Location: **12 mi. NE of Peterborough**

No. of Rooms: **3**
No. of Private Baths: **1**
Max. No. Sharing Bath: **4**

Double/pb: **$45**
Double/sb: **$40**
Single/sb: **$32**
Guest Cottage: **$55–$75; sleeps 2–4**
Open: **All year**
Reduced Rates: **Available**
Breakfast: **Full**

Pets: **No**
Children: **Welcome**
Smoking: **No**
Social Drinking: **Permitted**
Airport/Station Pickup: **Yes**
Foreign Languages: **French**

Windmere is located in the heart of the Kawartha Lakes, a water-skiers' and fishermen's paradise. Joan and Wally have an 1839 stone farmhouse, set amid shaded lawns and a large spring-fed swimming pond. The older part of the house has high-ceilinged rooms decorated with fine art and Victorian antiques. In the new wing, the accent is on wood, warmth, and informality. Freshly baked bran muffins and homemade jams are served each morning; in the evening, tea and a snack are offered in the family room. Your hosts can direct you to walking trails, art galleries, golf courses, and Petroglyphs Provincial Park, known for its Indian rock carvings.

Gretna Green ✪
5077 RIVER ROAD, NIAGARA FALLS, ONTARIO, CANADA L2E 3G7

Tel: **(416) 357-2081**
Hosts: **Stan and Marg Gardiner**
Location: **25 mi. NE of Buffalo, N.Y.**
No. of Rooms: **4**
No. of Private Baths: **4**
Double/pb: **$55**
Single/pb: **$45**

Open: **All year**
Reduced Rates: **10%, Oct. 1–Apr. 30**
Breakfast: **Full**
Pets: **No**
Children: **Welcome**
Smoking: **Permitted**
Social Drinking: **No**

Gretna Green is an easy stroll from the falls—the front porch of this 90-year-old brick home overlooks Niagara Gorge. With Marineland, the Imax Theatre, the local museums, and year-round festivals, this area is rich in diversions. But you won't miss out on your favorite shows because each bedroom has a TV. Marg loves to bake, and prides herself on the homemade muffins and scones she serves at breakfast.

Hiebert's Guest House
BOX 1371, 275 JOHN STREET, NIAGARA-ON-THE-LAKE, ONTARIO, CANADA L0S 1J0

Tel: **(416) 468-3687**
Hosts: **Otto and Marlene Hiebert**
Location: **10 mi. N of Niagara Falls**
No. of Rooms: **3**
Max. No. Sharing Bath: **3**
Double/sb: **$55**
Single/sb: **$50**

Open: **All year**
Reduced Rates: **$5 less, Jan.–Apr.**
Breakfast: **Full**
Pets: **No**
Children: **Welcome**
Smoking: **No**
Social Drinking: **No**

We wish we could share with you the many letters of reference attesting to "the cleanliness," "the warm Mennonite hospitality," "the delicious food," "the friendliness of the Hieberts." Their air-conditioned home is 10 miles from Niagara Falls, Ontario, and the U.S. border. The Shaw Festival Theatre and all of the area's points of interest are within walking distance. The breakfast muffins, served with homemade jams, are a special treat.

Ottawa Area Bed & Breakfast ✪
488 COOPER STREET, OTTAWA, ONTARIO, CANADA K1R 5H9

Tel: **(613) 563-0161**
Best Time to Call: **10 AM–10 PM**
Coordinators: **Robert Rivoire and R. G. Simmens**
States/Regions Covered: **Ontario, Ottawa**

Rates (Single/Double):
  Average: **$40**   **$50–$64**
Credit Cards: **No**

If you are seeking an interesting but inexpensive holiday, then Canada's capital, Ottawa, is the place for you. The city is packed with free activities including museums, the House of Parliament, art galleries, and historic sites. You can skate on the Rideau Canal or bike on miles of parkways and trails.

Toronto Bed & Breakfast (1987) Inc. ✪
BOX 269, 253 COLLEGE STREET, TORONTO, ONTARIO, CANADA M5T 1R5

Tel: **(416) 588-8800**
Best Time to Call: **9 AM–7 PM, Mon.– Fri.**
Coordinators: **Larry Page and Michael Coyne**
States/Regions Covered: **Toronto**

Rates (Single/Double):
  Modest: **$40**   **$50**
  Average: **$50**   **$55**
  Luxury: **$60**   **$85**
Credit Cards: **MC, VISA**
Minimum Stay: **2 nights, weekends**

Toronto, located on Lake Ontario, is a vibrant and sophisticated city, easily explored on foot. All of the homes on Larry and Michael's roster are convenient to excellent public transportation. The CN Tower, the Science Center, Yorkville, Eaton Centre, Harbourfront, and Casa Loma are just a few of the "must see" sights. Excellent restaurants abound at prices to suit every pocketbook.

PRINCE EDWARD ISLAND

Note: All prices listed in this section are quoted in Canadian dollars.

Woodington's Country Inn ✪
RR 2, KENSINGTON, PRINCE EDWARD ISLAND, CANADA C0B 1M0

Tel: **(902) 836-5518**	Open: **All year**
Best Time to Call: **Noon**	Reduced Rates: **10% after Sept. 15**
Hosts: **Marion and Claude "Woody" Woodington**	Breakfast: **Full**
	Other Meals: **Available**
No. of Rooms: **5**	Pets: **Welcome**
Max. No. Sharing Bath: **4**	Children: **Welcome**
Double/sb: **$44**	Smoking: **Permitted**
Single/sb: **$22**	Social Drinking: **Permitted**

Relax on the spacious lawns surrounding this immaculate Victorian farmhouse or stroll to the private beach. You'll feel at home immediately. Marion is a fabulous cook and her table reflects all that is fresh and wholesome. Woody hand-carves the most realistic duck decoys you've ever seen. Marion's spare time is spent making gorgeous quilts. A wood carving or quilt would make a memorable souvenir to take home.

Smallman's Bed and Breakfast
KNUTSFORD, O'LEARY, RR 1, PRINCE EDWARD ISLAND, CANADA C0B 1V0

Tel: **(902) 859-3469**	Suites: **$35**
Best Time to Call: **10 AM–noon; 6–10 PM**	Open: **All year**
	Breakfast: **Full**
Hosts: **Arnold and Eileen Smallman**	Other Meals: **Available**
Location: **7½ mi. from Rte. 2**	Pets: **Sometimes**
No. of Rooms: **4**	Children: **Welcome**
Max. No. Sharing Bath: **6**	Smoking: **Permitted**
Double/sb: **$25–$35**	Social Drinking: **No**
Single/sb: **$15–$20**	Airport/Station Pickup: **Yes**

This comfortable, split-level home is just 10 minutes from the beach. The kids will enjoy the backyard sandbox as well as a private track where the family racehorses train. Your host is a dedicated baker, always ready with coffee and a homemade snack. Breakfast specialties include homemade biscuits and cereals. Many local restaurants serve fresh lobster, clams, and oysters in season. Your hosts can direct you to the better buys in town, as well as the Gulf of St. Lawrence, golf courses, mills, and museums.

QUEBEC

Note: All prices listed in this section are quoted in Canadian dollars.

Bed & Breakfast à Montréal ✪
4912 VICTORIA, MONTREAL, QUEBEC, CANADA H3W 2N1

Tel: **(514) 738-9410**
Coordinator: **Marian Kahn**
States/Regions Covered: **Montreal,**
  Quebec City

Rates (Single/Double):
  Modest: **$30**   **$45**
  Average: **$40**   **$50–$60**
  Luxury: **$45–$60** **$65–$85**
Credit Cards: **AMEX, MC, VISA**

Marian established the province's first reservation service in 1980. Most of the fifty hosts in her group have been welcoming guests ever since and have seen many travelers return for repeat visits. Homes are located downtown, in the Latin Quarter, in fashionable Westmount, and in other attractive neighborhoods. Accommodations are in Victorian rowhouses, condo apartments, and even a contemporary ranchstyle house overlooking a golf course. Although the decor in each may differ, the standard of gracious hospitality is assured in all.

Bed & Breakfast—A Downtown Network ✪
3458 LAVAL AVENUE, MONTREAL, QUEBEC, CANADA H2X 3C8

Tel: **(514) 289-9749**
Best Time to Call: **8:30 AM–6 PM**
Coordinator: **Robert Finkelstein**
States/Regions Covered: **Montreal,**
  Outremont, Quebec City,
  Westmount

Rates (Single/Double):
  Modest: **$25**   **$35**
  Average: **$30–$40** **$45–$55**
  Luxury: **$55–$65** **$65–$75**
Credit Cards: **AMEX, MC, VISA**

Bob specializes in downtown accommodations with hosts ready to introduce you to good shopping, diverse restaurants, and places of special interest with an experienced eye on good value. After a day of hectic activity that might include a *calèche* ride through the cobbled streets of the Old Quarter, or a visit to the futuristic high-fashion urban area, and samples of excellent cuisine from all over the world, your hosts look forward to having you return to relax in their homes. There's a $5 surcharge for one-night stays.

Bed & Breakfast Bonjour Québec ✪
3765 BD MONACO, QUEBEC, CANADA G1P 3J3

Tel: **(418) 527-1465**
Best Time to Call: **7:30–11:30 AM; 7–8:30 PM**
Coordinators: **Denise and Raymond Blanchet**
States/Regions Covered: **Quebec City**

Rates (Single/Double):
Modest: **$35**   **$45**
Average: **$40**   **$60**
Luxury: **$85**   **$95**
Credit Cards: **No**

Denise and Raymond's accommodations are in the two districts that border Old Quebec. Their carefully selected hosts delight in making your visit a genuine French experience. The boulevard Grand-Allée is reminiscent of the Champs Élysée in Paris. Historic sites, the St. Lawrence River, charming restaurants, and shops are within easy reach of every B&B.

Appendix:
UNITED STATES AND CANADIAN TOURIST OFFICES

Listed here are the addresses and telephone numbers for the tourist offices of every U.S. state and Canadian province. When you write or call one of these offices, be sure to request a map of the state and a calendar of events. If you will be visiting a particular city or region, or if you have any special interests, be sure to specify them as well.

State Tourist Office

Alabama Bureau of Tourism and
  Travel
532 South Perry Street
Montgomery, Alabama 36104
(205) 261-4169 or (800) 252-2262
  (out of state) or (800) 392-8096
  (within Alabama)

Alaska Division of Tourism
P.O. Box E
Juneau, Alaska 99811
(907) 465-2010

Arizona Office of Tourism
1100 W. Washington Street
Phoenix, Arizona 85007
(602) 542-8687

Arkansas Department of Park and
  Tourism
1 Capitol Mall
Little Rock, Arkansas 72201
(501) 682-7777 or (800) 643-8383
  (out of state) or (800) 482-8999
  (within Arkansas)

California Office of Tourism
P.O. Box 189
Sacramento, California 95812-0189
(916) 322-1396 or (916) 322-1397
(800) 862-2543

Colorado Dept. of Tourism
1625 Broadway
Suite 1700
Denver, Colorado 80202
(303) 592-5410 or (800) 255-5550

Connecticut Department of Economic
  Development—Vacations
865 Brook Street
Rocky Hill, Connecticut 06067-3405
(203) 258-4290 or (800) 243-1685
  (out of state) or (800) 842-7492
  (within Connecticut)

Delaware Tourism Office
99 Kings Highway, P.O. Box 1401
Dover, Delaware 19903
(302) 736-4271 or (800) 441-8846
  (out of state) or (800) 282-8667
  (in Delaware)

Washington, D.C. Convention and
  Visitors' Association
1212 New York Avenue N.W.
1575 I Street, N.W.
Suite 600
Washington, D.C. 20005
(202) 789-7000

Florida Division of Tourism
Welcome Center, Plaza Level
New State Capitol Bldg.
126 W. Van Buren Street
Tallahassee, Florida 32399-2000
(904) 487-1462

Georgia Tourist Division
Box 1776
Atlanta, Georgia 30301
(404) 656-3590 or (800) 847-4842

Hawaii Visitors Bureau
2270 Kalakaua Ave.
Suite 801
Honolulu, Hawaii 96815
(808) 923-1811

Idaho Travel Council
700 W. State Street
Hall of Mirrors, 2nd floor
Boise, Idaho 83720
(515) 281-3100 or (800) 635-7820

Illinois Office of Tourism
310 South Michigan Avenue
Suite 108
Chicago, Illinois 60604
(312) 793-2094 or (800) 359-9294
   within Ill. or (800) 223-0121 out of
   state

Indiana Tourism Development
   Division
1 North Capitol, Suite 700
Indianapolis, Indiana 46204-2288
(317) 232-8860 or (800) 289-6646

Iowa Tourism Office
200 East Grand
Des Moines, Iowa 50309-2882
(515) 281-3679 or (800) 345-4692

Kansas Department of Economic
   Development—Travel and Tourism
   Division
400 West 8th Street, Suite 500
Topeka, Kansas 66603
(913) 296-2009 or (800) 252-6727
   (within Kansas)

Kentucky Department of Travel
   Development
Capitol Plaza Tower, 22nd floor
Frankfort, Kentucky 40601
(502) 564-4930 or (800) 225-8747
   (out of state)

Louisiana Office of Tourism
P.O. Box 94291
Baton Rouge, Louisiana 70804-9291
(504) 342-8119 or (800) 334-8626
   (out of state)

Maine Publicity Bureau
97 Winthrop St.
Hallwell, Maine 04347
(207) 289-2423 or (800) 533-9595

Maryland Office of Tourist
   Development
217 E. Redwood Ave.
Baltimore, Maryland 21202
(301) 333-6611 or (800) 543-1036

Massachusetts Div. of Tourism
100 Cambridge Street—13th Floor
Boston, Massachusetts 02202
(617) 727-3201 or (800) 447-MASS
   (out of state)

Michigan Travel Bureau
Dept. of Commerce
P.O. Box 30226
Lansing, Michigan 48909
(517) 373-1195 or (800) 543-2 YES

Minnesota Tourist Information Center
375 Jackson Street
Farm Credit Service Bldg.
St. Paul, Minnesota 55101
(612) 296-5029 or (800) 657-3700
   (out of state) or (800) 652-9747
   (in Minnesota)

Mississippi Division of Tourism
P.O. Box 849
Jackson, Mississippi 39205-0849
(601) 359-3297 or (800) 647-2290

Missouri Division of Tourism
P.O. Box 1055
Jefferson City, Missouri 65102
(314) 751-4133

Montana Promotion Division
1424 9th Avenue
Helena, Montana 59620
(406) 444-2645 or (800) 541-1447

Nebraska Division of Travel and
   Tourism
P.O. Box 94666
Lincoln, Nebraska 68509
(402) 471-3794 or (800) 228-4307 (out
   of state) (800) 742-7595 (within NB)

Nevada Commission on Tourism
Capitol Complex
5151 S. Carson St.
Carson City, Nevada 89710
(702) 687-4322 or (800) NEVADA 8

New Hampshire Office of Vacation
  Travel
P.O. Box 856
Concord, New Hampshire 03301
(603) 271-2343 or (800) 678-5040
  or (603) 271-2666

New Jersey Division of Travel and
  Tourism
C.N. 826
Trenton, New Jersey 08635
(609) 292-2470 or (800) 537-7397

New Mexico Travel Division
Joseph Montoya Building
1100 St. Francis Drive
Santa Fe, New Mexico 87503
(505) 827-0291 or (800) 545-2040
  (out of state)

New York State Division of Tourism
1 Commerce Plaza
Albany, New York 12245
(518) 474-4116 or (800) 225-5697
  (in the N.E. except Maine)

North Carolina Travel and Tourism
  Division
430 North Salisbury Street
Raleigh, North Carolina 27611
(919) 733-4171 or (800) VISIT NC
  (out of state)

North Dakota Tourism Promotion
Liberty Mem. Bldg.
604 E. Blvd.
Bismarck, North Dakota 58505
(701) 224-2525 or (800) 472-2100
  (within North Dakota) or (800)
  437-2077 (out of state)

Ohio Office of Tourism
P.O. Box 133
Columbus, Ohio 43216
(800) 848-1300 extension 8844
  or (800) 282-5393

Oklahoma Division of Tourism
P.O. Box 60,000
Oklahoma City, Oklahoma 73146
(405) 521-2409 or (800) 652-6552
  (in neighboring states) or
  (800) 522-8565 within OK

Oregon Economic Development
  Tourism Division
775 Summer St. N.E.
Salem, Oregon 97310
(503) 378-3451 or (800) 547-7842
  (out of state) or (800) 543-8838
  (within Oregon)

Pennsylvania Bureau of Travel
  Development
453 Forum Building, Dept. of
  Commerce
Harrisburg, Pennsylvania 17120
(717) 787-5453 or (800) 847-4872

Puerto Rico Tourism Co.
23rd Floor
575 Fifth Avenue
New York, New York 10107
(212) 599-6262 or (800) 223-6530
  or (800) 443-0266

Rhode Island Department of
  Economic Development
Tourism and Promotion Division
7 Jackson Walkway
Providence, Rhode Island 02903
(401) 277-2601 or (800) 556-2484
  (East Coast from Maine to Virginia,
  also W. Va. and Ohio)

South Carolina Division of Tourism
1205 Pendleton St.
Columbia, South Carolina 29201
(803) 734-0122

South Dakota Division of Tourism
Capitol Lake Plaza
711 Wells Avenue
Pierre, South Dakota 57501
(605) 773-3301 or (800) 843-1930
  (out of state); (800) 952-2217
  (in state)

Tennessee Tourist Development
P.O. Box 23170
Nashville, Tennessee 37202
(615) 741-2158

Texas Tourist Development
P.O. Box 12008, Capitol Station
Austin, Texas 78711
(512) 462-9191 or (800) 888-8839

Utah Travel Council
Council Hall
Capitol Hill
Salt Lake City, Utah 84114
(801) 538-1030

Vermont Travel Division
134 State Street
Montpelier, Vermont 05602
(802) 828-3236

Virginia Division of Tourism
202 North 9th Street
Suite 500
Richmond, Virginia 23219
(804) 786-4484 or (800) 847-4882

Washington State Tourism
    Development Division
101 General Administration Building
Olympia, Washington 98504
(206) 586-2088 or 586-2102
    or (800) 544-1800 (out of state)

Travel West Va.
2101 E. Washington Street
Charleston, West Virginia 25305
(304) 348-2286 or (800) CALL WVA

Wisconsin Division of Tourism
P.O. Box 7970-B
123 W. Washington
Madison, Wisconsin 53707
(608) 266-2161 or (800) 372-2737
    (within Wisconsin & neighboring
    states) or (800) 432-8747 (out of
    state)

Wyoming Travel Commission
I-25 and College Drive
Cheyenne, Wyoming 82002-0660
(307) 777-7777 or (800) 225-5996
    (out of state)

Canadian Province Tourist Office

Travel Alberta
15th Floor
10155 102 St.
Edmonton, Alberta, Canada T5J 4I6
(403) 427-4321 (from Edmonton area)
    or 800-222-6501 (from Alberta) or
    800-661-8888 (from the U.S. and
    Canada)

Tourism British Columbia
    1117 Wharf Street
Victoria, British Columbia, Canada
    V8V 1X4
(604) 387-1642 or (800) 663-6000

Travel Manitoba
Dept. 6020
7th Floor
155 Carlton Street
Winnipeg, Manitoba, Canada R3C
    3H8
(204) 945-4345 or 800-665-0040 (from
    mainland U.S. and Canada)

Tourism New Brunswick
P.O. Box 12345
Fredericton, New Brunswick, Canada
    E3B 5C3
(506) 453-8745 or 800-561-0123 (from
    mainland U.S. and Canada)

Newfoundland/Labrador Tourism
    Branch
Department of Development
P.O. Box 8700
St. John's, Newfoundland, Canada
    A1B 4J6
(709) 576-2830 (from St. John's area)
    or 800-563-6353 (from mainland
    U.S. and Canada)

Travel Arctic
Government of N.W. Territories
    Yellow Knife
Northwest Territories, Canada
    X1A 2L9
(403) 873-7200

Nova Scotia Tourism
P.O. Box 130
Halifax, Nova Scotia, Canada B3J 2M7
(902) 424-4247

Ontario Ministry of Tourism and
    Recreation
Customer Service
Queens Park
Toronto, Ontario, Canada M7A 2E5
(410) 965-4008 (within Canada) or
    (800) 668-2746 from mainland U.S.
    & Canada except Yukon & N.W.
    Territories

Department of Finance and Tourism
Visitor Services
P.O. Box 940
Charlottetown, Prince Edward Island,
    Canada C1A 7N5
(902) 368-4444 or (800) 565-7421 (from
    New Brunswick & Nova Scotia—
    May 15 to October 31) or (800) 565-
    9060

Tourism Quebec
C.P. 20 000
Quebec, Canada G1K 7X2
(800) 363-7777 (from 26 eastern states)
   or (514) 873-2015 (collect from all
   other U.S. locations)

Tourism Saskatchewan
1919 Saskatchewan Drive
Regina, Saskatchewan, Canada S4P
   3V7
(306) 787-2300 or (800) 667-7191
   (from Canada & mainland U.S.
   except Alaska) or (800) 667-7538 in
   Saskatchewan

Tourism Yukon
P.O. Box 2703
Whitehorse, Yukon, Canada Y1A 2C6
(403) 667-5340

BED AND BREAKFAST RESERVATION REQUEST FORM

Dear _____
    Host's Name

I read about your home in *Bed & Breakfast U.S.A. 1991,* and would
be interested in making reservations to stay with you.

My name: _____

Address: _____
        street

_____
    city   state   zip
Telephone: _____
        area code
Business address/telephone: _____

_____

Number of adult guests: _____

Number and ages of children: _____

Desired date and time of arrival: _____

Desired length of stay: _____

Mode of transportation: _____
(car, bus, train, plane)

Additional information/special requests/allergies: _____

_____

_____

_____

_____

_____

_____

I look forward to hearing from you soon.

                                    Sincerely,

APPLICATION FOR MEMBERSHIP
(Please type or print)
(Please refer to Preface, pages xxxvii–xxxviii for our membership criteria.)

Name of Bed & Breakfast: _____

Address: _____

City: _____ State: _____ Zip: _____ Phone: (   ) _____

Best Time to Call: _____

Host(s): _____

Located: No. of miles _____ compass direction _____ of Major

City _____ Geographic region _____

No. of miles _____ from major route _____ Exit: _____

No. of guest bedrooms with private bath: _____
No. of guest bedrooms that share a bath: _____
How many people (including *your* family) must use the shared bath? _____
How many bedrooms, if any, have a sink in them? _____

Room Rates:
$ _____ Double—private bath $ _____ Double—shared bath
$ _____ Single—private bath $ _____ Single—shared bath
$ _____ Suites
Separate Guest Cottage $ _____ Sleeps _____

Are you open year-round? ☐ Yes   ☐ No
If "No," specify when you are open: _____

How many rooms are wheelchair-accessible? _____

Do you require a minimum stay? _____

Do you discount rates at any time? ☐ No   ☐ Yes

Do you offer a discount to senior citizens? ☐ No   ☐ Yes: _____ %

Do you offer a discount for families? ☐ No   ☐ Yes: _____ %

Breakfast: Type of breakfast included in rate:
☐ Full ☐ Continental

Describe breakfast specialties: _____
_____

Are any other meals provided? ☐ No   ☐ Yes
Lunch ☐ cost: $ _____   Dinner ☐ cost: $ _____

Do you accept credit cards? ☐ No   ☐ Yes:
☐ AMEX ☐ DINERS ☐ DISCOVER ☐ MASTERCARD ☐ VISA

Will you GUARANTEE your rates from January through December 1992? ☐ Yes   ☐ No

Note: This Guarantee applies only to those guests making reservations having read about you in *Bed & Breakfast U.S.A., 1992*.

If you have household pets, specify how many:
☐ Dog(s)   ☐ Cat(s)   ☐ Other

Can you accommodate a guest's pet?
☐ No   ☐ Yes   ☐ Sometimes

Are children welcome? ☐ No   ☐ Yes   If "Yes," specify age restriction _____

Do you permit smoking somewhere inside your house?
☐ No   ☐ Yes

Do you permit social drinking? ☐ No   ☐ Yes

Guests can be met at ☐ Airport ____   ☐ Train ____   ☐ Bus ____

Can you speak a foreign language fluently? ☐ No   ☐ Yes
Describe: _____

GENERAL AREA OF YOUR B&B (i.e., Boston historic district; 20 minutes from Chicago Loop):

GENERAL DESCRIPTION OF YOUR B&B (i.e., brick Colonial with white shutters; Victorian mansion with stained-glass windows):

AMBIENCE OF YOUR B&B (i.e., furnished with rare antiques; lots of wood and glass):

THE QUALITIES THAT MAKE YOUR B&B SPECIAL ARE:

THINGS OF HISTORIC, SCENIC, CULTURAL, OR GENERAL INTEREST NEARBY (e.g., one mile from the San Diego Zoo; walking distance to the Lincoln Memorial):

YOUR OCCUPATION and SPECIAL INTERESTS (i.e., a retired teacher of Latin interested in woodworking; full-time host interested in quilting):

If you do welcome children, are there any special provisions for them (i.e., crib, playpen, high-chair, play area, baby-sitter)?

Do you offer snacks (i.e., complimentary wine and cheese; pretzels and chips but BYOB)?

Can guests use your kitchen for light snacks? ☐ No   ☐ Yes

Do you offer the following amenities? ☐ Guest refrigerator
☐ Air-conditioning   ☐ TV   ☐ Piano   ☐ Washing machine
☐ Dryer   ☐ Hot tub   ☐ Pool   ☐ Tennis court
Other _____

What major college or university is within 10 miles?
_____

Please supply the name, address, and phone number of three personal references from people not related to you (please use a separate sheet).

Please enclose a copy of your brochure along with color photos including exterior, guest bedrooms, baths, and breakfast area. Bedroom photos should include view of the headboard(s), bedside lamps and night tables. Please show us a typical breakfast setting. Use a label to identify the name of your B&B *on each*. If you have a black-and-white line drawing, send it along. If you have an original breakfast recipe that you'd like to share, send it along, too. (Of course, credit will be given to your B&B.) **Nobody can describe your B&B better than you. Limit your description to 100 words and submit it typed, double spaced, on a separate sheet of paper. We will of course reserve the right to edit.** As a member of the Tourist House Association of America, your B&B will be described in the next edition of our book, *Bed & Breakfast U.S.A.*, published by Plume, an imprint of New American Library, a division of Penguin USA, and distributed to bookstores and libraries throughout the U.S. The book is also used as a reference for B&Bs in our country by major offices of tourism throughout the world.

Note: The following will NOT be considered for inclusion in *Bed & Breakfast, USA:* B&Bs having more than 15 guestrooms. Rental properties or properties where the host doesn't reside on the premises. Rates starting at $95 or more. Rates exceeding $35 where 6 people share a bath. Rates exceeding $40 where 5 people share a bath. Beds without headboards, night tables, and adequate bedside reading lamps.

Note: If the publisher or authors receive negative reports from your guests regarding a deficiency in our standards of CLEANLINESS, COMFORT and CORDIALITY, and/or failure to honor the rate guarantee, we reserve the right to cancel your membership.

This membership application has been prepared by:

_____
(Signature)

Please enclose your $25 membership dues.   Date: _____

Yes! ☐ I'm interested in Group Liability Insurance.

No ☐ I am insured by _____ .

Return to:
Tourist House Association of America
RD 2, Box 355A
Greentown, Pennsylvania 18426

To assure that your listing will be considered for the 1992 edition of *Bed & Breakfast U.S.A.*, we MUST receive your completed application by March 31, 1991. Thereafter, listings will be considered only for the semiannual supplement. (See page 675.)

APPLICATION FOR MEMBERSHIP FOR A
BED & BREAKFAST RESERVATION SERVICE

NAME OF BED & BREAKFAST SERVICE: _____

ADDRESS: _____

CITY: _____ STATE: _____ ZIP: _____ PHONE:( ) _____

COORDINATOR: _____

BEST TIME TO CALL: _____

Do you have a telephone answering ☐ machine?   ☐ service?

Names of state(s), cities, and towns where you have hosts (in alphabetical order, please, and limit to 10):

Number of Hosts on your roster: _____

THINGS OF HISTORIC, SCENIC, CULTURAL, OR GENERAL INTEREST IN THE AREA(S) YOU SERVE:

Range of Rates:
Modest:	Single $ _____	Double $ _____
Average:	Single $ _____	Double $ _____
Luxury:	Single $ _____	Double $ _____

Will you GUARANTEE your rates through December 1992?
☐ Yes   ☐ No

How often do you reinspect listings? _____
Do you require a minimum stay? _____
Surcharges for one-night stay? _____
Do you accept credit cards? ☐ No   ☐ Yes:
☐ AMEX ☐ DINERS ☐ DISCOVER ☐ MASTERCARD
☐ VISA

Is the guest required to pay a fee to use your service?
☐ No   ☐ Yes—The fee is $ _____

Do you publish a directory of your B&B listings?
☐ No   ☐ Yes—The fee is $ _____

Are any of your B&Bs within 10 miles of a university? Which? __

Briefly describe a sample host home in each of the previous categories: e.g., A cozy farmhouse where the host weaves rugs; a restored 1800 Victorian where the host is a retired general; a contemporary mansion with a sauna and swimming pool.

Please supply the name, address, and phone number of three personal references from people not related to you (please use a separate sheet of paper). Please enclose a copy of your brochure.

This membership application has been prepared by:

_____
(Signature)

Please enclose your $25 membership dues.   Date: _____

If you have a special breakfast recipe that you'd like to share, send it along. (Of course, credit will be given to your B&B agency.) As a member of the Tourist House Association of America, your B&B agency will be described in the next edition of our book, *Bed & Breakfast U.S.A.*, published by Plume, an imprint of New American Library, a division of Penguin USA. Return to: Tourist House Association, RD 2, Box 355A, Greentown, PA 18426.

To assure that your listing will be considered for the 1992 edition, we must receive your completed application by March 31, 1991. Thereafter, listings will be considered only for the semiannual supplement. (See next page.)

INFORMATION ORDER FORM

We are constantly expanding our roster to include new members in the Tourist House Association of America. Their facilities will be fully described in the next edition of *Bed & Breakfast U.S.A.* In the meantime, we will be happy to send you a list including the name, address, telephone number, etc.

For those of you who would like to order additional copies of the book, and perhaps send one to a friend as a gift, we will be happy to fill mail orders. If it is a gift, let us know and we'll enclose a special gift card from you.

ORDER FORM

To:
Tourist House
Association—
Book Dept.
RD 1, Box 12A
Greentown, PA
18426

Date: _____

From: _____
(Print your name)
Address: _____

_____
City   State Zip

Please send:

☐ List of new B&Bs ($3.00), available July to December.

☐ _____ copies of *Bed & Breakfast U.S.A.* @ $12 each (includes 4th class mail)

Send to: _____

Address: _____

_____
City   State Zip

☐ Enclose a gift card from:

Please make check or money order payable to Tourist House Association.

WE WANT TO HEAR FROM YOU!

Name: _____

Address: _____
        street

        city   state   zip

Please contact the following B&Bs; I think that they would be great additions to the next edition of *Bed & Breakfast U.S.A.*

Name of B&B: _____

Address: _____
        street

        city   state   zip

Comments:

Name of B&B: _____

Address: _____
        street

        city   state   zip

Comments:

_____

The following is our report on our visit to the home of:

Name of B&B: _____ Date of visit: _____

Address: _____ I was pleased. ☐

_____ I was disappointed. ☐

Comments:

Just tear out this page and mail it to us. It won't ruin your book!

Return to:
Tourist House Association of America
RD 2, Box 355A
Greentown, Pennsylvania 18426